The Hindu Philosophy of Life, Ethics and Religion

Om-Tat-Sat

Srimad Bhagavadgita Rahasya

or

Karma=Yoga=Sastra

The Hindu Philosophy of Life, Ethics and Religion

Om-Tat-Sat

Srimad Bhagavadgita Rahasya

or

Karma=Yoga=Sastra

Including an External Examination of the Gita, the Original Sanskrit stanzas, their English translation, commentaries on the stanzas, and a comparison of Eastern with Western doctrines etc.

BY

BAL GANGADHAR TILAK, B.A., LL.B.,

LAW LECTURER, AND PLEADER, POONA; SOMETIME ADDITIONAL MEMBER OF THE COUNCIL OF H. E. THE GOVERNOR OF BOMBAY FOR MAKING LAWS, AUTHOR OF *Orion or Researches into the Antiquity of the Vedas, Arctic Home in the Vedas, Vedanga Jyotish and Vedic Chronology*, Founder of the 'Kesari' and the Maratha Newspapers Etc. Etc.

Translated By

BHALCHANDRA SITARAM SUKTHANKAR, M.A., LLB.,

Solicitor, High Court, Bombay,

Gibbs Prizeman; Petit Prizeman (Cercle Litteraire);

Dakshina Fellow; etc.

Vol. I

First Edition

GYAN

Published by

Gyan Publishing House
5, Ansari Road
Daryaganj, New Delhi-110002
Phone: 011-47034999, 9811692060
E-mail: books@gyanbooks.com

Distribution Network
gyanbooks.com
India, USA, Canada, UK, Australia, France

ISBN : **978-81-212-4059-8** (Set)
ISBN : 978-81-212-4969-0 **(PB)**
First Published, London, 1900

2nd Impression 2020

Printed at: Gyan Press, Delhi.

Srimad Bhagavadgita Rahasya or Karma=Yoga=Sastra Vol. I
Author: Bal Gangadhar Tilak

S'RĪ

BHAGAVADGĪTĀ-RAHASYA

OR

KARMA-YOGA-S'ĀSTRA

(English Translation)

FIRST EDITION

VOLUME I

Bhagavan

Shree Krishna

yada yada hi dharmasya glanir bhavati bharata
abhyutthanam adharmasya tad atmanam srjamy aham

(*Gita* 4. 7)

A PAGE FROM THE AUTHOR'S NOTE-BOOK

A fac-simile copy of an important memorandum entered by Lokamanya Tilak in his own hand-writing in a note-book, while in the Mandalay Jail, where the Gita-Rahasya was written.

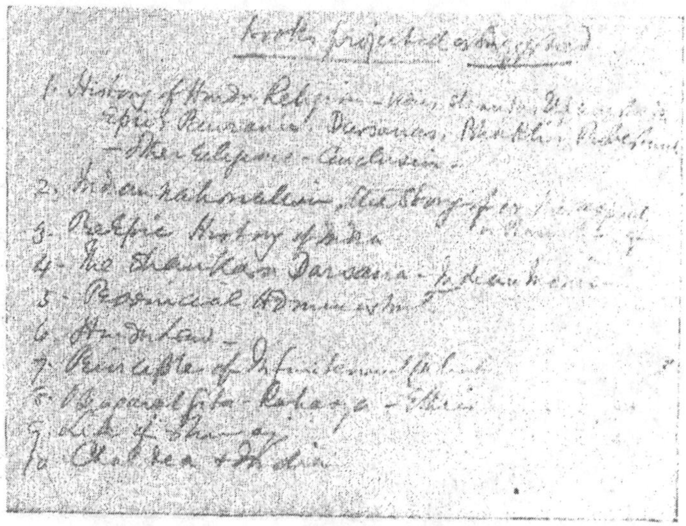

Out of the ten works mentioned in the above list, only the Gita-Rahasya was actually written, which incidentally shows the importance attached by the author to that subject. The other contemplated works have remained in the form of jotted notes.

The Hindu Philosophy of Life, Ethics and Religion.

OM-TAT-SAT

S'RĪMAD BHAGAVADGĪTĀ RAHASYA

OR

KARMA-YOGA-S'ĀSTRA

Including an external examination of the Gītā, the Original Sanskrit stanzas, their English translation, commentaries on the stanzas, and a comparison of Eastern with Western doctrines etc.

BY

BAL GANGADHAR TILAK, B.A., LL.B.,

LAW LECTURER, AND PLEADER, POONA; SOMETIME ADDITIONAL MEMBER OF THE COUNCIL OF H. E. THE GOVERNOR OF BOMBAY FOR MAKING LAWS, AUTHOR OF *Orion or Researches into the Antiquity of the Vedas*, *Arctic Home in the Vedas*, *Vedanga Jyotish* AND *Vedic Chronology*, FOUNDER OF THE '*Kesari*' AND THE *Maratha* NEWSPAPERS ETC. ETC.

TRANSLATED BY

BHALCHANDRA SITARAM SUKTHANKAR, M.A., LL.B.,

Solicitor, High Court, Bombay.

Gibbs Prizeman; Petit Prizeman (Cercle Littéraire); Dakshina Fellow; etc.

Vol. I.

FIRST EDITION

(10,000 Copies)

tasmād asaktaḥ satataṁ kāryaṁ karma samācara ।
asakto hy ācaran karma paramāpnoti pūruṣaḥ ॥ (Gītā, 3. 19).

ŚAKA YEAR 1857; 1936 A. D.

POONA.

Published for Tilak Bros. by :—R. B. Tilak, Lokamanya Tilak Mandir, 568, Narayan Peth, Poona City, (INDIA).

AND

Printed by S. V. Parulekar at the Bombay Vaibhav Press, Servants of India Society's Building, Sandhurst Road, Bombay, (INDIA).

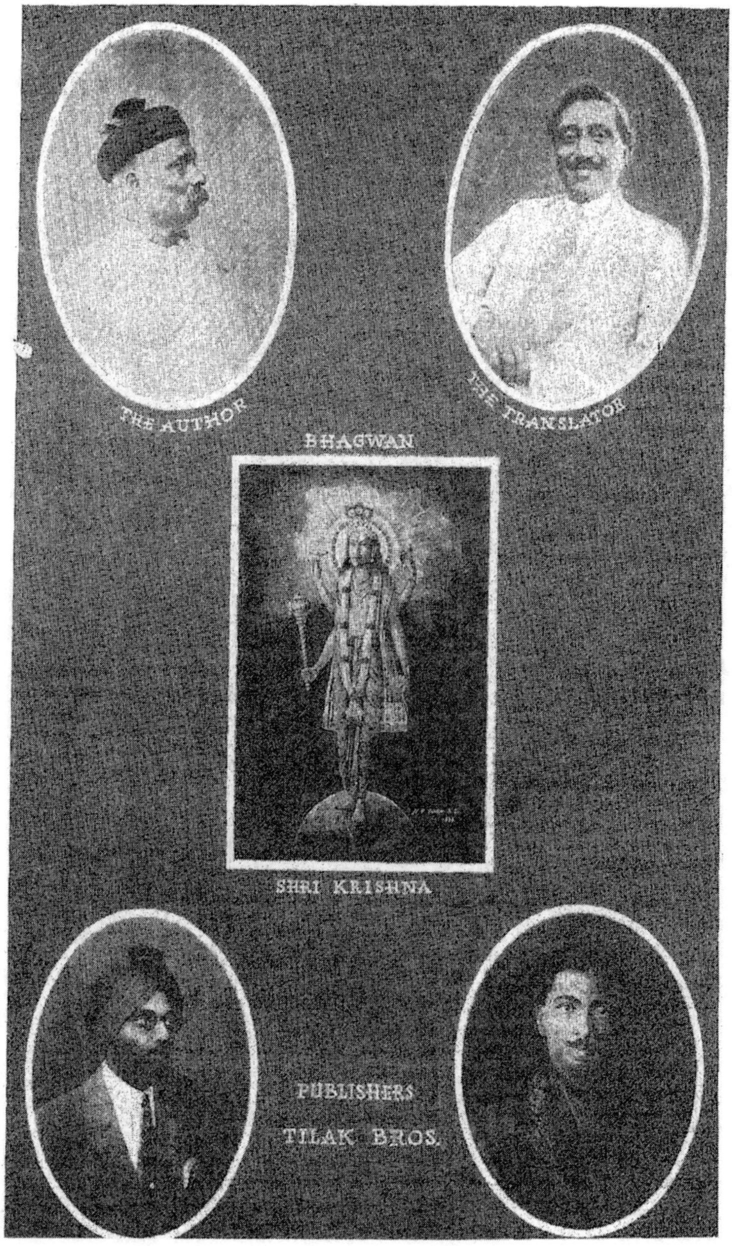
THE AUTHOR
THE TRANSLATOR
BHAGWAN
SHRI KRISHNA
PUBLISHERS
TILAK BROS.

Lokamanya Tilak's Residence in Poona

Various Vernacular Editions

OF THE

GĪTĀ-RAHASYA

MARATHI

First Edition, June 1915.
Second Edition, September 1915.
Third Edition, September 1918.
Fourth Edition, 1923.
First Edition in two parts, 1924–1926.

HINDI

First Edition, 1917.
Second Edition, 1918.
Third Edition, 1919.
Fourth Edition, 1924.
Fifth Edition, 1925.
Sixth Edition, 1928.
First Edition in two parts, 1926.
Seventh Edition, 1933.

GUJARATHI

First Edition, 1917.
Second Edition, 1924.

BENGALI

First Edition, 1924.

KANARESE

First Edition, 1919.

TELUGU

First Edition, 1919.

TAMIL

First Edition, (First Volume only).

Works of the Late LOK. B. G. TILAK.

1. The Arctic Home in the Vedas (In English).

2. The Orion, or Researches into the Antiquity of the Vedas (In English).

3. The Vedic Chronology and the Vedanga Jyotisha (In English).

4. THE GĪTĀ-RAHASYA.

Marathi, in two volumes.
Gujarathi, (cloth bound) in one volume.

Hindi,	,,	ditto.
Kanarese,	,,	ditto.
Bengali,	,,	ditto.

All the above books can be had of :—

Messrs. TILAK Bros.,
Lokamanya Tilak Mandir,
568, Narayan Peth,
Poona City (INDIA).

5. S'rīmad Bhagavadgītā, text, translation and important commentaries, in Hindi, Gujarathi, and Marathi.

6. Three-coloured portraits and pictures :—

Lokamanya Bal Gangadhar Tilak,
size 20″ by 27″, 8 as. each.
size 12″ by 18″, 4 as. each.

The Battle-field of Kuru-Kṣetra
size 20″ by 27″, 8 as. each.
size 12″ by 18″, 4 as. each.

PUBLISHER'S FOREWORD.

Lokamanya Bal Gangadhar Tilak, the author of the present work, had intended to publish an English translation of his work in order to give it an international circulation, which it would necessarily not have in its Marathi form as originally written out by him. It was his great ambition that the interpretation put by him on the doctrine preached by the Bhagavadgitā, should come before the eyes of learned philosophers, scholars, and *alumni*, all the world over, so that he could have the benefit of their views on the line of argument and interpretation adopted by him; and he had in his life-time made an attempt to get the work put into the English language. He was, however, unable to see this matter through on account of his numerous activities, and ultimately he suddenly fell ill and died, without seeing the realisation of his desire and ambition.

After his demise, we his two sons, as the publishers of his works, tried to carry out this his wish, but were unable to give the matter our whole-hearted attention, owing to being involved in heavy litigation arising out of the chaos resulting from the unfair advantage which certain interested parties took of his death. We spent a large sum of money in trying to get the work translated into English, but in spite of this expense, the matter remained incomplete; and in the meantime one of us, viz., my brother, Shridhar died, leaving this task unfinished. I am, therefore, now glad to announce that I have at last been able to successfully carry out the most cherished wish of my father, as also of my brother, and am publishing this volume on 1st August 1935, being the fifteenth anniversary of my father's death; and I shall feel that all the trouble which has been taken by me in bringing out this publication will be more than amply rewarded, if it gets into international circulation, and if I am thus enabled to fulfil the wishes of my late father, and brother; for, I shall then feel that I am free from my obligations to the deceased. I am writing this foreword on the seventh anniversary of my brother's death and I am dedicating this publication to his memory.

I am grateful to the various photographers, photographs taken by whom are reproduced in this publication; as also to the eminent writers and the publishers of works containing references to the Gītā, the Gītā-Rahasya, and to my late father, extracts from whose publications or writings, have been included in this publication.

My thanks are also due to a friend whose help was greatly responsible for this publication seeing the light of the day, and especially to Mr. A. V. Patvardhan, a member of the Servants of India Society, and the Manager of the Arya-Bhushan Press, Poona, who, out of regard for the late Lokamanya Tilak, undertook the printing of this work at the Bombay Vaibhava Press, without asking for any advance payment, and has agreed to receive all charges payable to the Press out of the sale proceeds of the book. In fact, but for this most generous accommodation, it would have been difficult for me to undertake and carry out such an expensive and ambitious project, at least in my present circumstances. I must also here acknowledge my gratitude to the Translator Mr. B. S. Sukthankar, who also has gladly consented to receive the amount payable to him for the translation, out of the sale proceeds of the book, in due course.

It is true that the price of the publication has been put a little high for moderate purses, as also that I have had to publish the book in two volumes, so as to partly meet the costs of the Press out of the sale proceeds of the first volume; but this has been done as there was no alternative course left to me.

Nevertheless, I have not made this division arbitrarily, as will appear from what follows. The book consists of two unequal parts, as written, the first part being the Philosophical Exposition, consisting of fifteen chapters and Appendices, and going over the first 588 pages of the original text, and the second consisting of the Gītā, with its translation, and the Commentary on such translation, stanza by stanza, which goes over about 360 pages. In publishing the book in two volumes I have included the first thirteen chapters of the Philosophical Exposition in the first volume, and chapters 14 and 15 of the

PUBLISHER'S DEDICATION

"Nay, the doctrine of the Gita has come into existence only in order to explain why a WISE MAN *must perform a particular act, notwithstanding that he sees before his eyes the terrible consequences of it ; and this is indeed the most important feature of the Gita." (Gita-Rahasya, chapter XI. page 417.)*

THIS PUBLICATION

IS

AFFECTIONATELY DEDICATED

TO

THE MEMORY OF MY LATE BROTHER

SHRIDHAR

one of the publishers of the late Lok. B. G. Tilak's Works,

WHOSE LAST WORDS

WERE

• • • • •

"I hope to be reborn in some poor, unknown peasant's hut to complete the mission of my life."

• • • • •

R. B. TILAK

[*P. T. O.*

Gaikwar Wada;
Poona City.
25th May 1928.

Sir,

Disappointed and tired of life, I am today committing suicide. I have always felt that I was born to serve my country, my society and my language. My parents never dreamt it otherwise. I was not born to be the helpless sport of lawyers and law-courts. But unfortunately, after the death of my father, the late Lokmanya B. G. Tilak, a gang of rascals, taking advantage of our ignorance and inexperience of the ways of the world cheated us and deprived us of the major portion of our family property, (viz. Press Papers Securities Bank-Cash &c). Almost till the end of the year 1923 my actions and writings were mostly guided by them, and whatever I signed published or executed during that period (1920 to 1923) was at their instance and under their influence. Our ignorance of Law and full confidence in them, was coolly exploited by them to carry out their own selfish and ambitious schemes detrimental to our own interests. All these complicated circumstances have at last driven matters to the Courts of Law. But to me, who am rather senti-mental, protracted litigation is virtually blood-curdling. The Court atmosphere is too stifling to me. I love freedom and my soul yearns for it. Suicide sets it free!

S. B. Tilak

2

I hope to be reborn in some poor, unknown peasant's hut to complete the mission of my life.

I have one more thing to communicate. Herewith annexed please find my letter of authority to my brother Mr. K. B. Tilak. Please produce this letter with its annexure before the Coroners Court, get it registered under the new Photo-system, preserve the original on Government Record and hand over certified copies of both to my said brother under your own seal and signature. I am confident the unseen hand of Providence will avenge the wrongs done to us, Tilak Brothers, sooner or later.

I have done. With due apologies for troubling your honour,

I remain,
Yours &c
P. G. Tilak

To

The District Magistrate,
Poona.

(one Enclosure)

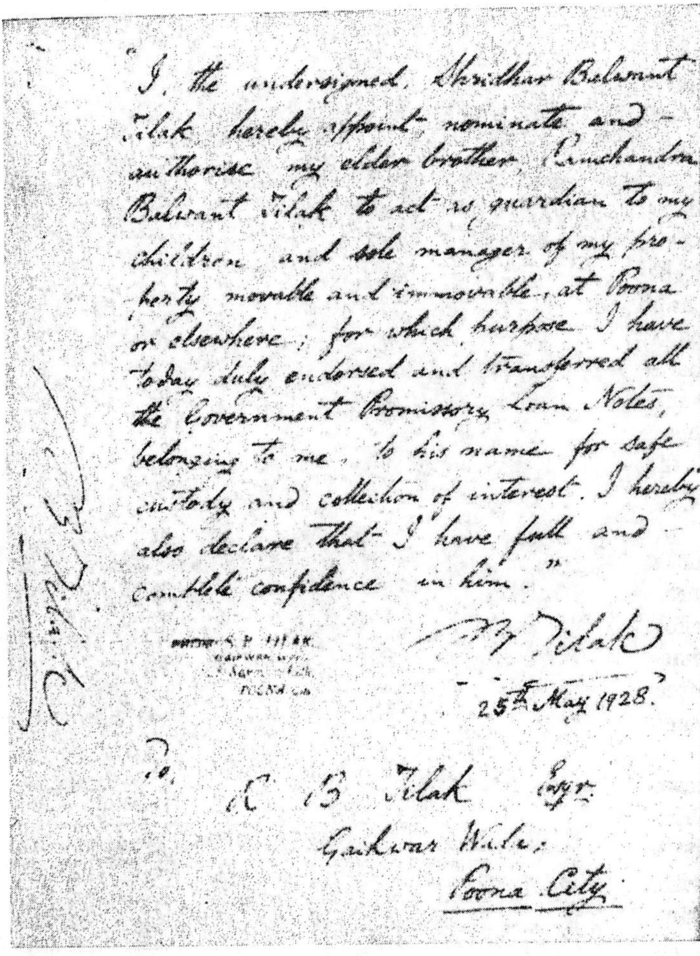

"I, the undersigned, Shridhar Balwant Tilak hereby appoint, nominate and authorise my elder brother, Ramchandra Balwant Tilak to act as guardian to my children and sole manager of my property movable and immovable, at Poona or elsewhere; for which purpose I have today duly endorsed and transferred all the Government Promissory Loan Notes, belonging to me, to his name for safe custody and collection of interest. I hereby also declare that I have full and complete confidence in him."

S. B. Tilak

25th May 1928.

To,

R. B. Tilak Esqr.

Gaikwar Wada;

Poona City.

Philosophical Exposition, and the Appendices together with the indices in the second volume, for the following reasons :—

(i) With the thirteenth chapter, the Exposition proper, comes to an end; the three remaining chapters, though an integral part of the Exposition, respectively contain only (*a*) an explanation about the continuity of the chapters of the Gītā, (*b*) the Summing up, or résumé, and (*c*) the Appendices; so that strictly speaking, the subject-matter does not suffer by my division (see the last words of the Author at the end of the thirteenth chapter, on p. 618).

(ii) In writing the book itself, the late Lokamanya wrote chapters I to VIII in one book, chapters IX to XIII, in the second book; chapters XIV and XV, and the External Examination (Appendices), and the translation of the first three Adhyāyas (chapters) of the Gītā in the third book; and the translation of the Adhyāyas four to eighteen of the Gītā and his Preface in the fourth book (see, Information regarding the original manuscript of the Gītā-Rahasya printed at p. xxviii following); thus, the first Volume as now published contains a translation of the subject-matter included in the first two books written by the Author.

(iii) The Volumes, as now published are more or less of the same size and price, so that from the point of view of the purchaser, it is easier for him to pay the purchase price of the whole book in two, more or less equal instalments, at different times. If the first Volume had been made to include the fifteen chapters and the Appendices, its price would have been much higher than as now fixed.

I have, however, implicit trust in the inherent spiritual power of this wonderful and well-known work of a recognised Oriental Scholar and Researcher, which enabled the first ten thousand copies of the Marathi publication to be sold off within a few months of its publication, and enabled it to go into several editions in Marathi, and to be translated into half a dozen Indian vernaculars; and I am sure that the same success will be met with by the present English translation.

Not only has the translator, Mr. B. S. Sukthankar, helped me by not putting any financial pressure on me, but he has put the translation through within a comparatively short space of time after it had been entrusted to him, by dint of untiring energy, in spare time, in spite of the numerous other taxes on his time and labour, apart from his professional work as an Attorney-at-Law, which ties him down most part of the day to his office; and he has put me under further obligations by personally carefully examining all the proofs. He has also to a certain extent given me financial accommodation for meeting such payments as had to be met in advance; and I may without exaggeration say that but for his sympathy, accommodation, enthusiasm, and help, it would have been difficult for me to bring out the present edition. A grateful mention must also be made of Dr. V. S. Sukthankar, of the Bhandarkar Oriental Research Institute, Poona, for the valuable help given by him in looking into the transliterated Sanskrit portions of the work, and making such valuable suggestions regarding the publication, as a man of his qualifications alone could make on account of his Continental experience of publications of similar works.

Last, but not least, my sincere thanks are due to Mr. B. M. Sidhaye, the Manager of the Bombay Vaibhav Press, who has ungrudgingly spared no pains to make the technical and difficult printing of this book as faultless and satisfactory as possible; and but for whose obliging help it would not have been possible to put this work through the press during that short space of time in which it has been actually printed.

I feel that in quoting this stanza, with which I am ending this Foreword, I am only voicing sentiments similar to those expressed by my revered father in the concluding remarks of his Preface to the original Marathi work, in parting with his precious thoughts and placing them into the hands of his readers :—

> " Go little book from this my solitude ;
> " I cast thee on the water, go thy ways ;
> " And if, as I believe, thy tone be good,
> " The world will find thee, after many days ".
>
> (Southey)

Bombay,
25th May 1935.

R. B. TILAK,
Publisher.

PROMINENT PERSONALITIES ON THE GĪTĀ, MR. TILAK, AND THE 'GĪTĀ-RAHASYA'.

1. SWAMI VIVEKANAND.

The Gita is a bouquet composed of the beautiful flowers of spiritual truths collected from the Upanishads.

2. Dr. ANNIE BESANT.

Among the priceless teachings that may be found in the great Hindu poem of the *Mahabharata*, there is none so rare and precious as this, "The Lord's Song". Since it fell from the divine lips of Shri Krishna on the field of battle, and stilled the surging emotions of his disciple and friend, how many troubled hearts has it quieted and strengthened, how many weary souls has it led to Him! It is meant to lift the aspirant from the lower levels of renunciation, where objects are renounced, to the loftier heights, where desires are dead, and where the Yogi dwells in calm and ceaseless contemplation while his body and mind are actively employed in discharging the duties that fall to his lot in life. That the spiritual man need not be a recluse, that union with the divine Life may be achieved and maintained in the midst of worldly affairs, that the obstacles to that union lie, not outside us, but within us, such is the central lesson of the BHAGAVAD-GITA.

It is a scripture of Yoga: now Yoga is literally Union; and it means harmony with the Divine Law, the becoming one with the Divine Life, by the subdual of all outward-going energies. To reach this, balance must be gained, as also equilibrium, so that self, joined to the Self, shall not be affected by pleasure or pain, desire or aversion, or any of the "pairs of opposites", between which untrained selves swing backwards and forwards. Moderation is, therefore, the key-note of the Gita and the harmonising of all the constituents of man, till they vibrate in perfect attunement with the One, the Supreme Self. This is the aim the disciple is to set before him. He must learn not to be attracted by the attractive, nor repelled by the repellent, but must see both as manifestations of the one

Lord, so that they may be lessons for his guidance, not fetters for his bondage. In the midst of turmoil, he must rest in the Lord of Peace, discharging every duty to the fullest, not because he seeks the results of his actions, but because it is his duty to perform them. His heart is an altar; love to his Lord, the flame burning upon it; all his acts, physical and mental, are sacrifices offered on the altar, and once offered, he has with them no further concern.

As though to make the lesson more impressive, it was given on a field of battle. Arjuna, the warrior-prince, was to vindicate his brother's title, to destroy a usurper who was oppressing the land; it was his duty as prince, as warrior, to fight for the deliverance of his nation and to restore order and peace. To make the contest more bitter, loved comrades and friends stood on both sides, wringing his heart with personal anguish, and making the conflict of duties as well as physical strife. Could he slay those to whom he owed love and duty, and trample on ties of kindred? To break family ties was a sin; to leave the people in cruel bondage was a sin; where was the right way? Justice must be done, else law would be disregarded; but how slay without sin? The answer is the *burden* of the book: Have no personal interest in the event; carry out the duty imposed by the position in life, realise that Ishvara, at once Lord and Law, is the doer, working out the mighty evolution that ends in bliss and peace; be identified with Him by devotion, and then perform duty as duty, fighting without passion or desire, without anger or hatred; thus Activity forges no bonds, Yoga is accomplished, and the Soul is free.

Such is the obvious teaching of this sacred book. But as all the acts of an Avatara are symbolical, we may pass from the outer to the inner planes, and see in the fight of Kurukshetra the battle-field of the Soul, and in the sons of Dhritarashtra, enemies it meets in its progress; Arjuna becomes the type of the struggling Soul of the disciple, and Shri Krishna is the Logos of the Soul. Thus, the teaching of the ancient battle-field gives guidance in all later days, and trains the aspiring soul in treading the steep and thorny path that leads to peace.

LOKAMANYA TILAK MANDIR

The author's residence, as now altered, showing the Memorial raised by his sons.

LOK. BAL GANGADHAR TILAK
while in England on the Indian
Home Rule Deputation.

To all such souls in the East and West come these divine lessons; for the path is one, though it has many names, and all Souls seek the same goal, though they may not realise their unity.

(From Mrs. Besant's Pocket Gita published by G. A. Natesan & Co. Madras.)

3. Pt. MADAN MOHAN MALAVIYA

I believe that in the whole history of mankind, the greatest outstanding personality having the deepest and the most profound knowledge and possessing super-human powers is Shri Krishna. I further believe that in all the living languages of the world, there is no book so full of truth-knowledge, and yet so handy as the *Bhagavadgita.*

This wonderful book of eighteen small chapters contains the essence of the Vedas and the Upanishads, and is a sure guide of the way to perfect happiness, here as well as hereafter. It preaches the three-fold way of Knowledge, Action, and Devotion, leading to the highest good of mankind. It brings to men the highest knowledge, the purest love and the most luminous action. It teaches self-control, the threefold austerity, non-violence, truth, compassion, obedience to the call of duty for the sake of duty, and putting up a fight against unrighteousness *(Adharma).*

Full of knowledge and truth and moral teaching, it has the power to raise men from the lowest depths of ignorance and suffering to the highest glories of divine beings. To my knowledge, there is no book in the whole range of the world's literature so high above all as the *Bhagavadgita,* which is a treasure-house of *Dharma,* not only for Hindus but for all mankind. Several scholars of different countries have by study of this book acquired a pure and perfect knowledge of the Supreme Being Who is responsible for the creation, preservation and destruction of the universe, and have gained a stainless, desireless, supreme devotion to His feet. Those men and women are very fortunate who have got this little lamp of light full of an inexhaustible quantity of the oil of love, showing the way out of the darkness and ignorance of the world. It is incumbent on such people to use it for all mankind groping in the darkness.

4. SIR VALENTINE CHIROL.

There is no more beautiful book in the sacred literature of the Hindus ; there is none in which the more enlightened find greater spiritual comfort.

It was a Hindu gentleman and a Brahmin who told me that if I wanted to study the psychology of the Indian unrest, I should begin by studying Tilak's career. "Tilak's onslaught in Poona upon Ranade, his alliance with the bigots of orthodoxy, his appeals to popular superstition in the new Ganapati celebrations, to racial fanaticism in the 'Anti-Cow-Killing movement', to Mahratta sentiment in the cult which he introduced of Shivaji, his active propaganda amongst schoolboys and students, his gymnastic societies, his preaching in favour of physical training, and last but not least his control of the Press, and the note of personal violence which he imparted to newspaper polemics, represent the progressive stages of a highly-organised campaign which has served as a model to the apostles of unrest all over India". This was a valuable piece of advice, for, if any one can claim to be truly the father of Indian unrest, it is Bal Gangadhar Tilak.

(From *Indian Unrest* by Sir Valentine Chirol.)

5. HON'BLE G. K. GOKHALE.

Tilak's natural endowments are first-rate. He has used them for the service of the country and although I did not approve of his methods, I never questioned his motives. There is no man who has suffered so much for the country, who has had in his life to contend against powerful opposition so much as Tilak ; and there is no man who has shown grit, patience and courage so rare, that several times he lost his fortune and by his indomitable will gathered it together again.

(From Dnyan-Prakash dated 2-2-1915).

6. MAHATMA M. K. GANDHI.

"Early in my childhood I had felt the need of a scripture that would serve me as an unfailing guide through the trials and temptations of life. The Vedas could not supply that need, if only because to learn them would require fifteen to sixteen years of hard study at a place like Kashi, for which

Silver articles & Caskets containing Public addresses & purses presented to the author in public meetings & processions throughout India (*Copyright*)

THREE GENERATIONS OF THE AUTHOR

A statue of the author erected by the Poona (City) Municipality in front of the Reay Market, Poona

I was not ready then. But the Gita, I had read somewhere, gave within the compass of its 700 verses the quintessence of all the Shastras and the Upanishads. That decided me. I learnt Sanskrit to enable me to read the Gita. To-day the Gita is not only my Bible or my Koran; it is more than that—it is my mother. I lost my earthly mother who gave me birth long ago; but this eternal mother has completely filled her place by my side ever since. She has never changed, she has never failed me. When I am in difficulty or distress, I seek refuge in her bosom.

It is sometimes alleged against the Gita that it is too difficult a work for the man in the street. The criticism, I venture to submit, is ill-founded. If you find all the eighteen chapters too difficult to negotiate, make a careful study of the first three chapters only. They will give you in a nutshell what is propounded in greater detail and from different angles in the remaining fifteen chapters.

Even these three chapters can be further epitomised in a few verses that can be selected from these chapters. Add to this the fact that at three distinct places, the Gita goes even further and exhorts us to leave alone all 'isms' and take refuge in the Lord alone, and it will be seen how baseless is the charge that the message of the Gita is too subtle or complicated for lay minds to understand.

The Gita is the universal mother. She turns away nobody. Her door is wide open to any one who knocks. A true votary of the Gita does not know what disappointment is. He ever dwells in perennial joy and peace that passeth understanding. But that peace and joy come not to the sceptic or to him who is proud of his intellect or learning. It is reserved only for the humble in spirit who brings to her worship a fullness of faith and an undivided singleness of mind. There never was a man who worshipped her in that spirit and went back disappointed.

The Gita inculcates the duty of perseverance in the face of seeming failure. It teaches us that we have a right to actions only but not to the fruit thereof, and that success and failure are one and the same thing at bottom. It calls upon us to dedicate ourselves, body, mind and soul, to pure duty, and not to become mental voluptuaries at the mercy of all chance desires and undisciplined impulses. As a "Satyagrahi", I can declare that the Gita is ever presenting me with fresh lessons. If somebody tells me that this is my delusion, my reply to him would be that I shall hug this delusion as my richest treasure.

I would advise every one to begin the day with an early morning recitation of the Gita. Take up the study of the Gita not in a carping or critical spirit, but in a devout and reverent spirit. Thus approached, she will grant your every wish. Once you have tasted of its sweet nectar, your attachment to it will grow from day to day. The recitation of the Gita verses will support you in your trials and console you in your distress, even in the darkness of solitary confinement. And, if with these verses on your lips you receive the final summons and deliver up your spirit, you will attain 'Brahma-Nirvana,' the Final Liberation.

The Gita enabled the late Lokamanya Tilak out of his encyclopædic learning and study, to produce a monumental commentary. For him it was a store-house of profound truths to exercise his intellect upon. I believe his commentary on the Gita will be a more lasting monument to his memory. It will survive even the successful termination of the struggle for Swarajya. Even then his memory will remain as fresh as ever on account of his spotless purity of life and his great commentary on the Gita. No one in his life time, nor even now, could claim deeper and vaster knowledge of the Shastras than he possessed. His masterwork commentary on the Gita is unsurpassed and will remain so for a long time to come. Nobody has yet carried on more elaborate research in the questions arising from the Gita and the Vedas."

Paying a glowing tribute to the memory of the Late Lokmanya Tilak, Gandhiji said "his vast learning, his immense sacrifices and his life-long service have won for him a unique place in the hearts of the people".

(From Speeches of Mahatma Gandhi at Benares and at Cawnpore).

7. BABU AUROBINDO GHOSE.

What is the message of the Gita and what its working value, its spiritual utility to the human mind of the present day, after the long ages that have elapsed since it was written and the great subsequent transformations of thought and experience? The human mind moves always forward, alters its view-point and enlarges its thought-substance, and the effect of these changes is to render past systems of thinking obsolete or, when they are preserved, to extend, to modify and subtly or visibly to alter their value. The vitality of an ancient doctrine consists in the extent to which it naturally lends itself to such a treatment; for that means that whatever may have been the limitations or the obsolescences of the form of its thought, the truth of substance, the truth of living vision and experience on which its system was built, is still sound and retains a permanent validity and significance. The Gita is a book that has worn extraordinarily well, and it is almost as fresh and still in its real substance quite as new, because always renewable in experience, as when it first appeared in or was written into the frame of the 'Mahabharata'. It is still received in India as one of the great bodies of doctrine that most authoritatively govern religious thinking; and its teaching is acknowledged as of the highest value if not wholly accepted by almost all shades of religious belief and opinion. Its influence is not merely philosophic or academic but immediate and living, an influence both for thought and action, and its ideas are actually at work as a powerful shaping factor in the revival and renewal of a nation and a culture. It has even been said recently by a great voice that all we need of spiritual truth for the spiritual life is to be found in the Gita. It would be to encourage the superstition of the book to take too literally that utterance. The truth of the spirit is infinite and cannot be circumscribed in that manner. Still it may be said that most of the main clues are there and that after all the later developments of spiritual experience and discovery, we can still return to it for a large inspiration and guidance. Outside India too it is universally acknowledged as one of the world's great scriptures, although in Europe its thought is better understood than its secret of spiritual practice.

Neither Mr. Tilak nor his works really require any presentation of foreword.

His Orion and his Arctic Home have acquired at once a world-wide recognition and left as strong a mark as can at all be imprinted on the ever-shifting sands of oriental research. His work on the Gita, no mere commentary, but an original criticism and presentation of ethical truths, is a monumental work, THE FIRST PROSE WRITING OF THE FRONT RANK IN WEIGHT AND IMPORTANCE IN THE MARATHI LANGUAGE, AND LIKELY TO BECOME A CLASSIC. This one book sufficiently proves that had he devoted his energies in this direction, he might easily have filled a large place in the history of Marathi literature and in the history of ethical thought, so subtle and comprehensive in its thinking, so great the perfection and satisfying force of its style. But it was psychologically impossible for Mr. Tilak to devote his energies in any great degree to another action than the one life-mission for which the Master of his works had chosen him. His powerful literary gift has been given up to a journalistic work, ephemeral as even the best journalistic work must be, but consistently brilliant, vigorous, politically educative through decades, to an extent seldom matched and certainly never surpassed. His scholastic labour has been done almost by way of recreation. Nor can anything be more significant than the fact that the works which have brought him a fame other than that of the politician and patriot, were done in periods of compulsory cessation from his life work,—planned and partly, if not wholly, executed during the imprisonments which could alone enforce leisure upon this unresting worker for his country. Even these by-products of his genius have some reference to the one passion of his life, the renewal, if not the surpassing, of the past greatness of the nation by the greatness of its future. His Vedic researches seek to fix its pre-historic point of departure; the Gita-rahasya takes the scripture which is perhaps the strongest and most comprehensive production of Indian spirituality and justifies to that spirituality by its own authoritative ancient message the sense of the importance of life, of action, of human existence, of man's labour for mankind which is indispensable to the idealism of the modern spirit.

Mr. Tilak himself, his career, his place in Indian politics are also a self-evident proposition, a hard fact baffling and dismaying in the last degree to those to whom his name has been anathema, and his increasing pre-eminence figured as a portent of evil. Yet is Mr. Tilak a man of various and no ordinary gifts, and in several lines of life he might have achieved present distinction or a pre-eminent and enduring fame. Though he has never practised, he has a close knowledge of law and an acute legal mind which, had he cared in the least degree for wealth and worldy position, would have brought him to the front at the bar. He is a great Sanskrit scholar, a powerful writer and a strong, subtle and lucid thinker. He might have filled a large place in the field of contemporary Asiatic scholarship. He is the very type and incarnation of the Maratha character, the Maratha qualities, the Maratha spirit, but with the unified solidity in the character, the touch of genius in the qualities, the vital force in the spirit which make a great personality readily the representative man of his people. The Maratha race, as their soil and their history have made them, are a rugged, strong and sturdy people; democratic in their every fibre; keenly intelligent and practical to the very marrow; following in ideas, even in poetry, philosophy and religion, the drive towards life and action; capable of great fervour, feeling and enthusiasm, like all Indian people, but not emotional idealists; having in their thought and speech, always a turn for strength, sense, accuracy, lucidity and vigour; in learning and scholarship, patient, industrious, careful, thorough and penetrating; in life, simple, hardy and frugal; in their temperament, courageous, pugnacious, full of spirit, yet with a tact in dealing with hard facts and circumventing obstacles; shrewd yet aggressive diplomatists, born politicians, born fighters. All this Mr. Tilak is with a singular and eminent completeness, and all on a large scale, adding to it all a lucid simplicity and genius, a secret intensity, and inner strength of will, a single-mindedness in aim of quite extraordinary force, which remind one of the brightness, sharpness and perfect temper of a fine sword hidden in a sober scabbard.

The indomitable will and the unwavering devotion have been the whole meaning of Mr. Tilak's life; they are the reason of his immense hold on the people. For he does not owe his pre-eminent position to wealth and great social position, professional success, recognition by Government, a power of fervid oratory or of fluent and telling speech; for he had none of these things to help him. He owes it to himself alone and to the thing his life has meant and because he has meant it with his whole mind and his whole soul. He has kept back nothing for himself or for other aims, but has given all himself to his country. As he emerged on the political field, his people saw more and more clearly in him their representative man, themselves in large, the genius of their type. They felt him to be of one spirit and make, with the great men who had made their past history, almost believed him to be a reincarnation of one of them returned to carry out his old work in a new form and under new conditions. They beheld in him the spirit of Maharashtra once again embodied in a great individual. He occupies a position in his province which has no parallel in the rest of India.

The landmarks of Mr. Tilak's life are landmarks also in the history of his province and his country.

His first great step associated him in a pioneer work whose motive was to educate the people for a new life under the new conditions, on the one side, a purely educational movement of which the fruit was the Ferguson College, fitly founding the reawakening of the country by an effort of which co-operation in self-sacrifice was the moving spirit, on the other, the initiation of the Kesari newspaper, which figured increasingly as the characteristic and powerful expression of the political mind of Maharashtra. Mr. Tilak's career has counted three periods each of which had an imprisonment for its culminating point. His first imprisonment in the Kolhapur case belongs to this first stage of self-development and development of the Maratha country for new ideas and activities and for the national future.

The second period brought in a wider conception and a profounder effort. For now it was to reawaken not only the political mind but the soul of the people by linking its future to its past; it worked by a more strenuous and popular propaganda which reached its height in the organisation of the Shivaji and the Ganapati festivals. His separation from the Social reform leader, Agarkar, had opened the way for the peculiar role which he has played as a trusted and accredited leader of conservative and religious India in the paths of democratic politics. It was this position which enabled him to effect the union of the new political spirit with the tradition and sentiment of the historic past and of both with the ineradicable religious temperament of the people of which these festivals were the symbol. The congress movement was for a long time purely occidental in its mind, character and methods, confined to the English-educated few, founded on the political rights and interests of the people read in the light of English history and European ideals, but with no roots either in the past of the country or in the inner spirit of the nation. Mr. Tilak was the first political leader to break through the routine of its somewhat academical methods, to bridge the gulf between the present and the past, and to restore continuity to the political life of the nation. He developed a language and a spirit and he used methods which indianised the movement and brought into it the masses. To his work of this period we owe that really living, strong and readily organised movement in Maharashtra which has shown its energy and sincerity in more than one crisis and struggle. This divination of the mind and spirit of his people and its needs and this power to seize on the right way to call it forth prove strikingly the political genius of Mr. Tilak; they made him the one man predestined to lead them in this trying and difficult period when all has to be discovered and all has to be reconstructed. What was done then by Mr. Tilak in Maharashtra has been initiated for all India by the Swadeshi movement. To bring in the mass of the people, to found the greatness of the future on the greatness of the past, to infuse Indian politics with Indian religious fervour and spirituality, are the indispensable conditions for a great and powerful political awakening in India. Others, writers, thinkers, spiritual leaders, had seen this truth. Mr. Tilak was the first to bring it into the actual field of practical politics. The second period of his labour for this country culminated in a longer and harsher imprisonment which was as it were the second seal of the divine hand upon his work; for there can be no diviner seal than suffering for a cause.

A third period, that the Swadeshi movement, brought Mr. Tilak forward prominently as an All-India leader: it gave him at last the wider field, the greater driving power, the larger leverage he needed to bring his life-work rapidly to a head, and not only in Maharashtra but throughout the country. From the inception of the Boycott Movement to the Surat catastrophe and his last and longest imprisonment. which was its equal, the name and work of Mr. Tilak are a part of Indian history.

These three imprisonments, each showing more clearly the moral stuff and quality of the man under the test and glare of suffering, have been the three seals of his career. The first found him one of a small knot of pioneer workers; it marked him out to be the strong and inflexible leader of a strong and sturdy people. The second found him already the inspiring power of a great awakening of the Maratha spirit; it left him an uncrowned king in the Deccan and gave him that high reputation throughout India, which was the foundation-stone of his commanding influence. The last found him the leader of an All-India party, the foremost exponent and head of a thorough-going Nationalism; it sent him back to be one of the two or three foremost men of India adored and followed by the whole nation. No prominent man in India has suffered more for his country; none has taken his sacrifices and sufferings more quietly and as a matter of course.

All the Indian provinces and communities have spoken with one voice, Mr. Tilak's principles of work have been accepted; the ideas which he had so much troubled to enforce have become the commonplaces and truisms of our political thought. The only question that remains is the rapidity of a new inevitable evolution. That is the hope for which Mr. Tilak still stands, a leader of all India.

BIRTH 23 JULY 1856. DEATH 1 AUG. 1920.

Bal Gangadhar Tilak

Mr. Tilak's name stands already for history as a Nation-builder, one of the half-dozen greatest political personalities, memorable figures, representative men of the nation in this most critical period of India's destinies, a name to be remembered gratefully so long as the country has pride in its past and hope for its future.

MR. TILAK ON THE GĪTĀ-RAHASYA.

Let me begin by telling you what induced me to take up the study of *Bhagvad Gita*. When I was quite a boy, I was often told by my elders that strictly religious and really philosophic life was incompatible with the hum-drum life of every day. If one was ambitious enough to try to attain Moksha, the highest goal a person could attain, then he must divest himself of all earthly desires and renounce this world. One could not serve two masters, the world and God. I understood this to mean that if one would lead a life which was the life worth living, according to the religion in which I was born, then the sooner the world was given up the better. This set me thinking. The question that I formulated for myself to be solved was: Does my religion want me to give up this world and renounce it before I attempt to, or in order to be able to, attain the perfection of manhood? In my boyhood I was also told that *Bhagvada Gita* was universally acknowledged to be a book containing all the principles and philosophy of the Hindu Religion, and I thought if this be so I should find an answer in this book to my query; and thus began my study of the *Bhagvad Gita*. I approached the book with a mind prepossessed by no previous ideas about any philosophy, and had no theory of my own for which I sought any support in the *Gita*. A person whose mind is prepossessed by certain ideas, reads the book with a prejudiced mind; for instance, when a Christian reads it, he does not want to know what the *Gita* says but wants to find out if there are any principles in the *Gita* which he has already met with in the Bible, and if so the conclusion he rushes to is that the *Gita* was copied from the Bible. I have dealt with this topic in my book *Gita Rahasya* and I need hardly say much about it here, but what I want to emphasise is this, that when you want to read and understand a book, especially a great work like the *Gita*—you must approach it with an unprejudiced and unprepossessed mind. To do this, I know, is one of the most difficult things. Those who profess to do it may have a lurking thought or prejudice in their minds which vitiates the reading of the book to some extent. However I am describing to you the frame of mind one must get into if one wants to get at the truth; and however difficult it be, it has to be done. The next thing one has to do is to take into consideration the time and the circumstances in which the book was written and the purpose for which the book was written. In short, the book must not be read devoid of its context. This is especially true about a book like *Bhagvad Gita.* Various commentators have put as many interpretations on the book, and surely the writer or composer could not have written or composed the book for so many interpretations being put on it. He must have put one meaning and one purpose running through the book, and that I have tried to find out. I believe I have succeeded in it, because having no theory of mine for which I sought any support from the book so universally respected, I had no reason to twist the text to suit my theory. There has not been a commentator of the *Gita* who did not advocate a pet theory of his own and has not tried to support the same by showing that the *Bhagvad Gita* lent him support. The conclusion I have come to is that the *Gita* advocates the performance of action in this world even after the actor has achieved the highest union with the Supreme Deity by Jnana (knowledge) or Bhakti (Devotion). This action must be done to keep the world going by the right path of evolution which the Creator has destined the world to follow. In order that the action may not bind the actor, it must be done with the aim of helping His purpose, and without any Attachment to the coming result. This I hold is a lesson of the *Gita.* Jnana-Yoga there is, yes. Bhakti-Yoga there is, yes. Who says not? But they are both subservient to the Karma-Yoga preached in the *Gita.* If the *Gita* was preached to desponding Arjuna to make him ready for the fight—for the Action—how can it be said that the ultimate lesson of the great book is Bhakti or Jnana alone? In fact, there is a blending of all these Yogas in the *Gita*; and as the air is not Oxygen or Hydrogen, or any other gas alone, but a composition of all these in a certain proportion, so in the *Gita* all these Yogas are blended into one.

I differ from almost all the commentators when I say that the *Gita* enjoins Action even after the perfection in Jnana and

Bhakti is attained and the Deity is reached through these mediums. Now, there is a fundamental unity underlying the Logos (Ishvara), man, and world. The world is in existence because the Logos has willed it so. It is His Will that holds it together. Man strives to gain union with God; and when this union is achieved, the individual will merges in the mighty Universal Will. When this is achieved, will the individual say: "I shall do no Action, and I shall not help the world"—the world which is, because the Will with Which he has sought union has willed it to be so? It does not stand to reason. It is not I who say so: the *Gita* says so. Shri Krishna himself says that there is nothing in all the three worlds that He need acquire, and *still* He acts. He acts because if He did not, the world will be ruined. If man seeks unity with the Deity, he must necessarily seek unity with the interests of the world also, and work for it. If he does not, then the unity is not perfect, because there is union between two elements out of the three (man and Deity) and the third (the world) is left out. I have thus solved the question for myself and I hold that serving the world, and thus serving His Will, is the surest way of Salvation; and this way can be followed by remaining *in* the world and not going away from it.

(A summary of the speech of Mr. Tilak, re: *Gita Rahasya*).

The Karma-Yoga which I preach is not a new theory; neither was the discovery of the Law of Karma made as recently as to-day. The knowledge of the Law is so ancient that not even Shri Krishna was the great Teacher who first propounded it. It must be remembered that Karma-Yoga has been our sacred heritage from times immemorial when we Indians were seated on the high pedestal of wealth and lore. Karma-Yoga or to put it in another way, the law of duty, is the combination of all that is best in spiritual science, in actual action and in an unselfish meditative life. Compliance with this universal law leads to the realisation of the most cherished ideas of man. Such was the doctrine taught by our forefathers, who never intended that the goal of life should be meditation alone. No one can expect Providence to protect one who sits with folded arms and throws his burden on others. God does not help the indolent. You must be doing all that you can to lift yourself up, and then only may you rely on the Almighty to help you. You should not, however, presume that you have to toil that you yourself might reap the fruit of your labour. That cannot always be the case. Let us then try our utmost and leave the generations to come to enjoy that fruit. Remember, it is not you who had planted the mango-trees the fruit whereof you have tasted. Let the advantage now go to our children and their descendants. It is only given to us to toil and work. And so, there ought to be no relaxation in our efforts, lest we incur the curse of those that come after us. Action alone must be our guiding principle, action disinterested and well thought out. It does not matter who the Sovereign is. It is enough if we have full liberty to elevate ourselves in the best possible manner. This is called immutable Dharma, and Karma-Yoga is nothing but the method which leads to the attainment of Dharma or material and spiritual glory. God has declared His will. HE has willed that self can be exalted only through its own efforts. Everything lies in your hands. Karma-Yoga does not look upon this world as nothing; it requires only that your motives should be untainted by selfish interest and passion. This is the true view of practical Vedanta, the key to which is apt to be lost in sophistry.

(Poona Sarvajanik Sabha Quarterly).

SOME INFORMATION REGARDING THE ORIGINAL MANUSCRIPT OF THE GĪTĀ-RAHASYA.

The original manuscript of the Gītā-Rahasya is contained in four manuscript books, about which the following detailed information is available :—

Book	Contents	Pages	Period of writing.
1.	Rahasya, Chap. 1–8	1–143	2nd November 1910 to 8th December 1910.
2.	„ Chap. 9–13	1–402	13th December 1910 to 15th January 1911.
3.	„ Chap. 14–15	1–147	15th January 1911 to 30th January 1911.
	External Examination.	151–244 401–412	
	Title page, Dedication,	245–247	
	Translation of stanzas in chapters 1–3 of the Gītā.	249–399	
4.	Translation of stanzas in chapters 4-18 of the Gītā.	1–340 344–374 385–407	10th March 1911 to 30th March 1911.
	and Preface.	341–343 375–384	Total, 108 days.

The contents of the book, the Dedication, as also the Preface was written by the late Lokamanya in jail; and he has given detailed instructions in various places as to which subject-matter was to be printed in continuation of which matter, and made the book complete in that way. This shows that he was not sure whether he would leave the jail alive, and that it was his most intense desire that, in case he did not do so, the information which he had collected with great labour, and the thoughts which had suggested themselves to him from that information, should come to the hands of the next generation and not be wasted. The Contents which were prepared by him were written out at the commencement of each of the first two manuscript books and referred only to those two books. The title-page and the Dedication is at pages 245–247 in the third manuscript book, and the Preface is at pages 341–343 and 375–384 of the fourth manuscript book. After his release from jail, some addition was made to the

Preface; but this addition consists only of the reference made by him to the individuals who were of use to him in the matter of the publication. This reference is contained in the second last pragraph of the Preface to the first editon; but the last paragraph of the Preface was written by him in jail.

The eight chapters in the first manuscript book were headed by him as '*pūrvārdha*' (earlier half). The second manuscript book has been headed '*uttarārdha*' first part, (first part of the latter half) and the third manuscript book has been headed '*uttarārdha*, second part' (second part of the latter half). From this, it would appear that it was his original intention to publish the book in two parts. Out of these, the manuscript book containing the first eight chapters was written within about a month, and these chapters are of extreme importance. From this, the readers will get a clear idea about the thorough preparedness and the unimpeded flow of writing of the Lokamanya. Tearing off pages from the manuscript or adding new pages was not permissible under the jail regulations. But there are to be found memoranda on the inner sides of the covers of the second and third manuscript books, that permission had been granted to him to insert pages containing new matter which had suggested itself to him after further consideration. The first three manuscript books seem to have been each written within the space of one month and the last manuscript books was written within only fifteen days. The principal subject-matter was written on the right-hand pages only and the subject-matter to be added to the opposite page was written on the blank back of the previous page. We think that the desire of readers for information about the original manuscript will be satisfied by this information.

That he was busy considering the subject-matter of this book before the book itself was written is sufficiently proved by two other books written by him. While fixing down the meaning of the stanza commencing with "*māsānāṁ mārgaśīrṣo 'ham*" (Gītā 10. 35), he dived into the ocean of the Vedas, and placed at the disposal of the public the jewel 'Orion'; and while travelling through the depths of the ocean of the Vedas, he discovered 'the Ancient Home of the Aryas'. Although the Gītā-Rahasya was the last book to be published in point of time, yet, greater importance must be attached to that book than to the two other books, if one bears in mind the history of the writing of those two books. These two books have come into existence only as a result of the investigations made by him into the import of the Gītā. In his introduction to 'Orion', he has made a reference to his study of the Gītā.

These two books were published in due course, and they were talked of all the world over; but the Lokamanya could not get a propitious moment for starting the writing of the Gītā-Rahasya until he went to jail for the third time. The ideas regarding the two other books were also conceived during his previous imprisonments. He could not be free from the burden of public work and get the necessary peace and leisure for writing the book until he was in jail; but, before he could actually start writing the book, he had to overcome many difficulties. It is best to describe these difficulties in his own words: "Three different orders were received at three different times regarding the book............After a few days, the order of leaving all my books with me was cancelled; and a new order was received, that only four books should be left with me at a time. When I complained about this to the Government of Burma, another order was received, that all the books should be left with me to enable me to write the book. At the date when I was released from jail, the number of books with me was between 350 and 400. I was given bound books (and not loose pages) for writing, after the pages in them had been counted and numbered on either side. I was not given ink for writing but only a lead pencil and that too, ready sharpened" (Interview with Lokmanya Tilak after his release from jail, published in the *Kesari* of 30th June 1914).

If the readers put some pressure on their imagination, they cannot but have before their eyes a clear picture of what difficulties had to be overcome by him and what trouble he experienced while he was writing the book. Despite all this, he got the manuscript of the book ready for printing in the winter of 1910. The fact of the rough draft of the book being ready for printing is mentioned by him in a letter written in the beginning of the year 1911; and that letter has been printed *in toto* in an issue of the *Maratha*, published in the month of March. In order that the Exposition of the Gītā made by him in the Gītā-Rahasya should be easier to follow for his readers, Lokamanya Tilak delivered four lectures during the Gaṇapati festival in the year 1914; after this the printing of the work was taken in hand, and the first edition of the book was published in June 1915. The subsequent history is well-known to everybody.

TRANSLATOR'S PREFACE.

In placing before the public this English translation of the GĪTĀ-RAHASYA (the Esoteric Import of the Gītā) by the late Lokamanya Bal Gangadhar Tilak, the object of the publishers has been to give this Exposition of the Message of the Gītā a far wider circulation than it could have in its original Marathi form. It is true that the work has been translated into some of the Indian vernaculars; but that circulation has necessarily been a limited one.

The late Lokamanya Bal Gangadhar Tilak was a spiritual and intellectual giant. He was a monumental figure in the history of India, and it is a question whether he was more a philosopher than a politician and statesman, in as much as his statesmanship and his political activities would appear to have been based on the Karma-Yoga and the principles of Ethics, which he believed to have been expounded in the Gītā. In fact, the Gītā and its teachings would seem to have been the guiding beacon of his life; and if one considers what he did for India, and compares it with what he has preached in the Gītā-Rahasya, one will come to believe that he has practised what he preached, (which few people do), and that his political activities were a concrete example of that 'universal welfare' (*lokasaṁgraha*), which according to him, was preached by the Gītā to be the basis of Karma-Yoga. And, one will not be far wide of the mark, if one looks upon him as a *maharṣi* in an age of National regeneration.

As a result of the various commentaries in ancient times on the Śrīmad Bhagavadgītā, this Divine Book has been considered by some as advocating the Path of Renunciation, whereas, others have interpreted it as advocating the Path of Devotion. Both these being paths of indifference to the world (*vairāgya*), the effect of these commentaries has been to emasculate the devotees of the Gītā, and to fill them with an apathy towards worldly affairs, and towards a spirited and active national existence.

The Lokamanya has, however, shown in this Exposition of the Esoteric Import of the Gītā, that the true path of life taught by the Gītā has been pure, righteous, and moral Action *in* the affairs of the world (as against Renunciation, or indifference to the world), based on the Spiritual Realisation of the identity and equality of the Soul or Self (Ātman) in all created beings, and in which intense Devotion to the Almighty is the most important factor. The Author has in effect proved that the Gītā does not support any individual mode of life, such as Renunciation purely, or Action purely, or Devotion purely, but that it preaches a fusion and harmony between all the three modes of life, and declares the best mode of life to be incessant Righteous Action ("*na ṛte śrāntasya sakhyāya devāḥ*", i. e., "the gods do not like any, except those who labour until they are tired"), based on an Equability of Reason arising from the Spiritual Realisation of the Absolute Self, combined with an intense Devotion to the Parameśvara (Almighty).

At the 18th Session of the Mahārāṣṭra Sāhitya Pariṣad (Maharashtra Literary Conference) held at Nagpur in the year 1933, I tabled a Resolution that: "This Conference is of opinion that there should be a Society for translating Marathi literature into English, in order to give international importance to the Marathi language". This Resolution was unanimously passed by the Conference, and pursuant to that Resolution, I framed the draft of a scheme for the establishment and registration of such a literary society.

While I was busy with this project, my friend and my office client, Mr. R. B. Tilak, the surviving son of the late Lokamanya Tilak, who had seen my English translations of some Marathi poems which had been published in certain Magazines, and who also knew of the Resolution passed at the Nagpur Conference, approached me with a request that I should undertake the translation into English of the Gītā-Rahasya, which is one of the most brilliant gems of Marathi literature, and thus place before the public a concrete example of the usefulness of the Resolution adopted at my instance by the Mahārāṣṭra Sāhitya Pariṣad. As the task set before me was a stupendous one, both on account of its volume and the labour involved, as also on account of the extremely difficult and involved style of the author, I was at first doubtful whether or not I should undertake the work. In fact, the task of getting this work translated into English had at first been attempted in the life-time of the late Lokamanya Tilak, and again after his death, by his sons, as has been mentioned by Mr. R. B. Tilak, in the Publisher's Foreword. Being inspired, however, by the "spiritual power of this wonderful and well-known work", which saw the sale of ten thousand copies of the first Marathi edition of it "within a few months of its being published" (as stated in the Publishor's Foreword), and being further inspired by the advice of Vidulā to her son that, "*muhūrtaṁ jvalitaṁ śreyo na ca dhūmāyitaṁ ciram*" (Ma. Bhā. U. 132. 15), that is, "it is better to shine like a flame for a little while, than to perpetually smoulder", I resolved that I would see this work through at any cost. In forming this resolve, I wanted to place before the Mahārāṣṭra public a concrete example of the usefulness of the Resolution, which I had tabled at the Mahārāṣṭra Sāhitya Pariṣad, as also to place the real message of the Gītā according to one of the most brilliant Indian philosophers as stated in the beginning of this Preface, before the world, which, to me, seems sadly in need of it at the present moment. Having regard to the hold which the English language has on the world, no better medium could be found for sending this message of the Gītā to every home in every corner of the world. There was a time when Indians considered it a sacrilege to put religious and philosophical lore into the hands of the unregenerate classes, and more so, into the hands of foreigners who would, of course, be far beyond the pale of these classes; but, in my humble opinion, it is the sacred duty of any one who possesses any kind of Knowledge, to place such Knowledge at the disposal of those who are inclined to purify themselves in the Flame of Knowledge; for, "*asaṁskṛtās tu saṁskāryāḥ bhratṛbhiḥ pūrvasaṁskṛtaiḥ*", i. e., "it is the duty of those who have been previously initiated, to initiate their brethren, who are uninitated". And, if this Message of the Gītā, which the late Lokamanya Tilak, placed before his, Maharashtriyan compatriots through this book, and which his sons circulated further into India itself through the medium of its vernacular translations, goes round the world, on the River of Time, spreading the inspiration given by the original text, I shall feel that I have discharged to a certain extent my obligations to my mother-land, and to my mother-tongue, by advancing to a certain extent the spiritual regeneration of the world.

To enable the reader to understand the method followed by me in this translation, I would like to draw his attention to the rules, printed immediately after this preface at p. xxxix, which I have attempted to follow.

As will be seen from the details about the original work which are given at p. xxviii, the whole book was written by the Author in the Mandalay jail within the period of about five months from 2nd November 1910 to 30th March 1911. So great has been my anxiety to place this wonderful interpretation of the philosophy of the Gītā before the world at large, that I have translated the whole of the book within about the same time, that is, from 20th May to 14th November 1934, by devoting every spare moment to the translation in spite of my other work. This was, of course, the first draft of the work which I prepared; and the same has been subsequently revised, re-cast, and even re-written by me in some places, as the printing was going on.

The translation of the first six chapters (about 147 pages of the original), had been prepared by another gentleman, and the type-written copy of it was placed by the publishers in my hands; but I have not made any use of it whatsoever, as I have preferred to have a homogeneous, and consistent style and method of translation for the whole text, which would be entirely mine.

In translating, I have attempted to be as faithful to the text as possible, as I have thought that in the case of a philosophical and technical book written by a genius like the late Lokamanya, it would be extremely wrong to take any liberty whatsoever with the text. The late Lokamanya, besides being a great philosopher, and a great statesman, was also a master of the Marathi language; and even an apparently insignificant word used by him has an immense modifying or limiting value, and the omission of even a small conjunction or the translation of an 'and' as an 'or,' would considerably injure the sense intended to be conveyed by the author. I have, therefore, not changed the text at all, but only altered the garb or the medium of expression; for, a translation is no translation, if it is not faithful. I have not even broken up long and involved sentences; for, though a sentence may be long and involved, each portion of it has a bearing and a limiting value on the remaining portions of the sentence; and breaking up such a sentence into several small sentences, would make it lose its cumulative force, and to that extent the meaning intended to be conveyed by the author would be disabled. In following this procedure, I have satisfied myself by thinking, that if there are persons in India, who can without difficulty understand the long and involved sentences in the original Marathi text, there cannot be a dearth of intelligent persons in the world, who will be able to understand the same sentences, with their long and involved construction, in the garb of the English language and character. Some readers will possibly find the sense being continually interrupted by the Sanskrit quotations. But the rendering of those quotations has been made in such a way, that if the reader reads only the English rendering without reading the quotation, he will find that the rendering fits into the sentence and that the sense runs on without any interruption.

I had at one time thought of omitting the quotations, and giving only the English rendering, but I realized that I would thereby be destroying the characteristic feature of the style of the Author, though it would have made reading easy.

As stated above, I have made this translation both as a national duty which I owe to my mother-tongue, as also with the idea of placing the immortal Spiritual Knowledge contained in the Gītā-Rahasya within the grasp of everyone, whose Destiny inspires him to study it with attention; and, I have no doubt that every reader who goes through these pages conscientiously and sincerely, and with an unbiassed, impartial, and Truth-seeking mind will be spiritually benefited by doing so.

Before concluding this foreword, I must express my appreciation of the sincere pains taken by the Manager and the staff of the Bombay Vaibhava Press for ensuring the correct printing of the press copy, which has been considerably troublesome on account of the Sanskrit quotations and words, which are printed in a transliterated form; and I have even been allowed, as an exceptional case, to make corrections when the form was on the machine ready for printing. My gratitude is due to my brother Dr. V. S. Sukthankar, the Chief Editor of the Bhandarkar Oriental Research Institute in charge of the Critical edition of the Mahābhārata, who has for some time looked into the transliterated portions and made very valuable suggestions regarding the translation. My thanks are similarly due to Professor A. B. Gajendragadkar of the Elphinstone College, Nyāya-Ratna Dhundiraj G. Vinod M. A., and Mr. S. A. Sabnis, Solicitor, for the suggestions occasionally made by them, and the encouragement I have received from them. My thanks are lastly due to Mr. P. B. Gothaskar, retired Librarian of the Bombay Branch of the Royal Asiatic Society, who on account of having been in touch with the publication of the Journal of that Society, was of great use to me in correcting the earlier proofs and who, in carefully revising those proofs, also drew my attention to such sundry inaccuracies, as he thought, had remained in the translation, so as to enable me to correct them, if necessary. The final proofs were corrected by me. Apart from the printer's devils which have inevitably crept in, it is necessary to mention the mistake in the heading of Chapter XII, in which the word 'Siddha-Vyavahārā' is wrong, and the correct word, as in the original, is only 'Vyavahāra.'

In concluding this Preface, I cannot but follow the injunction of the Blessed Lord that, "*yat karoṣi yad aśnāsi yaj juhoṣi.........tat kuruṣva mad arpaṇam*", (Gī. 9. 27), which has also been carried out by the Author himself (see foot-note to Author's Dedication); and I humbly dedicate this compilation to the Parameśvara in the shape of the Eternal Trinity of (i) Śrī Mahā Lakṣmī Indirā, the Goddess of Wealth, the consort of Śrī Viṣṇu, Who claimed my Devotion, and was the cause of my taking this work in hand and completing it, (ii) Śrī Mahā Kālī Pārvatī, the Goddess of Destruction, Who destroyed the Knot of Ignorance in my heart ("*ājñāna-hṛdaya-granthi*"—Śiva-Gītā, 13. 32), and opened my eyes to the Realities of Life, and kept my footsteps continually on the Path of Knowledge, and (iii) Śrī Mahā Sarasvatī Vidyā, the Goddess of Learning, Who has now claimed me for Her own, and compelled me to cast this Fruit of my Action (*karmaṇy evādhikāras te mā phaleṣu kadā ca na*—Gī. 2. 47), in the shape of this translation, on the River of Time, which circumscribes and goes round the whole world, and Who is verily my Mother (for I am a Sārasvat by birth !).

OM-TAT-SAT.

आतां प्रार्थना ऐका कमलापति । तुझे नामीं राहो माझी मती ।
हेंचि मागणें पुढता पुढतीं । परंज्योति व्यंकटेशा ॥

Bombay,
12th June 1935.

B. S. SUKTHANKAR.

GENERAL RULES REGARDING THE TRANSLATION.

(i) Wherever a philosophical Sanskrit word used in the Marathi text (not being a technical philosophical term which has been Anglicised), has been rendered by me into English, I have, wherever necessary, placed immediately after such rendering the actual word used by the author in the original, in italics, and within brackets; e. g., bodily (*kāyika*), Self-Realised (*ātma-jñānin*), occasional (*naimittika*), etc. This has been done to enable such of my readers as are acquainted with Sanskrit to understand what the author himself wanted to say, in case my rendering has not been correct.

(ii) If the word in the original text is a technical philosophical word, which has been Anglicised, I have used the word in Roman characters, beginning with a capital letter, e. g., Jīva, Parameśvara, Prakṛti, Paramātman, Ātman etc.

(iii) Diacritical signs have been used in order to ensure correct pronunciation by the reader, whose attention is drawn to the tabular statement at p. xl showing what diacritical sign has been used for indicating which sound.

(iv) Technical philosophical English words are used with an initial capital letter in order to distinguish them from when they are not so used, e. g., Real, Matter, Spirit, the Imperceptible, Knowledge, Mind, Consciousness, the Quality-less etc., unless they have been used as adjectives, or in a non-technical sense, e. g., the qualityless Brahman etc.

(v) If in the text itself, there is a Sanskrit word in brackets after another Sanskrit word, (which latter one has been rendered by me into English), the Author's word in brackets, though in Sanskrit, *has not been put into italics*, in order to distinguish the case from where I have put such words in italic characters, in brackets, after the rendering, as mentioned in (i) above.

(vi) If the Sanskrit word in the original has been retained in the translated text, its rendering in English is placed after it in brackets; e. g., the *kārya* (product), *karma* (Action) etc. This has been done only where the retention has been necessary on account of the context.

(vii) I have not added anything of my own in the translated text except as follows :-In almost all places where the Author has given a Sanskrit quotation, he has immediately afterwards translated this quotation or given a summary of it in Marathi; and this, of course, has been translated into English. In some places, however, the Author has not translated a Sanskrit quotation into Marathi; and in these cases, I myself have translated it into English, for the convenience of the reader not acquainted with Sanskrit; but, wherever this has been done, I have added the word "—Trans." after the translation. Any inaccuracies in such translations, would, of course, be mine. Where, however, such a quotation has been from the Gītā itself, I have rendered into English, the translation of that quotation, as made by the Author himself, in his translation of the stanzas of the Gītā (See Vol. II of this work).

SCHEME OF TRANSLITERATION OF SANSKRIT

अ	*a*	क	*k*	ठ	*ṭh*	ब	*b*
आ	*ā*	ख	*kh*	ड	*ḍ*	भ	*bh*
इ	*i*	ग	*g*	ढ	*ḍh*	म	*m*
ई	*ī*	घ	*gh*	ण	*ṇ*	य	*y*
उ	*u*	ङ	*ṅ*	त	*t*	र	*r*
ऊ	*ū*	च	*c*	थ	*th*	ल	*l*
ऋ	*ṛ*	छ	*ch*	द	*d*	व	*v*
ए	*e*	ज	*j*	ध	*dh*	श	*ś*
ऐ	*ai*	झ	*jh*	न	*n*	ष	*ṣ*
ओ	*o*	ञ	*ñ*	प	*p*	स	*s*
औ	*au*	ट	*ṭ*	फ	*ph*	ह	*h*

ं (*anusvāra*) *ṁ*, : (*visarga*) *aḥ*, क्ष............*kṣ*, ज्ञ............*jñ*

ऽ (*avagraha*) ... ...

EXPLANATION OF THE PICTORIAL MAP OF THE PROMINENT SCHOOLS OF INDIAN PHILOSOPHY mentioned in the GĪTĀ-RAHASYA.

Shown on the wrapper

and opp. page 18.

The river is the River of Time, on the banks which are the various Ages through which India has passed, namely, (1) the Vedic Age, (2) the Age of the Gita, (3) the Age of Buddha, (4) the Age of Shri Shankaracharya, (5) the Age Jnaneshvara, Tukarama and others being the Age of Devotion, (6) the Age of Shri Samartha Ramadasa, showing the revival of Action, and (7) the deputation of Indian Leaders at the gates of the Houses of Parliament and (8) Mahatma Gandhi, in the Present Age.

Nos. 1, 2, 6, 7 and 8 are the Ages of Action, or of Karma-Yoga starting with the Vedic Karma age, and ending with the present days, and forming a big L, which means the Lucky Ages, whereas Nos. 3, 4 and 5 are the Ages of Renunciation, which are only a small passing cloud on the Karma-Yoga tradition of India.

The narrow bed of the river in the Ages of Renunciation, spreads out as it flows down along the plains of the Ages of Action, suggesting the widening out of the view-point of Philosophy from the narrow Pass of Renunciation to the broad Fields of Action.

The two inset pictures in the form of the 'Svastika' show the five Pandavas on the Kuru field, and the five Indian leaders near the Houses of Parliament, in each case, on the Field of Action. The last picture is of Mahatma Gandhi, the latest Karma-Yogin of India.

R. B. TILAK.

AUTHOR'S DEDICATION.

(IN SANSKRIT VERSE)

How very profound is the importance of the Gītā, which was expounded in ancient times by wise men, and which was further explained in various ways by Ācārayas, and how limited is the scope of my intelligence? Still, I am impelled by my rashness to explain the same once more, keeping before my eyes the old Śāstras as well as notable modern ideas; and honourable people desiring to understand what is doable and what not-doable, deserve to hear this (new) explanation. Having made this request to revered persons in the sweet words of Kālidāsa, I, a Brahmin, (by name) Bāla, the son of Gaṅgādhara, born in the family of Tilaka, belonging to the clan (*gotra*) of the Ṛṣi Śāṇḍilya, and a resident of the town of Poona, situate in the Mahārāṣṭra, following the path of the Good, and with the words of Hari * in my mind, do dedicate this work to the Lord of Lakṣmī, the Soul of the World, in the Śalivāhana Śaka 1837. May the Blessed Lord, the Highest Puruṣa, be pleased by this dedication.

---

* "Whatever you do, or eat, or offer by way of sacrifice, or give, or perform by way of austerity, dedicate all that to Me, O, son of Kunti".

(Gītā 9. 27).

AUTHOR'S PREFACE.

I am only repeating the stale words uttered by Saints।
How can an insignificant man like me know this ? ॥

—Tukārāma.

Although in the beginning of this book, I have explained my reasons for publishing it, in spite of the fact that there are in existence many Sanskrit commentaries, or criticisms, or Prakrit translations, or exhaustive and universally accepted expositions of the Śrīmad Bhagavadgītā, yet, there is no better place than an Introduction for explaining all such things as cannot be included in the discussion of the subject-matter of the book itself. The first of these things is about the author himself. It is now nearly forty-three years since I made my first acquaintance with the Bhagavadgītā. In the year 1872, during the last illness of my father, the task of reading out to him a Prakrit commentary on the Bhagavadgītā called *Bhāṣā-vivṛtti* fell to my lot. At that date, that is, when I was only 16 years old, it was not possible for me to fully understand the import of the Gītā. Still, as the impressions made on the mind in young age are lasting, the liking for the Bhagavadgītā which then came into existence did not die out; and when I had later on made further studies in Sanskrit and English, I had occasion to read from time to time the Sanskrit commentaries and other criticisms, as also the expositions by many learned scholars in English and in Marathi on the Gītā. I was then faced by the doubt as to why the Gītā, which was expounded in order to induce to fight that Arjuna, who was dejected by the idea that it was a sin to war with one's own relatives, should contain an Exposition of the manner in which Release could be obtained by Knowledge (Jñāna) or by Devotion (Bhakti), that is to say, only of the '*mokṣa-mārga*'; and that doubt gradually gained ground, because, I could not find a satisfactory answer to that question in any commentary on the Gītā. It is quite possible that others too might have felt the same doubt. One cannot say no to that. When a person is engulfed in commentaries, he cannot find a different solution, though he may feel that the solution given in the commentary is not satisfactory. I, therefore, put aside all criticisms and commentaries, and independently and thoughtfully read the Gītā over several times. I then got out of the clutches of the commentators, and was convinced that the original Gītā did not preach the Philosophy of Renunciation (*nivṛtti*), but of Energism (Karma-Yoga); and that possibly, the single word '*yoga*' used in the Gītā had been used to mean Karma-Yoga. That conviction was strengthened by the study of the Mahābhārata, the Vedānta-Sūtras, the Upaniṣads and other Sanskrit and English treatises on Vedānta; and believing that by publishing that opinion, there would be a fuller discussion on the subject, and that it would be easier to arrive at the truth, I delivered public lectures on the subject on four or five occasions at different times. One of these was delivered at Nagpur in January 1902, and the other one at the Saṅkeśvara Maṭha in August 1904, in the presence of Jagadguru Śrī Śaṁkarācārya of the Karavīra and Saṅkeśvara Maṭha, and at his request. The summary of the lecture delivered at Nagpur was published in the newspapers at the time. With the same object, I also discussed the matter from time to time privately, whenever I had leisure, with some of my learned friends. One of these was the late Mr. Shripati Buva Bhingarkar. In his company, I had occasion to see some Prakrit treatises pertaining to the Bhāgavata cult, and some of the ideas explained in the Gītā-Rahasya were first fixed in the discussions between myself and the Buva. It is a matter of deep regret that he is not alive to see this work. Though my opinion that the creed preached in the Gītā was one of Action, had, in this way, become quite definite, and though I had decided to reduce it to writing, many years went by. But I thought that a considerable amount of misunderstanding would arise if I merely published in a book form, this moral of the Gītā, which had not been accepted in the commentaries, criticisms, or translations now commonly available, without assigning any reasons as to why I was unable to accept the conclusions arrived at by the former commentators. At the same time, as the work of dealing with the opinions of all the commentators, and exposing their incompleteness with reasons, and of comparing the religion expounded in the Gītā with other religions or philosophies was one entailing great labour, it was not possible for me to satisfactorily complete it, within a short period of time. Therefore, although my friends Daji Saheb Kharay and Dada Saheb Khaparday had, in anticipation and somewhat hastily, announced that I was shortly going to publish a treatise on the Gītā, yet, seeing that the material in hand was not sufficient, I went on putting off the work of writing the book. And later on, when in the year 1908, I was convicted and sent to Mandalay, in Burma, the chance of this book being written came practically to an end. But, when after sometime, Government was pleased to grant permission to take the books and other things essential for writing this book from Poona to Mandalay, the draft of this book was first made in the Mandalay Jail in the Winter of 1910–1911 (between Kartik Shuddha 1st and Falgun Vadya 30th of the Śaka Year 1832); and thereafter, the draft was improved upon from time to time, as things suggested themselves to me; and those portions which had remained incomplete as the necessary books had not been available, were completed after my release from jail. Nevertheless, I cannot even now say that this work is complete in every respect; because, the elementary principles of Release (*mokṣa*) and Moral Philosophy are very recondite, and they have been so exhaustively expounded by ancient and modern scholars, that it is very often difficult to correctly decide which portion of such expositions ought to be incorporated in this small book, without including too much. But, my physical condition is now becoming weak, as described by the great Mahārāṣṭra poet Moropanta in the following *āryā* stanza:–

> Old age, which is the spotless white banner carried by the
> army of attendants of Death, is already in sight ।
> And my body is exhausted in the struggle with diseases,
> which are the advance-guard of that army ॥;

and my contemporaries in life have passed on. So, having come to the conclusion that I should place before the public the information which I have gathered, and the ideas which have occurred to me, and that someone else possessed by the same inspiration (*samānadharmā*), will come to birth in the immediate or distant future, and develop and work them out, I have published this book.

Though I am not prepared to accept the opinion that the Gītā gives only an exposition of the paths of Release based on Renunciation, such as, 'the Knowledge of the Brahman' or 'Devotion', after proving worldly Action to be inferior and negligible, I must, at the outset, make it clear that I do not also say that there is no exposition at all in the Bhagavadgītā of the paths of obtaining Release. Nay; I too have shown in this book, that according to the philosophy of the Gītā, it is the primary duty of every human being in this world, to acquire the Knowledge of the pure form of the Parameśvara, and thereby to cleanse out and purify his own Reason as far as possible. But, that is not the principal subject-matter of the Gītā. At the commencement of the war, Arjuna was engulfed in a perplexity about what his duty was, namely, whether he should or should not take part in a war, which would ruin the welfare of his Ātman, in the shape of Release, as a result of his committing heinous sins like the destruction of his own clan, etc., though it was the duty of every Kṣatriya to fight. And I am of opinion that in order to clear this doubt, the Gītā has propounded the device of performing Action in such a way that one ultimately attains Release without committing sin, namely, the Karma-Yoga founded on Knowledge, in which Devotion is the principal factor, after it had fully expounded the Philosophy of Action and Non-Action, and also the various paths of attaining Release according to pure Vedānta Philosophy, and had established that no man is free from Action, and that Action should never be given up. This exposition of Action and Non-Action, or of Morality and Immorality is called 'Ethics' by modern purely Materialistic philosophers. It is not that I could not have made this exposition by following the usual procedure, and explained how this principle has been established by the Gītā, by commenting on the Gītā stanza by stanza. But, unless one is thoroughly conversant with the various philosophical doctrines, arguments and deductions pertaining to Vedānta, Mīmāṁsā, Sāṁkhya, the Doctrine of Causality (*karma-vipāka*) and

Devotion, on the authority of which the doctrine of Karma-Yoga has been established in the Gītā, and the reference to which is sometimes very succinct, the full purport of the exposition made in the Gītā is not easily understood. I have, therefore, scientifically divided all the various subjects or doctrines, which one comes across in the Gītā, into chapters, and briefly expounded them, together with the most important logical arguments relating to them; and I have, at the same time, consistently with the critical methods of the present day, compared in brief and as occasion arose, the most important doctrines propounded in the Gītā, with the doctrines propounded in other religions and philosophies. It may thus be said that the essay 'Gītā-Rahasya' (the Esoteric Import of the Gītā), which is published in the beginning of this book, is by itself an independent, though a small, book on the doctrine of Proper Action (Karma-Yoga). But, in any case, it was not possible to consider fully each individual stanza of the Gītā in a general exposition of this kind. I have, therefore, at the end of the book, translated the Gītā, stanza by stanza, and added exhaustive commentaries to the translations in different places, in order to explain the anterior and posterior context; or, in order to show how former commentators have stretched the meaning of some of the stanzas of the Gītā in order to support their own doctrines (See Gītā 3. 17-19; 6. 3; and 18. 2); or, in order to show which of the various doctrines enunciated in the Gītā-Rahasya appear how and where in the Gītā, according to the catechismal method of the Gītā. It is true that by following this method, some subject-matter has been repeated; but, as I felt convinced that I could not in any other way fully dissipate the misunderstanding, which now exists in the mind of the common reader as regards the import of the Gītā, I have separated the exposition of the Gītā-Rahasya (Esoteric Import of the Gītā) from the translation itself; and thereby, it has become easy for me (i) to show with authorities and with former history, where and in what manner, the doctrines of the Gītā with reference to Vedānta, Mīmāṁsā, Devotion etc., have appeared in the Bhārata, the Sāṁkhya system, the Vedānta-Sūtras, the Upaniṣads, the Mīmāṁsā and other original texts, (ii) to explain in a lucid way the difference between Renunciation (Saṁnyāsa) and Action (Karma-Yoga), as also (iii) to expound in a proper way the importance of the Gītā from the point of view of practical Action, by comparing the Gītā with other religious opinions or philosophies. If there had not been all sorts of commentaries on the Gītā, and if various persons had not interpreted the import of the Gītā, each in a different way, it would have been totally unnecessary for me to quote the original Sanskrit authorities which go to support the propositions laid down by me in my book. But such a thing cannot be done in the present times; and it is likely that many may doubt the correctness of the import of the Gītā or of the propositions, laid down by me. I have, therefore, everywhere pointed out the authorities which support what I say, and in important places, I have given the original Sanskrit text of the authorities with translations. As many of these dicta are usually accepted as proved truths in books on Vedānta, my secondary object in quoting them has been, that my readers should get acquainted with them in the course of reading, and find it easier on that account to remember the doctrines embodied in those statements. But, as it is not likely that all readers will be knowing Sanskrit, I have arranged my book on the whole in such a way that, if any reader who does not understand Sanskrit, reads the book, omitting the Sanskrit stanzas, there will not be any interruption anywhere in the sense; on this account, it has became necessary in many places, to remain satisfied with giving a mere summary of the Sanskrit stanza, instead of giving a literal translation of it. But as the original stanza is given in each case, there is no risk of any misunderstanding arising as a result of this procedure having been followed.

There is a story told about the Kohinoor diamond that after it had been taken from India to England, it was again cut there, and on that account, it began to look more brilliant. This law, which is true in the case of a diamond, also applies to a jewel in the shape of truth. It is true that the religion propounded by the Gītā is true and unshakeable. But, as the time at which and the form in which it was propounded, and the other attendant circumstances have considerably changed, it does not strike may as as brilliant as before. As the Gītā was propounded at a time, when 'whether to act or renounce' was considered a question of great importance, to be determined before arriving at a decision as to which act was good and which bad, many people look upon a considerable portion of it as now unnecessary; and, as that position has been further made worse by commentaries supporting the Path of Renunciation, the exposition of Karma-Yoga contained in the Gītā has become very difficult to understand for many in the present age. Besides, some of our new scholars are of opinion that as a result of the present growth of the Material sciences in the West, the deductions laid down in ancient times with reference to the Karma-Yoga, on the basis of the Philosophy of the Absolute Self, cannot possibly be fully applicable to modern conditions. In order to prove that this idea is wrong, I have briefly mentioned in various places in my exposition of the Gītā-Rahasya (Esoteric Import of the Gītā) the doctrines of Western philosophers, which are similar to those in the Gītā. Really speaking, the exposition of Ethics in the Gītā is in no way fortified by such a comparison. Yet, those people whose eyes are dazzled by the present unheard of growth of the Material sciences. or who have learnt to consider the Science of Ethics, only externally, that is to say, only in its Material aspect, as a result of the present one-sided methods of education, will be made to see clearly by means of this comparison that, not only has human knowledge not yet gone beyond the doctrines laid down on this subject by our philosophers, for the simple reason that Ethics and the science of Release are both beyond Material Knowledge, but, deliberations are still going on on these questions in the West, from the Metaphysical point of view, and the opinions of these Metaphysicians are not materially different from the doctrines laid down in the Gītā. This fact will be clearly borne out by the comparative exposition appearing in the different chapters of the Gītā-Rahasya. But, as this subject is very extensive, I must explain here, with reference to the summaries of the opinions of Western philosophers which I have given in various places, that, as my principal object has been only to expound the import of the Gītā, I have accepted as authoritative the doctrines laid down in the Gītā, and have mentioned the Western opinions only so far as was necessary in order to show to what extent the doctrines of Western moral philosophers or scholars tally with the doctrines in the Gītā; and this too has been done by me only to such an extent that the ordinary Marathi reader should experience no difficulty in grasping their import. It cannot, therefore, be disputed that those who wish to ascertain the minute differences between the two—and these differences are many—or to see the full argumentative exposition or developing-out of these theorems, must examine the original Western books themselves. Western scholars say that the first systematic treatise on the discrimination between Right and Wrong Action or on Morality was written by the Greek philosopher Aristotle. But in my opinion, these questions had been examined long before Aristotle in a more exhaustive and scientific manner in the Mahābhārata and in the Gītā; and no moral doctrine has yet been evolved, which is different from the doctrines metaphysically expounded in the Gītā. The solution given by Aristotle of the question whether it is better to spend one's life peacefully, in philosophical meditation, and living like a hermit, or to spend it in all sorts of political activities, is to be found in the Gītā; and the opinion of Socrates that whatever sin is committed by man, is committed by him only as a result of ignorance, is also to be found to a certain extent in the Gītā, because it is a doctrine of the Gītā that it is not possible for a man to commit any sin, after his Reason has become equable as a result of the Knowledge of the Brahman. The doctrine of the Epicureans and the Stoïcs that the conduct of the perfect Jñānin is a standard for everybody, from the moral point of view, is to be found in the Gītā; and the description of the perfect Jñānin, given by the philosophers belonging to these sects, tallies with the description of the Sthitaprajña (Steady-in-Mind) given in the Gītā. Similarly, the dictum of Mill, Spencer, Kant, and other Materialistic philosophers, that the highest peak or test of Morality consists in everybody acting so as to promote the welfare of the whole of mankind, is included in the external characteristic of a **Sthitaprajña** descibed in the Gītā in the words "*sarvabhūtahite-ratah*" (i. e., "one busy promoting the welfare of all created beings"—Trans.); and the arguments relating to Ethics, and the doctrines regarding Freedom of Will, enunciated by Kant and Green, are to be found mentioned in the Gītā, on the authority of the Knowledge contained in the Upaniṣads. If the Gītā had not contained anything more than this, it would still have commanded universal respect. But the Gītā does not stop there. After showing that the conflict between Release (*mokṣa)*, Devotion (*bhakti*), and Ethics (*nīti-dharma*) imagined by Materialistic philosophers, as also the conflict between Knowledge (*jñāna*) and Right Action (*karma*) imagined by the followers of the School of Renunciation (*saṁnyāsa*) were groundless, and also showing that the fundamental element in the *brahmavidyā* (science of the Brahman), and in *bhakti* (the Path of Devotion) is the foundation of Ethics and good behaviour, the Gītā has shown what path of life should be adopted by a man by properly harmonising Knowledge (*jñāna*), Renunciation (*saṁnyāsa*), Right Action (*karma*) and Devotion (*bhakti*). The Gītā is thus essentially a treatise on Right or Proper Action (Karma-Yoga); and that is why it has been given a position of supreme importance in all Vedic treatises, which refer to it as '*brahmavidyāntargata* (*karma-*) *yoga-śāstra* (i. e., "the Science of Right Action included in the Science of the Brahman"—Trans.) The saying "*gītā sugīta kartavyā kim anyaiḥ śāstra vistaraiḥ*", i.e., "it is quite enough if one thoroughly studies the Gītā; what is the use of dabbling in the other Śāstras?" is indeed correct; and, therefore, it is my earnest and respectful request to everyone, who wishes to become acquainted with the basic principles of the Hindu Religion and Morality, that he should first study this wonderful and unprecedented book; because, as the Gītā expounds the root principles of the present Vedic Religion, as also its final aspect, based on Knowledge and giving primary importance to Devotion, and preaching the Karma-Yoga (Right Action), which (aspect) it had assumed after Sāṁkhya, Nyāya, Mīmāṁsā, Upaniṣads, Vedānta and other ancient Śāstras, which dealt with the Perishable and the Imperishable (*kṣarākṣara*) and the Body and the Ātman (*kṣetra-kṣetrajña*) had come to as perfect a state as possible, it may well be said that there is no other work in the whole of Sanskrit literature, which explains the principles of the present Hindu Religion in as succinct and yet as clear and unambiguous a manner as the Gītā.

From what has been stated above, my readers will get an idea as to the general trend of the exposition contained in the Gītā-Rahasya. From the reference to the opinions of the earlier commentators on the Gītā, made in the beginning of the third chapter of the Śāṁkarabhāṣya on the Gītā, it would appear that these commentaries were in favour of Karma-Yoga (Right Action). These commentaries are not now available; therefore, there is no reason why this book of mine should not be called the first comparative exposition of the Gītā, in support of Right Action. The meanings of some stanzas given in this book are different from those given in the present commentaries, and I have also had to deal with many other subjects, which have nowhere been fully explained in the Marathi language. I have attempted to explain these subjects and the arguments in support of such explanation succinctly, but in as clear and easily intelligible a manner as possible; and notwithstanding repetition, I have purposely given, in many places, synonyms for various words, of which the meanings have not yet become current or commonly known in the Marathi language, side by side with those words; and I have also clearly shown in different places the most salient theorems in these subjects, by separating them from the exposition itself. Yet, it is always difficult to discuss scientific and difficult subjects in a few words; and the Marathi terminology of these subjects is also not yet definite. I am, therefore, alive to the fact that in this my new way of exposition, there may possibly creep in difficulty, unintelligibleness, or incompleteness, as a result of mental confusion, inadvertence, or for some other reasons. But the Bhagavadgītā is not something unknown to my readers. The Gītā is a book which is daily recited by many, and there are also many who have studied, or who are studying it scientifically. I have, therefore, to request such authoritative persons, that if this book comes to their hands, and they come across any flaws in it of the nature mentioned above, they will please draw my attention to them, so that I will consider the suggestions, and will also make the necessary corrections, if there is any occasion to bring out a second edition of this book. Some persons are likely to gather the impression that I have a particular system (*saṁpradāya*) of mine own, and that I have explained the Gītā in a special way, in support of that system. I must, therefore, make it clear here that the Gītā-Rahasya has not been written with reference to any particular person, or any particular system. I have put forward the clear meaning of the Sanskrit stanzas in the Gītā, according to my understanding. If, as a result of this straight-forward translation—and as Sanskrit is now widely understood, may people will easily see whether or not my translation is straight-forward—my exposition assumes a doctrine-supporting character, then such character is of the Gītā and not mine. As the clear request of Arjuna to the Blessed Lord was: "Do not confuse me by placing before me several courses of conduct, but point out to me definitely only one course, which is the proper course" (Gī. 3. 2 ; 5. 17), it is clear that the Gītā must be in support of one particular opinion (Gī. 3. 31); and I have set out to explain what that opinion is, by impartially interpreting the original Gītā. I have not preconceived a doctrine first, and then attempted to stretch the meaning of the Gītā, because the Gītā will not fit in with that doctrine. In short, my attempt is to popularise the true inner import of the Gītā with the devotees of the Gītā—to whatever doctrine such import may pertain—and I have come forward to make, so to say, such a Sacrifice of Knowledge (*jñāna-yajña*) as is referred to by the Blessed Lord at the end of the Gītā; and I am sanguine that my countrymen, and co-religionists, will willingly give me this charitable offering of information in order to make my attempt flawless.

I have explained at length in the Gītā-Rahasya the reasons for the difference between the Esoteric Import of the Gītā according to me, and that propounded by ancient commentators. But, though there may be such a difference of opinion as to the teaching of the Gītā, yet, as I have always made use more or less, of the various commentaries or criticisms on the Gītā, as also of the former or modern Prakrit translations of the Gītā, as occasion arose in writing the present book, I must here say that

I am deeply indebted to them. I must likewise express my gratitude towards those Western philosophers, to the theorems mentioned in whose works I have now and then referred. As it is doubtful whether it would have been possible for me to write this book without the help of all those works, I have quoted in the beginning of this introduction the following words of Tukārāma: "I am only repeating the stale words uttered by saints". That a work like the Gītā, which propounds Knowledge, untouched by Time, that is, equally true at all times, should, according to changing times, give fresh inspiration to human beings, is not a matter of surprise; because, that is the characteristic feature of such universal works. But, the labour spent on such works by ancient scholars is not, on that account, wasted. This same argument applies to the translations of the Gītā into English, German, and other languages made by Western scholars. Though these translations are based primarily on the ancient commentaries on the Gītā, some Western scholars have also started interpreting the Gītā independently. But, these expositions of the Western scholars are to a certain extent incomplete, and in some places undoubtedly misleading and wrong, whether because, they have not properly understood the principle of the true (Karma-) Yoga or the history of the Vedic religious systems, or because, they have principally inclined towards the external examination of the matter only, or, for some other similar reason. There is no occasion to consider or examine here in detail those works of Western scholars on the Gītā. In the Appendices to this book, I have stated what I have to say regarding the important questions raised by them. Nevertheless, I must in this Preface refer to some writings in English on the Gītā, which I have recently come across. One such writing is that of Mr. Brooks. Mr. Brooks is a Theosophist and he has maintained in his book on the Gītā, that the Bhagavadgītā is in favour of Action (Karma-Yoga); and he has expressed the same opinion in his lectures. The second thesis is by Mr. S. Radhakrishnam of Madras, which has appeared in the form of a small essay in the International Ethical Quarterly (July 1911) published in America. In this work, the similarity between the Gītā and Kant on questions of Ethics and

Freedom of Will has been shown. In my opinion, this similarity is even more comprehensive than has been shown in this essay; and the arguments of Green on the question of Ethics are even more consistent with the Gītā than those of Kant. But as both these questions have been dealt with by me in this book, I shall not repeat the same matter here. Pandit Sitanath Tatvabhushana has also recently published a book in English called *Kṛṣṇa and the Gītā*, which contains the twelve lectures delivered by that scholar on the Gītā. But, any one who reads those books will be sure to notice, that there is a great deal of difference between the arguments contained in these books or in the book of Brooks and those advanced in mine. But, these writings show that my ideas about the Gītā are not new-fangled; and, as these works are a propitious sign that people are paying more and more attention to the doctrine of Right Action (*karma-yoga*) in the Gītā, I am taking this opportunity of congratulating these modern writers.

It is true that this work was completed in the Mandalay Jail; but it had been written with a lead pencil, and it contained corrections and deletions in many places; so, when it had been returned to me after inspection by Government, it was necessary to make a fair copy of it for printing; and if I myself had to do that work, who knows how many months more would have passed before the work was published! But Messrs. Waman Gopal Joshi, Narayan Krishna Gogte, Ramkrishna Dattatraya Paradkar, Ramkrishna Sadashiva Pimputkar, Appaji Vishnu Kulkarni and other gentlemen, have willingly rendered assistance in this matter and quickly finished the work, for which I am grateful to them. Similarly Mr. Krishnaji Prabhakar Khadilkar, and especially Vedaśāstra-sampanna Dīkṣit Kāśināth Śāstri Lele, specially came here from Bombay, and took the trouble of reading the manuscript, and made many useful and critical suggestions, for which I am grateful to them. The reader, however, must not forget that the responsibility of the opinions expressed in this book is mine. In this way, the book was got ready for printing, but there was the risk of shortage of paper on account of the War. This difficulty was overcome by the timely supply of paper, which was good in my opinion, by Messrs D. Padamji & Son, proprietors of the Swadeshi Paper Mills in Bombay; and it became possible to publish a book on the Gītā on good Indian paper. Yet, as the book was found to be larger than estimated, while the printing was in progress, there was again shortage of paper; and, if that deficit had not been met by the proprietor of the Reay Paper Mills, Poona, my readers would have had to wait for a few months more for the publication of the book. Therefore, not only I, but also my readers, must feel grateful to the proprietors of these two mills. The task of correcting proofs still remained. This was undertaken by Messrs Ramkrishna Dattatraya Paradkar, Ramkrishna Sadashiva Pimputkar and Hari Raghunath Bhagvat. But of these, Mr. Hari Raghunath Bhagvat was alone attending to the work of verifying the references to other books made in different places, and of pointing out to me such defects as had remained. Needless to say, without the assistance of all these people, it would have been impossible for me to publish this book so soon. I, therefore, take this opportunity of sincerely thanking all these people. Finally, I must express my thanks to the owner of the Chitra-Shala Press, who undertook to publish this book carefully and as early as possible, and who has carried out his undertaking. Just as the assistance of many persons is necessary before the grain is turned into food for the eater, though there may be a harvest in the field, so also I may safely say, is the case with writers—at any rate, that was the case with me. And therefore, I once more sincerely thank all those persons who have helped me—whether or not I have specifically mentioned their names in the above list—and I end this preface.

The preface is over. Now, though I feel unhappy at the idea that that subject, in thinking on which I have spent many years, and the constant company of and meditation over which has brought so much satisfaction to my mind, and happiness into my heart, is now going to leave my hands in the shape of a book, yet, as these thoughts have come into my mind for the sole purpose of being handed down to coming generations—with interest, or at any rate, just as they are—I am placing this philosopher's stone, in the shape of a *rāja-guhya* (the king of mysticisms) of the Vedic religion into the hands of my promising readers, uttering the canon (*mantra*): "*uttiṣṭhata* | *jāgrata* | *prāpyavarān-nibodhata* !", that is, "Arise, awake, and understand these blessings (conferred by the Blessed Lord)", and with feelings of affection. In this (mysticism) lies the entire essence of Right and Wrong Action, and the Blessed Lord Himself has confidently given us the assurance, that the observance of this Religion, even to a small extent, delivers a person from great difficulties. What more can anybody want? Keep in mind the universal rule that, "Nothing happens, unless something is done", and devote yourselves to Desireless Action; that is all. The Gītā was not preached either as a pastime for persons tired out after living a worldly life in the pursuit of selfish motives, nor as a preparatory lesson for living such worldly life, but in order to give philosophical advice as to how one should live his worldly life with an eye to Release (*mokṣa*), and as to the true duty of human beings in worldly life. My last prayer to everyone, therefore, is, that one should not fail to thoroughly understand this ancient science of the life of a householder, or of worldly life, as early as possible in one's life.

Poona, Adhika Vaiśākha, Śaka Year, 1837. — BAL GANGADHAR TILAK.

CONTENTS OF VOLUME I.

(GENERAL).

Note :—Volume II will contain Chap. XIV and XV of the Exposition, the Appendices, the text of the Gītā with translation of each stanza and commentaries on such translation, and several indices.

Detailed Contents of Volume I with special reference to the subject-matter of chapters I to XIII

CHAPTER I—INTRODUCTORY.

CHAPTER·II. KARMA-JIJÑĀSĀ-

(THE DESIRE TO KNOW THE RIGHT ACTION)

CHAPTER III.

KARMA-YOGA-ŚĀSTRA.

(The Science of Right Action).

CHAPTER IV.

ĀDHIBHAUTIKA-SUKHAVĀDA.

(The Materialistic theory of Happiness).

CHAPTER V.

SUKHA-DUḤKHA-VIVEKA.

(The Consideration of Happiness and Unhappiness).

CHAPTER VI.

ĀDHIDAIVATA-PAKṢA AND KṢETRAKṢETRAJÑA-VICĀRA.

(The Intuitionist School and the Consideration of the Body and the Ātman).

CHAPTER VII.

KĀPILA-SĀMKHYA-ŚĀSTRA OR KṢARĀKṢARA-VICĀRA.

(The Kāpila-Sāṁkya Philosophy or the Consideration of the Mutable and the Immutable).

CHAPTER VIII.

THE CONSTRUCTION AND DESTRUCTION OF THE COSMOS.

CHAPTER IX.

ADHYĀTMA.

(The Philosophy of the Absolute Self)

Objections to the Duality of Matter and Spirit—the method of considering that which is beyond both—the Absolute Self (*paramātmā* or *para puruṣa*) is beyond both—the Trinity of Matter (Cosmos), Spirit (Jīva) and the Highest Īśvara (*Parameśvara*)—the description of the form of the Parameśvara as given in the Gītā—the Perceptible (*vyakta*) or Qualityful (*saguṇa*) form, and its inferiority—the Imperceptible, capable of Perception by Illusion (Māyā)—the three divisions of the Imperceptible into (i) qualityful (ii) qualityless and (iii) qualityful-qualityless—similar descriptions in the Upaniṣads—the methods of worship (*vidyā*) and symbols (*pratīka*) mentioned in the Upaniṣads for worship (*upāsanā*)—of the three imperceptible forms, the qualityless is the best—(p. 289)—the scientific exposition of the above doctrines—the moot meanings of the words 'Qualityful' (*saguṇa*) and 'Qualityless' (*nirguṇa*)—the natural idea of Immortality—how the Knowledge of the universe is acquired, and what it consists of—the description of the process of acquiring Knowledge, and definition of Names and Forms—the Appearance of Names and Forms, and the Thing-in-Itself (*vastu-tatva*)—the definition of the Real (*satya*); Names and Forms are unreal (*asatya*) because they are perishable, and the Thing-in-itself (*vastu-tatva*) is Real, because imperishable—the Thing-in-Itself is the imperishable Brahman, and Names and Forms are illusory—the meaning of the words Real (*satya*) and Illusory (*mithyā*) in Vedānta—the embodiment of Material Sciences is Names and Forms (p. 302)—the theory of *vijñāna* is not acceptable to Vedānta—the ancientness of the doctrine of Māyā—the form of the immutable (*nitya*) Brahman, clothed in Names and Forms, and of the Embodied (*śārira*) Ātman is the same—why both are said to be of the form of Consciousness (*cit*)—the identity of the Brahman and the Ātman is expressed by saying: "what is in the body (*piṇḍa*) is also in the Cosmos (*brahmāṇḍa*)"—the bliss of Realising the Brahman (*brahmānanda*)—the death of the Ego—the fourth state (*turīyāvasthā*)

CHAPTER X.

KARMA-VIPĀKA AND ĀTMA-ŚVĀTAMTRYA.

(The Effect of Karma and Freedom of Will).

CHAPTER XI.

SAMNYĀSA and KARMA-YOGA.

(Renunciation and Karma-Yoga.)

CHAPTER XII.

SIDDHĀVASTHĀ AND VYAVAHĀRA.

(The State of a Perfect, and Worldly Affairs)

CHAPTER XIII.

BHAKTI-MĀRGA.

(The Path of Devotion.)

acquiring Knowledge, Religious Faith (*śraddhā*) and Reason—both these are mutually dependent—the accomplishment of practical purposes by Faith—though one may acquire Knowledge of the Parameśvara by Faith, that is not enough—in order to be able to assimilate that Knowledge, it is necessary to contemplate on the Parameśvara with an intense and desireless love—this is called DEVOTION—the Contemplation of the Qualityful Imperceptible, is laborious and difficult of achievement—therefore, it is necessary to have some definite object for worship—the Path of Knowledge and the Path of Devotion lead to the same goal—nevertheless, Devotion cannot become a Niṣṭhā like Knowledge—the visible form of the Parameśvara, accessible by love, which is taken for Devotion—the meaning of the word '*pratīka*'—the meaning of the words '*rāja-vidyā*' and '*rāja-guhya*'—the lovingness in the Gītā (p. 586)—any one of the innumerable manifestations of the Parameśvara can be taken as a symbol (*pratīka*)—different symbols taken by different people and the resulting confusion—how that can be avoided—the difference between the symbol (*pratīka*) and the belief with which one worships the symbol—whatever the symbol is, the result obtained is according to one's belief about it—worship of different deities—but the One who gives the Fruit is the Parameśvara and not the deity—whichever deity is worshipped, that becomes an informal worship of the Parameśvara—the superiority of the Path of Devotion in the Gītā from this point of view—the purity or impurity of Devotion and Love—improvement takes place by gradual degrees, as a result of industry, and perfection is reached after many births—that man who has neither Faith nor Reason is lost—whether by Reason or by Devotion, the knowledge of the same Non-Dual Brahman is obtained (p. 601)—all the doctrines pertaining to the theory of Causality (*karma-vipāka-prakriyā*) and the Philosophy of the Absolute Self, also stand good in the Path of Devotion—See, for instance, the form of the Personal Self ('*jīva*'), and of the Parameśvara according to the Gītā—nevertheless, there is sometimes a verbal difference in these doctrines—for instance, Karma now becomes the same as the Parameśvara—dedication to the Brahman (*brahmārpaṇa*) and dedication to Kṛṣṇa

---

LIST OF ILLUSTRATIONS.

DETAILED

Contents of chapters XIV and XV and of the Appendices, which are included in the Second Volume of the Book.

—:o:—

CHAPTER XIV.

GITĀDHYĀYA-SAṀGATI.

(The Continuity of the chapters of the Gītā).

Two methods of proving a subject—scientific and catechistic —the good and bad aspects of the catechistic method—the beginning of the Gītā—the first chapter—in the second chapter, the subject-matter starts with only two Paths of life, namely, the Sāṁkhya and the Yoga—the exposition of Karma-Yoga in the third, fourth and fifth chapters—Equability of Reason (*sāmya-buddhi*) is better than Karma—it is impossible to get rid of Karma—Karma-Yoga is superior to Sāṁkhya-Niṣṭhā—the necessity of the control of all organs in order to attain Equability of Reason (*sāmya-buddhi*)—the method of control of the organs mentioned in the sixth chapter—it is not proper to divide the Gītā into the three parts, Action (*karma*), Devotion (*bhakti*) and Knowledge (*jñāna*)—Knowledge and Devotion are the means of attaining Equability of Reason, according to the Karma-Yoga—therefore, the Gītā cannot be divided into three six-chaptered parts, one part for '*tvam*,' one for '*tat*' and one for '*asi*'—the exposition of '*jñāna*' and '*vijñāna*' is given in chapters VII to XII, for the successful practice of Karma-Yoga, and not independently—a summary of chapters VII to XII—even in these chapters of the Gītā, Devotion and Knowledge have not been dealt with independently, but are intermingled with each other, and they have been given the single name '*jñāna-vijñāna*'—a summary of chapters XIII to XVII—the summing up in the eighteenth chapter is in support of Karma-Yoga—therefore, considering the introductory and final chapters (*upakrama-upsaṁhāra*) according to rules of the Mīmāṁsa, Karma-Yoga is seen to be the doctrine propounded by the Gītā—the four-fold goal of human life (*puruṣārtha*)— '*artha*' (wealth) and '*kāma*' (Desire) must be consistent with '*dharma*' (Morality)—but Release (*mokṣa*) is not in conflict with Morality (*dharma*)—how the Gītā came to be explained away as supporting Renunciation—Is not Sāṁkhya + Desireless Action = Karma-Yoga, to be found in the Gītā ?—nevertheless Karma-Yoga is the doctrine ultimately expounded—prayer to the followers of the Path of Renunciation.

CHAPTER XV.

UPASAṀHĀRA.

(Résumé or Summary)

Difference between the science of Karma-Yoga and the formulating of rules of Worldly Morality (*ācāra-saṁgraha*)—the erroneous idea that Ethics cannot be properly justified by Vedānta—Gītā does that very thing—the Exposition of the religion of the Gītā solely from the point of view of Ethics—Reason is superior to Karma—the Nakulopākhyāna—similar theorems in Buddhism and Christianity—comparison of the doctrine of Equability of Reason in the Gītā, with the two Western doctrines of 'greatest good of the greatest number' and 'Conscience'—similarity between Western Metaphysics and the Exposition in the Gītā—the doctrines of Kant and Green—Vedānta and Ethics—the reason why there are various codes of Ethics, and differences of opinion about the construction of the Body and the Cosmos—the important part of the Metaphysical exposition in the Gītā—the harmonising of Release (*mokṣa*), Ethics and worldly life—Renunciation according to Christianity—the Western idea of Action based on the search for Happiness—comparison of the same with the Karma-mārga in the Gītā—difference between the arrangement of the four castes and Ethics—the Western Karma-mārga is based on elimination of pain, and the Gītā religion is based on Desirelessness—a short history of the Karma-Yoga in the Kaliyuga—Jain and Buddhist monks—the Saṁnyāsin followers of Śaṁkarācārya—the Mahomedan rule—the Devotees of the Blessed Lord, the galaxy of saints, and Rāmadāsa—the livingness of the Gītā religion—the fearlessness, immutability, and equality of the Gītā religion—prayer to the Almighty.

APPENDICES.

An External Examination of the Gītā.

also of the Gītā—the combination of Spiritual Knowledge with Action in the Gītā is from the Upaniṣads, but there is the addition of Devotion—the ancient treatises on the Bhāgavata doctrine, the Gītā and the Nārāyaṇīyopākhyāna—the date of Śrī Kṛṣṇa and of the growth of the Sātvata or Bhāgavata religion is the same—that time, is about 700 to 800 years before Buddha, or about 1500 years before Christ—the reasons for thinking so—the impossible position arising out of a different conclusion—the original aspect of the Bhāgavata religion supports Inaction—the next aspect is Devotional—and the final aspect is for Qualified Monism (Viśiṣṭādvaita)—the original Gītā is about 900 years before Christ—PART V:—THE DATE OF THE PRESENT GĪTĀ—the date of the present Gītā is the same as of the present Mahābhārata—out of these, the present Mahābhārata is prior in point of time to Bhāsa, Aśvaghoṣa Aśvalāyana, Alexander, and the method of starting the year with the Sun in Aries (Meṣa), but subsequent to Buddha; so it is about 500 years prior to the Śaka era—the present Gītā is prior in point of time to Kālidāsa, Bāṇabhaṭṭa, the dramatist Bhāsa, the Purāṇas, Baudhāyana, and the Mahāyāna sect in Buddhism, that is, about 500 years before the Śaka era—PART VI: GĪTĀ and the BUDDHIST LITERATURE—the similarity between the description of the 'Sthitaprajña' in the Gītā and the 'Arhata' of Buddhism—the nature of the Buddhist religion, and its growth out of the previous Brahmin religion—Buddha has discarded the doctrine of the Ātman in the Upaniṣads, and has adopted only a course of conduct consistent with Renunciation (*nivṛtti*)—the visible reasons for this Path of life according to the Buddhist religion, or the four *ārya* truths—the similarity between the Vedic Smārta religion, and the duties of a householder according to Buddhism—all these ideas are originally from the Vedic religion—the reason, nevertheless, for considering the Mahābhārata and the Gītā independently—the improbability of the subsequent Devotional Buddhist religion having been evolved out of the original Renunciatory Buddhist religion, which denied the existence of the Ātman—the growth of the Mahāyāna Sect—reasons for concluding that the Path of Devotion based on Action (*pravṛtti*) in the Mahāyāna creed has been

Explanation of the Abbreviations used in the Gītā-Rahasya, and information about the treatises referred to by the Abbreviations.

———:o::o:———

NOTE :—These are not in the same order as in the original', as they have been re-arranged according to the English Alphabet, whereas in the original, they are arranged according to the Marathi Alphabet—Trans.).

Ai. Brā. *Aitareya Brāhmaṇa*; *pañcikā* and *khaṇḍa*, (Dr. Houda's Edition).

Ai. or Ai. U. } *Aitareyopaniṣad*; chapter, *khaṇḍa* and stanza (Anandasrama Edition).

Aṣṭā. *Aṣṭāvakragītā*; chapter and stanza, (*Gītā-Saṁgraha* published by Messrs Ashtekar & Co.)

Atharva. *Atharvaveda*; the figures after this show respectively, the *kāṇḍa*, the *sūkta*, and the *ṛcā*.

Bhāg. *Śrīmad Bhāgavatapurāṇa*, (Nirnaya-Sagara Edition).

Bhā. Jyo. *Bhāratīya Jyotiḥ Śāstra* (Written by the late Balkrishna Dikshit).

Bṛ. or Bṛha. } *Bṛhadāraṇyakopaniṣat*; *adhyāya*, *brāhmaṇa* and *mantra* (Anandasrama Edition). The usual reference is to the Kaṇvapāṭha, but in one place, there is a reference to the Mādhyandina-śākhā.

Bra. Sū. See. Ve. Sū. below.

Chān. *Chāndogyopaniṣat*; chapter, *khaṇḍa* and *mantra*. (Anandasrama Edition).

Dā. or Dāsa. } The *Dāsabodha* of Śrī Samartha (Edition of the Satkaryottejaka Sabha, Dhulia).

Gā. Tukārāma's *Gāthā* (Damodar Savlarama's Edition, 1900).

Gī. *Bhagavadgītā*, chapter and stanza; Gī. Śāṁ. Bhā.; *Gītā Śāṁkarabhāṣya*. Gītā. Rā. Bhā., *Gītā Rāmānujabhāṣya*. The Anandasrama Edition of the Gītā and of the *Śāṁkarabhāṣya* contains at the end a glossary, which I have found very useful; and I am very grateful for it to the compiler. The *Rāmānujabhāṣya* is the one printed in the Venkatesvara Press; The *Madhvabhāṣya* is the one printed by Krishnacharya of Kumbhakonam; The *Ānandagiri* Commentary, and the *Paramārtha-prapā*, are those printed in the Jagadhitecchu Press; the *Madhusūdana* Commentary is the one printed in the Native Opinion Press; the *Śrīdharī* and *Vāmanī* (Marathi) Commentaries are those printed in the Nirnayasagara Press; the *Paiśācabhāṣya* is the one printed in the Anandasrama Press; the *Tattvadīpikā* of the Vallabha school is the one printed in the Guzarati Printing Press; the *Nīlakaṇṭhī* is from the Bombay Mahābhārata; and the *Brahmānandī* is the one printed in Madras; these are the commentaries of which I have made use. But, as the Guzarati Printing Press has recently published together in one volume all these commentaries except the *Paiśācabhāṣya* and the *Brahamānandī*, as also the commentary of the Nimbārka School and some other commentaries, in all fifteen, that one volume is now sufficient for all needs.

Gī. Ra. or Gītā Ra. } *Gītā-Rahasya.* The first essay of this book.

Hari. *Harivaṁśa*; *parva*, chapter and stanza (Bombay Edition).

Īśā. *Īśāvāsyopaniṣat.* (Anandasrama Edition).

Jai. Sū. The *Mīmāṁsā-Sūtras* of Jaimini; chapter, *pāda*, and *sūtra*. (Calcutta Edition).

Jñā. *Jñāneśvarī* with translation; Indira Press Edition.

Ka. or Kaṭha. } *Kaṭhopaniṣat*; *vallī* and *mantra* (Anandasrama Edition).

Kai. *Kaivalyopaniṣat*; *khaṇḍa* and *mantra*; Twenty-eight Upaniṣads (Nirnaya-Sagara Edition).

Kauṣī. *Kauṣītakyupaniṣat* or *Kauṣītaki Brāhmaṇopaniṣat*; chapter and *khaṇḍa*; sometimes the first chapter of this Upaniṣad is referred to as the third chapter according to the order of the Brāhmaṇas; (Anandasrama Edition).

Kena. *Kenopaniṣat* (= *Talavakāropaniṣat*), *khaṇḍa* and mantra (Anandasrama Edition).

Ma. Bhā. *Śriman Mahābhārata.* The following letter shows the various Parvas, and the numbers are of the chapters and the stanzas. I have everywhere used the Sanskrit Edition published at Calcutta by Babu Pratapchandra Roy. If the same stanzas have to be referred to in the Bombay edition, they will be found a little in advance or behind.

Maitryu. *Maitryupaniṣat* or *Maitrāyaṇyupaiṣat*; *prapāṭhaka* and *mantra* (Anandasrama Edition).

Manu. *Manu-Smṛti*, chapter and stanza. (Dr. Jolly's Edition; but in the Mandalik's or in any other edition, these stanzas will mostly be found in the same places; the commentaries on Manu are from the Mandalik edition).

Matsya. *Matsya-Purāṇa* (Anandasrama Edition).

Mi. Pra. *Milinda Praśna*, Pali text, English translation. (Sacred Books of the East Series).

Muṇ. or Muṇḍa. *Muṇḍakopaniṣat*; *muṇḍaka*, *khaṇḍa* and *mantra* (Anandasrama Edition).

Nār. Pañ. *Nārada Pañcarātra*. (Calcutta edition).

Nā. Sū. *Nārada-Sūtras* (Bombay edition).

Nṛsiṁha. U. *Nṛsiṁhottara tāpanīyopaniṣat*.

Pañca. *Pañcadaśī* with commentary (Nirnaya-Sagara Edition).

Pātañjala-Sū. *Pātañjala-Yoga-Sūtras*. (Tukarama Tatya's Edition).

Praśna. *Praśnopaniṣat*; *praśna* and *mantra*. (Anandasrama Edition).

Ṛg. *Ṛg-veda*; *maṇḍala*, *sūkta*, and *ṛcā*.

Rāmapū. *Rāmapūrvatāpinyupaniṣat* (Anandasrama Edition).

S. B. E. *Sacred Books of the East Series*.

Sāṁ. Kā. *Sāṁkhya Kārikā* (Tukarama Tatya's Edition).

Śān. Sū. *Śāṇḍilya-Śūtras* (Bombay Edition).

Śiva. *Śiva-gītā*; chapter and stanza; *Gītā-Saṁgraha* of Messrs Ashtekar & Co.,

Sūrya. Gī. *Sūrya-Gītā*; chapter and stanza, (Madras Edition).

Śve. *Śvetāśvataropaniṣat*; chapter and *mantra* (Anandasrama Edition).

Tai. or Tai. U. *Taittirīya Upaniṣat*; *vallī*, *anuvāka*, and *mantra* (Anandasrama Edition).

Tai. Brā. *Taittirīya Brāhmaṇa*; *kāṇḍa*, *prapāṭhaka*, *anuvāka* and *mantra* (Anandasrama Edition).

Tai. Saṁ. *Taittirīya Saṁhitā*; *kāṇḍa*, *prapāṭhaka*, *anuvāka* and *mantra*.

Tukā. Gā. Tukārāma's *Gāthā*; See Gā. above.

Vāja. Saṁ. *Vājasaneyi Saṁhitā*; chapter and *mantra* (Bebar Edition).

Vālmīki Rā. or Vā. Rā. *Vālmīki Rāmāyaṇa*; *kāṇḍa*, chapter and stanza (Bombay Edition).

Ve. Sū. *Vedānta-Sūtras* or *Brahma-Sūtras*; chapter, *pāda*, and *sūtra*.

Ve. Sū. Śāṁ. Bhā. *Śāṁkarabhāṣya* on the *Vedānta-Sūtras*; the Anandasrama Edition has been used everywhere.

Viṣṇu. *Viṣṇu-Purāṇa*; *aṁśa*, chapter, and stanza (Bombay Edition).

Yājña. *Yājñavalkya-Smṛti*; chapter and stanza (Bombay Edition); I have in one or two places referred to the *Aparārka* commentary (Bombay Edition) on this.

Yo. or Yoga. *Yoga-Vāsiṣṭha*; chapter, *sarga*, and stanza. There are two sub-divisions, Pū. (*pūrvārdha*) and U. (*uttarārdha*) of the sixth chapter (Commentated Nirnaya-Sagara Edition).

NOTE:—Besides these, there are many Sanskrit, English, Marathi, and Pali treatises, which have been mentioned in various places; but as a general rule, the names of those books have been given in full, wherever they occur, or they have been mentioned in such a way as to be easily intelligible; and they have, therefore, not been mentioned in the above list.

THE LION OF INDIA

(Copyright)

"AN UNCROWNED KING IN THE DECCAN." (p. xxii)
"THE FATHER OF INDIAN UNREST." (p. xiv)
"THE LEADER OF AN ALL-INDIA PARTY." (p. xxii)

S'RĪ GANES'ĀYA NAMAH

OM TAT SAT

S'RĪMAD BHAGAVADGĪTĀ RAHASYA

OR

THE PHILOSOPHY OF ENERGISM (PROPER ACTION)

CHAPTER I

INTRODUCTORY

Nārāyaṇaṁ namaskṛtya naraṁ caiva narottamam ।
devīṁ Sarasvatīṁ Vyāsaṁ tato jayam udīrayet ॥ *

Mahābhārata (opening verse)

The S'rīmad Bhagavadgītā is one of the most brilliant and pure gems of our ancient sacred books. It would be difficult to find a simpler work in Sanskrit literature or even in all the literature of the world than the Gītā, which explains to us in an unambiguous and succint manner the deep and sacred principles of the sacred science of the SELF (Ātman), after imparting to us the knowledge of the human body and the cosmos, and on the authority of those principles acquaints every human being with the most perfect and complete condition of the Self, that is to say, with what the highest manhood is, and which further establishes a logical and admirable harmony between Devotion (*bhakti*) and Spiritual Knowledge (*jñāna*), and ultimately between both these and the duties of ordinary life enjoined by the *S'āstras*, thereby inspiring the mind, bewildered by the vicissitudes of life to calmly and, what is more, desirelessly adhere to the path of duty. Even

* This verse means that one should first offer obeisance to Nārāyaṇa, to Nara, the most excellent among men, to Devī Sarasvatī, and to Vyāsa and then begin to recite the "Jaya", that is, the Mahābhārata. The two Ṛṣis Nara and Nārāyaṇa were the two

if one examines the work looking upon it as a poem, this work, which simplifies to every reader, young or old, the numerous abstruse doctrines of Self-Knowledge in inspired language and is replete with the sweetness of Devotion plus Self-Realisation, will certainly be looked upon as an excellent poem. The pre-eminent worth, therefore, of a book which contains the quintessence of Vedic religion, uttered by the voice of the Blessed Lord can best only be imagined. It is stated at the commencement of the Anugītā, that after the Bhārata war was over, and S'rī Kṛṣṇa and Arjuna were one day chatting together, Arjuna conceiving the desire of hearing the Gītā again from the lips of the Blessed Lord, said to Śrī Kṛṣṇa :—" I have forgotten the advice you gave me when the war commenced; so, please repeat it to me." In reply the Blessed Lord said to him that even He could not repeat that advice in the same way, because on the previous occasion the advice had been given, when His mind was in the highest Yogic state (Ma. Bhā. As'vamedha. 16, stanzas 10-13). Really speaking, nothing was impossible for the Blessed Lord, but His answer that it would be impossible for Him to repeat the Gītā, clearly reveals the excellent worth of the Gītā. The fact that the Gītā is considered by all the different traditionary schools of the Vedic religion for over twenty-five centuries to be as venerable and authoritative as the Vedas themselves is due to the same

---

components into which the Paramātman had broken itself up and Arjuna and Śrī Kṛṣṇa were their later incarnations, as has been stated in the Mahābhārata (Ma. Bhā. U. 48. 7-9 and 20-22; and Vana. 12. 44-46). As these two Ṛṣis were the promulgators of the Nārāyaṇīya or the Bhāgavata religion, consisting of Desireless Action, they are first worshipped in all the treatises on the Bhāgavata religion. In some readings, the word *'caiva'* is used instead of *'Vyāsa'* as in this verse, but I do not think that is correct; because, although Nara and Nārāyaṇa were the promulgators of the Bhāgavata religion, yet I think it only proper that Vyāsa, who wrote both the Bhārata and the Gītā, which are the two principal works relating to this religion, should also be worshipped in the beginning of the book. "Jaya" is the ancient name for the Mahābhārata.

cause; and on the same account, this work, which is as old as the Smṛtis, has been appropriately, though figuratively described in the Gītā-dhyāna as follows:—

sarvopaniṣado gāvo dogdhā Gopālanandanaḥ ।
Pārtho vatsaḥ sudhīr bhoktā dugdhaṁ Gītāmṛtaṁ mahat ॥

that is:—" All the Upaniṣads are, so to say, cows, the Blessed Lord Śrī Kṛṣṇa is Himself the drawer of the milk (milk-man), the intelligent Arjuna is the drinker, the calf (which causes the flow of the milk in the cows), and (when these unprecedented circumstances have come about) the milk which has been drawn, is the Gītā-nectar of the highest order." It cannot, therefore, be a matter of surprise that any number of translations, commentaries, or expositions of this work have appeared in all the vernacular languages of India; but, after the Westerners have got acquainted with Sanskrit, there have been made any number of translations of the Gītā into Greek, Latin, German, French, English etc., and this wonderful work has now come to be known throughout the world.

Not only does this work contain the quintessence of all the Upaniṣads, but the full name of this work is "Śrīmad Bhagavadgītā Upaniṣat". The enunciative words, conveying that the chapter is closed, which are used at the end of each chapter of the Gītā contain the words "*iti śrīmad Bhagavadgītāsu Upaniṣatsu Brahmavidyāyāṁ yogaśāstre Śrī-Kṛṣṇārjuna-saṁvāde*" etc. *i.e.*, "thus the conversation between Śrī-Kṛṣṇa and Arjuna on the Karma-yoga science, (that is to say, on the science of the yoga based on the knowledge of the Brahman) in the Upaniṣad sung by the Blessed Lord." Although these enunciative words are not to be found in the original Bhārata, yet as we find them in all the editions of the Gītā, one may draw the inference that, that mode of enunciation must have come into vogue, when the Gītā was for the first time separated from the Mahābhārata for daily recital, that is to say, before any commentary was written on it; and I shall explain later on the importance of these words in determining the import of the Gītā from this point of view. For the present, it is necessary for us to consider only the words "*Bhagavadgītāsu Upaniṣatsu.*" Although the word "Upaniṣat" is of the neuter gender in the Marathi language, yet as it is of the feminine gender in Sanskrit, so the idea "the Upaniṣad sung, that is, told by the Blessed Lord" is conveyed, in Sanskrit, by the expression "*Śrīmad Bhagavadgītā Upaniṣat*", a compound of an adjective and a noun in the feminine gender; and although the work is singular in number, yet as it has become customary to refer to it in the plural number by way of respect, one comes across the plural seventh-case-ended form of "*S'rīmad Bhagavadgītāsūpaniṣatsu*". Even in the commentary (bhāṣya) written by Ṣ'aṁkarācārya, we come across the expression "*iti gītāsu*" in the plural number with reference to this work. But in contracting the expression, the affixes or words used for indicating respect and also the common-noun "Upaniṣat" at the end, indicative of a class, being dropped, the two first-case-ended singular words "*S'rīmad Bhagavadgītā*" and "*Upaniṣat*" have at first been changed into "*Bhagavadgītā*" and later on merely "*Gītā*", which is a feminine and extensively contracted form,—as has been the case with the names Kena, Kaṭha, Chāndogya etc., If the word "Upaniṣat" had not occurred in the original name, then the name of this work would have been contracted into the neuter form "Bhagavadgītaṁ" or merely "Gītaṁ" as has been the case with "Bhāgavataṁ" or "Bhārataṁ" or "Gopīgītaṁ", but as, instead of that, the word has remained in the feminine form as "Bhagavadgītā" or "Gītā," we must always take the word "Upaniṣat" as implied after it. The word "Anugītā" has been interpreted in the same way in the commentary of Arjunamiśra on the Anugītā.

But we find that the word "Gītā" is applied not only to the Bhagavadgītā of 700 verses but also in an ordinary meaning to many other works dealing with Spiritual Knowledge. For instance, in certain sundry chapters of the Mokṣaparva, included in the Śāntiparva of the Mahābhārata, we find that the names Piṅgalagītā, Śaṁpākagīta, Maṅkigītā, Bodhyagītā, Vicakkhyugītā, Hārītagītā, Vṛtragītā, Parāśaragītā, and Haṁsagītā have been used and one part of the Anugītā in the Aśvamedhaparva has been called by the separate and special name of "Brāhmaṇagītā". Besides these, there are also numerous other gītās which are well-known, such as the

Avadhūtagītā, Aṣṭāvakragītā, Īśvaragītā, Uttaragītā, Kapilagītā, Gaṇeśagītā, Devīgītā, Pāṇḍavagītā, Brahmagītā Bhikṣugītā, Yamagītā, Rāmagītā, Vyāsagītā, Śivagītā, Sūtagītā, Sūryagītā, etc. Some of these exist independently, whereas the others are to be found in different Purāṇas. For instance, the Gaṇeśagītā is to be found at the end of the Gaṇeśapurāṇa in the Krīḍākhaṇḍa in the 138th to 148th chapters and one may say that it is a faithful copy of the Bhagavadgītā, with slight verbal differences. The Īśvaragītā is to be found in the first eleven chapters in the Uttaravibhāga of the Kūrmapurāṇa, and the Vyāsagītā starts in the next chapter. The Brahmagītā is to be found in the first twelve chapters of the latter portion of the fourth i. e., the Yajña-vaibhava *khaṇḍa* of the Sūta-Saṁhitā included in the Skandapurāṇa and the Sūtagītā is in the subsequent eight chapters. There is to be found a Brahmagītā different from this Brahmagītā of the Skandapurāṇa, in the 173rd to 181st stanzas of the latter half of the chapter on "Nirvāṇa", in the Yogavāsiṣṭha. The Yamagītā is of three kinds. The first is to be found in the seventh chapter of the 3rd part (aṁśa) of the Viṣṇupurāṇa, the second one in the 381st chapter of the 3rd division (*khaṇḍa*) of the Agnipurāṇa and the third one in the 8th chapter of Nṛsiṁhapurāṇa. The same is the case with the Rāmagītā. The Rāmagītā which is in common acceptance in this part of the country is to be found in the fifth *sarga* of the Uttarakāṇḍa of the Adhyātma Rāmāyaṇa and this Adhyātma Rāmāyaṇa is looked upon as a part of the Brahmāṇḍapurāṇa. But there is also another Rāmagītā to be found in the work known as "Gurujñānavāsiṣṭha-tattvasārāyaṇa" which is well-known on the Madras side. This book deals with Vedānta philosophy and is divided into three divisions (*kāṇḍas*) called the Jñāna, Upāsanā, and Karma. In the first eighteen chapters of the second part (*pāda*) called the Upāsanākāṇḍa, we find the Rāmagītā and in the first five chapters of the third part (*pāda*) of the third kāṇḍa, called the Karmakāṇḍa, we find the Sūryagītā. The Śivagītā is said to be in the Pātālakhaṇḍa of the Padmapurāṇa. But, in the edition of this purāṇa which has been printed in the Anandashrama Press in Poona, we do not find the Śivagītā. Pandit Jwalaprasad has stated in his book called Aṣṭādaśapurāṇadarśana (Survey of the eighteen Purāṇas) that it is to be found in the Gauḍīya Padmottarapurāṇa, and in the table of contents of the Padmapurāṇa which is given along with those of other Purāṇas in the Nāradapurāṇa, we find a reference to the Śivagītā. Besides these, the Haṁsagītā is to be found in the 13th chapter of the 11th *skandha* of the Śrī Bhāgavatpurāṇa and the Bhikṣugītā is to be found in the 23rd chapter of the same *skandha*; and the Kāpileyopākhyāna contained in the chapters 23 to 33 of the third *skandha*, is also known as Kapilagītā. But I have seen an independent printed book by the name Kapilagītā. This Kapilagītā deals principally with the Haṭhayoga, and one finds it stated in it that it has been taken from the Padmapurāṇa; however, not only do we not find it in the Padmapurāṇa, but as we find in it in one place (4. 7) such words as "Jaina" "Jaṅgama" (liṅgāita), and "Sophi" (a Mahomedan saint), we have to say that it must have been written after the Mahomedan rule commenced. As in the Bhāgavatpurāṇa, so also in the Devībhāgavata, we find a Gītā from the 31st to the 40th chapters of the seventh *skandha*, and as that gītā is supposed to have come out of the mouth of the Devī, it is called the "Devīgītā". Besides these, a summary of the Bhagavadgītā itself is to be found in the 380th chapter of the third *khaṇḍa*, of the Agnipurāṇa as also in the 247th chapter of the *pūrvakhaṇḍa* of the Garuḍapurāṇa. In the same way, although it is stated that the work "Yogavāsiṣṭha" was recited by Vasiṣṭha to Rāma in the Rāma incarnation, yet we find a summary of the Bhagavadgītā, which was preached to Arjuna by the Blessed Lord in the subsequent Kṛṣṇa incarnation, reproduced in the last, that is, in the Nirvāṇa chapter, in which many verses are taken as they are from Bhagavadgītā, and it is given the name "Arjunopākhyāna" (Cf. Yoga. 6, Pū. Sarga. 52–58). I have stated above that the Śivagītā is not to be found in the Padmapurāṇa printed at Poona, but though that is so, yet a Bhagavadgītā-māhātmya is described from the 171st to the 188th chapters of the Uttarakhaṇḍa of this edition (of the Padmapurāṇa), and one chapter of this *māhātmya* is dedicated to each chapter of the Bhagavadgītā and it also contains traditionary stories about the same. There is besides one

Gitā-māhātmya in the Varāhapurāṇa and it is said that there is also a third Gītā-māhātmya in the Śaiva or Vāyupurāṇa. But I do not come across it in the Vāyupurāṇa printed in Calcutta. A small chapter of nine verses called "Gītā-dhyāna" is to be found printed in the beginning of the printed editions of the Bhagavadgītā, but I cannot say from where it has been taken. Nevertheless, the verse "*Bhīṣmadroṇa-taṭā Jayadratha-jalā*" (from these nine verses) is to be found, with slight verbal differences, at the very commencement of the recently published drama of Bhāsa called "Ūrubhaṅga". Therefore, it would seem that this Gītā-dhyāna must have come into vogue probably after the date of the dramatist Bhāsa. Because, it would be more proper to say that the Gītā-dhyāna has been prepared by borrowing different verses from different texts and writing some new verses, rather than to say that a well-known dramatist like Bhāsa has taken that verse from the Gītā-dhyāna. As the dramatist Bhāsa lived before Kālidāsa, his date cannot at most be later than Śaka 300. *

From what has been stated above, one can understand which and how many copies, and good or bad imitations, summaries and *māhātmyas* of the Gītā are to be found in the purāṇas. One cannot definitely say to what purāṇas some gītās like the Avadhūtagītā, the Aṣṭāvakragītā, etc., belong and if they do not form part of any purāṇas, then by whom and when they were independently written. Yet, if one considers the arrangement or the disposition of subject matters in all these gītās, one will see that all these works must have been written after the Bhagavadgītā had come into prominence and acquired general acceptance. Nay, one may even go further and say that these various gītās have been brought into existence with the idea that the sacred literature of a particular sect or a purāṇa does not become complete unless it contains a gītā similar to the Bhagavadgītā. As in the Bhagavadgītā, the Blessed Lord first showed to Arjuna his Cosmic Form and then preached to him the Divine Knowledge,

* Most of the above-mentioned Gītās and also several other Gītās (including the Bhagavadgītā) have been printed by Mr. Hari Raghunath Bhagwat.

so also is the case with the S'ivagītā and Devīgītā, or the Gaṇes'agītā; and in the S'ivagītā, Īs'varagītā, etc., we find many verses taken literally from the Bhagavadgītā. Considering the matter from the point of view of Spiritual Knowledge, these various gītās do not contain anything more than the Bhagavadgītā; but, what is more, the wonderful skill of establishing a harmony between the Realisation of the Highest Self (*adhyātma*) and Action (*karma*) which is seen in the Bhagavadgītā, is not to be found in any-one of these gītās. Somebody has subsequently written the Uttaragītā as a supplement to the Bhagavadgītā in the form of a conversation between Kṛṣṇa and Arjuna, in the belief that the Pātañjala-yoga or the Haṭha-yoga or the Philosophy of Renunciation (*saṁnyāsa*) by Abandonment of Action (*karma*) has not been sufficiently well described in the Bhagavadgītā, and the Avadhūta, the Aṣṭāvakra and some other gītās are purely one-sided, that is to say, they are only in support of the path of Renunciation; and the Yamagītā, Pāṇḍavagītā, and some other gītās are very small and purely devotional, like eulogistic hymns. It is true that the same is not the case with the Śivagītā, the Gaṇes'agītā and the Sūryagītā and they contain a skilful harmonising of Action and Spiritual Knowledge; yet, as that exposition in them has been more or less adopted from the Bhagavadgītā there is no novelty about them. Therefore, these paurāṇic stale gītās which have come into existence later on, fall into the shade before the profound and comprehensive brilliance of the Bhagavadgītā and the excellence of the Bhagavadgītā has been all the more established and enhanced by these imitation gītās; and the word "gītā" has come to mean Bhagavadgītā principally. Although the works Adhyātma Rāmāyaṇa and Yogavāsiṣṭha are more exhaustive, yet from their construction, they are evidently of a later date. The Gurujñānavāsiṣṭha-tattvasārāyaṇa of the Madras Presidency is a very ancient work according to some, but I am not of that opinion, because it contains a reference to 108 Upaniṣads and it cannot be said that all of them are ancient; and if one considers the Sūryagītā, we find in it a reference (see 3. 30) to Qualified-Monism (*viśiṣṭādvaita*), and in some places the arguments too seem to have been adopted from the Bhagavadgītā (1. 68), and therefore, one has to come to the conclusion that even this work was written much later on, possibly even after the date of S'rī S'aṁkarācārya.

Although there were many gītās, yet inasmuch as the Bhagavadgītā was of unquestionable excellence, as shown above, later philosophers, following the Vedic cult, thought it proper not to take much notice of the other gītās and to examine only the Bhagavadgītā and explain its import to their co-religionists. The examination of a work is of two kinds; there is the internal examination and the external examination. If one considers the book as a whole and extracts the inner meaning, the import, the implied meaning, or conclusions sought to be proved by it, that is called the "internal examination". Considering where a particular work was written, who wrote it, what kind of language is used in it, to what extent good sense or sweetness of sound are to be found in it from the poetical point of view, whether the diction of it is grammatically correct, or it contains any old archäic constructions, what opinions, places or personages are mentioned in it, and whether or not such references enable you to determine the date of the work or the social conditions availing at the time when the work was written, whether the ideas in the book are original or are borrowed from some one else, and if borrowed, then which they are, and from whom they are borrowed, etc.—which is an exposition of the purely external aspects of the book,—is called the "external examination" of the work. Those ancient commentators who have written commentaries (*bhāṣya*) or criticisms (*ṭīkā*) on the Gītā have not given much attention to these external aspects. Because, considering these matters, while examining a supernatural work like the Bhagavadgītā, would, in their opinion, be like wasting time in merely counting the petals of an excellent flower, instead of admiring its scent, colour or beauty or in criticising the combs of a honey-comb full of honey; but following the example of Western critics, modern scholars are now devoting much attention to the external examination of the Gītā. One of these has counted the archäic constructions in the Gītā and come to the conclusion that this work must have been written at least a few centuries before the birth of

Christ; and that, the doubt that the path of Devotion described in the Gītā may have been adopted from the Christian religion (which was promulgated at a later date) is absolutely without foundation. Another scholar has taken it for granted that the atheistic opinions which have been mentioned in the 16th chapter of the Gītā, must, most probably, be Buddhistic, and come to the conclusion that the Gītā must have come into existence after the date of Buddha. Another scholar says that as in the verse "*brahma-sūtra padaiś-caiva*" in the 13th chapter, the Brahma-Sūtras have been mentioned, the Gītā must have been written after the date of Brahma-Sūtras; on the other hand, several others say that as the Gītā has undoubtedly been taken as an authority in some places at least in the Brahma-Sūtras, one cannot imagine that the Gītā was later than the Brahma-Sūtras. Still other scholars say that there could have been no time for Śrī Kṛṣṇa to recite the Bhagavadgitā of 700 stanzas to Arjuna on the battle-field during the Bhārata war. In the hurry and scurry of the war, the most that Śrī Kṛṣṇa could have told Arjuna would be about 40 or 50 very important and crucial verses or the import of them and that the expansion of these verses must have been made later on when the story of the war was recited by Saṁjaya to Dhṛtarāṣṭra or by Vyāsa to Śuka or by Vaiśaṁpāyana to Janamejaya, or by Sūta to Śaunaka, or at least when the original Bhārata was expanded by some one into the 'Mahābhārata'. When such an idea has taken root in the mind regarding the construction of the Gītā, scholars have taken to diving into the ocean of the Gītā and some scholars have declared seven * and others twenty-eight or thirty-six or one hundred verses to be the original verses of the Gītā! Some

* At present, there is one Gītā which consists only of seven verses, namely, the following:—(1) "*Om ityekākṣaraṁ Brahma* etc." (Gī. 8. 13); (2) "*sthāne Hṛṣīkeśa tava prakīrtyā* etc." (Gī. 11. 36) (3) "*sarvataḥ pāṇipādaṁ tat*" etc. (Gī. 13. 13); (4) *kaviṁ purāṇam-anuśāsitāraṁ*" etc. (Gī. 8. 9); (5) "*ūrdhva mūlamadhaḥ śākhaṁ*" etc. (Gī. 15. 11); (6) "*sarvasya cāhaṁ hṛdi saṁniviṣṭo* etc." (Gī. 15. 15); (7) "*manmanā bhava madbhakto* etc" (Gī. 18. 65); and there are various other abbreviated editions of the Gītā based on the same sample.

have even gone to the length of saying that there was no occasion whatsoever for explaining to Arjuna the philosophy of the Brahman on the battle-field and that this excellent treatise on the Vedanta philosophy has been interpolated by some one later on into the Mahābhārata. It is not that these questions of external examination are totally useless. For instance, let us take the illustration of the petals of the flower or of the honey-comb which was mentioned above. In classifying vegetables, it is very necessary to consider the petals of their flowers; and it has now been proved mathematically that there are to be found combs for storage of honey in a honeycomb, which are made with the idea of economising as far as possible the quantity of wax and thereby reducing as far as possible the surface area of the external envelopes or combs without in any way reducing the cubic contents of the comb in weight of honey, and that thereby the inherent skill and intelligence of the bees can be proved. Therefore, taking into account these uses of such examination, I too have in the appendix at the end of this book, considered some important points arising in the external examination of the Gītā. But those who want to understand the esoteric import of any book, should not waste time in these external examinations. In order to show the difference between those who understand the hidden message of Vākdevī and those who formally worship her, the poet Murārī has given a very excellent illustration. He says:—

abdhir laṅghita eva vānarabhaṭaiḥ kiṁ tvasya gaṁbhīratām ।
āpātālanimagnapīvaratanur-jānāti manthācalaḥ ॥

If one wants to know of the immense depth of the ocean, whom should he ask of it? It is true that on the occasion of the war between Rāma and Rāvaṇa, powerful and agile monkey warriors crossed the ocean without difficulty and reached Ceylon (Laṅka); but how could these poor fellows have gained any knowledge of the immense depth of the ocean? The only one who can know truly of this depth is the great Mandarācala (Mandara mountain) rooted in pātāla, which was placed by the gods at the bottom of the ocean, in order to make of it a "*manthā*" or churner at the time of the churning of the ocean.

According to this logic of the poet Murārī, we must now take into account only the words of those scholars and learned persons who have churned the ocean of the Gītā in order to draw out its moral. The foremost of these writers is the writer of the Mahābhārata. One may even say that he is in a way the author of the present-day Gītā. I will, therefore, in the first place shortly explain what is the moral involved in the Gītā according to the writer of the Mahābhārata.

From the fact that the Gītā is called "Bhagavadgītā" or "the Upaniṣad sung by the Blessed Lord" one sees that the advice given in the Gītā to Arjuna is principally of the Bhāgavata religion, that is to say, of the religion promulgated by the Bhagavān, because, Śrī Kṛṣṇa is known by the name "Śrī Bhagavān" usually in the Bhāgavata religion. It is stated in the commencement of the fourth chapter of the Gītā (4. 1-3) that this religion was nothing new, but was something which had been preached by the Bhagavān to Vivasvān and by Vivasvān to Manu and by Manu to Ikṣvāku. And in the exposition of the Nārāyaṇīya or Bhāgavata religion at the end of the Śāntiparva of the Mahābhārata, after the tradition of the Bhāgavata religion in the various incarnations of Brahmadeva, that is, during the various *kalpas* has been described, it is stated in the description of the Tretāyuga out of the present life of Brahmadeva, that :—

Tretāyugādau ca tato Vivasvān Manave dadau ।
Manuś ca lokabhṛtyarthaṁ sutāyekṣvākave dadau ।
Ikṣvākuṇā ca kathito vyāpya lokānavasthitaḥ ॥

(Ma. Bhā. Śān. 348. 51-52).

i.e., "the Bhāgavata religion has been traditionally handed down by Vivasvān to Manu and by Manu to Ikṣvāku". These two traditions are consistent with each other (see my commentary on Gī. 4. 1). And in as much as the traditions of two different religions cannot be the same, one comes to the necessary conclusion, on seeing this unity of traditions, that the Gītā religion and Bhāgavata religion must be one and the same. But this matter does not depend on inference alone. Because, in the exposition of the Nārāyaṇīya or Bhāgavata religion which is to be found in the Mahābhārata itself, Vaiśampāyana has described the summary of the Gītā to Janamejaya in the following words ;–

evam eṣa mahān dharmaḥ sa te pūrvaṁ nṛpottama |
kathito Harigītāsu samāsavidhikalpitaḥ ||

(Ma. Bhā. Śān. 346. 10).

that is; "Oh excellent king, Janamejaya! this magnificent Bhāgavata religion together with its ritual was described by me to you concisely on a former occasion namely, in the Harigītā, that is, in the Bhagavadgītā." And in the second following chapter, it is clearly stated that this exposition of the Nārāyaṇīya religion :–

samupoḍheṣvanīkeṣu Kurupāṇḍavayor mṛdhe |
Arjune vimanaske ca gītā Bhagavatā svayam ||

(Ma. Bhā. Śān. 348. 8).

that is; "was made by the Blessed Lord when during the fight between the Kauravas and the Pāṇḍavas both the armies had become ready for war and Arjuna had become dejected *i.e.* '*vimanaska*.'" From this it follows beyond doubt that the word "Harigītā" in this place means the Bhagavadgītā and nothing else. Thus, the preceptorial tradition of these two religions is the same. This "Bhāgavata" or "Nārāyaṇīya" religion which has been twice mentioned in the Gītā as being the subject matter of exposition, has the other names of "Sātvata" or "Ekāntika" religion, and where that religion is being expounded in the Mahābhārata, its two-fold quality is described thus :–

Nārāyaṇaparo dharmaḥ punarāvṛttidurlabhaḥ |
pravṛttilakśaṇaś caiva dharmo Nārāyaṇātmakaḥ ||

(Ma. Bhā. Śan. 347. 80–81)

that is; "this Nārāyaṇīya religion is such as obviates re-birth (*punar-janma*) *i. e.* gives complete Release (*mokṣa*) and is also Energistic (*pravṛttipara*)" and then it is clearly explained how this religion is Energistic.

The word "Energism" (*pravṛtti*) is understood in popular acceptance as meaning, performing desirelessly the duties which pertain to one's status in life, according to the arrangement of the four castes, without taking up Asceticism (*saṁnyāsa*). It, therefore, follows that the sermon given in the Gītā to Arjuna is of the Bhāgavata religion and, in as much as that religion is Energistic, it also follows that the writer of the Mahābhārata looked upon that advice also as Energistic. Nevertheless, it is not that the Gītā contains only the Energistic Bhāgavata religion. Vais'aṁpāyana has further said to Janamejaya:

yatīnāṁ cāpi yo dharmaḥ sa te pūrvaṁ nṛpottama ।
kathito Harigītāsu samāsavidhikalpitaḥ ॥

(Ma. Bhā. S'ān. 348. 53).

that is :—" this Bhāgavata religion and side by side with it (*cāpi*) the renunciatory religion of ascetics (*saṁnyāsi*) together with the relative ritual has, O excellent King, been explained by me to you before in the Bhagavadgītā ". Still, although the renunciatory religion has in this way been mentioned in the Gītā side by side with the energistic religion of Action, yet the tradition of the Gītā religion of Manu, Ikṣvāku etc. which has been mentioned in the Gītā does not at all apply to the renunciatory religion; it is consistent only with the tradition of the Bhāgavata religion. It, therefore, follows from the statements referred to above that according to the writer of the Mahābhārata, the advice which has been given to Arjuna in the Gītā relates principally to the Energistic Bhāgavata religion traditionally handed down from Manu to Ikṣvāku etc., and that it contains a reference to the renunciatory path of ascetics only as a side reference. That this progressive or Energistic Nārāyaṇīya religion in the Mahābhārata and theBhāgavata religion of the Bhāgavata-Purāṇa are fundamentally one and the same, will be seen to be quite clear from the statements made by Pṛthu, Priyavrata, Prahlāda and other devotees of the Blessed Lord or from the other descriptions of the path of Desireless Action which are to be found elsewhere in the Bhāgavata (Bhāgavata. 4. 22. 51-52; 7. 10. 23 and 11. 4. 6). But the true purpose of the Bhāgavata-Purāṇa is not to justify the Energistic principles in favour of Action contained in Bhāgavata religion. This justification is to be found in the Mahābhārata or principally in the Gītā. But, it is stated in the earlier chapters of the Bhāgavata, that while justifying these principles, Śrī Vyāsa forgot to define the moral value of the devotional aspect of the Bhāgavata religion, and as Desireless Action (*naiṣkarmya*) by itself is useless without Devotion (Bhāgavata. 1. 5. 12), the Bhāgavata-Purāṇa had to be subsequently written to make up for this deficit. From this the real import of the Bhāgavata-Purāṇa becomes quite clear; and on that account, the Energistic aspect of the Bhāgavata religion has not been as forcefully emphasised in the Bhāgavata as the devotional aspect of devotion to the Blessed Lord, which has been explained by the recitation of numerous stories. Nay, the writer of the Bhāgavata says that all yoga of Energism (Karma-Yoga) is useless in the absence of Devotion (Bhāg 1. 5. 34). Therefore, the Bhāgavata-Purāṇa which lays stress on Devotion is not—although it relates to the Bhāgavata religion—as useful for determining the moral laid down in the Gītā as the Nārāyaṇīya Upākhyāna of the Bhārata itself which contains the Gītā; and if the Bhāgvata-Purāṇa is made use of for that purpose, then one must do so, bearing clearly in mind, that both the object and the time of the Bhārata and the Bhāgavata are quite different. The various questions as to what were the original forms of the renunciatory religion of monks and of the Energistic Bhāgavata religion, what the reasons were for this difference, in what respects the form of the original Bhāgavata religion has changed in present times etc. will be considered later on in detail.

I have so far dealt with what the moral of the Gītā is according to the writer of the Mahābhārata himself. Let us now see what the purport of the Gītā is according to those persons who have written commentaries (*bhāṣya*) and criticisms on the Gītā. Among these commentaries and criticisms, the *bhāṣya* on the Gītā of Śrī Śaṁkarācārya is considered to be the most ancient. But there is no doubt that there had been numerous other commentaries or criticisms on the Gītā before that date. These commentaries, however, are not now available and therefore, there are now no means for determining in what way the Gītā was interpreted in the interval between the date of the Mahābhārata and the birth of Śaṁkarācārya. Nevertheless, it is quite clear from the references to the opinions of these earlier critics which are to be found in the Śāṁkarabhāṣya itself (Gī. Śāṁ. Bhā. Introductions to Chap. 1 and 3) that the commentators who had come before Śaṁkarācārya had placed an Energistic interpretation on the Gītā, as combining Action with Spiritual Realisation, that is to say, to the effect that every man who had acquired spiritual knowledge had nevertheless to continue performing the duties pertaining to his particular status in life so long as he lived—as had been done by the writer of the Mahābhārata. But as this doctrine of the Vedic Karma-Yoga was not palatable to Śaṁkarācārya, he has in the commencement of the Bhāṣya, in the introduction, clearly stated that he had written the Bhāṣya with the sole intention of refuting that opinion and of explaining what the esoteric moral of the Gītā was according to himself. As a matter of fact, this is exactly what the word "*bhāṣya*" means. The two words "commentary" (*bhāṣya*) and "criticism" (*ṭīkā*) are, it is true, often used as being synonymous. But ordinarily "ṭīkā" means explaining the plain meaning of the original work and making the understanding of the words in it easy; but the writer of the "*bhāṣya*" does not remain satisfied with that; he critically and logically examines the entire work and explains what its purport is according to his opinion and how that work has to be interpreted consistently with that purport. That is the nature of the Śāṁkarabhāṣya on the Gītā. But the different way in which the Ācārya has interpreted the moral of the Gītā requires the previous history to be shortly mentioned before one understands the underlying reason for it. The Vedic religion was not purely ritualistic (*tāntrika*) and the Upaniṣads had minutely considered even in very ancient times the deep underlying import of it. But as these Upaniṣads have been written by different ṛṣis at different times, they contain various kinds of thought and some of them are apparently mutually contradictory. Bādarāyaṇācārya has reconciled these inconsistencies and he has in his Brahma-Sūtras harmonised all the Upaniṣads; and on that account, the Vedānta-Sūtras are considered to be as authoritative on this matter as the Upaniṣads themselves. These Vedānta-Sūtras are also known by the other names of "Brahma-Sūtras" or "Śārīraka-Sūtras". Yet the consideration of the philosophy of the Vedic religion does not end here. Because, as the spiritual knowledge in the Upaniṣads is primarily ascetical, that is renunciatory, and as the Vedānta-Sūtras have been written only with the intention of harmonising the Upaniṣads, we find nowhere even in the Upaniṣads any detailed and logical exposition of the Energistic Vedic religion. Therefore, when as stated above, the Energistic Bhagavadgītā for the first time supplemented the philosophy of the Vedic religion it became, as a supplement to the religious philosophy in the Vedas and in the Upaniṣads, a work as authoritative and acceptable as both; and later on, the Upaniṣads, the Vedānta-Sūtras and the Bhagavadgītā acquired the collective name of "Prasthāna-trayī" (the Trinity of Systems). "Prasthāna-trayī" means the three principal authoritative works or pillars of the Vedic religion which systematically and scientifically expounded the two paths of Renunciation (*nivṛtti*) and Energism (*pravṛtti*). When once the Bhagavadgītā came in this way to be included in the "Prasthāna-trayī" and the sovereignty of this "Prasthāna-trayī" came to be firmly established, all religious opinions or cults which were inconsistent with these three works or which could not find a place in them, came to be considered as inferior and unacceptable by the followers of the Vedic religion. The net result of this was that the protagonist Ācāryas of each of the various cults which came into existence in India after the extinction of the Buddhistic religion, such as, the Monistic *(advaita)*, the Qualified-Monistic (*viśiṣṭādvaita*), the Dualistic *(dvaita)* and and the Purely Monistic *(śuddhādvaita)* cults with the superadded principles of Devotion (*bhakti*) or Renunciation (*saṁnyāsa*) had to write commentaries on all the three parts of the Prasthāna-trayī (and, necessarily on the Bhagavadgītā also), and had somehow or other to prove that according to these three works, which had become authoritative and acceptable as Scriptures long before those cults came into existence, the particular cult promulgated by them was the correct cult, and that the other cults were inconsistent with those Scriptures. Because, if they had admitted that these authoritative religious treatises would support other cults besides those propounded by themselves, the value of their particular cult would to that extent suffer and that was not desirable for any of these protagonists. When once this rule of writing sectarian (*sāmpradāyika*) commentaries on the Prasthāna-trayī supporting a particular doctrine came into vogue, different learned writers began to propound in their criticisms their own interpretations of the moral of the Gītā on the authority of the commentaries pertaining to their particular doctrine and such criticisms began to gain authority in those particular sects. The commentaries or criticisms which are now available on the Gītā, are more or less all of this kind, that is to say, they are written by Ācāryas pertaining to diverse sects; and on that account, although the original Bhagavadgītā propounds only one theme, yet it has come to be believed that the same Gītā supports all the various cults. The first, that is the most ancient of these cults is that of Śrī Śaṁkarācārya, and from the point of view of philosophy, that cult has become the one most accepted in India. The first Śaṁkarācārya was born in the year 710 of the Śālivāhana era (788 A. D.) and in the 32nd year of his age, he entered the caves (Śaka. 710 to 742.) i. e. 788–820 A.D.* The Ācārya was a superman and a great sage and he had by his brilliant intellectual power refuted the Jain and the Buddhistic doctrines which had then gained ground on all sides and established his own Non-Dualistic (*advaita*) doctrine; and, as is well-known, he established four monastaries (*maṭha*) in the four directions of India for the protection of the Vedic religion contained in the Śrutis and Smṛtis and for the second time in the Kali-Yuga gave currency to the Vedic renunciatory doctrine or cult of Asceticism (*saṁnyāsa*). Whatever religious doctrine is taken, it naturally falls into two divisions; one is the philosophical aspect of it and the other, the actual mode of life prescribed by it. In the first part, the meaning of Release (*mokṣa*) is usually explained in a scientific and logical way after explaining what conclusions must be drawn as to the nature of the Parameśvara after a proper consideration of the material body (*piṇḍa*) in its relation to the Cosmos (*brahmāṇḍa*); in the other part, there is an explanation of how a man has to lead his life in this world, so that such mode of life should become a means for obtaining

* In my opinion, the date of the first Śaṁkarācārya must be pushed back by at least 100 years, and I have given my reasons for doing so in the Appendix.

The Pictorial map of the Prominent Schools of Indian Philosophy

Designed by:—R. B. TILAK

(Copyright)

that Release *(mokṣa)*. According to the first of these, that is to say, according to the philosophical aspects of the doctrine, Śaṁkarācārya says that (1) the multiplicity of the various objects in the world, such as, "I", "You", or all the other things which are visible to the eye, is not a true multiplicity, but that there is in all of them a single, pure, and eternal Highest Self *(Parabrahman)*, and various human organs experience a sense of multiplicity as a result of the Illusion *(māyā)* of that Parabrahman; (2) the Self *(Ātman)* of a man is also fundamentally of the same nature as the Parabrahman; and (3) that it is not possible for any one to obtain Release *(mokṣa)* except after the complete Realisation *(jñāna)* or personal experience of this identity of the Ātman and the Parabrahman. This is known as Non-Dualism *(advaita-vāda)*, because, the sum and substance of this doctrine is, that there is no other independent and real substance except one pure self-enlightened, eternal, and Released Parabrahman; that the multiplicity which is visible to the eyes is an optical illusion or an imaginary experience resulting from the effect of Illusion *(māyā)*; and that Māyā is not some distinct, real, or independent substance, but is unreal *(mithyā)*; and, when one has to consider only the philosophical aspect of the doctrine, it is not necessary to go deeper into this opinion of Śrī Śaṁkarācārya. But that does not end there. Coupled with the Non-Dualistic philosphy there is another proposition of the Śāṁkara doctrine relating to the mode of life, that, although it is necessary to perform the Actions pertaining to the state of a householder in order to acquire the capacity of realising the identity of the Brahman and the Ātman by the purification of the mind, yet it will be impossible to obtain Release unless one discontinues those actions later on and ultimately gives them up and takes up *saṁnyāsa* (asceticism); because, in as much as Action *(karma)* and Knowledge *(jñāna)* are mutually antogonistic like light and darkness, the knowledge of the Brahman does not become perfect unless a man has entirely conquered all root tendencies *(vāsanā)* and given up all Actions. This second proposition is known as the Path of Renunciation *(nivṛtti-mārga)*, or because in this path one ultimately gives up all Actions and remains steeped in Knowledge or Realisation it is also called "*saṁnyāsa-niṣṭhā*" (the Path of Renunciation) or "*jñāna-niṣṭhā*" (the Path of Realisation). It is stated in the Śāṁkarabhāṣya on the Upaniṣads and on the Brahmasūtras that not only the Non-Dualistic philosophy but also the Path of Renunciation, that is to say, both the aspects of the cult of Śaṁkara have been preached in those books; and in the Bhāṣya on the Gītā, a definite conclusion has been drawn that the teaching of the Bhagavadgītā is the same (Gī. Śaṁ. Bhā. Introduction; and Brahma-Sū. Śāṁ. Bhā. 2. 1. 14); and as authority for that, he has quoted such sentences from the Gītā as "*jñānāgniḥ sarva-karmāṇi bhasmasāt kurute*" i. e., "all Action (*karma*) is reduced to ashes in the fire of *jñāna*" (Gī. 4. 37) and "*sarva karmākhilaṁ Pārtha jñāne parisamāpyate*" i. e., "all Actions culminate in Realisation (*jñāna*)" (Gī. 4. 33). In short, the Śāṁkarabhāṣya has been written in order to show that the teaching of the Gītā is consistent with that particular Vedic path which—after proving it to be the most excellent one—was recommended by Śaṁkarācārya, after he had refuted the Buddhistic doctrines; and further, to show that the Gītā is not in favour of the combination of Knowledge with Action, which was prescribed by the previous commentators; and to show that the Blessed Lord has in the Gītā preached to Arjuna the doctrine of the Śāṁkara cult, that Action is only a means of acquiring Knowledge and is inferior and that Release is ultimately obtained only by Knowledge combined with Renunciation of Action. If there had been any commentary on the Gītā before the date of Śaṁkarācārya, interpreting it as favouring Asceticism, such a commentary is not now available. Therefore, we must say that the first attempt to deprive the Gītā of its Energistic form and to give it a Renunciatory doctrinal form was made by the Śāṁkarabhāṣya. Those commentators on the Gītā who came after Śrī Śaṁkarācārya and who followed his doctrines, such as, Madhusūdana and others, have in this matter principally adopted the procedure of the Ācārya. Yet, later on, there came into existence another queer idea, namely that the principal sacred canon enunciated in the Chāndogyopaniṣad, namely, "TAT TVAM ASI" i. e., "THAT (Parabrahman) ART THOU (Śvetaketu)", which is one of the sacred canons of the Non-Dualistic cult, is the canon which has been expatiated upon in the eighteen chapters of the Gītā, but that the Blessed Lord has changed the order of the three parts of that sacred canon and taken "*tvaṁ*" first and "*tat*" after that and "*asi*" last, and He has in this new order impartially allotted six chapters of the Gītā to each of these parts equally! The Paiśāca-bhāṣya on the Gītā does not pertain to any particular doctrine but is independent and it is believed to have been written by Hanumān i. e., by Mārutī. But such is not the case. This Bhāṣya has been written by the philosopher Hanumān, who has also written a criticism on the Bhāgavata and it supports the path of Renunciation and in it, in some places, interpretations have been copied verbatim from the Sāṁkarabhāṣya. In the same way, the older or modern Marathi translations of or commentaries on the Gītā principally follow the Śāṁkarabhāṣya; and the English translation of the Bhagavadgītā by the late Kashinath Trimbak Telang, published in the Sacred Books of East Series brought out by Professor Max Müller, is stated by him at the end of the introduction to that translation, to be as far as possible consistent with Śrī Śaṁkarācārya and the commentators of his school.

When once in this way, doctrinal commentaries on the Gītā and on the other two works out of the Prasthāna-trayī began to be written, the same course was later on followed by persons holding other doctrinal views. About 250 years after the coming to existence of the Śāṁkara tradition which maintained the theory of Illusion *(māyā)*, Non-Dualism *(advaita)* and Renunciation *(saṁnyāsa)*, Śrī Rāmānujācārya (born Śaka 938 i. e. 1016 A. D.) founded the Qualified-Monism *(viśiṣṭādvaita)* tradition; and in order to substantiate that cult he also, like Śrī Śaṁkarācārya, has written independent commentaries *(bhāṣya)* on the Prasthāna-trayī, including, of course, the Gītā. This school is of the opinion that the doctrines of the Unreality of Illusion *(māyā)* and Non-Dualism laid down by Śaṁkarācārya were not correct and that although the three principles of Consciousness *(jīva)*, Cosmos *(jagat)* and Īśvara were independent, yet in as much as *jīva*, i. e., consciousness *(cit)*, and the Cosmos (which is *acit* i. e., unconscious) were both the body of one and the same Īśvara, therefore, the *cit-acit*-bodied Īśvara was one and one alone and that out of this subtle '*cit*' and '*acit*' in the body of the Īśvara, the gross *cit* and the gross *acit* or the numerous forms of Life and the Cosmos came into existence later on; and Rāmānujācārya says that from the philosophical point of view, this is the doctrine which has been enunciated by the Upaniṣads and the Brahma-Sūtras (Gī. Rāmā. 2. 12; 13. 2). One may even say that the works of Rāmānujācārya were responsible for the Qualified-Monism doctrine finding its way into the Bhāgavata religion; because, the previous exposition of the Bhāgavata religion to be found in the Māhābhārata and in the Gītā is seen to be on the basis of the Non-Dualistic cult. As Rāmānujācārya belonged to the Bhāgavata religion, he ought to have naturally realised that the Gītā enunciated the Energistic path of Karma-Yoga. But as at the date of Rāmānujācārya, the Karma-Yoga of the original Bhāgavata religion had practically come to an end and it had acquired a Qualified-Monistic (*viśiṣṭādvaita*) form in its philosophical aspect, and principally a Devotional form from the point of view of the mode of life, Rāmānujācārya drew the further conclusions that although *jñāna, karma* and *bhakti* (Devotion) are all three referred to in the Gītā, yet the doctrine enunciated in the Gītā is in essence Qualified-Monistic from the point of view of philosophy, and of Devotion to the Vāsudeva from the point of view of mode of life; and that the Path of Action (*karma-niṣṭhā*) was something which led to Path of Knowledge (*jñāna-niṣṭhā*) and was not something independent (Gī. Rā. Bhā. 18. 1 and 3. 1). But although Rāmānujācārya had effected a change in the cult of Śaṁkara by substituting the Qualified-Monism for Non-Duality and Devotion for Renunciation, yet if Devotion is looked upon as the highest duty of man from the point of view of mode of life, then the lifelong performance of the worldly duties pertaining to one's particular status, becomes an inferior mode of life; and on that account the interpretation put on the Gītā by Rāmānujācārya must also be looked upon as in a way in favour of Renunciation of Action. Because, when once the mind has become purified as a result of an Energistic mode of life, and man has attained Realisation (*jñāna*), whether he, thereafter, adopts the fourth stage of life and remains steeped in the contemplation of the Brahman or he is steeped in the unbounded loving worship of the Vāsudeva is just the same from the point of view of Action *(karma)*; that is to say, both are Renunciatory. And the same objection applies to the other cults which came into existence after the date of Rāmānujācārya. Although Rāmānujācārya may have been right in saying that the theory of the Non-Reality of Illusion is wrong and that one ultimately attains Release only by devotion to the Vāsudeva, yet looking upon the Parabrahman and the Conscious Ego *(jīva)* as ONE in one way, and different in other ways is a contradiction in terms and an inconsistency. Therefore, a third school which came into existence after the date of Śrī Rāmānujācārya, is of the opinion, that both must be looked upon as eternally different from each other and that there never can be any unity between them, whether partial or total, and therefore, this school is known as the Dualistic school. The protagonist of this school was Śrī Madhvācārya, alias Śrīmadānandatīrtha. He died in Śaka 1120 (1198 A.D.) and according to the Madhva school, he was then 79 years old. But Dr. Bhandarkar has in the English Book "Vaiṣṇavism, Śaivism, and other sects" recently published by him, established on the authority of stone inscriptions and other books (see page 59) that Madhvācārya must be taken to have lived from Śaka 1119 to 1198 (1197 to 1276 A. D.). Madhvācārya has shown in his commentaries on the Prasthāna-trayī (which includes the Gītā) that all these sacred books are in favour of the theory of Duality. In his commentary on the Gītā, he says that although Desireless Action has been extolled in the Gītā, yet Desireless Action is only a means and Devotion is the true and ultimate cult, and that when once one has become perfect by following the Path of Devotion, whether one thereafter performs or does not perform Action is just the same. It is true that there are some statements in the Gītā such as, "*dhyānāt karmaphalatyāgaḥ*" ...i. e., "the abandonment of the fruit of the action (i. e., Desireless Action) is superior to the meditation on the Parameśvara (i. e., Devotion)" etc. which are inconsistent with this doctrine; but, says the Mādhvabhāṣya on the Gītā, such sentences are not to be understood literally but as mere expletives and unimportant (Gī. Mābhā. 12. 30). The fourth school is the school of Śrī Vallabhācārya (born in Śaka 1401 i. e. 1479 A. D.) This is also a Vaiṣṇava School like those of Rāmānuja and Madhvācārya. However, the opinions of this school regarding the Conscious Ego (*jīva*), Cosmos (*jagat*), and Īśvara are different from the opinions of the Qualified-Monism or the Dualistic Schools. This school accepts the doctrine that the Conscious Ego (*jīva*) when pure and unblinded by Illusion (*māyā*) and the Parabrahman are one, and are not two distinct things; and that is why, this school is known as the pure Non-Dualistic (*śuddhādvaita*), school. Nevertheless this School differs from the Śāṁkara school on account of the other doctrines pertaining to it, namely that, the Conscious Ego (*jīva*) and the Brahman cannot be looked upon as one and the same in the same sense as is done by Śrī Śaṁkarācārya but that the various Souls are particles of the Īśvara, like sparks of fire; that the Cosmos, which is composed of Illusion, is not unreal (*mithyā*) but Illusion is a Force which has separated itself from the Īśvara at the desire of the Parameśvara, that the Conscious Ego (*jīva*) which has become dependent on Illusion, cannot acquire the knowledge necessary for obtaining Release except by divine pleasure; and that, therefore, Devotion to the Blessed Lord is the most important means of obtaining Release. This pleasure of the Parameśvara is also known by the other names of '*puṣṭi*' '*poṣaṇa*' etc. and, therefore, this cult is also known as '*puṣṭi-mārga*'. In the books of this school on the Gītā, such as the *Tattvadīpikā* and others, it is laid down that in as much as the Blessed Lord has, after first preaching to Arjuna the Saṁkhya philosophy and the Karma-Yoga, ultimately made him perfect by treating him with the nectar of the philosophy of Devotion, Devotion but above all, the Devotion included in '*puṣṭi-mārga*'—which entails the abandonment of home and domestic ties—is the most concentrated moral of the Gītā and that on that account the Blessed Lord has in the end given the advice:—"*sarva-dharmān parityajya māmekaṁ śaraṇaṁ vraja*"—i. e., "give up all other religions and surrender yourself to Me alone" (Gī. 18. 66). Besides these, there is another Vaiṣṇava cult, entailing the worship of Rādhākṛṣṇa, which was promulgated by Nimbārka. Dr. Bhandarkar has established that this Ācārya lived after the date of Rāmānujācārya and before the date of Madhvācārya ; that is to say about Śaka. 1084 (1162 A. D.) The opinion of Nimbārkācārya regarding the Conscious Ego *(jīva)* the Cosmos *(jagat)* and the Īśvara is, that although these three are different from each other, yet the existence and activity of the Conscious Ego *(jīva)* and of the Cosmos are not independent but depend upon the desire of the Īśvara; and that the subtle elements of the Conscious Ego (jīva) and of the Cosmos are contained in the fundamental Īśvara. In order to prove this doctrine, Nimbārka has written an independent *bhāṣya* on the Vedānta-sūtras, and Keśava Kaśmīri Bhattācārya, who belongs to this school has written a commentary on the Bhagavadgītā called '*Tattvaprakāśikā*' and has shown in it that the moral laid down by the Gītā is consistent with the doctrines of this school. In order to differentiate this school from the Qualified-Monism school of Rāmānujācārya, one may refer to it as the Dual-Non-Dual *(dvaitādvaita)* school. It is quite clear that these different Devotional sub-cults of Duality and Qualified- Monism which discard the Śaṁkara doctrine of Māyā have come into existence because of the belief that Devotion, that is, the worship of a tangible thing, loses foundation and to a certain extent becomes forceless, unless one looks upon the visible objects in the world as real. But one cannot say that in order to justify Devotion, the theories of Non-duality or of Illusion have to be discarded. The saints in the Mahārāṣṭra have substantiated the doctrine of Devotion without discarding the doctrines of Illusion and Non-Duality ; and this course seems to have been followed from before the time of Śrī Śaṁkarācārya. In this cult, the doctrines of Non-Duality, the illusory nature of things, and the necessity of abandonment of Action which are the concomitant doctrines of the Śaṁkara cult are taken for granted. But the advice of the followers of this school, such as the Saint Tukārām, is that Devotion is the easiest of the means by which Release in the shape of realising the identity of the Brahman and the Ātman, can be obtained : "if you want to reach the Īśvara, then this is the easiest way" (Tukā. Gā. 3002. 2) ; and they say that the path of Devotion based on Non-Duality is the principal moral of the Gītā in as much as the Blessed Lord himself has first told Arjuna that *"kleśodhi-*

katarasteṣām avyaktāsaktacetasām " (Gī. 12. 5)...i. e., " concentrating the mind on the Intangible Brahman is more difficult " and subsequently told him that : " *bhaktāstetīva me priyāḥ* " i. e., " my devotees are most beloved of me " (Gī. 12. 20). The summing up of the Gītā which has been made by Śrīdhar Svāmī in his commentary on the Gītā (Gī. 18. 78) is of this kind. But, the most valuable work relating to this school, though in the Marathi language, is the Jñāneśvarī. In this work it is stated that the Doctrine of Karma is dealt with in the first four out of the 18 chapters of the Gītā, the Doctrine of Devotion in the next seven and the Doctrine of Jñana in the subsequent chapters and Jñāneśvara himself has at the end of his book said that he has written his commentary " after consulting the Bhāṣyakāras (Śaṁkarācārya)." But, as Jñāneśvara Mahārāja had the wonderful skill of expounding the meaning of the Gītā, by numerous beautiful illustrations and comparisons and also, as he has propounded the doctrines of Desireless Action and principally the doctrine of Devotion in a much better way than Śrī Śaṁkarācārya, the Jñāneśvarī must be looked upon as an independent treatise on the Gītā. Jñāneśvara Mahārāja himself was a *yogi*. Therefore, he has written a very detailed commentary on that verse in the sixth chapter of the Gītā which deals with the practice of the Pātañjala Yoga, and in it he has said that the words of the Blessed Lord at the end of the chapter namely : " *tasmādyogī bhavārjuna* "...i. e., "therefore, Oh Arjuna, become a Yogī, that is, become proficient in the practice of the Yoga " show that the Blessed Lord has declared the Pātañjala Yoga to be the '*pantharāja* ' i. e., the most excellent of all paths. In short, different commentators have interpreted the Gītā in their own ways by first declaring the Energistic path of Action (Karma-Yoga) preached by the Gītā to be inferior, that is to say, merely a means for Realisation *(jñāna)*, and then going on to say that the Gītā has preached the various philosophical doctrines, as also the highest duties from the point of view of Release, which are prescribed by their respective schools, such as: Non-Dualism based on the doctrine of Illusion, coupled with Renunciation of Action; or Qualified-Monism based on the reality of Illusion, coupled with Devotion to the Vāsudeva; or

Dualism, coupled with worship of the Viṣṇu; or pure Non-dualism, coupled with Devotion; or the Non-Dualism of the Śāṁkara cult, coupled with Devotion; or Pātañjala yoga, coupled with Devotion; or Devotion pure and simple; or Yoga pure and simple; or Realisation of the Brahman pure and simple,*—all of which are paths of Release, based on Renunciation. No one says that the Bhagavadgītā looks upon the Karma-Yoga as the most excellent path of life. It is not that I alone say so. Even the well-known Marathi poet Vāman Pandit is of the same opinion. In his exhaustive commentary on the Gītā, in the Marathi language known as *Yathārtha-dīpika*, he first says :— " But Oh, Blessed Lord, in this Kali-yuga each one interpretes the Gītā according to his own opinion ", and he goes on to say : " Everyone on some pretext or other gives a different meaning to the Gītā but I do not like this their doing, though they are great ; what shall I do, Oh, Blessed Lord ? " This is his complaint to the Blessed Lord. Seeing this confusion of the diverse opinions of the commentators, some scholars say that in as much as these various traditionary doctrines of Release are mutually contradictory and one cannot definitely say that any particular one of them has been recommended by the Gītā, one has to come to the conclusion that the Blessed Lord has on the battle-field at the commencement of the war described individually, precisely, and skilfully all these various means of attaining Release—and specially, the three paths of Action *(karma)*, Devotion *(bhakti)*, and Realisation *(jñāna)* and satisfied Arjuna in whose mind there had arisen a confusion about these diverse means of attaining Release. It is true that some commentators do maintain that these descriptions of the various means of Release are not several or unconnected with each other, but the Gītā has harmonised them with each other ; and finally, there are also to be found others who say that although the teaching of the Brahman in the Gītā is apparently easy, yet the true import of it is very deep and no one can

*The several commentaries on the Gītā by the Ācāryas of the various cults and the important criticisms pertaining to those cults in all fifteen, have been recently published at the Guzrathi Printing Press. This book is very useful for studying the opinions advanced by the various commentators side by side.

understand it except from the mouth of a preceptor (Gī. 4. 34.), and that though there may be numerous criticisms on the Gītā, yet, there is no other way to realise the true meaning of it, except from the mouth of a preceptor.

These numerous interpretations of the Bhagavadgītā, namely, the Energistic interpretation consistent with the Bhāgavata religion made by the writer of the Mahābhārata and the other purely Renunciatory ones made by several later Ācāryas, poets, yogis, or devotees of the Blessed Lord, consistently with the different traditionary schools to which they respectively belonged, are likely to cause confusion and one will naturally ask whether it is possible that all these mutually contradictory interpretations can be put on one and the same work; and if it is not only possible but even desirable, then why so? No one can entertain any doubt that these various Ācāryas who wrote the commentaries were learned, religious and extremely pure-minded. Nay, one may even say that the world has not to this day produced a philosopher of the calibre of Śrī. Śaṁkarācārya. Then why should there have been such a difference between him and the later Ācāryas? The Gītā is not such a pot of jugglery, that any one can extract any meaning he likes out of it. The Gītā had been written long before these various schools of thought came into existence, and it was preached by Śrī Kṛṣṇa to Arjuna not to increase his confusion but to remove it; and it contains a preaching of one definite creed to Arjuna (Gī. 5. 1, 2), and the effect of that advice on Arjuna has also been what it ought to have been. Then, why should there be so much confusion about the teaching of the Gītā? This question seems a really difficult one. But the answer of it is not as difficult as would appear, at first sight. Suppose, looking at a sweet and nice food-preparation, one says that it is made of wheat, and another one says it is made of ghee and a third one says, it is made of sugar, according to his own taste; then, which one of them will you call wrong? Each one is correct in his own way and ultimately the question what that food-preparation is, remains unsolved. Because, as it is possible to mix wheat, clarified butter, and sugar and to prepare from them various kinds of eatables such as 'ladūs,' 'jilebī', 'ghīwar' etc. the particular eatable cannot be sufficiently defined by saying that ghee or wheat or sugar is the principle element in it. Just as when the ocean was churned, though one person got nectar, another one got poison, and others got Lakśmī, Airāvata, Kaustubha, Pārijāta, and other articles, yet the real nature of the ocean was not thereby fixed, so also is the case of the commentators who have churned the ocean of the Gītā on a doctrinal basis, or one may even say that just as, the same Śrī. Kṛṣṇa Bhagavāna who had entered the Durbar at the time of the assasination of Kaṁsa, appeared to various persons in different forms, that is, he appeared to athletes like adamant and to women like the God of Beauty (*Madana*) and to parents like their own son etc. (Bhāg. 10. Pū. 43. 17), so also although the Bhagavadgītā is one and the same, people following different cults see it in a different light. Whatever religious cult may be taken, it is quite clear that ordinarily it must be based on some authoritative religious text or other; otherwise that cult will be considered to be totally without authority and will not be acceptable to people. Therefore, however numerous the different cults of the Vedic religion may be, yet with the exception of a few specified things, such as, the Īśvara, the Conscious Ego and the Cosmos and their mutual interrelations, all other things are common to all the various cults; and therefore, in the various doctrinal commentaries or criticisms which have been written on our authoritative religious texts, ninety per cent of the statements or stanzas in the original work are interpreted in more or less the same way. The only difference is as regards the remaining statements or doctrines. If these statements are taken in their literal meaning, they cannot possibly be equally appropriate to all the cults. Therefore, different commentators, who have propounded different doctrines, usually accept as important only such of these statements as are consistent with their own particular cult, and either say that the others are unimportant, or skilfully twist the meanings of such statements as might be totally inconsistent with their cults, or wherever possible, they draw hidden meanings or inferences favourable to themselves from easy and plain statements, and say that the particular work is an authority for their particular cult. For instance, see my commentary on Gītā 2. 12 and 16; 3. 19; 6.

3 and 18. 2. But it will be easily seen that laying down in this way that a book has a particular purport, and examining in the first place, without prejudice, the whole of the work, and drawing its implied purport without insisting that one's own cult is propounded by the Gītā, or on any such other thing, are two totally different things.

If one gives up the doctrinal method of determining the purport of a book as faulty, one must show what other means there are for determining the import of the Gītā. There is an old and more or less generally accepted rule on this matter in the form of a verse of the Mīmāṁsā writers, who were extremely skilful in determining the meanings of a particular book, chapter, or sentence. That verse is as follows;—

upakramopasaṁhārau abhyāso 'pūrvatā phalam ।
arthavādopapattī ca liṅgaṁ tātparyanirṇaye ॥

The Mīmāṁsā writers say that if one has to find out the purport of any particular writing, chapter, or book, then the seven things mentioned in the above verse are necessary (i. e., *liṅga*). and all these seven things have got to be considered. The first two out of these are '*upakramopasaṁhārau*', which mean the beginning and the end of the book. Every writer starts writing a book with some motive or other in his mind; and when that particular object has been achieved, he completes his book. Therefore, the commencement and the end of the work have first to be taken into account in determining the purport of the book. Geometry has defined a straight line as a line which goes from the point of commencement straight to the last point without swerving above or below or to the right or to the left. The same rule applies to the purport of a book. That purport which is properly fixed between the beginning and the end of the book and does not leave or divert from either of them, is the proper purport of it. If there are other roads for going from the beginning to the end, all those roads must be considered as crooked roads or bye-paths. When the direction of the purport of a work has in this way been fixed with due consideration for the commencement and the end, one should see what things are told repeatedly in it, that is to say, of what things an '*abhyāsa*' has been made. Because, whatever thing is intended by the writer of a book to be proved, he shows numerous reasons in support of it on numerous occasions and refers to it as a definite proposition over and over again, saying each time: "therefore, this thing is proved", or, "therefore, this particular thing has got to be done". The fourth and the fifth means for determining the purport of the work are the new-ness (*apūrvatā*) and the effect (*phala*) of it. '*Apūrvatā*' means something new. Unless the writer has something new to tell, he is usually not induced to write a new book; at any rate, that used to be so when there were no printing-presses. Therefore, before determining the purport of a book one has in the first instance to see what it contains which is new, particular, or not previously known. In the same way, if some particular result has been achieved by that writing or by that book, that is to say, if it has had some definite effect, then one must also take into account that result or effect. Because, in as much as the book has been written with the express intention that that particular result or effect should be achieved, the object of the writer becomes clearer from the effect which has been achieved. The sixth and the seventh means are '*arthavāda*' and '*upapatti*'. '*Arthavāda*' is a technical term of the Mimāṁsā school (Jai.-Sū. 1. 2. 1-18). Although the thing about which a statement is to be made or the fact which is to be proved is fixed, the writer nevertheless, deals with many other things as occasion arises, whether by way of illustration or by way of comparison in the course of the argument, and whether for showing consistency or for showing the similarity or the difference, or in order to support his own side by showing the faults of the opposite side, or for the sake of grace or as an exaggeration, or by way of stating the previous history of the question, or for some other reason, with the idea of supplementing the argument, and sometimes without any reason whatsoever. The statements, which are made by the writer on such occasions, are given by way of glorification merely or of further elucidation or are only supplemental, though they might not be totally irrelevant to the subject-matter to be proved; and therefore, it is not certain that such statements are always true. *

*If the statements made in the *arthavāda* are consistent with the actual state of things, it is called '*anuvāda*,' if inconsistent it is

One may even say that the writer is not particularly careful to see whether or not the statements made in the *arthavāda*, are literally true; and therefore, one is not justified in looking upon the statements made in an *arthavāda*, as authoritative, that is to say, as indicating the conclusions arrived at by the writer with reference to the various subject-matters in it. Looking upon them as pure glorifications, that is to say, as hollow, irrelevant, or mere praise, the Mimāṁsā writers call them '*arthavāda*', and they do not take into account these statements in determining the final conclusion to be drawn from the work. Even after all this, one has still to see ultimately the *upapatti*. '*Upapatti*' or '*upapādana*' is the name given to the refuting of all things which would prove the contrary case and the subsequent logical and systematic martialling of things, which support one's own case, when you are proving a particular point. When the two ends, being the *upakrama* and the *upasaṁhāra*, have once been fixed, the intervening line can be defined by the consideration of the *arthavāda* and the *upapatti*. As the *arthavāda* shows you what subject matter is irrelevant or merely auxilliary, the man who attempts to determine the conclusion of the book, does not touch the several bye-paths when once the *arthavāda* has been determined; and when once all the bye-paths have been abandoned and the reader or the critic takes to the correct path, the ladder of *upapatti* like the wave of the sea pushes him forward from stage to stage further and further from the beginning until at last he reaches the conclusion. As these rules of determining the purport of a book laid down by our ancient Mimāṁsā writers are equally accepted by learned persons in all countries, it is not necessary to further labour their usefulness or necessity. *

called '*guṇavāda*', and if it is neither, it is called '*bhutārthavāda*'. '*Arthavāda*' is a common word and these are the three sub-divisions of *arthavāda* according to the truth or false-hood of the statements made in it.

* These rules of determining the import of a book are seen to be observed even in English Courts of justice. For instance, if it is not possible to understand any particular judgment, such meaning is decided by considering the result (*phala*) of that

Here some one may ask : Did not the various Ācāryas, who founded the various cults, know these rules of Mimāṁsā ? And, if one finds these rules in their own works, then what reason is there for saying that the purport of the Gītā drawn by the Mimāṁsā school is one-sided ? To that, the only answer is, that once a man's vision has become doctrinal, he naturally adopts that method by which he can prove that the cult which he follows is the cult established by authoritative religious treatises. Because, doctrinal commentators start with this fixed pre-conceived notion regarding the purport of a book, that if it yields some purport, inconsistent with their own doctrine, that purport is wrong, and that some other meaning is intended ; and though some rule of the Mimāṁsā logic is violated when they attempt to prove that the meaning, which in their opinion is the proved correct meaning has been accepted everywhere, these commentators, as a result of this fixed pre-conviction are not in the least perturbed thereby. The works Mitākṣarā and Dāyabhāga etc. which deal with the Hindu Law, attempt to harmonise the Smṛti texts on this principle. But the books of Hindu Law are not unique in this respect. Even, the numerous sectarian writers belonging to the numerous subsequent sects of Christian and Mahomedan religions, twist in the same way the original works on those religions namely the Bible and Qurān, and it is on the same principle that the followers of Christ have ascribed meanings to some of the sentences in the Old Testament of the Bible, which are different from those given to them by the Jews. Nay, wherever the number of the authoritative treatises or writings on any subject is fixed in advance and one has to subsequently justify one's own position on the basis of these limited authoritative books, the same method of determining the meaning of any book is seen to be followed. This also accounts for the way in which present-day legislators, pleaders or judges, very often twist

judgment, namely, the Decree or order passed on it; and if the judgment contains any statements which are not necessary for determining the point at issue, these statements are not taken as authorities for the purpose of later cases. Such statements are known as "obiter dicta" or "useless statements", and strictly speaking this is one kind of "*arthavāda*".

one way or the other, former authoritative or legal treatises. If such be the case with purely worldly matters, what wonder is there that divergent commentaries based on different traditions have been written on the Upaniṣads and the Vedānta-Sūtras and side by side with them, on the third book out of the Prasthānatrayī, namely, the Bhagavadgītā ? But if one leaves aside this doctrinal method, and pays a little attention to the *upakrama, upasaṁhāra* etc., of the Bhagavadgītā, it will be seen that the Blessed Lord preached the Gītā to Arjuna at the critical moment before the Bhārata war was actually started, when the armies of both sides had formed themselves into ranks on the Kurukṣetra and were on the point of opening the fight, and that He has done so with the idea of inducing Arjuna,—who had become dejected and was on the point of renouncing the world,—to perform his duties as a warrior by preaching to him the gospel of the Brahman. When Arjuna began to see who had come to fight with him taking the part of the unjust Duryodhana, he saw the old ancestor Bhīṣma, the preceptor Droṇācārya, the preceptor's son Aśvatthāman, the Kauravas (who though antagonistic were yet his cousins), and his next-of-kin, relations, friends, maternal uncles, paternal uncles, brothers-in-law, kings, princes, etc. ; and realising that in order to win the kingdom of Hastināpura, he would have to kill these people and thereby incur the greatest of sins like the destruction of one's own clan, his mind suddenly became dejected. On the one hand, the religion of the warrior was saying to him : "Fight !", and on the other hand, devotion to his ancestors, devotion to his preceptors, love for his brethren, affection for his relatives, and other natural laws were pulling him backwards. If he fought, it would be a fight with his own people, and thereby he would incur the terrible sin of killing his ancestors, preceptors, relatives etc. ; and if he did not fight, he would be failing in his duty as a warrior ; and when in this way he was between the frying-pan and the fire, he was in the same position as a person caught between two fighting rams ! He was indeed a great warrior, but when he was suddenly caught in the moral net of righteousness and unrighteousness, he felt faint, his hair rose on end, the bow in his hand fell down and he suddenly flopped down in his chariot, crying: "I shall not fight!", and ultimately the distant feeling of his duty as a warrior was overcome by the naturally more proximate feeling of love for his brethren and he in self-deception began to think to himself:—"It would be better to beg in order to fill the pit of the stomach, rather than that I should win the kingdom by committing such terrible sins as killing ancestors or preceptors or brethren or relatives or exterminating even the whole clan. It does not matter one whit if my enemies, seeing me unarmed at this moment, come and cut my throat, but I do not wish to enjoy that happiness which is steeped in the blood of my own relatives killed in warfare, and burdened with their curses. It is true the warrior-religion is there, but if on that account I have to incur such terrible sins as killing my own ancestors, brethren, or preceptors, then, may that warrior-religion and warrior-morality go to perdition. If the other side, not realising this, have become cruel in heart, I ought not do the same thing; I must see in what consists the true salvation of my Self, and if my conscience does not consider it proper to commit such terrible sins, then, however sacred the warrior-religion may be, of what use is it to me in these circumstances?" When in this way his conscience began to prick him and he became uncertain as to his duty (*dharma-saṁmūḍha*) and did not know which path of duty to follow, he surrendered himself to Śrī Kṛṣṇa, who preached the Gītā to him and put him on the right path; and when Arjuna, wanted to back out of the fight, fearing that it would entail the death of Bhīṣma and others,—though it was his duty to fight—Śrī Kṛṣṇa made him take up the fight of his own accord. If we have to extract the true purport of the teaching of the Gītā, such purport must be consistent with this '*upakrama*' (beginning) and '*upasaṁhāra*' (conclusion). It would have been out of place here for Śrī Kṛṣṇa to explain how Release could be obtained by Devotion or by the Knowledge of the Brahman or by the Pātañjala-yoga, which were purely renunciatory paths or paths entailing asceticism and abandonment of Action. Śrī Kṛṣṇa did not intend to send Arjuna to the woods as a mendicant by making a *saṁnyāsin* of him, filling his mind with apathy (*vairāgya*), nor to induce him to go to the Himalayas as a *yogin* wearing a loin cloth (*kaupīna*) and eating the leaves of the nim-tree. Nor did the Blessed Lord intend to place in his hands cymbals and a drum and a harp instead of bow and arrows and to make him dance again like Bṛhannalā before the entire warrior community of India, on the sacred field of the Kuru, steeped in the beatific happiness of loudly reciting the name of the Blessed Lord with supreme devotion, to the tune of those musical instruments. The dance which Arjuna had to make on the battle-field of Kuru, after having finished his period of remaining incongnito *(ajñāta-vāsa)* was of quite a different nature. When the Blessed Lord was preaching the Gītā, He has in numerous places, and showing reasons at every step and using the conjunction *'tasmāt'* i. e., 'for this reason'—which is an important conjunction showing the reason—said :—"*tasmād yudhyasva Bhārata*"—i. e., "therefore, O Arjuna, fight" (Gī. 2. 18), or "*tasmād uttiṣṭha Kaunteya yuddhāya kṛtaniścayaḥ*"—i. e., "therefore, determine to fight and rise (Gī. 2. 37), or "*tasmād asaktaḥ satataṁ kāryaṁ karma samācara*"—i. e., "therefore, give up attachment, and do your duty" (Gī. 3. 19), or, "*kuru karmaiva tasmāt tvaṁ*"—i. e. "therefore, perform Action" (Gī. 4. 15), or "*tasmāt.............. mām anusmara yudhya ca*"—i. e., "therefore, think of me and fight" (Gī. 8. 7); "the doer and the causer of everything is I myself, and you are only the tool; and therefore, fight and conquer your enemies" (Gī. 11. 33); "it is proper that you should perform all Actions, which are your duties according to the Śāstras" (Gī. 16. 24)—all which is a preaching definitely Energistic; and in the eighteenth chapter of the *upasaṁhāra* (conclusion), He says again: "you must do all these duties" (Gī. 18. 6), as His definite and best advice; and ultimately asking Arjuna the question:—"Oh, Arjuna, has your self-deception, due to ignorance, yet been removed or not ?" (Gī. 18. 72), He has taken an acknowledgment from him in the following words :—

naṣṭomohaḥ smṛtir labdhā tvatprasādān mayācyuta ।
sthito'smi gatasaṁdehaḥ kariṣye vacanaṁ tava ॥

i. e., "my doubts and my ignorance about my duties, have now been removed; I shall now do as You say". And it is not that this acknowledgment was merely orally given by Arjuna, but thereafter, he did really fight and in the course of the fight arising on that occasion, he has actually killed Bhīṣma, Karṇa, Jayadratha, and others as occasion arose. The objection taken to this by some is that: the advice given by the Blessed Lord preached Realisation *(jñāna)* based on Renunciation *(saṁnyāsa)*, or Yoga or Devotion, and that that was the principal subject-matter of proof; but that as the war had already started, the Blessed Lord has here and there briefly praised in His preaching the worth of Action and allowed Arjuna to complete the war which had been started; that is to say, the completion of the war must not be looked upon as the central or the most important factor but something which was auxilliary or merely an *arthavāda*. But by such a spineless argument, the *upakrama*, *upasaṁhāra* and *phala* of the Gītā is not satisfactorily accounted for. The Blessed Lord had to show the importance and necessity of performing at all costs the duties enjoined by one's *dharma* while life lasts, and the Gītā has nowhere advanced any such hollow argument as the one mentioned above for doing so; and if such an argument had been advanced, that would never have appealed to such an intelligent and critical person like Arjuna. When the prospect of a terrible clan-destruction was staring him in the face, whether to fight or not, and, if fighting was the proper course, then how that could be done without incurring sin, was the principal question before him; and however much one tries to do so, it will be impossible to dismiss, as an *arthavāda*, the definite answer given to this principal question in the following words, namely:— "Fight with a disinterested frame of mind," or "Perform Action". Doing so would amount to treating the owner of the house as a guest. I do not say that the Gītā has not preached Vedānta, or Devotion or the Pātañjala Yoga at all. But the combination of these three subjects which has been made by the Gītā must be such that thereby Arjuna, who was on the horns of a terrible dilemma of conflicting principles of morality, and who had on that account become so confused about his proper duty as to say: "Shall I do this, or shall I do that?", could find a sinless path of duty and feel inclined to perform the duties enjoined on him by his status as a warrior. In short, it is perfectly clear that the proper preaching in this place would be of Energism *(pravṛtti,)* and that, as all other things are only supporting Energism, that is, as they are all auxilliary, the purport of the Gītā religion must also be to support Energism, that is, to support Action. But no commentator has properly explained what this Energistic purport is and how that implied moral can be authoritatively based on Vedānta philosophy. Whichever commentator is taken, he totally neglects the *upakrama* of the Gītā, that is, its first chapter and the concluding *upasaṁhāra*, and the *phala*, and becomes engrossed in discussing from a Renunciatory point of view how the preaching in the Gītā about the Realisation of the Brahman or about Devotion support their respective cults: as though it would be a great sin to link together a permanent union between Knowledge and Devotion on the one hand and Action *(karma)* on the other! The doubt mentioned by me was experienced by one of these commentators who said that the Bhagavadgītā must be interpreted keeping before one's eyes the life of Śrī Kṛṣṇa himself;* and the Non-Dualistic philosopher Paramahaṁsa Śrī Kṛṣṇānanda Svāmi, who has recently died at Kāśī (Benares) has in the short Sanskrit monograph written by him on the Gītā entitled *Gītārtha-parāmarṣa* made the definite statement that: *"tasmāt gītā nāma Brahmavidyāmūlaṁ nītiśāstram"*—i. e., "therefore, the Gītā is the philosophy of Duty, that is, the philosophy of Ethics based on the science of the Brahman *(brahmavidyā)*" † The German philosopher Prof. Deussen, in his work called *The Philosophy of the Upaniṣads* has given expression to the same thoughts in one place with reference to the Bhagavadgītā, and several other

* The name of this commentator and some extracts from his commentary were communicated to me many years ago by a respectable scholar, but I cannot trace that letter anywhere in the confusion of my papers; and I have also forgotten the name of the commentator; so I have to beg this respectable scholar to communicate that information to me again if he chances to read this book.

† Sri Kṛṣṇānanda Svāmi has written four monographs on this subject which are named *Śrī Gītā-Rahasya*, *Gītārtha-prakāśa* *Gītārtha-parāmarśa* and *Gītā-sāroddhāra*, and they have all been collected and published together at Rajkot. The above quotation is from the *Gītārtha-parāmarśa*.

Eastern and Western critics of the Gītā have expressed the same opinion. Nevertheless, none of these persons have thoroughly examined the Gītā or attempted to clearly and in detail show how all the statements, deductions, or chapters in it can be explained as being connected together on the basis of the philosophy of Energism *(karma)*. On the other hand, Prof. Deussen has said in his book that such a conclusion would be very difficult to justify. * Therefore, the principal object of this book is to critically examine the Gītā in that light and to show the complete consistency which is to be found in it. But before I do so, it is necessary to deal in greater detail with the nature of the difficulty experienced by Arjuna as a result of his having been caught on the horns of the dilemma of mutually contradictory ethical principles, for otherwise, the readers will not realise the true bearing of the subject-matter of the Gītā. Therefore, in order to understand the nature of these difficulties in the shape of having to decide between Action and Inaction and to explain how a man on many occasions becomes non-plussed by being caught in the dilemma of " Shall I do this, or shall I do that ? ", we shall now first consider the numerous illustrations of such occasions, which are come across in our sacred books and especially in the Mahābhārata.

---

* Prof. Deussen's *The Philosophy of the Upaniṣads*, P. 362, Eng. Trans. 1906.

CHAPTER II.

THE DESIRE TO KNOW THE RIGHT ACTION

(KARMA-JIJÑĀSĀ.)

kiṁ karma kim akarmeti kavayo'py atra mohitāḥ । *

Gitā. 4. 16.

The critical position in which Arjuna had found himself in the commencement of the Bhagavadgitā, as a result of being caught between two mutually contradictory paths of duty and become doubtful about his proper duty is not something unique. The cases of persons who, taking up Asceticism (*saṁnyāsa*), give up the world and live in the woods, or of self-centred weaklings who meekly submit to all kinds of injustice in the world without a murmer, are different. But those great and responsible persons, who have to live in society and to do their duties consistently with righteousness and morality often find themselves in such circumstances. Whereas Arjuna got confused and was filled with this desire to know his proper duty in the commencement of the war, Yudhiṣṭhira, was in the same position when he was later on faced with the duty of performing the *śrāddha* ceremonies of the various relatives who had been killed in the war; and the Sāntiparva has come to be written in order to pacify the doubts by which he was then puzzled. Nay, great writers have written charming poems or excellent dramas based on such puzzling situations of duty and non-duty which they have either found in history or imagined. For instance, take the drama *Hamlet* of the well-known English dramatist Shakespeare. The uncle of the Prince of Denmark, named Hamlet had murdered his ruling brother, that is, the father of Hamlet, and married his widow and seized the throne. This drama has portrayed in an excellent manner the state of mind of the young and tender-hearted Hamlet, who on this

---

* "What is doable (right action), and what it is not-doable (wrong action or inaction) is a question which puzzles even sages". In this place, the word "*akarma*" (not-doable) must be interpreted as meaning 'absence of action' or 'wrong action' according to the context. See my commentary on the verse.

occasion was faced with the puzzle as to whether he should put to death his sinful uncle and discharge his filial obligations towards his father, or pardon him, because he was his own uncle, his step-father, as also the ruling king; and how he later on became, insane because he did not find any proper path-shower and guardian like Śrī Kṛṣṇa; and how ultimately the poor fellow met his end while vacillating between "to be" and "not to be". Shakespeare has described another similar occasion in a drama of his called *Coriolanus*. Coriolanus was a brave Roman potentate, who had been driven out of Rome by the citizens of Rome and on that account had gone and joined hands with the enemies of Rome, whom he promised never to forsake. After sometime, the camp of the hostile army under his command came to be placed outside the gates of Rome itself, he having attacked and defeated the Romans and conquered territory after territory. Then, the women of Rome put forward the wife and the mother of Coriolanus and advised him as to his duty to his motherland, and made him break the promise given by him to the enemies of Rome. There are numerous other similar examples of persons being puzzled as to duty and non-duty in the ancient or the modern history of the world. But it is not necessary for us to go so far. We may say that our epic Mahābhārata is a mine of such critical occasions. In the beginning of the book (Ā. 2), while describing the Bhārata, Vyāsa himself has qualified it by the adjectives "*sukṣmārtha-nyāyayuktam*" (i. e., filled with the discrimination between subtle positions) and "*aneka samayānvitam*" (i. e., replete with numerous critical occasions), and he has further praised it by saying that, not only does it contain the philosophy of Ethics (*dharma-śāstra*), the philosophy of wealth (*artha-śāstra*) and the philosophy of Release (*mokṣa-śāstra*) but that in this matter, "*yad ihāsti tad anyatra yan nehāsti na tat kvacit*", i. e., "what is to be found here, is to be found everywhere and what cannot be found here can be found nowhere else". (Ā. 62. 53). It may even be said that the Bhārata has been expanded into the 'Mahābhārata' for the sole purpose of explaining to ordinary persons in the simple form of stories how our great ancient personages have behaved in numerous difficult circumstances of life; for, otherwise, it would not be necessary to write 18 *parvas* (cantos) for describing merely the Bhārata war or the history known as 'Jaya'.

Some persons may say: "Keep aside the case of Śrī Kṛṣṇa and Arjuna; why is it necessary for you or us to enter into such deep questions? Have not Manu and the other writers of the Smṛtis laid down in their own books, clear rules as to how persons should behave in worldly life? If one follows the ordinary commandments prescribed for everybody in all religions, such as: 'Do not commit murder', 'Do not hurt others', 'Act according to moral principles', 'Speak the truth', 'Respect your elders and your preceptors', 'Do not commit theft or adultery', etc., where is the necessity of entering into these puzzling questions?" But I will in reply ask them: "So long as every human being in this world has not started living according to these rules, should virtuous people, by their virtuous conduct, allow themselves to be caught in the nets spread by rascals or should they give measure for measure by way of retaliation and protect themselves?" Besides, even if these ordinary commandments are considered as unchanging and authoritative, yet responsible persons are very often faced with such situations, that two or more of these commandments become applicable simultaneously; and then, the man is puzzled as to whether he should follow this commandment or that commandment, and loses his reason. The situation into which Arjuna had found himself was such a situation; and the Mahābhārata contains in several places critical descriptions of similar circumstances having engulfed other illustrious persons besides Arjuna. For instance, let us take the precept of "Harmlessness" *(ahiṁsā)* which is one of the five eternal moral principles enjoined by Manu (Manu. 10. 63) as binding on all the four castes namely, *"ahiṁsā satyam asteyaṁ śaucam indriya-nigrahaḥ"* i. e., Harmlessness *(ahiṁsā)*, Truth *(satya)*, Not-stealing *(asteya)*, Purity of the body, the mind, and of speech *(śauca)*, and Control of the organs *(indriya-nigraha)*. *"Ahiṁsā paramo dharmaḥ"* i. e., "Harmlessness is the highest religion" (Ma. Bhā. Ā. 11. 13.), is a principle which has been accepted as pre-eminent not only in our Vedic religion but in all other religions. The religious commandments given in the Buddhistic and Christian sacred books have given the first place to the commandment 'Thou shalt not kill' as has been done by Manu. '*Hiṁsā*' does not mean only destroying life but also includes harming the minds or the bodies of others. Therefore, '*ahiṁsā*' means 'not harming in any way any living being'. Patricide, matricide, homicide, etc. are the most terrible forms of *hiṁsā* and this religion of Harmlessness is looked upon as the highest religion according to all people in the world. But, assuming for the sake of argument that some villain has come, with a weapon in his hands to kill you, or to commit rape on your wife or daughter, or to set fire to your house, or to steal all your wealth, or to deprive you of your immoveable property; and, there is nobody there who can protect you; then should you close your eyes and treat with unconcern such a villain (*ātatāyin*) saying: "*ahiṁsā paramo dharmaḥ*?" or should you, as much as possible, punish him if he does not listen to reason? Manu says:—

guruṁ vā bālavṛddhau vā brāhmaṇaṁ vā bahuśrutam ।
ātatāyinam āyāntaṁ hanyād evāvicārayan ॥

i.e., "such an *ātatāyin* that is, villain, should be killed without the slightest compunction and without considering whether he is a preceptor (*guru*) or an old man or a child or learned Brahmin". For the Śāstras say: on such an occasion, the killer does not incur the sin of killing, but the villain is killed by his own unrighteousness (Manu. 8. 350). Not only Manu, but also modern criminal law has accepted the right of self-defence with some limitations. On these occasions, self-protection is considered to be of higher importance than Harmlessness. The killing of tender infants (*bhrūṇa-hatyā*) is considered to be the most objectionable of murders; but, if the child is being born by transverse presentation, is it not necessary to cut the child and deliver the mother? The slaughter of animals for the purposes of ritualistic sacrifice (*yajña*) is considered blameless even by the Vedas (Manu. 5. 31); yet, that at least can be avoided by making an animal of flour for purposes of sacrifice (Ma. Bhā. Śān. 337; Anu. 115. 56). But how are you going to stop the killing of the numerous micro-organisms with which the air, water, fruit etc., and all other places are filled? Arjuna in the Mahābhārata says :—

sūkṣmayonīni bhūtāni tarkagamyāni kānicit |
pakṣmano 'pi nipātena yeṣāṁ syāt skandha-paryayaḥ ||
(Ma. Bhā. Śān. 15. 26).

i.e., "there are in this world so many micro-organisms invisible to the naked eye, of which the existence can, however, be imagined, that merely by the moving of one's eye-lids, their limbs will be destroyed"! Then, where is the sense of repeating orally "Thou shalt not kill, thou shalt not kill"? It is on the basis of this discrimination, that hunting has been justified in the Anuśāsanaparva (Anu. 116). In the Vana-parva, there is a story that a Brahmin, being urged by anger to destroy a virtuous woman, and being unsuccessful, surrendered himself to that woman; then, that woman sent him to a hunter in order to learn from him the true import of one's duties. This hunter earned his living by selling flesh and he was extremely devoted to his parents. Seeing the way in which the hunter was earning his living, this Brahmin was filled with intense surprise and sorrow. Then the hunter explained to him the true principle of Harmlessness and opened his eyes! Does not everybody eat everybody else in this world? "*Jīvo jīvasya jīvanam*" (Bhāga. 1. 13. 46) i.e., "life is the life of life", is an eternal truth; and it is stated not only in the Smṛtis (Manu. 5. 28; Ma. Bhā. 15. 21) but also in the Upaniṣads (Ve. Sū. 3. 4. 28; Chān. 5. 2. 1; Bṛ. 6. 1. 14) that in times of distress "*prāṇasyānnam idaṁ sarvaṁ*", i.e., "all this is the food for life". If every one becomes harmless, how is warriorship to continue? And when once warriorship has come to an end, subject-people will have no protectors and anybody will be in a position to destroy anybody else. In short, the ordinary rules of morality are not always sufficient, and even the most principle maxim of Ethics, namely that of Harmlessness, does not escape the necessity of discrimination between the duty and the non-duty.

The Śāstras have recommended the qualities of forgiveness, peace and kindness consistently with Harmlessness, but how will it be possible to practise peace on all occasions? Prahlāda in the Mahābhārata first points out to his grandson Bali, that people will not stop at openly running away with even the wife and children of an always peaceful man and he advises Bali as follows :–

na śreyaḥ satataṁ tejo na nityaṁ śreyasī kṣamā ।

....

tasmān nityaṁ kṣamā tāta paṇḍitair apavāditā ॥

i. e. "Forgiveness in all cases or warlikeness in all cases is not the proper thing. Therefore, O, my son ! the wise have mentioned exceptions to the law of forgiveness" (Vana. 28. 6, 8). Prahlāda has then described some of the occasions which would be proper occasions for forgiveness, but Prahlāda does not explain the principle by which these occasions are to be recognised; and if some one takes advantage of the prescribed exceptions, without knowing the occasions when they apply, he will be guilty of misbehaviour; therefore, it is extremely important to understand the principle by which these occasions are to be recognised.

There is another law which has become wholly authoritative and acceptable to everybody in the world, whether old or young, and male or female, in all countries, and among all religions, and that is the law of Truth. Who can sufficiently praise the worth of Truth ? '*Ṛtaṁ*' and '*satyaṁ*' came into existence before the world. The Vedas extol the worth of Truth by saying that it is *satya* which controls the firmament, the earth, the air and the other primordial elements. See the incantations : "*ṛtaṁ ca satyaṁ cābhīddhāt tapaso 'dhyajāyata*" (R. 10. 190. 1) i. e. "Law (*ṛtaṁ*) and Truth (*satyaṁ*) have been brought into existence after the performance of effulgent penance", and "*satyenottabhitā bhūmiḥ*" (R. 10. 85. 1) i.e. "the Earth has become dignified on account of Truth". The root meaning of the word '*satya*' is 'which exists,' that is, 'which never ceases to exist,' or 'which is not touched by the past, present or the future'; and therefore, the value of *satya* has been properly described by saying : "there is no religion like Truth, Truth is *Parabrahma*". The statement : "*nāsti satyāt paro dharmaḥ*" (Śān. 162. 24) i. e. "there is no religion higher than Truth", is found in many places in the Mahābhārata which also says :–

aśvamedha-sahasraṁ ca satyaṁ ca tulayā dhṛtam ।
aśvamedha-sahasrād dhi satyam eva viśiṣyate ॥

i. e. "when the respective merits of a thousand *aśvamedha yajñas* and of Truth were weighed in the scale, it was found that Truth weighed more" (Ā. 74. 102). This refers to the ordinary rule of Truth. Manu in addition says about speaking the truth that :-

vācy arthā niyatāḥ sarve vāṅmūlā vāgviniḥsṛtāḥ I
tāṁ tu yaḥ stenayed vācaṁ sa sarvasteya-kṛnnaraḥ II

(Manu. 4. 256).

i. e. "all the activities of mankind are carried on by speech; there is no other means like speech for the communication of thoughts; then, that man who sullies this fountain-head of speech, which is the basic foundation of all these activities, that is to say, the man who is false to his own speech must be said to be despoiling everything at one stroke". Therefore, says Manu: "*satyapūtāṁ vaded vācaṁ*" (Manu. 6. 46) that is, "Speak only that which has been purified by Truth." In the Upaniṣads also, the law of Truth has been given a higher place than all other laws, in the following words: "*satyaṁ vada I dharmaṁ cara I*" (Tai. 1. 11. 1) that is: "Speak the truth, do what is right"; and Bhīsma, who was lying on the bed of arrows, after having in the Śāntiparva and the Anuśāsanaparva taught to Yudhiṣṭhira all the various laws, has before yielding up his breath preached to every one the law of Truth as being the sum and substance of all laws, in the following words: "*satyeṣu yatitavyaṁ vaḥ satyaṁ hi paramaṁ balam*" i.e. "You should strive for Truth, in as much as Truth is the highest power." (Ma. Bhā. Anu. 167. 50). We find that the very same laws have been adopted into the Buddhistic and Christian religions.

Can any one dream that there can be exceptions to this eternally-lasting law of Truth, which is thus established on all hands? But life in this world, which is full of villains, is difficult. Suppose, you have seen some persons escaping from the hands of marauders and hiding in a thick forest; and the marauders, who follow them with naked swords in their hands, stand before you and ask you, where those people are! What answer will you give? Will you speak the truth or will you save the lives of unoffending and innocent people? I ask this question because, preventing the murder of innocent people is according to the Śāstras a religion, as highly important as Truth itself. Manu says:—"*nāpṛṣṭaḥ kasyacid brūyān na cānyāyena pṛcchataḥ*" (Manu. 2. 110; Ma. Bhā. Śān. 287. 34)—that is, "Do not speak to anyone unless he questions you, and if some one asks you a question unjustly, then, do not give a reply, even if you are questioned"; and, "*jānann api hi medhāvī jaḍaval loka ācaret*"—i.e. "even if you know the answer simply say: 'hm! hm!' like an ignorant person", and save the situation. Very well; but, is not saying merely: 'Hm! hm!' in effect speaking the untruth? It is stated in many places in the Bhārata itself that: *na vyājena cared dharmam*", i.e. "do not somehow satisfy yourselves by being false to morality; morality is not deceived, it is you who are deceived" (Ma. Bhā. Ā. 215. 34). But if you cannot save the situation even by saying: 'Hm! hm!', what is to be done? What will you do if a thief is sitting on your chest with a dagger in his hand and asking you where the money is, and you are sure to lose your life if you do not give a proper reply? The Blessed Lord Śrī Kṛṣṇa who understood the inner meaning of all laws says to Arjuna in the Karṇaparva (Ka. 69. 61), after giving him the illustration of highway robbers mentioned above, and later on in the Satyānṛtādhyāya, of the Śāntiparva, Bhīṣma also says to Yudhiṣṭhira:—"

akūjanena cen mokṣo nāvakūjet kathaṁcana ।
avaśyaṁ kūjitavye vā śaṅkeran vāpy akūjanāt ।
śreyas tatrānṛtaṁ vaktuṁ satyād iti vicāritam ॥

(Śān. 109. 15, 16.)

i.e. "if you can escape without speaking, then do not speak under any circumstances; but if it is necessary to speak, or if by not speaking you may rouse suspicion in the mind (of another), then, telling a lie has been found, after mature deliberation, to be much better than speaking the truth." Because, the law of Truth is not confined to speech, and that conduct which leads to the benefit of all, cannot be looked upon as objectionable merely on the ground that the vocal expression is untruthful. That by which everybody will be harmed is neither Truth nor Harmlessness. Nārada says to Śuka in the Śāntiparva on the authority of Sanatkumāra :-

satyasya vacanaṁ śreyaḥ satyād api hitaṁ vadet I
yad bhūta-hitam atyantam etat satyaṁ mataṁ mama II

(Ma. Bhā. Śān. 329. 13 ; 287. 19).

i. e., "speaking the truth is the proper thing; but rather than truth, speak that which will lead to the welfare of all; because, that in which the highest welfare of all consists is in my opinion the real Truth". Seeing the words '*yad bhūta-hitaṁ*', one will certainly think of the modern western Utilitarians, and these words may be looked upon as an interpolation. I, therefore, say that these words have appeared more than twice in the Vanaparva of the Bhārata in the conversation between the Brahmin and the hunter; and in one of those places, there is a verbal change as: "*ahiṁsā satya-vacanaṁ sarva-bhūta-hitaṁ param*" (Vana. 206. 73), and in another place, there is another verbal difference as: "*yad bhūta-hitam atyantaṁ tat satyam iti dhāraṇā*" (Vana. 208. 4). There is no other reason for the fact that the truthful Yudhiṣṭhira confused Droṇa by the ambiguous answer: "*naro vā kuñjaro vā*" i. e., "either the man (named Aśvatthāmā) or the elephant", and the same rule applies to other similar things. Our religion does not ask us to save the life of a murderer by telling a lie. Because, as the *Śāstras* themselves have prescribed the punishment of death for a murderer, such a person is certainly punishable or fit for death. All the Śāstras say that one who bears false witness on such or similar occasions, goes to hell personally, and also sends to the same place seven or more of his ancestors (Manu. 8. 89-99; Ma. Bhā. Ā. 7. 3). But what are you going to do when, as in the illustration of the highway robbers given above from the Karṇa-parva, speaking the truth will lead to innocent persons being unnecessarily killed? The English writer Green has in his book named *Prolegomena to Ethics* said that books on moral philosophy are silent on this question. It is true that Manu and Yājñavalkya look upon such situations as exceptions to the law of Truth. But as even according to them, untruthfulness is the less praiseworthy conduct, they have prescribed a penance for it in the following words :-

tat pāvanāya nirvāpyaś caruḥ sārasvato dvijaiḥ ॥

(Yājña. 2. 83 ; Manu. 8. 104-6).

i. e., "Brahmins should expiate that sin by offering the '*Sārasvata*' oblation".

Those learned Western philosophers who have not been surprised by the exceptions to the law of Harmlessness, have attempted to blame our law-givers on account of the exceptions to the law of Truth ! I will, therefore, explain here what authoritative Christian preachers and Western writers on Ethics have said on this subject. The following words of St. Paul who was a disciple of Christ namely : "for, if the truth of God hath more abounded through my lie unto His glory ; why yet am I also judged as a sinner ? " (The Romans 3. 7) are to be found in the New Testament of the Bible ; and Millman, who has written a history of the Christian religion says that ancient Christian preachers very often followed the same principle. Moralists will not in the present times, as a rule, consider it justifiable to delude people or to cheat them and convert them. Nevertheless, even they do not say that the law of Truth is without exception. Take, for instance, the book on Ethics written by the scholar Sidgwick, which is being taught in our colleges. Sidgwick decides questions of morality, where there are doubts as to what is doable and what not-doable, by the rule of the ' greatest happiness of the greatest number' ; and by the test of that principle he has ultimately laid down that : "We do not think that truth ought always to be told to children, or madmen, or invalids, or by advocates ; and we are not sure that we are bound to tell it to enemies or robbers, or even to persons who ask questions which they know they have no right to ask (if a mere refusal to answer would practically reveal an important secret)". (Sidgwick's *Methods of Ethics* Book III Chapter XI, Paragraph 6, p. 355, 7th Edition. Also see pp. 315-317). Mill has included this exception to the law of Truth in his book on Ethics. * Besides these exceptions,

* Mill's *Utilitarianism*, Chapter II, pp. 33-34 (15th Ed. Longman's 1907).

Sidgwick also says in his book that: "Again, though we esteem candour and scrupulous sincerity in most persons, we scarcely look for them in a diplomatist who has to conceal secrets, or in a tradesman describing his goods, (for purchasers can find out the defects of what they buy)". * In a third place, he says that similar exceptions are made in favour of Christian missionaries and soldiers. Leslie Stephen, another Western writer, who discusses Ethics from the material point of view, gives other similar illustrations and says ultimately that: "It seems to me that the known consequences of an action must always be relevant to its morality. If I were absolutely certain that a lie would do good, I should certainly hesitate before speaking the truth, and the certainty might be of such a kind as to make me think it a duty to lie". † Green, who has considered the subject of Ethics from the metaphysical (*adhyātma*) point of view, definitely says with reference to such occasions, that in these cases the principles of Ethics do not satisfy the doubts of men; and ultimately comes to the conclusion that: "A true Moral Philosophy does not recognise any value in conformity to the universal rule, simply as such, but only in that which ordinarily issues in such conformity, viz., the readiness to sacrifice every lower inclination in the desire to do right for the sake of doing it". ‡ The same is the opinion of other Western writers on Ethics, such as, Bain, Whewell, and others. §

If you compare the rules laid down by the Western philosophers mentioned above, with the rules laid down by our

---

* Sidgwick's *Methods of Ethics*, Book IV Chap. III, Para. 7. P. 454, 7th Ed. and Book II Chap. V Para. 3, P 169.

† Leslie Stephen's, *Science of Ethics* Cha. IX. Para 29, p. 369 (2nd Ed) "And the certainty might be of such a kind as to make me think it a duty to lie".

‡ Green's *Prolegomena to Ethics* Para 315 p. 379, 5th Cheaper Edition.

§ Bain's *Mental and Moral Science*, p. 445 (Ed. 1875); Whewell's *Elements of Morality*, Bk. II, Ch. XIII and XIV, (4th Ed. 1864).

lawgivers, you will clearly see who had greater respect for Truth. It is true that our religions texts (*Śāstras*) say :—

> *na narmayuktaṁ vacanaṁ hinasti*
> *na strīṣu rājan na vivāhakāle* ।
> *prāṇātyaye sarvadhanāpahāre*
> *pañcānṛtāny āhur apātakāni* ॥
> (Ma. Bhā. Ā. 82. 16).

i.e., "There is no sin in speaking the untruth on the following five occasions, namely, if in joke or while speaking with women or at the time of marriage, or if your life is in danger, or for protecting your own property." (See also Śān. 109 and Manu. 8. 110). But that does not mean that one must always speak the untruth in speaking with women, and these exceptions are to be understood in the same way in the Mahābhārata, as those mentioned by Prof. Sidgwick with reference to "children, or madmen or invalids". But Western philosophers, who have shelved the metaphysical as also the next-world view of the matter, have gone further and have barefacedly permitted even merchants to tell any lies they like for their own benefit, which is a thing our lawgivers have not done! It is true that where there is a conflict between Verbal Truth, that is to say, truthful speech, and Practical Truth, that is to say, the benefit of humanity, they have permitted that the situation may be saved by telling a lie, if, from the practical point of view, that is unavoidable. Nevertheless, as they look upon the moral laws of Truth etc. as permanent, that is to say, immutable under all circumstances, they have considered this speaking of untruth as a sin to a certain extent, from the next-world point of view, and have prescribed relative penances. Purely materialistic philosophers will say, that these penances are mere bug-bears. But as those who prescribed these penances or those for whom these penances were prescribed, were not of the same opinion, one has got to say that both these classes look upon these exceptions to the law of Truth as the less proper course of conduct; and the same moral has been conveyed by the relative traditional stories on this point. For instance, Yudhiṣṭhira, on a difficult occasion, half-heartedly and only once, uttered the words "*naro vā kuñjaro vā.*" But on that account his chariot, which till then used to move in the air about four inches above the surface of the earth began to move in contact with the earth like the chariots of other people, and he had also to spend a few hours in hell, as has been stated in the Mahābhārata itself (Droṇa. 191. 57, 58 and Svargā. 3.15). In the same way, as Arjuna killed Bhīṣma, taking shelter behind Śikhaṇḍi, though according to the laws of warfare, he had to suffer defeat later on at the hands of his son Babhruvāhana, as has been stated in the Aśvamedhaparva (Ma. Bhā. Aśva. 81. 10). From this it will be seen that these exceptions, which have been contigently permitted, are not to be treated as the rule or as authority, and that our religious writers have drawn the following ultimate philosophical proposition, namely :-

ātmahetoḥ parārthe vā narmahāsyāśrayāt tathā ।
ye mṛṣā na vadantīha te narāḥ svargagāminaḥ ॥

that is : " those persons alone attain heaven, who never speak the untruth in this world, whether for their own benefit, or for the benefit of others, or in joke ; " as was explained by Mahādeva to Pārvatī. (Ma. Bhā. Anu. 144. 19).

The law of Truth consists in performing one's promises or vows. Śrī Kṛṣṇa and Bhīṣma both said, that the Himalaya might move from its site, or fire itself would become cold, but what they had said would not be otherwise (Ma. Bhā. Ā. 103 and U. 81. 48) ; and even Bhartṛhari has described righteous persons in the following terms :-

tejasvinaḥ sukham asūn api saṁtyajanti ।
satyavratavyasanino na punaḥ pratijñām ॥

(Nītiśataka.110)

that is : " illustrious i.e. high-principled persons will willingly sacrifice their lives, but will not break a vow ". In the same way, the vows of Dāśarathi Ramchandra of being true to his speech and shooting only one arrow have become as famous as his vow of monogamy, as appears from : " *dviḥ śaraṁ nābhisaṁdhatte Rāmo dvir nābhibhāṣate* " i.e., " Śrī Rāma had not to draw an arrow twice nor did he prevaricate "—(Subhāṣita) ; and there are tales in the Purāṇas that Harishchandra served as a domestic, for drawing water in the home of a burner of dead bodies in order to carry out a promise which he had given in a dream. But, on the other hand, it is stated in the Vedas that even the gods themselves broke the pledges made by them with Vṛtra or found out some loop-holes in them and killed Vṛtra; and the murder of Hiraṇyakaśipu is justified in the Purāṇas on the same basis. Besides, some agreements made in ordinary life are such as are considered unlawful or unfit for observance according to law. A similar story is related in the Mahābhārata with reference to Arjuna. Arjuna had made a vow that he would immediately behead any person who asked him to surrender his Gāṇḍīva bow to another. Later on, when Karṇa had defeated Yudhiṣṭhira in the war, and Yudhiṣṭhira naturally said to him (Arjuna) in despair: "What has been the use of your Gāṇḍīva bow to us? Throw it away from your hands", Arjuna rose, sword in hand, to behead Yudhiṣṭhira. But as Śrī Kṛṣṇa was near him at the time, he critically expounded to him the religion of Truth from the philosophical point of view, and said to him: "You are a fool, you do not understand the subtle points of morality, and you must learn them from your elders; you have not learnt at the feet of elders—'*na vṛddhāḥ sevitās tvayā*'. If you wish only to be true to your vow, then deprecate Yudhiṣṭhira, because for respectable persons, deprecation is as painful as death, etc."; and he thus saved him from the sin of murder of an elder brother which he would have thoughtlessly committed, as has been stated in the Karṇaparva (Ma. Bhā. Karṇa. 69). The discrimination between Truth and Falsehood which was made by Śrī Kṛṣṇa on this occasion, has been subsequently preached by Bhīṣma to Yudhiṣṭhira in the Satyānṛtādhyāya of the Śāntiparva (Śān. 109); and all must bear it in mind in relation to the affairs of ordinary life. Yet, it is difficult to explain how to recognise these subtle exceptions, and my readers will readily notice that although the law of fraternity was in this particular case looked upon as superior to the law of veracity, yet, the occasion mentioned in the Gītā was just the oppposite, and there the warrior-religion has been pronounced to be superior to the law of fraternity.

If there is so much difference of opinion with reference to Harmlessness (*ahiṁsā*) and Veracity (*satya*), then why should one be surprised if the same line of reasoning is applied to the third common law, namely of Not-Stealing (*asteya*)? If stealing or taking away by force that wealth which a man has lawfully acquired is permitted, then people will stop accumulating wealth, and all will suffer; and chaos will reign as a result of the arrangement of society being broken up. But, there are exceptions to this rule. When such a calamity (*āpatti*) arises that food cannot be had, whether for money or by labour or for charity on account of a general famine, shall we look upon as a sinner, some person who thinks of saving his life by committing theft? There is a story in the Mahābhārata that when such a difficult contingency befell Viśvāmitra, as a result of famine for twelve consecutive years, he was on the point of saving his life by stealing a leg of dog's flesh hung up in the home of a butcher (Śān. 141), and by eating that uneatable food; thereupon, this butcher gave him much advice based on the Śāstras, not to commit the sin of eating such uneatable food, and that too by theft, and quoted: "*pañca pañcanakhā bhakṣyāḥ*" (Manu. 5. 18). * But Viśvāmitra rejected that advice, saying :–

pibanty evodakaṁ gāvo maṇḍūkeṣu ruvatsv api ı
na te 'dhikāro dharme 'sti mā bhūr ātmapraśaṁsakaḥ ॥

* Out of the animals who have five toes, such as, the dog, the monkey etc. Manu and Yājñavalkya have prescribed the porcupine (which has arrow-like hair), *salluka*, (this is a kind of a porcupine), the iguana, the tortoise, and the hare as edible (Manu 5. 18; Yājña. 1. 177) Manu has included in the list also the '*khaḍga*' that is, the rhinoceros; but commentators say that there is a doubt about that animal. If this doubtful case is omitted, only five animals remain, of which the flesh is edible, and this is what is meant by the words :–"*pañca pañcanakhā bhakṣyāḥ*" i. e., "it is only five five-toed animals which are edible". Still, the Mīmāṁsā writers interprete this as meaning that, those who are allowed to eat flesh should not eat the flesh of any five-toed animals except these; and not that one must necessarily eat the flesh of these animals. This technical interpretation is known as '*parisaṁkhyā*'. The rule "*pañca pañcanakhā bhakṣyāḥ*" is an illustration of this '*parisaṁkhyā*'. Where flesh-eating is itself unlawful, the eating of the flesh of these animals is also unlawful.

that is:–" O butcher!, cows do not stop drinking water, although frogs remonstrate. Keep quiet! you have no right to explain principles of morality to me, do not boast unnecessarily ". Viśvāmitra has on this occasion also said: "*jīvitaṁ maraṇāt śreyo jīvan dharmam avāpnuyāt*" i. e., " if one remains alive, then he can think of religion; and therefore, even from the point of view of religion, keeping alive is better than dying "; and Manu has given the illustration not only of Viśvāmitra but also of Ajigarta, Vāmadeva, and other ṛsis who have, in similar circumstances, behaved similarly (Manu. 10. 105-108). The English writer Hobbes says in his book that: "If in a great famine, he takes the food by force or stealth, which he cannot obtain for money nor charity; or, in defence of his life, snatch away another man's sword, he is totally excused for the reason next before alleged"; * and Mill has said that in such circumstances, it is the duty of every human being to save his own life even by commiting theft.

But are there no exceptions to this theory of Viśvāmitra that: 'Keeping alive is better than dying'? Keeping alive is not the only thing worth doing in this world! Even crows keep alive, for many years, by eating the *piṇḍa* offerings. Therefore, Vīrapatnī Vidulā says to her son that: "Rather than that you should rot in the bed or remain cooped up in the house for a hundred years, it is better that you show warrior-like prowess even for a few hours and then die"—"*muhūrtaṁ jvalitaṁ śreyo na ca dhūmayitaṁ ciram*" (Ma. Bhā. U. 132. 15). If one is bound to die either to-day or to-morrow or at any rate after a hundred years (Bhāg. 10. 1. 38; Gī. 2. 27), then why be afraid of it or cry or dread it or lament? From the metaphysical point of view, the Self *(Ātman)* is eternal and never dies. Therefore, in considering the question of death, all that one has to consider is the body which has fallen to one's lot according to one's destiny (*prārabdha*). This body is perishable in any case. But in as much as this perishable human body is the only means by which one can perform whatever is

* Hobbes' *Leviathan*, Part II Chap. XXVII P. 139, (Morley's Universal Library Edition); Mills' *Utilitarianism*, Chap. V. P. 95 (15th Ed.).—" Thus, to save a life, it may not only be allowable, but a duty to steal etc."

to be performed in this world for the benefit of the Ātman, even Manu says: "*ātmānaṁ satataṁ rakṣet dārair api dhanair api*"—i.e. "it is better first to protect one's Self (*ātman*) before protecting one's wife, children or property (7. 213). Yet, noble souls have willingly sacrificed their lives in the fire of duty, in order to obtain something much more permanent than this perishable human body, e.g. for their God or religion, or for the sake of truth, or for acting according to their avowed purpose or sacred vow, or their professed course of conduct, or for protecting their reputation, or for the sake of success, or for the benefit of the entire world! There is a story in the Raghuvaṁśa that Dilīpa, while offering his body to a lion in order to protect the cow of Vasiṣṭha from him, said to him: "People like me are indifferent towards the human body which is made up of the five elements; therefore, look at my virtuous body rather than at my physical body" (Raghu. 2. 57) and the story of Jimūtavāhana having sacrificed his own body to an eagle in order to protect the lives of serpents, is to be found in the *Kathāsaritsāgara*, as also in the *Nāgānanda* drama. In the *Mṛcchakaṭika* (10. 27) Cārudatta says:—

na bhīto maraṇād asmi kevalaṁ dūṣitaṁ yaśaḥ ।
viśuddhasya hi me mṛtyuḥ putrajanmasamaḥ kila ॥

that is: "I am not afraid of death; I am unhappy only because my reputation will be tarnished. If my reputation remains untarnished, then even if I have to suffer death, I will be as happy about it as if a son were born to me"; and on this same principle, the king Śibi, in order to protect a *kapota* bird, which had surrendered itself to him, took the form of a *syena* bird and cut off pieces of flesh from his own body and offered them to the Dharma who was hunting the *kapota* bird; and when a sword made out of the bones of a ṛṣi named Dadhīci was needed for killing Vṛtra, the enemy of the gods, all the gods went to that ṛṣi and said to him: "*śarīratyāgaṁ lokahitārthaṁ bhavān kartum arhati*" i. e. "O Ṛṣi, be pleased to give up your life for the sake of the benefit of all", and thereupon, that ṛṣi most willingly gave up his life and allowed the gods to take his bones. These stories are to be found respectively in the Vanaparva and the Śāntiparva of the Bhārata (Vana. 100 and 131; Śān. 342). When the god Sūrya (Sun) came to know that Indra was going to the most generous Karṇa in the form of a Brahmin for begging from him the shield and ear-ornaments (*kavaca-kuṇḍala*) with which he had come to birth, he (Sūrya), warned Karṇa not to part with the same by gift to anybody and said to him that though he (Karṇa) was known as a most magnanimous person, yet he should not part with the shield and ear-ornaments to anybody, as his life would be in danger if he did so; and "*mṛtasya kīrtyā kiṁ kāryam*" i. e. "once he was dead, fame would be of no use to him." Hearing this message of the Sun-god, Karṇa gave him the fearless reply that: "*jīvitenāpi me rakṣyā kīrtis tad viddhi me vratam*" i. e. "I do not care, if I lose my life, but protecting my reputation is my avowed purpose" (Ma. Bhā. Vana. 299. 38). I may even say that such warlike doctrines as: "If you die you will go to heaven and if you win, you will enjoy the wealth of the earth" (Gī. 2. 37) or "*svadharme nidhanaṁ śreyaḥ*" (Gī. 3. 35), i. e. "Even if you meet your death, in acting according to your own religion, yet there is virtue in that", are based on the same principle; and consistently with that principle Śrī Samartha Rāmadāsa Svāmi has preached that: "If you think of your reputation, you will have no happiness and if you pursue happiness, you will have to sacrifice your reputation" (Dāsa. 12. 10. 19; 19. 10. 25); and that therefore: "When you have shed your body, your renown should survive you; O my mind! righteous persons should act in this way". Nevertheless the questions: "What is the use of renown after you are dead, though it may be true that by doing good to others you obtain renown?" or, "Why should a righteous man prefer death to disgrace? (Gī. 2. 34), or prefer doing good to others to saving his own life?" will not be satisfactorily answered unless one enters into the consideration of the Self and the Non-self (*ātmānātma*); and even if these questions are answered otherwise, yet in order to understand on what occasions it is proper to sacrifice one's life and when it is not proper to do so, one has also to consider the question of the philosophy of Action and Non-Action (*karmākarma*); otherwise, far from acquiring the glory of having sacrificed one's life, one will have incurred the sin of having foolishly committed suicide.

The religion of worshipping and serving one's mother, father, preceptor, etc., who are worshipful persons, as if they were deities, is looked upon as an important religion out of the several general and generally accepted religions. Because, if such were not the case, the family, the *gurukula* and even society itself will not be properly arranged. Therefore, not only in the Smṛti treatises but also in the Upaniṣads, it is stated that each preceptor after first preaching "*satyaṁ vada* । *dharmaṁ cara* ।", i.e., "speak the truth, live righteously" to the disciple who left him to go home after finishing his instruction, used next to preach to him: "*mātṛdevo bhava* । *pitṛdevo bhava* । *ācāryadevo bhava* ।" i.e. "treat your mother, your father, and your preceptor as if they were gods" (Tai. 1. 11. 1. and 2); and that is the sum and substance of the chapter on the coversation between the Brahmin and the hunter in the Mahābhārata (Vana. 213). But even in this religion, unexpected difficulties arise. Manu has said:

upādhyāyān daśācāryaḥ ācāryāṇām śataṁ pitā ।
sahasraṁ tu pitṛn mātā gauraveṇātiricyate ॥

(Manu. 2. 145).

i. e. "the preceptor is more in worth than ten lecturers, the father is worth more than a hundred preceptors, and the mother is worth more than a thousand fathers". Yet, it is a well-known story that because his mother had committed a grievous sin, Paraśurāma, at the instance of his father, cut her throat (Vana. 116. 14); and in the Cirakārikopākhyāna of the Śānti-parva (Śān. 265) the question of the relative propriety of killing one's mother at the behest of one's father or of disobeying one's father, has been considered in all its bearings with arguments *pro* and *con* in a separate chapter by itself. From this it will be seen that the practice of discussing such subtle positions in life from the ethical point of view was fully in vogue at the date of the Mahābhārata. Every one is conversant with the story of Śrī Rāmacandra having at the behest of his father willingly accepted banishment into the forests for 14 years in order to give effect to the promise made by his father. But the principle which has been enunciated above with reference to the mother, has occasionally to be applied to the case of the father. For instance, if after a son has become a king by his own prowess, he has occasion to try some crime committed by his father, should he in his capacity as a king, punish his father or let him off because he is his father? Manu says:-

pitācāryaḥ suhṛn mātā bhāryā putraḥ purohitaḥ ।
nādaṇḍyo nāma rājño 'sti yaḥ svadharme na tiṣṭhati ॥

i. e. "May he be a father or a preceptor or a friend or a son or a priest, may she be a mother, or a wife, if he or she have not behaved according to their own duties, they are not unpunishable for the king; that is, the king must give them condign punishment" (Manu. 8. 335; Ma. Bhā. Śān. 121. 60). Because, in this situation, the religion of sonhood is inferior to the religion of kinghood. And it is stated both in the Bhārata and the Rāmāyaṇa, that the most illustrious King Sagara, belonging to the Sūryavaṁśa banished his son, acting on this principle, because he found that his son was unreasonable and ill-behaved and was harassing his subjects. (Ma. Bhā. 107; Rāmā. 1. 38). Even in the Manu-Smṛti, there is a story that a ṛṣi named Āngirasa, having acquired excellent knowledge already at a tender age, his uncles (paternal and maternal) and other elders began to learn at his feet; on one such occasion Āngirasa, in addressing them, naturally used the words: 'my children' which are used by a teacher in addressing his pupils-"*putr.kā iti hovāca jñānena parigṛhya tān*" i.e. "having imparted knowledge to them, he addressed them as 'my children'!"—Then what an uproar arose! All the old people became livid with anger, and were convinced that the boy had become arrogant; and they made a complaint to the gods that he should be properly punished. The gods listened to the pleadings on either side, and ultimately gave the decision that the words which Āngirasa had used in addressing them were perfectly proper; because:-

na tena vṛddho bhavati yenāsya palitaṁ śiraḥ ।
yo vai yuvāpy adhīyānas taṁ devāḥ sthaviraṁ viduḥ ॥

that is:-" if his hair have become white, a man does not on that account alone, become old; although a man may be young, yet if he is learned, the gods look upon him as old" (Manu. 2. 156; and also Ma. Bhā. Vana. 133. 11; Śalya. 51. 47). This principle has been accepted not only by Manu and Vyāsa but also by the Lord Buddha. Because, the first line of the above verse from the Smṛti has been adopted *verbatim* into the well-known Buddhistic treatise on Ethics, in the Pali language, known as the '*Dhammapada*' * (Dhammapada, 260); and later on it is said in the same book that the man who has become mature only by age, has lived in vain; and that in order that a person should become truly religious and old, he must have acquired the virtues of veracity, harmlessness etc.; and in another treatise named '*Cullavagga*', the Lord Buddha has himself permitted that even if the *bhikṣu* (mendicant) who may be preaching may be young, yet he should sit on a high pedestal and preach the religion to other *bhikṣus* who had been previously invested into the creed and may be older than him (Cullavagga, 6. 13. 1). The story of Prahlāda having disobeyed his father Hiraṇyakaśipu, and won the Blessed Lord mentioned in the Purāṇas is well-known; and from these stories it will be seen that as a result of other important considerations coming into existence, one has unavoidably to temporarily forget not only the relationship between the older and the younger in age, but also the universally accepted relationship between father and son. But if, when such an occasion has not arisen, an arrogant son begins to abuse his father, will he not be looked upon as a brute? Bhīṣma has

* The work '*Dhammapada*' has been translated into English in the Sacred Books of the East Series Vol. X and the *Cullavagga* has also been translated into English in the Volumes XVII and XX of the same series. Mr. Yadavarao Varvikar, has also translated the *Dhammapada* into Marathi, and that was first published in the *Kolhapur Granthamala* and later on as an independent book. The verse in Pali in the *Dhammapada* is as follows :-

na tena thero hoti yenassa palitaṁ siro |
paripakko vayo tassa mogha-jiṇṇo ti vuccati ||

The word '*thera*' is applied to Buddhist mendicants. It is a corruption from the Sanskrit word "*sthavira*".

said to Yudhiṣṭhira: "*gurur garīyān pitṛto mātṛtaś ceti me matiḥ*" (Śān. 108. 17), i. e. "the preceptor is superior even to the mother or the father." But it is stated in the Mahābhārata itself, that when the preceptor of the king Marutta had abandoned him for his selfish interests, Marutta said :–

guror apy avaliptasya kāryākāryam ajānataḥ ।
utpathapratipannasya nyāyyaṁ bhavati śāsanam ॥
(Ma. Bhā. Ā. 142. 52–53).

i. e. "Even a preceptor, who, disregarding what ought to be done and what ought not to be done, takes up arrogantly the wrong path, deserves punishment". This verse has appeared four times in the Mahābhārata. (Ma. Bhā. Ā. 142. 52-53; U. 179. 24; Śān. 57. 7; 140. 48). Out of these, the reading in the first reference is as above and in the other references, the fourth part of the verse reads: "*daṇḍo bhavati śāśvataḥ*" or "*parityāgo vidhīyate*". But where this verse has appeared in the Vālmiki Rāmāyaṇa (Rāmā. 2. 21. 13), the reading mentioned above is the only reading which has appeared; and, therefore, I have adopted it in this book. The fights between Bhiṣma and Parśurāmā and between Arjuna and Droṇa were justified on the same principle and when the preceptors of Prahlāda appointed by Hiraṇyakaśipu began to advise him against worshipping the Blessed Lord, he has disregarded their advice on the same principle. In the Śāntiparva, Bhīṣma himself says to Śrī Kṛṣṇa that, although a preceptor may be venerable yet he also must be bound by rules of Ethics; otherwise :–

samayatyāgino lubdhān gurūn api ca Keśava ।
nihaṁti samare pāpān kṣatriyaḥ sa hi dharmavit ॥
(Śān. 55. 16).

that is: "Oh Keśava, that kṣatriya is truly law-abiding, who kills such persons as break laws, ethical principles, or rules of proper conduct, or is greedy or sinful, notwithstanding that they occupy the position of preceptors." So also, in the Taittiriyopaniṣad, after first stating: "*ācāryadevo bhava*", i.e., "Treat your preceptor as a deity", it is immediately afterwards stated that: "*yāny asmākaṁ sucaritāni* । *tāni tvayopāsyāni* । *no itarāṇi* ॥" (Tai. 1. 11. 2), i.e., "Imitate only such of our actions as are good, and disregard the others". From this, it is quite clear that the net advice of the Upaniṣads is that, even if the elders are god-like, because they are preceptors, or parents, yet, do not become addicted to drink, because they were addicted to drink; because, the position of ethical principles or of laws is even higher than that of the mother or the father or the preceptor, etc. The statement of Manu that: "Follow your religion; if any one destroys his religion, that is to say, disregards it, that religion will, without fail, destroy him." (Manu. 8. 14-16), has been made on the same principles. The king is a deity who is even more worshipful than the preceptor (Manu. 7. 8, and Ma. Bhā. Śān. 68. 40). But, the Manu-Smṛti says that even he does not escape the binding force of laws, and that if he breaks them, he will be destroyed; and the same idea is conveyed by the histories of the two kings Vena and Khaninetra mentioned in the Mahābhārata (Manu. 7. 41 and 8. 128; Ma. Bhā. Śān. 59. 92-100 and Aśva. 4).

Control of the organs is placed on the same level with Harmlessness (*ahiṁsā*), Veracity (*satya*), and Not-stealing (*asteya*), in the ordinary general religions (Manu. 10. 63). All the Śāstras contain the advice that Desire (*kāma*), Anger (*krodha*) and Avarice (*lobha*) are the enemies of man, and that unless they are fully conquered, neither he nor society will in any way be benefitted; and it is stated in the Viduranīti, as also in the Bhagavadgītā, that :-

trividhaṁ narakasyedaṁ dvāraṁ nāśanam ātmanaḥ ।
kāmaḥ krodhas tathā lobhas tasmād etat trayaṁ tyajet ॥

i.e., "*Kāma*, *krodha* and *lobha* are the three gateways of hell; and as they are destructive agents, they must be eschewed" (Gī. 16. 21; Ma. Bhā. U. 32. 70). But the Blessed Lord has in the Gītā itself described his own form in the following words: "*dharmāviruddho bhūteṣu kāmo 'smi Bharatarṣabha*" (Gī. 7. 11), i.e., "O. Arjuna! I am that *kāma* (desire) which exists in the hearts of living things, being consistent with law (*dharma*)". Therefore, that *kāma* (desire) which is inconsistent with *dharma* is the gateway of hell and other kinds of *kāma* are not proscribed by the Blessed Lord; and even Manu has said: "*parityajed arthakāmau yau syātām dharmavarjitau*", i.e., "that wealth (*artha*) and desire (*kāma*) which are inconsistent with justice (*dharma*) should be eschewed" (Manu. 4. 176). If to-morrow all living beings decide to say good-bye to the Lord Kāma, and to observe celibacy the whole of their lives, the entire living creation will come to an end within fifty or at most one hundred years, and the silence of death will reign everywhere; and that creation, in order to save which from destruction, the Blessed Lord takes incarnations every now and then, will within a short time, be destroyed. *Kāma* and *krodha* are enemies, it is true, but when?: if you allow them to become uncontrolled. Even Manu and the other writers of the Śāstras have accepted the position that *kāma* and *krodha* are extremely essential, within proper limits, in order that the world should go on (Manu. 5. 56). The highest civilisation consists in putting a proper restraint on these powerful mental impulses, and not in totally destroying them. It is stated in the Bhāgavata that :-

loke vyavāyāmiṣamadyasevā
nityāsti jantor na hi tatra codanā |
vyavasthitis teṣu vivāhayajña-
surāgrahairāsu nivṛttir iṣṭā ||

(Bhāg. 11. 5. 11).

i. e. "In this world, it is not necessary to tell any one to indulge in the enjoyment of sexual intercourse or in eating flesh or drinking wine. These are things which human beings want naturally. And it is in order to systematise these three impulses, that is to say, in order to give them a systematic basis by subjecting them to limitations or restraint, that the writers of the Śāstras have ordained marriage, and the Soma-yāga and the Sautrāmaṇi-yajña respectively for them; but even with reference to these matters, the most excellent course is Renunciation (*nivṛtti*), that is to say, Desireless Action". Although the word '*nivṛtti*', when used in relation to fifth-case-ended nouns, means, 'renunciation of a particular thing' or 'giving up a particular Action altogether'; yet, as the adjective '*nivṛtta*' is in the Karma-Yoga applied to the noun '*karma*', the word '*nivṛtta-karma*', it must be borne in mind, means 'Action which is to be performed desirelessly'; and the word has been used clearly in those meanings in the Manu-Smṛti and in the Bhāgavata-purāṇa (Manu. 12. 89 ; Bhāg. 11. 10. 1 and 7. 15. 47). In speaking about anger (*krodha*) Bhāravi says in the Kirāta-kāvya (1. 33) that :-

amarṣaśūnyena janasya jantunā
na jātahārdena na vidviṣādaraḥ ॥

i. e., "if a man does not get angry or annoyed when he has been insulted, it is just the same whether he is your friend or whether he hates you !" Vidulā has said, that from the point of view of the warrior (*kṣatriya*) religion :-

etāvān eva puruṣo yad amarṣī yad akṣamī ।
kṣamāvān niramarṣaś ca naiva strī na punaḥ pumān ॥

(Ma. Bhā. U. 132. 33).

i. e., "he who gets angry (on account of injustice) and who does not submit (to insult), is truly a man. He who does not get angry or annoyed is neither a woman nor a man". It has already been stated above that in order that the world should go on, there must not be either anger or valour at all times, or forgiveness at all times. The same law applies to avarice (*lobha*) ; because, even if a man is a *saṁnyāsi* (ascetic) yet he wants Release (*mokṣa*).

Vyāsa has stated in various stories in the Mahābhārata, that the various virtues of valour, courage, kindness, probity, friendship, impartiality etc., are, in addition to their mutual oppositions, also limited by considerations of time and place. Whatever the virtue may be, it is not equally appropriate in all circumstances. Bhartṛhari says that :-

vipadi dhairyam athābhyudaye kṣamā
sadasi vākpaṭutā yudhi vikramaḥ ।

(Niti. 63).

that is : "Courage is a virtue in days of misfortune, forgiveness in days of power (that is, notwithstanding that you are in a position to punish), oratory in an assembly, and valour in warfare". In times of peace, there are not wanting mere talkers like Uttara; but although there may be many Hambirarāos who are courageous enough to shoot arrows through the nose-rings of their wives, it is only one of them who acquits himself with credit as an archer on the battle-field! Not only are courage and the other abovementioned virtues really appropriate in the respective circumstances mentioned, but they cannot even be properly tested except in such circumstances. There are not wanting shoals of school-friends; but, "*nikaṣagrāvā tu teṣāṁ vipat*", i.e. "adversity is their touchstone". Misfortune is the true test for trying them. The word 'circumstances' above includes considerations of worthiness and unworthiness, in addition to considerations of time and place. No virtue is greater than impartiality. The Bhagavadgītā itself clearly says that being: "*samaḥ sarveṣu bhūteṣu*", i.e., "impartial towards all created things", is a characteristic feature of a perfect being (*siddha*). But, what does this impartiality mean? If somebody showers charity on each and every one alike, that is to say, without considering their respective merits, shall we call him a wise man or a fool? This question has been answered in the Gītā itself in the following words: "*deśe kāle ca pātre ca tad dānaṁ sāttvikaṁ viduḥ*", i.e., "that charity which is made with proper regard for the place, the time, and the worthiness (of the party) is the pure (*sāttvika*) charity" (Gī. 17. 20). Considerations of time, are not limited to the present time. As times change, so also changes take place in the laws relating to worldly life; and therefore, if one has to consider the propriety or otherwise of any thing pertaining to ancient times, one has necessarily to consider also the ideas of righteousness or unrighteousness prevailing at that time. Manu (1. 85) and Vyāsa (Ma. Bhā. Śān. 259. 8) say :-

anye kṛtayuge dharmās tretāyāṁ dvāpare 'pare |
anye kaliyuge nṛṇāṁ yugahrāsānurūpataḥ ||

i. e., "the laws relating to the *Kṛta*, *Tretā*, *Dvāpara* and the *Kali-yuga* are all different according as the *yugas* (eras) change". And it is stated in the Mahābhārata itself that in ancient times, women were not restricted by marriage, and they were entirely independent and unchecked in that matter; but, when the evil effects of this kind of life manifested themselves later on, Śvetaketu laid down the limitation of marriage (Ma. Bhā. Ā. 122); and Śukrācārya was the first one to promulgate the prohibition against drink (Ma. Bhā, Ā. 76). Needless to say, there must be different standards for considering the laws pertaining to the times when these restrictions were not in vogue, than those relating to the times when they came into vogue; and in the same way, if the laws which are in force in the present age are changed in the future, then the consideration of the righteousness or unrighteousness of actions in the future will also be on a different basis. As there are considerations of time, so also are there considerations of the customs of the country, the customs of the family, as also the customs of the community; for. custom is the root of all religion. Nevertheless, there are inconsistencies even among customs. Bhīṣma has described the differences between customs in the following words:

na hi sarvahitaḥ kaścid ācāraḥ saṁpravartate ।
tenaivānyaḥ prabhavati so 'paraṁ bādhate punaḥ ॥

(Śān. 259. 17. 18).

that is: "One cannot find any custom, which is beneficial to everybody, at all times. If you take one custom, another one is better, and if you accept the second custom, it is again contrary to a third one"; and he has said that we have to discriminate between customs and customs.

If I go on solving in this way all the riddles about what should be done and what should not be done (*karmākarma*) and what is righteous and what unrighteous (*dharmādharma*), I shall have to write a second Mahābhārata myself. I have laboured on this subject so long only with the idea of impressing on the mind of my readers how the circumstances in which Arjuna found himself in the beginning of the Gītā as a result of a conflict between fraternal affection and a warrior's duties were not something out of the common; and how similar circumstances very often befall great and responsible persons in life, giving rise sometimes to a conflict between the principles of Harmlessness and Self-protection, or of Veracity and general welfare, or between the protection of one's person and one's reputation, or again between different duties arising out of different aspects of the same situation; and how, many exceptions thus arise, which are not provided for by ordinary and generally accepted moral laws; and lastly, how on such occasions, not only ordinary, but even very clever and learned persons, naturally feel the desire of finding out whether or not there is some definite formula or basis for determining what should be done and what not, or, what is one's duty and what is not one's duty. It is true that some concessions have been made in the Śāstras to meet calamities like a famine which are technically known as '*āpaddharma*'. For instance, the writers of the Smṛtis say that in such calamities (*āpatkāla*) a Brahmin incurs no sin, if he takes food in any place; and in the Chāndogyopaniṣad, there is even a story of Uṣasticākrāyaṇa having done so. (Yājña. 3. 41; Chān. 1. 10). But there is a world of difference between those circumstances and the circumstance mentioned above. In the case of famine, there is a conflict between religious principles on the one hand and hunger, thirst, and other bodily needs on the other, and the bodily organs drag you in one direction and religious principles in the opposite direction. But in many of the circumstances mentioned above, the conflict is not between bodily impulses and religious principles but there is an inter-conflict between two principles laid down in the Śāstras themselves and it becomes necessary to consider minutely whether to follow this religious precept or that; and though it may be possible for persons of ordinary intelligence to arrive at a decision on a few such occasions by considering what pure-minded persons have done in the past in similar circumstances, yet on other occasions, even sages are puzzled; because, the more one thinks about a particular matter, more and more of doubts and counter-arguments come into existence, and it becomes very difficult to arrive at a definite conclusion; and if a proper decision is not arrived at, there is a risk of one's committing an unlawful thing or even a crime. Considering the matter from this point of view, it will be seen that the discrimination between the lawful and the unlawful or between the doable and the not-doable becomes an independent science by itself, which is even more difficult than the sciences of logic or grammar. In old Sanskrit treatises, the word '*nīti-śāstra*' (Ethics) used to be applied principally to regal jurisprudence (*rāja-nīti*) and the doable and the not-doable used to be technically called '*dharma-śāstra*'. But as the word '*nīti*' includes both duty and good conduct, I have in this book referred to the discussion of the questions of righteousness and unrighteousness or of what ought to be done and what ought not be done, by the name '*nīti-śāstra*'. In order to show that this science, which expounds Ethics, or shows what is doable and what is not-doable, or what is righteous and what unrighteous, is indeed a very difficult science, the sentence "*sūkṣmā gatir hi dharmasya*", i.e., "the true nature of righteousness, that is to say, of the Ethics of worldly life, is very subtle", occurs several times in the Mahābhārata. It is extremely difficult to satisfactorily answer such questions as:—How did five Pāṇḍavas marry one Draupadi? or, Why did Bhīṣma, Droṇa and others sit quiet, as if with a dead heart, when attempts were made to denude Draupadi?, or, Whether the principle; "*arthasya puruṣo dāsaḥ dāsas tv artho na kasyacit*" i.e., "man is the servant of wealth (*artha*), wealth is the servant of nobody" (Ma. Bhā. Bhī. 43. 35), enunciated by Bhīṣma and Droṇa, in justification of their having sided with the wicked Duryodhana in the civil war is or is not correct? or, if service is looked upon as dog-like, as is shown by the words: "*sevā śvavṛttir ākhyātā*", i.e., "servitude is said to be the tendency of a dog" (Manu. 406) and is accordingly considered eschewable, then why did Bhīṣma and others not give up the service of Duryodhana, rather than becoming the slaves of wealth? Because, on such occasions different persons arrive at different inferences or decisions according to different circumstances. Not only are the principles of justice extremely subtle ("*sukṣmā gatir hi dharmasya*", Ma. Bhā. Anu. 10. 70), but, as is stated later on in the Mahābhārata itself, there are numerous branches to those principles and the inferences which can be drawn from them are numerous ("*bahuśākhā hy anantikā*", Ma. Bhā. Vana. 208. 2). Tulādhāra also, where he is discoursing on questions of morality, in the Tulādhāra-Jājali conversation, says: "*sūkṣmatvān na sa vijñātuṁ śakyate bahunihnavaḥ*", i. e., "as morality is subtle and complicated, one very often does not know what it is" (Śān. 261. 37). The writer of the Mahābhārata was fully conversant with these subtle occasions, and he has collected together different traditionary stories in the Mahābhārata in order to explain how great men behaved in the past in those circumstances. But it was necessary to scientifically examine all these subjects and to enunciate the universal principle underlying them, in a religious work like the Mahābhārata. Vyāsa has explained this underlying principle in the Bhagavadgītā, taking his stand on the advice given in the past by Śrī Kṛṣṇa to Arjuna on the pretext of removing his doubts about his duty; and, therefore, the Gītā has become the mystic Upaniṣad and the crown jewel of the Mahābhārata, and the Mahābhārata has become an illustrated and detailed lecture on the fundamental principles of Right Action (Karma-Yoga) which have been enunciated in the Gītā. I have to suggest to those who imagine that the Gītā has been subsequently interpolated into the Mahābhārata that they should pay close attention to this fact. Nay, the uniqueness and special feature of the Gītā consists in this very thing. Because, although there are numerous treatises like the Upaniṣads etc. which deal with the pure science of Release (*mokṣa*) that is, with Vedānta, or like the Smṛtis which merely enunciate rules of righteous conduct such as Harmlessness etc., yet there is not to be found, at least in these days, another ancient work in the Sanskrit literature like the Gītā which discriminates between the doable and the not-doable (*kāryākārya-vyavasthiti*) on the authority of the extremely recondite philosophy of the Vedānta. Devotees of the Gītā need not be told that the word '*kāryākārya-vyavasthiti*' has not been coined by me, but is from the Gītā itself (Gītā. 16. 24). In the Yoga-vāsiṣṭha, Vasiṣṭha has ultimately preached to Śrī Rāma, the path of Energism (Karma-Yoga) based on Self-Realisation (*jñāna*), as has been done in the Gītā; but such works, which have been written after the date of the Gītā, and which are only imitations of it, do not in any way detract from the uniqueness of the Gītā, to which I have referred above.

CHAPTER III

THE SCIENCE OF RIGHT ACTION

(KARMA-YOGA-ŚĀSTRA)

tasmād yogāya yujyasva yogaḥ karmasu kauśalam । *

Gītā 2. 50.

If a man is not actuated by the desire of acquiring the knowledge of a particular science, he is unfit to study that science, and explaining such a science to such an unfit person is like pouring water on an obverse vessel. Not only is the disciple not benefited by it, but even the preceptor wastes his labour, and both waste their time. Therefore, the aphorisms "*athāto dharmajijñāsā*" and "*athāto brahmajijñāsā*" appear at the beginning of both the Jaimini and the Bādarāyaṇa-Sūtras. Just as the teaching of the Brahman is best imparted to a '*mumukṣu*' (one who is desirous of Release) or as the teaching of Law or justice is best imparted to one who seeks that knowledge, so also is the teaching of the Science of of Right Action (Karma) most properly given to the person who has been inspired with the '*jijñāsā*' (desire of knowing) how to rightly perform Action while leading a worldly life; and that is why I have disposed of the '*athāto*' in the first chapter and have outlined the nature of '*karmajijñāsā*' and the importance of the science of Karma-Yoga in the second chapter. Unless a man has by experience found where his difficulty lies, he does not realise the importance of the science of getting over that difficulty; and if this importance is not realised, a science which has been learnt merely by rote, is later on found difficult to remember. Therefore, good teachers first ascertain whether or not the disciple has been inspired with desire for the knowledge, and if there is no such inspiration, they attempt to rouse the desire. The Science of Right Action (Karma-Yoga) has been expounded in the Gītā on this

* "Therefore, take shelter in the Yoga; 'Yoga' is the name given to the skill, the wisdom or the gracefulness of performing Action (*Karma*)": such is the definition or connotation of the term 'Yoga', which has been more fully dealt with later on in this chapter.

basis. When, being beset with the doubt whether or not he should take part in a war in which he would be responsible for the slaughter of ancestors and preceptors and also of all kings and brethren, Arjuna was inspired by the desire to give up the war and renounce the world, and when he was not satisfied by the ordinary arguments that abandoning a duty which had befallen him was a foolish and weak act and that by doing so, far from obtaining heaven he would on the other hand, suffer disgrace, Śrī Kṛṣṇa preached to him the science of Karma-Yoga, after in the first instance seeming to ridicule him by saying: "*aśocyān anvaśocas tvaṁ prajñāvādāṁś ca bhāṣase*" i. e., "you lament those for whom you ought not to lament and at the same time, tell me big tales about the knowledge of the Brahman". I have shown in the last chapter that the doubt by which Arjuna had been beset, was not groundless, and that even great sages are in certain circumstances, puzzled as to 'what to do and what not to do'. But the starting advice of Śrī Kṛṣṇa to Arjuna is: that it is not proper to give up Action (*karma*) on the ground that numerous difficulties arise in the consideration of what should be done and what should not be done; that, a wise man should practise such a '*yoga*' or device whereby instead of Actions being done away with in the world, one will only escape their evil effects or binding force, and that: "*tasmād yogāya yujyasva*" i. e., "therefore, you, should do the same". This 'Yoga' is the science of 'KARMA-YOGA'; and in as much as, the circumstances in which Arjuna found himself were not unique, but every one of us comes across small or big difficulties of the same nature in worldly life, it is necessary that we should all profit by the exposition of this Karma-Yoga science which has been made in the Bhagavadgītā. But whichever science is taken, it is necessary to properly define the important words occurring in its exposition so that their meanings are properly understood, and to first precisely explain the fundamental outline of the exposition of that science; otherwise, many misunderstandings or difficulties subsequently arise. Therefore, following this usual practice, I shall first examine and explain the meanings of some of the important words which occur in this science.

The first of these words is 'KARMA'. The word '*karma*' comes from the root '*kṛ*', and means 'doing', 'affairs', or 'activity'; and that same ordinary meaning is intended in the Bhagavadgītā. My only reason for explaining this is, that the reader should not be confused by the limited and restricted meanings in which this word has been used in the Mīmāṁsā philosophy or in other places. Whichever religion is taken, it prescribes some Action or other for reaching the Īśvara. According to the ancient Vedic religion, this Action was sacrificial ritual; and the Pūrva-Mīmāṁsā of Jaimini has been written with the sole purpose of showing how the various different and sometimes apparently contradictory statements which are to be found in the Vedic treatises regarding the performance of this sacrificial ritual can be reconciled with each other. According to Jaimini, the performance of this Vedic or *Śrauta* (prescribed by the *Śrutis*) sacrificial ritual was the principal and the ancient religion. Whatever a man does, must be taken to have been done by him for the purpose of the '*yajña*' (sacrifice). If he earns money, he must earn it for the sake of the *yajña*; and if he collects grain, that also must be understood to have been done for the *yajña* (Ma. Bhā. Śān. 26. 25). In as much as the Vedas themselves have enjoined the performance of the *yajñas*, any Action done for the purpose of the *yajña* cannot of itself be a source of bondage to man; it is a means for the *yajña* and not an independent object; and therefore, the effect of that Action is included in the result to be achieved by the *yajña*; it has no independent effect. But although these Actions, which are performed for the purpose of the *yajña*, may not have an independent effect, yet the *yajña* itself leads to heaven (which, according to the Mīmāṁsa school, is a kind of happiness), and the performer of the *yajña* performs it willingly, only in order to attain heaven. Therefore, the performance *(karma)* of the *yajña* itself falls into the category of '*puruṣārtha*' (something which a man desires). Any particular thing which a man likes and which he desires to attain is called '*puruṣārtha*' (Jai. Sū. 4. 1. 1 and 2). '*Kratu*' is a synonym for '*yajña*' and therefore, the word '*kratvartha*' is also used in place of the word '*yajñārtha*' and therefore, all Actions fall into the two divisions of '*yajñārtha*' ('*kratvartha*') that is, Actions which do not give any independent fruit or benefit and are, therefore, non-binding, and *'puruṣārtha'* that is, Actions performed for the benefit of the doer and, therefore, binding. The Saṁhitās and the Brāhmaṇas contain nothing else but a description of sacrificial ritual. It is true that in the Ṛg-Veda-saṁhitā there are verses *(sūkta)* in praise of Indra and the other gods; but as these are to be used only at the time of the *yajña*, the Mīmāṁsa writers say that all Śruti treatises preach only the *yajña* and other sacrificial ritual. These orthodox ritual-masters, and pure *karma-vādins* say that heaven can be attained only by performing the sacrificial ritual prescribed by the Vedas and not otherwise; and that, that is so, whether you perform the *yajñas* ignorantly or after Realising the Brahman. Although this sacrificial ritual is accepted by the Upaniṣads, yet their worth is declared to be lower than that of the Knowledge of the Brahman, and the Upaniṣads say that though heaven may be attained by the *yajñas*, Realisation of the Brahman *(brahma-jñāna)* is necessary for attaining the true Release. The desire-prompted Actions in the shape of sacrificial ritual, described in the second chapter of the Bhagavadgītā by the words " *vedavādaratāḥ Pārtha nānyadastīti vādinaḥ* " (Gī. 2. 42) are the above-mentioned sacrificial ritual, performed without having realised the Brahman. In the same way, the sentence *yajñārthāt karmaṇo 'nyatra loko 'yaṁ karmabandhanaḥ*" i. e., " Actions performed for the purpose of the *yajña*, do not create bondage; all other Actions have a binding force " (Gī. 3. 9) is only a repetition of the opinion of the Mīmāṁsā school. Besides- this sacrificial ritual, (being the Actions prescribed by the Vedas and the *Śrutis*), there are other Actions, necessary from the point of view of religion, which have been prescribed by the Manu-Smṛti and other religious treatises, having regard to the division of society into the four castes. For instance, fighting has been prescribed for the warrior *(kṣatriya)*, trade for the merchant *(vaiśya)* etc.; and, as these have been for the first time systematically prescribed in the Smṛti writings, they are referred to as *'Smārta'* (prescribed by the Smṛtis) Actions or *yajñas.* There are besides these Actions prescribed by the Śrutis and the Smṛtis, other religious Actions, e.g., fasting, austerities etc., which have for the first time been described in detail in the Purāṇas, and these may, therefore, be described as '*paurāṇika karma* (Actions). All these Actions are again sub-divided into everyday *(nitya)*, occasional *(naimittika)*, and for-a-particular-purpose *(kāmya)* Actions. Such Actions as must be performed every day, such as bathing and offering prayers at twilight, are called *nitya-karma*. By performing these, no special purpose *(artha-siddhi)* is achieved; but if they are not performed, one incurs sin. *Naimittika* (occasional) Actions are such as have to be performed because some occasion necessitating them has arisen, such as, the pacification of unauspicious stars, penances etc. If that occasion for which we perform this pacification or penance had not come into existence, there would be no necessity for performing this Action. In addition to these, there are certain other Actions which we very often perform because we desire a particular thing and for acquiring that thing, as enjoined by the Śāstras. These Actions are *kāmya* (desire-prompted) actions; e.g., sacrificial ritual for causing rain or for obtaining a son. In addition to these everyday, occasional, and desire-prompted Actions, there are other Actions such as, drinking etc. which have been pronounced to be totally objectionable by the Śāstras and therefore, they are named *niṣiddha* (objectionable) actions. Which Actions are everyday Actions, which occasional, which desire-prompted and which objectionable has been laid down by our religious treatises; and if any person versed in religion is asked whether a particular act performed by a particular person is sinful or virtuous, he will consider whether that particular Action is *yajñārtha* or *puruṣārtha* or *nitya* or *naimittika* or *kāmya* or *niṣiddha* according to the directions of the Śāstras and give his opinion accordingly. The view-point of the Bhagavadgītā is more exhaustive than this or may even be said to be beyond this. It may be that a particular Action has not been pronounced as objectionable by the Śāstras; nay, it may even have been prescribed as proper, e.g., in the case in point, the warrior-religion was the 'prescribed' *(vihita)* thing for Arjuna; but on that account, it does not follow that one should always perform that Action, nor also that it will always be certainly beneficial; and the injunctions of the Śāstras are very often mutually contradictory, as has been shown in the previous chapter. The subject-matter of the Gītā is to show whether or not there are any means for ascertaining what course should be followed by a person on such an occasion and if so, what those means are. It is not necessary for the purpose of this exposition to pay any special attention to the divisions of '*karma*' mentioned above. In order to explain to what extent the doctrines laid down by the Mīmāṁsā school regarding the sacrificial ritual etc. prescribed by the Vedas or the other duties prescribed for the four castes are consistent with the Karma-Yoga advocated in the Gītā, their theories have been examined in the Gītā as occasion arose; and in the last chapter, the question whether or not a Self-Realised (*jñānin*) man should perform sacrificial ritual has been precisely answered (Gī. 18. 6). But in as much as the principal subject-matter of the Gītā is more exhaustive than this, the word 'Karma' as used in the exposition made in the Gītā must not be taken in the restricted meaning of Actions prescribed by the Śrutis or the Smṛtis, but in a more comprehensive meaning. In short, all the Actions which a man performs, e.g., eating, drinking, playing, sitting, rising, residing, breathing, smiling, weeping, smelling, seeing, speaking, hearing, walking, giving, taking, sleeping, waking, killing, fighting, meditating or contemplating, commanding, or objecting, giving, performing sacrificial ritual, agriculture or commerce, desiring, deciding, keeping quiet, etc., etc., etc., are all included in the word 'Karma' as used in the Bhagavadgītā, whether those Actions are bodily (*kāyika*) or vocal (*vācika*) or mental (*mānasika*) (Gītā 5. 8-9). In short, even the remaining alive or the dying of the body itself, are Actions, and as occasion arises, it becomes necessary to consider which of the two actions of 'remaining alive' or 'dying' is to be chosen. When this consideration arises, the word 'karma' (Action) can also be understood in the meaning of Duty (*kartavya-karma*) or proper action (*vihita-karma*) (Gī. 4. 16). We have so far considered the actions of human beings. Going beyond this, the word 'karma' is also applied to the activities of the moveable and immoveable world, that is to say, even of lifeless things. But that matter will be considered in the subsequent chapter on Cause and Effect (*karma-vipāka-prakriyā*).

The word "YOGA" is even more complicated in its meaning than the word '*karma*'. The present-day ordinary meaning of this word is 'controlling the mental impulses of the organs by means of *prāṇāyāma*, i.e., 'control of the breath' or 'the Yoga of mental absorption or meditation prescribed by the Pātañjala-Sūtras', and the word has been used in the same meanings also in the Upaniṣads (Kaṭha. 6. 11). But it must first be borne in mind that this restricted meaning is not the meaning in which it has been used in the Bhagavadgītā. The word '*Yoga*' comes from the root '*yuj*' which means 'to join', and its root meaning is 'the state of union', 'combination', 'addition' or 'co-existence' or 'staying together', and later on, it has also come to mean the 'means', 'device' or 'method' or 'thing to be done', that is, the '*Karma*' (Action) which is necessary for acquiring that state, and the Amarakośa has given all these meanings of the word in the following sentence: "*yogaḥ sannahanopāya-dhyāna-saṁgati-yuktiṣu*" (3. 3. 22). In practical astrology, if some planets have become propitious or unpropitious, we say that they are forming a propitious or unpropitious '*yoga*', and the word '*yoga*' in the phrase '*yoga-kṣema*' means 'acquiring such things as one has not got' (Gī. 9. 22). On seeing that Droṇācārya would not be vanquished in the Bhārati war, Śrī Kṛṣṇa has, in the following words said that: "there was only one '*yoga*' (means or 'trick') for vanquishing him":— "*eko hi yogo 'sya bhaved vadhāya*", i.e., "he can be killed only by one trick" (Ma. Bhā. Dro. 181. 31) and later on He has narrated how He had killed Jarāsaṁdha and other kings for the protection of the Religion by means of '*yoga*'. It is stated in the Udyoga parva that after Bhīṣma had taken away the damsels Ambā, Ambikā and Ambālikā, the other kings pursued him crying: "Yoga, Yoga" (U. 172), and the word '*yoga*' has been used in the same meaning in numerous other places in the Mahābhārata. In the Gītā, the words '*yoga*', '*yogi*' or other compounds from the word '*yoga*' have occured about 80 times. But nowhere except in at most four or five places has it been used in the meaning of 'Pātañjala-yoga' (Gī. 6. 12 and 23). We find almost everywhere the word used more or less in the meaning of 'means', 'skilful device,' 'method', 'the thing to be done', 'union', etc., and it must be said that this is one of the comprehensive words used in the Gītā-science. Still, it is not enough even to say in a general way that '*yoga*' means 'means', 'skilful device' or 'method'. Because, according as the speaker may wish, it may be a means of Renunciation *(saṁnyāsa)* or Action *(karma)* or mental control *(citta-nirodha)* or of Release *(Mokṣa)* or of something else. For instance, the word '*yoga*' has been used in the Gītā itself, in three or four places, to signify the divine skill or wonderful power of the Blessed Lord in creating the variegated perceptible creation (Gī. 7. 25; 9. 5; 10. 7; 11. 8) and on that account, the Blessed Lord has been referred to as '*Yogeśvara*' (Gī. 18. 75). But this is not the principal meaning of the word '*yoga*' in the Gītā. Therefore, in order to explain what particular skill, means, method or process is principally signified in the Gītā by the use of the word '*yoga*', this word has intentionally been clearly defined in the Gītā itself as: "*yogaḥ karmasu kauśalam*" (Gī. 2. 50) i.e. "'yoga' means some special skill, device, intelligent method, or graceful way of performing Actions"; and in the Śāṁkara-bhāṣya on this phrase, the phrase '*karmasu kauśalam*' has been interpreted as meaning: "the device of eliminating the natural tendency of *karma* to create a bondage". Normally, there are numerous '*yoga*' or means of performing one and the same action, but the best of all these methods is specially referred to as 'yoga'. For instance, the earning of money can be achieved by theft or deceit or by begging or by service or by borrowing or by physical labour, and many other such ways; and although the word '*yoga*' can be applied to each of these ways, according to the root meaning of the word, yet, 'earning money by one's own labour without sacrificing one's independence' is principally referred to as "the *yoga* of acquiring wealth" *(dravya-prāpti-yoga)*.

If the Blessed Lord Himself has intentionally and specifically defined the word '*yoga*' in the Gītā itself as: "*yogaḥ karmasu kauśalam*" i.e., "'Yoga' means a special device of performing Actions", then, there should strictly speaking remain no doubt whatsoever about the primary meaning of this word in the Gītā. But, as several commentators have extracted various hidden meanings from the Gītā by twisting the meaning of this word, disregarding this definition of the word given by the Blessed Lord Himself, it is necessary here to go deeper into the meaning of the word '*yoga*', in order to clear that mis-interpretation. The word '*yoga*' appears for the first time in the second chapter of the Gītā and at that very place the meaning of that word is explained. After having justified the war on the authority of the Sāṁkhya philosophy, the Blessed Lord goes on to say that He will next give Arjuna the justification of the war on the authority of the Yoga (Gī. 2. 39), and He, to begin with, describes how the minds of persons continually engrossed in desire-prompted Action like sacrificial ritual, become disintegrated on account of the desire for the reward (Gī. 2. 41–46). He then goes on to say that Arjuna should not allow his mind to be disintegrated in this way, and should "give up all attachments (*āsakti*), but not think of giving up Action", and He has further said to him: "become steeped in the yoga (*yogastha*) and perform Actions" (Gī. 2. 48) and in the same place the word '*yoga*' has been to begin with clearly defined as meaning: "'Yoga' means equability of mind towards success or failure". Then, He goes on to say: "this 'yoga' of equability of mind is better than performing Actions with the desire for the fruit" (Gī. 2. 49) and that "when the mind is equable, the doer is not affected by the sin or the virtue of the Action, and, therefore, acquire this Yoga". Immediately thereafter, He again defines the nature of 'Yoga' by the words: "*yogaḥ karmasu kauśalam*" (Gī. 2. 50). From this, it becomes clear that the special device mentioned to start with by the Blessed Lord for the sinless performance of Actions, namely an equable mind, is what is known as '*kauśala*' (skilful device) and that performing Actions by this '*kauśala*' or device is, in the Gītā, known as '*yoga*'; and this very meaning of that word has further been made perfectly clear by Arjuna who says: "*yo 'yaṁ yogas tvayā proktaḥ sāmyena Madhusūdana*" (Gī. 6. 33), i.e., "this yoga of equality, that is, of an equable frame of mind which has been prescribed by you to me". There are two ways in which the Self-Realised man should live in this world which have been prescribed by the Vedic religion in existence long before the date of Śrī Śaṁkarācārya. One of these ways is the literal abandonment (*saṁnyāsa*) or giving up (*tyāga*) of all Action after Self-Realisation, and the other way is of not giving up Actions even after Self-Realisation, but going on performing them while life lasts, in such a way that one does not thereby incur either sin or merit. It is with reference to these two paths that the words '*saṁnyāsa*' and '*karma-yoga*' have been used later on in the Gītā (Gī. 5. 2). '*saṁnyāsa*' means 'give up' and '*yoga*' means 'stick to'; therefore, these are two independent paths of the giving up or the sticking to Action. The two words '*sāṁkhya*' and '*yoga*' (*Sāṁkhya-yogau*) are two abbreviated terms, which are used later on with reference to these two paths (Gī. 5. 4). It is true that the sixth chapter of the Gītā contains a description of the postures *(āsanas)* of the Pātañjala-yoga necessary for steadying the mind; but for whom has that description been given? Not for the ascetic, but for the Karma-Yogi, i. e., for the person who continues skilfully performing Actions, and, in order that he might thereby acquire an equable frame of mind. Otherwise, the sentence "*tapasvibhyo 'dhiko yogi*", i.e., "the yogi is superior to the ascetic" is meaningless. Also, the advice given to Arjuna at the end of this chapter in the terms "*tasmād yogī bhavārjuna*" (6. 46), i.e., "therefore, O Arjuna, become a yogi", does not mean "take to the practice of Pātañjala-Yoga" but has to be taken as meaning "become a yogi, who performs Actions skilfully or a Karma-Yogi", in which meaning that word has been used in the phrases: "*yogasthaḥ kuru karmāṇi*" (2. 48) i.e., perform Action, having become a yogi", or after that: "*tasmād yogāya yujyasva yogaḥ karmasu kauśalam* (Gī. 2. 50), i.e., "therefore, take shelter in *yoga*; '*yoga*' means the skill of performing Action", or at the end of the fourth chapter, "*yogam ātiṣṭhottiṣṭha Bhārata*" (4. 42), i.e., "take shelter in the yoga, O, Bhārata, and stand up". Because, His saying "follow the Pātañjala-yoga and stand up and fight" would be impossible and even improbable. It has been clearly stated previously that: *karmayogena yogināṁ*" (Gī. 3. 3) i.e., "yogis are persons who perform Actions"; and in the exposition of the Nārāyaṇīya or the Bhāgavata religion in the Mahābhārata, it is stated that persons belonging to that religion do not abandon worldly affairs but perform them skilfully (*"suprayuktena karmaṇā"*) and attain the Parameśvara (Ma. Bhā. Śān. 348. 56). From this it follows, that the words '*yogi*' and '*karma-yogi*' have been used synonymously in the Gītā and that they mean: "a person who performs Action according to a particular device." Yet, instead of using the long word '*karma-yoga*', its abbreviated form '*yoga*' has been more frequently used both in the Gītā and in the Mahābhārata. The word '*yoga*', which has been used by the Blessed Lord three times in succession in the stanza: "this *yoga* which I have explained to you had been taught by me before to Vivasvān (Gī. 4. 1); Vivasvān taught it to Manu, but as this *yoga* subsequently ceased to exist, I had once more to-day to explain that *yoga* to you", has not been intended to mean the Pātañjala-yoga; and one has to understand it as meaning "a particular kind of device, method, or process of performing Action". In the same way, the reference by Sañjaya to the conversation between Śrī Kṛṣṇa and Arjuna as '*yoga*' (Gī. 18. 75) means the same thing. Although Śrī Śaṁkarācārya himself followed the path of Renunciation, yet he has in the beginning of his Gītā-bhāṣya pointed out the two divisions of the Vedic Religion into '*pravṛtti*' and '*nivṛtti*' and the word '*yoga*' has been interpreted by him in some places according to the definition given by the Blessed Lord as "*samyag darśanopāya karmānuṣṭhānam*" (Gī. Bhā. 4. 42) and in other places as "*yogaḥ yuktiḥ*" (Gī. Bhā. 17. 7). In the same way also in the Mahābhārata, these two words have been clearly defined in the Anugītā in the phrase "*pravṛtti lakṣaṇo yogaḥ jñānaṁ saṁnyāsa lakṣaṇam*" i. e., "*yoga* means the path of Energism (*pravṛtti-mārga*) and *jñāna* means the path of Renunciation (*saṁnyāsa* or *nivṛtti-mārga*) (Ma. Bhā. Aśva. 43. 25) and even in the Nārāyaṇīyopākhyāna at the end of the Śāntiparva the words '*sāṁkhya*' and '*yoga*' have occurred on numerous occasions in these two senses, and it is explained how and why these two paths were created by the Blessed Lord in the beginning of the creation itself (Ma. Bhā. Śān. 240 and 348). That this Nārāyaṇīya or Bhāgavata religion has been propounded in the Bhagavadgītā will become perfectly clear from the quotation from the Mahābhārata which has been given at the beginning of the first chapter. Therefore, one has to say that the meanings of '*sāṁkhya*' as '*nivṛtti*' and of '*yoga*' as '*pravṛtti*', which are their ancient technical meanings according to the Nārāyaṇīya religion, are also their meanings in the Gītā; and, if anybody has any doubts about this, these doubts ought to be fully cleared by the definition of that word given in the Gītā as: "*samatvaṁ yoga uccyate*", i.e., "'yoga' is the name given to equability" or "*yogaḥ karmasu kauśalam*", i. e., "'yoga' means skill in Action," as also by such phrases used in the Gītā as "*karma-yogeṇa yoginām*" etc.; and, it is established beyond argument that the word '*yoga*' has been used in the Gītā in the sense of only the path of Energism *(pravṛtti-mārga)* i. e., the "KARMA-YOGA". Not only in the Vedic religious treatises, but also in the Buddhistic religious treatises in Pali and in Sanskrit, the word Yoga is found to have been used in this meaning. For instance, in the Pali work, named *Milinda-praśna* written about Śake 200, we come across the word "Pubba-yoga (*pūrva-yoga*)" where its meaning has been defined as "*pubbakamma*" *(pūrva-karma)* (Mi. Pra. 1. 4); and in the 50th verse of the first canto *(sarga)* of the Sanskrit poem *Buddha-carita* written by the poet Aśvaghoṣa in the beginning of the Śālivāhana era, we find the following statement:—"*ācāryakaṁ yogavidhau dvijānām–aprāptam-anyair–Janako jagāma*" i. e. "The king Janaka had become an *ācārya* (preacher) for teaching the Yoga methods (*yoga-vidhi*) to Brahmins, and such a preceptorship had not been acquired by any one before him." In this place, the word '*yoga-vidhi*' has to be interpreted as meaning "the method *(vidhi)* of the Desire-less Karma-Yoga". Because, the Gītā and all the other works emphatically say that that was the true bearing of the mode of life of Janaka, and Aśvaghoṣa has in the *Buddha-carita* (9. 19–20) given the illustration of Janaka himself in order to show "how Release can be obtained notwithstanding that one leads the life of a house-holder". When it has been in this way proved that even according to the Buddhistic treatises, this path of Action prescribed by Janaka was known as 'yoga', one has to understand the word '*yoga*' used in the Gītā also in the same meaning; because, the Gītā itself says that the path prescribed by Janaka is the very path it advocates (Gī. 3. 20). We will later on consider in greater detail the two paths of 'Sāṁkhya' and 'Yoga'. The matter under consideration at present is in what meaning the word '*yoga*' has been used in the Gītā.

When the principal meanings of the words '*yoga*', namely, 'Karma-Yoga', and '*yogī*', namely 'Karma-Yogī', have in this way been established, it is not necessary to say in so many words what the subject-matter of the Bhagavadgītā is. The Blessed Lord Himself refers to the advice given by Him as '*yoga*' (Gī. 4. 1–3). Not only that, but as I have already stated above, Arjuna in the sixth chapter (Gī. 6. 33), and Sañjaya in the conclusion (*upasaṁhāra*) at the end of the Gītā (Gī. 18. 75) have characterised the preaching of the Gītā as '*yoga*'. In the same way, in the enunciatory words used at the end of each chapter of the Gītā signifying the conclusion of the chapter (which is technically called *saṁkalpa*), it is clearly stated that the Science of Yoga (*yoga-śāstra*) is the subject-matter of the Gītā; but none of the commentators on the Gītā, seem to have paid any attention to this meaning of the word in the *saṁkalpa*. After the the two opening words "*Śrīmad-Bhagavadgītāsu upaniṣastu*"in this *saṁkalpa*, come the two words "*brahma-vidyāyāṁ yoga-śāstre*". Out of these, the first two words mean "in the Upaniṣat sung by the Blessed Lord" and it is quite clear from the following two words that "the *Yoga-Śāstra* which is one of the *Brahma-Vidyās*", that is, the KARMA-YOGA-ŚĀSTRA, is the subject matter of the Gītā. '*Brahma-vidyā*' means 'Knowledge of the Brahman' (*Brahmajñāna*); and when that has been acquired, the Self-Released man has two cults or paths open before him (Gī. 3. 3). One is the Sāṁkhya path or the *saṁnyāsa* (Renunciation) path, that is, the path of abandoning all wordly affairs or Actions after Self-Realisation, and living like an apathetic (*virakta*) person; and the other path is the path of Yoga or of Karma-Yoga, that is to say, of not giving up wordly affairs but continuing to perform them in such a way that they do not create any difficulty in the matter of obtaining Release. Out of these two paths, the first one is also known as the 'path of Self-Realisation' (*jñāna-niṣṭhā*) and an exposition of that will be found to have been made by many *ṛṣis* in the Upaniṣads and other writers. But there is no scientific exposition anywhere, except in the Gītā, of the Karma-Yoga, which is included in the *Brahma-vidyā*. Therefore, it now becomes quite clear that those persons who first prepared that *saṁkalpa*—and, as I have stated above, it must have been there before any of the commentaries on the Gītā were written, since it is to be found in all the editions of the Gītā—must have added the words *"brahma-vidyāyām yoga-śāstre"* in this *saṁkalpa* on proper authority, and intentionally, for emphasising the uniqueness of the subject-matter of the Gītā-śāstra, and not uselessly or frivolously; and at the same time, we also easily understand what the import of the Gītā was understood to be before any commentaries in support of particular cults came to be written on it. It is our great fortune that this work of preaching the Karma-Yoga was taken on his own shoulders by Śrī Kṛṣṇa Bhagavān, who was the promulgator of this path of Yoga and who was the personified 'Īśvara of all yogas' ('*Yogeśvara*' is '*yoga*' plus '*Īśvara*'), and who has explained the esoteric import of it to Arjuna for the benefit of the whole world. It is true that the words '*karma-yoga*' and '*karma-yoga-śāstra*' are longer than the words '*yoga*' and '*yoga-śāstra*' used in the Gītā; but in order that there should no more be any doubts as to what the Gītā preaches, I have intentionally given the name "Karma-Yoga-Śāstra" to this work and to this chapter.

That science by means of which we can decide such questions as: Which is the best and purest of the several 'yogas', means, or processes in which a particular Action can be performed; whether it can be always followed; if not, what are the exceptions to it, and how they arise; why is that path which we call good, really good, or that which we call bad, really bad, and on the strength of what, is this goodness or badness to be decided and who is to do so or what is the underlying principle in it etc. is known as the 'KARMA-YOGA-ŚĀSTRA' (science of Karma-Yoga) or, as expressed briefly in the Gītā 'YOGA-ŚASTRA' (the science of Yoga). 'Good' or 'bad' are words in ordinary use and the following other words: propitious and unpropitious, or beneficial and harmful, or meritorious and non-meritorious, or sin and virtue, or righteous and unrighteous, are used in the same sense. The same is the meaning conveyed by the word-couples doable and not-doable (*kārya* and *akārya*), duty and non-duty (*kartavya* and *akartavya*), just and unjust (*nyāyya* and *anyāyya*). Nevertheless, as the various persons who have used these words have different ideas about the formation of the universe, there have also come into existence, different ways in which the 'Karma-Yoga' science has been expounded. Whatever science is taken, the subject-matter of it can be discussed ordinarily in three ways:—(1) considering the various objects in the physical world from the point of view that they really are as they are perceived by our organs, and that there is nothing beyond, is the first of these methods, which is known as "*ĀDHI-BHAUTIKA*" (positive or materialistic) way of considering them. For instance, when you look upon the Sun not as a deity, but as a round-mass of gross matter made up of the five primordial elements, and examine its various properties, such as its heat, or light, or weight, or distance, or power of attraction, etc., that becomes the positive or material examination of the Sun. Take the tree as another illustration. If we do not consider the internal force in the tree which is responsible for its getting leaves etc., but consider the tree purely externally, that is, consider only the facts that when the seed is put into the earth, it takes root and becomes a sprout, which grows later on and goes through the visible changes of leaves, flowers, fruits etc., that is a purely material examination of the tree. The examination of the subject-matter in Chemistry or Physics or the science of electricity or other modern sciences is of this kind. Nay, materialists imagine, that when they have examined in this way the visible properties of any object, that is all they need to do and that it is useless to further examine the objects in the world. (2) When we discard this point of view, and examine what there is at the root of the object in the material world and whether the activities of these objects are due to some inherent properties in them or there is some other power or principle behind those activities, then one has to transcend the material examination of the object. For instance, if we believe that in the gross or lifeless globe of the Sun, made up of the five primordial elements, there exists a deity called the 'Sun' which dwells within it, and that this deity carries on the activities of the material Sun, such examination is called an *ĀDHI-DAIVIKA* (Theological) examination of the object. According to this point of view, there are in the tree, water, air, etc., innumerable deities, which are distinct from those objects, and which activate those objects. (3) But, when instead of believing in this way that there are millions and millions of independent deities in all the various objects in the gross world, we believe that there exists in this world some Spiritual Force, i.e., factor of consciousness *(cicchakti)* imperceptible to the organs, which carries on all the activities of the external world; and that this Spiritual Force exists in the human body in the shape of an Ātman and acquaints the human being with the entire creation; and that this cosmos is kept going by that force, such consideration of the object is called an *ĀDHYATMIKA* (metaphysical) examination of the object. For instance, metaphysicians believe that the movements of the Sun and the Moon or even of the leaves of the tree are inspired by this unimaginable Power and that there are not different and independent deities in the Sun or in other objects. These three ways of examining any subject-matter have been in existence from times immemorial and they seem to have been followed even in the Upaniṣads. For instance, in the Bṛhadāraṇyaka and other Upaniṣads, while considering whether the organs of perception (*Jñānendriya*) or the vital force (*prāṇa*) is superior, their respective strengths are considered, once from the point of view that they have deities like Agni etc., and again by considering their subtle (metaphysical i. e., *ādhyātmika*) forms (Bṛ. 1. 5. 21 and 22; Chān. 1. 2 and 3; Kauṣi 2. 8); and the consideration of the form of the *Īśvara* at the end of the seventh chapter and in the beginning of the eight chapter of the Gītā is also from this point of view. Out of these three methods, our religious writers attach a higher importance to the metaphysical (*ādhyātmika*) method of consideration than to others, relying on the authority "*adhyātma-vidyā vidyānām*" (Gī. 10. 32) i. e. "the metaphysical science is the highest of all sciences". But in modern times, the meanings of these three words are to a certain extent changed and the well-known French Materialist Comte * has given the highest importance

* Auguste Comte was a great philosopher who lived in France in the last century. He wrote a very important book on Sociology and has shown for the first time how the constitution of

to the Positive (material) exposition. He says that there is no sense in trying to find out the fundamental element, if any, which exists at the root of the world; and in as much as this element is always unknowable (*agamya*) it is neither possible nor proper to found on it the edifice of a science. When the aboriginal man for the first time, saw trees, clouds, volcanoes and other moving objects, he credulously began to believe that they were all deities. According to Comte, this was the Theological consideration of the universe. But man very soon gave up this idea and began to think that there must be some element in the shape of an Ātman in all these objects. According to Comte, this is the second stage of the progress of human knowledge; and this stage is called by him the Metaphysical stage. But when even after considering the universe in this way, actual practical scientific knowledge did not grow, man ultimately began to examine deeper and deeper only the visible properties of the objects in this world; and on that account, man has now begun to exercise greater control over the external world, as a result of his having been able to invent steam-engines, telegraphs etc. Comte calls this the Positive *ādhibhautika)* consideration and he has come to the conclusion that this method of consideration of any science or object is the most profitable one. According to Comte, we must adopt this method for scientifically considering Sociology or the science of Karma-Yoga; and after a careful consideration of the history of the world, this philosopher has drawn the following conclusion regarding the science of wordly life, from that point of view, namely that: the highest religion of

society can be scientifically considered. He has come to the conclusion after considering numerous sciences, that whichever science is taken, the consideration of it is first Theological and then Metaphysical and that, lastly it attains the Positive form. These three systems have been respectively given by me the ancient names of '*ādhidaivika*' '*ādhyātmika*' and '*ādhibhautika*' in this book. Comte has not invented these methods. They are old methods, but he has fixed a new historical order for them and the only discovery made by him is that of all the three, the positive (*ādhibhautika*) system of consideration is the best. The most important of the works of this writer have been translated into English.

every human being is to love the whole human race and to continually strive for the benefit of everybody. Mill, Spencer and other English philosophers may be said to support this opinion. On the other hand, Kant, Haegel, Schaupenhaur and other German philosophers, have proved that this positive method of considering Ethics is inefficient and they have recently revived in Europe the method of basing Ethics on Metaphysics adopted by our Vedānta philosophers. This matter, however, will be dealt with in greater detail later on.

The reason why different writers have used the different words '*kārya*' and '*akārya*' (doable and not-doable), '*dharmya*' and '*adharmya*' (moral and immoral) in the meaning of 'good' and 'bad' although they all convey the same meaning, is that every one has his own different way or view of dealing with a particular subject-matter. The question of Arjuna was whether or not that war in which he would have to kill Bhīṣma, Droṇa, etc., was meritorious (Gī. 2. 7); and if a Materialist had to answer this question, he would have critically considered the palpable profit or loss of it to Arjuna personally, as also the results of it on the entire society and would have declared whether the fight was just (*nyāyya*) or unjust (*anyāyya*); because, these Materialists do not admit of any other test for determining the goodness or badness of any particular Action except the material, that is, the actual, external results of that Action on the world. But such an answer would not have satisfied Arjuna; his vision was more comprehensive; what he wanted was to know whether that war would in the end benefit his Self (*ātman*), not in this world alone, but from the next-world point of view. He had no doubt as to whether or not he would acquire the kingdom or material happiness as a result of the death of Bhīṣma and Droṇa or whether his rule would be more beneficial to people than the rule of Duryodhana. In short, he had to see whether or not what he did was '*dharmya*' (moral) or '*adharmya*' (immoral), '*puṇya*' (non-sin) or '*pāpa*' (sin); and the exposition in the Gītā has been made from that point of view. Not only in the Gītā but also in other places in the Mahābhārata has the examination of *karma* (Action) and *akarma* (non-Action) been made from this next-world and Metaphysical point of view and in it, the two words '*dharma*' and '*adharma*' have been primarily used in order to show the goodness or badness of any particular act. But as the word '*dharma*' and its opposite correlative '*adharma*' are likely to create confusion on account of their very comprehensive meaning, it is necessary to discuss here in greater detail the meanings in which those words have been principally used in the science of Karma-Yoga.

The word 'DHARMA' is in ordinary practice very often used to imply only the path leading to next-world happiness. When we ask some one "What is your *dharma* (religion)"? our intention is to ask him by what path he goes—whether Vedic, Buddhist, Jain, Christian, Mahomedan or Parsi—for acquiring happiness in the next world; and the reply which he gives is also from the same point of view. In the same way, where the subject-matter of the Vedic *yajñas* and *yāgas* instrumental to the acquisition of heaven is being considered, the word '*dharma*' is used in the same meaning, as in the canon "*athāto dharmajijñāsā*" etc. but the word '*dharma*' is not to be understood in such a restricted meaning, and it is very often used for indicating the limitations of worldly morality, as in the phrases, '*rājadharma*' (the duty of kings), '*prajādharma*' (the duty of subjects), '*deśadharma*' (the duty of a country), '*jñatidharma*' (the duty pertaining to a caste), '*kuladharma*' (the duty pertaining to clan or family), '*mitradharma*' (one's duty as a friend) etc. If these two meanings of the word '*dharma*' are to be individually explained, the *dharma* relating to the life after death may be called '*mokṣadharma*' or simply '*mokṣa*' and the *dharma* relating to this worldly life, i. e., Ethics may be given the name of '*dharma*' simply. For instance, in enumerating the four ideals of manhood *(puruṣārtha)*, we say '*dharma*' (morality), '*artha*' (wealth), '*kāma*' (desire), '*mokṣa*' (Release). If '*mokṣa*' is meant to be included in the first word '*dharma*', then it would not be necessary to mention '*mokṣa*' as an independent ideal at the end. Therefore, we must say that the writers of our scriptures use the word '*dharma*' in this place as meaning the numerous ethical duties which form part of our worldly life. The same meaning is conveyed by the words *kartavya-karma* (duty), '*nīti*' (Ethics), '*nītidharma*' (morality) or "*sadācaraṇa*' (good conduct) used now-a-days. But in ancient Sanskrit treatises, the words '*nīti*' or '*nītiśāstra*' were used principally with reference to regal jurisprudence *(rājanīti)* and therefore, the ordinary exposition of duty *(kartavya-karma)* or good conduct *(sad-vartana)* used to be called the 'exposition of *dharma*' *(dharma-pravacana)* instead of the 'exposition of *nīti*' *('nīti-pravacana')*. But this technical distinction between the two words *nīti*' and '*dharma*' has not been adopted in all Sanskrit treatises; and, therefore, I too, have used the terms '*nīti*', '*kartavya*' or simply '*dharma*' as synonymous; and, where the subject of Release *(mokṣa)* has to be considered, I have used the independent terms '*adhyātma*' (Metaphysics) or '*bhakti-mārga*' (Path of Devotion). The word '*dharma*' has appeared on numerous occasions in the Mahābhārata, and whenever it has been said there that a particular person is bound to do a particular thing according to his '*dharma*', the word '*dharma*' means ethical science *(kartavya-śāstra)* or the then sociology *(samāja-vyavasthā-śāstra)*; and wherever there has been occasion to refer to the paths leading to next-world happiness, in the latter half of the Śānti-parva, the specific word '*mokṣa-dharma*' has been used. So also in the Manu-Smṛti and other Smṛti texts, in mentioning the specific duties of the four castes, Brahmin, kṣatriya, vaiśya, and śūdra, the word '*dharma*' has been used on many occasions and in many places; and even in the Bhagavadgītā the word '*dharma*' has been used as meaning 'the duties of the four castes in this world' in the expression "*svadharmam api cāvekṣya*" (Gī. 2. 31) where the Blessed Lord is telling Arjuna to fight, having regard to what his '*dharma*' is, and also later on in the expression: "*svadharme nidhanaṁ śreyaḥ paradharmo bhayāvahaḥ*" (Gī. 3. 35), i.e., "it is better to die performing one's caste duties; following the duties enjoined on another caste is dangerous". The ancient *ṛṣis* had created the institution of the four castes—which was in the nature of a division of labour—in order that all the affairs of society should go on without a hitch, and that society should be protected and maintained on all sides, without any particular person or group of persons having to bear the whole burden. Later on, people belonging to this society became '*jātimātropajīvī*' that is "persons, who forgetting their respective caste duties, belonged to a particular caste merely by reason of birth" and became mere nominal Brahmins, kṣatriyas, vaiśyās, or śudras; but let us keep that thing aside for a time. Originally, this institution had been made for the maintenance of society and it is quite clear that if any one of the four castes had given up the *'dharma'* i. e., duties allocated to it, or if any particular caste had totally ceased to exist and its place had not been taken by some other persons, the entire society would to that extent have been disabled and would later on have either been gradually destroyed or at least have sunk to a very low stage. There are numerous societies in the Western hemisphere, which have come to prominence notwithstanding that they do not have the institution of the four castes. But we must not forget that although the institution of the four castes may not be in existence among them, yet all the duties of the four castes are seen being performed in those societies, if not in the shape of castes, at any rate by some other arrangement in the shape of professional divisions or classes. In short, when we use the word *'dharma'* from the worldly point of view, we consider in what way society will be maintained *(dhāraṇā)* and benefited. Manu has said that that *'dharma'* which is *'asukhodarka'*, that is to say, 'from which unhappiness ultimately results' should be given up (Manu. 4. 176); and Bhīṣma says in the Satyānṛtodhyāya of the Śāntiparva (Śān. 109. 12), where the exposition of *'dharma'* and *'adharma'* is made, and before that, Śrī Kṛṣṇa also says in the Karṇaparva (Ma. Bhā. Karṇa. 69. 59), that :-

dhāraṇād dharmam ity āhur dharmo dhārayate prajāḥ ।
yat syād dhāraṇa sañyuktaṁ sa dharma iti niścayaḥ ॥

that is, "the word *Dharma* comes from the root *dhṛ*, i. e., to hold or uphold, and all human beings are held together by *dharma*. That by which the holding together (of all human beings) takes place is *dharma* ". Therefore, when this *dharma* ceases to be observed, the binding-ropes of society may be said to have become loose, and when these binding ropes are loosened, society will be in the same position as the planetary system consisting of the Sun and the planets would be in the sky without the binding force of gravitation or as a ship would be on the ocean without a rudder. Therefore, Vyāsa in the Bhārata gives the advice that, in order that society should not come to an end by reaching such a lamentable state, money *(artha)* if it has to be acquired, must be acquired by *'dharma'*, that is, without disturbing the arrangement of society; and if the desires, such as the sex impulses *(kāma)* etc. have to be satisfied, that should also be done consistently with *'dharma'*; and he says at the end of the Bhārata that :–

ūrdhvabāhur viraumy eṣaḥ na ca kaścic chṛṇoti mām |
dharmād arthaś ca kāmaś ca sa dharmaḥ kiṁ na sevyate ||

i. e., "Oh people I am haranguing you with raised hands, (but) no one listens to me ! if both wealth *(artha)* and desires *(kāma)* can be acquired by *dharma*, (then) why do you not follow such a *dharma?*" My readers will from this understand the chief meaning in which the word *'dharma'* has been used in the expression *dharma-saṁhitā*, when the Mahābhārata, from the point of view of *'dharma'*, is looked upon as the fifth Veda or *dharma-saṁhitā*; and for the same reason, namely, on the ground that it is a *dharma-grantha*, has the Mahābhārata been included among the religious texts prescribed for daily recital in the *Brahma-yajña* (ritual for Brahmins)—as is shown by the use of the symbolical words : " *Nārāyaṇaṁ namaskṛtya* "—along with the two treatises Pūrva-Mīmāṁsa and Uttara-Mīmāṁsa (which deal with the question of next-world happiness).

Reading the exposition made by me above of what is *dharma* and what is *adharma*, some one may object : if you accept these principles of 'the maintenance of society' *(samāja-dhāraṇā)* and 'general welfare' *(sarva-bhūta-hitaṁ)*, as mentioned in the second chapter when discussing the question of Truth and Falsehood *(satyānṛta)*, then there is no difference between your point of view and the Materialistic point of view; because, both these principles are outwardly real, that is Materialistic. This question has been dealt with by me in detail in the next chapter. For the present, I will only say that although we accept maintenance of society as being the chief outward use of *dharma*, yet we never lose sight of the Redemption of the Ātman *(ātma-kalyāṇa)* or Release *(mokṣa)* which is the highest ideal according to the Vedic or all other religions and which is the special feature of our view-point. Whether it is maintenance of society or the general material welfare of everybody, if these externally useful principles obstruct the Redemption of the Ātman, we do not want them. If even our works on medicine maintain that the medical science is a useful science, because it serves as a means for obtaining Release (*mokṣa*), by protecting the body, then it is absolutely impossible that our religious writers would divorce the Karma-Yoga-Śāstra, which considers the most important subject of the performance of various worldly Actions, from the Metaphysical philosophy of Release. And therefore, we look upon that Action which is favourable to our Metaphysical betterment as '*puṇya*' (religiously meritorious), '*dharma*' (moral), or '*śubha*' (good) and that which is unfavourable to it, as '*pāpa*' (sinful), '*adharma*' (immoral), or '*aśubha*' (bad). It is for this very reason that we use the words '*dharma*' and '*adharma*' (notwithstanding that they have a double meaning and are to a certain extent ambiguous) in place of the words '*kartavya*' (duty) '*akartavya*' (non-duty) and '*kārya*' (doable) and '*akārya*' (non-doable). Even when the worldly affairs or activities in the external world are primarily to be considered, we consider whether or not these activities are conducive to Ātmic * benefit, simultaneously with considering their external effects. If a Materialist is asked why I should sacrifice my own benefit for the benefit of others, what answer can he give except by saying: "That is ordinary human nature"? The writers of our Śāstras have seen further than this and the science of Karma-Yoga has been considered in the Mahābhārata from this comprehensive Metaphysical standpoint, and Vedānta has for the same reason been dealt with in the Bhagavadgītā. Even the ancient Greek philosophers were of the opinion that one has to take 'the greatest benefit' or 'the climax of virtue' as the highest ideal of mankind and dealt with the question of the doable and the not-doable from that point of view; and Aristotle has in his book on Ethics said that all these things are included in the Ātmic benefit (1. 7, 8). Yet, Aristotle has not given due importance to Ātmic benefit. That is not the case with our philosophers. They have laid down, that Ātmic benefit or

[*This word 'Ātmic' (i. e., of the 'Ātman') has been coined by me on the analogy 'Vedic'.—Trans.]

Metaphysical perfection is the first and the highest duty of every man; that the question of the doable and the not-doable must be considered on the basis that Ātmic benefit is more important than any other benefit; and that, it is not proper to consider that question without reference to Metaphysical philosophy. The same position seems to have been accepted in modern times by some Western philosophers, in dealing with the question of the doable and the not-doable. For instance, the German philosopher Kant first wrote the metaphysical book *Critique of Pure Reason*, that is, of '*vyavasāyātmika*', (i.e., pure) '*buddhi*' (i.e., Reason), and subsequently the book *Critique of Practical Reason*, that is, of '*vāsanātmaka*' (i.e., practical) '*buddhi*' (i.e., Reason). * And even in England, Green has started his book entitled *Prolegomena to Ethics* with the consideration of the Ātman, which is the bed-rock of the entire universe. But, as the works of purely materialistic philosophers on Ethics are principally taught in our colleges the fundamental principles of the Karma-Yoga mentioned in the Gītā, are not well understood even by learned persons among us, who have had an English education.

It will be clear from the exposition made by me above why we apply the common word 'DHARMA' chiefly to wordly morality or to systems laid down for the maintenance of society. Not only in the Sanskrit treatises, Mahābhārata and Bhagavadgītā, but also in vernacular works is the word '*dharma*' always used as meaning worldly duties or laws. We understand the words *kuladharma* and *kulācāra* as synonymous. The Marathi poet, Moropant, has used the word '*dharma*' in this sense, in describing the incident in the Bhārata war when Karṇa had got out of his chariot for raising the wheel of his chariot which had sunk into the earth, and Arjuna was on the point of killing him. Karṇa then said: "It is not the ethics of warfare (*yuddhadharma*) to kill an enemy when he is unarmed," and Śrī Kṛṣṇa retaliated by reminding him of the previous incidents of the attempted

* Kant was a German philosopher, and he is looked upon at the father of modern philosophy. Two of his works, the *Critique of Pure Reason* and the *Critique of Pratical Reason* are well-known. The work written by Green is known as *Prolegomena to Ethics*.

denuding of Draupadī, or the murder of Abhimanyu, when alone, by a number of persons, and asking him: "Where was then your *dharma*, Oh, Rādhāsuta?" with reference to all those incidents; and even in the Mahābhārata the word '*dharma*' has been used in relating this incident in the expression "*kva te dharmās tadā gataḥ*", i.e., "where did your '*dharma*' (morality) go then?", and it is shown that it is morally right to give measure for measure to such immoral persons. In short, as it has become usual, whether in Sanskrit or in Prakrit literature, to use the word '*dharma*' as indicating the rules of morality which have been laid down by high and reverend persons, with reference to various matters, for the maintenance of society, I have adopted the same word in this book. These rules, which have been laid down by reverend people (*śiṣṭa*) and which have become acceptable on all hands and are known as 'respectable behaviour' (*śiṣṭācāra*), are, from this point of view, the root of morality (*dharma*); and therefore, in the Mahābhārata (Anu. 104. 157) and also in the Smṛti treatises there are such statements as: '*ācāraprabhavo dharmaḥ*", i.e., "morality springs from custom" or: "*ācāraḥ paramo dharmaḥ*", i.e., "rules of custom are the highest morality" (Manu. 1. 108), or (where the origin of morality is mentioned), "*vedaḥ smṛtiḥ sadācāraḥ svasya ca priyamātmanaḥ*", (Manu. 2. 12), i.e., 'the Vedas, the Smṛtis, good conduct and that which we ourselves desire." But that is not enough for the science of Karma-Yoga, and, as has been stated by me before in the second chapter, it is necessary to fully and critically consider what causes led to a particular *ācāra* or code of conduct being fixed.

We must also here consider another definition of the word '*dharma*' which is come across in ancient treatises. This is the definition given by the Mīmāṁsa school. That school says: "*codanālakṣaṇo 'rtho dharmaḥ*" (Jai. Sū. 1. 1. 2) '*Codanā*' means 'inspiring,' that is, some authoritative person saying or ordering: "Do this" or "Do not do this". So long as no one has laid down such a limitation or such a limitation has not come into existence, one is at liberty to do what he likes. This means that *dharma* originally came into existence as a result of such limitations, and this definition of morality is to a certain extent similar to the opinions of the well-known English writer Hobbes. The human being, in the aboriginal condition behaved according to the particular frame of mind ruling at the time. But when he later on found out that such unrestricted behaviour was not beneficial on the whole, he came to the definite conclusion that it was in the best interests of everybody to lay down and observe certain restrictions on the self-inspired actions of the organs, and every human being began to observe these limitations, which have gained ground on account of general acceptance (*śiṣṭācāra*), or for some other reason, as if they were laws ; and when such limitations grew in number, they formed themselves into a code. I have mentioned in the previous chapter that the institution of marriage was not at first in vogue, but was brought into existence by Śvetaketu, and also that the prohibition against drink was first laid down by Śukrācārya. In defining the word *dharma* as: "*codanālakṣaṇo 'rtho dharmaḥ*" only the fact of such restrictions having been dictated by these law-givers has been taken into account and the motives of Śvetaketu or of Śukrācārya in laying down these limitations has been lost sight of. Even in the case of a rule of morality (*dharma*), some one first realises its importance and then it is promulgated. It is not necessary to ask anyone to eat, drink, and make merry, because, those are the inherent tendencies of the physical organs. That is what is meant by Manu when he says: "*na māṁsabhakṣaṇe doṣo na madye na ca maithune*" (Manu. 5. 56), i. e., "Eating flesh or drinking wine or enjoying sexual intercourse, is not sinful.", that is, there is nothing in them which is contrary to the rules of nature. All these things are the inherent desires, not only of men but of every living being ——"*pravṛttir eṣa bhūtānām*", i. e., "these are the tendencies of created beings". Morality consists in putting proper limitations on an unrestricted course of life resulting from passions in the interest of the maintenance of society or of general welfare. Because :—

āhāranidrā bhayamaithunaṁ ca
sāmānyam etat paśubhir narāṇām ।
dharmo hi teṣām adhiko viśeṣo
dharmeṇa hīnāḥ paśubhiḥ samānāḥ ॥

i. e. "eating, sleeping, fear, and sexual relations are the heritage of men, same as of animals ; *dharma*, (that is, restraining them by rules of morality), is the difference between man and beast ; and those who are not governed by this code of morality may be looked upon as beasts." There is in the Śāntiparva of the Mahābhārata, a similar verse (Śān. 294. 29) and the verse in the Bhāgavata, which prescribes limitations on the desires of hunger etc. has been quoted in the previous chapter. In the same way what the Blessed Lord is referring to, is the nature of morality to lay down limitations on unrestricted mental impulses, where in the Bhagavadgītā, He says to Arjuna :—

indriyasyendriyasy ārthe rāga dveṣau vyavasthitau ।
tayor na vaśam āgacchet tau hy asya paripanthinau ॥

i.e. "the attractions and repulsions between the organs of sense on the one hand and the various objects which are pleasurable or repulsive to them on the other are unchangingly inherent. One should not become their slaves, because, both love and hate are enemies". The organs of a man urge him to behave like a beast, and his intelligence pulls him in the opposite direction. Those persons who redeem themselves by sacrificing the animal tendencies rampant in their bodies into the fire of this warfare are the true sacrificers, and are indeed blessed.

Call *dharma*, '*ācāra-prabhava*' (born of custom), or call it '*dhāraṇāt*' (something which upholds or keeps together), or call it '*codanālakṣaṇa*' (some precept which has been dictated), whichever definition of *dharma* (worldly morality) is accepted, none of them is much useful for coming to a definite conclusion, when one has to decide between what is moral and what immoral. The first definition only tells us what the fundamental form of *dharma* is. The second definition tells us what its external use is, and the third definition tells us that moral restrictions were laid down in the beginning by some persons or other. Not only is there much difference between customs and customs but, as there are numerous consequences of one and the same act, and also as the '*codanā*' i.e., precepts of different *ṛṣis* are also different, we have to look out for some other way of determining what the *dharma* is, when there are doubts in the matter. When Yakṣa asked Yudhiṣṭhira what this other way was, Yudhiṣṭhira replied:-

tarko 'pratiṣṭhaḥ śrutayo vibhinnāḥ
naiko ṛṣir yasya vacaḥ pramāṇam ।
dharmasya tattvaṁ nihitaṁ guhāyāṁ
mahājano yena gataḥ sa panthāḥ ॥

(Ma. Bhā. Vana. 312. 115).

that is: "inferential logic is uncertain, i. e., it is such that it will give birth to various inferences according to different degrees of keenness of intelligence in men; the Śrutis, that is, the precepts of the Vedas, are all mutually conflicting; and, as regards the Smṛtis, there is not a single ṛṣi (sage) whose precept we can look upon as more authoritative than that of others. Well, if we seek the fundamental principle of this (worldly) *dharma*, it is lost in darkness, that is to say, it is such as cannot be understood by a man of ordinary intelligence. Therefore, the path which has been followed by venerable persons is the path of *dharma*". Very well! but who are the venerable persons (*mahājanaḥ*)? That word '*mahājanaḥ*' cannot be interpreted to mean 'a large (*mahā*) collection of persons (*janaḥ*)'. Because, following the path which has been laid down by ordinary persons (or collection of persons), whose minds are never troubled by considerations of what is right and what is wrong, will be like playing a blind man's buff or like "*andhenaiva nīyamānā yathāndhāḥ*", i. e., "the blind being led by the blind", as stated in the Kaṭhopaniṣad. If you interprete the word '*mahājanaḥ*' as meaning 'erudite and venerable persons'—and that is the meaning conveyed in the above verse—then, where is there any uniformity in their behaviour? The sinless Rāmacandra discarded his wife, though she had passed through the ordeal of fire, merely on the ground of public criticism; and the same Rāmacandra, in order that Sugrīva should be on his side, entered into an offensive and defensive alliance with him, by making him '*tulyārimitra*', i. e., 'with common friends and enemies', and killed Vāli who had in no way wronged him! Paraśurāma murdered his own mother at the behest of his father!, and as regards the Pāṇḍavas, five of them had only one wife! If you consider the gods in the heavens, then some of them are the paramours of Ahilyā, whereas others are seen lying in the sky with mutilated bodies, being wounded by the arrows of Rudra, as was Brahmadeva because he ran after his own daughter in the form of a stag (Ai. Brā. 3. 33). With these things before his mind's eye, Bhavabhūti has put the words: "*vṛddhās te na vicāraṇīyacaritāḥ*", i. e., "one must not attach too much importance to the doings of these old people" in the mouth of Lava in the *Uttararāmacaritra*. A writer, who has written in English the history of the Devil, has said in his book that if one considers the history of the warfare between the supporters of the gods and of the Devil, we see that very often the gods (*devas*) have cheated the non-gods (*daityas*); and in the same way, in the Kauṣītakī-Brāhmaṇopaniṣad (See, Kauṣī. 3. 1 as also Ai. Brā. 7. 28), Indra says to Pratardana: "I have killed Vṛtra (although he was a Brahmin); I have torn into pieces the ascetic Arunmukha, and thrown the carrion to wolves; and, breaking all the various treaties which had been made by me, I have killed the friends and clansmen of Prahlāda and also killed the demons named Pauloma and Kālakhañja; yet on that account, "*tasya me tatra na loma ca mamīyate*", i. e., "not a hair of my head has been touched". If some one says: "You have no occasion to consider the evil doings of these venerable persons, but, as stated in the Taittiriyopaniṣad (Taitti. 1. 11. 2), imitate only their good actions, and neglect the rest; for instance, obey your father, as was done by Paraśurāma, but do not kill your mother", then, the primary question of how good actions are to be differentiated from bad actions again arises. Therefore, after having described his various deeds as mentioned above, Indra says to Pratardana: "Bearing in mind that that man who has fully Realised his Self is not prejudicially affected by patricide, matricide, infanticide, theft, or any other sinful actions, try and realise in the first instance what the Ātman is, so that all your doubts will be answered"; and he has thereafter explained to Pratardana the science of the Ātman. In short, although the precept "*mahājano yena gataḥ sa panthāḥ*" may be easy to follow for ordinary persons, yet it does not meet all possible contingencies; and thoughtful persons have ultimately to enter into the Philosophy of the Ātman *(ātma-jñāna)* and ascertain the true principle underlying the actions of the venerable persons *(mahājanah)*, however deep that principle may be. It is for this reason that the advice: "*na devacaritaṁ caret*", i. e., "one must not follow only the external actions of gods", is given. Some persons have hit upon an easier way for determining the doable and the not-doable. They say that whatever virtue is taken, we must always take care against excess of it, for such excess turns a virtue into a vice. Charity is a virtue; but, "*atidānād balir baddhaḥ*", i. e., "because of too much charity, Bali was undone". The well-known Greek philosopher Aristotle has in his book on Ethics prescribed the same test for distinguishing between the doable and the not-doable; and he has clearly shown how every virtue, in excess, is the cause of one's undoing. Even Kālidāsa has come to the conclusion (see Raghuvaṁśa 17. 47) that courage, pure and simple, is like the cruel behaviour of an animal like a tiger; and morality, pure and simple, is nothing else but cowardice; and that the king Atithi, used to rule by a judicious admixture of the sword and regal jurisprudence. If a man speaks too much, he is talkative, if he speaks too little, he is reserved; if he spends too much, he is a spendthrift, if he spends too little, he is a miser; if he is too advanced, he is wayward, and if he lags behind, he is a laggard; if he insists on anything too much, he is obstinate, and if he insists too little, he is fickle; if he is too accommodating, he makes himself cheap, and if he remains stiff, then he is proud: this is how Bhartṛhari and others have described some good and bad qualities. However, such a rule of the thumb does not overcome all difficulties, because, who is to decide what is 'too much', and what is 'moderate'? What may be 'too much' for one or on any particular occasion, may be too little for another person or on another occasion. Jumping into the firmament at the moment of his birth in order to catch hold of the Sun was as nothing to Māruti (Vā. Rāmā. 7. 35). Therefore, as the *śyena* bird advised the King Śibi, every man, when faced with the discernment between the duty *(dharma)* and the non-duty *(adharma)* should on every occasion consider the relative merits and the importance or unimportance of mutually conflicting duties, and intelligently arrive at a conclusion as to the true duty or proper Action :—

avirodhāt tu yo dharmaḥ sa dharmaḥ satyavikrama ।
virodhiṣu mahīpāla niścitya gurulāghavam ।
na bādhā vidyate yatra taṁ dharmaṁ samupācaret ॥

(Ma. Bhā. Vana. 131. 11. 12 and Manu. 9. 299).

i. e., "Oh, Satyavikrama ! that is *dharma* (duty) in which there is no contradiction ; Oh, King !, if there is such a contradiction, then come to a decision as to the relative worth of the act and the opposition, and follow that path of duty in which there is no opposition;". But one cannot, on that account only, say that the true test of determining the proper conduct on a doubtful occasion is to discriminate between the duty and the non-duty. Because, as we often see in ordinary life, different learned people discriminate in different ways according to their own lights, and arrive at several different decisions as regards the morality of a particular act ; and this is what is meant by the words, "*tarko 'pratiṣṭhaḥ*" in the quotation above. We must, therefore, now see whether or not there are any other means for arriving at a correct solution of these doubtful points about the duty and the non-duty ; and if so, what those means are ; and if there are more than one ways, then, which is the best way of all. This is what science has to determine for us. The true characteristic feature of a science is : "*anekasaṁśayocchedi parokṣārthasya darśakam*", i. e., "it must remove confusion regarding matters which the mind cannot at first grasp on account of numerous doubts which spring up, and make their meaning free from doubt and easy, and, even give a proper insight into matters which might not be actually before the eyes or which may be matters of the future"; and the fact that by learning astronomy, one can predict the occurrence and the time of future eclipses justifies the words "*parokṣārthasya darśakam*" used in the latter part of the above definition. But in order that all these various difficulties should be solved, one has first to see what these difficulties are. And, therefore, ancient as also modern writers, before dealing with the subject-matter to be proved by a science first enumerate all the other existing aspects of the same subject-matter, and show the faults or insufficiency in them. Following this method, I shall, before mentioning the YOGA or device established or preached in the Gītā for determining the doability or non-doability of any particular Action, first consider the more well-known of the other devices which are prescribed by philosophers for the same purpose. It is true that these other devices were not very much in vogue in India but were promulgated principally by Western philosophers. But it cannot, on that account, be said that I should not consider them in this book; because, it is necessary to be acquainted with these other devices, if even to a small extent, not only for the purpose of comparison, but also in order to understand the true importance of the Metaphysical (*ādhyātmika)* Karma-Yoga expounded in the Gītā.

CHAPTER IV.

THE MATERIALISTIC THEORY OF HAPPINESS

(ĀDHIBHAUTIKA SUKHAVĀDA)

duḥkhād uddvijate sarvaḥ sarvasya sukham īpsitam । *

Mahābhārata. Śānti. 139. 61.

As we have seen that stock precepts like : '*mahājano yena gataḥ sa panthāḥ*', i. e. 'follow the path which has been followed by venerable persons', or, '*ati sarvatra varjayet*', i. e., 'do too much of nothing', do not satisfactorily explain : (i) why Manu and the other legislators laid down the rules of '*ahiṁsā satyamasteya*' (Non-Violence, Veracity, Not-stealing) etc., (ii) whether those rules are mutable or immutable, (iii) what their extent or the fundamental principle underlying them is, and (iv) which precept should be followed when two or more of them are equally in point and yet conflict with each other, it is now necessary for us to see whether or not there are any definite means for properly determining these questions, and deciding which is the most beneficial or meritorious path of duty, as also, in what way and from what point of view we can determine the relative importance or the greater or less worth of mutually conflicting principles of morality. I have in the last chapter explained that there are three ways of considering the questions involved in the exposition of Action and Non-Action, namely, the Positive, (*ādhibhautika*), the Theological (*ādhidaivika*), and the Metaphysical (*ādhyātmika*), just as in the case of the scientific exposition of other matters. According to our philosophers the most excellent of these ways is the Metaphysical way. But, as it is necessary to carefully consider the other two methods in order to fully understand the importance of the Metaphysical method, I have in this chapter first considered the fundamental Materialistic principles underlying the examination of the question of Action and Non-Action. The positive physical sciences, which have had an immense growth in modern times have to deal principally with the external or visible properties of tangile objects.

* that is .—"Every one is unwilling to suffer pain and every-one wants happiness".

Therefore, those persons who have spent their lives in studying the physical sciences, or who attach much importance to the critical methods particular to these sciences, get into the habit of always considering only the external effects of things ; and their philosophical vision being thereby to a certain extent narrowed, they do not, in discussing any particular thing, attach much importance to causes which are Metaphysical, or intangible, or invisible, or which have reference to the next world. But, although on that account, they leave out of consideration the Metaphysical or the next-world point of view, yet, as codes of morality are necessary for the satisfactory regulation of the mutual relations of human beings and for public welfare, even these philosophers, who are indifferent about life after death or who have no faith in intangible or Metaphysical knowledge, (and also necesssarily no faith in God), look upon the science of Proper Action (Karma-Yoga) as a most important science ; and, therefore, there has been in the past and there is still going on, a considerable amount of discussion in the West, as to whether the science of Proper and Improper Action can be satisfactorily dealt with in the same way as the physical sciences, that is to say, by means of arguments based on purely worldly and visible effects. As a result of this discussion, modern Western philosophers have made up their minds that the science of Metaphysics is of no use whatsoever for the consideration of Ethics, that the goodness or badness of any particular Action must be determined by considering only those of its external effects which are actually visible to us, and that we can do so. Any act which a man performs, is performed by him either for obtaining happiness, or for warding off unhappiness. One may even say that 'the happiness of all human beings' is the highest worldly goal, and if the ultimate visible resultant of all Action is thus definite, the correct method of deciding Ethical problems, is to determine the moral value of all Actions by weighing the greater or lesser possibilities of each Action producing happiness or preventing unhappiness. If one judges the goodness or badness of any particular object in ordinary life by considering its external usefulness, e. g., if we decide that that cow which has short horns and which is docile, and at the same time gives a large quantity of milk is the best cow, then on the same principle, we must also consider that Action as the most meritorious one, from the ethical point of view, of which the external result of producing happiness or preventing unhappiness is the highest. If it is possible to decide the ethical value of any particular act in such an easy and scientific way, namely, by considering the greater or less value of its purely external and visible effects, one should not trouble about entering into the discussion of the Self and Non-Self (*ātmānātma*); "*arke cen madhu vindeta kimarthaṁ parvataṁ vrajet*",* i. e., "if one can get honey near at hand where he sits, then where is the sense of going into the hills to look for honey-combs?" I call this method of determining the morality of any particular Action by considering merely its external results the '*ādhibhautika sukhavāda*' (the Materialistic Theory of Happiness), because, the happiness to be considered for determining the morality of any Action is, according to this theory, actually visible and is external—that is, is such as arises from the contact of the organs with external objects, and consequently Materialistic (*ādhibhautika*)—and this school has likewise been brought into existence by those philosophers who consider the world from the purely positive or Materialistic point of view. But, it is not possible to fully discuss this theory in this book. It would be necessary to write an independent book to even merely summarise the opinions of the different writers. I have, therefore, in this chapter collected together and given as precisely as possible as much general information about this Materialistic school of Ethics as is absolutely necessary for fully understanding the nature and importance of the science of Proper Action expounded in the Bhagavadgītā. If any one wants to go deeper into the matter, he must study the original works of the Western philo-

* The word '*arka*' in this stanza has been interpreted by some as meaning the '*rui*' tree (swallow-wart or calotropis gigantea). But, in his commentary on the Śāṁkarabhāṣya on the Brahma-Sūtras 3. 4. 3, Ānandagiri has defined the word '*arka*' as meaning 'near.' The other part of this verse is "*siddhasy ārthasya saṁprāptau ko vidvān yatnam-ācaret*", i.e., if the desired object is already achieved, what wise man will make further efforts?

sophers. From my statement above, that Materialistic philosophers are apathetic about the science of the Ātman or about the next world, one must not draw the conclusion that all the learned persons who subscribe to this path, are selfish, self-centred or immoral. There belong to this school high-minded philosophers like Comte, Spencer, Mill, and others, who most earnestly and enthusiastically preached that striving for the benefit of the whole world by making at least one's worldly outlook as comprehensive as possible (if one does not believe in the next world), is the highest duty of every man; and as their works are replete with the most noble and deep thoughts, they ought to be read by every one. Although the paths of the science of Proper Action are many, yet, so long as one has not given the go-bye to the external ideal of 'the benefit of the world', one must not ridicule a philosopher on the ground that his method of dealing with the philosophy of Ethics is different from one's own. I shall now precisely and in their proper order, consider the various divisions into which the modern or ancient Materialistic philosophers fall, as a result of differences of opinion between them as to whether the external material happiness which has to be considered for determining the ethical propriety or impropriety of an action is one's own happiness or the happiness of another, and whether of one person or of several persons; and I shall also consider to what extent these opinions are proper or faultless.

The first of these classes is of those who maintain the theory of pure selfish happiness. This school of thought says that there is no such thing as life after death or as philanthropy; that all Metaphysical sciences have been written by dishonest people to serve their own ends; that the only thing which is real in this world is one's own interest; and that, that act by which this self-interest can be achieved or whereby one can promote one's own material happiness is the most just, the most proper, and the most meritorious act. This opinion was, at a very early date, vociforously proclaimed in India by Cārvāka. and the mischievous advice given by Jābāli to Śrī Rāma at the end of the Ayodhyākāṇḍa of the Rāmāyaṇa, as also the Kaṇikanīti in the Mahābhārata (Ma.

Bhā. Ā. 142), pertains to this school of thought. The opinion of the illustrious Cārvāka was that when the five primordial elements are fused together, they acquire the quality of an Ātman, and when the body is burnt, the Ātman is burnt with it; therefore, a wise man should not bother about the Ātman, but should enjoy himself so long as life lasts, even borrowing money for the purpose, if necessary; one should "*ṛṇaṁ kṛtvā ghṛtaṁ pibet*", i. e., "borrow money and drink clarified butter", because there is nothing after death. As Cārvāka was born in India, he satisfied himself with prescribing the drinking of clarified butter (*ghṛtaṁ pibet*) otherwise, this canon would have been transformed into '*ṛṇaṁ kṛtvā surāṁ pibet*', i. e., 'borrow money and drink wine'. This school says: "What is this *dharma* and this charity? All the objects which have been created in this world by the Parameśvara,—what did I say? I have made a mistake! Of course, there is no Parameśvara—all the things which I see in this world have come into existence only for my enjoyment, and as I can see no other purpose for them, there is, of course, no such purpose. When I am dead, the world is over; and therefore, so long as I am alive, I shall acquire all the various things which can be acquired, acquiring this to-day and that to-morrow, and thereby I shall satisfy all my desires. If at all I go in for any religious austerity or charity, that will be only to increase my reputation and worth; and if I make a *rājasūya yajña* or an *aśvamedha yajña*, that too will be for the sole purpose of establishing that my power is unchallenged in all directions. In short, the EGO, the 'I' is the only focus of this world, and this 'I' is the sum and substance of all morality; all the rest is false". The description of godless endowment (*āsurī saṁpatti*) given in the 16th chapter of the Gītā in the words: "*īśvaro 'ham ahaṁ bhogī siddho'haṁ balavān sukhī*" (Gī. 16. 14), i. e., "I am the Īśvara, I am the one who enjoys, and I am the *siddha* (perfect), the all-powerful, and the happy", applies quite appropriately to the opinions of persons who follow this philosophy. If instead of Śrī Kṛṣṇa, there had been some person like Jābāli belonging to this sect for advising Arjuna, he would, in the first place, have slapped Arjuna on the face, and then said to him: "What a fool are you! When you have without effort got this golden opportunity of fighting and conquering everybody and enjoying all kinds of royal enjoyment and happiness, you are uttering the most foolish things, being lost in the futile confusion of 'shall I do this, or shall I do that'! You will not get such a chance again. What a fool are you to think of the Ātman and of relatives! Strike! and enjoy the empire of Hastināpura after having removed all the thorns from your path! In this lies your truest happiness. Is there anything in this world except one's visible material happiness?" But, Arjuna was not anxious to hear such a disgustingly selfish, purely self-centred, and ungodlike advice; and he had, already in advance, said to Śrī Kṛṣṇa :

etān na hantum icchāmi ghnato 'pi Madhusūdana ।
api trailokyarājyasya hetoḥ kiṁ nu mahīkṛte ॥

(Gī. 1. 36).

that is, "If I had to acquire for myself (by this war), the kingdom even of the three worlds—to say nothing of the kingdom of this world—(that is, such physical pleasures), I do not desire for that purpose to kill the Kauravas. I do not mind if they slit open my throat". Even a mere reference to this ungodlike self-centred and entirely selfish doctrine of material happiness, which Arjuna had, in this way, denounced in advance, would amount to a refutation of it. This extremely low stage reached by the school of Material Happiness, which looks upon one's own physical pleasures as the highest ideal of man, and throws religion and morality to the winds, and totally disregards what happens to other people, has been treated by all writers on the science of Proper Action, and even by ordinary people, as extremely immoral, objectionable and disdainable. Nay!, this theory does not even deserve the name of Ethics or of an exposition of morality; and therefore, instead of wasting more time in considering this subject, we will now turn to the next class of Materialistic philosophers.

Pure and naked selfishness or self-centredness never succeeds in the world; because, although physical and material pleasures may be desirable to every one, yet, as is a matter of actual experience, if our happiness interferes with the happiness of others, those others will certainly do us harm. Therefore other Materialistic philosophers maintain that although one's happiness or selfish purposes may be one's goal, yet, in as much as it is not possible for one to acquire such happiness, unless one makes some sacrifices for other people similar to those one oneself wants from them, one must long-sightedly take into account the happiness of others in order to obtain one's own happiness. I put these Materialistic philosophers in the second class. It may be said that the Materialistic exposition of Ethics truly begins at this point. Because, instead of saying like Cārvāka, that no ethical limitations are necessary for the maintenance of society, persons belonging to this school have made an attempt to explain their own view as to why these limitations must be observed by everybody. These people say that, if one minutely considers how the theory of Harmlessness came into this world, and why people follow that doctrine, there is no other reason at the root of it except the fear based on selfish considerations that, 'if I kill others, others will kill me, and then I will lose my happiness', and that all other moral precepts have come into existence as a result of this selfish fear in the same way as this law of Harmlessness. If we suffer pain, we cry, and if others suffer pain, we feel pity for them. But why? Because the fear that we in our turn may have to suffer the same pain, that is, of course, the thought of our possible future unhappiness comes to our minds. Charity, generosity, pity, love, gratefulness, humbleness, friendship, and other qualities which at first sight appear to be for the benefit of others are, if we trace them to their origin, nothing but means of acquiring our own happiness or warding off our own unhappiness in another form. Everybody-soever helps others or gives in charity with the internal motive that if he found himself in the same position, other people should help him; and we love others, only in order that others should love us. At any rate, the selfish idea that other people should call us good is at the back of our minds. The expressions 'doing good to others' and 'the welfare of others' are words based on confusion of thought. What is real, is one's own selfish purpose; and one's own selfish purpose means obtaining one's own happiness or warding off one's own unhappiness. This amounts to saying that a mother suckles her baby not on account of love, but she does this selfish act in order to ease herself (as her breasts are full of milk and she feels the inconvenience of the pressure), or in order that the child, after growing up, should love her and give her happiness. The fact that people of this school of thought admit that it is necessary to long-sightedly observe such moral principles as will permit of the happiness of others—though that may be for obtaining one's own happiness—is the important difference between this school of thought and the school of Cārvāka. Nevertheless, the idea that a human being is nothing but a statue cast into the mould of selfish physical desires, which is the opinion of the Cārvāka school, has been left untouched by this school. This opinion has been supported in England by Hobbes and in France by Helvetius. But there are not to be found many followers of this school in England or anywhere else. After the exposition of Ethics by Hobbes had been published, it was refuted by philosophers like Butler, * who proved that human nature as a whole is not absolutely selfish, and that there exist in a human being from birth such other qualities as humanity, love, gratitude etc., to a greater or less extent, side by side with selfishness; and therefore, in considering any act or any dealing from the ethical point of view, one should instead of considering only the qualities of selfishness or even of long-sighted selfishness, always consider the two inherent distinct tendencies of human beings, namely, 'selfishness', (*svārtha*) and the 'unselfishness', (*parārtha*). If even a cruel animal like a tigress is prepared to sacrifice her life for the sake of her cubs, it follows that saying that the emotions of love and philanthrophy come into existence in the human mind merely out of selfishness is futile, and that weighing between the duty and the non-duty merely from the point of view of long-sighted selfishness is

---

* The opinion of Hobbes has been given in the book called *Leviathan*; and the opinions of Butler are to be found in his Essay called *Sermons on Human Nature*. Morley has given the summary of the book of Helvetius in his (Morley's) book on *Diderot*, (Volume II, Chap. V).

scientifically incorrect. Our ancient writers had not lost sight of the fact that persons, whose intelligence has remained unpurified on account of their having remained wholly engrossed in family life, very often do whatever they do in this world for others, only with an eye to their own benefit. The saint Tukārām has said: "the daughter-in-law weeps for the mother-in-law, but the motive in her heart is quite different" (Gā. 2583. ·2); and some of our philosophers have gone even beyond Helvetius. For instance, in commenting on the proposition laid down by Śrī Śaṁkarācārya in his Brahma-Sūtrabhāṣya (Ve. Sū.Śāṁ. Bhā. 2. 2. 3) on the authority of the Gautama-Nyāyasūtra (1. 1, 18) '*pravartanā lakṣaṇā dosāḥ*', i. e., 'all human activity, whether selfish or unselfish, is faulty', Ānandgiri says that: " We practise kindness or benevolence towards others only in order to remove that pain which results from the emotion of pity awakening in our hearts." This argument of Ānandgiri is to be found in almost all our books on the Path of Renunciation, and all that is principally attempted to be proved from it is, that all Actions are selfish, and, therefore, non-performable. But in the conversation between Yājñavalkya and his wife Maitreyi, which appears twice in the Bṛhadāraṇyakopaniṣad (Bṛ. 2. 4; 4. 5), this very argument has been made use of in another and a strange way. In answering the question of Maitreyi: "How can one acquire immortality ? ", Yājñavalkya says to her: "O Maitreyi, the husband is loved by the wife, not for the sake of the husband, but for the sake of her own *ātman;* in the same way, the son is not loved by us for his own sake; we love him for our own sake.* The same law applies to wealth, animals, and all other objects. '*ātmanastu kāmāya sarvaṁ priyaṁ bhavati*', i, e., 'We like all things for the sake of our Self (*ātman*)'. and if all love is in

* "What say you of natural affection ? Is that also a species of self-love? Yes; all is self-love. *Your* children are loved only because they are yours. *Your* friend, for a like reason. And *your* country engages you only so far as it has a connection with *yourself*": this is the way in which Hume has referred to this line of argument in his book *Of the Dignity or Meanness of Human Nature.* Hume's own opinion in the matter is different.

this way based on Self, must we not, in the first place, find out what our *ātman* (Self) is?" And, therefore, the concluding advice of Yājñavalkya is: "*ātmā vā are draṣṭavyaḥ śrotavyo mantavyo nididhyāsitavyaḥ*", i. e., "See (first) what the *ātman* (Self) is, hear the *ātman*, and meditate and contemplate on the *ātman*". When the true form of the Ātman has in this way been realised by following this advice, the whole world becomes Self-ised (*ātma-maya*), and the distinction between selfishness (*svārtha*) and unselfishness (*parārtha*) in the mind ceases to exist. Although this argument of Yājñavalkya is apparently the same as that of Hobbes, yet, as can be easily seen, the inferences drawn by them respectively from that advice are contrary to each other. Hobbes attaches higher importance to selfishness, and, looking upon all philanthrophy as long-sighted selfishness, says that there is nothing in this world except selfishness; whereas Yājñavalkya, relying on the word '*sva*' (one's own) in the phrase '*svārtha*' (selfishness), shows, on the authority of that word, that from the Metaphysical point of view, all created beings are harmoniously comprised in our Ātman and our Ātman is likewise harmoniously comprised in all created beings; and he, in that way, gets rid of the apparently dualistic (*dvaita*) conflict between the interest of oneself and the interest of others. These opinions of Yājñavalkya and of the school of Renunciation will be considered in greater detail later on. I have referred here to the opinions of Yājñavalkya and others only for the purpose of showing how our ancient writers have more or less praised or accepted as correct the principle that 'the ordinary tendency of human beings is selfish, that is, is concerned with their own happiness', and drawn from it inferences which are quite contrary to those drawn by Hobbes.

Having thus proved that human nature is not purely selfish and is not governed wholly by the *tamas* quality, nor totally ungodly (as has been maintained by the English writer Hobbes and the French writer Helvetius), and that a benevolent (*sāttvika*) mental impulse forms part of human nature from birth along with the selfish impulse, and that doing good to others is not long-sighted selfishness, one has to give equal importance to the two principles of *svārtha*, i. e., one's own happiness and *parārtha*, i. e., the happiness of others, in building up the science of the doable and the not-doable (*kāryākārya-vyavasthiti*). This is the third division of Materialistic philosophers. Nevertheless, the Materialistic view that both *svārtha* and *parārtha* deal only with worldly happiness, and that there is nothing beyond worldly happiness, is also held by this school. The only difference is that people who belong to this school consider it their duty to take into account both self-interest (*svārtha*) and other's-interest (*parārtha*) in determining questions of morality, because they look upon the impulse of doing good to others as, as much an inherent impulse, as the selfish impulse. As normally there is no conflict between self-interest and other's-interest, all the Actions which a man performs are primarily also beneficial to society. If one man accumulates wealth, that ultimately benefits the whole society; because, society being a collection of numerous individuals, if each individual in it benefits himself without harming others, that is bound to benefit the whole society. Therefore, this school of philosophers has laid down that if one can do good to others without neglecting one's own happiness, it is one's duty to do so. But, as this school does not admit the superiority of other's-interest and advises that one should each time, according to one's own lights, consider whether one's own interests or the interests of others are superior, it is difficult to decide to what extent one should sacrifice one's own happiness for the happiness of others when there is a conflict between self-interest and other's-interest, and there is very often a chance of a man falling a prey to considerations of his own interests. For instance, if self-interest is considered to be as important as other's-interest, it is difficult to decide by reference to the doctrines of this school of thought, whether or not one should, for the sake of truth, suffer considerable financial loss—to say nothing of the much more serious question whether or not one should, for the sake of truth, sacrifice one's life or lose one's kingdom. Persons belonging to this school may possibly praise a benevolent man who sacrifices his life for the advantage of another, but if they are themselves faced with a similar situation, these philosophers, who habitually sit on the two stools of self-interest and other's-interest, will certainly be dragged towards self-interest. This school believes that they do not look upon other's-interest as a long-sighted variety of selfishness (as was done by Hobbes), but that they minutely weigh self-interest and other's-interest in a scale, and very skilfully decide in what self-interest lies; and, on that account, they glorify their doctrine by calling it the path of 'enlightened' (*udātta*) or 'wise' self-interest (but self-interest in any case!) * But see what Bhartṛhari says :—

eke satpuruṣāḥ parārthaghaṭakāḥ svārthān parityajya ye ।
sāmānyāstu parārtham udyamabhṛtaḥ svārthā 'virodhena ye ।
te'mī mānavarākṣasāḥ parahitaṁ svārthāya nighnanti ye ।
ye tu ghnanti nirarthakaṁ parahitaṁ te ke na jānīmahe ॥

(Nī. Śa. 74)

that is, "those who do good to others, sacrificing their own interests are the truly good persons; those who strive for the good of others, without sacrificing self-interest, are ordinary persons; those who harm others, for their self-interest, must be looked upon not as human beings but as godless beings (*rākṣasāḥ*); but I do not know how to describe those who are worse than these, that is, those who needlessly harm the interests of others". In the same way in describing the most excellent form of regal morality, Kālidāsa says :—

svasukhanirabhilāṣaḥ khidyase lokahetoḥ ।
pratidinam athavā te vṛttir evaṁ vidhaiva ॥

(Śākuntala 5. 7).

that is, "you strive every day for the welfare of others without considering your own happiness, or it may be said that such is your natural instinct or vocation". Neither Bhartṛhari nor Kālidāsa had to see how to discriminate between Right Action or Wrong Action *(karmākarma)* or righteousness and unrighteousness *(dharmādharma)* by adopting both the principles of self-interest and other's-interest into a science of Right Action (Karma-Yoga), and judiciously weighing them. Nevertheless,

* This is called in English 'enlightened self-interest'. I have translated the word 'enlightened' into Marathi as '*udātta*' or '*śahāṇā*'.

the highest place which has been given by them to persons who sacrifice self-interest for other's-interest is justifiable even from the point of view of Ethics. Persons belonging to this school of thought say, that although other's-interest may be superior to self-interest from the philosophical point of view, yet, in as much as we have not to consider what ideally pure morality is, but only how 'ordinary' persons should act in the ordinary affairs of the world, the prominence given by us to 'enlightened self-interest' is proper from the worldly point of view. * But in my opinion, there is no sense in this argument. The weights and measures used in commerce are as a rule more or less inaccurate; but if, taking advantage of that fact, the greatest possible accuracy is not maintained in the standard weights and measures kept in public offices, shall we not blame the persons in authority? The same rule applies to the philosophy of Karma-Yoga. Ethics has been formulated only in order to scientifically define the pure, complete, and constant form of morality; and, if any science of Ethics does not do this, it must be said to be useless. Sidgwick is not wrong in saying that 'enlightened self-interest' is the path of ordinary people. Bhartṛhari says the same thing. But if one examines what the opinion of these ordinary people about the highest morality is, it will be seen that, even in their opinion, the importance given by Sidgwick to enlightened self-interest is wrong, and the path of spotless morality or the path followed by saints, is looked upon by them as something much better than the ordinary selfish path; and, that is what is intended to be conveyed by the stanzas of Bhartṛhari quoted above.

I have so far dealt with the three divisions of the School of Material happiness, namely, the purely selfish, the long-sighted selfish, and the enlightened selfish (which is both the former ones combined), and I have pointed out what the

* Sidgwick's *Methods of Ethics* Book I, Chap. II, § 2, pp. 18–29; also Book IV Chap. IV, § 3 p. 474. Sidgwick has not invented this third path; but ordinary well-educated English people usually follow this path of morality which is also known as 'Common sense morality'.

principal short-comings of their respective systems are. But this does not exhaust all the divisions of the Material happiness school. The next division, that is to say, the best division of this school is the one of the benevolent *(sāttvika)* Materialistic philosophers, who maintain that: one should decide the ethical doability or non-doability of all Actions by judiciously weighing the Material happiness of not only one human being, but of the entire human race.* It is not possible that one and the same act will cause happiness to all persons in the world or in a society at one and the same time. If one person looks upon a particular thing as productive of happiness, it produces unhappiness to another person. But, just as light is not considered objectionable on the ground that the owl does not like it, so also if a particular thing is not profitable to some persons, it cannot be said, even according to the Karma-Yoga science, that it is not beneficial to all; and on that account, the words 'the happiness of all persons' *(sarvabhūtahita)* have to be understood as meaning the 'greatest happiness (good) of the greatest number'. In short, the opinion of this school is that, "we must consider only such acts as ethically just and fit to be performed, as are conducive to the greatest good of the greatest number; and that, acting in that way is the true duty of every human being in this world." This doctrine of the school of Material happiness is acceptable to the Metaphysical school. Nay, I may even say that this principle was propounded by the Metaphysicians in very ancient times, and the Materialistic philosophers have now turned it to use in a particular way. It is a well-known fact, as has been said by the Saint Tukārām that, "saintly persons come to life only for the benefit of the world; they suffer in body in order to do good to others". Needless to say, there is no dispute about the correctness or the propriety of this principle. Even in the Bhagavadgītā, in describing the characteristic features of saints (*jñānin*) who practise the perfect Yoga—of course, the Karma-Yoga—the words "*sarvabhūtahite ratah*" i. e., "they are engrossed in doing good to all created beings"

* Bentham, Mill etc. are the protagonists of this School. I have translated the words 'greatest good of the greatest number' as the 'greatest happiness of the greatest number', in this book.

have been clearly used twice (Gī. 5. 25; 12. 4); and it becomes quite clear from the statement from the Mahābhārata quoted in the second chapter above: "*yad bhūtahitam atyantaṁ tat satyam iti dhāraṇā*". (Vana 208. 4), i. e., "that is Truth according to *dharma* in which the highest benefit of all lies," that our ancient writers used to take into account this principle in deciding what is just (*dharma*) and what unjust (*adharma*). But, looking upon the promotion of the welfare of all created beings as the external characteristic feature of the conduct of *jñānins*, and occasionally making use of that principle in a broad way for determining what is just and what unjust, is something absolutely different from taking for granted that that is the substance of Ethics, and disregarding everything else, and erecting an immense structure of the science of Ethics on that foundation alone. Materialistic philosophers accept the latter course and maintain that Ethics has nothing to do with Metaphysics. It is, therefore, necessary for us to see now to what extent they are correct. There is a great deal of difference between the meanings of the two words 'happiness' (*sukha*) and 'benefit' (*hita*); but, although for the moment that difference is not taken into consideration and the word '*sarvabhūtahita*' is taken as meaning 'the greatest happiness of the greatest number', yet it will be seen, that numerous important difficulties arise, if we rely only on this principle for distinguishing the doable from the not-doable. Suppose, a Materialist follower of this principle was advising Arjuna: what would he have told him? Would he not have said: If as a result of your becoming victorious in the Bhāratīya war, you bring about the greatest happiness of the greatest number, then it is your duty to fight, even if you might kill Bhīṣma. Apparently, this advice seems very easy. But, if we go a little deeper, we realise its insufficiency and the difficulties involved in it. 'Greatest number' means how much? The Pāṇḍava army was of seven *akṣauhiṇīs* (a unit for measuring the numbers of soldiers). But, the Kaurava army was of eleven *akṣauhiṇīs*. Can one, therefore, argue that the Pāṇḍavas were in the wrong, on the ground that if the Pāṇḍavas had been defeated these eleven Kaurava *akṣauhiṇīs* would have become happy? To decide questions of morality merely on the basis of numbers would be wrong on any number of occasions, to say nothing of the Bhāratīya war. Even in ordinary life everyone believes, that that act which pleases even one good man is more truly a good act than the act which gives happiness to a hundred thousand evil-doers. In order to justify this belief, the happiness of one saint has to be given a higher value than the happiness of a hundred thousand evil-doors, and if one does that, the fundamental principle that 'the greatest external happiness of the greatest number is the only test of morality' becomes, to that extent, weak. One has, therefore, to say that numbers have no fixed bearing on morality. It must also be borne in mind that some thing which is ordinarily considered as productive of happiness by all persons is, by a far-sighted person, seen to be disadvantageous to all. Take for example the cases of Socrates and Jesus Christ. Both of them were preaching to their countrymen what, in their respective opinions, was ultimately beneficial. But their countrymen denounced them as 'enemies of society', and put them to death. The people, as also their leaders, were acting on the principle of the 'greatest good of the greatest number'; but, we do not now say that what the ordinary people then did was just. In short, even if we for a moment admit that 'greatest good of the greatest number' is the only fundamental principle of Ethics, yet, we do not thereby solve to any extent the questions, in what lies the happiness of millions of persons, how that has to be ascertained, and by whom. On ordinary occasions, the task of finding this out may be left to those persons whose happiness or unhappiness is under consideration. But, as it is not necessary to go so deep into the matter on ordinary occasions, and, as ordinary persons do not possess the mental grasp to understand and decide faultlessly in what their happiness lies on extraordinary and difficult occasions, putting into the hands of such uneducated persons the solitary ethical principle of 'the greatest good of the greatest number' is like placing a fire-brand into the hands of an evil spirit, as is apparent from the illustrations of the two leaders given above. There is no sense in the repartee: "Our ethical principle is correct; what can we do if ignorant persons have wrongly applied it?" Because, although the principle may be correct, one must at the same time explain who are the proper persons to give effect to it, and when and how these persons do so, and other similar limitations of the principle. Otherwise, ordinary people will needlessly indulge in the fond belief that they are as capable of determining questions of morality as Socrates, and serious consequences are likely to follow.

This theory is open to other objections which are more serious than the two objections: (i) questions of morality cannot be properly decided by reference to numbers alone and (ii) there is no definite external measure for logically proving in what lies the greatest good of the greatest number, which I have mentioned above. For instance, only a little consideration will show that it is very often impossible to fully and satisfactorily decide whether a particular Action is just or unjust by considering merely its external effects. It is true that we decide whether a particular watch is good or bad, by seeing whether or not it shows correct time; but before applying this rule to human actions, one must bear in mind, that man is not merely a watch or a machine. It is true that all saints strive for the benefit of the world. But we cannot draw the definite converse conclusion that every person who strives for the benefit of the world must be a saint. One must also see what that man's frame of mind is. This is the great difference between a man and a machine; and therefore, if some one commits a crime unintentionally or by mistake, it is legally considered a pardonable offence. In short, we cannot arrive at a correct decision as to whether a particular act is good or bad, just or unjust, or moral or immoral by considering merely its external result or effect, that is, by considering whether or not that act will produce the greatest good of the greatest number. One has also necessarily to consider at the same time, the reason, the desire, or the motive of the doer of the act. There was once an occasion to construct a tramway for the benefit and happiness of all the citizens of a big city in America. But there were delays in obtaining the requisite sanction from the proper authorities. Thereupon, the directors of the tramway company gave a bribe to the persons in authority, and the necessary sanction was immediately obtained; and, the construction of the tramway being complete soon afterwards, all the people in the city were in consequence considerably convenienced and benefited. Some time after that, the bribery was found out, and the manager of the tramway was criminally prosecuted. There was no unanimity in the first jury, so a second jury was empanelled and the second jury having found the manager guilty, he was convicted. In such a case, the principle of the greatest good of the greatest number is useless by itself. The external effect of the bribery, namely, that the tramway came to be constructed because the bribe was given, was the greatest good of the greatest number; yet, on that account, the fact that the bribe was given does not become legal.* Though the external effects of the two several acts of giving in charity desirelessly in the belief that it is one's duty to do so (*dātavyaṁ*), and of giving in charity for the sake of reputation or for some other purpose are the same, yet, even the Bhagavadgītā distinguishes between the two by saying, that the first gift is *sāttvika* (benevolent) and that the second gift is *rājasa* (desire-prompted) (Gī. 17. 20-23); and the same gift, if made to an unworthy person is said to be *tāmasa* and objectionable. Even ordinary people consider a poor man's giving a few pies for a charitable purpose as of the same moral value, as the gift of a hundred rupees by a rich man. But, if the matter be considered by an external test like 'the greatest good of the greatest number', we will have to say that these two gifts are not of the same moral value. The great drawback of the Materialistic ethical principle of the 'greatest good of the greatest number' is, that it does not attach any importance to the motive or the reason of the doer, and if one says that the inner motive has to be taken into account, then the fundamental condition of the greatest external good of the greatest number being the only test of morality is not satisfied. As the Legislative Council or Assembly is a collection of many individuals, it is not necessary to ascertain what the state of their conscience was, when we consider whether or not the laws made by them are proper; and it is enough if one considers only the external

* This illustration is taken from the book, *The Ethical Problem* of Dr. Paul Carus, (pp. 58 and 69, 2nd Edition).

aspect of the laws, namely, whether or not the greatest good of the greatest number will result from them. But, as will be clear from the illustrations given above, the same test does not apply to other cases. I do not say that the principle of 'the greatest good or happiness of the greatest number' is utterly useless. One cannot have a more excellent principle for considering external matters; but in considering whether a particular thing is morally just or unjust, it is very often necessary to consider several other things besides this external principle; and therefore, one cannot safely depend on this principle alone for determining questions of morality; and all that I say is, that it is necessary to ascertain and fix upon some principle, more definite and faultless than this. The same moral is conveyed by the statement: "The Reason (*buddhi*) is of greater importance than the Action" (Gī. 2. 49), made in the very beginning of the Gītā. If one considers only the external Action, it is often misleading. It is not impossible for a man to be subject to excessive anger, notwithstanding that he continues to perform his external Actions of religious austerities. But on the other hand, if the heart is pure, the external act becomes immaterial, and the religious or moral value of an insignificant external act like the giving of dried boiled rice by Sudāmā to Śrī Kṛṣṇa is considered by people to be as great as the public distribution of tons of food, which will give great happiness to a great number. Therefore, the well-known German philosopher Kant * has treated the weighing of the external and visible effects of an act as of minor importance and has started his exposition of Ethics with a consideration of the purity of mind of the doer. It is not that this shortcoming of the Materialistic theory of happiness was not noticed by the principal supporters of that theory. Hume has clearly said that in as much as the acts of a person are considered a test of his morality as being the index of his disposition, it is impossible to decide that they are praiseworthy or unworthy merely from their external effects; † and even Mill

* Kant's *Theory of Ethics* (Tran. by Abbott) 6th Ed. p. 6.

† "For as actions are objects of our moral sentiment, so far only as they are indications of the internal character, passions, and affections, it is impossible that they can give rise either to

accepts the position that 'the morality of any act depends entirely upon the motive of the doer, that is to say, upon the reasoning on which he bases that act.' But, in order to support his own point of view, Mill has added a rider to this principle that, 'so long as the external act is the same, its moral value remains the same, whatever may have been the desire which prompted it'. * This argument of Mill is only doctrinal. Because, if the Reason (*buddhi*) is different, then, though two acts may be the same in appearance, yet they can never have the same value essentially. And Green, therefore, objects that the limitation: 'so long as there is no difference in the (external) act' etc. laid down by Mill, itself falls to the ground †. The same is the opinion expressed in the Gītā. Because, the Gītā says that even if two persons have given the same amounts for the same charitable purpose—that is, even when their external act is just the same—it is possible that one gift will be *sāttvika*, and the other one will be *rājasa* or even *tāmasa* if the two persons have different reasons for the gift. But I shall deal in greater detail with this question later on, when I compare the Eastern and the Western opinions in the matter. All that I have to prove at the moment is, that even this refined form of the Materialistic theory of happiness,—which depends only on the external results of an Action—falls short on the mark in determining questions of morality; and Mill's admission quoted above is, in my opinion, the best possible proof of that fact.

---

praise or blame, where they proceed not from these principles but are derived altogether from external objects". Hume's *Inquiry concerning Human Understanding*. Section VIII Part II (p. 368 of Hume's *Essays*. The World Library Edition).

* 'Morality of the action depends entirely upon the intention, that is, upon what the agent *wills to do*. But the motive, that is, the feeling which makes him will so to do, when it makes no difference in the act, makes none in the morality."

Mill's *Utilitarianism* p. 39 (27 ?).

† Green's '*Prolegomena to Ethics*' § 292 Note. p. 348 (5th Cheaper Ed.).

The greatest drawback of the theory of 'the greatest good of the greatest number' is that it does not take into consideration the Reason (*buddhi*) of the doer. Because, the writings of Mill himself show that, even if his arguments are accepted, this principle of determining questions of morality merely by external results, is applicable only within specified limits, that is, is one-sided, and cannot be equally applied to all cases. But, there is a further objection to this theory, namely that, as the entire argument of the theory has been developed on the basis that other's-interest is superior to self-interest, without explaining why or how it is so, the theory of 'enlightened self-interest' gets a chance of pushing itself forward. If both self-interest and other's-interest have come into existence with man, why should one look upon the good of the greatest number as more important than one's own interest? The answer, that other's interest should be protected because it involves the greatest good of the greatest number is not satisfactory; because the question itself is why I should bring about the greatest good of the greatest number. It is true that this question does not always arise, since one's interest, as a general rule, lies in promoting the interests of others. But, the difference between this last and fourth stage of the Materialistic theory of happiness and its third stage is, that the followers of this last school believe that where there is a conflict between self-interest and other's-interest, the duty of everybody is to sacrifice self-interest and to strive for other's-interest, instead of following the path of 'enlightened self-interest.' Is not some explanation due in support of this particular feature of this Materialistic theory of happiness? As one learned Materialistic philosopher belonging to this school realised this difficulty, he has examined the activities of all living beings, from the minutest organisms to the human race, and come to the conclusion that in as much as the quality of maintaining one's own progeny or community just as one maintains oneself, and of helping one's fellows as much as possible without harming any one, is to be seen being gradually more and more developed from the stage of minute organisms to the human race, we must say that that is the principle feature of the mode of life of the living world.

This feature is firstly noticed in the living world in the production of progeny and protecting it. In those minute organisms in which the difference of the sexes has not been developed, the body of one organism is seen to grow until it breaks into two organisms; or, it may even be said, that this minute organism sacrifices its own life for the sake of its progeny, that is to say, for the sake of another. In the same way, animals of both sexes in grades of life higher than that of these organisms, are seen to willingly sacrifice their own interests in the living world for the maintenance of their progeny; and this quality is seen to be always growing; so that, even in the most aboriginal societies, man is seen willingly helping, not only his own progeny, but also his tribe; and therefore, the highest duty in this world of man, who is the crown jewel of the living world, is to attempt to permanently do away with the present apparent conflict between self-interest and other's-interest by further developing this tendency of created beings of finding happiness in other's-interest as if it was self-interest, which is observed to become stronger and stronger in the rising grades of creation.* This argument is correct. There is nothing new in the principle that, as the virtue of philanthrophy is to be seen even in the dumb world in the shape of protection of progeny, it is the highest duty of enlightened man to carry that virtue to its perfection. Only, as the knowledge of the material sciences has now considerably increased, it is now possible to develope more systematically the Materialistic demonstration of this principle. Although the point of view of our philosophers was Metaphysical, yet, it has been stated in our ancient treatises that:

aṣṭādaśa purāṇānāṁ sāraṁ sāraṁ samuddhṛtam ।
paropakāraḥ puṇyāya pāpāya parapīḍanam ॥

that is, "doing good to others is meritorious, and doing harm to others, sinful; this is the sum and substance of the eighteen

* This argument is to be found in the *Data of Ethics* written by Spencer. Spencer has explained the difference between his opinions and the opinions of Mill in his letters to Mill, and this book contains extracts from this correspondence. See pp 57 and 123. Also see Bain's *Mental and Moral Science*, pp. 721 and 722, (Ed. 1875).

Purāṇas"; and, even Bhartṛhari says that: "*svārtho yasya parārtha eva sa pumān ekaḥ satām agraṇīḥ*", i. e., "that man with whom other's-interest has become self-interest is the best of good men". But, when we consider the scale of life gradually rising from the minutest organisms to the human race, another question also arises, namely: is the virtue of philanthrophy the only virtue which has been fully developed in the human race, or have other benevolent (*sāttvika*) virtues, such as justice, kindness, wisdom, far-sightedness, logic, courage, perseverance, forgiveness, control of the organs, etc., also been developed in man? When one thinks of this, one has to say that all virtues have been more fully developed in the human race than in any other living being. We will for the present refer to this aggregate of *sāttvika* qualities as 'humanness'. When in this way 'humanness' is seen to be superior to philanthrophy, one has, in determining the propriety or impropriety or the morality of any particular Action, to examine that Action from the point of view of its 'humanness'—that is, from the point of view of all those various qualities which are seen to be more developed in the human race than in other living beings—rather than from the point of view of its philanthropicalness. We must, therefore, come to the conclusion, that it is better to call that Action alone virtuous, or to say that that alone is morality, which will enhance the state of being human or the 'humanness', of all human beings, or which will be consistent with the dignity of such 'humanness', instead of merely relying on the virtue of philanthrophy, and somehow or other getting rid of the matter. And when one accepts this comprehensive view-point, the consideration of 'the greatest good of the greatest number', becomes only an insignificant part of such view-point, and the doctrine that the righteousness or unrighteousness of all Actions has to be tested only by that test falls to the ground, and we see that we have also to take 'humanness' into account. And when one considers minutely in what 'humanness', or 'the state of being human' consists, the question "*ātmā vā are draṣṭavyaḥ*" naturally crops up, as stated by Yājñavalkya. An American writer, who has written an exposition of Ethics, has given this comprenensive quality of 'humanness' the name of 'Ātmā'.

From what has been stated above, one will see how even the upholders of the theory of Material happiness have to rise from the lowest stage of pure selfishness or pure physical happiness of one's self to the higher stage of philanthrophy, and ultimately to that of humanness. But, as even in the idea of humanness, the upholders of the Material happiness theory attach importance solely to the external physical happiness of all human beings, even this final stage of Materialism, which disregards internal purity and internal happiness, is not flawless in the eyes of our Metaphysicians. Although we may accept in a general way that the whole struggle of mankind is directed towards obtaining happiness or preventing unhappiness, yet, until one has in the first place satisfactorily solved the question as to whether true and permanent happiness is material, that is, lies in the enjoyment of worldly physical pleasure or in something else, one cannot accept as correct any Materialistic theory. Even Materialistic philosophers admit that mental happiness stands on a higher footing than physical happiness. If one promises to a human being all the happiness which it is possible for a beast to enjoy, and asks him whether he is prepared to become a beast, not a single human being will say yes. In the same way, an intelligent person need not be told that that particular peace of mind which results from deep meditation on philosophical problems is a thousand times better than material wealth, or the enjoyment of external pleasures. And even considering the general opinion on the matter, it will be seen that people do not accept as wholly correct the doctrines that morality depends on numbers, that whatever a human being does is for Material happiness, and that Material happiness is the highest ideal of a human being. We believe that the humanness of a human being lies in possessing such an amount of mental control as to be able to sacrifice external happiness and even one's own life in order to act up to such moral principles as Veracity etc., which are of greater importance than life or external happiness from the Metaphysical point of view; and also Arjuna had not asked Śrī Kṛṣṇa how much happiness would result to how many persons by his taking part in the war, but he had said: "Tell me in what lies my highest benefit, that is the highest benefit of my Ātman" (Gī. 2. 7; 3. 2). This constant benefit or happiness of the Ātman lies in the peace (*śānti*) of the Ātman; and it is stated in the Bṛhadāraṇyakopaniṣad (Bṛ. 2. 4. 2) that however much of material happiness or wealth one might obtain, there is no hope of obtaining by that alone the happiness or peace of the Ātman—"*amṛtatvasya tu naśāsti vittena*"; and in the Kaṭhopaniṣad, it is stated that although Death (Mṛtyu) was ready to bestow on Naciketa, sons, grand-sons, animals, grain, money and other kinds of material wealth, he gave to Mṛtyu the definite reply: "I want the knowledge of the Ātman, I do not want wealth"; and after differentiating between '*preya*', i. e., that worldly happiness which is pleasing to the organs, and '*śreya*', i. e. the true benefit of the Ātman, it is stated:—

śreyaś ca preyaś ca manuṣyam etas
tau saṁparītya vivinakti dhīraḥ ।
śreyo hi dhīro 'bhipreyaso vṛṇīte
preyo mando yogakṣemād vṛṇīte ॥

(Kaṭha. 1. 2. 2)

that is, "when man is faced with '*preya*' (transient external pleasure of the organs) and '*śreya*' (true and permanent benefit), he elects between the two. He who is wise prefers *śreya* to *preya*, and the weak-minded man prefers *preya*, that is, external happiness to the benefit of the Ātman". It is, therefore, not correct to believe that the highest goal of man in this world is the physical happiness obtainable through the organs in worldly life, and that whatever a man does is done by him merely for the sake of obtaining external, that is, Material happiness or for preventing unhappiness.

Not only is the internal happiness obtainable through Reason, or Metaphysical happiness of greater worth than the external happiness obtained through the medium of the organs, but the physical pleasure which exists to-day comes to an end to-morrow, i. e., is transient. The same is not the case with rules of Ethics. Non-violence, Veracity and other moral principles are looked upon by people as independent of external circumstances, that is, of external happiness or unhappiness and as being constant in their application at all times and in all circumstances, that is to say, they are looked upon as permanent by everybody. Materialism cannot satisfactorily explain the reason why moral principles have this permanence which does not depend on external matters, nor how it comes into existence. For, whatever general doctrine is laid down by reference to happiness or unhappiness in the external world, yet, in as much as all happiness or unhappiness is inherently transient, all doctrines of morality founded on such a transient foundation are equally weak, i.e., non-permanent; and, on that account, the ever-lasting permanence of the law of Truth seen in one's being ready to sacrifice one's life in the interests of Truth, irrespective of considerations of happiness or unhappiness, cannot be based on the doctrine of the 'greatest happiness of the greatest number'. Some persons advance the argument, that if in ordinary life even responsible persons are seen taking shelter behind falsehood when faced with the problem of sacrificing their lives, and if we see, that in such circumstances even philosophers are not punctillious, then it is not necessary to look upon the religion of Truth etc, as eternal; but this argument is not correct. Because, even those people who have not got the moral courage or do not find it convenient to sacrifice their lives for the sake of Truth, admit by their own mouths the eternal nature of this principle of morality. On this account, in the Mahābhārata, after all the rules of ordinary life which lead to the acquisition of wealth (*artha*), desires (*kāma*) etc. have been dealt with, Vyāsa ultimately in the Bhārata–Sāvitri, (and also in the Viduranīti), has given to everybody the following advice namely :—

na jātu kāmān na bhayān na lobhād
dharmaṁ tyajed jīvitasyāpihetoḥ ।
dharmo nityaḥ sukhaduḥkhe tv anitye
jīvo nityoḥ hetur asya tv anityaḥ " ॥

(Ma. Bhā. Sva. 5. 6; U. 39.12, 13),

that is: "although happiness and unhappiness is transient, yet morality is constant; therefore, one should not abandon moral principles, whether for desire of happiness or out of fear, or avarice, or even if life itself is threatened. Life is fundamentally eternal and its objects, such as, happiness, or unhappiness, etc., are transient." And that, therefore, instead of wasting time in thinking of transient happiness or unhappiness, one should link eternal life with eternal religion. In order to see how far this advice of Vyāsa is correct, we have now to consider the true nature of happiness and unhappiness and to see what permanent happiness is.

CHAPTER V

THE CONSIDERATION OF HAPPINESS AND UNHAPPINESS

(SUKHA-DUḤKHA-VIVEKA)

sukham ātyantikaṁ yat tat buddhigrāhyam atīndriyam I *

Gītā. 6. 21.

Our philosophers have accepted the position that every human being in this world is continually struggling in order to obtain happiness, or to increase the amount of happiness which he has obtained, or to obviate or reduce his unhappiness. In the Śāntiparva, Bhṛgu says the Bhāradvāja (Ma. Bhā. Śān. 190. 9) that:-"*iha khalu amuṣmiṁś ca loke vastupravṛttayaḥ sukhārtham abhidhīyante na hy ataḥparaṁ viśiṣṭataraṁ asti*", i. e., "in this world or elsewhere, all activity is for obtaining happiness, there is no other goal except this for *dharma, artha,* or *kāma.*" But, our philosophers say, though a man is suddenly seized by the hand of death, while he is grabbing a false coin in the belief that it is true because he does not understand in what true happiness lies, or while he is spending his life in the hope that happiness will come sometime or other, his neighbour does not become any the wiser on that account, and follows the same mode of life; and the cycle of life goes on in this way, nobody troubling to think in what true and permanent happiness lies. There is a great deal of difference between the opinions of Eastern and Western philosophers as to whether life consists only of unhappiness, or is principally happy or principally unhappy. Nevertheless, there is no difference of opinion about the fact that whichever position is accepted, the advantage of a man lies in obtaining the highest measure of happiness by preventing unhappiness to the greatest possible extent. The words '*hitaṁ*' (advantage), or '*śreyas*' (merit), or '*kalyāṇam*' (benefit) are ordinarily more often used than the word '*sukhaṁ*' (happiness); and I shall later on explain what the difference between them is. Yet, if one takes for granted that the word 'happiness' includes all kinds of benefits, then the

* "That happiness is the most beatific happiness which being obtainable only by means of Reason (*buddhi*), is independent of the organs (*indriyam*)."

proposition that ordinarily every human being strives to obtain happiness may be said to be generally accepted. But, on that account, the definitions of pain and happiness given in the Parāśaragītā included in the Mahābhārata, (Ma. Bhā. Śān. 295. 27) namely : "*yad iṣṭaṁ tat sukhaṁ prāhuḥ dveṣyaṁ duḥkham iheṣyate*", i. e., "that which is desired by us is happiness, and that which we dislike, or which we do not desire is unhappiness", do not become entirely faultless from the philosophical point of view. Because, the word '*iṣṭa*' in this definition can also be interpreted to mean 'a desirable thing or object'; and if that meaning is accepted, one will have to refer to a desirable object as 'happiness'. For example, although we might desire water when we are thirsty, yet water, which is an external object, cannot be called 'happiness'. If that were so, one will have to say that a person who is drowned in the waters of a river, has been drowned in happiness! That organic satisfaction which results from the drinking of water is happiness. It is true that men desire this satisfaction of the organs or this happiness, but we cannot, on that account, lay down the broad proposition, that all that is desirable must be happiness. Therefore, the Nyāya school has given the two definitions: "*anukūlavedanīyaṁ sukham*", i. e., "desirable suffering is happiness", and "*pratikūlavedanīyaṁ duḥkham*", i.e., "undesirable suffering is unhappiness", and it has treated both pain and happiness as some kind of suffering. As these sufferings are fundamental, that is to say, as they start from the moment of birth, and as they can be realised only by experience, it is not possible to give better definitions of pain or happiness than these given by the Nyāya school. It is not that these sufferings in the shape of pain and happiness result only from human activity; but, sometimes the anger of deities gives rise to intractable diseases, and men have to suffer the resulting unhappiness; therefore, in treatises on Vedānta, this pain and happiness is usually divided into '*ādhidaivika*' (god-given), '*ādhibhautika*' (physical), and '*ādhyātmika*' (metaphysical). Out of these, that pain or happiness which we suffer as a result of the blessings or the anger of deities is known as '*ādhidaivika*', and that pain or happiness, in the shape of warmth or cold, which results from the contact of the human organs with the external objects in the world composed of the five primordial elements (such as the earth etc.), is called '*ādhibhautika*'; and all pain and happiness which arises without any such external contact, is called '*ādhyātmika*'. When this classification of pain and happiness is accepted, pain, like fever etc., when it results from the disturbance of the internal ratio of wind, bile etc. in the body, and the peaceful health, which results from that internal ratio being correct, fall into the category of Metaphysical (*ādhyātmika*) pain and happiness. Because, although this pain and happiness is bodily, that is to say, although it pertains to the gross body made up of the five primordial elements, yet, we cannot always say that it is due to the contact of the body with external objects. And therefore, even Metaphysical pain and happiness have, according to Vedānta philosophy, to be further sub-divided into bodily-metaphysical, and mental-metaphysical pain and happiness. But, if pain and happiness is, in this way further divided into bodily and mental divisions, it is no more necessary to recognise the *ādhidaivika* pain and happiness as a distinct class. Because, as is clear, the pain or happiness which arises as a result of the blessings or the anger of deities, has ultimately to be borne by man through his body or through his mind. I have, therefore, not followed the three-fold division of pain and happiness made in Vedānta terminology, but have adopted only the two divisions, external or bodily (*bāhya* or *śārir*), and internal or mental (*abhyantara* or *mānasika*); and I have in this book called all bodily pain and happiness '*ādhibhautika*' (physical) and all mental pain and happiness '*ādhyātmika*' (Metaphysical). I have not made a third division of *ādhidaivika* (god-given) pain and happiness, as has been done in books on Vedānta philosophy, because, in my opinion, this two-fold classification is more convenient for dealing scientifically with the question of pain and happiness; and this difference between the Vedānta terminology and my terminology must be continually borne in mind in reading the following pages.

Whether we look upon pain and happiness as of two kinds or of three kinds, nobody wants pain; therefore, it is stated both in the Vedānta and the Sāṁkhya philosophies (Sāṁ. Kā. 1: Gī. 6. 21, 22), that preventing every kind of pain to the greatest possible extent, and obtaining the uttermost and the permanent happines is the highest goal of man. When in this way, the uttermost happiness has become the highest goal of man, we have naturally to consider the questions: what is to be called the uttermost, the real, and the permanent happiness, whether or not it is possible to obtain it, and if so, when and how it can be obtained etc.; and when you begin to consider these questions, the next question which arises is, whether pain and happiness are two independent and different kinds of sufferings, experiences, or things, as defined by the Nyāya School, or whether the absence of the one can be referred to as the other, on the principle that 'that which is not light, is darkness'. After saying that: "When our mouth becomes dry on account of thirst, we drink sweet water in order to remove that unhappiness; when we suffer on account of hunger, we eat nice food in order to alleviate that suffering; and, when the sexual desire is roused and becomes unbearable, we satisfy it by sexual intercourse with a woman", Bhartṛhari in the last line of the stanza says:-

pratikāro vyādheḥ sukham iti viparyasyati janaḥ ı

that is, "when any disease or unhappiness has befallen you, the removal of it is, by confusion of thought, referred to as 'happiness'"! There is no such independent thing as happiness which goes beyond the removal of unhappiness. It is not that this rule applies only to the selfish activities of men. I have in the last chapter referred to the opinion of Ānandagiri, that even in the matter of doing good to others, the feeling of pity invoked in our hearts on seeing the unhappiness of another becomes unbearable to us, and we do the good to others only in order to remove this our suffering in the shape of our being unable to bear it. If we accept this position, we will have to accept as correct the definitions of pain and happiness given in Mahābhārata in one place, namely:—

tṛṣṇārtiprabhavaṁ duḥkhaṁ duḥkhārtiprabhavaṁ sukham ı
(Śān. 25. 22; 174. 19).

that is, "some Thirst first comes into existence; on account of the suffering caused by that Thirst, unhappiness comes into existence; and from the suffering caused by that unhappiness, happiness subsequently follows". In short, according to these philosophers, when some Hope, Desire, or Thirst has first entered the human mind, man thereby begins to suffer pain, and the removal of that pain is called happiness; happiness is not some independent thing. Nay, this school has even gone further and drawn further inferences that all the tendencies of human life are Desire-impelled or Thirst-prompted; that Thirst cannot be entirely uprooted, unless all the activities of worldly life are abandoned; and that, unless Thirst is entirely uprooted, true and permanent happiness cannot be obtained. This path has been advocated as an alternative path in the Bṛhadāraṇyaka (Bṛ. 4. 4. 22; Ve. Sū. 3. 4. 15); and in the Jābāla, Saṁnyāsa and other Upaniṣads, it has been advocated as the principal path. This idea has also been adopted in the Aṣṭāvakragītā (9. 8; 10. 3–8) and in the Avadhūtagītā (3. 46). The ultimate doctrine of this school is that the man who desires to obtain the highest happiness or Release, must give up worldly life as early as possible, and follow the path of Renunciation (*saṁnyāsa*); and the path of the Abandonment of the Actions which have been prescribed by the Śrutis and the Smṛtis (*śrauta-smārta-karma-saṁnyāsa*), described in the Smṛti treatises, and which was established in the Kali era by Śrī Śaṁkarācārya is based on this principle. If there is no such real thing as happiness, and, if whatever is, is unhappiness, and that too based on Thirst, then it is clear, that all the bother of self-interest or other's-interest will be obviated and the fundamental equable frame of mind (*śānti*) will be the only thing to remain, when these diseases in the shape of Thirst etc. are in the first place entirely uprooted; and for this reason, it is stated in the Pingalagītā in the Śāntiparva of the Mahābhārata, as also in the Mankigītā, that:–

> *yac ca kāmsukhaṁ loke yac ca divyaṁ mahat sukham* ।
> *tṛṣṇākṣayasukhasyaite nārhataḥ ṣodaśīṁ kalām* ॥
>
> (Śān. 174. 48; 177. 49)

i. e., "that happiness which is experienced in this world, by the satisfaction of desires (*kāma*), as also the greater happiness which is to be found in heaven, are neither worth even one-sixteenth of the happiness which results from the destruction of Thirst". The Jain and the Buddhistic religions have later on copied the Vedic path of Renunciation; and therefore, in the religious treatises of both these religions, the evil effects and discardability of Thirst have been described as above, or possibly in even more forcible terms. (For example, see the Tṛṣṇāvagga in the *Dhammapada*). In the treatises of the Buddhistic religion to be found in Tibet, it is even stated that the above-mentioned stanza from the Mahābhārata was uttered by Gautama Buddha when he attained the Buddha-hood. *

It is not that the above-mentioned evil effects of Thirst have not been acknowledged by the Bhagavadgītā. But, as the doctrine of the Gītā is that the total abandonment of Action is not the proper course for obviating those evil effects, it is necessary to consider here somewhat minutely the above explanation of the nature of pain and happiness. We cannot, in the first place, accept as totally correct the dictum of the Saṁnyāsa school, that all happiness arises from the preventing of pain, such as Thirst etc. Wishing to experience again something, which one has once experienced (seen, heard, etc.) is known as Desire (*kāma, vāsanā, or icchā*). When this desire becomes stronger as a result of the pain due to one's not obtaining soon enough the desired object, or when the obtained happiness being felt to be insufficient, one wants more and more of it, this desire becomes a Thirst (*tṛṣṇā*). But if Desire is satisfied before it has grown into Thirst, we cannot say that the resulting happiness arises from the removal of the unhappiness of Thirst. For instance, if we take the case of the food which we get every day at a stated time, it is not our experience that we feel unhappiness every day before taking food. If we do not get food at the proper time, we will suffer unhappiness as a result of hunger, but not otherwise. But

* See Rockhill's *Life of Buddha*, p. 33. This stanza has appeared in the Pali book called *Udāna* (2. 2); but, it is not stated there that it was uttered by Buddha when he attained the 'Buddha-hood', from which it can be clearly seen that these stanzas could not have been originally uttered by Buddha.

even if we do not in this way distinguish between Thirst and Desire, and say that both are synonymous, the doctrine that the root of all happiness is Thirst is seen to be incorrect. For instance, if we suddenly put a piece of sugar-candy into the mouth of a child, the happiness which it experiences cannot be said to have resulted from the destruction of a previous Thirst. Similarly, if while walking along the road, one comes across a beautiful garden and hears the melodious notes of a cuckoo, or coming across a temple on the way, one sees in it the beautiful image of the deity, one thereby experiences happiness, though there had been no previous desire of obtaining those particular objects. If we think over these illustrations, we have to abandon the above-mentioned definition of happiness of the Saṁnyāsa school, and say that our organs have an inherent capacity for feeding on good or bad objects, and that when they are in that way carrying on their various activities, they come into contact sometimes with a desirable and sometimes an undesirable object, and we, thereupon, experience either pain or happiness, without having had any previous Desire or Thirst for it. With this purport in mind, it is stated in the Gītā (Gī. 2. 14), that pain and happiness arises as a result of '*mātrāsparśa*', that is, of contact with cold or warm objects etc. The external objects in the world are technically known as '*mātrā*', and the above statement in the Gītā means that the contact (*sparśa*), i. e., the union of these external objects with our organs results in the suffering (*vedanā*) of pain or happiness. That is also the doctrine of the science of Karma-Yoga. Nobody can satisfactorily explain why a harsh sound is undesirable to the ear, or why a sweet drink is pleasurable to the tongue, or why the light of the full moon is pleasing to the eyes. All that we know is that when the tongue gets a sweet liquid to taste, it is satisfied. As Material Happiness is, by its very nature, wholly dependent on the organs, happiness is very often experienced by merely carrying on the particular activities of the organs, whatever the ultimate result of our doing so may be. For instance, the words which sometimes naturally escape our lips when some idea enters our mind, are not uttered by us with the idea of acquainting someone else with our thoughts. On the other hand, there is sometimes even a risk of some hidden design or scheme in our minds being divulged by these automatic activities of the organs, and of our being thereby harmed. When little children first learn to walk, they aimlessly walk about the whole day, because they then experience happiness by the mere act of walking. Therefore, the Blessed Lord, instead of saying that all happiness consists of the absence of unhappiness, says that :–"*indriyasyendriyasyārthe rāga dveṣau vyavasthitau*" (Gī. 3. 34), i. e., the attraction and repulsion which exists between the organs of the sense on the one hand, and their relative objects, such as, sound, touch, etc., on the other hand, are both '*vyavasthita*', i.e., fundamentally self-existing ; and His advice is that all that we have to see is how these activities will become beneficial or can be made by us beneficial to our Ātman; and that therefore, instead of attempting to destroy the natural impulses of the mind, or of the organs, we should keep our mind and organs under control in order that those impulses should be beneficial to us, and not let the impulses get out of control. This advice, and saying that one should destroy Thirst and along with Thirst all other mental impulses, are two diametrically opposite things. The message of the Gītā is not that one should do away with all activity or prowess in the world; but, on the other hand, it is stated in the 18th Chapter of the Gītā (18. 26) that the doer must, side by side with equability of mind, possess the qualities of perseverance and enthusiasm. But we will deal with this matter in greater detail later on. All that we have to see for the present is whether pain and happiness are two independent states of mind or whether one of them is merely the absence of the other; and what the opinion of the Bhagavadgītā on this matter is will be easily understood by my readers from what has been stated above. Not only have '*sukham*' (happiness) and '*duḥkham*' (pain) been independently dealt with in describing what the '*kṣetra*' (field) is (Gī. 13. 6), but (Gī. 14.6,7), Happiness is said to be the sign of *sattvam* (purity) and Thirst of *rajas* (passion), and *sattvam* and *rajas* are considered two independent qualities. From this also it is clear, that pain and happiness have, in the Bhagavadgītā, been considered as two mutually opposite and distinct frames of mind. The fact that the Gītā looks upon *rājasa-tyāga* (abandonment based on passion) as inferior, as is shown by the words: "One does not derive the result of Abandonment by abandoning some Action on the ground that it leads to unhappiness; for such an abandonment is *rājasa*" (Gī. 18. 1), also refutes the doctrine that all happiness is based on the destruction of Thirst.

Even if we believe that happiness does not consist of the destruction of Thirst or of the absence of unhappiness, and that happiness and unhappiness are two independent things, yet, in as much as both these sufferings are mutually opposite or contrary to each other, we are next faced with the question whether it is possible for a man to experience the pleasure of happiness, if he has never suffered unhappiness. Some philosophers say that unless unhappiness has in the first instance been experienced, it is impossible to realise the pleasure of happiness. Others, on the other hand, pointing at the perpetual happiness enjoyed by deities in heaven, say that previous experience of unhappiness is not at all necessary for realising the pleasure of happiness. One can experience the sweetness of honey, jaugery, sugar, the mango-fruit or the plantain before having previously tasted any saltish object. In the same way, since happiness also is of various kinds, one can, without any previous experience of unhappiness, experience perpetual happiness without getting tired of it, by enjoying in succession diverse kinds of happiness, e. g., by moving from a mattress of cotton on to a mattress of feathers, or from a fixed palanquin to the more comfortable swinging palanquin. But, if one considers the ordinary course of life in this world, it will be seen that all this argument is useless. As the Purāṇas show cases of even gods coming into difficulties, and as even heavenly happiness comes to an end after one's acquired merit has been exhausted in due course of time, the illustration of heavenly happiness is not appropriate; and even if it were appropriate, what use is the illustration of heavenly happiness to us? Although we may believe that: "*nityam eva sukhaṁ svarge*", i. e., "in heaven there is permanent happiness", yet, it is stated immediately afterwards that :—

"*sukhaṁ duḥkham ihobhayam*" (Ma. Bhā. Śān. 190. 14), i. e., "in this world, pain is mixed with happiness"; and consistently with that position even Rāmdāsa Svāmi has described his own personal experience as follows: "Who is there in this world who is wholly happy? Consult your mind, search and see". And, as is actually experienced by us in this life, we have also to admit the correctness of the following advice given by Draupadī to Satyabhāmā, namely :—

sukhaṁ sukheneha na jātu labhyaṁ
duḥkhena sādhvī labhate sukhāni ı

(Ma. Bhā. Vana. 233. 4)

that is, "happiness never comes out of happiness; in order that a saintly woman should experience happiness, she must suffer unhappiness or trouble". Because, though a fruit may be placed on your lips, you have still to take the trouble of pushing it into the mouth, and if it falls into your mouth, you have still to take the trouble of chewing it. At any rate, this much is unquestionable, that there is a world of difference between the sweetness of the happiness which comes after unhappiness, and the sweetness of the happiness which is experienced by a man who is always engrossed in the enjoyment of the objects of pleasure. Because, by continually enjoying happiness, the keenness of the appreciative power of the organs which enjoy the happiness is dulled, and as is well-known :—

prāyeṇa śrīmatāṁ loke bhoktuṁ śaktir na vidyate ı
kāṣṭhāny api hi jīryante daridrāṇāṁ ca sarvaśaḥ ıı

(Ma. Bhā. Śān. 28.59)

that is, "rich people do very often not have even the power of enjoying tasteful food, and poor people can appreciate and digest even uncooked wood". Therefore, in considering worldly life, it is uselss to consider further whether it is possible to enjoy continual happiness without unhappiness. "*sukhasyānantaraṁ duḥkhaṁ duḥkhasyānantaraṁ sukham*" (Vana. 260. 40; Śān. 25.23), i. e., "unhappiness follows on the steps of happiness, and similarly happiness comes in the wake of unhappiness", or as has been described by Kālidāsa in the *Meghadūta* :–

> *kasyaikāntaṁ sukham upanataṁ duḥkham ekāntato va* ।
> *nīcair gacchaty upari ca daśā cakranemikrameṇa* ॥

that is, "no one experiences continual happiness or continual unhappiness; pain and happiness always move alternately up and down like the points on the circumference of a wheel". Such is the case, whether because this unhappiness has been created in order to increase the sweetness of happiness or because it has some other purpose in the scheme of activity of Matter (*prakṛti*). It may not be quite impossible to continually obtain one object of pleasure after another, without getting tired of enjoyment; but it is absolutely impossible, at any rate in this *karma-bhūmi*, i. e., world of Action (destiny ?) to totally abolish unhappiness and continually experience nothing but happiness.

If worldly life does not consist only of happiness, but is always a mixture of pain and happiness, the third question which naturally arises in due course is, whether there is more of happiness or of unhappiness in life. Many Western philosophers, who look upon Material Happiness as the highest goal of life say, that if there were more of pain than of happiness in life, many, if not all, persons would not have troubled to live worldly life, but would have committed suicide. But, in as much as man does not seem to be tired of living, he must be experiencing more of happiness than of unhappiness in life, and therefore, happiness must be looked upon as the highest goal of man, and the question of morality and immorality must also be solved by that standard. But, making suicide depend in this way on worldly happiness in not, really speaking, correct. It is true that sometimes a man, getting tired of life, commits suicide; but people look upon him as an exception, that is, as a lunatic. From this it is seen that ordinarily people do not connect committing or not committing suicide with worldly happiness, but look upon it as an independent thing by itself; and, the same inference follows if one considers the life of an aborginy, which would be looked upon as extremely arduous by civilised persons. The well-known biologist Charles Darwin, while describing in his

Travels the aboriginies he came across in the extreme south of South America says, that these aboriginies, men and women, remain without clothes all the year round, even in their extremely cold country; and, as they do not store food, they have for days together to remain without food; yet, their numbers are continually increasing.* But, from the fact that these aboriginies do not commit suicide, no one draws the inference that their mode of life is full of happiness. It is true that they do not commit suicide; but if one minutely considers why that is so, one will see that each one of these persons is filled with extreme happiness by the idea that "I am a human being and not a beast"; and he considers the happiness of being a human being so much greater than all other happiness, that he is never prepared to lose this superior happiness of being a man, however arduous his life may be. Not only does man not commit suicide, but even birds or beasts do not do so. But can one, on that account, say that their life is full of happiness? Therefore, our philosophers say, that instead of drawing the mistaken inference that the life of a man or of a bird or beast is full of happiness from the fact that they do not commit suicide, the only true inference which can be drawn from that fact is that: whatever the nature of a man's life, he does not set much store by it, but believes that an incomparable happiness lies in having become a living being (*sacetana*) from a lifeless being (*acetana*), and more than anything else, in having become a man. It is on that basis that the following rising grades have been described in the Śāstras :—

bhūtanāṁ prāṇinaḥ śreṣthaḥ prāṇinām buddhijīvinaḥ ।
buddhimatsu narāḥ śreṣṭhā nareṣu brāhmaṇāḥ smṛtāḥ ॥
brāhmaṇeṣu ca vidvāṁsaḥ vidvatsu kṛtabuddhayaḥ ।
kṛtabuddhiṣu kartāraḥ kartṛṣu brahmavādinaḥ ॥

(Manu. 1. 96. 97; Ma. Bhā. Udyo. 5. 1 and 2).

that is, "the living being is superior to the dead; the intelligents are superior among the living; men are superior among the intelligent; Brahmins, among men; learned Brahmins among Brahmins; doers, among the enligtened-minded, and

* Darwin's *Naturalist's Voyage round the World*, Chap. X.

brahmavādin (those who belong to the cult of the Brahman), among the doers"; and on the same basis, it is stated in vernacular treatises, that out of the 84 lakhs of forms of life (*yoni*) the human life is the most superior; that among men, he who desires Release (*mumukṣu*) is most superior; and, that among *mumukṣus*, the perfect (*siddha*) is the most superior. That is also the purport of the proverb "life is dearer than anything else", (*sabase jīva pyāra*); and for this very reason, if someone commits suicide, finding life full of unhappiness, people look upon him as insane, and the religious treatises count him as a sinner (Ma. Bhā. Karṇa. 70. 28); and an attempt to commit suicide is looked upon as a crime by law. When in this way it has been proved that one cannot, from the fact that a man does not commit suicide, properly draw the conclusion that life is full of happiness, we must, in deciding the question whether life is full of happiness or unhappiness, keep aside for the time being the natural blessing of having been born a human being on account of previous destiny, and consider only the events of the post-natal worldly life. The fact that man does not commit suicide or continues to live is accounted for by the Energistic principle of life; it is not any proof of the preponderance of happiness in worldly life as stated by Materialistic philosophers. Or, saying the same thing in other words, we must say that the desire not to commit suicide is a natural desire; that this desire does not arise as a result of the weighing of the happiness and unhappiness in life; and that therefore, one cannot from that fact draw the conclusion that life is full of happiness.

When in this way we do not, by confusion of thought, mix up the blessing of being born a human being with the nature of his subsequent life, and recognise 'being a human being' and 'the ordinary life or the usual activities of men' as two distinct things, there remain no other means for deciding the question whether there is more of happiness or of unhappiness in worldly life for the being which has taken the superior human form, than considering how many of the 'present' desires of every man are satisfied and how many disappointed. The reason for saying 'present' desires is that, those things which have become available to all persons in civilised life, become every-day happenings, and we forget the happiness they produce; and we decide the question of the happiness or unhappiness of worldly life by considering only how many of the things, which have newly become necessities, are obtained by us. There is a world of difference between (i) comparing the means of happiness which are available to us to-day with how many of them were available to us a hundred years ago, and (ii) considering whether or not I am happy to-day. For instance, anybody will admit that the present-day travelling by train is much more comfortable than travelling by bullock-cart, which was in vogue a hundred years ago. But we have now forgotten this happiness of train-travel, and we are unhappy only if some day a train gets late, and we receive our mail late. And therefore, the 'present' happiness or unhappiness of man is usually considered by thinking of his present needs and disregarding all the means of happiness which have already become available; and, if we try to consider what these needs are, we see that there is no end of them. If one desire is satisfied to-day, another new desire takes its place to-morrow, and we want to satisfy this new desire; and as human desire is thus always one step ahead of life, man is never free from unhappiness. In this place, we must bear carefully in mind the difference between the two positions that 'all happiness is the destruction of desire' and that 'however much of happiness is obtained, man is still unsatisfied'. Saying that 'all happiness is not the absence of unhappiness, but pain and happiness are two independent kinds of organic sufferings' is one thing, and that 'one is dissatisfied, because new kinds of happiness are wanted, without taking into account the happiness which may at any time already be part of one's life', is another thing. The first of these two dicta deals with the actual nature of happiness; and the second, with whether or not a man is fully satisfied by the happiness he has obtained. As the desire for objects of pleasure is a continually increasing desire, a man wants to enjoy over and over again the same happiness which he has already enjoyed. though he may not get new kinds of happiness everyday, and thus human desire is never controlled. There is a story told of a Roman Emperor named Vitalius that in order to experience over and over again the pleasure of eating tasteful food, he used to take medicines for vomitting the food which he had already eaten, and dine several times every day! But the story of the repentant king Yayāti is even more instructive than this. After the king Yayāti had become old as a result of the curse of Śukrācārya, the latter, by a pang of kindness, gave him the option of giving his old age to another person and taking in exchange his youth. Thereupon, he took the youth of his son Puru in exchange for his own oldness, and, having enjoyed all objects of pleasure for a thousand years, he found by experience that all the objects in the world were incapable of satisfying the desire for happiness of even one human being; and Vyāsa has stated in the Ādiparva of the Mahābhārata that Yayāti then said:

na jātu kāmaḥ kāmānām upabhogena śāmyati ।
haviṣā kṛṣṇavartmeva bhūya evābhivardhate ॥

(Ma. Bhā. Ā. 75.49)

that is, "by enjoying objects of pleasure, the desire for the objects of pleasure is not satisfied, but on the other hand this desire grows more and more, just as fire burns more and more by sacrificial offerings being thrown into it"; and the same stanza is to be found in the Manu-Smṛti (Manu. 2. 94). The inner reason for this is that, notwithstanding the abundance of means of pleasure, the desire for happiness is never quenched only by enjoying happiness, in as much as the hunger of the organs is always on a rising scale, and it has to be restrained in some other way; and this principle has been fully accepted by our religious writers who have in the first place prescribed that every one must put a restraint on the enjoyment of pleasure. If those who say that enjoyment of objects of pleasure is the highest goal in this world apply their mind to this doctrine which is based on experience, they will easily realise the absurdity of their beliefs. This doctrine of the Vedic religion has also been accepted in the Buddhistic religion and there is a statement in the Buddhistic treatises that the following words came out of the mouth of the king named Māndhātā mentioned in the Purāṇas (instead of Yayāti) at the moment of his death:—

na kahāpaṇavassena titti kāmesu vijjati ।
api dibbesu kāmesu ratiṁ so nādhigacchati ॥

(Dhammapada, 186–187).

that is, "although coins called '*kārṣāpaṇa*' fall as a shower of rain, there is no satisfaction (*titti* means *tṛpti*) of Desire, and the desires of a desirer are not satisfied even by getting the happiness of heaven". As it is thus imposible that the happiness of enjoying objects of pleasure can ever be considered sufficient, every man thinks that 'I am unhappy', and when this mental frame of mankind is taken into account then, as stated in the Mahābhārata :—

sukhād bahutaraṁ duḥkhaṁ jīvite nāsti saṁśayaḥ ।

(Śān. 305. 6; 330. 16).

that is, "in this life (*saṁsāra*), unhappiness is more than happiness"; or as stated by the Saint Tukārām: "if you consider happiness, it is as small as a grain; and if you consider unhappiness, it is as big as a mountain (Tukā. Gā. 2986). The same is the doctrine laid down by the writers of the Upaniṣads (Maitryu 1. 2–4), and it is stated also in the Gītā that the life of man is inconstant and the 'home of unhappiness', and that life in the world is not lasting and is 'devoid of happiness' (Gī. 8. 15 and 9. 3). The same is the opinion of the German philosopher Schopenhauer, and he has made use of a very curious illustration for proving it. He says that we measure the happiness of a man by considering how many of his desires for happiness, out of the total possible desires for happiness, are satisfied; and if the enjoyment of happiness falls short of the desire for happiness, we say that the man is to that extent unhappy. If this ratio is to be explained mathematically we have to divide the enjoyment of happiness by the desire for happiness and show it in the form of a fraction, thus: $\frac{\text{enjoyment of happiness.}}{\text{desire for happiness}}$ But this is such a queer fraction that its denominator, namely, the desire for happiness, is always increasing in a greater measnre than its numerator, namely, the enjoyment of happiness; so that, if this fraction is in the beginning ½ it becomes later on 3/10, that is to say, if the numerator increases three times, the denominator increases five times, and the fraction becomes more and more incomplete. Thus, it is futile to entertain the hope of a man becoming fully happy. In considering how much there was of happiness in ancient times, we consider only the numerator of this fraction by itself and do not pay any attention to the fact that the denominator has now increased much more than the numerator. But when we have to consider only whether a human being is happy or unhappy without reference to time, we must consider both the numerator and the denominator; and we see that this fraction will never become complete. That is the sum and substance of the words of Manu: "*na jātu kāmaḥ kāmānām*" etc. (2. 94). As there is no definite instrument like a thermometer for measuring happiness and unhappiness, this mathematical exposition of the mutual ratio of pain and happiness might not be acceptable to some; but if this argument is rejected, there remains no measure for proving that there is a preponderance of happiness in life for man. Therefore, this objection, which applies as much to the question of happiness as of unhappiness, leaves untouched the general proposition in the above discussion, namely, the theorem proved by the uncontrollable growth of the desire for happiness beyond the actual enjoyment of happiness. It is stated in Mahomedan history, that during the Mahomedan rule in Spain, a just and powerful ruler named Abdul Rahiman the third * had kept a diary of how he spent his days and from that diary he ultimately found that in a rule of 50 years he had experienced unalloyed happiness only for 14 days; and another writer † has stated that if one compares the opinions of ancient and modern philosophers in the world and especially in Europe, the number of those who say that life is full of happiness is seen to be about the same as of those who say that life is full of unhappiness. If to these numbers we add the numbers of the Indian philosophers, I need not say which way the scale will turn.

* *Moors in Spain* p. 128 (Story of the Nations Series).

† Macmillan's *Promotion of Happiness* p. 26.

Reading the exposition made above regarding the happiness and unhappiness of worldly life, some follower of the Saṁnyāsa school will retaliate: "although you do not accept the doctrine that there can be no peace unless one gives up all Thirst-prompted Actions on the ground that happiness is not some actual entity, yet, if even according to yourselves, dissatisfaction arises from Thirst and unhappiness later on springs from dissatisfaction, why do you not say that man should give up Thirst and, along with Thirst, all wordly Actions—whether those Actions are for his own good or for the good of others—at any rate for removing this dissatisfaction, and then remain perpetually satisfied ?". In the Mahābhārata itself, we find statements like: "*asaṁtoṣasya nāsty antas tuṣṭis tu paramaṁ sukham*", i. e., "there is no end to dissatisfaction, and contentment is the soul of bliss." (Ma. Bhā Vana. 215. 22); and both the Jain and Buddhistic religions are based on the same foundation; and in the Western countries, Schopenhauer has maintained * the same opinion. But on the other hand, one may ask whether one should cut off the tongue altogether because it sometimes utters obscene words, and whether people have discontinued the use of fire and given up cooking food on the ground that houses sometimes catch fire. If we make use of electricity, to say nothing of fire, in daily life, by keeping them under proper control, it is not impossible for us to dispose of Thirst or dissatisfaction in the same way. It would be a different matter, if this dissatisfaction was wholly and on all occasions disadvantageous; but on proper consideration we see that such is not the case. Dissatisfaction does not mean merely craving or weak-kneedness. Such a kind of dissatisfaction has been discountenanced even by philosophers. But the dissatisfaction which is at the root of the desire not to remain stagnant in the position which has fallen to one's lot, but to bring it to as excellent a condition as possible by gradually improving it more and more, with as peaceable and equable a frame of mind

---

* Schopenhauer's *World as Will and Representation* Vol. II Chap. 46. The description given by him of the unhappiness of worldly life is excellent. The original work is in the German language, and it has been translated into English.

as possible, is not a dissatisfaction which ought to be discountenanced. It need not be said that a society divided into four castes will soon go to rack and ruin if the Brāhmins give up the desire for knowledge, the Kṣatriyas for worldly prosperity, and the Vaiśyas for property. With this purport in view, Vyāsa has said to Yudhiṣṭhira:— "*yajño vidyā samutthānam asaṁtoṣaḥ śriyaṁ prati*" (Śān. 23. 9), i. e., "sacrifice, learning, effort, and dissatisfaction in the matter of worldly acquisitions", are virtues in the case of Kṣatriyas. In the same way, Vidulā in advising her son says: "*saṁtoṣo vai śriyaṁ hanti*" "(Ma. Bhā. U. 132. 33), i. e.," by contentment, worldly prosperity is destroyed"; and there is also a statement on another occasion that: "*asaṁtoṣaḥ śriyo mūlaṁ*" (Ma. Bhā. Sabhā. 55. 11)*, i. e., "dissatisfaction is the root of prosperity". Although contentment is referred to as a virtue in the case of Brāhmins, it only means contentment with reference to wealth or worldly prosperity, according to the four-caste arrangement. If a Brāhmin says that the knowledge which he has acquired is enough for him, he will bring about his own undoing, and the same will be the case with the Vaiśyas or the Śūdras, if they always remain satisfied with what they have acquired according to their own status in life. In short, discontent is the seed of all future prosperity, effort, opulence and even of Release; and, it must always be borne in mind by everybody, that if this discontent is totally annihilated, we will be nowhere, whether in this world or in the next. In the Bhagavadgītā itself, in listening to the advice of Śrī Kṛṣṇa, Arjuna has said: "*bhūyaḥ kathaya tṛptir hi śṛṇvato nāsti me 'mṛtam*" (Gī. 10. 18), i. e., "I am not satisfied with what I have heard of your nectar-like speech, therefore, describe to me more and more of your manifestations"; and then the Blessed Lord has again started enumerating his manifestations. He did not say to him: "restrain your desire, dissatisfaction or discontent is improper". From this it follows that even the Blessed Lord Himself considered it proper that one should entertain discontent about a good or beneficial matter, and there is a

* cf: "Unhappiness is the cause of progress." Dr. Paul Carus in *The Ethical Problem* p. 251 (2nd Ed.)

stanza of Bhartrhari that: "*yaśasi cābhirucir vyasanaṁ śrutau*" etc., i. e., "there ought to be liking or desire, but that should be for success; and one must also have a vice, but that should be of learning; that vice is not prohibited". Still, we must control discontent, in the same way as Desire, Anger etc., because if it becomes uncontrolled, it will clearly end in our undoing; and therefore, the endowment (*saṁpatti*) of those persons who continually run after worldly happiness piling thirst on thirst and hope on hope with the sole object of enjoying objects of pleasure is referred to as "ungodly endowment" (*āsura saṁpat*) in the 16th Chapter of the Gītā. Not only are the pure (*sāttvika*) tendencies in the human mind destroyed by such greediness and the man undone, but, in as much as it is impossible that Thirst should ever be quenched, the desire for enjoyment of objects of pleasure grows continually, and man's life is ended in the greed. But on the other hand, giving up all kinds of Thirst, and with it, all Actions, in order to escape this evil effect of Thirst or discontent is also not the pure (*sāttvika*) path. As has been stated above, Thirst or discontent is the seed of future prosperity: and therefore, instead of attempting to kill an innocent man out of fear for a thief, one has to carefully consider what Thirst or discontent causes unhappiness, and adopt the skilful middle path of giving up only that particular hope, thirst or discontent which produces unhappiness, and it is not necessary for that purpose to give up all kinds of Action whatsoever. This device or skill (*kauśalaṁ*) of giving up only that hope which causes unhappiness and performing one's duties according to one's status in life is known as Yoga or Karma-yoga (Gī. 2. 50.); and, as that is the Yoga which has been principally dealt with in the Gītā, I shall consider here in a little more detail what kind of hope has been looked upon by the Gītā as productive of unhappiness.

In describing above the actual nature of human pain and unhappiness, I have stated that a man hears by his ears, feels by his skin, sees by his eyes, tastes by his tongue, and smells by his nose; and that a man is happy or unhappy according as these activities of his organs are consistent with their natural tendencies. But, the question of pain and happiness is not completely exhausted by making this definition. Although it is necessary that the organs should, in the first instance, come into contact with external objects in order that Material pain or happiness should arise, yet, if one considers in what way this pain or happiness is subsequently experienced by man, it will be seen that a man has ultimately to perform the function of realising, that is, of taking on himself, this pain or happiness, which results from the activities of the organs, by means of his Mind (*manas*). '*cakṣuḥ paśyati rūpāṇi manasā na tu cakṣuṣā*', i. e., "the function of seeing is not performed solely by the eyes : the assistance of the mind is absolutely necessary for it" (Ma. Bhā. Śān. 311. 17); and it is stated in the Mahābhārata that if that mind is in pain, then even having seen is as if you have not seen, and even in the Bṛhadāraṇyakopaniṣad, there are such statements as : "*anyatramanā abhūvaṁ nādarśam*", i. e., "my mind was elsewhere, and therefore, I did not see", or, "*anyatramanā abhūvaṁ nāśrauṣam*", i. e., "my mind was elsewhere, and therefore, I did not hear" (Bṛ. 1. 5. 3). From this it becomes clear, that in order to experience Material pain or happiness, the organs are not sufficient by themselves, but require the assistance of the Mind ; and as regards Metaphysical pain or happiness, it is purely mental. It, therefore, follows that all experience of pain or happiness ultimately depends on the Mind ; and if this is true, it naturally follows that it is not impossible to control the experience of pain or happiness if one controls the mind. With regard to these facts, Manu has described the characteristics of pain and happiness in a different way than the Nyāya school. He says :

sarvaṁ paravaśaṁ duḥkhaṁ sarvam ātmavaśaṁ sukham ।
etad vidyāt samāsena lakṣaṇaṁ sukhaduḥkhayoḥ ॥

(Manu. 4. 160).

that is, "all that which is subject to the control of others (external objects) is unhappiness, and all that which is subject to the control of oneself (of one's mind) is happiness ; these are in brief the characteristic features of pain and happiness". The word 'suffering' (*vedanā*) used in the connotation of pain and happiness given by the Nyāya school, includes both physical and mental suffering, and it also shows the actual external nature of pain and happiness ; and when one bears in mind that Manu is referring principally to the internal experience of pain and happiness, there remains no inconsistency between these two definitions. When in this way, we do not make the experience of pain or happiness depend on the organs:

bhaiṣajyam etad duḥkhasya yad etan nānucintayet ।

that is, "not brooding on one's unhappiness, becomes the most potent medicine for doing away with unhappiness" (Ma. Bhā. Śān. 205. 2); and we find numerous illustrations in history, of people having hardened their minds, and willingly sacrificed their lives for the sake of their Religion or of Truth. Therefore, says the Gītā, when one does what one has to do with perfect mental control and after giving up the DESIRE FOR THE RESULT *(phalāśā)* and with a frame of mind which is equal towards pain and happiness, there remains no fear or possibility of experiencing the unhappiness of Actions, and it does not become necessary to give them up. Giving up the desire for the result does not mean giving up the resulting benefit, if it has been acquired, nor entertaining a desire that no one should ever get that benefit. In the same way, there is a world for difference between the desire for the result and the Desire, Hope, or Motive for performing Action, or employing a particular means for obtaining a particular result. There is a difference between merely desiring to move one's hands and feet and desiring to move one's hands for catching or one's feet for kicking some one else. The first desire extends merely to the doing of the act and there is no other motive behind it; and if we give up this desire, all Action will come to an end. Besides having this desire, a man must also have the knowledge that every act is sure to have some result or consequence; and not only must he have that knowledge, but he must entertain the desire of doing a particular act with the intention of thereby producing some particular result; otherwise, all his Actions will be as pointless as those of a madman. All of these desires, motives, or arrangements do not ultimately produce pain; nor does the Gītā ask you to give them up. But if one goes much further than that, and allows his mind to be afflicted by the

ATTACHMENT (*āsakti*), ambition, pride, self-identification, or insistence of MINE-NESS (*mamatva*), which exists in the mind of the doer with reference to the result of the Action in the shape of the feeling that: "whatever action is performed by ME is performed by ME with the intention that 'I' should necessarily get a particular benefit from a particular act of MINE"; and if thereafter there is any obstruction in the matter of getting the desired result or benefit, the chain of misery starts. If this obstruction is inevitable and is an act of Fate, man only suffers from despair; but, if it is the handiwork of another person, it gives rise later on to anger or even hate, and this hate leads to evil action, and evil action leads to self-destruction. This attachment, in the shape of MINE-NESS, for the result of the Action, is also known as '*phalāśā*' (hope of benefit), '*saṁga*' (fondness), '*ahaṁkāra-buddhi*' (egoism), and '*kāma*' (desire); and in order to show that the chain of unhappiness in life really starts at this point, it is stated in the second chapter of the Gītā, that Desire springs from Attachment for objects of pleasure, Anger (*krodha*) from Desire, Mental Confusion (*moha*) from Anger, and ultimately, the man himself is destroyed (Gī. 2. 62, 63). When I have thus established that Actions in the gross material world, which are lifeless in themselves, are not themselves the root of unhappiness, but that the true root of unhappiness is the Hope for result, Desire, or Attachment with which man performs those Actions, it naturally follows that in order to prevent this unhappiness, it is quite enough if a person, by controlling his mind, gives up the Attachment, Desire or Hope of result entertained by him towards the objects of pleasure; and it follows logically that it is not necessary to give up all objects of pleasure, or Actions, or Desires as prescribed by the Saṁnyāsa school. Therefore, it is next stated in the Gītā (Gī. 2. 64), that that man who partakes of the objects of pleasure he comes across in the world, with a desireless and unattached frame of mind, without entertaining any hope of result, is the true '*sthitaprajña*' (steady-in-mind). The activity of Action in the world never comes to an end. Even if man ceases to exist in this world, Matter (*prakṛti*) will carry on its activities according to its constituent qualities (*guṇa-dharma*). Gross Matter would not in any way be happy or unhappy on that account. Man arrogates to himself an undue importance, and becomes attached to the activities of Matter, and in that way suffers pain and happiness. But if he gives up this attachment, and performs all his Actions in the belief that '*guṇā guṇeṣu vartante*', i. e., "all activities are going on according to the constituent qualities of Matter" (Gī. 3. 28), there will remain no unhappiness in the shape of discontent. Therefore, Vyāsa has advised Yudhiṣṭhira that instead of lamenting that worldly life is principally unhappy, and attempting to give up such life, one should believe that Matter is carrying on its own activities, and that:—

sukhaṁ vā yadi vā duḥkhaṁ priyaṁ vā yadi vāpriyam ।
prāptaṁ prāptam upāsita hṛdayenāparājitaḥ ॥

(Ma. Bhā. Śān. 25. 26).

that is, "one should put up with whatever takes place, whenever it takes place, without being disheartened, (that is to say, without becoming dejected, and giving up one's duty), whether it causes happiness or unhappiness, and whether it is pleasurable or unpleasant." The full importance of this advice will be appreciated when one bears in mind that one has to perform some duties in life, even suffering the pain which they cause. In the Bhagavadgītā itself, the characteristic features of the *sthitaprajña* are described in the words: "*yaḥ sarvatrānabhisnehas tat tat prāpya śubhāśubham*" (2. 57), i. e., "that man who, when anything favourable or unfavourable happens, always remains unattached, and neither welcomes it nor dislikes it, is the true *sthitaprajña*"; and in the fifth chapter it is stated that, "*na prahṛṣyet priyaṁ prāpya nodvijet prāpya cāpriyam*" (5. 20), i. e., "when you experience happiness, you should not on that account become excited; and when you experience unhappiness, you should also not on that account become dejected"; and it is stated in the second chapter, that this pain and happiness must be borne with a desireless frame of mind (2. 14, 15); and the same advice has been repeatedly given in various other places (Gī. 5. 9; 13. 9). In the terminology of Vedānta Philosophy, doing this is called 'dedicating all Actions to the Brahman' (*Brahmārpaṇa*), and in the Path of Devotion, the word '*Kṛṣṇārpaṇa*' (dedication to Kṛṣṇa) is used instead of '*Brahmārpaṇa*' (dedication to the Brahman); and this is the sum and substance of the whole of the preaching of the Gītā.

Whatever the nature of the Action, when one does not give up the Desire to do it, nor also one's activity, but goes on performing whatever one wants to do, being equally prepared for the resulting pain or happiness, with an aloof frame of mind, and without entertaining the hope for the result, not only does one escape the evil effects due to non-control of Thirst or discontent, but also the danger of the world becoming desolate as a result of Action being destroyed in the attempt to destroy Thirst; and all our mental impulses remain pure and become beneficial to all created beings. It is clear beyond doubt that in order in this way to be able to give up the hope for the result, one must obtain perfect control over the mind and over the organs by means of Apathy (*vairāgya*). But, there is a world of difference between (i) keeping one's organs under control and allowing them to perform their various activities, not for a selfish purpose, but apathetically and desirelessly and for the welfare of others, on the one hand, and (ii) deliberately destroying all Actions, that is to say, all the activities of the various organs in order to kill Thirst, as prescribed by the Path of Renunciation, on the other hand. The Apathy and Control of the organs prescribed by the Gītā is of the first kind and not of the second kind; and in the same way, in the conversation between Janaka and the Brahmin in the Anugītā (Ma. Bhā. Aśva. 32. 17-23) the king Janaka says to Dharma, who had appeared to him in the form of a Brahmin that:

> *śṛṇu buddhiṁ ca yāṁ jñātvā sarvatra viṣayo mama* ||
> *nāham ātmārtham icchāmi gāndhān ghrāṇagatān api* |
> ....
> *nāham ātmārtham icchāmi mano nityaṁ manontare* |
> *mano me nirjitaṁ tasmād vaśe tiṣṭhati sarvadā* ||

that is, "I will describe to you that apathetic frame of mind (*vairāgya*) with which I enjoy all objects of pleasure. I do not 'for myself' smell any scent, nor do I not 'for myself' see anything with my eyes etc; and I do not also put to use my mind for my Self *(atmārtha)*, that is, for my own benefit; therefore, I have conquered my nose (eyes etc.) and my mind, and they are all under my control". This is what is meant by the statement in the Gītā (Gī. 3. 6, 7) that he who merely chokes up the impulses of the organs but contemplates objects of pleasure by his mind is a hypocrite, and he who conquers the desiring frame of mind by means of mental control, and allows all his mental impulses to carry on their various activities for the benefit of the world is the real superman. The external world, or the activities of the organs are not something which we have brought into existence, but they are self-created; and however self-controlled a *saṁnyāsi* may be, yet, when his hunger becomes uncontrollable, he goes out to beg for food (Gī. 3. 33); or when he has sat for a considerable length of time in one place, he gets up and stands for some time. If we see that however much there is of mental control, one cannot escape the inherent activities of the organs, then the wisest course is seen to be not to perversely attempt to destroy the impulses of the organs, and at the same time all Actions and all kinds of Desire or Discontent (Gī. 2. 47; 18. 59), but to give up the hope for the result by controlling the mind, and to look upon pain and happiness as alike (Gī. 2. 38), and to perform all Actions desirelessly and for the benefit of the world as prescribed by the Śāstras. Therefore, the Blessed Lord first tells Arjuna in the following stanza:

karmaṇy evādhikāras te mā phaleṣu kadācana |
mā karmaphalahetur bhūḥ mā te saṅgo 'stvakarmaṇi ||
(Gī. 2. 47).

that, in as much as you have been born in this world of Action, therefore, "your authority extends only to the performance of Actions"; but bear in mind that this your authority extends only to the performance of Action which ought to be performed (that is, to *kartavya)*. The word *'eva'* which means 'only', clearly shows that the authority of man does not extend to anything other than *karma*, that is, to the result of the *karma*. But the Blessed Lord does not leave this important matter to be understood merely by inference, and He again, and in perfectly clear words, says in the second quarter of the stanza, that "your authority never extends to the result of the Action", because, getting or not getting the result of the Action is not a matter which is within your control, but is always in the gift of the Parameśvara or is dependent on the entire Effect of Causes (*karma-vipākā*) in the world. Hoping that a particular thing which is not within one's control should take place in a particular way, is a sign of madness. But the Blessed Lord has not left even this third thing for inference, and has in the third quarter of the stanza said: "therefore, do not perform any Action, keeping in mind the hope for the result of the Action"; whatever may be the result of your Action according to the general law of Cause and Effect, will be its effect; it is not possible that such result should be more or less, or take place earlier or later, according to your desires, and by entertaining any such desire, it is only you who suffer unnecessary pain and trouble. But here some persons—especially those who follow the Path of Renunciation—will object: "Is it not better to give up Action (*karma*) altogether rather than engaging in the useless procedure of performing Actions and giving up the hope of the result?" And therefore, the Blessed Lord has in the last quarter of the stanza made the definite statement that "do not insist upon not performing Action," but perform Action according to the authority which you possess, though without entertaining any hope for the result. These doctrines are so important from the point of view of Karma-Yoga, that the four quarters of the above stanza may be said to be the four aphorisms (*catuḥ-sūtri*) of the science of Karma-Yoga or of the Gītā religion.

If worldly activity is not to be given up, although happiness and unhappiness always befall you alternatively in life, and although it is an established fact that the sum total of unhappiness is greater than that of happiness, then some persons are likely to think, that all human efforts towards the total elimination of unhappiness and the acquisition of total happiness are futile; and if one considers only Material Happiness, that is to say, happiness in the shape of the enjoyment of external objects of pleasure through the medium of the organs, this their objection will have to be admitted to be substantial. Just as the Moon never comes within the grasp of the little children who spread out their little hands towards the heavens in order to catch hold of it, so also those persons, who run after Material Happiness in the hope of reaching the highest form of happiness, will in any case find it very difficult to reach the highest form of happiness. But as Material Happiness is not the only kind of happiness, it is possible to find out the way of acquiring the highest and the constant form of happiness, even in this difficult position. As has been stated above, when happiness is divided into the two divisions of physical and mental happiness, one has to attach a higher importance to the activities of the mind than to the activities of the body or of the organs. Even the well-known Materialist philosopher Mill has admitted in his book on Utilitarianism, * that the theorem that the merit of Mental happiness is higher than that of bodily (i. e., Material) happiness, which has been laid down by scients (*jñānin*), is not made by them as a result of any arrogance about their own knowledge but because the true greatness or appropriateness of the superior human birth consists in Knowledge. Dogs, pigs, oxen etc. also like the happiness of the organs in the same way as human beings; and if the human race was of the opinion that enjoyment of objects of pleasure is the only true happiness in the world, then man would be ready to become a beast. But in as much as nobody is willing to become a beast, notwithstanding that he can thereby obtain all the physical happiness which can be got by beasts, it is clear that there is something more in a human being than in a beast. When one begins to consider what this something is, one has to investigate into the nature of that Ātman which acquires the knowledge of one's Self and of the external world by means of the Mind and of the Reason (*buddhi*); and when one has once begun to think of this matter, one naturally comes to the conclusion that, that happiness

* "It is better to be a human being dissatisfied than a pig satisfied; better to be Secrates dissatisfied than a fool satisfied. And if the fool, or the pig, is of a different opinion, it is because they only know their own side of the question". *Utilitarianism* p. 14 (Longman's, 1907).

which is to be found in the extremely noble activities and in the purest state of the Mind and of the Reason is the highest or the most ideal happiness of mankind, as compared with the happiness of the enjoyment of objects of pleasure, which is common to man and beast. This kind of happiness is self-controlled, that is, it can be acquired without depending on external objects, and without reducing the happiness of others, and by one's own exertions; and as a man becomes better and better, the nature of this happiness becomes more and more pure and unalloyed. Bhartṛhari has said that "*manasi ca parituṣṭe ko'rthavān ko daridraḥ*", i. e., "when the mind is satisfied, the begger is the same as the rich man", and the well-known Greek philospher Plato has maintained that Mental Happiness is superior to bodily (that is, external or Material) happiness, and that, that happiness which can be realised only by means of the Reason, (which is the highest Metaphysical Happiness), is superior even to Mental Happiness. * Therefore, even if we for the time being keep aside the question of Release, the fact that that Reason alone can obtain the highest happiness, which is engrossed in the contemplation of the Ātman, is definitely proved; and therefore, after happiness has been divided in the Bhagavadgītā into the three divisions of *sāttvika*, *rājasa* and *tāmasa*, it is first stated that "*tat sukhaṁ sāttvikaṁ proktaṁ ātmabuddhi-prasādajam*", i. e., "that Metaphysical Happiness which is the result of the contentedness of the Self-engrossed Reason (that is, of the Reason which having realised the true nature of the Ātman, namely, that there is only one Ātman in all created beings, is engrossed in that idea) is the *sāttvika* (placid), that is, the most superior kind of happiness (Gī. 18. 37); and the Gītā goes on to say that the Material Happiness arising from the organs and the objects of the organs is of a lower grade, that is, is *rājasa* (Gī. 18. 38); and that the happiness which arises from sleep, or idleness or which confuses the mind is the most inferior form, that is, is *tāmasa*. That is the meaning which is conveyed by the stanza from the Gītā which has been quoted at the commencement of this chapter, and the Gītā itself says (Gī. 6. 25) that when a man has once

* *Republic* (Book IX).

experienced this beatific happiness, he is not shaken from this peaceful mental frame, whatever the magnitude of the misfortune which subsequently befalls him. This beatific happiness is not to be found even in the enjoyment of heavenly objects of pleasure, and the Reason of a man has in the first instance to become absolutely contented before he can experience it. He who is always engrossed in the enjoyment of the objects of pleasure, without seeing how he can keep his frame of mind contented, experiences happiness, which is temporary and inconstant. Because, that organic happiness which exists to-day, ceases to exist tomorrow; and what is more, that thing which our organs look upon as productive of happiness to day, becomes for some reason or other, productive of unhappiness tomorrow. For instance, the same cold water which is desirable in summer, becomes undesirable in winter; and even if one acquires the happiness, the desire for happiness, as has been mentioned above, is never fully quenched. Therefore, although the world 'happiness' can be applied comprehen-sively to all kinds of happiness, yet, one has to differentiate between happiness and happiness. In ordinary practice, the word 'happiness' means principally 'organic happiness'. But when it becomes necessary to differentiate between the happiness of the enjoyment of objects of pleasure from that happiness which is beyond the organs, that is, which is beyond organic happiness, and which can be realised only by the self-engrossed Reason, the Material Happiness which consists of the enjoyment of objects of pleasure, is called simply 'happiness' (*sukham* or *preyas*), and the Metaphysical Happiness which is born of Self-Realisation (*ātma-buddhi-prasādaja*) is called 'beatific happiness' (*śreyas*), blessing (*kalyāṇam*), amelioration (*hitam*), beatitude (*ānanda*), or peace (*śānti*). The distinction made between '*preyas*' and '*śreyas*' by Naciketa in the sentence from the Kaṭhopaniṣad quoted at the end of the last chapter, has been made on this basis. Mṛtyu (Death) had already in the beginning explained to him the esoteric secrets of Fire (*agni*). But, when after having acquired that happiness, Naciketa asked for the blessing of being explained what was meant by the Knowledge or Realisation of the Atman (*ātmajñāna*), Mṛtyu tempted him with many other kinds of worldly happiness instead. But Naciketa was not tempted by these transient Material kinds of happiness, or things which appeared pleasing (*preyas*) on the face of them, and extending his vision, he insisted on having, and ultimately succeeded in acquiring, that philosophy of the Ātman which led to the blessing (*śreyas*) of his Ātman (Self) and was ultimately beneficial. In short, our philosophers have been looking upon that Reason-born happiness or Metaphysical beatitude, which results from the Realisation of the Ātman, as the most superior happiness and their advice is that this happiness is such as can be obtained by everybody, in as much as it is self-controlled, and that everybody should try to acquire it. That wonderful and special happiness which belongs to mankind in addition to its beastly qualities is this happiness; and this happiness of the Ātman (*ātmānanda*) is the most constant, the most independent and the most excellent of all happiness, in as much as it is independent of external circumstances. This peace is called in the Gītā (Gī. 6. 15) by the name of the Peace (*śānti*) of Emancipation (*nirvāṇa*); and it is also the climax of happiness which pertains to the Brāhmi state of the *sthitaprajña* (steady-in-mind) described in the Gītā (Gī. 2. 71; 6. 28; 12. 12; 18. 62).

In this way, we have proved that the peace or happiness of the Ātman is the most excellent of all happiness, and that as it is self-controlled, it is such as can be acquired by everybody. But by proving that gold is the most valuable of all metals, iron and other metals do not cease to be useful; and though sugar is sweet, one cannot do without salt; and the same is the case with the happiness of the Ātman or of Peace (*śānti*). At any rate, it cannot be disputed that Material objects are necessary for the protection of the body, along with this Peace; and therefore, in the phrases used for blessing, one does not say simply: "*śāntirastu*" (May there be *śānti*!, i. e., Peace), but say: "*śāntiḥ puṣṭis tuṣṭiś cāstu*", that is, 'May there also be *puṣṭi* (Material Happiness), and *tuṣṭi* (contentedness) along with *śānti* (peace)'. If our philosohpers had been of the opinion that one ought to acquire contentedness (*tuṣṭi*) by having merely Peace (*śānti*), there would have been no occasion to add to this phrase, the word '*puṣṭi*'. Nevertheless, it is also not proper to have an inordinate desire for increase of Material Happiness (that is, *puṣṭi*). Therefore, this phrase means: "May you have Peace, Material happiness and also Contentedness in proper proportions, and that you must obtain them". The same is the moral of the Kaṭhopaniṣad. The only matter which has been described in detail in this Upaniṣad is that after Naciketa had gone to the sphere of Yama, that is, of Death, Yama asked him to ask for three blessings, and that Yama accordingly gave him the three blessings which he had asked for. But after Mṛtyu had asked Naciketa to ask for blessings, Naciketa did not in the first place ask for the blessing of Brahman-Realisation (*Brahmajñāna*), but first said: "My father has got angry with me; may he become propitious to me"; and then, "teach me the science of Fire (*agni*), that is, of all sacrificial ritual which will give me material opulence"; and, when he had acquired these blessings, he asked for the third blessing saying: "teach me the Knowledge of the Ātman". But when Mṛtyu began to say to him that he would give him (Naciketa) additional happiness instead of this third blessing, Naciketa has insisted: "now explain to me that Brahmajñāna which will lead to *śreyas*", instead of aspiring for possessing more of the knowledge of sacrifical ritual than was necessary for obtaining *preyas*. In short, as stated in the last *mantra* of this Upaniṣad, Naciketu obtained both the '*Brahma-vidyā*' (knowledge of the Brahman), and '*yoga-vidhi*' (sacrificial ritual), and he was emancipated (Kaṭha 6. 18). From this it follows, that the combination of *jñāna* and *karma* is the summary of the preaching of this Upaniṣad. There is also a similar story about Indra. Not only had Indra himself acquired fully the Knowledge of the Brahman, (*Brahmajñāna*) but he had taught the science of the Ātman (*ātmavidyā*) to Pratardana, as has been stated in the Kauṣitakyupaniṣad. Yet, after Indra had lost his kingdom and Prahlāda had become the king of the three spheres, Indra went to Bṛhaspati, the preceptor of the gods, and asked him to explain to him in what *śreyas* lay. Then Bṛhaspati taught the dethroned Indra the *Brahmavidyā*, that is, the Knowledge of the Ātman, (*ātmajñāna*) and said to him that that was all which was *śreyas* (*etāvac chreya iti*). But Indra was not satisfied and again asked the question: "*ko viśeṣo bhavet?*", i. e., "Is there anything more?"; thereupon Bṛhaspati sent him to Śukrācārya. There, there was a repetition of the same process, and Śukrācārya said to him: "That something more is known to Prahlād." Then at last Indra went to Prahlāda in the form of a Brahmin and became his disciple, and after some time had passed, Prahlāda explained to him that '*śīlam*', (the habit of behaving consistently with Truth and Morality) was the master-key for gaining the kingdom of the three spheres, and that that was also known as *śreyas*. Then, when Prahlāda said to him: "I am very much pleased by your service, I shall give you whatever blessing you may ask", Indra, in the form of the Brahmin, said to him: "Give me your '*śīlam*'". When Prahlāda consented, the deity '*śīlam*', and after it Morality (*dharmam*), Veracity (*satyam*), good conduct (*vṛtta*), and ultimately opulence (*śrī*) and other deities left the body of Prahlāda and entered the body of Indra, and in this way Indra regained his kingdom: such is the ancient story which has been told by Bhīṣma to Yudhiṣṭhira in the Śāntiparva (Śān. 124). Although the Knowledge of the Brahman by itself may be worth more than prosperity (*aiśvaryam*) by itself, yet, in as much as whoever has to live in this world is under the obligation and has also the moral right to acquire material prosperity for himself or for his own country in the same way as it is possessed by others or by other countries, the highest ideal of man in this world, as is apparent from this beautiful story, is seen to be the combination of Peace (*śānti*), and Material Happiness (*puṣṭi*), or of desired things (*preyas*) and true and lasting benefit (*śreyas*), or of Knowledge (*jñānam*) and prosperity (*aiśvaryam*), according to our Karma-Yoga science. Has that Bhagavān than Whom there is none higher in this world, and Whose path is followed by others (Gī. 3. 33), Himself given up prosperity and wealth? The word '*bhaga*' has been defined in the Śāstras as:

aiśvaryasya samagrasya dharmasya yaśasaḥ śriyaḥ |
jñānavairāgyayoś caiva ṣaṇṇāṁ bhaga itīraṇā ||

(Viṣṇu. 6. 5. 74).

that is, "the word '*bhaga*' includes the followings six things: namely, complete Yogic prosperity, righteousness, success, property, knowledge, and apathy". The word '*aiśvaryam*' in this stanza is usually taken to mean '*Yogaiśvaryam*' (Yogic prosperity), because the word '*śrī*', that is, wealth, appears later on. But as ordinarily, the word '*aiśvaryam*' is used to mean and include authority, success, and wealth, and the word '*jñānam*' includes apathy and righteousness, we may say that in ordinary parlance, the entire meaning conveyed by the above stanza is included in the two words '*jñānam*' and '*aiśvaryam*'; and in as much as the Blessed Lord has Himself accepted the combination of *jñānam* and *aiśvaryam*, other persons should consider that as proper and act accordingly (Gī. 3. 21; Ma. Bhā. Śān. 341. 25). The doctrine that the knowledge of the Ātman is the only ideal of man in this world is a doctrine of the school of Renunciation, which says that, as worldly life is full of unhappiness, it should be given up; it is not a doctrine of the Karma-Yoga science, and it is not proper to mix up these doctrines of different schools of thought and pervert the meaning of the Gītā. And as the Gītā itself says that mere prosperity without Knowledge is a godless prosperity (*āsura sampatti*), it follows that we must always maintain the union of *jñānam* with *aiśvaryam*, or of *aiśvaryam* with *jñānam*, or of *śānti* with *puṣṭi*. When it is admitted that *aiśvayram* is necessary, though along with *jñānam*, it necessarily follows that Action must be performed. Manu has said that: "*karmāṇy ārabhamāṇaṁ hi puruṣaṁ śrīr niṣevate*" (Manu. 9. 300), i. e., "in this world, only those persons who perform Action, acquire *śrī* (prosperity)". The same thing is established by our personal experience, and the same is the advice given in the Gītā to Arjuna (Gī. 3. 8). Some persons take the objection to this position that in as much as Action is not necessary for Release, all Action must be given up ultimately, that is, after the acquisition of Knowledge. But, as I am at present considering the question only of pain and happiness, and also as I have not yet gone into the examination of the natures of Action (*karma*) and Release (*mokṣa*), I shall not here answer that exception. I shall explain in detail in the ninth and tenth chapters what Metaphysics, and the Theory of Cause and Effect are, and then in the eleventh chapter, I will prove that even this objection is groundless.

I have so far shown that pain and happiness are two independent and different sufferings; that, as it is impossible to satisfy the desire for happiness by the enjoyment of happiness, we find that in ordinary life the sum total of unhappiness is always greater; that, in order to escape this unhappiness, the most meritorious thing to do is not to totally destroy Thirst or Discontent and at the same time Action itself, but to continue the performance of all Actions without entertaining any hope for the result; that, the happiness of enjoying objects of pleasure is in itself a happiness, which is always insufficient, inconstant, and beastly, and that the true ideal of man, who is endowed with Reason, must be higher than such happiness; that, this true ideal is the happiness of the peace (*śānti*) which results from Self-Realisation; but that, although Metaphysical Happiness is, in this way, superior to Material Happiness, yet, one must possess with it also a proper quantity of worldly objects; and that therefore, we must also make Effort, that is, perform Action, desirelessly. When these conclusions have been firmly established by the Karma-Yoga science, I need not further say that it is wrong to decide questions of Morality by the consideration of the external effects of Actions in the shape of pain and happiness on the basis that Material Happiness is the highest ideal of man—even looking at the question from the point of view of Happiness merely. Because, looking upon a thing which can never by itself reach the state of perfection, as the 'highest' ideal, is misusing the word 'highest' (*parama*), and is as unreasonable as believing that water exists, where there is only a mirage. If one's highest ideal is itself inconstant and incomplete, then, what else, except something inconstant can one acquire, by keeping that ideal before one's eyes? This is what is meant by the words: "*dharmo nityaḥ sukhaduḥkhe tv anitye*", i. e., "morality is immutable; pain and happiness are mutable". There is much difference of opinion among Materialistic philosophers themselves as to how the word 'happiness', in the phrase 'the greatest happiness of the greatest number', is to be understood. Some of these philosophers are of opinion that, in as much as man is very often willing to sacrifice his life for the sake of Veracity, or of his Religion, casting aside all Material Happiness, it is not proper to say that his desire is always to acquire Material Happiness; and they have, therefore, maintained that we must use the word 'benefit' (*hitam*), or the word 'good' (*kalyāṇam*) instead of the word 'happiness' (*sukham*), and change the phrase 'greatest happiness of the greatest number' into the phrase 'greatest good or benefit of the greatest number'. But, even doing so, the objection that the Reason (*buddhi*) of the doer has not been taken into account, as also several other objections apply to this point of view. If one says that Mental Happiness must be taken into account, along with Material Happiness, then, the fundamental theorem that the morality of any particular Action must be decided by its external effects, is falsified, and one, to a certain extent, accepts the Metaphysical aspect of the matter. But, if in this way, you cannot escape accepting the Metaphysical aspect of the matter, then where is the sense of accepting it only half way? Therefore, our philosophy of Karma-Yoga has ultimately come to the conclusion that the doctrines of 'the benefit of everybody', or 'the greatest happiness of the greatest number', or 'the highest development of humanness' or other such external tests or Materialistic methods of determining questions of Morality are inferior tests, and that what is Right Action, and what Wrong Action or Non-Action must be determined by the Metaphysical tests of beatific happiness in the shape of Self-Realisation, and the attendant Pure Reason of the doer. The case is different, of course, of those persons who have sworn not to enter into the philosophy of things beyond the external world, under any circumstances. Otherwise, it only logically follows that one has got to go beyond Mind and Reason, and look upon the permanent benefit of the permanent Ātman as the most predominant factor, even in the Karma-Yoga science. The belief of some persons that when one enters into Vedānta, everything becomes Brahmised (*Brahma-maya*), and the necessity of worldly life cannot satisfactorily be accounted for, is wrong. As the various works on Vedānta, which can ordinarily be read now-a-days have been written principally by followers of the Path of

Renunciation, and as in the Path of Renunciation, worldly life in the shape of Thirst is looked upon as totally insipid, it is true that the science of Karma-Yoga has not been properly expounded in their works. Nay, these writers, who are intolerant of rival cults, have foisted the arguments of the Path of Renunciation on the Karma-Yoga, and attempted to create the belief that Saṁnyāsa (Renunciation) and Karma-Yoga, are not two independent paths for obtaining Release (*mokṣa*), but that Saṁnyāsa is the only correct Path according to the Śāstras. But such a view is incorrect. The Path of Karma-Yoga has been independently followed from times immemorial, side by side with the Path of Renunciation, according to the Vedic religion; and the promulgators of this path have very satisfactorily expounded the science of Karma-Yoga, without departing from the elementary principles of Vedānta. The Bhagavadgītā is a work pertaining to this Path of Karma-Yoga. But, leaving aside the Gītā for the moment, it will be seen that the system of expounding the science of the doable and the not-doable from the Metaphysical point of view was started, even in England itself, by writers like Green, * and long before him, in Germany. However much one may consider the visible world, so long as one has not properly understood who is the HE who sees this visible world, or who performs these Actions, the consideration of the highest duty of man in this world will always remain incomplete from the philosophical point of view. Therefore, the advice of Yājñavalkya: "*ātmā vā are draṣṭavyaḥ śrotavyo mantavyo nididhyāsitavyaḥ* ", is literally applicable to the present case. If even after the examination of the external world, one ultimately comes to basic principles like philanthropy, then, we must say that by such examination, the importance of the science of the Highest Self (*adhyātma*) is not in any way belittled, but that this is one more proof of there being only one Ātman in all created things. If Materialistic philosophers cannot transcend the limitations which they have placed on themselves, there is no help for it. Our philosophers have

* *Prolegomena to Ethics*, Book I; and Kant's *Metaphysics of Morals* (trans. by Abbott, in Kant's *Theory of Ethics*).

extended their sight far beyond that, and have fully justified the science of Karma-Yoga on the basis of Metaphysics. But, in as much as it is necessary to consider another contrary view *(pūrva-pakṣa)*, which deals with the subject of Right Action and Wrong Action or Non-Action, I shall deal with that view before explaining how that justification has been made.

CHAPTER VI.

THE INTUITIONIST SCHOOL AND THE CONSIDERATION OF THE BODY AND THE ĀTMAN.

(ĀDHIDAIVATA-PAKṢA AND KṢETRA-KṢETRAJÑA-VICĀRA).

satyapūtām vaded vācam manaḥpūtam samācaret *

Manu. 6. 46.

There is another method of the consideration of the question of Action, Non-Action, and Wrong Action, besides the Positive or Material method, namely, the Intuitionist (*ādhidaivata*) method. Those who belong to this school say that, when a man decides as to what is Action, Non-Action, or Wrong Action, or as to the doability or non-doability of any particular Action, he never troubles to find out how pain or happiness will result from any particular Action, and whether the sum total of happiness caused by it is greater than that of unhappiness, nor does he enter into the consideration of the Ātman and the Non-Ātman; and many persons do not understand these intricate questions. Nor even does everybody do every particular act for his own happiness. Whatever arguments may be advanced by Materialist philosophers, if one considers minutely for a moment what the state of mind of a person is in determining the righteousness or unrighteousness of any particular Action, it will be seen that inherent and noble mental impulses like pity, kindness, philanthropy etc. impel him to do any particular act on the spot. For instance, when a man sees a beggar, his mind is inspired by the feeling of pity before the thought as to what benefit will be acquired by his Self or by his giving the beggar something in charity enters it, and he gets rid of the matter by giving the beggar whatever he can; in the same way, when her child begins to cry, the mother does not stop to consider

---

* "Speak that which has been purified (become *pūta*) by *satyam* (veracity); and behave in that way which your Mind considers as pure".

how much how many people will be benefitted by her feeding it, but she at once begins to feed it. Therefore, the true foundations of the science of Karma-Yoga are these noble mental impulses. These mental impulses have not been given to us by anybody, but they are Nature-born or inherent, or, in a sense, self-created deities. When a judge is seated in his judicial chair, he is inspired by the deity of Justice when he administers justice, and if he defies this inspiration, he administers injustice. The inherent mental impulses of kindness, pity, philanthropy, gratitude, love for one's duty, courage and other virtues, are deities just like the deity of Justice. Every one by nature knows what the true forms of these deities are. If he defies the inspirations of these deities on account of avarice, hate, or jealousy, or for some such other reason, what can these deities do? Now, it is true that there is sometimes a conflict between these deities themselves; then, we are in doubt as to the inspiration of which deity we should consider as predominant in doing a particular Action; and then it becomes necessary for us to consider some other power besides the deities of Justice, Kindness, etc. in order to satisfy this doubt. But even if, on these occasions, we do not enter into the intricacies of Metaphysical considerations, or of the weighing of pain or happiness, but only consult our Mental Deity (*manodevatā*), that is, our Conscience, that deity immediately shows us which path is the more meritorious one; and therefore, Conscience is superior to all deities. The word 'Conscience' (*manodevatā*) is not to be understood as meaning and including desire, anger, avarice, or the other emotions which inhabit the mind, but as meaning, in the present context, the God-given or inherent power which every one possesses of choosing between good and bad. This very power has got the high-sounding name of "Power of discriminating between the good and the bad" (*sad-asad-viveka-buddhi*), * and if a person, on any occasion of doubt, thinks for a moment quietly and with a peaceful mind, this deity which discriminates between the right and the wrong (*sad-asad-vivecana-devatā*)

* This '*sad-asad-viveka-buddhi*' means 'Conscience' in English; and the '*ādhidaivata-pakṣa*' is the Intuitionist School.

will never fail him. Nay, on such occasions, we say to other persons: "Consult your own mind". What importance to attach to what virtue is ready listed with this sovereign deity which immediately gives you her decision on any matter in accordance with this list, as occasion arises. Suppose, there is an occasion when there is a conflict between the principles of Self-protection and Harmlessness, such as a famine, when we are in doubt as to whether or not to eat uneatable food; then, we should consult our Conscience, and immediately it will come out with the decision: "Eat the uneatable food". Similarly, if there is a conflict between Self-interest, and philanthropy, that situation too must be solved by the help of this Mental Deity. One writer has after peaceful thought stumbled on this list of the relative values of righteous and unrighteous actions prepared by the deity of Conscience, and he has published it in his book. * In this list, the highest place has been given to the feeling of Reverence combined with Humility; and Kindness, Gratitude, Generosity, Affection etc. are given the consecutive lower grades. This writer is of the opinion that when there is a conflict between a virtue of a lower order, and a virtue of a higher order, one must attach higher importance to the virtue of the higher order. According to this writer, there is no other proper way of determining the doability or non-doability or the righteousness or unrighteousness of any Action; because, even if we extend our vision as far as possible, and decide in what the 'greatest good of the greatest number' lies, yet in as much as our discriminating Reason does not possess the power or authority to order us to do that in which the good of the greatest number lies, the question whether or not one should do that which is beneficial to the greatest number ultimately remains unsolved, and again the whole matter remains in abeyance. The decision of the doability or non-doability of an Action arrived at after a far-sighted consideration of pain and happiness

* This writer is James Martineau, and he has published this list in his work entitled *"Types of Ethical Theory"* (Vol. II. p. 266; 3rd Ed.). Martineau calls his school the Idio-psychological School. But I include this school in the Intuitionist School.

will meet the same fate as that of a decision which may have been given by a judge who has not received proper authority from the king. Mere far-sightedness cannot tell a person to do something, or that he must do some particular thing; because, far-sightedness being a human product, it cannot control human beings. On such occasions, there must be some one else having a higher authority than ourselves who gives the command; and this function can be satisfactorily discharged only by this God-given Conscience, which is superior to man, and therefore, in a position to exercise authority over man. As this deity is self-created it is also usual, in ordinary parlance to say: "My Conscience *(manodevatā)* tells me a particular thing". The fact that when a man has committed a sinful action, he is subsequently ashamed of it, and that his inner consciousness bites him, is nothing else but the punishment of this Mental Deity; and that proves the existence of this independent Mental Deity. For otherwise, we cannot, according to this school of thought, explain why our Conscience pricks only ourselves.

The summary given above is of the opinions of the Intuitionist School in the Western countries. In these countries, this body of thought has been principally promulgated by Christian preachers; and in their opinion, this God-given method is superior to, and easier to follow than the purely Materialistic methods for determining the righteousness or unrighteousness of an Action, and is, therefore, the method which should be acted upon. Although in India there was no such independent section of the science of Karma-Yoga in ancient times, yet we come across similar opinions in many places in our ancient treatises. We find in many places in the Mahābhārata that the various mental impulses have been given the forms of deities. I have referred in the foregoing pages to the story of the deities of Morality *(dharmam)*, Prosperity *(śri)* etc. having left the body of Prahlāda and entered the body of Indra. This deity who discriminates between doability and non-doability, or righteousness and unrighteousness is called '*Dharmam*', and there are stories that this deity had manifested himself in the form of a *syena* bird for testing the truthfulness of the King Sibi, and first in the form of a *yakṣa* and later on in the form of a dog for testing Yudhiṣṭhira. Even in the Bhagavadgītā (10. 34), Fame *(kīrti)*, Opulence *(śrī)*, Speech *(vāk)*, Memory *(smṛti)*, Acumen *(medhā)*, Perseverance *(dhṛti)*, and Forgiveness *(kṣamā)* are called deities; and out of these, memory, acumen, perseverance, and forgiveness are qualities of the mind. The Mind itself is a deity, and the worship of it has been prescribed in the Upaniṣads, as being a symbol of the Parabrahman (Tai. 3. 4; Chān. 3. 18). When Manu says: "*manaḥpūtaṁ samācaret*" (6. 46), i. e., "Do what the Mind believes to be pure", he may be said to have intended the Mental Deity by the word '*manas*' (Mind). In ordinary affairs, we say instead: "Do as the Mental Deity (*manodevatā*) pleases. In the Marathi language, the word '*manaḥpūta*' has acquired quite the contrary meaning; and on many occasions, when a person does whatever he likes, he is said to behave '*manaḥpūta*'. But the true meaning of this phrase is that: 'One should do only that which the Mind considers as sacred or pure'. In the fourth chapter of the *Manu-Saṁhitā*, Manu himself has made the meaning clearer by saying:

yat karma kurvato 'sya syāt paritoṣon 'tarātmanaḥ ।
tat prayatnena kurvīta viparītaṁ tu varjayet ॥

(Manu-Saṁh. 4. 161).

that is, "One should perform by efforts that Action by which one's innermost Ātman is satisfied; and one shonld give up whatever is disliked by it". So also, Manu, Yājñavalkya, and the other Smṛti-writers, in mentioning the fundamental rules of practical morality such as the rules of Morality applicable to the four castes, etc. have said:

vedaḥ smṛtiḥ sadācāraḥ svasya ca priyam ātmanaḥ ।
etac caturvidhaṁ prāhuḥ sākṣād dharmasya lakṣaṇam ॥

(Manu. 2. 12).

that is, "the Vedas, the Smṛtis, good behaviour, and the satisfaction of one's Ātman, are the four fundamental elements of righteousness (*dharmam*). The meaning of the words 'the satisfaction of the Ātman' is, 'that which one's Mind looks upon as pure'; and it is quite clear that where the righteousness or unrighteousness of any particular Action could not be decided by consulting the Śrutis, the Smṛtis, and the principles of good behaviour (*sadācāra*), the fourth means of deciding the matter was considered to be its '*manaḥ-pūtatā*', i. e., its 'being considered as pure by the Mind'. In the Mahābhārata, Dhṛtarāṣṭra, after relating the stories of Prahlāda and Indra mentioned in the last Chapter, has said in describing '*śīlam*', that :

yad anyeṣāṁ hitaṁ na syād ātmanaḥ karma pauruṣam ।
apatrapeta vā yena na tat kuryāt kathaṁcana ॥
(Ma. Bhā. Śān. 124. 66).

that is, "That Action of ours which is not beneficial to others, or of which we ourselves would feel ashamed, should not be performed in any case. My readers will notice that by using the expressions 'is not beneficial to others' and 'feel ashamed', this verse has included in the same place both the doctrines of 'the greatest good of the greatest number' and the 'Mental Deity'. Even in the Manu-Smṛti, that Action for having done which or when doing which one feels ashamed, is referred to as '*tāmasa*', and that Action of doing which one does not feel ashamed, and whereby our innermost self (*antarātman*) remains happy, is referred to as '*sāttvika*' (Manu. 12. 35. 37); and these ideas are to be found also in the Buddhistic treatise *Dhammapada* (See Dhammapada, 67 and 68). Kālidāsa says that when there is a doubt as to the doability or non-doability of any Action :

satāṁ hi saṁdehapadeṣu vastuṣu
pramāṇam antaḥkaraṇapravṛttayaḥ ।
(Śākun. 1. 20).

that is, "saintly persons always consider as authoritative the dictates of their own Conscience". Controlling the mental impulses by concentrating the mind on a single object is the province of the Pātañjala Yoga, and as this Yoga-Śāstra has been in vogue in India from very ancient times, it was at no time necessary to teach our people the method of making the mind peaceful and quiet, and doing that which the Mind considered as proper, whenever there was any doubt about any matter. It is stated in the various Smṛtis at the very commencement, that the Ṛṣis who wrote them, used always to define righteousness and unrighteousness after first completely concentrating their minds (Manu. 11); and the method of thus consulting the dictates of Conscience on any matter also seems at first sight extremely easy. But when one minutely considers what is meant by a 'pure mind' from the philosophical point of view, this facility of the matter disappears; and on that account, our philosophers have not based the edifice of Karma-Yoga on it. We must now consider what this philosophical point of view is; but before I do so, I will here explain briefly how the Western Materialistic philosophers have refuted this Intuitionist theory. Because, although the reasons adduced by the Materialists and the Metaphysicians may be different, yet as the result arrived at by both is the same, I shall first deal with the arguments of the Materialists, in order that the importance and the propriety of the arguments of the Metaphysicians should be the better understood by my readers.

As the Intuitionist School has, as mentioned above, given the highest place to Conscience Pure, it is clear that the objection against the Materialistic philosophy or morals, namely, that they do not attach any importance to the Reason of the doer, does not apply to the Intuitionist theory. But when one minutely considers what is to be called the 'Pure Conscience' in the shape of a Mental Deity which discriminates between the Right and the Wrong (*sad-āsad-viveka-buddhiḥ*), it will be seen that other unconquerable difficulties arise with reference to this theory also. Nobody need be told that whatever thing is taken, considering it in all its bearings, and finding out whether or not it is performable or unperformable, doable or not-doable, or whether or not it will be advantageous or pleasant, is a thing which is not done by the nose or the eyes or any other organs, and that there is an independent organ, namely, the Mind, which serves that purpose. Therefore, doability or non-doability, righteousness or unrighteousness are things which must be determined by the Mind, whether you call it an organ or a deity. If that were all that the Intuitionist school said, nobody would find any fault with it. But, Western Intuitionists have gone far beyond that. They say that deciding whether a thing is good or bad (*sat* or *asat*), just or unjust, righteous or unrighteous, is quite different from deciding whether a particular object is heavy or light, white or black, or whether a calculation is correct or incorrect. The Mind can, by logical methods, decide matters which fall within the second category; but the Mind itself is incapable of deciding on the matters mentioned in the first category, and that is a thing which can be done only by the Mental Deity in the shape of the Power of discrimination between good and bad. They explain this by saying that in determining whether a particular calculation is correct or incorrect, we first examine the additions or multiplications involved in it, and then arrive at a decision, that is to say, before determining this question, the Mind has to go through some other actions or activities; but the same is not the case in the matter of the discrimination between good and bad. As soon as we hear that somebody has murdered somebody else, we immediately utter the words: "What a bad thing has been done by him!", and we have not to think about the matter at all. As the decision which we arrive at without any consideration, and the one which we arrive at after consideration, cannot both be said to be the functions of one and the same mental capacity, we must say that Conscience is an independent Mental Deity. As this power or deity is equally awake in the hearts of all human beings, every one looks upon murder as a crime, and nobody has to be taught anything about the matter. This Intuitionist argument is answered by Materialistic philosophers by saying, that from the fact that we can spontaneously arrive at a decision on any matter, we cannot draw the conclusion that such matter must be different from another matter as to which we come to a decision after proper consideration. Doing a thing quickly or slowly is a matter of practice. Take the case of calculations. Merchants quote the rate for the seer immediately on being given the rate for the khandy, by mental calculation. But on that account, their deity of calculation does not become different from the same deity of the best mathematicians. By habit, something becomes so much part and parcel of oneself, that one does it easily and without the slightest consideration. An excellent marksman easily shoots and kills birds on the wing; but no one, on that account, says that there is some independent deity of marksmanship. Not only that, but no one, on that account, considers the science of marksmanship or of calculating the speed of flying birds or other scientific calculations as unnecessary. There is a story told of Napoleon Buonaparte, that as soon as he stood on the battle-field and cast only one glance all round, he could immediately find out the weakest point of the enemy. But, on that account, nobody said that the science of warfare is an independent deity, and that it is in no way connected with other mental faculties. It may be that one man has a greater aptitude for a particular thing than another. But on that account, we do not say that the two have two different kinds of intelligence. Besides, it is not that the decision on questions of doability or non-doability, or of righteousness or unrighteousness is made instantaneously on all occasions. Because, if such were the case, there would never have been any doubt as to whether 'a particular thing ought to be done or ought not to be done'. Not only is such doubt occasionally experienced by every one, but, what is more, the decisions given by different persons as to the doability or non-doability of the same Action are different. If there is only one self-created deity in the form of 'Conscience', why should there be this difference? Therefore, we have to say that a man comes to a decision on any particular matter, according as his mind is evolved or educated. There are many aboriginal tribes who do not consider murder a crime, but even eat human flesh with pleasure! But if we for a moment leave aside the case of uncivilised human beings, yet, according to the customs of different countries, something which is considered objectionable in one country is wholly acceptable in another country. Marrying a second wife when the first one is alive, is considered a crime in England; but nobody thinks much of it in India. Indians would feel ashamed of sitting in an assembly without their turbans on; but in England people consider taking off one's hat as a sign of respect! If it were true that one feels ashamed of a wrong act as a result only of

God-given or inherent Conscience, should not every one feel equally ashamed of the same act? Even marauders consider it disgraceful to draw a sword against a person whose food they have eaten; but, even powerful civilised nations in the West consider it a sign of patriotism to murder people who are subjects of a neighbouring nation!!. If there is only one deity in the shape of Conscience, why should there be this difference? And if one admits different kinds of Conscience, according to civilization or according to the customs of countries, then the self-created immutability of Conscience itself suffers. As man leaves the uncivilised state and is gradually more and more civilised, so also are his Mind and Reason developed; and when in this way, the Reason has developed, man becomes capable of spontaneously conceiving such ideas as he would have been incapable of conceiving in his former uncivilised condition. We may even say that the Reason being developed in this way is a sign of civilisation. Just as a civilised or educated person's not asking for everything which he casts his eyes on is a sign of the control over the organs which has become ingrained in him, so also has the mental faculty of choosing between good and evil gradually grown in mankind, and it has now become so much part of human nature that we give our decision as to the morality of a thing spontaneously and without consideration. If we have to see things which are near or which are far, we have to contract the muscles and tendons of the eyes to a greater or lesser extent, and this is done so quickly that we never realise it; but has any one, on that account, looked upon the consideration of the reasons for this process as useless? In short, the Mind or the Reason of man are the same at all times and with reference to all matters. It is not that we decide between black and white by one kind of Reason and between good and evil by another kind of Reason. The only difference is that the Reason of a particular person may be more developed, whereas the Reason of another person may be uneducated or incompletely developed. Western Materialistic philosophers have thus drawn the conclusion that when we bear in mind this difference, and also take into account our experience that being able to do any particular thing quickly is only a matter of habit or practice, we have no reason for imagining that there is an independent and wonderful power like Conscience in addition to the natural faculties of the Mind.

The ultimate decision of our ancient philosophers on this matter is similar to that of the Western Materialistic philosophers. They admit the principle that it is necessary to consider any particular matter quietly and with a peaceful mind. But they do not accept the position that there is one kind of Reason which decides the question of righteousness and unrighteousness and another kind of Reason which decides whether a particular thing is black or white. The Mind arrives at a correct or incorrect decision according as it has been educated. They, therefore, say that everybody must make an effort to develop his Mind; and they have also given rules explaining what this development is and how it is to be made. But they do not accept the position that the power of discrimination between good and bad (*sad-asad-vivecana-śakti)* is some independent heavenly gift which is different from the ordinary Reason of a man. The question as to how a man acquires knowledge and how the activities of his Mind and Reason are carried on, have been very minutely examined in ancient times. This examination is technically known as "the consideration of the Body and the Ātman" *(kṣetra-kṣetrajña-vicāra)*. '*kṣetra*' means the body and '*kṣetrajña*' means the Ātman. This *kṣetra-kṣetrajña-vicāra* is the foundation of Metaphysics; and as it is impossible to look upon the Power of discrimination between good and bad or any other Mental Deity as higher than the Ātman when once one has properly understood this science of the Body and the Ātman, it becomes perfectly clear how the Intuitionist arguments are insufficient. I shall, therefore, in this place briefly consider the science of the Body (*kṣetra* or Field) and the Ātman (*kṣetrajña)*. Thereby, my readers will be able to properly understand the correct meanings of many of the doctrines of the Bhagavadgītā.

The body of man (*piṇḍa, kṣetra,* or *śarīra*) may be said to be a great factory. As in any factory raw material is first taken in from outside, and then all the material is selected or arranged, and having determined which of the material is useful for the factory and which not, the raw material taken in is manufactured into different articles and sent out, so also are there numerous activities going on every moment in the human body. The first of the means man has for acquiring the knowledge of the various objects in the world made up of the five primordial elements, are his organs. The true or fundamental form of the objects in the world cannot be realised by any one by means of his organs. Materialists say that such form is the same as it appears to our organs; but if tomorrow a human being acquires another new organ, then, from his point of view the qualities of the different objects in the world will be different. Human organs are of two kinds, namely, organs of Action (*karmendriya*) and organs of perception (*jñanendriya*). The hands, the feet, the voice, the anus and the generative organs are the five organs of Action. All the Actions which we perform by means of our body are performed through these five organs. Besides these, there are the five organs of perception, namely, the nose, the eyes, the ears, the tongue and the skin. We perceive colour by the eyes, taste by the tongue, sound by the ears, smell by the nose, and touch by the skin. All the knowledge that we acquire of any external object, is the effect of its colour, taste, sound, smell or touch, and nothing else. For instance, take a piece of gold. It looks yellow, it seems heavy to the touch, and it is elongated on being hammered. These and its other qualities which we perceive by means of our organs, is what is 'gold' in our eyes; and when these qualities are seen to recur in any particular object, then such object becomes an independent physical object named 'gold' in our opinion. Just as there are doors in a factory for taking material in from outside and for sending out the material which is inside, so also, the organs of perception are the doors of the human body for taking material inside and the organs of action are the doors for sending that material out. When the rays of the Sun fall on any object and enter our eyes on being reflected, our Ātman perceives the colour of that object; and when the minute atoms of scent, emanating from that object come and strike our olfactory nerves, we smell it. The functions of the other organs of perception are carried on in the same way; and when the organs perception are functioning in this way, we become aware of the external objects in the world through their medium. But the organs of perception do not themselves acquire the knowledge of the activities which they carry on; and therefore, these organs of perception are not called '*jnātā*' (Knower), but they have been referred to as the portals for taking in material from outside. When external material has come inside through these doors, the dealing with it afterwards is the function of the Mind. For instance, when at noon the clock strikes twelve, it is not the ears which understand what o'clock it is. Just as each stroke falls, aerial vibrations come and strike the ears, and when each of these strokes has in the first place created a distinct effect on the mind, we mentally calculate the sum of all these phenomena and decide what o'clock it is. Even the beasts have got the organs of perception, and as each stroke of the clock falls, it causes an effect on their mind through their ears. But their mind is not sufficiently developed to be able to total up the number of strokes and to understand that it is twelve o'clock. Explaining this in technical language, it is said that although a beast is capable of perceiving individual phenomena by themselves, yet, it is not able to perceive the unity which results from that diversity. In the Bhagavadgitā, this is explained by saying: "*indriyāṇi parāṇy āhuḥ indriyebhyaḥ paraṁ manaḥ*", (Gī. 3. 42), i.e., "the organs are superior to the external objects, and the Mind is superior to all the organs". As has been stated above, if the Mind is not in its proper place, we do not see anything although the eyes may be open, nor do we hear anything though the ears may be open. In short, the external material comes into the factory of the Body through the organs of perception to the clerk called 'Mind', and this clerk subsequently examines that material. We will now consider how this examination is done, and how it becomes necessary to further sub-divide that which we have so far been broadly referring to as the 'Mind', or how one and the same Mind acquires different names according to difference in its functions.

All the impressions which are created on the mind through the organs of perception have first to be placed together in one place and by comparing them with each other, one has first to decide which of them are good and which bad, which acceptable and which objectionable, which harmful and which beneficial; and when this examination has been made, we are induced to do that thing which is good, beneficial, proper, or doable. This is the ordinary course. For instance, when we go into a garden, impressions of the various trees and flowers in it are made on our minds through our organs of perception. But unless our Ātman has acquired the knowledge of which of these flowers have a good smell and which a bad one, we do not get the desire of possessing a particular flower, and consequently perform the Action of plucking it. Therefore, all mental activity falls into the following three broad divisions, namely: (1) having acquired the knowledge of external objects by means of the organs of perception, arranging all these impressions, or carefully classifying them for purposes of comparison, (2) after this classification has been made, critically examining the good or bad qualities of the different objects and deciding which object is acceptable and which not; and (3) when the decision has been made, feeling the desire to acquire the acceptable and reject the unacceptable, and getting ready for appropriate action. It is not that these three functions must take place immediately one after the other, and without there being any interval of time between them. We may in the present feel the desire of acquiring some object which we may have seen in the past; nevertheless we cannot, on that account, say that any one of these three functions is unnecessary. Just as though the Court of Justice is one and the same, the work in it is divided in the following way, namely, the two parties or their respective pleaders first place their respective evidence and witnesses before the Judge, and the Judge gives his decision after considering the evidence on either side, and the Sheriff ultimately carries out the decision which has been given by the Judge, so also are the activities of that clerk whom we have so far broadly referred to as the 'Mind', divided. Out of these activities, the function of considering discriminatingly all the various objects which are perceived, and deciding that a particular thing is of a particular kind (*evameva*) and not of another kind (*nānyathā*), that is to say, the function of a Judge, belongs to the organ called 'Reason' (*buddhiḥ*); and all the mental functions referred to above, except the functions of this faculty of discriminating between good and evil, are carried out by the organ called 'Mind' (*manas*), according to the terminology of both the Vedānta and the Sāṁkhya philosophies (Sāṁ. Kā. 23 and 27). This (minor) Mind, like a pleader, places before the Reason the various ideas that a particular thing is like this (*saṁkalpam*) or is like that (*vikalpam*) etc., for decision; and therefore, it is called an organ which is '*saṁkalpa-vikalpātmakam*', that is, which merely forms ideas without arriving at any decision. The word '*saṁkalpam*' is sometimes made to include also the factor of decision (Chāndogya. 7. 4. 1.). But in this particular place, the word '*saṁkalpam*', has been used to mean and include merely realising, or believing, or taking for granted, or understanding that a particular thing is of a particular kind, or such activities as planning some Action, desiring, thinking, or conceiving, without arriving at any decision (*niścayaḥ*). But the function of the Mind is not exhausted after placing various ideas for decision before the Reason in this way like a pleader. When the Reason has decided on the goodness or badness of any particular act, and has decided what is acceptable, the Mind has also to perform the Registrar's function of bringing about, through the organs of Action, that thing which has been found acceptable, that is to say, of carrying into execution the decisions of Reason; and therefore, the Mind can also be defined in another way. It is true that considering how to carry into execution the decision which has been arrived at by the Reason is in a sense *saṁkalpa-vikalpātmaka*; nevertheless that process has been given the independent name '*vyākaraṇam*', that is, 'development', in the Sanskrit language; all the other mental activities except these are the functions of Reason. The Mind does not discriminate between the various ideas in the mind. Discriminating between them and giving to the Ātman the accurate knowledge of any particular object, or deciding that a particular thing is only of a particular kind after proper classification, or arriving at a definite inference, and deciding as to the doability or non-doability of any particular Action after inferentially determining the relation of Cause and

Effect between two things, are all functions of the Reason and are known in Sanskrit as '*vyavasāyaḥ*' or '*adhyavasāyaḥ*'. Therefore, these two words have been defined in the Mahābhārata in the following way in order to show the difference between the Reason and the (minor) Mind, namely:—

"*vyavasāyātmikā buddhiḥ mano vyākaraṇātmakam*"

(Ma. Bhā. Śān. 251. 11).

that is, "the '*buddhiḥ*' (Reason) is an organ which does the '*vyavasāyaḥ*, that is, which discriminates and arrives at a decision, and the Mind (minor) is an organ which does the *vyākaraṇam*, that is, carries out the development or the further arrangements. In short, the Reason is *vyavasāyātmikā* and the mind is *vyākaraṇātmakam*". Even the Bhagavadgītā contains the words "*vyavasāyātmikā buddhiḥ*" (Gī. 2. 44); and in that place, the word *buddhiḥ* means the organ which discriminates and decides. The *buddhiḥ* is like a sword. Its function is only to cut whatever comes before it or is brought before it. It has no other quality or function (Ma. Bhā. Vana. 181. 26). Planning, desiring, wanting, memory, perseverance, faith, enthusiasm, kindness, interestedness, affection, pity, gratitude, sexual impulses, shame, joy, fear, love, attachment, hate, avarice, arrogance, jealousy, anger etc., are all qualities or faculties of the Mind (Bṛ. 1. 5. 3; Maitryu. 6. 30), and man is prompted to perform any particular act, according to the particular mental impulse which has sprung into the Mind. However reasonable a man may be, and even if he fully understands how poor people suffer, yet, if the feeling of pity is not aroused in his heart, he will never be inspired by the desire to help the poor; or, though he might feel the desire to fight, he will not fight if he is wanting in courage. The Reason only tells us what the result will be of those things which we want to do. But as desire, courage etc., are not the faculties of the Reason, Reason by itself, that is, without the help of the Mind, never inspires the organs to do anything. On the other hand, though the Mind can inspire the organs when under the sway of Anger etc., yet an Action which may have been performed without the discrimination of the Reason and merely by the inspiration of the mental impulses, will not necessarily be morally pure. For instance, if something is given in charity without exercising the Reason and merely under the impulse of the feeling of pity, there is a chance of its having evil effects if the charity is given to an undeserving person. In short, the mental impulses by themselves are blind without the help of Reason. Therefore, in order that any good Action should be performed by a man, there must be a combination of a Reason which is pure, that is to say, such as will arrive at a correct decision between good and bad, a Mind which will act according to the dictates of the Reason, and organs which are subject to the control of Mind. Besides the words '*buddhiḥ*' and '*manas*', the other words '*antaḥkaraṇam*' and '*cittam*' are also in vogue. As the word *antaḥkaraṇam* out of these means the internal (i. e., *antaḥ*) organ (i. e., *karaṇam* or *indriyam*), it usually includes the *manas* (Mind), *buddhiḥ* (Reason), *cittam* (Consciousness) and *ahaṁkāram* (Egoism) etc; and when the Mind first contemplates external objects, it becomes *cittam*, (i. e., Consciousness), (Mā. Bhā. Śān. 274. 17). But, as in ordinary parlance these words are used as being synonymous, there is very often a confusion as to what meaning is intended in which place. In order that such a confusion should not arise, only the two words Mind and Reason, out of the various words mentioned above, are used in scientific terminology in the specific meanings mentioned above. When in this way a differentiation has been made between the Mind and the Reason, the Reason in its capacity of a judge, necessarily becomes superior to the Mind, and the Mind becomes the clerk of the Reason. This is the purport of the following words used in the Gītā, namely, "*manasas tu parā buddhiḥ*", i. e., "the Reason is superior to or beyond the Mind" (Gī. 3. 42). Nevertheless, even this clerk has, as mentioned above, to perform two different functions; the first of these is to properly arrange all the impressions which have come from outside, through the medium of the organs of perception, and to place those impressions before the Reason for decision; and the second one is to carry the order or the message of the Reason to the organs of Action after the Reason has arrived at a decision, and make these organs perform those external Actions which are necessary to be performed for carrying out the decision of the Reason. Just as very often in a shop, the duty of purchasing merchandise for the shop and also the duty of sitting in the shop and selling the goods are both carried out by one and the same clerk, so also is the case with the Mind. Suppose, you see a friend of yours and being inspired with the desire of calling him, you say to him 'hullo!' ; then, let us see what are the various functions which are carried out in your *antaḥkaraṇam.* First, your eyes, that is, the organ of perception, have sent a message to the Reason through the medium of the Mind that your friend is near you, and that knowledge is conveyed through the Reason to your Ātman. Here, the first function, namely, of the acquisition of knowledge, is over. Then the Ātman, through the medium of the Reason decides to call the friend; next, the desire to speak springs into the Mind in order to execute the decision of the Reason, and the Mind causes the word 'hullo!' to be uttered by the organ of Action. In the *Śikṣā-grantha* of Pāṇini, the function of the utterance of words has been described on that basis as follows :—

ātmā buddhyā sametyārthān mano yuṅkte vivakṣayā ।
manaḥ kāyāgnim āhanti sa prerayati mārutam ।
mārutas tūrasi caran mandraṁ janayati svaram ॥

that is, "the Ātman in the first place grasps all things through the medium of the Reason, and creates in the Mind the desire to speak; then the Mind sets in action the bodily heat (*kāyāgni*) which in turn sets the breath in motion; then this breath entering the chest, creates the lowest sound; and this sound ultimately comes out of the mouth in the shape of labial, guttural, or other sounds." The last two lines of the above stanza are also to be found in the Maitryupaniṣad (Maitryu. 7. 11.); and from this it is clear, that this stanza must be older than Pāṇini. * '*kāyāgni*' is known in present-day medical

* Max Müller has said that Maitryupaniṣad must be earlier in point of time than Pāṇini. See Sacred Books of the East Series Vol. XV pp. xlvii—li. This matter has been more fully dealt with by me in the Appendices.

science as 'nerves'. But according to that science, the nerves which bring in the perception of external objects are different from those which carry the message of the Reason to the organs of Action through the medium of the Mind; and therefore, according to Western medical scientists, we must have two kinds of Mind. Our philosophers have not thought that there are two kinds of Mind; they have differentiated between the Reason and the Mind, and have said that the Mind is dual, that is to say, where the organs of Action are concerned it acts according to the organs of Action, and where the organs of perception are concerned, it acts according to those organs. Both these ideas are essentially the same. According to the points of view of both, the Reason is the judge who decides, and the Mind becomes *saṁkalpa-vikalpātmakam*, that is, performs the function of conceiving ideas in relation to the organs of perception, and becomes *vyākaraṇātmakam*, that is, executive, in relation to the organs of Action, that is to say, it becomes the actual provocator of the organs of Action. Nevertheless, in developing (i. e., making the *vyākaraṇam* of) anything, the Mind has very often to conceive ideas (that is, make *saṁkalpam* and *vikalpam*) in order to see in what way the dictates of the Reason can be carried out. Therefore, in defining the Mind, it is usual to say simply "*saṁkalpa-vikalpātmakaṁ manaḥ*"; but, it must not be forgotten, that even according to that definition, both kinds of functions of the Mind are included.

The definition of Reason given by me above, namely, that it is the organ which discerns, is intended only for the purpose of minute scientific discussions. But, these scientific meanings of words are always fixed subsequently. It is, therefore, necessary to consider here also the practical meanings which the word '*buddhiḥ*' had acquired before this scientific meaning had been fixed. We cannot acquire the knowledge of anything unless it has been identified by the Pure Reason (*vyavasāyātmikā buddhiḥ*); and unless we have acquired the knowledge of that object, we do not conceive the intention or the desire of obtaining it. Therefore, just as in ordinary parlance, the word 'mango' is applied both to the mango-tree and the mango-fruit, so also ordinary people very often use ths single word '*buddhiḥ*' (Reason) for signifying the Pure Reason (*vyavasāyātmikā buddhiḥ*), as also the fruits of that Reason in the shape of Desire etc. For instance, when we say that the *buddhiḥ* of a particular person is evil, we intend to say that his 'Desire' is evil. As 'Intention' or 'Desire' are both faculties of the Mind from the scientific point of view, it is not correct to refer to them by the word '*buddhiḥ*'. But, before the word '*buddhiḥ*' had been scientifically analysed, the word '*buddhiḥ*' had begun to be used in ordinary parlance in the two meanings of (i) the organ which discerns and (ii) the Intention or Desire which subsequently arises in the human mind as a result of the functioning of that organ. Therefore, just as the additional word 'tree' or 'fruit' is used when it is intended to show the two different meanings of the word 'mango', so also, when it is necessary to differentiate between the two meanings of the word '*buddhiḥ*', the '*buddhiḥ*' which discriminates, that is to say, the technical '*buddhiḥ*' is referred to by qualifying it by the adjective '*vyavasāyātmikā*' and Desire is referred to as simply '*buddhiḥ*' or at most as '*vāsanātmikā buddhiḥ*'. In the Gītā the word '*buddhiḥ*' has been used in both the above meanings (Gī. 2. 41, 44, 49 and 3. 42); and in order to properly understand the exposition of the Karma-Yoga, both these meanings of the word '*buddhiḥ*' have to be continually kept before the mind. When man begins to do any particular act, he first considers whether it is good or bad, doable or not-doable etc., by means of his Pure Reason (*vyavasāyātmikā buddhiḥ*), and when the Desire or Intention (that is, the *vāsanātmikā buddhiḥ*) of doing that act enters his mind, he becomes ready to perform the act. This is the order of the mental functions. When that *buddhiḥ* out of the two (namely the *vyavasāyātmikā*) which has to decide between the doability and the non-doability of any particular Action is functioning properly, the Mind is not polluted by improper Desires (*buddhiḥ*) entering it. Therefore, the first theorem of the Karma-Yoga preached in the Gītā is that the *vyavasāyātmikā buddhiḥ* (Pure Reason) must be made pure and steady (Gī. 2. 41). Not only the Gītā, but also Kant has differentiated between two kinds of *buddhiḥ* and he has described the functions of the *vyavasāyātmikā buddhiḥ* (Pure Reason) and of the *vyavahārikā* or *vāsanātmikā buddhiḥ* (Practical Reason) in two different books.* Really speaking, steadying the Pure Reason is the subject-matter of the Pātañjala Yoga-Śāstra, and not of the Karma-Yoga Śāstra. But in considering any particular act, one must, according to the doctrine of the Gītā, first consider the desire or the *vāsanātmikā buddhiḥ* of the doer of the act, before one looks at the effect of the act (Gī. 2. 49); and in the same way when one considers the question of Desires it will be seen that the man whose pure Reason has not become steady and pure, conceives different shades of desire in his mind, and therefore, it is not certain that these desires will be always pure or holy (Gī. 2. 41). And if the desires themselves are not pure, how will the resulting Action be pure? Therefore, one has to consider in detail, even in the science of Karma-Yoga, the methods or means which have to be employed to keep the *vyavasāyātmikā buddhiḥ* pure, and therefore, the Pātañjala Yoga has been described in the sixth chapter of the Bhagvadgītā as one of the means by which the *vyavasāyātmikā buddhiḥ* can be made pure. But some doctrinal commentators have disregarded this fact and drawn the inference that the Gītā supports and preaches the Pātañjala Yoga! From this it will be clear to my readers how necessary it is to bear in mind the above-mentioned two meanings of the word '*buddhiḥ*' and their mutual relation.

I have in this way explained what the respective functions of the Mind and the Reason are, after explaining the internal working of the human mind, and I have also mentioned the other meanings of the word '*buddhiḥ*'. Having in this way differentiated between the Mind and the '*vyavasāyātmikā buddhiḥ*' (Pure Reason), let us see how this aspect affects the question of the deity which discerns between good and evil (*sad-asad-viveka-devatā*). As the only purpose which this deity serves is to choose between good and evil, it cannot be included in the (minor) Mind; and as there is only one

* Kant calls the *vyavasāyātmikā buddhiḥ* Pure Reason; and the *vāsanātmikā buddhiḥ* Practical Reason; and he has dealt with these two kinds of Reason in two separate books.

'*vyavasāyātmikā buddhiḥ*' (Pure Reason) which considers all matters and comes to a decision on them, we cannot give an independent place for the *sad-asad-vivecana śakti* (power of discriminating between good and evil). There may be numerous matters about which one has to think, discriminate, and come to a conclusion. In commerce, war, civil or criminal legal proceedings, money-lending, agriculture, and other trades, there arise any number of occasions on which one has to discriminate. But, on that account, the *vyavasāyātmikā buddhiḥ* in each case does not become different. The function of discrimination is common to all these cases; and therefore, the *buddhiḥ* (Reason) which makes that discrimination or decision must also be one only. But in as much as the *buddhiḥ* is a bodily faculty (*śārira-dharma*) just like the Mind, it can be *sāttviki*, *rājasi*, or *tāmasi* according to previous Actions, hereditary impressions, or education or for other reasons; and therefore, a thing which might be acceptable to the *buddhiḥ* of one person may be looked upon as unacceptable to the *buddhiḥ* of another person. But on that account, we cannot say that the organ of *buddhiḥ* is different in each case. Take for instance, the case of the eye. Some people have squint eyes, while others have half-closed eyes, and others one eye only, and some have dim vision, while others have a clear vision. But, on that account, we do not say that the eye is a different organ in each case, but say that the organ is one and the same. The same argument must be applied to the case of the *buddhiḥ*. That same *buddhiḥ* which differentiates between rice and wheat, or between a stone and a diamond, or which distinguishes between black and white, or sweet and bitter, also discriminates between what is to be feared and what not, what is good and what evil, what is profitable and what disadvantageous, what is righteous and what unrighteous, or what doable and what not-doable, and comes to a final decision in the matter. However much we may glorify it in ordinary parlance by calling it a 'Mental Deity' yet from the philosophical point of view, it is one and the same *vyavasāyātmikā buddhiḥ* (pure Reason). That is why in the 18th Chapter of the Gītā, one and the same *buddhiḥ* has been divided into the three kinds of *sāttvikī*, *rājasī*, and *tāmasi* and the Blessed Lord first says to Arjuna :—

pravṛttiṁ ca nivṛttiṁ ca kāryākārye bhayābhaye |
bandhaṁ mokṣaṁ ca yā vetti buddhiḥ sā Pārtha sāttvikī ||
(Gī. 18. 30)

that is, "that *buddhiḥ* which (properly) understands which Action should be begun and which not, which is proper to be performed and which not, what should be feared and what not, what leads to bondage and what to Release (*mokṣa*), is the *sāttvikī buddhiḥ* ";

and then He goes on to say :—

yayā dharmam adharmaṁ ca kāryaṁ cākāryam eva ca |
ayathāvat prajānāti buddhiḥ sā Pārtha rājasī ||
(Gī. 18. 31)

that is, "that *buddhiḥ* which does not make a proper discrimination between the *dharmam* (righteous) and the *adharmam* (unrighteous), or between the doable and the not-doable, that *buddhiḥ* is *rājasī* ";

and He lastly says :—

adharmaṁ dharmam iti yā manyate tamasāvṛtā |
sarvārthān viparītāṁś ca buddhiḥ sā Pārtha tāmasī ||
(Gī. 18. 32)

that is, "that *buddhiḥ* which looks upon that as righteous (*dharmam*) which is unrighteous (*adharmam*), that is to say, which gives a totally perverse, that is, contrary verdict on all matters is the *tāmasī buddhiḥ*". From this explanation, it will be clear that the theory that there is an independent and distinct deity of which the function is *sad-asad-vivekaḥ*, (i. e., discrimination between good and evil) is not accepted by the Gītā. That does not mean that there can never exist a *buddhiḥ* (Reason) which will always choose the right thing. What is meant is that the *buddhiḥ* is one and the same, but the *sāttvika* quality of choosing only the right thing is acquired by it by previous impressions, or by education, or by control of the organs, or by the nature of the food which a man eats etc., and in the absence of such factors as previous impressions etc., that same *buddhiḥ* becomes *rājasī or tāmasī*, not only in the matter of the discrimination between the doable and the not-doable but also in all other matters. Such is the import of the above stanzas. The facts of the difference between the *buddhiḥ* of a thief and that of an honest man, or of persons belonging to different countries is explained by this theory in a satisfactory way, in which it cannot be explained by looking upon the Power of discrimination between good and evil (*sad-asad-vivecana-śakti*) as an independent deity. Making one's *buddhiḥ, sāttvikī*, is what one oneself can do; and it cannot be done without the control of the organs. So long as the *vyavasāyātmikā buddhiḥ* acts only according to the dictates of the organs, without discriminating between or examining what promotes one's true benefit, it cannot be called Pure (*śuddha*); therefore, one must not allow the *buddhiḥ* to become the slave of the Mind and the organs, but one must on the other hand arrange it so that the Mind and the organs are under its control. This principle has been enunciated in numerous places in the Bhagavadgītā (Gī. 2. 67, 68; 3. 7, 41; 6. 24, 26) and, on that account, the body has been compared to a chariot in the Kaṭhopaniṣad, and it is metaphorically stated that in order that the horses in the shape of the organs which pull that chariot should be properly guided in the path of the enjoyment of objects of pleasure, the charioteer in the shape of the *vyavasāyātmikā buddhiḥ* has to courageously keep taut and steady the reins in the shape of the Mind (Kaṭha. 3. 3. 9); and in the Mahābhārata also, the same simile has been adopted in two or three places with some slight difference (Ma. Bhā. Vana 210. 25; Strī. 7. 13; Aśva. 51. 5). This simile is so proper for describing the function of the control of the organs, that the famous greek Philosopher Plato has in his book (*Phoedrus*. 246) made use of the same illustration in describing the control of the organs. This illustration does not appear literally in the Bhagavadgītā. Yet, the description of the control of the organs in the above-mentioned stanzas has been made keeping this illustration in mind, as cannot but be noticed by anybody who keeps in sight the previous and posterior context of this subject-matter. Ordinarily, that is, when it is not necessary to make subtle scientific distinctions, this is known as '*manonigraha*' (control of the Mind); but when, as mentioned above, a distinction is made between the *manas* (Mind) and the *buddhiḥ* (Reason), the function of control falls to the share, not of the Mind, but of the pure (*vyavasāyātmikā*) Reason. In order this *vyavasāyātmikā buddhiḥ* should become pure, the principle that there is only one Ātman in all human beings, must be deeply impressed on the mind by realising the true nature of the Parameśvara whether by the mental absorption (*samādhi*) taught in the Pātañjala Yoga, or by Devotion or by Knowledge (*jñāna*) or by Meditation (*dhyāna*). This is what is known as Self-devoted (*ātma-niṣṭha*) *buddhiḥ*. When the *vyavasāyātmikā buddhiḥ* has in this way become Self-devoted (*ātmaniṣṭha*), and the Mind and the organs have learnt to act according to its directions as a result of mental control, Desire, Intention, or other mental functions (*manodharma*) or the *vāsanātmikā buddhiḥ* (Practical Reason), naturally become pure and chaste, and the bodily organs naturally tend towards *sāttvika* actions. From the Metaphysical point of view, this is the foundation of all good actions, that is to say, the esoteric teaching (*rahasya*) of the science of Proper Action (Karma-Yoga).

My readers will now have realised why our philosophers have not accepted Conscience as an independent deity, in addition to the ordinary functions of the Mind and the Reason. From their point of view, there is no objection to looking upon the Mind or the Reason as deities by way of glorification; but they have come to the conclusion that considering the matter scientifically, there is no third element like Conscience which is distinct from and in addition to the two things which we call *manas* (mind), and *buddhiḥ* (Reason) and which is inherent. We now clearly see the propriety of the word *satām* having been used in the phrase '*satām hi saṁdeha padeṣu*' etc. Those whose minds are pure and Self-devoted (*ātmaniṣṭha*), need not at any time be afraid of consulting their Conscience (*antaḥkaraṇa*). We may even say that they should purify their Mind as much as possible before performing any Action, and consult their Conscience. But, there is no sense in dishonest people saying: "We do the same thing", because, the Conscience of both is not the same, and whereas the Conscience of saints is *sāttvika*, that of thieves is *tāmasa*. In short, that which the Intuitionist School refers to as 'the Deity which discerns between Good and Evil' (the *sad-asad-viveka-devatā*), is seen not to be an independent deity when the matter is considered from the philosophical point of view, but to be only the Self-devoted and the *sāttvika* form of the *vyavasāyātmikā buddhiḥ*. This is the theory of our philosophers, and when this theory is accepted, the Intuitionist point of view naturally falls to the ground.

When we have thus seen that the Materialistic aspect is one-sided and insufficient, and also that the easy device found out by the Intuitionist school is ineffective, it becomes necessary for us to see whether or not there is some other way for justifying the doctrine of Karma-Yoga. This way is the Metaphysical aspect of the matter; because, when we have once come to the conclusion that there is no such independent and self-created (*svayambhū*) deity like the *sad-asad-viveka-buddhiḥ* (Conscience), notwithstanding the fact that the Reason is superior to external Action, it becomes necessary to consider, even in the science of Karma-Yoga, how one can keep one's Reason pure in order that one should be able to perform pure Action, what is meant by Pure Reason, and how the Reason can be made pure; and the consideration of these questions cannot be complete unless one leaves aside the Material sciences which deal only with the external physical world, and enters into Metaphysics. Our philosophers have laid down the ultimate doctrine, in this matter, that the Reason which has not fully realised the true and all-pervading nature of the Parameśvara, is not pure; and the science of the Highest Self (*adhyātma*) has been expounded in the Gītā solely in order to explain what this Self-devoted Reason (*ātmaniṣṭha buddhiḥ*) is. But, disregarding this anterior and posterior context, some doctrinal commentators on the Gītā have laid down the conclusion that Vedānta is the principal subject-matter of exposition in the Gītā. It will be shown later on exhaustively that this conclusion arrived at by these commentators as to the subject-matter expounded in the Gītā, is not correct. I have for the time being only to show how it is necessary to consider the question of the Ātman when one wishes to find out how the

Reason is to be purified. This question of the Ātman has to be considered from two points of view :—(1) the first method of exposition is to examine one's own body, (*piṇḍaḥ*, *kṣetra*, or *śarīram*), as also the activities of one's Mind, and to explain how as a result of such examination, one has to admit the existence of the Ātman in the shape of a *kṣetrajña*, or an owner of the Body (Gī. Chap. 13). This is known as the *śārīraka-vicāra* or the KṢETRA-KṢETRAJÑA-VICĀRA (the Consideration of the Body and the Ātman); and that is why the Vedānta-Sūtras are known as *śārīraka* (dealing with the Body) *sūtras*. When in this way we have examined our Body and our Mind, we have next to consider (2) whether the elementary principle which is arrived at by such examination, and the principle which is arrived at by the examination of the *brahmāṇḍam* or the visible world around us, are the same or are different. The examination of the world made in this way is known as the KṢARĀKṢARA-VICĀRA or the VYAKTĀVYAKTA-VICĀRA (the consideration of the Mutable and the Immutable, or the consideration of the Perceptible and the Imperceptible). The '*kṣara*' or '*vyakta*' is the name of all the mutable objects in the world, and *akṣara* or *avyakta* is the name of the essential and eternal element in the mutable objects in this creation (Gī. 8. 21; 15. 16). The fundamental Element which we discover by further examining these two elementary principles arrived at by the consideration of the Body and the Ātman and of the Mutable and the Immutable, and which is the Element from which both these elements have been evolved, and which is beyond (*para*) both of them, and is the Root Element of everything, is called the Absolute Self (*Paramātman*) or the *Puruṣottamaḥ* (Gī. 8. 20). All these ideas are to be found in the Bhagavadgītā, and the science of Proper Action has been expounded in it by showing how the *buddhiḥ* is ultimately purified by the Realisation (*jñānam*) of this Element in the shape of the Paramātman, which is the Root Cause of everything. If, therefore, we have to understand this method of exposition, we must also follow the path which has been followed in the Gītā. Out of these two subject-matters, the knowledge of the *brahmāṇḍam* or the consideration of the Mutable and the Immutable (*kṣarākṣara*) will be dealt with in the next chapter. I shall now complete the science of the *piṇḍa*, or the consideration of the Body and the Ātman which I had commenced in this chapter in order to explain the true nature of the Conscience, and which has remained incomplete.

I have finished my exposition of the gross Body made up of the five primordial elements, the five organs of Action, the five organs of Perception, the five objects of these five organs of Perception in the shape of sound, touch, colour, taste, and smell, the Mind which is the conceiver of ideas (*saṁkalpa-vikalpa*), and the Pure Reason (*vyavasāyātmikā buddhiḥ*). But that does not exhaust the consideration of the Body. The Mind and the Reason are the means or the organs for thought. If the gross Body does not possess movement (*cetanā*) in the form of Vitality (*prāṇaḥ*) in addition to these, it will be just the same whether the Mind and the Reason exist or not. Therefore, it is necessary to include one more element in the Body in addition to these other things, namely, Movement (*cetanā*). The word '*cetanā*', is sometimes also used as meaning the same thing as '*caitanyam*' (Consciousness). But one must bear in mind that the word *cetanā* has not been used in the sense of *caitanyam* in the present context. '*cetana*' here means the movement, activity, or the vital motion of the Life forces seen in the gross Body. That *cicchaktiḥ* (Power of Consciousness) by means of which movement or activity is created even in Gross Matter, is known as *caitanyam*; and we have now to consider what that Power is. That factor which gives rise to the distinction between "mine", and "other's" which is to be seen in the Body in addition to its Vital activity or Movement, is a different quality altogether; because, in as much as the Reason is only an organ which comes to a decision after proper consideration, Individuation (*ahaṁkāraḥ*), which is at the root of the distinction between one's and another's, must be looked upon as something different from Reason. Like and dislike, pain and happiness, and other correlative couplets (*dvandvam*) are the properties of the Mind. But as the Nyāya school looks upon these as properties of the Ātman, Vedānta philosophy includes them among the properties of the Mind in order to clear that misunderstanding. In the same way, that fundamental element in the shape of Matter (*prakṛti*), from which the five primordial elements have sprung, is also included in the Body (Gī. 13. 5, 6). That Power by which all these elements are controlled or kept steady, is again a different power (Gī. 18. 33), and it is called '*dhṛti*' (co-hesion). That amalgamated product which results from the combination of all these things is scientifically called the '*savikāra śarīra*' (activated Body), or '*kṣetra*'; and this is what we, in ordinary parlance, call the activated (*savikāra*) human body, or the *piṇḍa*. I have defined the word '*kṣetra*' in this way, consistently with the Gītā. But in mentioning the qualities Desire, Hate etc., this definition is sometimes more or less departed from. For instance, in the conversation between Janaka and Sulabhā, in the Śānti-parva (Śān. 320), the five organs of Action have not been mentioned in the definition of the Body, but instead of them the six qualities of Time-feeling (*kāla*), Realisation of Good and Evil (*sad-asad-bhāvaḥ*), Method (*vidhiḥ*), Vitality (*śukram*), and Strength (*bala*) have been mentioned. According to this classification, the five organs of Action have to be included in the five primordial elements, whereas according to the classification adopted in the Gītā, we are to include Time in the Ether (*ākāśam*), and Method, Vitality, Strength etc., in the five primordial elements or in Matter. Whatever may be the case, the word '*kṣetra*' conveys only one meaning to everybody. That collection of mental and bodily elements or qualities in the shape of *prāṇaḥ* (Life force), which has specific activities (*viśiṣṭa-cetanā*), is known as '*kṣetra*'. As the word '*śarīra*' is also applied to dead bodies, the different word '*kṣetra*' has been used in this particular place. '*kṣetra*' originally means 'field', but in the present context, it has been used metaphorically as meaning the 'activated (*savikāra*) and living (*sajīva*) human body'. That which has been referred to by me above as a great factory is this '*kṣetra*'. The organs of Perception, and the organs of Action, are the portals of this factory for taking in material from outside and for sending out the manufactured products respectively and, the Mind, the Reason, Individuation (*ahaṁkāra*), and Activity (*cetanā*) are the workmen in this factory; and all the functions carried on or caused to be carried on by these workmen, are referred to as the activities (*vyāpārāḥ*), feelings (*vikārāḥ*), or properties (*dharmāḥ*) of this Body.

When in this way, the meaning of the word '*kṣetra*' has been defined, the next question which naturally arises is, to whom does this *kṣetra* or field belong, is there or is there not some owner for this factory? Although the word 'Ātman' is very often used in the meaning of 'Mind' or 'Conscience' or 'one's Self', yet, its principal meaning is 'the owner of the Body (*kṣetrajña*)'. Whatever functions are performed by man, and whether they are mental or bodily, are carried on by his internal organs such as *buddhiḥ* etc., his organs of Perception such as the eyes etc., and his organs of Action, such as hands, feet, etc. In the whole of this group, the Mind and the Reason are the most superior. But although they may, in this way, be superior to the other organs, yet they are both fundamentally the manifestations (*vikārāḥ*) of Matter (*prakṛti*) or of the gross Body, just like the other organs. (See the next chapter.) Therefore, although the Mind and the Reason may be the highest of all the organs, yet they cannot do anything beyond their particular functions, and it is not possible that they should be able to do anything else. It is true that the Mind thinks and the Reason decides. But, knowing this, we do not arrive at a conclusion as to for whom the Mind and the Reason perform these functions, or as to who performs that synthesis which is necessary for obtaining a synthetic knowledge of the diverse activities carried on by the Mind and the Reason on various occasions, or as to how all the organs subsequently receive the directions to perform their various functions consistently with that synthesis. It cannot be said that all this is done by the gross Body of man. Because, when '*cetanā*' or activity leaves this gross Body, this gross Body is unable to perform these functions although it remains behind; and as the component parts of the gross Body, namely, the flesh, the muscles, etc., are the result of food, and these are continually worn out and continually re-formed, it cannot be said that the feeling of sameness by which a person realises, that "I", who saw a particular thing yesterday, am the same as the 'I' who see a different thing to-day, is the property of the continually changing gross Body. If, however, one leaves aside the gross Body, and says that *cetanā* (Activity) is the owner of the body, then, in deep sleep, one does not continue to possess the 'I' feeling although such activities or *cetanā* as breathing or blood-circulation are going on. (Bṛ. 1. 1. 15–18). It, therefore, follows that Activity or the functioning of Life forces, is a specific quality which has been acquired by the gross Body, and is not the controlling factor, owner or power which synthesizes all the activities of the organs (Kaṭha. 5. 5). The possessive case adjectival forms 'mine' or 'another's' prove to us the existence of the quality of Individuation (*ahaṁkāraḥ*). But by knowing that, we do not come to a conclusion as to who this '*aham*' or 'I' is. If you say, that this 'I' is a pure illusion, then the experience of everybody is just the contrary; and imagining something which is inconsistent with this personal experience of everybody, would place one in the position described by Śrī Samartha Rāmadāsa as: "saying something which is inconsistent with experience is wholly tiresome; it is as useless as opening one's mouth wide and crying" (Dāsa. 9. 5. 15); and even if we do this, the fact of the synthesis of the activities of the organs is not satisfactorily explained. Some go so far as to say that there is no such individual thing as 'I' but that the name 'I' should be given to the conglomeration or the fusion of all those elements, such as, the Mind, Reason, Activity, gross Body etc., which are included in the word '*kṣetra*'. But we see by our own eyes, that by merely piling a piece of wood on another piece of wood, we cannot make a box; nor is motion created in a watch by merely putting together all its various wheels. We cannot, therefore, say that activity arises by mere juxta-position. Nobody need be told that the various activities of the *kṣetra* are not purely foolish activities and that there is some specific intention or object in them. Who is it that gives this direction to the various workmen, such as, *buddhiḥ* etc., in the factory of the Body? Juxta-position (*saṁghātaḥ*) means merely putting together. Although several things may be put together, it is necessary to thread them together in order that they should form one whole. Otherwise, they will become disorganised at any moment. We have now to see what this thread is. It is not that the Gītā does not accept the principle of conglomeration *(saṁghātaḥ)*; but that is looked upon as part of the *kṣetra* (Gī. 13. 6). We do not thereby get an idea as to who the *kṣetrajña* or the owner of the Body is. Some persons think, that conglomeration gives rise to some new quality. But this opinion itself is not correct; because, philosophers have after mature consideration come to the conclusion that that which was not in existence before, in some form or other, cannot come into existence anew (Gī. 2. 16). But even if we keep this doctrine aside for a moment, the next question which naturally springs up is why should we not look upon the new quality which arises in the conglomeration, as the owner of the Body? To this, some Materialist philosophers reply, that a substance cannot be different from its qualities, and that the qualities want some superintendence *(adhiṣṭhānam)*, and therefore, instead of looking upon the property acquired by the Aggregate as the owner of the Body, we look upon the Aggregate itself as such owner. Very well; then why do you not say 'wood' instead of 'fire', or 'cloud' instead of 'electricity', or 'the earth' instead of 'the gravity of the earth' in ordinary parlance? If it is not disputed that there must be in existence some Power which is distinct from the Mind and the Reason in order that all the activities of the Body should be carried on systematically and according to some proper arrangement, then can we, because the seat of that Power is still unknown to us, or because we cannot properly explain the full nature of that Power or of that seat, say that that Power does not exist at all? No person can sit on his own shoulders; in the same way, it is absurd to say that an Aggregate *(saṁghātaḥ)* gives to itself the knowledge of itself. Therefore, we come to the emphatic conclusion even from the logical point of view, that THAT THING for the enjoyment or the benefit of which, the various functions of the Aggregate of the bodily organs etc. are carried on, must be something which is quite distinct from the Aggregate itself. It is true that this Element which is distinct from the Aggregate, is an element which cannot become an object of perception *(jñeya)* or become visible to itself like other objects in the creation, since it is self-enlightened. But, on that account, the fact of its existence cannot come into question; because, there is no rule that all objects must fall into the single category of the 'perceivable' *(jñeya)*. All objects fall into two categories, namely, the '*jñātā*' and the '*jñeya*', i. e., the Perceiver, and That which is perceived by the Perceiver, and if some thing does not fall into the second category, it can come into the first category and its existence is as fully established as the existence of the Perceivable. Nay, we may go further and say that in as much as the Ātman, which is beyond the Aggregate *(saṁghāta)* is itself a Knower, there is no wonder that it does not become the subject-matter of the knowledge which it acquires; and therefore, Yājñavalkya has said in the Bṛhadāraṇyakopaniṣad, that "*vijñātāram are kena vijānīyāt*", i. e., "Oh! how can there be some one else, who can know That which knows everything?" (Br. 2. 4. 14). Therefore, one has to come to the ultimate conclusion, that there exists in this activated living Body some comprehensive and potent Power which is more powerful and more comprehensive than the various dependent and and one-sided workmen in the Body who work in grades rising from organs like the hands and feet to Life, Activity, Mind and Reason; that this Power remains aloof from all of them, and synthesizes the activities of all of them and fixes for them the direction in which they are to act, and is an ever-awake witness of all their activities. This doctrine has been accepted both by the Sāṁkhya and Vedānta philosophies, and the modern German philosopher Kant has shown by minutely examining all the activities of Reason that this is the doctrine which one arrives at. The Mind, the Reason, Individuation or Activity are all qualities or component parts of the Body, that is, of the '*kṣetra*'. The inspirer of these components is different from them, independent of them, and beyond them. "*yo buddheḥ paratas tu saḥ*" (Gī. 3. 42), i. e., "It is beyond the grasp of the Reason". This is what is known in the Sāṁkhya philosophy as '*puruṣa*', and in Vedānta philosophy as '*kṣetrajña*', that is to say, the Ātman which knows or controls the Body; and the actual experience which every one has of the feeling that 'I am', is the most excellent proof of the existence of this Knower of the Body (Ve-Sū. Śāṁ. Bhā. 3. 3. 53, 54). Not only does nobody think that 'I am not', but even if a person by his mouth utters the words: 'I am not', he thereby inferentially acknowledges the existence of the Ātman or the 'I' which is the subject of the predicate 'am not'. The Vedānta philosophy has been propounded only in order to explain as clearly as possible the fundamental, pure, and qualityless form of this *kṣetrajña* or Ātman, which manifests itself in this way in the body in the individuated and qualified form 'I' (Gī. 13. 4); nevertheless this conclusion is not arrived at by merely considering the Body, that is to say, the *kṣetra*. I have stated before that we have to see what can be ascertained by considering the Cosmos (*brahmāṇḍam*) that is to say, the external world, in addition to consideration of the Body and the Ātman. This consideration of the Cosmos is known as '*kṣarākṣara-vicāra*'. By considering the Body and the Ātman, we come to know the fundamental element (*kṣetrajña* or Ātman) which exists in the *kṣetra* (the Body, or the *piṇḍa*) and by considering the Mutable and the Immutable (*kṣarākṣara*), we understand the fundamental element in the Cosmos (*brahmāṇḍa*), that is, in the external creation. When in this way, the fundamental elements of the Body (*piṇḍa*) and of the Cosmos (*brahmāṇḍa*) have been definitely and severally fixed, Vedānta philosophy, after further consideration comes to the conclusion that both these are uniform or one and the same,—or that WHATEVER IS IN THE BODY (PIṆḌA), IS ALSO IN THE COSMOS (BRAHMĀṆḌAM).* This is the ultimate truth of the moveable and the

---

* The classification made in our philosophy of *kṣarākṣara-vicāra* and *kṣetra kṣetrajña-vicāra* was not known to Green. Yet the exposition of Metaphysics made by him in the commencement of his book called *Prolegomena to Ethics*, has been made by him in a twofold way, namely, regarding the 'Spiritual Principle in Nature' and the 'Spiritual Principle in Man'; and later on, he has shown the identity between the two. The *kṣetra-kṣetrajña-vicāra* includes such mental philosophies as Psychology etc., and the *kṣarākṣara-vicāra* includes such sciences as Physics, Metaphysics etc. and even Western philosophers have accepted the position that the nature of the Ātman has to be arrived at, after taking into consideration all these things.

immoveable Cosmos. When we realise that this kind of examination has been made even in the Western countries, and that the doctrines advanced by Western philosophers like Kant etc. are very much akin to the doctrines of Vedānta philosophy, we cannot but feel a wonder about the supermanly mental powers of those persons, who laid down these doctrines of Vedānta by mere introspection, in an age when the Material sciences were not so advanced as they are in the present day; but we must not stop with feeling wonder about this matter, —we must feel proud of it.

CHAPTER VII.

THE KĀPILA SĀṀKHYA PHILOSOPHY OR THE CONSIDERATION OF THE MUTABLE AND THE IMMUTABLE.

(KĀPILA SĀṀKHYA-ŚĀSTRA OR KṢARĀKṢARA-VICĀRA).

prakṛtiṁ puruṣaṁ caiva viddhyanādī ubhāv api *

Gītā. 13. 19.

I have stated in the last chapter, that simultaneously with the consideration of the Body and the Lord or Superintendent of the Body—the *kṣetra* and the *kṣetrajña*—one must also consider the visible world and the fundamental principle in it—the '*kṣara*' (mutable) and the '*akṣara*' (immutable)—and then go on to the determination of the nature of the Ātman. There are three systems of thought which scientifically consider the mutable and the immutable world. The first of these is the Nyāya school and the second one is the Kāpila Sāṁkhya school. But the Vedānta philosophy has expounded the form of the Brahman in a third way altogether, after proving that the propositions laid down by both of those systems of thought are incomplete. Therefore, before considering the arguments advanced in the Vedānta philosophy, it is necessary for us to see what the ideas of the Nyāya school and of the Sāṁkhya school are. In the Vedānta-Sūtras of Bādarāyaṇācārya, the same method has been adopted, and the opinions of the Nyāya school and of the Sāṁkhya school have been refuted in the second chapter. Although the whole of this subject-matter cannot be given here, yet, I have in this and the next chapter given as much information about it as is necessary for understanding the mystic import of the Bhagavadgītā. The propositions laid down by the Sāṁkhya school are of greater importance than those laid down by the Nyāya school. Because, as Bādarāyaṇācārya has said (Ve. Sū. 2. 1. 12 and 2. 2. 17), though no respectable and

* "Know that both the *prakṛti* (Matter) and the *puruṣa* (Spirit) are eternal".

leading Vedānta philosopher has accepted as correct the Nyāya doctrines laid down by the followers of Kaṇāda, yet, as many of the propositions of the Kāpila Sāṁkhya-śāstra are to be found in the Smṛti writings of Manu and others and also in the Gītā, my readers must first become acquainted with them. Nevertheless, it must be stated right in the beginning that though many ideas of the Sāṁkhya philosophy are to be found in the Vedānta philosophy, yet the readers must not forget that the ultimate doctrines laid down by the Sāṁkhya school and the Vedānta school are extremely different from each other. There has also been raised an important question, namely, whether the Vedāntists or the Sāṁkhya philosophers are the originators of those ideas which are common to the Vedānta and the Sāṁkhya philosophy. But it is not possible to go so deep into that subject-matter in this book. Possibly, the Upaniṣads (Vedānta) and the Sāṁkhya philosophy grew up side by side like two children, and the doctrines found in the Upaniṣads, which are similar to the Sāṁkhya doctrines, may have been independently arrived at by the writers of the Upaniṣads; or on the other hand, the writers of the Upaniṣads may have borrowed some of these doctrines from the Sāṁkhya philosophy; or thirdly, Kapilācārya may have improved upon the doctrines laid down by the ancient Upaniṣads according to his own opinions, and formulated the Sāṁkhya philosophy. All these three positions are possible. But taking into account the fact that though the Upaniṣads and the Sāṁkhya philosophy are both ancient, the Upaniṣads are the more ancient (Śrauta) of the two, the last supposition seems to be the most credible of the three. Whatever may be the truth, when one has once become acquainted with the doctrines laid down by the Nyāya and the Sāṁkhya schools of philosophy, it becomes easier to grasp the principles of Vedānta, especially of the Vedānta in the Gītā. Therefore, let us first consider what the opinions of these two Smārta śāstras about the formation of the universe are.

Some persons have a wrong idea that the only object of Nyāya (i. e., Logic) is to decide what conclusions can subsequently be drawn by inference from some desired or given data and which of these inferences are correct, and which wrong, and why.

Proving by means of inference etc. is a part of Logic. But that is not the most important part; classifying or enumerating the various things in the world, that is to say, the subject-matter of proof (apart from the question of proving them), finding out what are the fundamental classes or things under which all the substances in the world can be classified, as a result of the gradual evolution of things in the lower orders into things in the higher orders, finding out what their nature and qualities are, and how other things came into existence out of these things, and how all these things can be proved, and all such other questions are included in Logic. Nay, one may go further and say that this science has come into existence only for this purpose, and not merely for considering the question of inference. It is in this way that the Nyāya-sūtras of Kaṇāda are begun and worked out. The followers of Kaṇāda are known as Kāṇādas. In their opinion the root cause of the world is Atoms. The definition of atoms given by Kaṇāda and the one given by Western natural scientists is the same. When after dividing and sub-dividing things you come to the stage when division is no more possible, you have reached the atom or '*paramāṇu*' (*parama* + *aṇu*), that is, the ultimate entity. As these atoms coalesce, they acquire new qualities as a result of the union, and new things are created. There are also atoms of the Mind and of the Body, and when these unite, life results. The atoms of the earth, water, fire and air are fundamentally different from each other. The fundamental atoms of the earth, have four qualities, namely, form, taste, smell, and touch; those of water have three such qualities, those of fire, two, and those of air, only one. In this way the entire cosmos is from the very beginning filled with permanent and subtle atoms. There is no other root cause of the world except the atoms. The commencement (*āraṁbha*) of the mutual coalition or union of the original and permanent atoms results in all the perceptible things in the world coming into existence. This theory propounded by the Nyāya school regarding the creation of the perceptible universe is technically known as '*āraṁbha-vāda*' (Theory of Commencement), and some followers of that school never go beyond this. There is a story about one of them, that when those who were around him at the moment of his death, asked him to take the name of God, he uttered the words: "*pīlavaḥ! pīlavaḥ! pīlavaḥ!*"– "atoms! atoms! atoms!". Nevertheless, other followers of the Nyāya school believe that Īśvara is responsible for bringing about the fusion or union of atoms and they in that way complete the chain of the creation of the universe; and these are known as theistic Logicians. In the second sub-division of the second chapter of the Vedānta-Sūtras (2. 2. 11–17), this Atomic theory, and immediately thereafter, also the theory that the Īśvara is merely the immediate cause (2. 2. 37–39) has been refuted.

Reading what is stated above regarding this Atomic theory, those of my readers who have studied English will at once think of the Atomic theory advanced by the modern chemist Dalton. But in the Western countries, the Atomic theory of Dalton has now been put into shade by the Evolution theory of the well-known biologist Darwin. In the same way, in India in ancient times, the Sāṁkhya philosophy has put into the background the theories of Kaṇāda. Not only can the Kaṇāda school not explain satisfactorily how Activity was first imparted to atoms, but their theories cannot also explain how the rising gradation of living things like trees, animals, and men came into existence, nor also how that which was lifeless became living, and several other things. This explanation was given in the 19th Century in the Western countries by Lamarque and Darwin, and in our country in ancient times by Kapila. The summary of the opinions of both these schools is that the Cosmos or universe came to be created by the bursting forth of the constituents of one original substance; and on this account, the Atomic theory lost ground in India in ancient times, and now in the Western countries. Similarly, modern physicists have now also proved that the atom is not indivisible. It was not possible in ancient times to prove the Atomic theory or the Evolution theory by analysing and examining various material objects in the world by means of physics and other natural sciences. Experimenting again and again on the various objects in the world, or determining their qualities by analysing them in various ways, or making a comparison between the organs of the bodies of numerous present and former living things in the living world, and such other present day devices of the natural sciences were not available to Kaṇāda or to Kapila. They have deduced their propositions from whatever material was before their eyes at the time. Still it is a matter of great surprise that the philosophical propositions laid down by the Sāṁkhya philosophers as to how the growth or formation of the universe must have come about are not much different from the scientific propositions laid down by modern natural scientists. As the knowledge of biology has grown, the material proof of these opinions can now be given more logically, and by the growth of knowledge of the natural sciences, human beings have undoubtedly benefited to a considerable extent from the Material point of view. But in order to impress on the minds of my readers that the modern natural scientists cannot tell us much more than Kapila as to how diverse perceptible created things came into existence out of one Imperceptible *prakṛti* (Matter), I have in various places later on referred shortly to the propositions laid down by Haeckel for comparison side by side with the propositions of the Kāpila Sāṁkhya school. These propositions were not for the first time promulgated by Haeckel, and he has himself clearly admitted in his works that he was expounding his propositions on the authority of the works of Darwin, Spencer, and other previous natural scientists. Yet Haeckel has for the first time described succinctly and in an easily intelligible way all these various propositions, after properly co-ordinating them, in his book known as *The Riddle of the Universe*; and I have, therefore, for the sake of convenience, taken Haeckel as the protagonist of all these natural scientists, and referred principally to his opinions in this and the next Chapter. I need not say that this reference is only brief, because it is not possible to consider those propositions in this book in greater detail, and those who want further information about them must refer to the original works of Spencer, Darwin, Haeckel and other scholars.

Before considering the Kāpila Sāṁkhya philosophy, it must be mentioned that the word 'Sāṁkhya' is used in two different meanings. The first meaning is the Sāṁkhya philosophy expounded by Kapilācārya, and that meaning has been adopted in this Chapter and in one place in the Bhagavadgītā (Gī. 18. 13). But besides this specific meaning, it is usual to include philosophy of every kind in the general name 'Sāṁkhya', and it also includes the Vedānta philosophy. In the phrase '*Sāṁkhya-niṣṭhā*' or '*Sāṁkhya-yoga*' this ordinary meaning of the word '*Sāṁkhya*' is intended; and wherever the scients who follow this *niṣṭhā* (doctrine) have been referred to as '*Sāṁkhya*' in the Bhagavadgītā later on (Gī. 2. 39; 3. 3; 4. 5; and 13. 24), not only the followers of the Kāpila Sāṁkhya school, but also the Vedāntists who have abandoned all Actions by *ātmānātma-vicāra* (by considering what does and what does not pertain to the Self); and who are lost in the contemplation of the *Brahman*, are intended. As the word 'Sāṁkhya' comes from the root '*Saṁ-khyā*' (calculation), its primary meaning is 'one who counts'; and etymologists say that, as the fundamental elements according to the Kapila philosophy are just twenty-five, the followers of that philosophy originally got the specific name of 'Sāṁkhya' (in the sense of "counters"), and later on the word 'Sāṁkhya' acquired the comprehensive meaning of philosophy of every kind. I, therefore, think that after the practice of referring to Kāpila ascetics as 'Sāṁkhya' had first come into vogue, Vedānta ascetics also later on came to be known by that name. Whatever may be the case, in order that confusion should not arise as a result of this double meaning of the word 'Sāṁkhya', I have used the elongated heading of 'Kāpila Sāṁkhya-Śāstra' for this chapter. There are *sūtras* (Aphorisms) in the Kāpila Sāṁkhya-Śāstra just as in the Kāṇāda Nyāya philosophy. But as neither Gauḍapāda nor Śrī Śaṁkarācārya, who wrote the *Śārīra-bhāṣya*, have taken these *sūtras* as authorities in their works, many scholars are of opinion that they could not be ancient. The *Sāṁkhya-Kārikā* written by Īśvarakṛṣṇa is considered to be older than them. Gauḍapāda, the chief preceptor of Śaṁkarācārya, has written a *bhāṣya* (Commentary) on that work and even in the *Śāṁkarabhāṣya* itself, extracts have been taken from these Kārikās, and the translation of that work into the Chinese language made before 570 A. D.

is now available.* Īśvarakṛṣṇa has stated at the end of these Kārikās, that he has in his work given a summary in seventy couplets in the *āryā* metre of a previous extensive book of sixty chapters called *Ṣaṣṭi-Tantra* (omitting some chapters). The work *Ṣaṣṭi-Tantra* is now not available, and I have, therefore, considered the fundamental propositions of the Kāpila Sāṁkhya-Śāstra on the authority of these Kārikās. In the Mahābhārata, the Sāṁkhya doctrines have been mentioned in many chapters. But as in that work, the Vedānta doctrines have been always mixed up with the Sāṁkhya doctrines, it becomes necessary to consider other treatises in order to decide what the pure Sāṁkhya philosophy was; and for that purpose, no work older than the Sāṁkhya-Kārikās is at present available. The pre-eminent worth of Kapila becomes clear from the following words of the Blessed Lord in the Gītā: "*siddhānām Kapilo muniḥ*" (Gī. 10. 26), that is, "from among the Siddhas, I am the Kapila muni". Nevertheless, it is not known where and when Kapila Ṛṣi lived. There is a statement in the Śāntiparva of the Mahābhārata that Sanatkumāra, Sanaka, Sanandana, Sanatsujāta, Sana, Sanātana and Kapila were the seven Mind-born sons of Brahmadeva, and that they were born with Knowledge (340.67); and in another place (Śān. 218), we find the Sāṁkhya

* Much information is now available about Īśvarakṛṣṇa from Buddhistic works. The preceptor of the Buddhistic scholar Vasubandhu was a contemporary opponent of Īśvarakṛṣṇa and the history of this Vasubandhu written by Paramārtha (449 to 569 A. D.) in the Chinese language has now been published. Dr. Takakasu has, on the strength of this, come to the conclusion that Īśvarakṛṣṇa must have lived about 450 A. D. (See *Journal of the Royal Asiatic Society of Great Britain and Ireland*, 1905, p. 33 to 53). But according to Dr. Vincent Smith, Vasubandhu himself must be placed somewhere in the 4th century (about 280–360 A. D.), because a translation of his works has been made in 404 A. D. into the Chinese language. When the date of Vasubandhu is in this way pushed back, the date of Īśvarakṛṣṇa is also pushed back to the same extent, that is to say, by about 200 years; and must be taken at about 240 A. D. (See Vincent Smith's *Early History of India*, 3rd Edition, p. 328.).

philosophy explained to Janaka by Āsuri, the disciple of Kapila, and Pañcaśikha, the disciple of Āsuri. Again in the Śāntiparva (301. 108, 109) Bhīṣma also says, that the science which was once propounded by Sāṁkhya about the formation of the universe is everywhere to be found "in the Purāṇas, in history and in books on political economy and other places". Nay, it may even be said that: "*jñānaṁ ca loke yad ihāsti kiṁcit Sāṁkhyāgataṁ tac ca mahan mahātman*", that is, "all the knowledge in this world originates in the Sāṁkhya philosophy" (Ma. Bhā. Śān. 301. 109). When one considers in what way the Evolution theory is being everywhere taxed into commission by the Western writers, one should not be surprised if every one of our writers has to some extent or other drawn upon our ancient Sāṁkhya philosophy, which is a match for the Evolution theory. Stupendous ideas like the theory of gravity of the earth, or the *utkrānti-tattva* * (Evolution theory) in the science of the creation, or the theory of the unity of Brahman and the Ātman, come into the mind of some superman once in a way in thousands of years. Therefore, the practice of expounding one's own arguments, on the authority of any universal doctrine or comprehensive theory accepted at the time, is seen followed in books in all countries.

This introduction has become necessary because the study of the Kāpila Sāṁkhya philosophy is now out of date. Let us now consider what the principal propositions of the Kāpila Sāṁkhya philosophy are. The first proposition of the Sāṁkhya philosophy is that nothing new comes into existence in this world; because, only *śūnya* (nothing) and nothing else can be produced by *śūnya* (that is, which did not exist before). Therefore, it must always be taken for granted that all the

* I have used the word '*utkrānti-tattva*' here as meaning 'the Evolution theory' because it is used in that sense now-a-days. But '*utkrānti*' means 'death' in Sanskrit. Therefore, in my opinion it would be more proper to use the expressions '*guṇavikāsa*' (the expansion of the constituents), '*guṇotkarṣa*' (the diffusion or growth of the constituents), *guṇapariṇāma*' (the development of the constituents) used in the Sāṁkhya philosophy for denoting the 'Evolution theory' instead of the term '*utkrānti-tattva*'.

qualities which are to be seen in the created products (*kārya*) must be found at least in a subtle form in the *kāraṇa* from which the products were created (Sāṁ. Kā. 9). According to the opinions of Buddhists and of Kaṇāda, one thing is destroyed and out of it another thing comes into existence; for instance, the seed is destroyed, and from that the sprout comes into existence, the sprout is destroyed, and from that the tree comes into existence, and so on. But the Sāṁkhya and the Vedānta philosophers do not accept this proposition. They maintain that those elements which existed in the seed of the tree are not destroyed, but they have absorbed other elements into themselves from the earth and from the air, and thereby the new form or state of a sprout is taken up by the seed (Ve. Sū. Śāṁ. Bhā. 2. 1. 18). Similarly, even if wood is burnt, it is only transformed into smoke, ashes etc., and not that the elements in the wood are totally destroyed and a new thing in the form of smoke comes into existence. It is stated in the Chāndogyopaniṣad that: "*katham asataḥ saj jāyeta?*", i. e., "how can something which exists come out of something which never existed?" (Chān. 6. 2. 2). The fundamental Cause of the universe is sometimes referred to as '*asat*' in the Upaniṣads (Chān. 3. 19. 1; Tai. 2. 7. 1). But Vedānta philosophy has laid down that that word is not to be interpreted as meaning '*a-bhāva*' (non-existing) but as indicating only the non-existence of such a perceptible state as can be denoted by name or form (Ve. Sū. 2. 1. 16, 17). Curds can be made only out of milk, not from water; oil comes out of 'til' (sesamum), not out of sand; from these and other actual experiences, one must draw the same conclusion; because, if one accepts the position that those qualities which do not exist in the *kāraṇa* (cause) can arise independently in the *kārya* (product), one cannot explain why it should not be possible to produce curds from water. In short, that which is now in existence cannot have come into existence out of something which originally did not exist. Therefore, the Sāṁkhya philosophers have laid down the proposition, that whatever product you may take, its present concomitants and qualities must in some form or other have been in existence in its original cause. This proposition is known as '*satkārya-vāda*' (theory of something being produced out of something which existed). Even modern natural scientists have laid down the proposition that the gross elements and the potential energy in all things are permanent, and whatever changes of form anything may go through, yet in the end the sum total of all material concomitants and of all potential energy in the world is always the same. For instance, even if we see a lamp burning and the oil disappearing, yet the atoms of oil are not totally destroyed, but continue to exist in the form of soot, smoke, or other subtle components; and, if all these subtle components are taken together and weighed, their weight will be the same as the total weight of the oil and of all those other matters from the air which were mixed with it when it was burning; and it has now been proved that the same rule applies to potential energy. But although these two propositions of modern physics and of the Sāṁkhya philosophy may be apparently similar, yet it must not be forgotten that the proposition of the Sāṁkhya philosophy has reference only to the fact of one thing being created out of another thing, that is to say, it refers specifically to the theory of Causes and Effects, whereas the proposition of modern physics is much more comprehensive. The very important difference between these two propositions which has now been proved by actual experiments and mathematics, is that no quality in any product can arise out of any quality which was not in the cause, and what is more, that the material elements and the potential energy in the causes are in no way destroyed by reason of their having been transformed into products, and that the sum total of the weights of the material elements and the potential energy of any product in its various states is always the same, and is neither increased nor decreased. Looking at the matter from this point of view, it will be seen that the propositions which have been given at the commencement of the second chapter of the Bhagavadgītā (Gī. 2. 16), such as: "*nāsato vidyate bhāvaḥ*", i. e., "that which is not, will never come into existence" etc., have greater similarity with the proposition of modern physics, than with the mere *satkāryavāda* which deals with causes and products, though they apparently look like *satkāryavāda*. The purport of the above quotation from the Chāndogyopaniṣad is also the same. In short, the doctrine of of *satkāryavāda* is acceptable to the Vedānta philosophy. Nevertheless, according to the Monistic (*advaita*) Vedānta philosophy, this proposition does not apply to anything beyond the qualified (*saguṇa*) universe, and how the qualified universe appears to have come into exsistence out of the qualityless (*nirguṇa*) must be explained in some other way. This theory of the Vedānta will be fully dealt with later on in the chapter on Metaphysics (*adhyātma*). As in this place we have to consider only how far the Sāṁkhya philosophers have gone, we will take for granted the doctrine of *satkāryavāda* and see how the Sāṁkhya philosophers have made use of it in dealing with the question of the Mutable and the Immutable.

When once this *satkāryavāda* is taken as proved, then, according to the Sāṁkhya science, the theory that the visible universe came into existence out of *śūnya*, there having been nothing whatsoever in existence before, naturally falls to the ground. Because, *śūnya* means non-existing, and that which exists can never come into existence out of that which does not exist. Therefore, it becomes absolutely clear that the universe must have come into existence out of some substance or other, and that all those constituents (*guṇas*) which we now see in the universe must have also been in this original substance. Now, if you look at the universe, many objects in it, such as trees, animals, men, stones, gold, silver, diamonds, water, air etc., are perceptible to our organs, and their forms and qualities are all different. The Sāṁkhya doctrine is that this diversity or difference is neither permanent nor fundamental and that the fundamental substance in all things, or Matter, is only one. Modern chemists had analysed various objects and had originally arrived at 62 fundamental elements. But as the Western natural scientists have now proved that these 62 elements are not eternal and that there must have been some one fundamental substance from which the sun, the moon, the earth, the stars, and the rest of the universe was created, it is not necessary to further labour this proposition. This original or fundamental substance at the root of all the things in the universe is known in Sāṁkhya philosophy as

'PRAKṚTI'. *Prakṛti* means 'fundamental' and all things which subsequently arise out of *prakṛti* are called '*vikṛti*' or the *vikāras* (transformations) of the fundamental substance.

But though there is only one fundamental substance in all things, if this substance had also only one constituent quality, then according to the *satkāryavāda*, other qualities could not have arisen out of this one quality; whereas, looking at the stones, earth, water, gold, and various other things in the world, we find that they have numerous qualities. Therefore, the Sāṁkhya philosophers have first carefully considered the constituents of all the various things and divided these constituents into three classes, namely, the *sattva*, the *rajas* and the *tamas*, (the placid, the active and the ignorant). Because, whatever object may be taken, it naturally has two states, namely, its pure, unadulterated, or perfect state and the opposite of it, its imperfect state; and it is seen that its tendency is to move from its imperfect state to its perfect state. Out of these three states, the state of perfection is called by the Sāṁkhya philosophers the *sāttvikī* state, the inperfect state is called the *tāmasī* state, and the state of progression is called the *rājasī* state; and according to them the three qualities, *sattva, rajas* and *tamas*, are to be found from the very beginning in Matter (prakṛti), which is the fundamental substance of all things. Nay, it may even be said, that these three constituents together make up Matter. In as much the strength of each of these qualities is the same in the beginning, Matter is originally equable. This equability existed in the beginning of the world and will come again when the world comes to an end. In this equability, there is no activity and everything is at rest; but, later on, when these three constituents begin to vary in intensity, various things spring out of Matter as a result of the progressive constituent, and the creation begins. Here the question arises as to how the difference arises in the intensity of the three constituents, *sattva, rajas* and *tamas*, which were originally equal in intensity. To this the reply of the Sāṁkhya philosophers is, that that is the inherent characteristic of Matter (Sāṁ. Kā. 61). Though Matter is gross, yet it carries out all this activity of its own accord. Out of these three constituents, knowledge or intelligence is the sign of the *sattva*, and the *rajas* constituent has an inspirational tendency, that is to say, it inspires a person to do some good or evil act. These three constituents can never exist by themselves independently. In everything, there is a mixture of all the three constituents; and in as much as the mutual ratio of the three constituents in this mixture always varies, the fundamental Matter, though originally one, assumes the various forms of gold, earth, iron, water, sky, the human body etc. as a result of this diversity in constituents. As the intensity or proportion of the *sattva* constituent is higher than that of the *rajas* and *tamas* constituents in the object which we consider as *sāttvika*, all that happens is that these constituents being kept in abeyance are not noticed by us. But strictly speaking, it must be understood that the three constituents *sattva*, *rajas* and *tamas* are to be found even in those objects which are *sāttvika* by nature. There does not exist a single object which is purely *sāttvika*, or purely *rājasa*, or purely *tāmasa*. In each object, there is an internal warfare going on between the three constituents, and we describe a particular object as *sāttvika*, *rājasa*, or *tāmasa* according to that one of these three constituents which becomes predominant. (Sāṁ. Kā. 12; Ma. Bhā. Aśva-Anugītā-36 and Śān. 305). For instance, when in one's own body the *sattva* constituent assumes preponderance over the *rajas* and *tamas* constituents, Knowledge comes into being in our body and we begin to realise the truth about things and our mind becomes peaceful. It is not that in this mental condition, the *rajas* and the *tamas* constituents cease to exist in the body; but as they are repressed, they do not produce any effect. (Gī. 14. 10). If instead of the *sattva* constituent, the *rajas* constituent assumes preponderance, then avarice arises in the human heart, and the man is filled with ambition and he is inspired to do various actions. In the same way, when the *tamas* constituent assumes preponderance over both the *sattva* and the *rajas* constituents, faults like sleep, idleness, confused memory etc. arise in the body. In short, the diversity which exists among the various objects in the world, such as gold, iron, mercury etc. is the result of the mutual warfare or diversity in intensity of the three constituents, *sattva*, *rajas* and *tamas*. The consideration as to how this diversity arises when there is only one fundamental Matter is known as '*vijñāna*'; and this includes all the natural sciences. For example, chemistry, the science of electricity, physics etc. are all diverse kinds of *jñāna*, that is, they are *vijñāna*.

This fundamental Matter, which is in an equable state, is 'AVYAKTA', that is, not perceptible to the organs; and all the various objects which come into existence as a result of the mutual internal warfare of its *sattva*, *rajas* and *tamas* constituents, and become perceptible to the organs, that is to say, all which we see or hear or taste or smell, or touch, goes under the name of '*vyakta*' according to the Sāṁkhya philosophy. 'VYAKTA' means all the objects which are definitely perceptible to the organs, whether they become perceptible on account of their form, or colour, or smell, or any other quality. Perceptible objects are numerous, and out of them, trees, stones etc. are GROSS (*sthūla*); whereas others like the Mind, Reason, Ether etc., though perceptible to the organs, are SUBTLE (*sūkṣma*). The word *sūkṣma* does not here have its ordinary meaning of 'small'; because, though ether is *sūkṣma*, it has enveloped the entire universe. Therefore, *sūkṣma* is to be taken to mean the opposite of '*sthūla*', or even thinner than air. The words 'gross' or 'subtle' give one an idea about the conformation of the body of a particular thing; and the words '*vyakta*' (perceptible) and '*avyakta*' (imperceptible) show whether or not a particular thing can be perceived by us in reality. Therefore, although two different things may both be subtle, yet one of them may be perceptible and the other imperceptible. For instance, though the air is subtle, yet as it is perceptible to the sense of touch, it is considered to be *vyakta*; and *prakṛti* (Matter), the fundamental substance of all things, being much more subtle than air itself, is not perceptible by any of the organs and is, therefore, *avyakta*. Here a question arises, namely : if *prakṛti* is not perceptible to any organ, then, what evidence is there that it exists ? To this the reply of the Sāṁkhya philosophers is, that by considering the various objects, it is proved by inference by the law of '*satkāryavāda*' that the root of all of them, though not actually perceptible to the organs, must nevertheless be in existence in a subtle form (Sāṁ. Kā. 8); and the Vedānta philosophers have accepted the same line of argument for proving the existence of the Brahman. (See the Sāṁkarabhāṣya on Kaṭha. 6. 12, 13). When you once in this way acknowledge *prakṛti* to be extremely subtle and imperceptible, the atomic theory of the Nyāya school naturally falls to the ground. Because, even if atoms are considered imperceptible and innumerable, yet, in as much as each atom is, according to the Nyāya theory, an independent entity or part, the question as to what matter any two atoms are composed of still remains. Therefore, the doctrine of the Sāṁkhya philosophy is, that in *prakṛti* there are no different parts in the shape of atoms, that it is consistent and homogeneous or unbroken in any part, and that it perpetually pervades everything in a form which is *avyakta* (that is, not perceptible to the organs) and inorganic. In describing the Parabrahman, Śrī Samartha Rāmadāsa Svāmī says in the *Dāsabodha* (Dā. 20. 2. 3.):-

"In whichever direction you see, it is endless; there "is no end or limit anywhere; there is one independent "homogeneous substance; there is nothing else".

The same description applies to the *prakṛti* of the Sāṁkhya philosophy. Matter, made up of three constituents, is imperceptible, self-created, and homogeneous, and it eternally saturates everything on all sides. The Ether, the air, and other different things came into existence afterwards; and although they may be subtle, yet they are perceptible; and '*prakṛti*' which is the fundament or origin of all these is imperceptible, though it is homogeneous and all-pervading. Nevertheless, there is a world of difference between the *Parabrahman* of Vedānta philosophy and the *prakṛti* of Sāṁkhya philosophy; because, whereas the *Parabrahman* is vitalising and unqualified, *prakṛti* is inactive (gross) and is qualified, since it possesses the *sattva*, *rajas* and *tamas* qualities. But this subject-matter will be more fully considered later on. For the moment, we have only to consider what the doctrines of the Sāṁkhya philosophy are. When the words *sūkṣma*, *sthūla*, *vyakta*, and *avyakta* have been defined as above, one comes to the inevitable conclusion that in the beginning of the universe, every object is in the form of subtle and imperceptible *prakṛti* and that it afterwards becomes *vyakta* (perceptible to the organs), whether it is subtle or gross; and that at the time of *pralaya* (total destruction of the universe), when this its perceptibtle form is destroyed, it again becomes merged into imperceptible Matter and becomes imperceptible. And the same opinion has been expressed in the Gītā (Gī. 2. 28 and 8. 18). In the Sāṁkhya philosophy, this imperceptible Matter is also known as '*akṣara*' (Immutable) and all things which are formed out of it are known as '*kṣara*' (Mutable). '*kṣara*' is not to be understood as meaning something which is totally destroyed, but only the destruction of the perceptible form is here meant. '*prakṛti*' has also other names, such as, '*pradhāna*' (fundamental), '*guṇa-kṣobhiṇī*' (stirrer up of the constituents), '*bahudhānaka*' (many-seeded), and '*prasava-dharmiṇī*' (generative). It is '*pradhāna*' (fundamental), because, it is the fundamental root of all objects in the universe; it is '*guṇakṣobhiṇī*' (stirrer up of constituents), because, it of its own accord breaks up the equable state of its three constituents (*guṇas*); it is '*bahudhānaka*' (many-seeded), because, it contains the germs of differentiation between various objects in the shape of the three constituents; and it is '*prasava-dharmiṇī*" (generative), because, all things are born or come into existence out of it. That is why these different names are given to Matter. This *prakṛti* is known in Vedānta philosophy as '*Māyā*' (Illusion) or an illusory appearance.

When all things in the world are classified under the two divisions of 'Perceptible' and 'Imperceptible' or 'Mutable' and 'Immutable', the next question which arises is into what categories the Ātman, the Mind, Intelligence, Individuation, and the organs, which have been mentioned in the last chapter on the *kṣetra-kṣetrajña-vicāra*, are to be put according to Sāṁkhya philosophy. The *kṣetra* and the organs being gross, they will of course be included in the category of the Perceptible. But how is one to dispose of the Mind, Individuation, Intelligence, and especially of the Ātman? The modern eminent European biologist Haeckel says in his books that the Mind, Intelligence, Individuation and the Ātman are all faculties of the body. We see that when the brain in a man's head is deranged, he loses memory and even becomes mad. Similarly, even if any part of the brain is deadened on account of a blow on the head, the mental faculty of that part is seen to come to an end. In short, mental faculties are only faculties of gross Matter and they can never be separated from gross Matter. Therefore, the mental faculties and the Ātman must be classified along with the brain in the category of the Perceptible. When you have made this classification, the imperceptible and gross Matter is ultimately the only thing which remains to be disposed of, because all perceptible objects have sprung out of this fundamental imperceptible. There is no other creator or generator of the world except *prakṛti*. When the Energy of the fundamental Matter (*prakṛti*) gradually increases, it acquires the form of *caitanya* (consciousness) or of the Ātman. This fundamental *prakṛti* is governed by fixed laws or rules like the *satkāryavāda*, and in accordance with those laws, the entire universe, as also man, is acting like a prisoner. Not only is the Ātman not something different from Matter, but it is neither imperishable nor independent; then, where is the room for salvation ?. The idea which a person has that he will do a particular thing according to his own will is a total illusion; he must go where *prakṛti* (Matter or Nature) drags him. In short, as the late Mr. Shankar Moro Ranade has stated in the 'Dhrupad' (stanza) at the commencement of the drama *Kalahapuri* :-

> "The world is a vast prison, all created beings are
> "prisoners, the inherent qualities of Matter are
> "shackles which nobody can break".

Haeckel's opinion is that this is the way in which the existence of the living and the non-living world goes on. And because according to him the universe originates from a single, gross, and imperceptible *prakṛti*, he has named his doctrine '*advaita*' (non-dualism) *. But in as much as this *advaita*

* Haeckel's original word is 'Monism', and he has written an independent work on it.

doctrine is based on something which is gross, and as it incorporates everything within gross Matter, I have named it '*jaḍādvaita*' (Gross Non-dualism) or Non-dualism based on the Natural sciences.

But the Sāṁkhya philosophy does not accept this Gross Non-dualism. They accept the position that the Mind, Reason and Individuation are qualities of Gross Matter which consists of the five primordial elements and consequently it is stated in the Sāṁkhya philosophy that Reason, Individuation, and other qualities gradually spring out of the fundamental imperceptible Matter. But according to the Sāṁkhyas, it is impossible that consciousness *(caitanya)* should spring out of gross Matter; not only that, but the words "I know a particular thing" cannot come to be used unless the one who knows, understands, or sees Matter, is different from Matter, in the same way as no one can sit on his own shoulders; and looking at the affairs of the world, it is the experience of every one that whatever he knows or sees is different from himself. The Sāṁkhya philosophers have, therefore, come to the conclusion that the one who knows (*jñātā*) and that which is to be known (*jñeya*), the one who sees and that which is to be seen, or the one who sees *prakṛti* and Gross *prakṛiti* must be two fundamentally different things (Sāṁ. Kā.17). The one which has been described in the last chapter as the *kṣetrajña*, or the Ātman, is the one which sees, knows or enjoys, and it is known in the Sāṁkhya philosophy as PURUṢA (Spirit), or '*jña*' (*jñātā*). As this Knower is different from Matter, it follows that the Knower is inherently quality-less, that is, beyond the three constituents of *prakṛti*, namely, *sattva*, *rajas* and *tamas*; that the Knower does not go through any change of form and does nothing else except seeing and knowing, and that all the activity which is going on in the world is only the activity of *prakṛti*. In short, the doctrine of the Sāṁkhya philosophers is that if MATTER (*prakṛti*) is *acetana* (lifeless), SPIRIT (*puruṣa*) is *sacetana* (vitalised); if Matter is responsible for all activity, Spirit is apathetic and non-active; if Matter has three constituents, Spirit is unconstituted; if Matter is blind, Spirit is seeing; and that these two different elements in this world are eternal, independent, and self-created. And it is with reference to this doctrine that the Bhagavadgītā first says: "*prakṛtiṁ puruṣaṁ caiva viddhy anādī ubhāv api*", that is, "*prakṛti* and *puruṣa* are both without a beginning and are eternal" (Gī. 13. 19), and then goes on to say: "*kāryakāraṇa kartṛtve hetuḥ prakṛtir ucyate*", i.e., the activities of the body and of the organs are carried on by *prakṛti*: and that, "*puruṣaḥ sukhaduḥkhānāṁ bhoktṛtve hetur ucyate*", i. e., "the *puruṣa* is responsible for our experience of pain and happiness". But although the doctrine, that *prakṛti* and *puruṣa* (Matter and Spirit) are both eternal, is acceptable to the Gītā, yet it must be borne in mind that the Gītā does not look upon these two elements as independent and self-created, as is done by Sāṁkhya philosophers. Because, in the Gītā itself the Blessed Lord has referred to Matter as his Illusion (Gī. 7. 14; 14. 3); and as regards the Spirit, he has said: "*mamaivāṁśo jīvaloke*" (Gī. 15. 7), i. e., "It is a part of me". Therefore, the Gītā has gone further than the Sāṁkhya philosophy. But we will keep aside this aspect for the time being, and consider further what pure Sāṁkhya philosophy says.

According to Sāṁkhya philosophy, all the objects in the world are divided into three classes:–the *avyakta* (the fundamental Matter or nature), the *vyakta* (the forms taken by it), and the *puruṣa* (*jña*), the Spirit or the Knower. But in as much as the form of perceptible objects out of these is destroyed at the time of *pralaya* (total destruction), imperceptible Matter (*prakṛti*) and Spirit (*puruṣa*) are the only two elements which remain in the end; and in as much as it is a proposition of the Sāṁkhya philosophers, that these two fundamental principles are eternal and self-created, they are called '*dvaiti*' (those who accept TWO principles). They do not accept any other fundamental principle besides Matter and Spirit, such as Īśvara, Time, inherent Nature or anything else.* Because, in as much as

* **Īśvarkṛṣṇa was a total atheist (*nirīśvaravādi*). He has stated in the last three summarising *āryā* couplets of his *Sāṁkhya-Kārikā*, that there were 70 *āryās* (couplets) in the *Sāṁkhya-kārikā* on the principal subject-matter. But in the Edition which has been printed in Bombay by Tukārām Tātyā, which contains the translations of Colebrooke and Wilson, there are only 69 *āryās* on the principal**

according to that philosophy the qualified Īśvara, Time, or inherent Nature are all perceptible, they are included in the perceptible objects which arise out of imperceptible Matter; and if you look upon the Īśvara as qualityless, then having regard to the law of *satkāryavāda*, Matter with its three constituents cannot spring out of a qualityless fundamental element. Therefore, they have definitely laid down that there is no third fundamental element in addition to *prakṛti* and *puruṣa* as a cause of the universe; and having in this way defined only two fundamental elements, they have according to their own opinion worked out how the entire universe was created out

---

subject. Therefore, Mr. Wilson was necessarily faced with the question which this 70th couplet was; but that couplet not having been available to him, his difficulty has remained unsolved. In my opinion, this couplet must be after the present 61st couplet. Because, the commentary of Gauḍapāda on the 61st couplet is not on one couplet, but on two couplets. And if the symbolical phrases in this commentary are taken and a verse is written, it will run as follows :

> *kāraṇam īśvaram eke bruvate kālam pare svabhāvaṁ vā* ।
> *prajāḥ kathaṁ nirguṇato vyaktaḥ kālaḥ svabhāvaś ca* ॥

And this verse fits in with the anterior and posterior context. I think that some one has subsequently omitted this *āryā*, as it supports atheism. But as this ultra-critical man who has omitted the original couplet, forgot to delete the commentary on the verse which was omitted, we can now reconstruct that verse. For this, we must be grateful to this officious man. It would appear from the first hymn of the sixth chapter of the Śvetāśvataropaniṣad, that in ancient times, people used to look upon Inherent Nature and Time as the fundamental causes of the world and the Vedāntists used to go further and to look upon the 'Īśvara' as such cause. That hymn is as follows :—

> *svabhāvam eke kavayo vadanti kālaṁ tathānye parimuhyamānāḥ* ।
> *devasyaiṣa mahimā tu loke yenedaṁ bhrāmyate brahmacakram* ॥

And in order to show that not even one of these three were accepted by the Sāṁkhya philosophers as a fundamental Cause, Īśvarakṛṣṇa put the couplet mentioned above after the 61st couplet.

of these two fundamental elements. They say that though the qualityless *puruṣa* (Spirit) is unable to do anything itself, yet, in the same way as the cow gives milk for its calf, or iron acquires the quality of attraction by the proximity of a magnet, so also immediately on the *puruṣa* coming into union with *prakṛti*, *prakṛti* which was originally imperceptible begins to place before the *puruṣa* the subtle and the gross perceptible diffusion of its own constituents (Sāṁ. Kā. 57). Although the *puruṣa* may be *sacetana* (vitalised) and a *jñātā* (knower), yet, in as much as it is *kevala* (isolated), that is, qualityless, it has not got the necessary perquisites for performing actions itself; and although *prakṛti* can perform actions, yet, in as much as it is gross and *acetana* (lifeless), it cannot understand what to do and what not to do. Therefore, just as when there is a partnership between a blind man and a lame man, the lame man sits on the shoulders of the blind man, and both of them begin to follow the road, so also when lifeless Matter becomes united with the vitalised Spirit, all the activities in the world come into existence (Sāṁ. Kā. 21); and just as in a drama an actress once takes one part and after some time again another part and performs her dance for the entertainment of the audience, so also *prakṛti* for the benefit of the *puruṣa* (for '*puruṣārtha*'), and though the *puruṣa* gives nothing in return, takes up numerous parts in the drama by changing the mutual ratio of the *sattva*, *rajas*, and *tamas* constituents, and continually performs its dance before the *puruṣa* (Sāṃ. Kā. 59). But so long as the Spirit, being entranced by this dance of Matter or by false pride (Gī. 3. 37) unjustifiably arrogates to itself this activity of Matter, and enmeshes itself in the strands of pain and happiness, it will never attain salvation. But on that day, when the Spirit realises that Matter with its three constituents is different and that it, the Spirit, is something different, the Spirit may well be said to be released. (Gī. 13. 29, 30; 14. 20). Because, strictly speaking, the Spirit is fundamentally neither a doer nor is it bound. It is independent and by its very nature isolated, that is, it is non-active. Whatever happens is being done by Matter. Nay, in as much as the Mind and even Reason are manifestations of Matter, whatever knowledge is acquired by Reason is the result of the activity of Matter. This knowledge is three-fold, namely, *sāttvika*, *rājasa* and *tāmasa* (Gī. 18. 20-22). Out of these, when Reason acquires the *sāttvika* kind of knowledge, the Spirit realises that it is different from Matter. The *sattva, rajas* and *tamas* constituents are the constituents of Matter, not of the Spirit. The Spirit is qualityless and *prakṛti* with its three constituents, is its mirror (Ma. Bhā. Śān. 204. 8.). When this mirror becomes clear, that is to say, when the Reason, which is a manifestation of Matter, becomes *sāttvika*, then the Spirit sees in this clear mirror its own clear identity, namely, that it is different from Matter, and Dame Matter, becoming shamefaced, stops her dance before the Spirit. When this state is acquired, the Spirit is released from all bonds and attains its inherent isolation. Isolation *(kaivalya)* means the state of being '*kevala*' (isolated), that is, being single and not being joint with Matter; and it is this natural state of the Spirit which is called *mokṣa* (Release) or salvation by the Sāṁkhya philosophers. But some Sāṁkhya philosophers have raised the delicate question whether in this state, it is the Spirit which abandons Matter or Matter which abandons the Spirit. This question is of the same type as the question whether the wife is too tall for the husband or the husband too short for the wife, and some may think it is equally useless. Because when two things are divorced from each other, there is no point in considering who has left whom, as we see that both leave each other. But if one gives this question of the Sāṁkhya philosophers deep consideration, it will be seen not to be improper from their point of view, in as much as according to the Sāṁkhya philosophy, the Spirit being without qualities, non-active, and apathetic, the performance of the actions of 'giving up' or 'sticking to' cannot technically speaking be ascribed to the Spirit (Gī. 13. 31, 32). Therefore, the Sāṁkhyas have come to the conclusion that it is Matter, (which has got the quality of activity), which must be said to leave the Spirit, that is to say, it is "*prakṛti*" which obtains its own Release from the Spirit (Sāṁ. Kā. 62 and Gī. 13. 34). In short, Release is not an independent state which results to the Spirit from some outside agency, nor is it a state which is different from its fundamental and inherent state; just as the outer skin of a stick of grass is different from the internal stock, or as the fish in water is different from the water, so are Matter and Spirit relationed towards each other. Ordinary persons, being steeped in ignorance as a result of the constituents of Matter, do not realise this distinction and remain tied up within the periphery of family affairs. But he who has realised this distinction may well be said to be released. It is stated in the Mahābhārata that such a person is called a 'knower' or '*buddha*' (wise) or '*kṛtakṛtya*', i. e., one who has done whatever ought to have been done by him. (See Ma. Bhā. Śān. 194. 58; 248. 11 and 306. 308). And the meaning of the word '*buddhimān*' (intelligent) in the sentence "*etad buddhvā buddhimān syāt*", i. e., "by understanding this, a man becomes '*buddhimān*' or '*buddha*', that is, becomes a knower" (Gī. 15. 20) is the same. The true form of Release even according to the science of the Ātman *(adhyātma)* is also the same. (Ve. Sū. Śāṁ. Bhā. 1. 1. 4). But the *advaita* (Monistic) Vedānta philosophers give a different explanation about it: instead of saying that the Spirit is inherently isolated, they say that in as much as the Ātman is fundamentally of the form of the *Parabrahman* (Supreme Spirit), *Mokṣa* is the realisation by the Ātman of its fundamental form, namely, of the *Parabrahman*. This difference between the Sāṁkhya philosophy and the Vedānta philosophy will be made clear in the next chapter.

Although the *advaita* (Monistic) Vedānta philosophy fully accepts the Sāṁkhya theory that the Spirit is qualityless, apathetic, and inactive, yet the other doctrine of the Sāṁkhya philosophy, namely, that there are fundamentally innumerable independent Spirits which see the dance of one and the same Matter is not acceptable to the Vedāntists (Gī. 8. 4; 13. 20-22; Ma. Bhā. Śān. 351; and Ve. Sū. Śāṁ. Bhā. 2. 1. 1). According to the Vedānta philosophy, living beings appear different as a result of difference of environment; but, as a matter of fact everything is Brahman. According to the Sāṁkhya philosophers, in as much as the life and death and the family of every man is different, and in as much as one comes across this difference in the world that one man is happy and another man is unhappy, every Ātman or *puruṣa* must be originally different from another, and their number is innumerable (Sāṁ. Kā. 18). It is true that Matter and Spirit are the two fundamental principles of the entire universe; but the Sāṁkhya philosophers interpret the word 'Spirit' as meaning a collection of innumerable Spirits. They say that the world goes on as a result of the union between these innumerable Spirits and Matter with its three constituents. When each Spirit becomes united with Matter, it places before that Spirit the diffusion of its constituents, and the Spirit goes on enjoying it. After this has gone on for a long time, when in the case of a particular Spirit, the activity of *prakṛti* takes the *sāttvika* (placid) form, that Spirit alone (not all Spirits) acquires true knowledge, and the activity of Matter comes to an end so far as it is concerned, and it reaches its fundamental isolated state. But even if it attains salvation, the worldly life of the other Spirits continues. Some people are likely to think that when a Spirit reaches the state of isolation, it must at once escape from the meshes of Matter. But according to the Sāṁkhya philosophers such is not the case, and the body and the organs which are the manifestations of Matter do not leave it till the body dies. The reason given by the Sāṁkhya philosophers for this is: "in the same way as the wheel of the potter goes on revolving for some time as a result of previous motion, even after the pot on it has been finished and taken away from it, so also does the body of even that man who has attained the state of isolation continue to exist for some time". (Sāṁ. Kā. 67). But the man who has attained that isolated state is not in any way obstructed, nor does he experience either pain or pleasure, on account of his body; because, in as much as this body, which is a manifestation of gross or lifeless Matter, is in itself gross or lifeless, he looks upon both pain and pleasure or happiness as the same; and if you say that the Spirit will be affected by pain or pleasure, then, as it has realised that it is different from the activity of Matter, and that the entire activity is of Matter and not its own, it remains apathetic, howmuchsoever active Matter may continue. That man who has not acquired this knowledge by transcending the three constituents of Matter, does not escape the cycle of birth and death; then he may take birth in the sphere of gods, as a result of the preponderance of the *sattva* constituent or in the sphere of humans, as a result of the preponderance of the *rajas* constituent, or in the sphere of animals, as a result of the preponderance of the *tamas* constituent (Sāṁ. Kā. 44, 54). These results, in the shape of the cycle of birth and death, befall a man as a result of the preponderance or minimisation of the *sattva*, *rajas* and *tamas* constituents in the Matter which envelopes him, that is, in his Reason. It is stated even in the Gītā (Gī. 14. 18), that:- "*ūrdhvaṁ gacchanti sattvasthāḥ*", that is, "persons in whom the *sāttvika* constituent predominates go to heaven", and *tāmasa* persons go to perdition. But these resulting states in the shape of heaven etc., are non-permanent. For that Spirit which wishes to become released from the cycle of birth and death, or according to the terminology of the Sāṁkhya philosophy, which has to maintain its difference or isolation from Matter, there is no other way except transcending the three constituents and becoming *virakta* (desireless). Kapilācārya had acquired this asceticism and Knowledge from his very birth. But it is not possible that every man can be in this state from the moment of his birth. Therefore, everyone must by means of the discrimination of fundamental principles realise the difference between Matter and Spirit and try to purify his Reason. When by such efforts, the Reason becomes *sāttvika*, there arise in that Reason itself the qualities of Realisation (*jñāna*), Asceticism (*vairāgya*), and Power (*aiśvarya*), and the man ultimately reaches isolation. The word '*aiśvarya*' (power) is used here in the sense of the Yogic power of acquiring whatever may be desired. According to the Sāṁkhya philosophy, Righteousness (*dharma*) is included in the *sāttvika* constituent; but Kapilācārya has ultimately made the distinction, that by mere *dharma* one acquires only heaven, whereas Knowledge and Asceticism give Release or Isolation, and effect a total annihilation of the unhappiness of a man. That man who, as a result of the preponderance of the *sāttvika* constituent in his bodily organs and in his Reason, has realised that he is distinct from Matter with its three constituents, is called *triguṇātīta* (one who has transcended the *sattva rajas* and *tamas* constituents) by the Sāṁkhyas. In this state of a *triguṇātīta*, neither the *sattva*, nor the *rajas*, nor the *tamas* constituent continues to exist; therefore, considering the matter minutely, one has to admit that this state is different from either the *sāttvikī*, or *rājasī*, or *tāmasī* states of mind; and following this line of argument the Bhāgavata religion, after dividing Devotion *(bhakti)* into ignorant, progressive, or placid, has described the disinterested and non-differentiating devotion of the man who has transcended the three constituents as *nirguṇa*, that is, unaffected-by-quality (Bhāg. 3. 29. 7-14). But it is not proper to extend the principle of division beyond the three divisions of placid, progressive, and ignorant. Therefore, the Sāṁkhya philosophers include the *triguṇātīta* state of transcending the three constituents in the placid (*sāttvika*) state on the basis that it results from the highest expansion of the placid constituent; and the same position has also been accepted in the Gītā. For instance, the non-differentiating knowledge that every thing is one and the same is, according to the Gītā, placid knowledge (Gī. 18. 20); and where the description of the *sāttvikī* state of mind is given in the fourteenth chapter of the Gītā, the description of the state of transcending the three constituents is given later on at the end of the same chapter. But it must be borne in mind that in as much as the Gītā does not accept the duality of Matter and Spirit, the words '*prakṛti*', '*puruṣa*', '*triguṇātīta*', which are technical terms of Sāṁkhya philosophy are always used in a slightly different meaning in the Gītā; or in short, the Gītā permanently keeps the rider of the monistic (*advaita*) Parabrahman on the Dualism (*dvaita*) of the Sāṁkhya philosophy. For instance, the difference between Matter and Spirit according to the Sāṁkhya philosophy has been described in the 13th chapter of the Gītā (Gī. 13. 19–34). But there the words '*prakṛti*' and '*puruṣa*' are synonymous with the words '*kṣetra*' and '*kṣetrajña*'. Similarly, the description in the 14th chapter of the state of transcending the three constituents (Gī. 14. 22–27) is of the *siddha* or released man who, having escaped the meshes of Māyā (Illusion) with its three constituents, has realised the Paramātman (Supreme Spirit) which is beyond both Matter and Spirit, and not of a Sāṁkhya philosopher, who looks upon Matter and Spirit as two distinct principles and who looks upon the isolation of the Spirit as the state of transcending the three constituents of Matter. This difference has been made perfectly clear by me in the subsequent chapter on *adhyātma* (philosophy of the Highest Self). But as the Blessed Lord has, while supporting the *adhyātma* or Vedānta philosophy in the Gītā, in many places made use of the Sāṁkhya terminology and arguments, one is likely to get the wrong idea, while reading the Gītā, that it accepts as correct the pure Sāṁkhya philosophy. Therefore, I have repeated here this difference between the Sāṁkhya philosophy and the propositions similar to it in the Gītā. Śaṁkarācārya has stated in the *Vedānta Sūtra-bhāṣya*, that he is prepared to accept all the propositions of the Sāṁkhya philosophy but not to give up the *advaita* theory of the Upaniṣads that there is only one fundamental principle in the world, namely, the Parabrahman (Supreme Spirit), which is beyond both Matter and Spirit and from which the entire creation, including Matter and Spirit, has sprung (Ve. Sū. Śāṁ. Bhā. 2. 1. 3); and the same line of argument applies to the arguments in the Gītā.

CHAPTER VIII.

THE CONSTRUCTION AND THE DESTRUCTION OF THE COSMOS.

guṇā guṇeṣu jāyante tatraiva niviśanti ca । *

Mahābhārata, Śānti. 305. 23.

I have so far dealt with the nature of the two independent fundamental principles of the world according to the Kāpila Sāṁkhya philosophy, namely, Matter and Spirit, and have described how one has to release one's Self from the network of the constituent qualities of Matter which it places before one's eyes, as a result of its union with Spirit. But the explanation of how this 'Saṁsāra' (worldly illusion) is placed by Matter before the Spirit—this its diffusion, or its drama which Marathi poets have given the vivid name of 'saṁsṛticā piṁgā' (the fantastic dance of worldly life), and which is called "the Mint of Matter" by Jñāneśvara Mahārāja—and in what way the same is destroyed, has still to be given; and I shall deal with that subject in this chapter. This activity of Matter is known as "the Construction and Destruction of the Cosmos", because, according to the Sāṁkhya philosophy, *prakṛti* (Matter) has created this world or creation for the benefit of innumerable Spirits. Śrī Samartha Rāmadāsa has in two or three places in the *Dāsabodha* given a beautiful description

---

* "Constituents (*guṇas*) are born out of constituents, and are merged in them".

of how the entire Cosmos is created from Matter, and I have taken the phrase "Construction and Destruction of the Cosmos" from that description. Similarly, this subject-matter has been dealt with principally in the seventh and eighth chapters of the Bhagavadgītā, and from the following prayer of Arjuna to Śrī Kṛṣṇa in the beginning of the eleventh chapter, namely: *bhavāpyayau hi bhūtānāṁ śrutau vistaraśo mayā*" (Gī. 11. 2), i. e., "I have heard (what You have said) in detail about the creation and the destruction of created beings; now show me actually Your Cosmic Form, and fulfill my ambition", it is clearly seen that the construction and the destruction of the Cosmos is an important part of the subject-matter of the Mutable and the Immutable. The Knowledge by which one realises that all the perceptible objects in the world, which are more than one (are numerous), contain only one fundamental imperceptible substance, is called 'jñāna' (Gī. 18. 20); and the Knowledge by which one understands how the various innumerable perceptible things severally came into existence out of one fundamental imperceptible substance is called '*vijñāna*'; and not only does this subject-matter include the consideration of the Mutable and the Immutable, but it also includes the knowledge of the Body and the Ātman and the knowledge of the Absolute Self.

According to the Bhagavadgītā, Matter does not carry on its activities independently, but has to do so according to the will of the Parameśvara (Gī. 9. 10). But, as has been stated before, Kapila Ṛṣi considered Matter as independent. According to the Sāṁkhya philosophy, its union with Spirit is a sufficient proximate cause for its diffusion to commence. Matter needs nothing else for this purpose. The Sāṁkhyas say that as soon as Matter is united with Spirit, its minting starts; and just as in spring, trees get foliage and after that, leaves, flowers, and fruits follow one after the other (Ma. Bhā. Śān. 231. 73; and Manu. 1. 30), so also is the fundamental equable state of Matter disrupted, and its constituents begin to spread out. On the other hand, in the Veda-Saṁhitās, the Upaniṣads, and the Smṛti texts, the Parabrahman is looked upon as fundamental instead of Matter, and different descriptions are found in those books about the creation of the Cosmos from that Parabrahman (Highest Brahman), namely that: "*hiraṇyagarbhaḥ samavartatāgre bhūtasya jātaḥ patir eka āsīt*", i. e., "the Golden Egg first came into existence" (Ṛg. 10. 121. 1), and from this Golden Egg, or from Truth, the whole world was created (Ṛg. 10. 72; 10. 190); or first, water was created (Ṛg. 10. 82. 6; Tai. Brā. 1. 1. 3. 7; Ai. U. 1. 1. 2), and from that water, the Cosmos; or that when in this water an egg had come into existence, the Brahmadeva was born out of it, and either from this Brahmadeva, or from the original Egg, the entire world was later on created (Manu. 1. 8–13; Chān. 3. 19); or that the same Brahmadeva (male) was turned, as to half of him, into a female (Bṛ. 1. 4. 3; Manu. 1. 32); or that Brahmadeva was a male before water came into existence (Kaṭha. 4. 6); or that from the Parabrahman only three elements were created, namely, brilliance, water and the earth (food), and that later on, all things were created as a result of the intermixture of the three (Chān. 6. 2–6). Nevertheless, there is a clear conclusion in the Vedānta-Sūtras (Ve. Sū. 2. 3. 1–15), that the five primordial elements, namely, Ether *(ākāśa)* etc., came into existence in their respective order from the fundamental Brahman in the shape of the Ātman (Tai. U. 2. 1); and there are clear references in the Upaniṣads to *prakṛti*, *mahat*, and other elements, e. g., see Kaṭha (3. 11), Maitrayaṇī (6. 10), Śvetāśvatara (4. 10; 6. 16) etc. From this it can be seen that though according to Vedānta philosophy, Matter is not independent, yet after the stage when a transformation makes its appearance in the Pure Brahman in the shape of an illusory Prakṛti, there is an agreement between that philosophy and the Sāṁkhya philosophy about the subsequent creation of the Cosmos; and it is, therefore, stated in the Mahābhārata that: "all knowledge which there is in history or in the Purāṇas, or in economics has all been derived from Sāṁkhya philosophy" (Śān. 301. 108, 109). This does not mean that the Vedāntists or the writers of the Purāṇas have copied this knowledge from the Kāpila Sāṁkhya philosophy; but only that everywhere the conception of the order in which the Cosmos was created is the same. Nay, it may even be said that the word 'Sāṁkhya' has been used here in the comprehensive meaning of 'Knowledge'. Nevertheless,

Kapilācārya has explained the order of the creation of the Cosmos in a particularly systematic manner from the point of view of a science, and as the Sāṁkhya theory has been principally accepted in the Bhagavadgītā, I have dealt with it at length in this chapter.

Not only have modern Western materialistic philosophers accepted the Sāṁkhya doctrine that the entire perceptible Cosmos has come out of one *avyakta* (imperceptible to the organs), subtle, homogeneous, unorganised, fundamental substance, which completely pervades everything on all sides, but they have come to the further conclusions that the energy in this fundamental substance has grown only gradually, and that nothing has come into existence suddenly and like a spout, giving the go-bye to the previous and continuous order of creation of the universe. This theory is called the Theory of Evolution. When this theory was first enunciated in the Western countries in the last century, it caused there a great commotion. In the Christian Scriptures, it is stated that the Creator of the world created the five primordial elements and every living being which fell into the category of moveables one by one at different times, and this genesis was believed in by all Christians before the advent of the Evolution Theory. Therefore, when this doctrine ran the risk of being refuted by the Theory of Evolution, that theory was attacked on all sides, and that opposition is still more or less going on in those countries. Nevertheless, in as much as the strength of a scientific truth must always prevail, the Evolution Theory of the creation of the Cosmos is now becoming more and more acceptable to all learned scholars. According to this theory, there was originally one subtle, homogeneous substance in the Solar system, and as the original motion or heat of that substance gradually became less and less, it got more and more condensed, and the Earth and the other planets gradually came into existence, and the Sun is the final portion of it which has now remained. The Earth was originally a very hot ball, same as the Sun, but as it gradually lost its heat, some portion of the original substance remained in the liquid from, while other portions became solidified, and the air and water which surround the earth and the gross material earth under them, came gradually into existence; and later on, all the living and non-living creation came into existence as the result of the union of these three. On the line of this argument, Darwin and other philosophers have maintained that even man has in this way gradually come into existence by evolution from micro-organisms. Yet, there is still a great deal of difference of opinion between Materialists and Metaphysicians as to whether or not the Soul (Ātman) should be considered as an independent fundamental principle. Haeckel and some others like him maintain that the Soul and Vitality have gradually come into existence out of Gross Matter, and support the *jaḍādvaita* (Gross Monistic) doctrine; on the other hand, Metaphysicians like Kant say that in as much as all the knowledge we get of the Cosmos is the result of the synthetic activity of the Soul, the Soul must be looked upon as an independent entity. Because, saying that the Soul which perceives the external world is a part of the world which is perceived by it, or that it has come into existence out of the world, is logically as meaningless as saying that one can sit on one's own shoulders. For the same reason, Matter and Spirit are looked upon as two independent principles in the Sāṁkhya philosophy. In short, it is even now being maintained by many learned scholars in the Western countries that however much the Materialistic knowledge of the universe may grow, the consideration of the form of the Root Principle of the Cosmos must always be made from a different point of view. But my readers will see that as regards the question of the order in which all perceptible things came to be created from one Gross Matter, there is not much difference of opinion between the Western Theory of Evolution, and the Diffusion-out of Matter described in the Sāṁkhya philosophy; because, the principal proposition that the heterogeneous perceptible Cosmos (both subtle and gross) came to be gradually created from one imperceptible, subtle, and homogeneous fundamental Matter, is accepted by both. But, as the knowledge of the Material sciences has now considerably increased, modern natural scientists have considered as prominent the three qualities of motion, heat and attraction, instead of the three qualities of *sattva*, *rajas*, and *tamas* of the Sāṁkhya philosophy.

It is true that from the point of view of the natural sciences, it is easier to realise the diversity in the mutual strength of heat or attraction than the diversity in the mutual intensity of the three qualities of *sattva*, *rajas*, and *tamas*. Nevertheless, the principle: "*guṇā guṇeṣu vartante*" (Gī. 3. 28), i. e., "constituents come out of constituents", which is the principle of the diffusion or expansion of constituent qualities, is common to both. Sāṁkhya philosophers say that in the same way as a folding-fan is gradually opened out, so also when the folds of Matter in its equable state (in which its *sattva*, *rajas*, and *tamas* constituent qualities are equal) are opened out, the whole perceptible universe begins to come into existence; and there is no real difference between this conception and the Theory of Evolution. Nevertheless, the fact that the Gītā, and partly also the Upaniṣads and other Vedic texts have without demur accepted the theory of the growth of the *guṇas* (constituents) side by side with the Monistic Vedānta doctrines, instead of rejecting it as is done by the Christian religion, is a difference which ought to be kept in mind from the point of view of the Philosophy of Religion.

Let us now consider what the theory of the Sāṁkhya philosophers is about the order in which the folds of Matter are unfolded. This order of unfoldment is known as '*guṇotkarṣa-vāda*' (the theory of the unfolding of constituent qualities), or '*guṇa-pariṇāma-vāda*' (the theory of the development of qualities). It need not be said that every man comes to a decision according to his own intelligence to perform an act or that he must first get the inspiration to do an act, before he commences to do the act. Nay, there are statements even in the Upaniṣads, that the universe came to be created after the One fundamental Paramātman was inspired with the desire to multiply, e. g., "*bahu syāṁ prajāyeya*" (Chān. 6. 2. 3; Taī. 2. 6). On the same line of argument, imperceptible Matter first comes to a decision to break up its own equable state and to create the perceptible universe. Decision means '*vyavasāya*', and coming to a decision is a sign of Reason. Therefore, the Sāṁkhya philosophers have come to the conclusion that the first quality which comes into existence in Matter is Pure (deciding) Reason (*vyavasāyatmikā buddhi*). In short, in the same way as a man has first to be inspired with the desire of doing some particular act, so also is it necessary that Matter should first be inspired with the desire of becoming diffuse. But because man is vitalised, that is to say, because in him there has taken place a union between the Reason of Matter and the vitalised Spirit (Ātman), he understands this deciding Reason which inspires him; and as Matter itself is non-vital or Gross, it does not understand its own Reason. This is the great difference between the two, and this difference is the result of the Consciousness which Matter has acquired as a result of its union with the Spirit. It is not the quality of Gross Matter. When one bears in mind that even modern Materialistic natural scientists have now begun to admit that unless one credits Matter with some Energy which, though non-self-intelligible *(asvayaṁvedya)*, is yet of the same nature as human intelligence, one cannot reasonably explain the mutual attraction or repulsion seen in the material world in the shape of gravitation, or magnetic attraction or repulsion, or other chemical actions, * one need not be surprised about the proposition of the Sāṁkhya philosophy that Reason is the first quality which is acquired by Matter. You may, if you like, give this quality which first arises in Matter the name of Reason which is non-vitalised or non-self-perceptible

* "Without the assumption of an atomic soul, the commonest and the most general phenomena of Chemistry are inexplicable. Pleasure and pain, desire and aversion, attraction and repulsion, must be common to all atoms of an aggregate; for the movements of atoms which must take place in the formation and dissolution of a chemical compound can be explained only by attributing to them *Sensation* and *Will*"—Haeckel in the *Perigenesis of the Plastidule* cited in Martineau's *Types of Ethical Theory*, Vol. II p. 399, 3rd Ed. Haeckel himself explains this statement as follows: "I explicitly stated that I conceived the elementary psychic qualities of *sensation* and *will* which may be attributed to atoms to be *unconscious*—just as unconscious as the elementary memory which I, in common with the distinguished psychologist Ewald Hering, consider to be a common function of all organised matter, or more correctly the living substances"—*The Riddle of the Universe*, Chap. IX p. 63 (R. P. A. Cheap. Ed.).

(*asvayamvedya*). But it is clear that the desire which a man gets and the desire which inspires Matttar belong originally to one and the same class; and, therefore, both are defined in the same way in hoth the places. This Reason has also such other names as '*mahat*', '*jñāna*', '*mati*', '*āsurī*', '*prajñā*' '*khyāti*' etc. Out of these, the name '*mahat*' (first person singular masculine, *mahān*, i. e., 'big') must have been given because Matter now begins to be enlarged, or on account of the importance of this quality. In as much as this quality of '*mahān*' or Reason is the result of the admixture of the three constituent qualities of *sattva*, *rajas*, and *tamas*, this quality of Matter can later on take diverse forms, though apparently it is singular. Because, though the *sattva*, *rajas* and *tamas* constituents are apparently only three in number, yet, in as much as the mutual ratio of these three can be infinitely different in each mixture, the varieties of Reason which result from the infinitely different ratios of each constituent in each mixture can also be infinite. This Reason, which arises from imperceptible Matter, is also subtle like Matter. But although Reason is subtle like Matter, in the sense in which the words 'perceptible', 'imperceptible', 'gross', and 'subtle' have been explained in the last chapter, yet it is not imperceptible like Matter, and one can acquire Knowledge of it. Therefore, this Reason falls into the category of things which are '*vyakta*' (i. e., perceptible to human beings); and not only Reason, but all other subsequent evolutes (*vikāra*) of Matter are also looked upon as perceptible in the Sāṁkhya philosophy. There is no imperceptible principle other than fundamental Matter.

Although perceptible Discerning Reason thus enters imperceptible Matter, it (Matter) still remains homogeneous. This homogeneity being broken up and heterogeneity being acquired is known as 'Individuation' (*pṛthaktva*) as in the case of mercury falling on the ground and being broken up into small globules. Unless this individuality or heterogeneity comes into existence, after Reason has come into existence, it is impossible that numerous different objects should be formed out of one singular Matter. This individuality which subsequently arrives as a result of Reason is known as 'Individuation' (*ahaṁkāra*), because, individuality is first expressed by the words 'I—you', and saying 'I—you' means '*ahaṁkāra*', that is, saying '*aham*' '*aham*' ('I' 'I'). This quality of Individuation which enters Matter may, if you like, be called a non-self-perceptible (*asvayaṁvedya*) Individuation. But the Individuation in man, and the Individuation by reason of which trees, stones, water, or other fundamental atoms spring out of homogeneous Matter are of the same kind; and the only difference is that as the stone is not self-conscious, it has not got the knowledge of '*aham*' ('I'), and as it has not got a mouth, it cannot by self-consciousness say 'I am different from you'. Otherwise, the elementary principle of remaining separate individually from others, that is, of consciousness or of Individuation is the same everywhere. This Individuation has also the other names of '*taijasa*', '*abhimāna*', '*bhutādi*', and '*dhātu*'. As Individuation is a sub-division of Reason it cannot come into existence, unless Reason has in the first instance come into existence. Sāṁkhya philosophers have, therefore, laid down that Individuation is the second quality, that is, the quality which comes into existence after Reason. It need not be said that there are infinite varieties of Individuation as in the case of Reason, as a result of the differences of the *sattva*, *rajas* and *tamas* constituents. The subsequent qualities are in the same way also of three infinite varieties. Nay, everything which exists in the perceptible world falls in the same way into infinite categories of *sāttvika*, *rājasa* and *tāmasa*; and consistently with this proposition, the Gītā has mentioned the three categories of qualities and the three categories of Devotion (Gi. Chap. 14 & Chap. 17).

When Matter, which originally is in an equable state, acquires the perceptible faculties of Discerning Reason and Individuation, homogeneity is destroyed and it begins to be transformed into numerous objects. Yet, it does not lose its subtle nature, and we may say that the subtle Atoms of the Nyāya school now begin to come into existence. Because, before Individuation came into existence, Matter was unbroken and unorganised. Reason and Individuation by themselves are, strictly speaking, only faculties. But, on that account the above proposition is not to be understood as meaning that they exist independently of the substance of Matter. What is meant is, that when these faculties enter the fundamental, homogeneous, and unorganised Matter, that Matter itself acquires the form of perceptible, heterogeneous, and organised substance. When fundamental Matter has thus acquired the faculty of becoming transformed into various objects by means of Individuation, its further development falls into two categories. One of these is the creation consisting of life having organs, such as trees, men etc., and the other is of the world consisting of unorganised things. In this place the word 'organs' is to be understood as meaning only 'the faculties of the organs of organised beings'. Because, the gross body of organised beings is included in the gross, that is, unorganised world, and their Ātman falls into the different category of 'Spirit'. Therefore, in dealing with the organised world, Sāṁkhya philosophy leaves out of consideration the Body and the Ātman, and considers only the organs. In as much as there can be no third substance in the world besides organic and inorganic substances, it goes without saying that Individuation cannot give rise to more than two categories. As organic faculty is more powerful than inorganic substance, the organic world is called *sāttvika*, that is, something which comes into existence as a result of the preponderance of the *sattva* constituent; and the inorganic world is called *tāmasa*, that is something which comes into existence as a result of the preponderance of the *tamas* constituent. In short, when the faculty of Individuation begins to create diverse objects, there is sometimes a preponderance of the *sāttvika* constituent, leading to the creation of the five organs of Perception, the five organs of Action, and the Mind, making in all the eleven fundamental organs of the organic world; and at other times, there is a preponderance of the *tamas* constituent, whereby the five fundamental Fine Elements *(tanmātra)* of the inorganic world come into existence. But in as much as Matter still continues to remain in a subtle form, these sixteen elements, which are a result of Individuation, are still subtle elements.*

* If I were to convey this import in the English language, I would say:–

The Primeval matter (*Prakriti*) was at first *homogeneous*. It *resolved* (*Buddhi*) to unfold itself, and by the *principle of differentiation*

The Fine Elements (*tanmātras*) of sound, touch, colour, taste and smell—that is to say, the extremely subtle fundamental forms of each of these properties which do not mix with each other—are the fundamental elements of the inorganic creation, and the remaining eleven organs, including the Mind, are the seeds of the organic creation. The explanation given in the Sāṁkhya philosophy as to why there are only five of the first kind and only eleven of the second kind deserves consideration. Modern natural scientists have divided the substances in the world into solid, liquid, and gaseous. But the principle of classification of substances according to Sāṁkhya philosophy is different. Sāṁkhya philosophers say that man acquires the knowledge of all worldly objects by means of the five organs of Perception; and the peculiar construction of these organs is such that any one organ perceives only one quality. As the eyes cannot smell, the ears cannot see, the skin cannot distinguish between sweet and bitter, the tongue does not recognise sound, and the nose cannot distinguish between black and white. If the five organs of Perception and their five objects, namely, sound, touch, sight, taste, and smell, are in this way fixed, one cannot fix the number of the properties of matter at more than five. Because, even if we imagine that there are more than five such properties, we have no means to perceive them. Each of these five objects of sense can of course be sub-divided into many divisions. For example, though sound is only one object of sense, yet, it is divided into numerous kinds of sound, such as small, large, harsh, hoarse, broken or sweet; or, as described in the science of music, it may be the note B or E or C etc.; or according to grammar, it may be guttural, palatal, labial etc.; and similarly, though taste is in reality only one object of sense, yet, it is also divided into many kinds such as, sweet, pungent, saltish, hot, bitter, astringent, acid etc; and although

(*Ahamkara*) became *heterogeneous*. It then branched off into *two* sections–one *organic* (*Sendriya*) and the other *inorganic* (*Nirindriya*). There are *eleven* elements of the organic and *five* of the inorganic creation. *Purusha* or the observer is different from all these and falls under none of the above categories.

colour is in reality only one object of sense, it is also divided into diverse colours such as white, black, green, blue, yellow, red etc; similarly even if sweetness is taken as a particular kind of taste, yet, the sweet tastes of sugarcane, milk, jaggery, or sugar are all different divisions of sweetness; and if one makes different mixtures of different qualities, this diversity of qualities becomes infinite in an infinite number of ways. But, whatever happens, the fundamental properties of substance can never be more than five; because, the organs of Perception are only five in number and each of them perceives only one object of sense. Therefore, although we do not come across any object which is an object of sound only or of touch only, that is, in which different properties are not mixed up, yet, according to Sāṁkhya philosophy, there must be fundamentally only five distinct subtle *tanmātra* modifications of fundamental Matter, namely, merely sound, merely touch, merely colour, merely taste, and merely smell—that is, the fine sound element *(śabda-tanmātra)*, the fine touch element *(sparśa-tanmātra)*, the fine colour element (*rūpa-tanmātra)*, the fine taste element (*rasa-tanmātra*) and the fine smell element (*gandha-tanmātra*). I have further on dealt with what the writers of the Upaniṣads have to say regarding the five Fine Elements or the five primordial elements springing from them.

If, after having thus considered the inorganic world and come to the conclusion that it has only five subtle fundamental elements, we next consider the organic world, we likewise come to the conclusion that no one has got more than eleven organs, namely, the five organs of Perception, the five organs of Action and the Mind. Although we see the organs of hands, feet etc., only in their gross forms in the Gross Body, yet, the diversity of the various organs cannot be explained, unless we admit the existence of some subtle element at the root of each of them. The western Materialistic theory of Evolution has gone into a considerable amount of discussion on this question. Modern biologists say that the most minute fundamental globular micro-organisms have only the organ of skin, and that from that skin other physical organs have come into existence one by one. They say, for instance, that the eye came into existence as a result of the contact of light with the skin of the original micro-organism; and that, similarly, the other gross organs came into existence by the contact of light etc. This doctrine of Materialistic philosophers is to be found even in Sāṁkhya philosophy. In the Mahābhārata, there is a description of the growth of the organs consistent with the tenets of Sāṁkhya philosophy, as follows :—

śabdarāgāt śrotram asya jāyate bhāvitātmanaḥ ।

rūparāgāt tathā cakṣuḥ ghrāṇaṁ gandhajighṛkṣayā ॥

(Ma. Bhā. Śān. 213. 16).

that is, "When the Ātman in a living being gets the desire of hearing sound, the ears come into existence; when it gets the desire of perceiving colour, the eyes are formed; when it gets the desire of smelling, the nose is created". But the Sāṁkhya philosophers say that though the skin may be the first thing to come into existence, yet, how can any amount of contact of the Sun's rays with the skin of micro-organisms in the living world give rise to eyes—and that too in a particular portion of the body—unless fundamental Matter possesses an inherent possibility of different organs being created? Darwin's theory only says that when one organism with eyes and another organism without eyes have been created, the former lives longer than the latter in the struggle for existence of the material world, and the latter is destroyed. But the Western Materialistic science of biology does not explain why in the first place the eyes and other physical organs at all come into existence. According to the Sāṁkhya philosophy, these various organs do not grow one by one out of one fundamental organ, but when Matter begins to become heterogeneous as a result of the element of Individuation, such Individuation causes the eleven different faculties or qualities, namely, the five organs of Perception, the five organs of Action and the Mind, to come into existence in fundamental Matter, independently of each other and simultaneously (*yugapat*); and thereby, later on, the organic world comes into existence. Out of these eleven organs, the Mind is dual, that is, it performs two different functions, according to the difference in the organs with which it works, as has been explained before in the sixth chapter: that is to say, it is discriminating and classifying (*saṁkalpa-vikalpātmaka*) in co-operation with the organs of Perception and arranges the various impressions experienced by the various organs, and after classifying them, places them before Reason for decision; and it is executive (*vyākaraṇātmaka*) in co-operation with the organs of Action, that is to say, it executes the decisions arrived at by Reason with the help of the organs of Action. In the Upaniṣads, the organs themselves are given the name of 'Vital Force' (*prāṇa*); and the authors of the Upaniṣads (Muṇḍa 2. 1 .3), like the Sāṁkhya philosophers, are of the opinion that these vital forces are not the embodiment of the five primordial elements, but are individually born out of the Paramātman (Absolute Self). The number of these vital forces or organs is stated in the Upaniṣads to be seven in some places and to be ten, eleven, twelve, or thirteen in other places; but Śrī Śaṁkarācārya has proved on the authority of the Vedānta-Sūtras, that if an attempt is made to harmonise the various statements in the Upaniṣads, the number of these organs is fixed at eleven (Ve. Sū. Śāṁ. Bhā. 2. 4. 5, 6); and in the Gītā it has been clearly stated that "*indriyāṇi daśaikaṁ ca*" (Gī. 13. 5), i. e., "the organs are ten plus one, or eleven". In short, there is no difference of opinion on this point between the Sāṁkhya and the Vedānta philosophy.

According to the Sāṁkhya philosophy, after the eleven organic faculties or qualities, which are the basis of the organic world, and the five subtle elementary essences (*tanmātras*) which are the basis of the inorganic world have thus come into existence as a result of *sāttvika* and *tāmasa* Individuation respectively, the five gross primordial elements (which are also called '*viśeṣa*'), as also gross inorganic substances, come into existence out of the five fundamental subtle essences (*tanmātras*); and when these inorganic substances, come into contact with the eleven subtle organs, the organic universe comes into existence.

The order in which the various Elements come out of fundamental Matter according to Sāṁkhya philosophy, and which has been so far described, will be clear from the genealogical tree given below :—

THE GENEALOGICAL TREE OF THE COSMOS.

SPIRIT →(Both self-created and eternal)←MATTER.

- SPIRIT (Quality-less.) (Synonyms ; *jña*, Observer etc.)
- MATTER. (Imperceptible and Subtle) (Possesses the *sattva*, *rajas*, and *tamas* constituents) (Synonyms : *pradhāna*, *avyakta*, *māyā*, *prasava-dharmiṇī* etc.)
  - MAHĀN OR REASON (Perceptible and Subtle) Synonyms : *āsuri*, *mati*, *jñāna*, *khyāti*, (etc.)
    - AHAMKĀRA (Individuation) (Perceptible and Subtle) (Synonyms : *abhimāna*, *taijasa*, etc.)
      - SĀTTVIKA CREATION (i.e., Perceptible & Subtle organs)
        - Five organs of PERCEPTION.
        - Five organs of ACTION.
        - MIND.
      - TĀMASA CREATION (i.e., Inorganic world)
        - Five TANMĀTRAS (Subtle)
          - Five PRIMORDIAL ELEMENTS or VIŚEṢAS (Gross).

(Bracket from MAHĀN to Five TANMĀTRAS:) The (subtle) LINGA-ŚARĪRA made up of EIGHTEEN elements.

There are thus twenty-five elementary principles, counting the five gross primordial elements and Spirit. Out of these, the twenty-three elements including and after Mahān (Reason), are the evolutes (*vikāras*) of fundamental Matter. But even then, the subtle Tanmātras and the five gross primordial elements are substantial (*dravyātmaka*) evolutes and Reason, Individuation, and the organs are merely faculties or qualities. The further distinction is that whereas these twenty-three elements are perceptible, fundamental Matter is imperceptible. Out of these twenty-three elements, Cardinal Directions (east, west etc.,) and Time are included by Sāṁkhya philosophers in Ether (*ākāśa*), and instead of looking upon Vital Force (*prāṇa*) as independent, they give the name of Vital Force to the various activities of the organs, when these activities have once started (Sāṁ. Kā. 29). But this opinion is not accepted by Vedāntists, who consider Vital Force as an independent element (Ve. Sū. 2. 49). Similarly, as has been stated before, Vedāntists do not look upon either Matter or Spirit as self-created and independent, but consider them to be two modifications (*vibhūti*) of one and the same Parameśvara. Except for this difference between the Sāṁkhyas and the Vedāntists, the other ideas about the order of creation of the Cosmos are common to both. For instance, the following description of the Brahmavṛkṣa or Brahmavana, which has occurred twice in the Anugītā in the Mahābhārata (Ma. Bhā. Aśva. 35. 20-23 and 47. 12-15) is in accordance with the principles of Sāṁkhya philosophy :-

avyaktabījaprabhavo buddhiskandhamayo mahān ।

mahāhaṁkāraviṭapaḥ indriyāntarakoṭaraḥ ॥

mahābhūtaviśākhaś ca viśeṣapratiśākhavān ।

sadāparṇaḥ sadāpuṣpaḥ śubhāśubhaphalodayaḥ ॥

ājīvyaḥ sarvabhūtānāṁ brahmavṛkṣaḥ sanātanaḥ ।

enaṁ chittvā ca bhittvā ca tattvajñānāsinā budhaḥ ॥

hitvā saṅgamayān pāśān mṛtyujanmajarodayān ।

nirmamo nirahaṁkāro mucyate nātra saṁśayaḥ ॥

that is: "the Imperceptible (Matter) is its seed, Reason (*mahān*) is its trunk, Individuation (*ahaṁkāra*) is its principal foliage, the Mind and the ten organs are the hollows inside the trunk, the (subtle) primordial elements (the five *tanmātras*) are its five large branches, and the Viśeṣas or the five Gross primordial elements are its sub-branches, and it is always covered by leaves, flowers, and auspicious or inauspicious fruit, and is the fundamental support of all living things; such is the ancient gigantic Brahmavṛkṣa. By cutting it with the philosophical sword and chopping it up into bits, a scient should destroy the bonds of Attachment (*saṁga*) which cause life, old age, and death, and should abandon the feeling of mine-ness and individuality; in this way alone can he be released". In short, this Brahmavṛkṣa is nothing but the 'dance of creation' or the 'diffusion' of Matter or of Illusion. The practice of referring to it as a 'tree' is very ancient and dates from the time of the Ṛgveda, and it has been called by the name 'the ancient Pipal Tree' (*sanātana aśvatthavṛkṣa*) in the Upaniṣads (Kaṭha. 6. 1). But there, that is, in the Vedas, the root of this tree (*Parabrahman*) is stated to be above and the branches (the development of the visible world) to be below. That the description of the Pipal tree in the Gītā has been made by harmonising the principles of Sāṁkhya philosophy with the Vedic description has been made clear in my commentary on the 1st and 2nd stanzas of the 15th chapter of the Gītā.

As the Sāṁkhyas and the Vedāntists classify in different ways the twenty-five elements described above in the form of a tree, it is necessary to give here some explanation about this classification. According to the Sāṁkhyas, these twenty-five elements fall into the four divisions of (i) fundamental *prakṛti*, (ii) *prakṛti-vikṛti*, (iii) *vikṛti* and (iv) neither *prakṛti* nor *vikṛti*. (1) As Prakṛti is not created from anything else, it is called fundamental *prakṛti* (Matter). (2) When you leave this fundamental Matter and come to the second stage, you come to the element Mahān. As Mahān springs from Prakṛti, it is said to be a *vikṛti* or an evolute of fundamental Matter; and as later on, Individuation comes out of the Mahān element, this Mahān is the *prakṛti* or root of Individuation. In this way this Mahān (Reason) becomes the *prakṛti* or root of Individuation on the one hand, and the *vikṛti* (evolute) of the fundamental Prakṛti (Matter) on the other hand. Therefore, Sāṁkhya philosophers have classified it under the heading of '*prakṛti-vikṛti*'; and in the same way Individuation (*ahaṁkāra*), and the five Tanmātras are also classified under the heading of '*prakṛti-vikṛti*'. That element which, being itself born out of some other element, i. e., being a *vikṛti*, is at the same time the parent (*prakṛti*) of the subsequent element is called a '*prakṛti-vikṛti*'. Mahat (Reason) Individuation, and the five Tanmātras, in all seven, are of this kind. (3) But the five organs of Perception, the five organs of Action, the Mind, and the five Gross primordial elements, which are in all sixteen, give birth to no further elements. On the other hand, they themselves are born out of some element or other. Therefore, these sixteen elements are not called '*prakṛti-vikṛti*', but are called '*vikṛti*' (evolutes). (4) The Spirit (Puruṣa) is neither *prakṛti* nor *vikṛti*; it is an independent and apathetic observer. This classification has been made by Īśvarakṛṣṇa, who has explained it as follows:-

mūlaprakṛtir avikṛtiḥ mahadādyāḥ prakṛtivikṛtayaḥ sapta ।

ṣoḍaśakastu vikāro na prakṛtir na vikṛtiḥ puruṣaḥ ॥

that is: "The fundamental Prakṛti is '*a-vikṛti*', that is, it is the *vikāra* (evolute) of no other substance; Mahat and the others, in all seven—Mahat, Ahaṁkāra and the five Tanmātras are *prakṛti-vikṛti*; and the eleven organs, including the Mind, and the five gross primordial elements, making in all sixteen, are called merely *vikṛti* or *vikāra* (evolutes). The Puruṣa (Spirit) is neither a *prakṛti* nor a *vikṛti*" (Sāṁ. Kā. 3). And these twenty-five elements are again classified into the three classes of Imperceptible, Perceptible and Jña. Out of these, fundamental Matter is imperceptible, the twenty-three elements, which have sprung from Matter are perceptible, and the Spirit is 'Jña'. Such is the classification according to Sāṁkhya philosophy. In the Purāṇas, the Smṛtis, the Mahābhārata and other treatises relating to Vedic philosophy, these same twenty-five elements are generally mentioned (See Maitryu. 6. 10: Manu 1. 14, 15). But in the Upaniṣads, it is stated that all these are created out of the Parabrahman, and there is no further discussion or classification. One comes across such classification in treatises later than the Upaniṣads, but it is different from the Sāṁkhya classification mentioned above. The total number of elements is twenty-five. As sixteen elements out of these are admittedly Vikṛtis, that it, as they are looked upon as created from other elements, even according to Sāṁkhya philosophy, they are not classified in these treatises as *prakṛti* or fundamental substances. That leaves nine elements:-(1) Spirit, (2) Matter, (3-9) Mahat, Ahaṁkāra and the five subtle elements (Tanmātras). The Sāṁkhyas call the last seven, after Spirit and Matter, '*prakṛti-vikṛti*'. But according to Vedānta philosophy, Matter is not looked upon as independent. According to their doctrine, both Spirit and and Matter come out of one Parameśvara (Absolute Īśvara). If this proposition is accepted, the distinction made by Sāṁkhya philosophers between fundamental Prakṛti and *prakṛti-vikṛti* comes to an end; because, as Prakṛti itself is looked upon as having sprung from the Parameśvara, it cannot be called the Root, and it falls into the category of '*prakṛti-vikṛti*'. Therefore, in describing the creation of the Cosmos, Vedānta philosophers say that from the Parameśvara there spring on the one hand the Jīva (Soul), and on the other hand, eight-fold Prakṛti (i. e., Prakṛti and seven *prakṛti-vikṛtis*, such as Mahat etc.,) (Ma. Bhā. Śān. 306. 29, and 310. 10). That is to say, according to Vedānta philosophers, keeping aside sixteen elements out of twenty-five, the remaining nine fall into the two classes of 'Jīva' (Soul) and the 'eight-fold Prakṛti'. This classification of Vedānta philosophers has been accepted in the Bhagavadgītā; but therein also, a small distinction is ultimately made. What the Sāṁkhyas called 'Puruṣa' is called 'Jīva' by the Gītā, and the Jīva is described as being the '*parā-prakṛti*' or the most sublime form of the Īśvara, and that which the Sāṁkhyas call the 'fundamental Prakṛti' is referred to in the Gītā as the '*apara*' or inferior form of the Parameśvara (Gī. 7. 4, 5.). When in this way, two main divisions have been made, then, in giving the further sub-divisions or kinds of the second main division, namely, of the inferior form of the Īśvara, it becomes necessary to mention the other elements which have sprung from this inferior form, in addition to that inferior form. Because, the inferior form (that is, the fundamental Prakṛti of Sāṁkhya philosophy) cannot be a kind or sub-division of itself. For instance, when you have to say how many children a father has, you cannot include the father in the counting of the children. Therefore, in enumerating the sub-divisions of the inferior form of the Parameśvara, one has to exclude the fundamental Prakṛti from the eight-fold Prakṛti mentioned by the Vedāntists, and to say that the remaining seven, that is to say, Mahān, Ahaṁkāra, and the five Fine Elements are the only kinds or sub-divisions of the fundamental Prakṛti; but if one does this, one will have to say that the inferior form of the Parameśvara, that is, fundamental Prakṛti is of seven kinds, whereas, as mentioned above, Prakṛti is of eight kinds according to the Vedāntists. Thus, the Vedāntists will say that Prakṛti is of eight kinds, and the Gītā will say that Prakṛti is of seven kinds, and an apparent conflict will come into existence between the two doctrines. The author of the Gītā, however, considered it advisable not to create such a conflict, but to be consistent with the description of Prakṛti as 'eight-fold'. Therefore, the Gītā has added the eighth element, namely, Mind, to the seven, namely Mahān, Ahaṁkāra, and the five Fine Elements, and has stated that the inferior form of the Parameśvara is of eight kinds (Gī. 7. 5). But, the ten organs are included in the Mind, and the five primordial elements are included in the five Fine Elements. Therefore, although the classification of the Gītā, may seem different from both the Sāṁkhya and the Vedāntic classification, the total number of the elements is not, on that account, either increased or decreased. The elements are everywhere twenty-five. Yet, in order that confusion should not arise as a result of this difference in classification, I have shown below these three methods of classification in the form of a tabular statement. In the thirteenth chapter of the Gītā (13. 5), the twenty-five elements of the Sāṁkhyas are enumerated one by one, just as they are, without troubling to classify them; and that shows that though the classification may be different, the total number of the elements is everywhere the same :-

CLASSIFICATION
of the twenty-five
FUNDAMENTAL ELEMENTS.

Sāṁkhya classification.	Elements.	Vedānta classification.	Gītā classification.
1. Neither prakṛti nor vikṛti.	1 SPIRIT.	(1) The superior form of Parabrahman	(1) *parā* Prakṛti.
1. Fundamental prakṛti.	1 PRAKṚTI.	(8) The inferior form of Parabrahman (*eight-fold*).	(1) *aparā* Prakṛti. (8) These are *eight* sub-divisions of the *aparā* Prakṛti.
7. *Prakṛti-vikṛti.*	1 Mahān. 1 Ahaṁkāra. 5 Tanmātras.		
16. Vikāras.	1 MIND 5 Organs of Perception. 5 Organs of Action 5 Primordial Elements.	(16) These *sixteen* Elements are not looked upon as Fundamental Elements by Vedāntists, as they are *vikāras*) (evolutes).	(15) These *fifteen* Elements are not looked upon as Fundamental Elements by the Gītā, as they are *vikāras* (evolutes).
25	25	25	25

I have thus concluded the description of how the homogeneous, inorganic, imperceptible, and gross Matter, which was fundamentally equable, acquires organic heterogeneity as a result of Individuation after it has become inspired by the non-self-perceptible 'Desire' (*buddhi*) of creating the visible universe, and also how, later on, as a result of the principle of the Development of Constituents (*guṇapariṇāma*), namely that, "Qualities spring out of qualities" (*guṇā guṇeṣu jāyante*), the eleven *sāttvika* subtle elements, which are the fundamental elements of the organic world come into existence on the one hand, and the five subtle Fine Elements (*tanmātras*), which are the fundamental elements of the *tāmasa* world come into existence on the other hand. I must now explain in what order the subsequent creation, namely, the five gross primordial elements, or the other gross material substances which spring from them, have come into existence. Sāṁkhya philosophy only tells us that the five gross primordial elements or Viśeṣas have come out of the five Fine Elements, as a result of *guṇa-pariṇāma*. But, as this matter has been more fully dealt with in Vedānta philosophy, I shall also, as the occasion has arisen, deal with that subject-matter, but after warning my readers that this is part of Vedānta philosophy and not of Sāṁkhya philosophy. Gross earth, water, brilliance, air and the ether are called the five primordial elements or Viśeṣas. Their order of creation has been thus described in the Taittirīyopaniṣad:—"*ātmanaḥ ākāśaḥ saṁbhūtaḥ । ākāśād vāyuḥ । vāyor agniḥ । agner āpaḥ । adbhyaḥ pṛthivī । pṛthivyā oṣadhayaḥ ।*" etc. (Tai. U. 2. 1). From the Paramātman, (not from the fundamental Gross Matter as the Sāṁkhyas say), ether was first created; from ether, the air; from the air, the fire; from the fire, water; and from water, later on, the earth has come into being. The Taittirīyopaniṣad does not give the reason for this order. But in the later Vedānta treatises, the explanation of this order of creation of the five primordial elements seems to be based on the *guṇapariṇāma* principle of the Sāṁkhya system. These later Vedānta writers say that by the law of "*guṇā guṇeṣu vartante*" (qualities spring out of qualities), a substance having only one quality first comes into existence, and from that substance other substances having two qualities, three qualities etc., subsequently come into existence. As ether out of the five primordial elements has principally the quality of sound only, it came into existence first. Then came into existence the air, because, the air has two qualities, namely, of sound and touch. Not only do we hear the sound of air, but we feel it by means of our organ of touch. Fire comes after the air, because, besides the qualities of sound and touch, it has also the third quality of colour. As water has, in addition to these three qualities, the quality of taste also, water must have come into existence after fire; and as the earth possesses the additional quality of smell besides these four qualities, we arrive at the proposition that the earth must have sprung later on out of water. Yāska has propounded this very doctrine (Nirukta 14. 4). The Taittirīyopaniṣad contains the further description that when the five gross primordial elements had come into existence in this order, "*pṛthivyā oṣadhayaḥ* । *oṣadhibhyo'nnam* । *annāt puruṣaḥ* ।" (Tai. 2. 1), i. e., "from the earth have grown vegetables; from the vegetables, food; and from food, man. This subsequent creation is the result of the mixture of the five primordial elements, and the process of that mixture is called '*pañcī-karaṇa*' in the Vedānta treatises. Pañcī-karaṇa means the coming into existence of a new substance by the mixture of different qualities of each of the five primordial elements. This union of five (*pañcīkaraṇa*) can necessarily take place in an indefinite number of ways.

In the ninth *daśaka* (collection of ten verses each) of the *Dāsabodha*, it is stated:

By mixing black and white । we get the grey colour ।
By mixing black and yellow । we get the green colour ॥
(9. 6. 40)

And in the 13th *daśaka*, it is stated as follows:-

In the womb of that earth ।
there is a collection of an infinite number of seeds ॥

When water gets mixed with the earth ।
sprouts come out ॥

Creepers of variegated colours ।
with waving leaves and flowers are next born ॥

After that come into existence ।
fruits of various tastes ॥

... ...

The earth and water are the root ।
of all oviparous, viviparous, steam-engendered,
and vegetable life ॥

Such is the wonder ।
of the creation of the universe ॥

There are four classes and four modes of voice ।
eighty-four lakhs * of species of living beings ॥

Have come into existence in the three worlds ।
which is the Cosmic Body" ॥

(Dāsabodha 13. 3. 10–15).

This description in the Dāsabodha given by Samartha Rāmadāsa is based on this idea. But it must not be forgotten that by the union of five (*pañcikaraṇa*) only gross objects or gross bodies come into existence, and this gross body must become united first with subtle organs and next with the Ātman or the Spirit before it becomes a living body.

I must also make it clear here that this union of five, which has been described in the later Vedānta works, is not to be found in the ancient Upaniṣads. In the Chāndogyopaniṣad, these Tanmātras or primordial elements are not considered to be five; but brilliance, water and food (earth) are the only three which are considered as subtle fundamental elements, and the entire diverse universe is said to have come into existence by the

* This idea of 84 lakhs of births is from the Purāṇas, and it is quite clear that it is only approximate. Nevertheless, it is not totally without foundation. Western natural scientists believe, according to the Theory of Evolution, that the human being has come into existence by evolution from one subtle micro-organism in the form of a living nodule at the beginning of the universe. From this idea, it becomes quite clear how many generations of each subsequent species (*yoni*, must have come into existence and passed away in order that this subtle nodule should have become a gross nodule, and that this gross nodule should in its turn have been transformed into a living bacillus and this bacillus been evolved into the next subsequent living organism. From this an English biologist has worked out a calculation, that for the smallest fish in water to develop its qualities and ultimately assume the form of a human being, there must have been at least 53 lakhs and 75 thousand generations of intermediate species and that the number of these generations may as well be ten times as much. These are

mixture of these three, that is, by '*trivṛtkaraṇa*'; and it is stated in the Śvetāśvataropaniṣad that: "*ajām ekāṁ lohitaśuklakṛṣṇām bahvīḥ prajāḥ sṛjamānāṁ sarupāḥ*" (Śvetā. 4. 5), i. e., "this she-goat (*ajā*) is red, or of the nature of fire; and white, or of the nature of water; and black, or of the nature of earth; and is thus made of three elements of three colours, and from it all creation (*prajā*) embodied in Name and Form has been created. In the 6th chapter of the Chāndogyopaniṣad has been given the conversation between Śvetaketu and his father. In it, the father of Śvetaketu clearly tells him: "O, my son! in the commencement of the world, there was nothing except '*ekam evādvitīyaṁ sat*' (single and unseconded *sat*), that is to say, nothing else except one homogeneous and eternal Parabrahman. How can '*sat*' (something which exists) come into existence out of '*asat*' (something which does not exist)? Therefore, in the beginning *sat* pervaded everything. Then that *sat* conceived the desire of becoming multifarious, that is, heterogeneous, and from it grew one by one, brilliance (*tejas*), water (*āpa*) and food (*pṛthvī*) in their subtle forms. Then, after the Parabrahman had entered these three elements in the form

the species ranging from the small aquatic animals upto the human being. If, to this are added the number of minute aquatic organisms lower down in the scale of life, it is impossible to ascertain how many more lakhs of generations will have to be counted. From this it will be clear to what extent the idea of these generations in the purāṇa of Materlialistic scientists has exceeded the idea of 84 lakhs of species in our Purāṇas. The same law applies to the calculation of time. Geo-biologists say that it is impossible to form even a rough idea of the date when living micro-organisms first came into existence on the earth, and that aquatic micro-organisms must have come into exi-tence crores of years ago. If further concise information is required about this matter, the reader is referred to *The Last Link* by Ernst Haeckel, with notes etc. by Dr. H. Gadow (1898). The above particulars have been taken from the appendices. The 84 lakhs of generations mentioned in the Purāṇas are to be counted as follows:— 9 lakhs for aquatic animals, 10 lakhs for birds, 11 lakhs for germs, 20 lakhs for beasts, 30 lakhs for immoveable things and 4 lakhs for mankind (See Dāsabodha 20. 6).

of Life, all the various things in the universe which are identified by Name and Form came into existence as a result of the union of those three (*trivṛtkaraṇa*). The red (*lohita*) colour, which is to be found in the gross fire or the Sun or in electricity, is the result of the subtle fundamental element of brilliance; the white (*śukla*) colour, of the fundamental subtle element of water; and the black (*kṛṣṇa*) colour, of the fundamental subtle element of earth. In the same way, subtle fire, subtle water, and subtle food (*pṛthvī*) are the three fundamental elements which are contained even in the food which man eats. Just as butter comes to the surface when you churn curds, so when this food, made up of the three subtle elements enters the stomach, the element of brilliance in it, creates gross, medium and subtle products in the shape of bones, marrow and speech respectively; and similarly, the element of water (*āpa*) creates urine, blood and Vital Force; and the element of earth (*pṛthvī*) creates the three susbstances, excrement, flesh and mind" (Chān. 6. 2–6). This system of the Chāndogyopaniṣad of not taking the primordial elements as five, but as only three, and of explaining the creation of all visible things by the union of these three substances (*trivṛtkaraṇa*) has been mentioned in the Vedānta-Sūtras (2. 4. 20), and Bādarāyaṇācārya does not even mention the word 'Pañcīkaraṇa'. Nevertheless, in the Taittirīya (2. 1), Praśna (4. 8), Bṛhadāraṇyaka (4. 4. 5) and other Upaniṣads, and in the Śvetāśvatara itself (2. 12) and in the Vedānta-Sūtras (2. 3. 1–14) and lastly in the Gītā (7. 4; 13. 5), five primordial elements are mentioned instead of three; and in the Garbhopaniṣad, the human body is in the very beginning stated to be '*pañcātmaka*', that is, made up of five; and the Mahābhārata and the Purāṇas give clear descriptions of Pañcīkaraṇa (Ma. Bhā. Śān. 184–186). From this it becomes quite clear, that the idea of the 'union of five' (*pañcīkaraṇa*) becomes ultimately acceptable to all Vedānta philosophers and that although the 'union of three' (*trivṛtkaraṇa*) may have been ancient, yet, after the primordial elements came to be believed to be five instead of three, the idea of Pañcīkaraṇa was based on the same sample as the Trivṛtkaraṇa, and the theory of Trivṛtkaraṇa went out of vogue. Not only is the human body formed of the five primordial elements, but the meaning of the word Pañcīkaraṇa has been extended to imply that each one of these five is divided in five different ways in the body. For instance, the quinary of skin, flesh, bone, marrow, and muscles grows out of earth etc. etc. (Ma. Bhā. Śān. 186. 20-25; and Dāsabodha 17. 8). This idea also seems to have been inspired by the description of Trivṛtkaraṇa in the Chāndogyopaniṣad mentioned above. There also, there is a statement at the end that brilliance, water, and earth are each to be found in three different forms in the human body.

The explanation of how the numerous inactive (*acetana*), that is to say, lifeless or gross objects in the world, which can be distinguished by Name and Form, came into existence out of the fundamental imperceptible Matter—or according to the Vedānta theory, from the Parabrahman—is now over. I shall now consider what more the Sāṁkhya philosophy tells us about the creation of the *sacetana* (that is, active) beings in the world, and later on, see how far that can be harmonised with the Vedānta doctrines. The body of living beings comes into existence when the five gross primordial elements sprung from the fundamental Matter are united with the subtle organs. But though this body is organic, it is still gross. The element which activates these organs is distinct from Gross Matter and it is known as Spirit (*puruṣa*). I have, in the previous chapter, mentioned the various doctrines of the Sāṁkhya philosophy that this Spirit is fundamentally inactive, that the living world begins to come into existence when this Spirit is united with fundamental Matter, and that when the Spirit acquires the knowledge that "I am different from Matter", its union with Matter is dissolved, failing which it has to peregrinate in the cycle of birth and death. But as I have not, in that chapter, explained how the Ātman—or according to Sāṁkhya terminology, the Puruṣa—of the person, who dies without having realised that the Ātman is different from Matter, gets one birth after another, it is necessary now to consider that question more in detail. It is quite clear that the Ātman of the man who dies without having acquired Self-Realisation does not escape entirely from the meshes of Matter; because, if such were the case, one will have to say with Cārvāka, that every man escapes from the tentacles of Matter or attains Release immediately after death; and Self-Realisation or the difference between sin and virtue will lose its importance. Likewise, if you say that after death, the Ātman or the Spirit alone survives, and that it, of its own accord, performs the action of taking new births, then the fundamental theorem that Spirit is inactive and apathetic, and that all the activity is of Matter is contradicted. Besides, by acknowledging that the Ātman takes new births of its own accord, you admit that to be its property, and fall into the impossible position that it will never escape from the cycle of birth and death. It, therefore, follows that though a man may have died without having acquired Self-Realisation, his Ātman must remain united with Matter, in order that Matter should give it new births. Nevertheless, as the Gross Body is destroyed after death, it is quite clear that this union cannot continue to be with Matter composed of the five gross primordial elements. But it is not that Matter consists only of the five gross primordial elements. There are in all twenty-three elements which arise out of Matter, and the five gross primordial elements are the last five out of them. When these last five elements (the five primordial elements) are subtracted from the twenty-three, eighteen elements remain. It, therefore, follows as a natural conclusion that though a man, who dies without having acquired Self-Realisation, escapes from the Gross Body made up of the five gross primordial elements, that is to say, from the last five elements, yet, his death does not absolve him from his union with the remaining eighteen elements arising out of Matter. Reason (Mahān) Individuation, Mind, the ten organs, and the five Fine Elements are these eighteen elements. (See the Geneological tree of the Cosmos given at page 2[illegible]3). All these elements are subtle. Therefore, that Body which is formed as a result of the continued union of Spirit (*puruṣa*) with them is called the 'Subtle Body', or the 'Liṅga-śarīra' as the opposite of the Gross Body or 'Sthūla-śarīra' (Sāṁ. Kā. 40). If any person dies without having acquired Self-Realisation, this his Subtle Body, made up of the eighteen elements of Matter, leaves his Gross Body on his death along with the Ātman, and compels him to take birth after birth. To this, an objection is raised by some persons to the following effect: when a man dies, one can actually see that the activities of Reason, Individuation, Mind, and the ten organs come to an end in his Gross Body along with life; therefore, these thirteen elements may rightly be included in the Subtle Body; but there is no reason for including the five Fine Elements in the Subtle Body along with these thirteen elements. To this the reply of the Sāṁkhya philosophers is, that the thirteen elements, pure Reason, pure Individuation, the Mind and the ten organs are only qualities of Matter, and in the same way as a shadow requires the support of some substance or other, or as a picture requires the support of the wall or of paper, so also must these thirteen elements, which are only qualities, have the support of some substance in order that they should stick together. Out of these, the Ātman (*puruṣa*), being itself qualityless and inactive, cannot by itself become the support for any quality. When the man is alive, the five gross primordial elements in his body form the support for these thirteen elements. But after his death, that is, after the destruction of the Gross Body, this support in the shape of the five primordial elements ceases to exist. Therefore, these thirteen elements, which are qualities, have to look for some other substance as a support. If you say that they can get the support of fundamental Matter, then, that is imperceptible and in an unevolved condition, that is to say, eternal and all-pervasive; and therefore, it cannot become the support of qualities like Reason etc., which go to form one small Subtle Body. Therefore, the five Fine Elements, which are the bases of the five gross primordial elements, have to be included in the Subtle Body side by side with the thirteen qualities, as a support for them in the place of the five gross primordial elements which are the evolutes of fundamental Matter (Sāṁ Kā. 41). Some writers belonging to the Sāṁkhya school imagine the existence of a third body, composed of the five Fine Elements, intermediate between the Subtle Body and the Gross Body, and maintain that this third body is the support for the Subtle Body. But that is not the correct interpretation of the forty-first couplet of the Sāṁkhya Kārikā, and in my opinion these commentators have imagined such a third body merely by confusion of thought. In my opinion this couplet has no use beyond explaining why the five Fine Elements have to be included in the Subtle Body along with the thirteen other elements, namely, Reason etc *.

Anybody can see after a little thought, that there is not much of a difference between the Subtle Body made up of eighteen elements described in the Sāṁkhya philosophy and the Subtle Body described in the Upaniṣads. It is stated in the Bṛhadāraṇyakopaniṣad that: "just as a leech (*jalāyukā*) having reached the end of a blade of grass, places the anterior part of its body on the next blade (by its anterior feet), and then draws up the posterior part, which was placed on the former blade of grass, in the same way, the Ātman leaves one body and enters the other body" (Bṛ. 4. 4. 3). But from this single illustration, the two inferences that (i) only the Ātman enters another body and that (ii) it does so immediately after leaving the first body, do not follow. Because, in the Bṛhadāraṇyakopaniṣad itself, there is another statement further on (Bṛ. 4. 4. 5), that the five subtle elements, the Mind, the organs, Vital Force and a man's righteous or unrighteous record, all leave the body along with the Ātman, which goes according to its mundane Actions to different spheres, where it remains for sometime. (Bṛ. 6. 2. 14 and 15). In the same way, it becomes quite clear from the description of the course

---

* It can be seen from a verse in the book of Bhatta Kumarila known as *Mīmāṁsā-śloka-vārtika* (Ātma-vāda, stanza 62), that he interprets this couplet in the same way as myself. That verse is as follows:—

antarābhavadeho hi neṣyate vindhyavāsinā ।
tadastitve pramāṇam hi na kiṁcid avagamyate ॥ 62 ॥

that is, "Vindhyavāsin did not accept the existence of an *antarābhava*, that is to say, of a '*deha*' or Body which is intermediate between the Subtle Body and the Gross Body. There is no authority for saying that there is such an intermediate body". Īśvarakṛṣṇa used to live in the Vindhya mountains; that is why he was known as 'Vindhyavāsin'. The *antarābhava* (intermediate) Body is also known as 'gandharva'. (See Amarakośa 3. 3. 132, and the commentary on it by Kṣīrasvāmi, published by Mr. Krishnaji Govind Oak and p. 8 of the introduction to that work.)

followed by Jīva along with the fundamental element of water (*āpa*) in the Chāndogyopaniṣad (Chān. 5. 3. 3; 5. 9. I) as also from the interpretation put thereon in the Vedānta-Sūtras (Ve. Sū. 3. 1. 1–7) that the Chāndogyopaniṣad included the three fundamental elements, viz., water (*āpa*) and along with it brilliance (*tejas*) and food (*anna*) in the Subtle Body. In short, it will be seen that when one adds Vital Force and '*dharmādharma*' (i. e. righteous and unrighteous actions) or Karma to the Sāṁkhya Subtle Body of eighteen elements, one gets the Vedāntic Subtle Body. But in as much as Vital Force (*prāṇa*) is included in the inherent tendencies of the eleven organs, and righteous and unrighteous action (*dharmādharma*) are included in the activities of Reason and Mind, one may say that this difference is merely verbal, and that there is no real dfference of opinion about the components of the Subtle Body between the Vedānta and the Sāṁkhya philosophies. It is for this reason that the description of the Subtle Body according to the Sāṁkhyas as "*mahadādi sūkṣmaparyantam*" has been repeated, as it is, in the words "*mahadādyaviśeṣāntam*,' in the Maitryupaniṣad (Maī. 6. 10). * In the Bhagavadgītā, the Subtle Body is described as consisting of "*manaḥ-ṣaṣṭhānīndriyāṇi*" (Gī. 15. 7), that is, of "the mind and the five organs of Perception"; and further on there is a description that life, in leaving the Gross Body, takes with itself this Subtle Body in the same way as the breeze carries scent from the flowers: "*vāyur gandhān ivāśayāt*" (Gī. 15. 8). Nevertheless in as much as the metaphysical knowledge in the Gītā has been borrowed from the Upaniṣads, one must say that the

---

* In the copy of the Maitryupaniṣad included in the Anandashrama Edition of *Dvātriṁśadupaniṣad* (thirty-two Upaniṣads), the reading of the hymn referred to above has been given as: "*mahadādyaṁviśeṣāntam*", and the same has been accepted by the commentators. If this reading is accepted then the 'Mahat' element which is at the beginning of the list has to be included in the Subtle Body and the 'Viśeṣas' or five primordial elements, indicated by the words '*viśeṣāntam*', have to be left out. That is to say, you have to interpret it as meaning that the '*mahat*' out of "*mahadādyaṁ*" has to be taken, and the '*viśeṣa*' out of '*viśeṣāntam*' has to be left out. But, where the beginning and the end are both mentioned, it is

Blessed Lord has intended to include the five organs of Action, the five Fine Elements, Vital Force, and sin and virtue, in the words "the six organs including the mind". There is a statement also in the Manu-Smṛti that after a man dies, he acquires a Subtle Body made up of the five Fine Elements in order to suffer the consequences of his virtuous or evil actions (Manu. 12. 16, 17). The words "*vāyur gandhān ivāśayāt*" in the Gītā, prove only that this body must be subtle; but they do not convey any idea as to the size of that body. But from the statement in the Sāvitryupākhyāna in the Mahābhārata (Ma. Bhā. Vana. 296. 16), that Yama took out a Spirit as large as a thumb from the (gross) body of Satyavāna—"*aṅguṣṭhamātraṁ puruṣaṁ niścakarṣa yamo balāt*"—it is clear that this Subtle Body was in those days, at least for purposes of illustration, taken to be as big as a thumb.

I have so far considered what inferences lead one to the conclusion that the Subtle Body exists, though it might be invisible to the eyes, as also what the component parts of that Subtle Body are. But it is not enough to merely say that the Subtle Body is formed by the combination of eighteen elements excluding fundamental Matter and the five gross primordial elements. There is no doubt that wherever this Subtle Body exists, this combination of eighteen elements will, according to its inherent qualities, create gross parts of the body, like hands and feet or gross organs, whether out of the gross bodies of parents, or later on, out of the food in the gross material world; and that it will maintain such a body. But, it remains to be explained why this Subtle Body, made up by the combination of eighteen elements, creates different bodies,

---

right to take both or to omit both. Therefore, according to Prof. Deussen, the nasal 'ṁ' at the end of the word '*mahadādyaṁ*' should be omitted and the hymn should be read as "*mahadādya viśeṣāntam*" (*mahadādi + aviśeṣāntam*). If that is done, the word '*aviśeṣa*' comes into existence, and the same rule becoming applicable to the '*mahat*' and to the '*avisesa*', that is, both to the beginning and the end, both get included in the Liṅga śarīra. This is the peculiarity of this reading; but, it must be borne in mind, that whichever reading is accepted, there is no difference in the meaning.

such as, animals, birds, men etc. The elements of consciousness in the living world are called 'Puruṣa' by the Sāṁkhyas, and according to them, though these 'Puruṣas' are innumerable, yet, in as much as each Puruṣa is inherently apathetic and inactive, the responsibility of creating different bodies, such as, birds, beasts etc. cannot rest with the Puruṣa. According to Vedānta philosophy, these differences are said to arise as a result of the sinful or virtuous Actions performed during life. This subject-matter of Karma-Vipāka (the effects caused by Actions) will be dealt with later on. According to Sāṁkhya philosophy, Karma cannot be looked upon as a third fundamental principle which is different from Spirit and Matter; and in as much as Spirit is apathetic, one has to say that Karma (Action) is something evolved from the *sattva*, *rajas*, and *tamas* constituents of Matter. Reason is the most important element out of the eighteen of which the Subtle Body is made up; because, it is from Reason that the subsequent seventeen elements, namely, Individuation, etc. come into existence. Therefore, that which goes under the name of 'Karma' in Vedānta philosophy is referred to in Sāṁkhya philosophy as the activity, property, or manifestation of Reason resulting from the varying intensity of the *sattva*, *rajas* and *tamas* constituents. This property or propensity of Reason is technically called 'Bhāva', and innumerable Bhāvas come into existence as a result of the varying intensity of the *sattva*, *rajas* and *tamas* constituents. These Bhāvas adhere to the Subtle Body in the same way as scent adheres to a flower or colour to cloth (Sāṁ. Kā. 40). The Subtle Body takes up new births according to these Bhāvas, or—in Vedāntic terminology—according to Karma; and the elements, which are drawn by the Subtle Body from the bodies of the parents in taking these various births, later on acquire various other Bhāvas. The different categories of gods or men or animals or trees, are the results of the combination of these Bhāvas (Sāṁ. Kā. 43–55). When the *sāttvika* constituent becomes absolute and pre-eminent in these Bhāvas, man acquires Self-Realisation and apathy towards the world, and begins to see the difference between Matter and Spirit; and then the Spirit reaches its original state of Isolation *(kaivalya)*, and the Subtle Body being discarded, the pain of man is absolutely eradicated. But, if this difference between Matter and Spirit has not been realised, and merely the *sattva* constituent has become predominant, the Subtle Body is re-born among gods, that is, in heaven; if the *rajas* quality has become predominant, it is re-born among men, that is, on the earth; and if the *tamas* quality has become predominant, it is re-born in the lower *(tiryak)* sphere (Gī. 14. 18). When in this way it has been re-born among men, the description of how a *kalala* (state of the embryo a short time after conception), a *budbuda* (bubble), flesh, muscles, and other different gross organs grow out of a drop of semen has been given in Sāṁkhya philosophy on the basis of the theory of "*guṇā guṇeṣu jāyante*". (Sāṁ. Kā. 43: Ma. Bhā. Śān. 320). That description is more or less similar to the description given in the Garbhopaniṣad. Although the above-mentioned technical meaning given to the word 'Bhāva' in Sāṁkhya philosophy may not be found in Vedānta treatises, yet, it will be seen from what has been stated above, that the reference by the Blessed Lord to the various qualities "*buddhir jñānam asaṁmohaḥ kṣamā satyāṁ damaḥ śamaḥ*" by the use of the word 'Bhāva' in the following verse (Gī. 10. 4, 5; 7. 12) must primarily have been made keeping in mind the technical terminology of Sāṁkhya philosophy.

When, in this way, all the living and non-living perceptible things in the universe have come into existence one after the other out of fundamental imperceptible Matter (according to the Sāṁkhya philosophy), or out of fundamental Parabrahman in the form of Sat (according to the Vedānta philosophy), all perceptible things are, both according to the Sāṁkhya and Vedānta philosophies, re-merged either into imperceptible Matter or into fundamental Brahman in a way which is the reverse of the order of development of constituents mentioned above, when the time for the destruction of the Cosmos comes (Ve. Sū. 2. 3. 14; Ma. Bhā. Śān. 232); that is to say, earth, out of the five primordial elements, is merged into water, water into fire, fire into air, air into ether, ether into the Fine Elements, the Fine Elements into Individuation, Individuation into Reason, and Reason or Mahān into Matter and—according to the Vedānta philosophy—Matter becomes merged into the fundamental Brahman. What period of time lapses between the creation of the universe and its destruction or merging is nowhere mentioned in the Sāṁkhya Kārikā. Yet, I think that the computation of time mentioned in the Manu-Saṁhitā (1. 66–73), Bhagavadgītā (8. 17), or the Mahābhārata (Śān. 231) must have been accepted by the Sāṁkhya philosophers. Our Uttarāyaṇa, that is, the period when the Sun seems to travel towards the North is the day of the gods, and our Dakṣiṇāyana, when the Sun seems to travel towards the South, is the night of the gods; because, there are statements not only in the Smṛtis, but also in astronomical treatises that the gods live on the Meru Mountain, that is to say, on the north pole, (Sūrya-Siddhānta, 1. 13; 12. 35. 67). Therefore, the period made up of the Uttarāyaṇa and the Dakṣiṇāyana, which is one year according to our calculations, is only one day and one night of the gods, and three hundred and sixty of our years are three hundred and sixty days and nights or one year of the gods. We have four yugas called, Kṛta, Tretā, Dvāpara and Kali. The periods of the yugas are counted as four thousand years for the Kṛta, three thousand years for the Tretā, two thousand years for the Dvāpara and one thousand years for the Kali. But one yuga does not start immediately after the close of the previous one, and there are intermediate years which are conjunctional. On either side of the Kṛta yuga, there are four hundred years; on either side of the Tretā, three hundred; on either side of the Dvāpara, two hundred; and on either side of Kali there are one hundred. In all, these transitional periods of the four yugas amount to two thousand years. Adding these two thousand years to the ten thousand years over which the Kṛta, Tretā, Dvāpara and Kali yugas extend, we get twelve thousand years. Now, are these twelve thousand years of human beings or of the gods? If these are considered to be human years, then, as more than five thousand years have elapsed since the commencement of the Kali yuga, not only is the Kali yuga of a thousand human years over, but the following Kṛta yuga is also over, and we must believe that we are now in the Tretā yuga. In order to get over this difficulty, it has been stated in the Purāṇas that these twelve thousand years are of the gods. Twelve thousand years of the gods mean 360 × 12000 = 43,20,000, that is, forty-three lakhs and twenty thousand years. The fixing of the yuga in our present almanacs is based on that method of calculation. This period of twelve thousand years of the gods is one mahāyuga of human beings, or one cycle of four yugas of the gods. Seventy-one such cycles of yugas of the gods make up one 'manvantara', and there are fourteen such manvantaras. But, at the commencement and the end of the first manvantara and subsequently at the end of each manvantara, there is a conjunctional period equal to one Kṛta yuga, that is to say, there are fifteen such conjunctional periods. These fifteen conjunctional periods and fourteen manvantaras make up one thousand yugas of the gods or one day of Brahmadeva (Sūrya-Siddhānta 1. 15–20); and one thousand more such yugas make up one night of Brahmadeva, as has been stated in the Manu-Smṛti and in the Mahābhārata (Manu. 1. 69–73 and 79; Ma. Bhā. Śan. 231. 18–31 and the Nirukta by Yāska 14. 9). According to this calculation, one day of Brahmadeva amounts to four hundred and thirty-two crores of human years, that is to say, 4,320,000,000 years. And this is called a 'kalpa'*. When this day of Brahmadeva or kalpa starts:–

avyaktād vyaktayaḥ sarvāḥ prabhavanty aharāgame I
rātryāgame pralīyante tatraivāvyaktasaṁjñake II

(Gī. 8. 18).

that is, "all the perceptible things in the universe begin to be created out of the Imperceptible; and when the night of Brahmadeva starts, the same perceptible things again begin to be merged in the Imperceptible", as has been stated in the Bhagavadgītā (Gī. 8. 18 and 9. 7), as also in the Smṛti treatises, and elsewhere in the Mahābhārata. There are besides this, other descriptions of Cosmic Destruction (*pralaya*) in the Purāṇas. But as in those pralayas the entire universe,

* A calculation of yugas etc. according to astrological science has been made by the late Shankar Balkrishna Dikshit in his work *Bhāratiya Jyotiḥśāstra* in various places to which the reader is referred. See pages 103 to 105 and p. 193 etc.

including the Sun and the Moon, are not destroyed, they are not taken into account in the consideration of the creation and the destruction of the Cosmos. One kalpa means one day or one night of Brahmadeva and 360 such days and 360 such nights make up one of his years, and taking the life of Brahmadeva at one hundred such years, one half of his life is now over and the first day of the second half of his life, that is, of his fifty-first year, or the Śvetavārāha kalpa has now started; and there are statements in the Purāṇas that out of the fourteen manvantaras of this kalpa, six manvantaras are over, as also 27 mahāyugas out of the seventy-one mahāyugas of the seventh manvantara called Vaivasvata, and that the first *caraṇa* or quarter of the 28th mahāyuga of the Vaivasvata manvantara is now going on (See Viṣṇu-Purāṇa 1. 3). In the Śaka year 1821, exactly five thousand years of this Kaliyuga were over; and according to this calculation, there were in the Śaka year 1821, three lakhs and ninety-one thousand years still in hand for the pralaya in the Kaliyuga to take place; therefore, the consideration of the Mahāpralaya to take place at the end of the present kalpa is a far, far, distant thing. The day of Brahmadeva, made up of four hundred and thirty-two crores of human years, is now going on and not even the noon of that day, that is to say, seven manvantaras are yet over.

As the description which has been given above of the creation and the destruction of the Cosmos is consistent with Vedānta philosophy—and if you omit the Parabrahman, also consistent with Sāṁkhya philosophy—this tradition of the order of formation of the universe has been accepted as correct by our philosophers, and the same order has been mentioned in the Bhagavadgītā. As has been stated in the beginning of this chapter, we come across other ideas regarding the creation of the universe in some places in the Śrutis, the Smṛtis, and the Purāṇas, namely, that the Brahmadeva or Hiraṇyagarbha first came into existence, or that water first came into existence and a Golden Egg was born in that water from the seed of the Parameśvara etc. But all these ideas are looked upon as inferior or merely descriptive; and when there is any occasion to explain them, people say that Hiraṇyagarbha or Brahmadeva is the same as Matter. Even the Blessed Lord has in the Bhagavadgītā called this Matter of three constituents by the name 'Brahma' in the words "*mama yonir mahad brahma*" (Gī. 14. 3), and He has said that from this His seed, numerous beings are created out of Matter, as a result of three constituents. Vedānta treatises say that the description found in different places that Dakṣa and other seven mind-born sons, or the seven Manus, were born from Brahmadeva, and that they thereafter created the moveable and immobile universe (Ma. Bhā. Ā. 65-67; Ma. Bhā. Śān. 207; Manu. 1. 34-63). which is once referred to also in the Gītā (Gī. 10. 6), can be made consistent with the above-mentioned scientific theory of the creation of the Cosmos, by interpreting Brahmadeva as meaning Matter; and the same argument is also applicable in other places. For instance, in the Śaiva or Pāśupata Darśana, Śiva is looked upon as the actual creator and five things, causes, products etc. are supposed to have come into existence from him; and in the Nārāyaṇīya or Bhāgavata religion, Vāsudeva is supposed to be the primary cause, and it is stated that Saṁkarṣaṇa (Jīva or Soul) was first born from Vāsudeva, Pradyumna (Mind) from Saṁkarṣaṇa, and Aniruddha (Individuation) from Pradyumna. But as, according to the Vedānta philosophy, Jīva (Soul) is not something which comes into existence anew every time, but is a permanent or eternal part of a permanent or eternal Parameśvara, the above-mentioned doctrine of the Bhāgavata religion regarding the birth of Jīva has been refuted in the second portion of the second chapter of the Vedānta-Sūtras (Ve. Sū. 2. 2. 42-45); and it is stated there that this doctrine is contrary to the Vedas, and, therefore, objectionable; and this proposition of the Vedānta-Sūtras has been repeated in the Gītā (Gī. 13. 4; 15. 7). In the same way, Sāṁkhya philosophers believe that there are two independent principles, Prakṛti and Puruṣa. But Vedānta philosophy does not accept this dualism, and says that both Prakṛti and Puruṣa are manifestations of one eternal and qualityless Absolute Self (Paramātman); and this doctrine has been accepted in the Bhagavadgītā (Gī. 9. 10). But, this matter will be more fully dealt with in the next chapter. I have to state here only this, that although the Bhagavadgītā accepts the principle of the devotion to Vāsudeva and the theory of Action (*pravṛtti*) propounded in the Nārayaṇīya or Bhāgavata religion, it does not accept the further doctrine of that religion, that Saṁkarṣaṇa (Jīva) was first created out of Vāsudeva, and Pradyumna (Mind) out of Saṁkarṣaṇa, and Aniruddha (Individuation) out of Pradyumna; and the words Saṁkarṣaṇa, Pradyumna, or Aniruddha are nowhere come across in the Gītā. This is the important difference between the Bhāgavata religion mentioned in the Pāncarātra, and the Bhāgavata religion mentioned in the Gītā. I have expressly mentioned this fact here in order that one should not draw the mistaken conclusion that the creed of devotional schools like the Bhāgavata school regarding the creation of the Cosmos or the the Jīva-Parameśvara is acceptable to the Gītā, from the mere fact that the Bhāgavata religion has been mentioned in the Bhagavadgītā. Let us now consider whether or not there is some element or principle at the root of the perceptible and imperceptible or mutable and immutable universe, which is beyond the Prakṛti and Puruṣa mentioned in Sāṁkhya philosophy. This is what is known as Adhyātma (the philosophy of the Absolute Self) or Vedānta.

CHAPTER IX.

THE PHILOSOPHY OF THE ABSOLUTE SELF.

(ADHYĀTMA)

paras tasmāt tu bhāvo 'nyo 'vyakto 'vyaktāt sanātanaḥ |
yaḥ sa sarveṣu bhūteṣu naśyatsu na vinaśyati ‖ *

(Gī. 8. 20).

The sum and substance of the last two chapters was that what was referred to as the *kṣetrajña* (Owner of the Body) in the consideration of the Body and the Ātman is known in Sāṁkhya philosophy as 'Puruṣa'; and that when one considers the question of the construction and the destruction of the mutable and immutable or the moveable and immoveable world, one arrives finally, according to the Sāṁkhyas, at only two independent and eternal fundamental elements, namely, Matter and Spirit; and that it is necessary for the Spirit to realise its difference from Matter, that is, its isolation, and transcend the three qualities (become *triguṇātīta*) in order to obtain the total annihilation of its pain and attain Release Modern natural scientists explain the order in which Matter places its evolution before Spirit, after its union with Spirit, in a way slightly different from the Sāṁkhyas; and, as the natural sciences are further developed, this order is likely to be improved. But the fundamental proposition that all perceptible objects have come into existence in a gradual order out of one imperceptible Matter as a result of the development of the constituents, cannot possibly be altered. Nevertheless, looking upon this as the subject-matter of other sciences, the lion of Vedānta does not enter into any dispute about it. That lion wants to go beyond all these sciences, and determine what Absolute Element is at the root of the Cosmic Body, and how a man should be merged in It; and in this its province it will not be out-roared by any other science. As jackals become

* "That second imperceptible substance, which is higher than the (Sāṁkhya) Imperceptible, and which is eternal, and which is not destroyed even when all other living things are destroyed", is the ultimate goal.

mute in the presence of the lion, so do all other sciences in the presence of Vedānta; therefore, an ancient classical writer has appropriately described Vedānta in the following words:—

tāvat garjanti śāstrāṇi jambukā vipine yathā ।

na garjati mahāśaktiḥ yāvad vedāntakesarī ॥

that is: "other sciences howl like jackals in the woods, so long as the lion of Vedānta, the all-powerful, does not roar". The 'Observer' which has been located after the consideration of the Body and the Ātman, namely, the Puruṣa (Spirit) or Ātman (Self), and imperceptible Matter with its *sattva, rajas* and *tamas* constituents which has been located after the consideration of the Mutable and the Immutable, are both independent according to the Sāṁkhyas, who say that, on that account, the fundamental Element of the world must be looked upon as dual. But Vedānta goes further, and says that in as much as the spirits of the Sāṁkhyas are innumerable (though they are qualityless), it would be prima facie better and more proper from the logical point of view (i) to carry to its logical conclusion and without exception, the theory of the unifying tendency of Knowledge, described in the words "*avibhaktaṁ vibhakteṣu*", which is seen rising from lower grades to higher grades, and as a result of which tendency all the various perceptible objects in the universe can be included in one imperceptible Matter, and (ii) to include both Matter and these innumerable Spirits finally and without division in the Absolute Element, than to believe that fundamental Matter is capable of first ascertaining in what the good of each one of these innumerable Spirits lies, and of behaving accordingly (Gī. 18. 20-22). Diversity is the result of Individuation, and if Spirit is qualityless, these innumerable Spirits cannot possess the quality of remaining distinct from each other; or, one has to say that they are not fundamentally innumerable, but that this innumerability has arisen in them as a result of their contact with the quality of Individuation possessed by Matter. There arises also another question, namely, is the union which takes place between independent Spirit and independent Matter real or illusory ?. If you say it is real (permanent), then, in as much as it can never be got rid of, the Ātman can never attain Release according to the Sāṁkhya doctrines; and if you say it is illusory, then, the statement that Matter begins to place its evolution before Spirit, as a result of its union with Spirit, falls to the ground. Even the illustration that Matter keeps up a continual dance for the benefit of Spirit, in the same way as the cow gives milk for the benefit of its calf, is inappropriate; because, you cannot explain away the relation between Matter and Spirit in the same way as you can explain the love of the cow for her calf on the ground that it has come out of her womb (Ve. Sū. Śāṁ. Bhā. 2. 2. 3). According to Sāṁkhya philosophy, Matter and Spirit are fundamentally extremely different from each other and whereas one is gross *(jaḍa)*, the other is self-conscious *(sacetana)*. If these two substances are extremely different and independent of each other at the commencement of the world, why should one act for the benefit of the other? Saying that such is their inherent quality is not a satisfactory answer. If one has to rely on an inherent quality, why find fault with the Gross-Non-Dualism *(jaḍādvaita)* of Haeckel?. Does not Haeckel say that in the course of the growth of the constituents of fundamental Matter, it acquires the Self-consciousness of looking at itself or of thinking of itself? But if the Sāṁkhyas do not accept that position, and if they differentiate between the 'Observer' and the 'visible world', why should one not make further use of the logic by which one arrives at this differentiation? Howmuchsoever one may examine the visible world, and come to the conclusion that the sensory nerves of the eye possess particular properties, yet, the one who has ascertained this, remains a separate entity. When in this way the Spirit which sees the visible world is found to be different from the visible world which it sees, then, is there or is there not some way for us for ascertaining who this 'Observer' is, as also whether the real form of the visible universe is as we perceive it by our organs, or different from it? Sāṁkhya philosophers say that, as these questions can never be solved, one is driven to look upon Matter and Spirit as two fundamentally different and independent elements; and if we consider the matter purely from the point of view of natural sciences, this opinion of the Sāṁkhyas cannot be said to be incorrect; because, the 'Observer', or what is known in Vedānta as the 'Ātman', cannot at any time become perceptible to the organs of the Observer, that is, to its own organs, as a separate entity, in the same way as we can examine the properties of the other objects in the universe as a result of their having become perceptible to our organs; and how can human organs examine such a substance which is incapable of perception by the organs, that is, beyond the reach of the organs (*indriyātīta*)? The Blessed Lord has himself described the Ātman in the Bhagavadgītā in the following words;—

nainaṁ chindanti śastrāṇi nainaṁ dahati pāvakaḥ ।
na cainaṁ kledayanty āpo na śoṣayati mārutaḥ ॥
(Gī. 2. 23).

that is, "it, that is, the Ātman cannot be cut by weapons, it cannot be burnt by fire, it cannot be wetted by water or dried up by wind". Therefore, the Ātman is not such a thing that it will be liquified like other objects by pouring on it a liquid substance like sulphuric acid, or that we will be able to see its interior by cutting it by sharp instruments in a dissecting room, or that by holding it over fire it will be turned to gas, or that it will be dried up by wind!" In short, all the devices which natural scientists have got for examining worldly objects fall flat in this case. Then, how is the Ātman to be examined? The question does appear to be difficult; but if one ponders a little over the matter, it will be seen to be not difficult. How have even the Sāṁkhyas determined that Spirit is qualityless and independent? Have they not done that by experience got by their own consciousness? Then, why not make use of the same method for determining the true nature of Matter and Spirit? Herein lies the great difference between Materialistic philosophy and the philosophy of the Absolute Self. The subject-matter of Materialistic philosophy is perceptible to the organs, whereas that of the philosophy of the Absolute Self is beyond the organs, that is, it is self-perceptible, or something which one oneself alone can realise. It may be argued that if the Ātman is self-perceptible, then let each person acquire such knowledge of it as he himself can: where is the use of the philosophy of the Absolute Self? This objection will be proper, if the Mind or the Conscience of each man were equally pure. But, as we know by experience that the purity or strength of everybody's mind is not the same, we have to accept as authoritative in this matter the experience of only those persons whose minds are extremely pure, clean, and broad. There is no sense in carrying on a foolish argument that 'I think like this' or 'you think like that' etc. Vedānta does not ask you to abandon logic altogether. All that it says is that since the subject-matter of the philosophy of the Absolute Self is self-perceptible, that is, as it is not capable of discernment by Materialistic methods, those arguments, which are inconsistent with the personal and direct experience which supermen, possessing an extremely pure, clean, and broad mind, have described regarding the Absolute Self, cannot be taken as correct in the consideration of that philosophy. Just as in Materialistic sciences, inferences inconsistent with physical experience are considered useless, so in the philosophy of the Absolute Self, personal experience or something which one's Ātman has realised is considered of higher value than technical skill. That teaching which is consistent with such self-experience is acceptable to the Vedāntists. Śrīmat Śaṁkarācārya has laid down this very principle in his commentary on the Vedānta-Sūtras, and those who wish to study the philosophy of the Absolute Self must always bear it in mind. There is an ancient saying that:-

acintyāḥ khalu ye bhāva na tāṁs tarkeṇa sādhayet ।
prakṛtibhyaḥ paraṁ yat tu tad acintyasya lakṣaṇam ॥

that is, "one should not, by mere imagination or inference, draw conclusions about those objects on which it is impossible to contemplate as they are beyond the reach of the organs; that substance which is beyond Matter, (which is the fundamental substance of the entire universe), is, in this way, incapable of contemplation"; and this stanza has been adopted in the Mahābhārata (Ma. Bhā. Bhīṣma 5. 12) and also in the commentary of Śrī Śaṁkarācārya on the Vedānta-Sūtras, but with the reading '*yojayet*' instead of '*sādhayet*'. (Ve. Sū. Śāṁ. Bhā. 2. 1. 27). It is similarly stated in the Muṇḍakopanisad and the Kaṭhopaniṣad, that knowledge of the Absolute Self cannot be got merely by imagination (Mun. 3. 2. 3; Kaṭha. 2. 8. 9 and 22). That is why the Upaniṣads have an important place in the philosophy of the Absolute Self. Much attention had been paid in India in ancient times to the question of concentrating the mind, and there was developed in our country an independent science on that subject which is known as the (Pātañjala) Yoga science. Those venerable Ṛṣis who, being experts in that science, had besides minds which were naturally very pure and broad, have described in the Upaniṣads the experience gained by them by introspection about the nature of the Ātman, or all that with which their pure and peaceful minds were inspired. Therefore, for drawing any conclusion about any Metaphysical principle, one cannot but refer to these Śruti texts (Kaṭha. 4. 1). One may find various arguments which support and justify this self-experience according to one's own acumen; but thereby, the authoritativeness of the original self-experience does not suffer. It is true that the Bhagavadgītā is a Smṛti text; but, I have explained in the very beginning of the first chapter, that it is considered to be as authoritative in the matter as the Upaniṣads. I have, therefore, in this chapter first explained with authorities, but simply—that is, without giving reasons—the doctrines propounded in the Gītā and in the Upaniṣads about this unimaginable Substance which is beyond Matter, and I have considered later on in the chapter in what way those theories can be scientifically supported.

The Bhagavadgītā does not accept the Sāṁkhya dualism of Matter and Spirit, and the first doctrine of the philosophy of the Absolute Self in the Gītā, as also in Vedānta, is that there is at the root of the moveable and immoveable world, a third Principle which is all-pervading, imperceptible and imperishable, and which is beyond both Matter and Spirit. Although the Sāṁkhya Prakṛti is imperceptible, it is qualityful (*saguṇa*), because, it is composed of the three constituents. But whatever is qualityful is perishable. Therefore, that something else which, being imperceptible, still survives after this qualityful imperceptible Matter has been destroyed, is the real and permanent Principle of the entire Cosmos—as has been stated in the Gītā in the course of the discussion on Matter and Spirit in the stanza (Gī. 8. 20) quoted at the beginning of this chapter; and later on, in the fifteenth chapter, after referring to the Mutable and the Immutable—the Perceptible and the Imperceptible—as the two Sāṁkhya elements, the Gītā says:—

uttamaḥ puruṣas tv anyaḥ paramātmety udāhṛtaḥ ।
yo lokatrayam āviśya bibharty avyaya īśvaraḥ ॥

that is, "that Puruṣa, which is different from both these (Matter and Spirit) is the Super-Excellent, the One which is known as the Absolute Ātman, the Inexhaustible and the All-Powerful; and, pervading the three-sphered universe, It protects it." As this Spirit is 'beyond' both the Mutable and the Immutable, that is, beyond the Perceptible and the Imperceptible, it is properly called (See Gī. 15. 18) 'the Absolute Spirit' (*puruṣottama*). Even in the Mahābhārata, Bhṛgu has said to Bhāradvāja as follows in defining the word 'Paramātman':

ātmā kṣetrajña ity uktaḥ saṁyuktaḥ prākṛtair guṇaiḥ ।
tair eva tu vinirmuktaḥ paramātmety udāhṛtaḥ ॥

(Ma. Bhā. Śān. 187. 24).

that is, "when the Ātman is imprisoned within the body, it is called Kṣetrajña (or Jīvātman, i. e. personal Self); and when the same Ātman is released from these '*prākṛta*' qualities, that is, from the qualities of Matter or of the body, it is known as the Paramātman (Absolute Self)". One is likely to think that these two definitions of the 'Paramātman' are different from each other; but really speaking, they are not so. As there is only one Paramātman, which is beyond the Mutable and Immutable Cosmos, and also beyond the Jīva (or, beyond both imperceptible Matter and Spirit, according to the Sāṁkhya philosophy) a two-fold characteristic or definition of one and the same Paramātman can be given, by once saying that It is beyond the Mutable and the Immutable, and again saying that It is beyond Jīva (Soul) or the Jīvātman (i. e. Puruṣa). Bearing this aspect in mind, Kālidāsa has described the Parameśvara in the *Kumārasaṁbhava* in the following words: "You are the Matter which exerts itself for the benefit of the Spirit, and You are also the Spirit which, apathetic Itself, observes that

Matter" (Kumā. 2. 13). So also, the Blessed Lord has said in the Gītā: "*mama yonir mahadbrahma*", i. e., "Matter is My generative principle (*yoni*) or only one of My forms" (14. 3) and that "Jīva or Soul is a part of Me" (15. 7); and in the seventh chapter, the Blessed Lord says :—

bhūmir āpo 'nalo vāyuḥ khaṁ mano buddhir eva ca ।
ahaṁkāra itīyaṁ me bhinnā prakṛtir aṣṭadhā ॥

(Gī. 7. 4).

that is, "the earth, water, fire, air, ether, the Mind, Reason, and Individuation is My eightfold Prakṛti"; besides this (*apareyam itastv anyām*), "that Jīva (Soul) which is maintaining the whole of this world is also My second Prakṛti" (Gī. 7. 5). The twenty-five Sāṁkhya elements have been referred to in many places in the Mahābhārata. Nevertheless, it is stated in each place that there is beyond these twenty-five elements an Absolute Element (*paramatattva*), which is the twenty-sixth (*ṣadviṁśa*) Element, and that a man does not become a 'buddha' (scient) unless he has realised It (Śān. 308). Our world is nothing but that knowledge which we get of all the objects in the world by means of our organs of Perception; that is why Matter or Creation is sometimes referred to as '*jñāna*' (Knowledge), and from this point of view, the Spirit becomes 'the Knower' i. e., *jñātā* (Śān. 306. 35-41). But the real TO BE KNOWN (*jñeya*) is beyond both Matter and Spirit, that is, beyond both Knowledge and Knower, and, that is what is known as the Absolute Spirit (*paramapuruṣa*) in the Gītā (Gī. 13. 12). Not only the Gītā, but also all the works on Vedānta philosophy are repeatedly exhorting us to realise that *parama* or *para* (that is, Absolute) Spirit which pervades the entire Cosmos and eternally maintains it; and they say that It is One, that It is Imperceptible, that It is Eternal, and that It is Immutable. The adjectives '*akṣara*' (Immutable) and '*avyakta*' (Imperceptible) are used in Sāṁkhya philosophy with reference to Prakṛti (Matter), because, it is one of the Sāṁkhya doctrines that there is no other fundamental cause of the Cosmos which is more subtle than Prakṛti (Sāṁ. Kā. 61). But—and my readers must bear this in mind—as, from the point of view of Vedānta, the Parabrahman alone is *a-kṣara*, that is, something which is never destroyed, and also *a-vyakta*, that is, imperceptible to the organs, the same terms '*akṣara*' and '*avyakta*' are used in the Gītā for referring to the form of the Parabrahman which is beyond Matter (Gī. 8. 20; 11. 37; 15. 16, 17). It is true that when this point of view has been accepted, it would be incorrect to refer to Matter as *akṣara* (imperishable or immutable) though it may be *avyakta* (imperceptible); but as the Gītā accepts the doctrines of the Sāṁkhya system regarding the order of creation of the Cosmos to such extent as they can be accepted without prejudicing the omnipotence of this Third Element (Absolute Spirit) which is beyond both Matter and Spirit, the Perishable and the Imperishable or the Perceptible and the Imperceptible Cosmos has been described in the Gītā without departing from the fixed terminology of the Sāṁkhyas; and therefore, when there is occasion to describe the Parabrahman, it becomes necessary for the Gītā to refer to it as the Imperceptible (*avyakta*) beyond the (Sāṁkhya) imperceptible, or the Immutable (*akṣara*) beyond the (Sāṁkhya) immutable. See, for instance, the stanza given at the commencement of this chapter. In short, in reading the Gītā, one must always bear in mind that the words '*avyakta*' and '*akṣara*' are both used in the Gītā, sometimes with reference to the Prakṛti (Matter) of Sāṁkhya philosophy, and at other times with reference to the Parabrahman of Vedānta philosophy, that is, in two different ways. That further Imperceptible, which is beyond the imperceptible of the Sāṁkhyas, is the Root of the Cosmos according to Vedānta. I shall later on explain how, as a result of this difference between Sāṁkhya and Vedānta philosophy regarding the Root Element of the world, the form of Mokṣa according to the philosophy of the Highest Self is also different from that according to Sāṁkhya philosophy.

When you once reject the Sāṁkhya dualism of Matter and Spirit, and say that there is a Third Element which is eternal, and which is at the root of the world in the form of a Parameśvara or a Puruṣottama, the further questions which necessarily arise are: what is the form of this third fundamental Element, and what is the nature of its relation to both Spirit and Matter? The three, Matter, Spirit, and

Absolute Īśvara are respectively called Cosmos, Jīva and Parabrahman in Metaphysics (i. e., the philosophy of the Absolute Self). The main object of Vedānta philosophy is to determine the exact nature of, and the mutual relationship between, these three substances; and one finds this subject-matter discussed everywhere in the Upaniṣads. Nevertheless, there is no unanimity of opinion amongst Vedāntists on this point; some of them say that these three substances are fundamentally one, while others say that the Jīva (personal Self) and the Cosmos are fundamentally different from the Parameśvara, whether to a small or a large extent; and on that account, the Vedāntists are divided into Advaitins (Monists), Viśiṣṭādvaitins (Qualified-Monists), and Dvaitins (Dualists).

All are unanimous in accepting the proposition that all the activities of the Jīva and of the Cosmos are carried on according to the will of the Parameśvara. But some believe that the form of these three substances is fundamentally homogenous and intact like ether; whereas, other Vedāntists say that since the Gross can never become homogeneous with the self-conscious, the personal Self (*jīva*) and the Cosmos must be looked upon as fundamentally different from the Parameśvara, though they are both included in one Parameśvara, in the same way as the unity of a pomegranate is not destroyed on account of there being numerous grains in it; and whenever there is a statement in the Upaniṣads that all the three are 'one', that is to be understood as meaning 'one like the pomegranate'. When in this way, diversity of opinion had arisen as regards the form of the Self (*jīva*), commentators supporting different creeds have stretched the meanings not only of the Upaniṣads, but also of the words in the Gītā, in their respective commentaries. Therefore, the subject-matter really propounded in the Gītā has been neglected by these commentators, in whose opinion the principal subject-matter to be considered in the Gītā has been whether the Vedānta of the Gītā is Monistic or Dualistic. However, before considering this matter further, let us see what the Blessed Lord has Himself said in the Gītā about the mutual relationship between the Cosmos (*prakṛti*), Jīva (*ātman* or *puruṣa*), and Parabrahman (Paramātman or Puruṣottama, i.e.,

Absolute Ātman or Absolute Spirit). My readers will see from what follows that there is unanimity on this matter between the Gītā and the Upaniṣads, and all the ideas in the Gītā are to be found in the Upaniṣads, which were earlier in point of time.

In describing the Puruṣottama, Para-puruṣa, Paramātman or Parabrahman, which is beyond both Matter and Spirit, the Bhagavadgītā has first said that it has its two forms, namely the *vyakta* and the *avyakta* (that is, the one which is perceptible to the eyes, and the one which is imperceptible to the eyes). It is clear that the *vyakta* form out of these two, that is to say, the form which is perceptible to the organs, must be possessed of qualities (*saguṇa*). Then remains the imperceptible form. It is true that this form is *avyakta*, that is, it is not perceptible to the organs; but from the fact that it is imperceptible to the organs, it does not follow that it must be qualityless; because, though it might not be perceptible to the eyes, it can still possess all kinds of qualities in a subtle form. Therefore, the Imperceptible also has been further subdivided into *saguṇa* (possessed of qualities), *saguṇa-nirguṇa* (qualified and qualityless) and *nirguṇa* (qualityless). The word '*guṇa*' is here intended to mean and include all the qualities which can be perceived not only by the external organs, but also by the Mind. As the Blessed Lord Śrī Kṛṣṇa, who was a living incarnation of the Parameśvara, was personally standing in front of Arjuna to advise him, He has indicated Himself in the first person by referring to His perceptible form in the following phrases in various places in the Gītā. "Prakṛti is My form" (9. 8); "the Jīva (Self) is a part of Me" (15. 7); "I am the Ātman inhabiting the heart of all created things" (10. 20); "all the various glorious (*śrīmat*) or magnificent (*vibhūtimat*) beings which exist in the world have been created out of a part of Me" (10. 41); "keep your mind fixed on Me and become My devotee" (9. 34); "in that way, you will come to be merged in Me. I am telling you this confidently, because you are dear to Me" (18. 65); and after having satisfied Arjuna by showing him His Cosmic Form that all the moveable and the immoveable Cosmos was actually contained in His perceptible form, He has ultimately advised Arjuna, that, as it was easier to worship the perceptible form than to worship the imperceptible form, he should put faith in Him (Gī. 12. 8), and that He was the fundamental repository of the Brahman, of perennial Release, of eternal Religion and of beatific happiness (Gī. 14. 27). Therefore, one may safely say that the Gītā from beginning to end describes only the perceptible form of the Blessed Lord.

But one cannot, on that account, look upon as correct the opinion of some followers of the Path of Devotion or of some commentators, that a perceptible Parameśvara is considered to be the ultimate object of attainment in the Gītā; because, side by side with the descriptions referred to above of His perceptible form, the Blessed Lord has Himself stated that it is illusory, and that His imperceptible form, which is beyond (*para*) that perceptible form, and which is not cognisable by the organs, is His principal form. For instance, He says:

avyaktaṁ vyaktimāpannaṁ manyante mām abuddhayaḥ ।
paraṁ bhāvam ajānanto mamāvyayam anuttamam ॥

that is, "whereas I am imperceptible to the organs, ignorant people consider Me as perceptible and do not take cognisance of My superior and imperceptible form which is beyond the perceptible form" (7. 24); and further on, in the next verse (7. 25), He has said: "as I am clothed in My YOGA-MĀYĀ (illusory form), ignorant people do not recognise Me". In the same way, He has given the explanation of His perceptible form in the fourth chapter (4. 6) as follows: "although I am not subject to birth and am eternal, yet I embody Myself in My own Prakṛti and take birth, that is, become perceptible by My own MĀYĀ (*svātmamāyayā*)". He has said later on in the seventh chapter that: "Matter made up of three constituents is my DIVINE ILLUSION, those who conquer that ILLUSION become merged in Me; and those low-natured fools whose perception is destroyed by it, are not merged in Me. (7. 14, 15); and He has ultimately in the eighteenth chapter advised Arjuna as follows: "O Arjuna ! the Īśvara resides in the hearts of all living beings in the form of Self (*jīva*), and he controls the activities of all created beings by his ILLUSION as if they were machines". It is stated in the Nārāyaṇīya chapter in the Śāntiparva in the Mahābhārata that the Blessed Lord had shown to Nārada also that Cosmic Form which He had shown to Arjuna (Śān. 339); and I have explained already in the first chapter that the Gītā advocates the Nārāyaṇīya or the Bhāgavata religion. After the Blessed Lord had thus shown to Nārada His Cosmic Form with its myriad eyes, colours and other visible qualities, He says to him :

māyā hyeṣā mayā sṛṣṭā yan māṁ paśyasi nārada ।
sarvabhūtaguṇair yuktaṁ naivaṁ tvaṁ jñātum arhasi ॥
(Ma. Bhā. Śān. 339. 44).

that is, "that My form which you see is an ILLUSION (*māyā*) created by Me; but do not, on that account, carry away the impression that I am possessed of the same qualities as are possessed by created things"; and then He goes on to say: "My real form is all-pervasive, imperceptible, and eternal and that form is realised by the Released." (Śān. 339. 48). We must, therefore, say that the Cosmic Form, which had been shown to Arjuna as stated in the Gītā, was illusory. In short, although the Blessed Lord has attached importance to His perceptible form for purposes of worship, the doctrine laid down by the Gītā will, from the above statements, be clearly seen to be that (i) the excellent and superior form of the Parameśvara is His imperceptible form, that is, the form which is not cognisable by the organs; (ii) that His changing from the Imperceptible to the Perceptible is His MĀYĀ (Illusion); and (iii) that unless a man conquers this Māyā, and realises the pure and imperceptible form of the Parameśvara, which is beyond the Māyā, he cannot attain Release. I will consider later on in detail what is meant by MĀYĀ. It becomes quite clear from the statements quoted above that the theory of Māyā was not an invention of Śrī Śaṁkarācārya, and that even before his time it was an accepted theory in the Bhagavadgītā, the Mahābhārata, and also in the Bhāgavata religion. Even in the Śvetāśvataropaniṣad, the creation of the Cosmos is described as follows: "*māyāṁ tu prakṛtiṁ vidyān māyinaṁ tu maheśvaram*" (Śvetā. 4. 10), that is, "Māyā is the Prakṛti (the Sāṁkhya Prakṛti) and the Lord of that Māyā is the Parameśvara; that Parameśvara creates the universe by His Māyā (Illusive Force)".

Although it is thus clear that the superior form of the Parameśvara is not perceptible, but is imperceptible, yet, it is necessary to consider whether this imperceptible form has qualities or is qualityless; because, we have before ourselves the example of a qualityful imperceptible substance in the form of the Sāṁkhya Prakṛti which, being imperceptible, is at the same time possessed of qualities, that is, which possesses the *sattva*, *rajas*, and *tamas* qualities; and according to some persons, the imperceptible and superior form of the Parameśvara must also be considered qualityful in the same way. These people say that in as much as the imperceptible Parameśvara creates the perceptible Cosmos, though He may do so by His Māyā (Gī. 9. 8), and as He also resides in the heart of everybody and makes them carry on their various activities (18. 61); in as much as He is the recipient and the Lord of all sacrifices (9. 24); in as much as all the Bhāvas (that is, rational activities) in the shape of pain and happiness of all living beings spring from Him (10, 5); in as much as He is the one who creates devotion in the hearts of living beings; and as "*labhate ca tataḥ kāmān mayaiva vihitān hi tān*" (7. 22), that is, as "He is the giver of the result of the desires of living beings"; therefore, though He may be imperceptible, that is, though He may not be perceptible to the organs, yet He must be looked upon as possessed of the qualities of mercy, potentiality etc., that is, possessed of qualities (*saguṇa*). But on the other hand, the Blessed Lord Himself says: "*na māṁ karmāṇi limpanti*", that is, "I am never polluted by Action" or, which is the same thing, by qualities (4. 14); foolish people suffer from MOHA (ignorance) as a result of the qualities of Prakṛti, and look upon the Ātman as the doer (3. 27; 14. 19); as this eternal and non-active Parameśvara inhabits the hearts of living beings in the form of Jīva (13. 31), people, who are overwhelmed by ignorance, become confused, though the Parameśvara is really speaking untouched by their activity or action (5. 14, 15). It is not that the forms of the Parameśvara who is imperceptible, (that is, imperceptible to the organs) have thus been described as only two, namely, qualityful (*saguṇa*) and qualityless (*nirguṇa*); but in some places both the forms are mixed up in describing the imperceptible Parameśvara. For instance, there are mutually contradictory *saguṇa-nirguṇa* descriptions of the Parameśvara in the ninth chapter of the Gītā where it is stated that: "*bhūtabhṛt na ca bhūtastho*" (9. 9), that is, "I am the fundamental support of all created things, and yet, I am not in them", and in the thirteenth chapter, where it is stated that: "the Parabrahman is neither *sat* (real) nor *asat*, i.e., illusory" (13. 12), "It appears to be possessed of all organs, yet, is devoid of organs, and is qualityless, and at the same time the experiencer of the qualities" (13. 14); "It is distant, and yet It is near" (13. 15); "It is undivided, and yet It appears to be divided" (13. 16). Nevertheless, in the beginning of the Gītā, already in the second chapter, it is stated that "this Ātman is imperceptible, unimaginable (*acintya*) and immutable, i. e., *avikārya*" (2. 25); and there is in the thirteenth chapter, a description of the superiority of the imperceptible form of the Parameśvara, which is pure, qualityless (*nirguṇa*), unorganised (*niravayava*), unchanging (*nirvikāra*), unimaginable (*acintya*) and eternal (*anādi*), in the following words:—"this absolute Ātman (Paramātman) is eternal, qualityless, and inexhaustible, and therefore, though It might reside in the body, It does nothing and is not effected by anything" (13. 31).

As in the Bhagavadgītā, so also in the Upaniṣads is the form of the imperceptible Parameśvara found described in three ways, that is, sometimes as being *saguṇa* (qualityful), sometimes as *saguṇa-nirguṇa* (qualityful and qualityless), and sometimes as *nirguṇa* (qualityless). It is not that one must always have a visible icon before oneself for purposes of worship. It is possible to worship a form which is indefinite (*nirākara*), that is, which is imperceptible to the eyes and the other organs of Perception. But, unless that which is to be worshipped is perceptible to the Mind, though it might be imperceptible to the eyes and other organs of perception, its worship will be impossible. Worship means contemplation, visualising by the Mind (*manas*) or meditation; and unless the Mind perceives some other quality of the object of contemplation—even if it cannot perceive its form—how can the Mind contemplate on it? Therefore, wherever the contemplation, mental visualisation or meditation of or on the imperceptible Parameśvara, that is, on the Parameśvara who is not visible to the eyes, has been mentioned in the Upaniṣāds, He has been considered as possessed of qualities *(saguṇa)*. These qualities which are imagined to exist in the Parameśvara are more or less comprehensive or more or less *sāttvika* according to the merit of the worshipper, and everyone gets the result of his worship in the measure of his faith. It is stated in the Chāndogyopaniṣad (3. 14. 1) that "man (*puruṣa*) is the embodiment of his determination (i. e., he is *kratumaya*), and he gets his meed after death, according to his '*kratu*' (determination)"; and it is also stated in the Bhagavadgītā that: "those who worship deities are merged in the deities, and those who worship ancestors are merged in the ancestors (Gītā 9. 25), or "*yo yacchraddhaḥ sa eva saḥ*", that is, "every one obtains results according to his own faith (17. 3). Necessarily, therefore, different qualities of the imperceptible Parameśvara to be worshipped have been described in the Upaniṣads according to the difference in the spiritual merit of the worshipper. This portion of the Upaniṣads is technically called 'VIDYĀ'. Vidyā means the path (in the form of worship) of reaching the Īśvara, and any chapter in which such path is described has the suffix 'vidyā' placed at the end of its name. Many forms of worship are described in the Upaniṣads, such as Śāndilya–vidyā (Chān. 3. 14), Puruṣa–vidyā (Chān. 3. 16, 17), Paryaṁka–vidyā (Kauṣī. 1), Prāṇopāsanā (Kauṣī. 2) etc., etc., and all these forms have been dwelt upon in the third section of the third chapter of the Vedānta–Sūtras. In these chapters, the imperceptible Parameśvara has been described as qualityful in the following terms: e. g., '*manomaya*' (mind-embodied), '*prāṇaśarīra*' (embodiment of Vital Force), '*bhārūpa*' (of shining appearance), '*satyasaṁkalpa*' (Truth-formed), '*ākāśātmā*' (ether-like), '*sarvakarmā*' (all-capable), '*sarvakāma*' (fulfiller of all desires), '*sarvagandha*' (embodiment of all scents), and '*sarvarasa*', i.e., embodiment of all tastes (Chān. 3. 14. 2); and in the Taittirīyopaniṣad (Tai. 2. 1–5; 3. 2–6) the worship of the Brahman in a rising scale has been described as the worship of food, life, mind, practical knowledge (*vijñāna*), and joy (*ānanda*); and in the Bṛhadāraṇyaka, Gārgya

Bālāki has prescribed to Ajātaśatru the worship of the Spirit in the Sun, the Moon, ether, the air, fire, water, or the cardinal points, as being the form of the Brahman; but Ajātaśatru has told him that the true Brahman is beyond all these, and ultimately maintained that the worship of Vital Force (*prāṇopāsanā*) is the highest. But this list does not end here. All the forms of the Brahman mentioned above are technically called '*pratīka*' (symbols), that is to say, an inferior form of the Brahman adopted for worship, or some sign indicating the Brahman; and when this form is kept before the eyes in the shape of an idol, it becomes a '*pratimā*' (icon). But all the Upaniṣads lay down the doctrine that the real form of the Brahman is different from this (Kena 1. 2. 8). In some places, this Brahman is defined so as to include all qualities in only three qualities, as in the following expressions: "*satyaṁ jñānam anantaṁ brahma*" (Taitti. 2. 1), or "*vijñānam ānandaṁ brahma*" (Bṛ. 3. 9. 28), or that the Brahman is of the form of *satya* (*sat*), *jñāna* (*cit*), *ānanda* (joy), or is '*saccidānanda*' in form. And in other places, there are descriptions which include mutually contradictory qualities, in the same way as in the Bhagavadgītā, like the following: "the Brahman is neither *sat* (real) nor *asat*, i. e., illusory" (Ṛg. 10. 129), or is "*aṇor aṇīyān mahato mahīyān*", that is, smaller than an atom and larger than the largest (Kaṭha 2. 20), or "*tad ejati tannaijati tad dūre tad antike*", that is, "It does not move and yet It moves, It is far away and yet It is near (Īśa 5; Muṇ. 3. 1. 7), or "It has the appearance of possessing the qualities of all organs" (*sarvendriyaguṇābhāsa*), and yet is '*sarvendriyavivarjita*', i. e., devoid of all organs (Śvetā. 3. 17). Mṛtyu, in advising Naciketa, has kept aside all these descriptions, and said that the Brahman is something which is beyond righteousness, beyond that which is done and that which has not been done, and beyond that which has happened and that which is capable of happening, i. e., 'bhavya' (Kaṭha 2. 14); and similar descriptions are given by Brahmadeva to Rudra in the chapter on the Nārāyaṇīya religion in the Mahābhārata (Ma. Bhā. Śān. 351. 11.); and by Nārada to Śuka in the chapter on Mokṣa (331. 44). Even in the Bṛhadāraṇyakopaniṣad (Bṛ. 2. 3. 2), it is stated in the beginning that there are three iconical forms of the Brahman, namely, earth, water, and fire and two non-iconical forms, namely, air and ether; and it is then stated that the forms or colours of the ether-formed (*sārabhūta*) spirits into which these non-iconical forms are transformed, change; and it is ultimately stated that "*neti, neti*", that is, "It is not this", "It is not this", that is to say, whatever has been described so far, is not the Brahman; the Parabrahman is something which is beyond (*para*) this non-iconical or iconical substance (which can be identified by Name and Form), and is '*agṛhya*', i. e., incomprehensible, and '*anirṇanīya*', i. e., indescribable (Br. 2. 3. 7 and Ve. Sū. 3. 2. 22). Nay, the Brahman is that which is beyond all objects whatsoever which can be named; and the words "*neti, neti*", that is, "It is not this, It is not this" have become a short symbol to show the imperceptible and qualityless form of that Brahman: and the same description has appeared four times in the Bṛhadāraṇyakopaniṣad (Bṛha. 3. 2. 29; 4. 2. 4; 4. 4. 22; and 4. 5. 15); and in the same way, there are also descriptions in other Upaniṣads of the qualityless and unimaginable form of the Parabrahman, such as, "*yato vāco nivartante aprāpya manasā saha*" (Taitti. 2. 9), or "*adreśyam (adṛṣya), agrāhyam*" (Muṇ. 1. 1. 6), or "*na cakṣuṣā gṛhyate na 'pi vācā* (Muṇ. 3. 1. 8), that is, "That which is not visible to the eyes, and which cannot be described by speech", or:

aśabdam asparśam arūpam avyayaṁ
tathā 'rasaṁ nityam agandhavac ca yat ।
anady anantaṁ mahataḥ paraṁ dhruvaṁ
nicāyya taṁ mṛtyumukhāt pramucyate ॥

that is, It does not possess the five qualities of sound, touch, colour, taste, and smell, which are possessed by the five primordial elements, and is without beginning, without end, and imperishable (See Ve. Sū. 3. 2. 22-30). In the description of the Nārāyaṇīya or Bhāgavata religion in the Śāntiparva of the Mahābhārata, the Blessed Lord has described His real form to Nārada as being "invisible, unsmellable, untouchable, qualityless, inorganic (*niṣkala*), unborn, eternal, permanent and inactive (*niṣkriya*); and said that such His form is known as '*vāsudeva paramātman*' (Vāsudeva, the Absolute Ātman); and that He is the Parameśvara who has transcended the three constituents, and who creates and destroys the universe (Ma. Bhā. Śān. 339. 21-38).

Not only in the Bhagavadgītā but also in the Bhāgavata or Nārāyaṇīya religion described in the Mahābhārata, and even in the Upaniṣads, the imperceptible form of the Parameśvara is considered to be superior to His perceptible form, and this imperceptible form is again described in three ways, that is, as being qualityful, qualityful-qualityless and qualityless, as will appear from the quotations above. Now, how is one going to harmonise these three mutually contradictory forms with the superior and imperceptible form of the Paramesvara? Out of these three forms, the qualityful-qualityless or dual form may be looked upon as a step between the *saguṇa* (qualityful) and the *nirguṇa* (qualityless) or the *ajñeya* (unknowable); because, one can realise the qualityless form only by, in the first place, realising the qualityful form, and then omitting quality after quality; and it is in this rising grade that the worship of the symbol of the Brahman has been described in the Upaniṣads. For instance, in the Bhṛguvallī in the Taittirīyopaniṣad, Bhṛgu has said to Varuṇa in the first place that *anna* (food) is Brahman, and thereafter he has in a gradual order explained to him the other forms of the Brahman, namely, Vital Force *(prāṇas)*, Mind *(manas)*, diverse knowledge *(vijñāna)* and joy i. e. *ānanda* (Taitti. 3. 2-6). Or, it may even be said that, since that which has no qualities cannot be described by adjectives showing quality, it is necessary to describe it by mutually contradictory adjectives; because, when you use the words 'distant' or 'real (*sat*) our mind gets inferentially the idea that there is some other thing, which is near or illusory *(asat)*. But, if there is only one Brahman to be found on all sides, what can be called near or illusory, if one calls the Parameśvara distant or real *(sat)*? Therefore, one cannot but use such expressions as, 'It is neither distant nor near, It is neither real nor illusory' and thereby get rid of mutually dependent quality-couplets like distant and near, or illusory and real; and one has to take advantage of these mutually contradictory adjectives in ordinary conversation for showing that, that which remains, and which is qualityless, and is such as exists everywhere and at all times, in an unrelated and independent state, is the true Brahman (Gī. 13. 12). In as much as whatever is, is Brahman, it is distant and it is also near, it is real or existent, and, at the same time, it is unreal or illusory; and looking at the matter from another point of view, the same Brahman may be defined at the same time by mutually contradictory adjectives (Gī. 11. 17; 13. 15). But though, in this way, one justifies the dual qualification of 'qualityful-qualityless' yet, it still remains to explain how the two mutually contradictory qualifications of 'qualityful' and 'qualityless' can be applied to the same Parameśvara. When the imperceptible Parameśvara takes up a perceptible (*vyakta*) form which is cognisable by the organs, that may be said to be His Māyā or illusion; but when He changes from the Qualityless to the Qualityful without becoming perceptible to or cognisable by the organs, and remains imperceptible, how is He to be called? For instance, one and the same indefinite Parameśvara is looked upon by some as qualityless, and is described by the words "*neti, neti*", that is, "It is not this, It is not this"; whereas others consider him qualityful, that is, as possessing all qualities and being the doer of all things, and being kind. Then it becomes necessary to explain, what the reason for this is, and which is the more correct description, as also to explain how the entire perceptible universe and all living beings came into existence out of one qualityless and imperceptible Brahman. To say that the imperceptible Parameśvara, who brings all projects to a successful conclusion, is, as a matter of fact, qualityful, and that His description in the Upaniṣads and in the Gītā as 'qualityless' is an exaggeration or meaningless praise, would be like cutting at the very root of the philosophy of the Absolute Self; because, characterising as an exaggeration the conscious self-experience of great Ṛṣis, who, after concentrating their minds and after very minute and peaceful meditation, have expounded the doctrine, that that is the true form of the Brahman which: "*yato vāco nivartante aprāpya manasā saha*" (Tai. 2. 9), that is, "is unrealisable by the mind, and which cannot be described by speech"; and saying that the true Brahman must be qualityful, because our minds cannot grasp the idea of an eternal and qualityless Brahman, would be as reasonable as saying that one's own candle-light is superior to the Sun! It would be different, of course, if this qualityless form of the Parameśvara had not been explained and justified in the Upaniṣads or in the Gītā; but such is not the case. The Bhagavadgītā does not rest with saying that the superior and true form of the Parameśvara is imperceptible, and that His taking up the form of the perceptible Cosmos is His MĀYĀ (Gī. 4. 6). The Blessed Lord has said to Arjuna in clear and unmistakable terms that: "as a result of MOHA (ignorance) arising from the qualities of Prakṛti, FOOLISH PEOPLE consider the (imperceptible and qualityless) Ātman as the performer of Actions" (Gī. 3. 27-29); the Īśvara does nothing, and people are deceived as a result of IGNORANCE (Gī. 5. 15); that is to say, though the imperceptible Ātman or the Absolute Īśvara is fundamentally qualityless (Gī. 13. 31), people as a result of 'confusion' or 'ignorance' foist on Him, qualities like activity etc., and make Him qualityful and imperceptible (Gī. 7. 24). From this, it follows that the true doctrines of the Gītā about the form of the Parameśvara are that :—(1) though there is any amount of description of the perceptible form of the Parameśvara in the Gītā, yet, His fundamental and superior form is imperceptible and qualityless, and people look upon Him as qualityful by IGNORANCE or MOHA; (2) the Sāṁkhya Prakṛti is His perceptible diffusion that is to say, the whole of this cosmos is the ILLUSION of the Parameśvara; and (3) the Sāṁkhya Puruṣa, that is, the personal Self, is fundamentally of the same form as the Parameśvara, and is qualityless and inactive like the Parameśvara, but people consider him as a doer *(kartā)* as a result of IGNORANCE. The same are the doctrines of Vedānta philosophy. But in later Vedānta treatises, some amount of distinction is made between Māyā (illusion) and Avidyā (ignorance) in enunciating these doctrines. For instance, in the *Pañcadaśī*, it is stated in the beginning, that the Ātman and the Parabrahman are originally identical, that is, are both of the form of the Brahman, and that when this Brahman, in the form of Consciousness *(cit)* is reflected in the form of Māyā (Illusion), Prakṛti composed of the *sattva*, *rajas* and *tamas* constituents (the Sāṁkhya fundamental Prakṛti) comes into existence. But later on, this Māyā is subdivided into '*māyā*' (illusion) and '*avidyā*' (ignorance); and it is stated that we have pure *māyā* when the pure *(śuddha) sattva* component, out of the three components of this Māyā is preponderant, and the Brahman which is reflected in this pure *māyā*, is called the qualityful or perceptible Īśvara (Hiraṇya-garbha); and, if this *sattva* component is impure *(aśuddha)*, that Māyā becomes '*avidyā*' (ignorance), and the Brahman which is reflected in it is given the name of '*jīva*' (Pañca. 1. 15–17). From this point of view, it is necessary to make a two-fold distinction between one and the same Māyā, by looking upon *māyā* as the cause of the 'perceptible Īśvara' springing out of the Parabrahman, and '*avidyā*' as the cause of the 'Jīva' springing out of the Parabrahman. But, this distinction has not been made in the Gītā. The Gītā says that the Jīva becomes confused (7. 4–15) as a result of the same Māyā by means of which the Blessed Lord takes up his perceptible or qualityful form (7. 25), or by means of which the eight-fold Prakṛti, that is, all the various objects in the world are born from Him (4. 6). The word '*avidyā*' does not occur anywhere in the Gītā, and where it appears in the Śvetāśvataropaniṣad, it is used to signify the diffusion of Māyā (Śvetā 5. 1). I shall, therefore, disregard the subtle difference made in later Vedāntic treatises between *avidyā* and *māyā* in relation to the Jīva and the Īśvara, merely for purposes of facility of exposition, and take the words *māyā*, *avidyā* and *ajñāna* as synonymous, and shortly and scientifically deal with the question as to what is ordinarily the elementary form of this Māyā with its three constituents or of *avidyā*, *ajñāna*, or *moha*, and also how the doctrines of the Gītā or of the Upaniṣads can be explained with reference to that form.

Although the words *nirguṇa* and *saguṇa* are apparently insignificant, yet, when one considers all the various things which they include, the entire Cosmos verily stands in front of one's eyes. These two small words embrace such numerous and ponderous questions as: how has the unbroken entity of that enternal Parabrahman, which is the Root of the Cosmos, been broken up by its acquiring the numerous activities or qualities which are perceptible to human organs, though it was originally ONE, inactive, and apathetic?; or, how is that, which was fundamentally homogeneous, now seen to be transformed into distinct, heterogeneous, and perceptible objects?; how has that Parabrahman, which is *nirvikāra* (immutable), and which does not possess the various qualities of sweetness, pungency, bitterness, solidity, liquidity, heat or cold, given rise to different kinds of tastes, or to more or less of solidity or liquidity, or to numerous couples of opposite qualities, such as, heat and cold, happiness and pain, light and darkness, death and immortality?; how has that Parabrahman, which is peaceful and undisturbed, given rise to numerous kinds of voices or sounds?; how has that Parabrahman, which does not know the difference of inside or outside, or distant or near, acquired the qualities of being here or further away, near or distant, or towards the East or towards the West, which are qualities of directions or of place?; how has that Parabrahman, which is immutable, unaffected by Time, permanent and immortal been changed into objects, which perish in a longer or shorter space of time?; or how has that Parabrahman, which is not affected by the law of causes and products, come before us in the form of a cause and a product, in the shape of earth and the earthenware pot? Or, to express the same thing in short, we have now to consider how that which was ONE, acquired diversity; how that which was non-dual, acquired duality; how that which was untouched by opposite doubles (*dvandva*), became affected by these opposite doubles; or, how that which was unattached (*asaṅga*), acquired attachment (*saṅga*). Sāṁkhya philosophy has got over this difficulty by imagining a duality from the very beginning, and by saying that qualityful Prakṛti with its three constituents, is eternal and independent, in the same way as the qualityless and eternal Puruṣa (Spirit). But, not only is the natural tendency of the human mind, to find out the fundamental Root of the world, not satisfied by this duality, but it also does not bear the test of logic. Therefore, the writers of the Upaniṣads have gone beyond Prakṛti and Puruṣa, and laid down the doctrine that the qualityless (*nirguṇa*) Brahman, which is even higher than the *saccidānanda* Brahman, i. e., the Brahman possessed of the qualities of eternal Existence (*sat*), Consciousness (*cit*), and Joy (*ānanda*), is the root of the world. But, I must now explain how the Qualityful (*saguṇa*) came out of the Qualityless (*nirguṇa*); because, it is a doctrine of Vedānta, as of Sāṁkhya philosophy, that that which is not, is not; and that that which is, can never come into existence out of that which is not. According to this doctrine, the Qualityful (*saguṇa*), that is, the qualityful objects in the world cannot come into existence out of the Brahman which is qualityless (*nirguṇa*). Then, whence has the Qualityful come? If one says that the Qualityful does not exist, then, one can see it before one's eyes; and, if one says that the Qualityful is Real (existing), in the same way as the Qualityless, then, in as much as the forms of qualities like, sound, touch, form, taste etc., which are perceptible to the organs, are one to-day and different to-morrow, that is, are ever-changing, or in other words, are perishable, mutable, and inconstant, one has to say, that the all-pervading Parameśvara is, so far at least as this qualityful part of Him is concerned, (imagining of course, the Parameśvara to be divisible), perishable. And how can one give the name of Parameśvara to something, which is divisible and perishable, and which always acts in a dependent way, and subject to the rules which regulate the creation? In short, whether you imagine that all qualityful objects, which are perceptible to the organs, have sprung out of the five primordial elements, or whether you imagine with the Sāṁkhyas or the material scientists, that all objects have been created from one and the same imperceptible but qualityful fundamental Matter, whichever position you take up, so long as this fundamental Prakṛti (Matter) has not been divested of perishable qualities, one certainly cannot describe these five primordial elements or this fundamental substance in the shape of Prakṛti as the imperishable, independent, or immortal element of the world. Therefore, he who wants to accept the theory of Prakṛti, must either give up the position that the Parameśvara is eternal, independent and immortal, or he must try to find out what lies beyond the five primordial elements, or beyond the fundamental qualityful Prakṛti known as 'Prakṛti'; and there is no third alternative. In the same way, as it is impossible to quench thirst by a mirage, or to get oil out of sand, so also is it futile to hope that immortality can ever come out of that which is palpably perishable; and, therefore, Yājñavalkya has definitely told Maitreyī that, however much of wealth one may acquire, yet, "*amṛtatvasya tu nāśāsti vittena*" (Bṛ. 2. 4. 2), i. e., "Do not entertain the hope of obtaining immortality by such wealth". Well; if you say that immortality is unreal, then, every man entertains the hope that the reward which he wishes to obtain from a king should be available for enjoyment after his death to his sons, grand-sons etc., so long as the Sun and the Moon last; or, we even find that, if there is a chance for a man to acquire long-standing or permanent fame, he does not care even for life. Not only are there prayers of the ancient Ṛṣis like: "O Indra! give us '*akṣita śrava*', that is, imperishable fame or wealth" (Ṛg. 1. 9. 7) or, "O Soma! make me immortal in the sphere of Vaivasvata (Yama)" (Ṛg. 9. 133. 8) to be found in extremely ancient works like the Ṛgveda, but even in modern times, pure Materialists like Spencer, Kant, and others are found maintaining that "it is the highest moral duty of mankind in this world to try to obtain the permanent happiness of the present and future generations, without being deluded by transient happiness". From where has this idea of permanent happiness, beyond the span of one's own life, that is to say, of immortality come? If one says that it is inherent nature, then, one is bound to admit that there is some immortal substance beyond this perishable body; and, if one says that such an immortal substance does not exist, then, one cannot explain in any other way that mental tendency which one oneself actually experiences. In this difficulty, many Materialists advise that, as these questions can never be solved, we should not attempt to solve them, or allow our minds to travel beyond the qualities or objects which are to be found in the visible world. This advice seems easy to follow; but, who is going to control the natural desire for philosophy which exists in the human mind, and how?; and, if this unquenchable desire for knowledge is once killed, how is knowledge to be increased? Ever since the day when the human being came into this world, he has been continually thinking of what the fundamental immortal principle at the root of this visible and perishable world, is; and, how he will reach it; and, however much the Material sciences are developed, this inherent tendency of the human mind towards the knowledge of the immortal principle will not be lessened. Let the material sciences be developed as much as they can, philosophy will always pocket all the knowledge of Nature contained in them, and run beyond! That was the state of things three or four thousand years ago, and the same state of things is now seen in Western countries. Nay, on that day when this ambition of a human being comes to an end, we will have to say of him "*sa vai mukto 'thavā paśuḥ*", that is, "he is either a Released soul, or a brute!"

No philosophers from any other country have yet found an explanation, which is more reasonable than the one given in our ancient treatises, about the existence of an Element, which is unbounded by time or place, and is immortal, eternal, independent, homogeneous, sole, immutable, all-pervasive, and qualityless, or as to how the qualityful creation came into existence out of that qualityless Element. The modern German philosopher Kant has minutely examined the reasons why man acquires a synthetic knowledge of the heterogeneity of the external universe, and he has given the same explanation as our philosophers, but in a clearer way and according to modern scientific methods; and although Haegel has gone beyond Kant, yet his deductions do not go beyond those of Vedānta. The same is the case with Schaupenhaur. He had read the Latin translation of the Upaniṣads, and he himself has admitted that he has in his works borrowed ideas from this "most valuable work in the world's literature". But it is not possible to consider in a small book like this, these difficult problems and their pros and cons, or the similarity and dissimilarity between the doctrines of Vedānta philosophy, and the doctrines laid down by Kant and other Western philosophers, or to consider the minute differences between the Vedānta philosophy appearing in ancient treatises like the Upaniṣads and the Vedānta-Sūtras, and that expounded in later works. Therefore, I have in this book broadly referred to only that portion of them to which it is necessary to refer in order to impress on the minds of my readers the veracity, the importance, and the reasons for the Metaphysical doctrines in the Gītā, on the authority principally of the Upaniṣads, and the Vedānta-Sūtras, and of the Bhāṣyas (commentaries) of Śrī Sāṁkarācārya on them. In order to determine what lies beyond the Sāṁkhya Dualism of Matter and Spirit, it is not sufficient to stop with the distinction made by Dualists between the Observer of the world and the visible world; and one has to consider minutely the form of the knowledge which the man who sees the world gets of the external world, as also how that knowledge is acquired, and what that knowledge consists of. Animals see the objects in the external world in the same way as they are seen by men. But, as man has got the special power of synthesising the experience impressed on his mind through organs of Perception like the eyes, ears, etc., he has got the special quality that he acquires the knowledge of the objects in the external world. It has already been explained by me in the chapter on the Body and the Ātman, that that power of synthesis, which is responsible for this special feature in man, is a power which is beyond Mind and Reason, that is to say, is a power of the Ātman. Man acquires the knowledge, not of only one object, but also and in the same way, of the various relations in the shape of causes and products, between the diverse objects in the world—which are known as the laws or principles of Creation; because, although the various objects in the world might be visible to the eyes, yet, the relation of causes and products between them is not a thing which is actually visible; and that relation is determined by the intellectual activity of the one who sees. For instance, when a particular object has passed before our eyes, we decide that he is a soldier by seeing his form and his movement, and that impression remains fixed in our minds. When another similar object passes before our eyes in the wake of the first object, the same intellectual process is repeated, and our Reason decides that that object is a second soldier; and when, in this way, we, by our memory, remember the various impressions, which our mind has received one after the other, but at different moments or times, and synthesise them, we get the synthetical knowledge of these various impressions that an 'army' has been passing in front of our eyes. When the mind has decided by looking at the form of the object which comes after the army, that he is a 'king', the former impression about the army, and the new impression about the king, are once more synthesised by our mind, and we say that the procession of the king is passing. From this, it becomes necessary for us to say, that our knowledge of the world is not some gross object which is actually perceived by the organs, but that 'knowledge' is the result of the synthesis of the various impressions received by the mind, which is made by the 'Observing Ātman'; and for the same reason Knowledge (Jñāna) has been defined in the Bhagavadgītā by the words: "*avibhaktam vibhakteṣu*", that is, by saying that: "that is true knowledge by means of which we realise the non-diversity or unity in that which is diverse or different" (Gī. 18. 20).* But if one again minutely considers what that is of which impressions are first received on the mind through the medium of the organs, it will be seen that though by means of the eyes, ears, nose etc., we may get knowledge of the form, sound, smell or other qualities of various objects, yet, our organs cannot tell us anything about the internal form of that substance which possesses these external qualities. We see that wet earth is manufactured into a pot, but we are not able to know what the elementary fundamental form of that substance which we call 'wet earth', is. When the mind has severally perceived the various qualities of stickiness, wetness, dirtiness of colour, or rotundity of form in the earthenware pot, the 'Observing' Ātman synthesises all these various impressions, and says: "this is wet earth"; and later on when the Mind perceives the qualities of a hollow and round form or appearance, or a firm sound, or dryness of this very substance (for there is no reason to believe that the elementary form of the substance has changed), the 'Observer' synthesises all these qualities and calls the substance a 'pot'. In short, all the change or difference takes place only in the quality of '*rūpa*' or '*ākāra*', that is, 'form', and the same fundamental substance gets different names

---

* Cf. "Knowledge is first produced by the synthesis of what is manifold". Kant's *Critique of Pure Reason*, p. 64, Max Müller's translation, 2nd Edition.

after the 'Observer' has synthesised the impressions made by these various qualities on the Mind. The most simple examples of this are the sea and the waves, or gold and ornaments; because the qualities of colour, solidity or liquidity, and weight, in these various objects, remain unchanged and the '*rūpa*' (form) and name are the only two things which change; and, therefore these easy illustrations are always mentioned in Vedānta philosophy. The gold remains the same; but the 'Observer', who synthesises the impressions received by the Mind, through the organs, of the changes which have taken place at different times in its form, gives to this fundamentally one and the same substance different names at different times, e. g., once 'necklace', at another time 'armlets'; once 'bangles', and at another time a 'necklet'; once 'rings', and at another time a 'chandrahāra' etc. These various NAMES which we give to objects from time to time, and the various FORMS of those objects by reason of which those names changed, are referred to in the Upaniṣads as 'NĀMA-RŪPA' (Name and Form) and this technical term also includes all other qualities (Chān. 6. 3 and 4; Bṛ. 1. 4. 7); because, whatever quality is taken, it must have some Name or Form. But although these NAMES and FORMS change every moment, yet, there is underlying them some substance, which is different from that Name and Form, and which never changes; and it becomes necessary for us to say, that numerous films in the shape of Name and Form have come on this fundamental substance, in the same way as some floating substance (*taraṅga*) comes on the surface of water. Our organs cannot perceive anything except Name and Form; therefore, it is true that our organs cannot realise that fundamental substance which is the substratum of these Names and Forms, but is different from them. But, though this Elementary Substance, which is the foundation of the entire universe, may be imperceptible, that is, uncognisable by the organs, yet, our Reason has drawn the definite inference that it is '*sat*', that is, really and eternally to be found in and under this Name and Form, and never ceases to exist; because, if you say, that there is fundamentally nothing beyond the Name and Form which is perceptible to our organs, then a 'necklace' and 'bangles' will become different objects, and there will be no foundation for the knowledge acquired by us, that both are made of one and the same substance, gold. All that we will be able to say is: 'this is a necklace', 'these are bangles'; but we will not be able to say that 'the necklace is of gold'. It, therefore, logically follows that that gold, with which we connect the necklace or chain embodied in a Name and Form by means of the words 'is of' in the sentences 'the necklace *is of* gold', 'the chain *is of* gold', etc., is not non-existent like the horn of the hare; and that the word 'gold' gives one the idea of that substance which has become the foundation of all golden ornaments. When the same logical argument is applied to all the various objects in the world, we come to the conclusion that the various objects having Names and Forms which we come across, such as, stones, pearls, silver, iron, wood, etc., have come into existence as a result of different Names and Forms having been super-imposed on one and the same eternal substance; that all the difference is only in the Name and Form and not in the fundamental substance; and that there permanently exists at the bottom of all Names and Forms only one homogeneous substance. 'Existing at all times in a permanent form in all substances' in this way, is technically known in Sanskrit as '*sattā-sāmānya*'.

This doctrine of our Vedānta philosophy has been accepted as correct by modern Western philosophers like Kant and others; and this invisible substance, which is different from all Names and Forms, and which is the root of the universe embodied in Name and Form, is in their books referred to as 'Thing-in-itself' *(vastu-tattva)*; and the Name and Form which becomes perceptible to the eyes and the other organs is called by them "external appearance" * But it is usual in Vedānta philosophy to refer to this everchanging external Appearance embodied in

* This subject-matter has been considered in the Critique of Pure Reason by Kant. He has named the fundamental substance underlying the world as "*Ding an sich*" (the Thing-in-itself); and I have translated those words by '*vastu-tattva*'; the external appearance of Name and Form has been named by Kant as '*Erschsinung*' (Appearance). According to Kant, the 'Thing-in-itself' cannot be known.

Name and Form as '*mithyā*' (illusory), or '*nāśavanta*' (perishable); and to refer to the Fundamental Element as '*satya*' (Real) or '*amṛta*' (immortal). Ordinary people define the word '*satya*' by saying '*cakṣur vai satyaṁ*', that is, "that which is seen by the eyes is real"; and if one considers the ordinary course of life, it is needless to say that there is a world of difference between seeing in a dream that one has got a lakh of rupees, or hearing about a lakh of rupees, and actually getting a lakh of rupees. Therefore, the dictum '*cakṣur vai satyam*' (i. e., that is Real, which is seen by the eyes) has been enunciated in the Bṛhadāraṇyakopaniṣad (Bṛ. 5. 14. 4) in order to explain whether one should trust more one's eyes or one's ears, if one has merely heard something by mere hearsay, or if one has actually seen it. But, what is the use of this relative definition of '*satya*' (Reality) for a science by which one has to determine whether the rupee which goes under the visible Name of 'rupee' or is recognised by its Form, namely, by its round appearance, is Real? We also see in the course of ordinary affairs, that if there is no consistency in what a man says, and if he now says one thing and shortly afterwards another thing, people call him false. Then, why should not the same argument be applied to the Name and Form called 'rupee' (not to the underlying substance) and the rupee be called false or illusory? For, we can take away the Name and Form, 'rupee' of a rupee, which our eyes see to-day, and give it to-morrow the Name and Form of 'chain' or 'cup'; that is to say, we see by our own eyes that Names and Forms always change, that is, are not constant. Besides, if one says that nothing else is true except what one sees by one's eyes, then, we will be landed in the position of calling that mental process of synthesis by means of which we acquire the knowledge of the world, and which is not visible to our eyes, unreal or false; and, thereby, we will have to say that all knowledge whatsoever which we acquire is false. Taking into account this and such other difficulties, the ordinary and relative definition of '*satya*' namely, "that alone is '*satya*' (Real) which can be seen by the eyes", is not accepted as correct; and the word '*satya*' has been defined in the Sarvopaniṣad as meaning something which is imperishable, that is, which does not cease to exist, though all other things have ceased to exist: and in the same way, *satya* has been defined in the Mahābhārata as:

satyaṁ nāmā 'vyayaṁ nityaṁ avikāri tathaiva ca I *

(Ma. Bhā. Śān. 162. 10)

that is, "that only is Real which is *avyaya* (i.e., never destroyed), *nitya* (i. e., always the same), and *avikāri* (i. e., of which the form is never changed)". This is the principle underlying the fact that a person who now says one thing and shortly afterwards another thing is called 'false' in common parlance. When we accept this non-relative definition of the Real (*satya*), one has necessarily to come to the conclusion that the Name and Form which constantly changes is false, though it is seen by the eyes; and that the immortal Thing-in-itself (*vastu-tattva*), which is at the bottom of and is covered by that Name and Form, and which always remains the same, is Real, though it is not seen by the eyes. The description of Brahman which is given in the Bhagavadgītā in the following words, namely, "*yaḥ sa sarveṣu bhūteṣu naśyatsu na vinaśyati*" (Gī. 8. 20; 13. 27), that is, "that is the immutable (*akṣara*) Brahman which never ceases to exist, although all things, that is, the bodies of all things encased in Name and Form are destroyed", has been given on the basis of this principle; and the same stanza has again appeared in the description of the Nārāyaṇīya or Bhāgavata religion in the Mahābhārata with the different reading "*bhūtagrāmaśarīreṣu*" instead of "*yaḥ sa sarveṣu bhūteṣu*" (Ma. Bhā. Śān. 339. 23). In the same way, the meaning of the 16th and 17th stanzas of the second chapter of the Gītā is the same. When, in Vedānta philosophy, the ornament is referred to as '*mithyā*' (illusory) and the gold as '*satya*' (real), one has not to understand that comparison as meaning that the ornament is useless, or invisible to the eyes, or totally false, that is, mere earth to which gold foil has been attached, or not in existence at all. The word '*mithyā*' has been used there with reference to the qualities of colour, form etc., and of appearance

* In defining the word 'real' (*sat* or *satya*), Green has said: "whatever anything is *really*, it is *unalterably*" (*Prolegomena to Ethics*, § 25.) This definition of Green and the definition in the Mahābhārata are fundamentally one and the same.

of an object, that is, to its external appearance, and not to the fundamental substance; because, as must be borne in mind, the fundamental substance is always '*satya*' (Real). The Vedāntist has to ascertain what the fundamental substance underlying the covering of Name and Form of various objects is; and that is the real subject-matter of philosophy. Even in ordinary life, we see that although a large sum may have been spent by us on labour for manufacturing a particular ornament, yet, if one is forced to sell that ornament to a merchant in adverse circumstances, the merchant says to us: "I do not take into account what expenses you have incurred per tola for manufacturing the ornament; if you are prepared to sell me this ornament as gold by weight, I will buy it"! If the same idea is to be conveyed in Vedānta terminology, we will have to say that, "the merchant sees the ornament to be illusory, and only the gold to be real". In the same way, if one wishes to sell a newly built house, the purchaser pays no attention to what amount has been spent for giving that house prettiness (*rūpa*=form), or convenience of arrangement (*ākṛti*=construction), and says that the house should be sold to him by the value of the timber and other material which has been used in constructing the house. My readers will get a clear idea from the above illustrations about the meaning of the reference by Vedāntists to the Name-d and Form-ed (*nāmarūpātmaka*) world as illusory and to the Brahman as real. When one says that the visible world is '*mithyā*' (illusory), one is not to be understood as meaning that it is not visible to the eyes; the real meaning is that the numerous appearances of various objects in the world resulting from Time or Space and diversified by Name and Form are perishable, that is, '*mithyā*' and that that imperishable and immutable substance which exists eternally under the cloak of this Name and Form is permanent and real. The merchant considers bangles, anklets, chain, armlets, and other ornaments as '*mithyā*' (illusory) and gold alone as *satya* (real). But in the factory of the goldsmith of the world, various Names and Forms are given to one and the same Fundamental Substance, and such various ornaments as gold, stone, timber, water, air etc. are formed out of that Substance. Therefore, the Vedāntist goes a little deeper than the ordinary merchant, and looks upon all Names and Forms, such as, gold, silver, or stone etc. as *mithyā* (illusory), and looks upon the Fundamental Substance being the substratum of all those objects, that is, the Thing- in-itself (*vastu-tattva*) as '*satya*' (immutable or real). As this Thing-in-itself has no qualities of Name, Form etc., it is impossible that it should ever become perceptible to the organs like eyes etc. But not only can one form a definite inference, by means of one's Reason, that it must exist in an imperceptible form, though it is invisible to the eyes, or unsmellable by the nose, or untouchable by the hand, but one has also to come to the conclusion that the immutable 'THAT' in this world is the real Thing-in-itself. This is what is known as the Fundamental Real in the world. But, some foolish foreign scholars and some local scholars considered as 'philosophers', without taking into account these technical Vedāntic meanings of the words '*satya*' and '*mithyā*', or taking the trouble to see whether or not it is possible for the word '*satya*' to have a meaning different from what they think, ridicule Vedānta by saying: "that world which we actually see with our own eyes is called '*mithyā*' (illusory) by the Vedāntists! Now, what is to be done?" But as Yāska has said it, a pillar is not to blame because a blind man does not see it! It has been stated over and over again in the Chāndogya (6. 1 and 7. 1), Bṛhadāraṇyaka (1. 6. 3), Muṇḍaka (3. 2. 8), Praśna. (6. 5), and other Upaniṣads that the ever-changing (that is, perishable) Names and Forms are not real, and that he who wishes to see the Real (that is, permanent) Element, must extend his vision beyond these Names and Forms; and these Names and Forms have in the Kaṭha (2. 5) and Muṇḍaka (1. 2. 9) been referred to as '*avidyā*', and ultimately in the Śvetāśvataropaniṣad as '*māyā*' (Śve. 4. 10). In the Bhagavadgitā, the same meaning is conveyed by the words '*māyā*' '*moha*', and '*ajñāna*'. That which existed in the commencement of the world was without Name and Form, that is, it was qualityless and imperceptible; and the same thing later on becomes perceptible and qualityful, as a result of its acquiring Names and Forms (Bṛ. 1. 4. 7; and Chān. 6. 1. 2, 3). Therefore, the mutable and perishable Name and Form is given the name 'Māyā' and the visible or qualityful world is said to of the illusory Māyic drama or '*līlā*' of the Īśvara. From this point of view, the Sāṁkhya Prakṛti is nothing but Māyā composed of the *sattva*, *rajas* and *tamas* constituents, that is to say, Māyā possessing Name and Form, though it might be imperceptible; and the creation or extension of the perceptible universe, described in the eighth chapter as having sprung from this Prakṛti, is also the evolution of that Māyā embodied in qualityful Names and Forms; because, whatever quality may be taken, it is bound to be visible to the organs, that is to say, to be embodied in Name and Form. All the Material sciences fall in this way into the category of Māyā. Take History, Geology, Electricity, Chemistry, Physics or any other science; all the exposition to be found in it is only of Names and Forms, that is to say, only of how a particular substance loses one Name and Form and acquires another Name and Form. For instance, these sciences only consider how and when that which is known as 'water' acquires the name of 'steam', or how various aniline dyes, having the red, green, blue, or various other colours, which are only differences of Name and Form, are formed from one black substance called coal-tar, etc. Therefore, by studying these sciences which are engrossed in Names and Forms, one cannot acquire the knowledge of the Real Substance, which is beyond Names and Forms; and it is clear that he who wishes to find the form of the Real Brahman must extend his vision beyond these Material sciences, that is to say, beyond these sciences which deal only with Names and Forms. And the same meaning is conveyed by the story at the commencement of the seventh chapter of the Chāndogyopaniṣad. In the beginning of the story, Nārada went to Sanatkumāra, that is, to Skanda, and said: "Give me knowledge of the Ātman". In reply, Sanatkumāra said to him: "Tell me what you have learnt, so that I will tell you what comes next". Nārada said: "I have learnt all the Vedas, namely, the Ṛg. and the other Vedas, in all four, as also History and Purāṇas (which is the fifth Veda), and also Grammar, Mathematics, Logic, Fine Arts, Ethics, subsidiary parts of the Vedas (*vedāṅga*), Morality, Black Magic, Warfare (*kṣatra-vidyā*), Astrology, the science of Serpents, Deities etc.; but I have not thereby acquired the knowledge of the Ātman, and I have, therefore, come to you".

In reply to that, Sanatkumāra said: "All that you have learnt deals only with Names and Forms and the true Brahman is far beyond this Nāma-Brahma (the Brahman qualified by Names)"; and he has afterwards gradually described to Nārada the Immortal Element in the form of the Absolute Spirit, which is beyond Names and Forms, that is to say, beyond the Sāṁkhya imperceptible Prakṛti, as also beyond Speech, Hope, Project, Mind, Reason (*jñāna*) and Life(*prāṇa*), and is superior to all of them.

All that has been said before may be summarised by saying that though the human organs cannot actually perceive or know anything except Names and Forms, yet, there must be some invisible, that is, imperceptible, eternal substance which is covered by this cloak of non-permanent Names and Forms; and that, it is on that account that we get a synthetic knowledge of the world. Whatever knowledge is acquired, is acquired by the Ātman; and therefore, the Ātman is called the 'Jñātā' (Knower). Whatever knowledge is acquired by this Knower, is of the Cosmos defined by Name and Form; and, therefore, this external Cosmos defined by Name and Form is called 'Jñāna' (Ma. Bhā. Śān. 306. 40); and the Thing-in-itself (*vastu-tattva*) which is at the root of this Name-d and Form-ed (*nāmarūpātmaka*) Cosmos is called the 'Jñeya'. Accepting this classification, the Bhagavadgītā says that the '*kṣetrajña ātmā*' is the Jñātā and the eternal Parabrahman, uncognisable by the organs is the Jñeya (Gī. 13. 12–17); and dividing Jñāna (Knowledge) subsequently into three parts, the Knowledge of the world arising on account of diversity or mani-manifoldness, is called *rājasa* knowledge, and the synthetic knowledge ultimately obtained from this diversity is called *sāttvika* knowledge (Gī. 18. 20, 21). To this an objection is raised by some to the effect that it is not proper for us to make the three-fold division of Jñātā, Jñāna, Jñeya (the Knower, Knowledge, and the To-Be-Known); and that there is no evidence before us for saying that there is anything in the world except that of which we get knowledge. The visible things, such as, cows, horses, etc., which are seen by us are nothing but the Knowledge which we have acquired; and although this Knowledge is Real, yet, as there is no means except

Knowledge itself for describing that of which this Knowledge has been acquired, we cannot say that there are any external objects besides this Knowledge which are independent substances, nor that there is some other independent substance, which is at the root of all these external objects; because, if there is no Knower, then there is no world which can be known. Looking at the matter from this point of view, the third division of Jñeya out of Jñātā, Jñāna, and Jñeya drops out, and the Jñātā and the Jñāna which he acquires, are the only two things which remain: and if this logic is carried a little further, then, in as much as the 'Knower' or 'Observer' is also a kind of Jñāna (Knowledge), nothing else except Jñāna (Knowledge) remains. This is known as 'Vijñāna-vāda': and that has been accepted as correct by the Buddhists following the Yogācāra path, who have laid down the doctrine that there is nothing independent in this world except the Jñāna (Knowledge) or the Jñātā (Knower); nay, that even the world itself does not exist, and that whatever is, is nothing but the Knowledge of mankind. Even among Western writers, there are some who support this doctrine, like Hume and others; but Vedānta philosophy does not accept this doctrine, which has been refuted by Bādarāyaṇācārya in the Vedānta-Sūtras (Ve. Sū. 2. 28–32), and by Śrīmat Śaṁkarācārya in his Bhāṣya (commentary) on those Sūtras. It is true that a man realises ultimately only the impressions made on his Mind; and this is what we call 'Jñāna'; but if there is nothing else except this Jñāna, how can one account for the diversity which is realised by our Reason in the various kinds of Jñāna, e. g., between the 'cow' being a different Jñāna, the 'horse' being a different Jñāna, or 'I' being a different Jñāna? The mental process of acquiring knowledge is everywhere the same, and if there is nothing else except such Jñāna, then, how have the differences between a cow, a horse etc. arisen? If some one says that the Mind creates these different divisions of Knowledge at its sweet will like a dream-world, one cannot explain this somewhat of consistency which is to be found in the Jñāna acquired in a waking state, which is different from the dream-world (Ve. Sū. Śaṁ. Bhā. 2. 2. 29; 3. 2. 4). Besides, if you say that there is no other thing except Jñāna, and that the Mind of the 'Observer' creates all the various things, then each 'Observer' must get the ego-ised knowledge that "my mind, that is, I myself, am the pillar" or "I myself am the cow". But since such is not the case, and everyone gets the experience that he himself is something different and that the pillar, the cow etc. are substances which are different from himself, Śaṁkarācārya has adduced the doctrine that there must be some other independent external things, in the external world, which are the foundation of the Knowledge acquired by the Mind of the Observer (Ve. Sū. Śāṁ. Bhā. 2. 2. 28). Kant is of the same opinion, and he has clearly said that although the synthetical process of human Reason is necessary for acquiring the knowledge of the world, yet, this knowledge is not something self-created, that is, unfounded or new which has been spun out by human Reason, but is always dependent on the external things in the world. Here an objection may be raised that: "What! your Śaṁkarācārya once says that the external world is Mithyā (illusory); and for refuting the Buddhistic doctrines, the same Śaṁkarācārya maintains that the existence of the external world is as real as the existence of the Observer! How are you going to reconcile these two things?" This question has already been answered before. When the Ācārya calls the external world '*mithyā*' (illusory) or '*asatya*' (unreal), he is to be understood as saying that the visible Name and Form of the external universe is unreal, that is to say, perishable. But although the external appearance embodied in Name and Form is said to be illusory, yet, one does not thereby prejudice the doctrine that there is some Real substance at the bottom of it, which is beyond the reach of the organs. In short, just as we have laid down the doctrine in the chapter on the Body and the Ātman, that there is some permanent Ātman-Element at the root of the perishable Names and Forms, like the bodily organs etc., so also, have we to come to the conclusion that there is some permanent substance at the root of the external universe clothed in Names and Forms. Therefore, Vedānta philosophy has laid down the doctrine that there is under the ever-varying (that is, illusory) appearance both of the physical organs and of the external world, some permanent (*nitya*), that is, Real *(satya)* substance. The next question is whether the two fundamental substances in these two cases are one and the same or are different. But before considering that question, I shall first consider precisely the allegation which is sometimes made as regards the modernity of that doctrine.

Some persons say that although the Vijñānavāda of the Buddhists is not acceptable to Vedānta philosophy, yet, in as much as the opinion of Śrī Śaṁkarācārya that the Name-d and Form-ed *(nāmarūpātmaka)* appearance of the external world, which is visible to the eyes, is illusory, and that the imperishable substance underlying it is Real—which is known as the 'MĀYĀ-VĀDA'—is not to be found in the ancient Upaniṣads, it cannot be considered as part of the original Vedānta philosophy. But, if one carefully considers the Upaniṣads, he will easily see that this objection is totally without foundation. I have already stated before that the word '*satya*' (Real) is applied in ordinary parlance to those things which are actually visible to the eyes. Therefore, in some places in the Upaniṣads, the word '*satya*' has been used in this its ordinary meaning, and the Name-d and Form-ed external objects, visible to the eyes, have been called '*satya*'; and the Fundamental Substance which is clothed by those Names and Forms is called '*amṛta*'. For instance, in the Bṛhadāraṇyakopaniṣad (1. 6. 3), it is stated that "*tadetadamṛtaṁ satyenacchannam*", that is, "that *amṛta* is covered by *satya*"; and the words *amṛta* and *satya* have been immediately afterwards defined as: "*prāṇo vā amṛtaṁ nāmarūpe satyaṁ tābhyām ayaṁ prāṇaśchannam*", that is, "*prāṇa* (Vitality) is *amṛta* (eternal) and Name and Form is *satya* (Real); the *prāṇa* is clothed by this *satya* in the shape of Name and Form". The word *prāṇa* is here used in the meaning of the Parabrahman in the form of *prāṇa*. From this it is seen that those things which are known as '*mithyā*' and '*satya*' in the later Upaniṣads, were originally respectively known as '*satya*' and '*amṛta*'. In some places, this *amṛta* is referred to as '*satyasya satyam*', that is, "the ultimate *satya* (Reality), which is at the core of the *satya* (Reality) visible to the eyes" (Bṛ. 2. 3. 6). But, the abovementioned objection does not become substantiated by reason of the fact merely that the visible universe has been referred to as *satya* in some places in the Upaniṣads; because, in the Bṛhadāraṇyaka itself, the final proposition stated is that everything else except the Ātman-formed Parabrahman is '*ārtam*', that is, perishable (Bṛ. 3. 7. 23). When the search for the Fundamental Substance underlying the world was first started, the world which was visible to the eyes was first looked upon as *satya*, and the investigators began to find out what other subtle *satya* was at its core. Then it was found that the form of that visible world which was being called *satya*, was perishable; and that there was at its core, some other imperishable, that is, *amṛta* substance. As it became more and more necessary to define clearly this difference between the two, the two words '*avidyā*' and '*vidyā*' came to be used in place of the words '*satya*' and '*amṛta*', and ultimately, the terminology '*māyā*' and '*satya*' or '*mithyā*' and '*satya*' came into vogue; because, as the root meaning of the word '*satya*' is, 'eternally lasting', people began latterly to consider it improper to refer to perishable and ever-changing Names and Forms as '*satya*'. But, though the words '*māyā*' or '*mithyā*' may have thus come into vogue subsequently, yet, the ideas that the appearance of worldly objects which is visible to one's eyes is perishable and *asatya*, and that the 'Elementary Substance' which underlies it, is alone *sat* or *satya*, have been in vogue from ancient times; and even in the Ṛg-veda, it is stated that: "*ekaṁ sad viprā* BAHUDHA *vadanti*" (1. 164. 46 and 10. 114. 5) —"that which is fundamentally one and permanent (*sat*), is given different NAMES by the *viprāḥ* (scients)"——that is to say, one and the same Real and eternal thing appears in different appearances as a result of Names and Forms. The word '*māyā*' has also been used in the Ṛg-veda to mean "making one form to appear as numerous"; and there is a statement in it that "*indro māyābhiḥ pururūpaḥ īyate*", that is, "Indra takes up various shapes by his Māyā" (Ṛg. 6. 47. 18). The word '*māyā*' has been once used in the Taittirīya Saṁhitā in the same sense (Tai. Saṁ. 1. 11), and ultimately in the Śvetāśvataropaniṣad, the word '*māyā*' has been applied to Names and Forms. But although the practice of applying the word '*māyā*' to Names and Forms first came into vogue at the date of the Śvetāśvataropanisad, yet, the idea that Names and Forms are non-permanent (*anitya*), and unreal (*asatya*), is prior in point of time; and it is clearly not an idea, which has been invented by Śaṁkarācārya by perverting the meaning of the word '*māyā*'. Those who have not got the moral courage to fearlessly call the appearance of the Name-d and Form-ed universe '*mithyā*' as has been done by Śrī Śaṁkarācārya, or those who are even afraid to use the word '*māyā*' in the same sense, as has been done by the Blessed Lord in the Bhagavadgītā, may, if they wish, use the Bṛhadāraṇyakopaniṣad terminology of '*satya*' and '*amṛta*' without any objection. Whatever may be said, the proposition that a distinction was made between Names and Forms as '*vināśī*' (perishable) and the Fundamental Substance underlying them as '*amṛta*' or '*avināśī*' (imperishable), even in the times of the ancient Vedas, does not thereby suffer.

The province of Adhyātma (the philosophy of the Absolute Self) does not end after deciding that in order that the Ātman should acquire the Knowledge, which it acquires, of the various Name-d and Form-ed objects in the external world, there must be, in the external world, at the root of these various objects, some 'some thing' in the shape of a fundamental and permanent substance, which is the foundation or counterpart of such Knowledge, and that otherwise it is impossible to acquire that Knowledge. Vedāntins call this Permanent Substance, which is at the root of the external world, 'Brahman'; and, it is necessary to determine the form of this Brahman, if it is possible to do so. As this Eternal Substance, which is at the root of all Name-d and Form-ed things is imperceptible, its form can clearly not be perceptible, or *sthūla* (gross), like the form of objects embodied in Name and Form. But if you omit objects which are perceptible and gross, yet, there are numerous other objects which are imperceptible, such as, the Mind, Memory, Desire, Life, Knowledge etc.; and it is not impossible that the Parabrahman is of the form of any one of them. Some say that the Parabrahman is of the same form as Prāṇa (Vital Force). The German philosopher Schaupenhaur has come to the decision that the Parabrahman is the embodiment of Desire. As Desire is a faculty of the Mind, the Brahman may, according to this opinion, be said to be made up of Mind (Tai. 3. 4). But, from what has been stated so far, one may say that: '*prajñānaṁ brahma*' (Ai. 3. 3), or "*vijñānaṁ brahma*" (Tai. 3. 5), i. e., "Brahman is the knowledge acquired by us of the diversity in the gross material world". Haegel's doctrine is of that kind. But in the Upaniṣads, the form of the Brahman has been made to include *sat*, that is, the common quality of Existence possessed by all things in the world (or their '*sattāsāmānyatva*') as also *ānanda* (Joy), along with Knowledge in the form of Consciousness (i. e.. *cidrūpi jñāna*); and the Brahman is said to be '*saccidānanda*' in form. Another form of the Brahman is the OM-kāra. The explanation of this form is as follows:-All the eternal Vedas first came out of the OM-kāra; and in as much as Brahmadeva created the entire universe from the eternal words in the Vedas, after the Vedas had come into existence (Gī. 17. 23; and Ma. Bhā. Śān. 231. 56--58), it is clear that there was nothing in the beginning except the OM-kāra, and, therefore, the OM-kāra is the true form of the Brahman (Māṇḍūkya. 1: Taitti. 1. 8). But, if you consider the matter from the purely Metaphysical point of view, all these forms of the Parabrahman possess more or less the character of Name and Form; because, all these forms are perceptible to human organs, and all that men come to know in this way, falls into the category of Names and Forms. Then, how is one going to determine the true form of that eternal, all-pervasive, homogeneous, permanent, and immortal Element (Gī. 13. 12-17), which is the foundation of these Names and Forms? Some Metaphysicians say that this Element must for ever remain uncongnisable by our organs; and Kant has even given up the further consideration of this subject-matter. In the Upaniṣads also, the uncognisable form of the Parabrahman has been described by saying "*neti, neti*"-that is, It is not something about which something can be told—the Brahman is beyond that; It is not visible to the eyes; and "*yato vāco nivartante aprāpya manasā saha*", that is, "It is beyond speech and also beyond the Mind". Nevertheless, the philosophy of the Absolute Self has come to the conclusion that even in this difficult position, man can, by his Reason, determine the nature of the form of Brahman. We must first find out which one is the most superior and comprehensive of the various imperceptible things mentioned above, namely, Desire, Memory

Determination, Hope, Life, Knowledge etc., and look upon the highest of them all as the form of the Parabrahman; because, it is an indisputable fact that the Parabrahman is the highest of all imperceptible substances. When one considers Desire, Memory, Hope, Determination etc. from this point of view, one sees, as has been shown in the chapter on the Body and the Ātman, that these are all natural faculties of the Mind; that the Mind is, therefore, higher than them all; that knowledge is higher than the Mind; that Reason is higher than Knowledge, as Knowledge is only an inherent faculty of Reason; and that ultimately that Ātman of which the Reason is a servant, is the highest of all (Gī. 3. 42). If the Ātman is higher than Desire, the Mind and the other imperceptible substances, it naturally follows, that the Ātman must be the form of the Parabrahman. The same argument has been adopted in the seventh chapter of the Chāndogyopaniṣad, and Sanatkumāra has said to Nārada, that the Mind is higher (*bhūyas*) than speech, Knowledge is higher than the Mind, and Strength (*bala*) is higher than Knowledge; and in as much as, going up in this way, the Ātman is the highest of all (*bhūman*), the Ātman must be the true form of the Parabrahman. From among English writers, Green has accepted this doctrine; but as his arguments are slightly different in nature, I will concisely mention them here in Vedāntic terminology. Green says that there must be some substance uniformly underlying the various Names and Forms in the external universe, which (substance) is the counterpart of the Knowledge created by the Ātman by synthesising the various impressions of Names and Forms made on the Mind through the organs; otherwise, the Knowledge resulting from the synthesis made by the Ātman will be self-conceived and without foundation, and will fall flat like the Vijñāna-vāda. We call this 'Something', Brahman; but Green accepts the terminology of Kant, and calls it the Thing-in-itself (*vastu-tattva*): this is the only difference between us and Green. In any case, the *vastu-tattva* (Brahman) and the Ātman remain ultimately the only two correlative things. Out of these, although the Ātman cannot be grasped by the Mind or by Reason, that is to say, although it is beyond the reach of the organs, yet, taking as correct one's self-experience, we come to the conclusion that the Ātman is not Gross, but is Thought-formed (*cidrūpī*), or of the form of Consciousness (*caitanya-rūpī*). Having in this way determined the form of the Ātman, we have next to determine the form of the Brahman. That Brahman or *vastu-tattva* is either (1) of the same form as the Ātman or (2) is different in form from the Ātman; these two things alone are possible; because, there is no third thing which now remains except the Brahman and the Ātman. But, it is our experience that if any two objects are different in form, then their effects and products must also be different. Therefore, in any science, we determine whether two things are the same or different, by considering their effects. For instance, if the roots, rootlings, bark, leaves, flowers, fruits etc. of two trees are the same, we come to the conclusion that they are the same; and if they are different, we say that the trees are different. When the same argument is applied in the present case, we see that the Ātman and the Brahman must be uniform; because, as has been mentioned above, the synthesis of the impressions created on the Mind by the various objects in the world, which (synthesis) results from the activity of the Ātman, must be the counterpart of the synthesis of all the objects in the world made by the Brahman or *vastu-tattva* (which is the Root of those objects) by breaking up their diversity; if not, all Knowledge will be without foundation and will fall flat. And, it now follows as a natural conclusion that though these two Elements, which arrive at two exactly similar syntheses may be in two different places, they cannot be different from each other; and that, the form of the Brahman must be the same as the form of the Ātman. * In short, from whichever point of view one considers the matter, it now follows that not only is the Brahman-Element underlying the Names and Forms in the external world, not gross like Matter embodied in Names and Forms, but also the various forms of the Brahman, which are embodiments respectively of Desire, Mind, Knowledge, Life, Vital Force, or the logos OM-kāra, are forms of a lower order, and the true form of the Brahman is beyond all of them and superior to

* Green's *Prolegomena to Ethics*, §§ 26 to 36.

all of them, that is to say, is of the form of the pure Ātman. And it also follows from what has been stated in various places in the Gītā on this subject, that the doctrine of the Gītā is the same (Gī. 2. 20; 7. 7; 8. 4; 13. 31; 15. 7, 8). But, it must not be thought that this doctrine of the identity of the Brahman and the Ātman was found out by our Ṛsis merely by some such logic; because, as has been stated in the beginning of this chapter, no proposition can be definitely laid down in the philosophy of the Absolute Self by means of Reason alone and it must always be supported by self-experience. We also see even in the Material sciences, that we first get an experience and later on come to know or find out the reasons for it. For the same reason, hundreds of years before the rational explanation for the identity of the Brahman and the Ātman was found out, our ancient Ṛṣis had first come to the conclusion that: "*neha nānāsti kiṁcana*" (Bṛ. 4. 4. 19; Kaṭha. 4. 11), i. e., "the diversity which is visible in this world is not real", and that there is at the bottom of that diversity an Element which is one in all directions, immortal, imperishable, and permanent (Gī. 18. 20); and had, by introspection, arrived at the ultimate conclusion that the Imperishable Element clothed in Names and Forms in the external world and the Ātman-element to be found in our bodies, which is beyond Reason, are one and the same, that is, they are both homogeneous, immortal, and inexhaustible; or that whatever element is in the Cosmos (*brahmāṇḍa*) also resides in the human body (*piṇḍa*); and in the Bṛhadāraṇyakopaniṣad, Yājñavalkya says to Maitreyī, to Gārgī, Vāruṇi and others, and to Janaka that this is the mystic import of Vedānta (Bṛ. 3. 5-8, 4. 2-4). It has been stated earlier in the same Upaniṣad, that he who has understood that "*ahaṁ brahmāsmi*", i. e., "I am the Para-brahman", has understood everything (Bṛ. 1. 4. 10); and in the sixth chapter of the Chāndogyopaniṣad, the father of Śvetaketu has explained to him this elementary principle of the Monistic (*advaita*) Vedānta in various ways. In the beginning of the chapter Śvetaketu said to his father:-" In the same way as one knows all the Name-d and Form-ed transformations of mud when he once knows what there is in a ball of mud, tell me that one thing by knowledge of which I will come to know about all things; because, I do not know that one thing". His father then explained to him by nine different illustrations, namely, of rivers, the sea, water, salt, etc. that: "that Element *(tat)* which is at the root of the visible world and thou *(tvam)*, that is to say, the Ātman in thy body, are one and the same thing; that is, "*tat tvam asi*"; and when thou hast understood what thy Ātman is, thou wilt of thy own accord understand what is at the root of the Cosmos"; and everytime, the canon "*tat tvam asi*" —— "thou art that" —— is repeated (Chān. 6. 8-16). "*tat tvam asi*" is one of the important canons of Monistic Vedānta, and that is translated into Marathi by "*jeṁ piṇḍīṁ teṁ brahmāḍīṁ*", i. e., "that which is in the Body, is also in the Cosmos".

We have, in this way, proved that the Brahman is the same in form as the Ātman. But, some are likely to think that because the Ātman is believed to be of the form of Consciousness (*cidrūpi*), the Brahman is also of that form (i. e., *cidrūpi*). It is, therefore, necessary to give here some further explanation of the true nature of the Brahman, and at the same time of the true nature of the Ātman. *cit* or *jñāna* (Knowledge) is a quality acquired by Reason—which is gross in nature—by contact with the Ātman; but in as much as it is not proper to arrogate this quality of Reason to the Ātman, one must, from the philosophical point of view, look upon the fundamental form of the Ātman as qualityless and unknowable. Therefore, though the Brahman is of the same nature as the Ātman, it is, according to some, to some extent improper to say that both or either of these is of the same nature as *cit* (Consciousness or Knowledge). It is not that their objection extends only to the Brahman and Ātman being conscious in form; but, it naturally follows, that it is also not proper according to them to apply the adjective *sat* (Real) to the Parabrahman; because, *sat* and *asat* (Reality and Illusion) are two qualities, which are contrary to each other, and always mutually dependent, and which are usually mentioned with reference to two different things. He who has never seen light, can never get an idea of darkness; and what is more, he cannot even imagine the couple *(dvaṁdva)* of light and darkness. The same argument applies to the couple of *sat* and *asat* (Real and Illusory). It is quite clear that when we notice that some objects are destroyed, we begin to divide all things into two classes of *asat* (perishable) and *sat* (non-perishable); or, in other words, in order that the human mind should conceive the two ideas of *sat* and *asat*, it is necessary that these two opposite qualities should come before the human eyes. But, if there was only one substance in the beginning, how can one apply to this Fundamental Substance the two mutually dependent words *sat* and *asat*, which came into existence by being applied to two different substances after duality had first come into existence? Because, if you call that fundamental substance, *sat*, then the question arises whether at that time (that is, before duality had come into existence) there was in existence something else by the side of it. Therefore, in the Nāsadīya-Sūkta of the Ṛg-Veda, no adjective is applied to the Parabrahman and the Fundamental Element of the universe is described by saying: "in the commencement of the world, there was neither *sat* nor *asat*, but whatever there was, was one", and that the couples of *sat* and *asat* came into existence afterwards (Ṛg. 10. 129); and it is stated in the Gītā that he whose Reason has become free from the doubles of *sat* and *asat*, hot and cold, etc. reaches the *nirdvaṁdva* (beyond-doubles) sphere of the Brahman, which is beyond these doubles (Gī. 7. 28; 2. 45). From this it will be seen how difficult and subtle are the ideas in the philosophy of the Absolute Self. If one considers the matter merely from the logical point of view, one is forced to admit this unknowability of the Parabrahman or of the Ātman. But although the Parabrahman may, in this way, be qualityless and unknowable, that is, beyond the reach of the organs, yet, as every man has a self-experience of his own Ātman, it is possible for us to get the self-experience that the indescribable form of this qualityless Ātman which we realise by means of a visionary experience (*sākṣātkāra*), is the same as of the Parabrahman; and therefore, the proposition that the Brahman and the Ātman are uniform does not become meaningless. Looking at the matter from this point of view, it is impossible to say more about the form of the Brahman than that: "the Brahman is the same in form as the Ātman"; and one has to depend for all other things on one's own self-experience. But, in a scientific exposition which has to appeal to Reason, it is necessary to give as much explanation as is possible, by the use of words. Therefore, although the Brahman is all-pervasive, unknowable, and indescribable, yet, in order to express the difference between the Gross World and the Brahman-Element (which is the same in nature as the Ātman), the philosophy of the Absolute Self considers the quality of *caitanya* (Consciousness), which becomes visible to us in Gross Matter after its contact with the Ātman, as the pre-eminent quality of the Ātman, and says that both the Ātman and the Parabrahman are *cidrūpi* or *caitanya-rūpi* (Conscious or Knowing, in form); because, if you do not do so, then, in as much as both the Ātman and the Brahman are qualityless, invisible, and indescribable, one has, in describing them either to sit quiet, or, if someone else gives some description of them by means of words, one has to say : "*neti neti* । *etasmād anyat param asti* । ", i. e., "It is not this, this is not It (Brahman), (this is a Name and Form), the true Brahman is something else, which is quite beyond that", and in this way, do nothing else except restricting oneself to negatives (Bṛ. 2. 3. 6). It is, therefore, that *cit* (Knowledge), *sat* ('*sattāmātratva*' or Existence) and *ānanda* (Joy) are commonly mentioned as the attributes of the Brahman. There is no doubt that these attributes are much higher than all other attributes; nevertheless, these attributes have been mentioned for the only purpose of acquainting one with the form of the Brahman, as far as it is possible to do so by words; and it must not be forgotten that the true form of the Brahman is qualityless, and that one has to get a self-experience *(aparokṣānubhava)* of it in order to understand it. I shall now concisely explain what our philosophers have said regarding the way in which this self-experience can be had, that is to say, in what way and when this indescribable form of the Brahman is experienced by the *brahma-niṣṭha* (the devotee of the Brahman).

The identification of the Brahman with the Ātman is described in Marathi by saying "what is in the *piṇḍa* (Body), is also in the *brahmāṇḍa* (Cosmos); and it logically follows that when once a man has experienced this identity of the

Brahman and the Ātman, there can no more remain any difference between the *jñātā* or observing Ātman, and the *jñeya* or the subject-matter to be seen. But, a doubt is likely to arise that if a man does not escape from his eyes and other organs, so long as he is alive, how can one get over the fact that these organs are different from the objects which are perceptible to the organs?; and, if one does not get rid of this difference, how is one to realise the identity of the Brahman and the Ātman? And, if one considers the matter only from the point of view of the organs, these doubts do not at first sight seem improper. But, if you consider the matter deeply, it will be seen that the organs do not perform the function of seeing external objects of their own accord. "*cakṣuḥ paśyati rūpaṇi manasā na tu cakṣuṣā*" (Ma. Bhā. Śān. 311.17)—in order to see anything (and also in order to hear anything etc.), the eyes (as also the ears etc.) require the help of the Mind. It has been stated before that if the Mind is vacant, objects in front of the eyes are not seen. When one takes into account this common experience, one sees that if the Mind is taken out of the organs, the dualities in the objects of the senses become non-existent to us, though they might exist in the external world, notwithstanding that the organs of eyes etc. are perfectly in order; and it is easy to draw the inference that the Mind will in this way become steeped in the Ātman or in the Ātman-formed Brahman, and one will begin to get a visionary experience (*sākṣātkāra*) of the identity of the Brahman and the Ātman. That man who has attained this mental state by meditation, mental isolation, worshipping in solitude, or by intense contemplation of the Brahman, will not perceive the dualities or differences in the visible world, although they may be before his eyes; and then he realises the form of the sole (*advaita*) Brahman of his own accord. In this beatific ultimate state, which is the result of the fullest Realisation of the Brahman, the three-fold difference, that is, *triputi* of Knower, Knowable, and Knowledge, or the dual difference of worshipper and worshipped ceases to exist. Therefore, this state of the mind cannot be described by one person to another person; because, it is clear that immediately on uttering the word 'another', this state of mind is destroyed, and the man returns from the *advaita* (non-dual) into the *dvaita* (dual). Nay, it is even difficult for anybody to say that he himself has experienced this state of mind! Because, as soon as you utter the word 'I', there arises in the mind the idea of a difference from others, and such an idea is obstructive to the realisation of the identity between this Brahman and the Ātman. It is for this reason that Yājñavalkya has described this state of beatitude in the Bṛhadāraṇyaka as follows :—"*yatra hi dvaitam iva bhavati tad itara itaraṁ paśyati.........jighrati.........śṛnoti......... vijānāti*।......*yatra tvasya sarvam ātmaivābhūt tat kena kaṁ paśyet.........jighret.........sṛṇuyāt......vijānīyāt*।...*vijñātāram are kena vijānīyāt*। *etāvad are khalu amṛtatvam iti*। i. e., "so long as the duality of the Observer and the observed existed, the one was seeing the other, smelling the other, hearing the other, and knowing the other; but when everything assumes the form of the Ātman, (that is, when there no more remains the difference between oneself and another), then, who is to see, smell, hear or know whom? O man! how can there be another one to know him who is himself the Knower?" (Bṛ. 4. 5. 15; 4. 3. 27). When everybody is in this way merged in the Ātman or in the Brahman, or becomes *ātmabhūta* or *brahmabhūta*, the doubles of pain and happiness, or fear, lamentation etc. cease to exist (Īśa. 7); because, in order that one should feel fear, or lament, the one to be feared or lamented must be different from oneself, and there is no room for a difference of this kind, when one has realised the identity of the Brahman and the Ātman. This state of being free from pain, lamentation etc. is called the '*ānandamaya*' state (the beatific state); and, it is stated in the Taittirīya Upaniṣad, that this *ānanda* (joy or beatitude) is Brahman (Tai. 2. 8; 3. 6). But, even this description is not perfect; because, where does the experiencer of this beatitude now remain any more? It is, therefore, stated in the Bṛhadāraṇyakopaniṣad that Self-beatitude (*ātmānanda*) is something by far stranger than ordinary joy (Bṛ. 4. 3. 32). Having regard to this insufficiency of the word '*ānanda*' (beatitude), which occurs in the description of the Brahman, the person who has realised the Brahman (*brahma-vettā*) is, in some other places, described only as "*brahma bhavati ya evaṁ veda*" (Bṛ. 4. 4. 25) or "*brahma veda brahmaiva bhavati*" (Muṇ. 3. 2. 9)——"he, who has realised the Brahman, has become the Brahman", that is to say, omitting the word '*ānanda*', from the description. In the same way as, after a lump of salt has been dissolved in water, the difference that one part of the water is saltish and another of it is not saltish does not remain, so also, once a man has realised the identity of the Brahman and the Ātman, everything becomes merged in the Brahman. This beatific condition of the mind has been described in the Upaniṣads as above (Bṛ. 2. 4. 12; Chān. 6. 13). But that saint Tukārāma about whom was said "*jayāci vade nitya vedānta vāṇī*", (i. e., " one whose voice always uttered Vedānta ") has described his self-experience in the following words by taking the sweet illustration of jaggery instead of this other saltish illustration :—

As jaggery is sweet । so has God come to be verywhere ॥
Now whom shall I worship । God is inside as also outside ॥
(Tu. Gā. 3627).

This is what is meant by saying, that though the Parabrahman is imperceptible to the organs and unrealisable by the mind, yet it is '*svānubhavagamya*', that is, it can be realised by every man by his self-experience. The unknowability of the Parabrahman which is spoken of, belongs to the stage in which there is a Knower and a To-Be-Known; it does not belong to the phase of the Realisation of Non-dualism. So long as one has the feeling that he is something different from the world, it is not possible for a man, whatever he may do, to fully realise the identity of the Brahman and the Ātman. But, although a river cannot swallow the sea, yet, it can fall into the sea and become merged into it; so also, may a man dive into the Parabrahman and realise it; and then he reaches the Brahm-ised (*brahmamaya*) state of "*sarvabhūtastham ātmānaṁ sarvabhūtāni cātmani*" (Gī. 6. 29), i. e. "all created beings are within himself, and he is within all created things." In order to explain that the full Realisation of the Brahman depends on one's own self-experience, the form of the Parabrahman has been skilfully and paradoxically described as follows: "*avijñātaṁ vijānatāṁ* *vijñātam avijānatām*" (Kena. 2. 3), " those who say that they have Realised the Parabrahman have not really Realised It; they alone have Realised It, who do not Realise that they have Realised It"; because, when a person says that he has Realised the Parabrahman, there is clearly in his mind the dual feeling that he (the Jñātā) is something different from the Brahman (the Jñeya) which he has known, and, therefore, his non-dual Realisation of the identity of the Ātman and the Brahman is, at this stage, to that extent, upripe or incomplete. Therefore, one who says this, admits by his own mouth that he has not really Realised the Brahman. On the other hand, when the dual feeling of 'I' and 'Brahman' has disappeared, and the identity of the Brahman and the Ātman has been fully Realised, the words "I have understood That" (that is, necessarily, something which is different from me) cannot be used. Therefore, when a man is in this condition, that is to say, when the Realiser (*jñānī*) is unable to say that he has Realised the Brahman, he may be said to have Realised the Brahman. That a Realiser should be thus totally merged, engrossed, totally dissolved, saturated or dead into the Parabrahman, as a result of a total annhiliation of the feeling of duality, would commonly be looked upon as difficult. But our philosophers have after personal experience come to the conclusion that this state of '*nirvāṇa*' (dissolution), which at first sight appears difficult, can ultimately be reached by a man by practice *(abhyāsa)* and by renunciation (*vairāgya)*. Some people raise an objection that in as much as the dual feeling of egoism is destroyed or dies in this state of mind, this is a kind of self-destruction. But any one can see that this objection is without foundation, when one realises that though a man cannot describe this state when he is experiencing it, yet, he can afterwards remember it.* But even a

* This feeling of non-duality or of non-differentiation which results from meditation and concentration is also experienced by smelling a chemical gas called nitrous-oxide. This gas is known as 'laughing gas' (See *Will to Believe and Other Essays on Popular Philosophy* by William James, pp. 294-298). But the great difference between the two is, that this state is artificial, whereas

stronger illustration than that is the experience of saints. Leave aside the self-experiences of ancient *siddha* (released) souls. Even in modern times, Tukārāma, that highest among the devotees of the Blessed Lord, has said :

> I saw my death by my own eyes ।
> that spectacle was incomparable ।
>
> (Gā. 3579).

in describing this state of ultimate bliss in figurative language, and with great exuberation and appreciation. By the worship of, and meditation on, the qualityful perceptible or imperceptible Brahman, the devotee gradually rises and ultimately reaches such a state that he Realises the identity of the Brahman and the Ātman, which is described by the words "*ahaṁ brahmāsmi*" (Bṛ. 1. 4. 10), i. e., "I am the Brahman" ; and then he becomes steeped to such an extent in that state, that he does not think of what state he is in, or of what he is experiencing. In as much as he has not ceased to be awake, this his state cannot be called the dream-state or the sleeping-state ; and, it cannot be called a waking-state, as all the activities based on duality, which are carried on in the waking-state, are stopped. Therefore, this state is referred to as the '*turīya*' (fourth) state, which is different from the ordinary dreaming (*svapna*), sleeping (*suṣupti*) or waking (*jāgṛti*) states : and as the '*nirvikalpa*' (i. e., in which there is not the slightest feeling of duality) form of meditation has been prescribed by the Pātañjala Yoga as the principal means for reaching this state, it is stated in the Gītā that one should spare no pains for acquiring by practice this '*nirvikalpa-samādhi-yoga*' (Gī. 6. 20-23). This feeling of the identity of the Brahman and the Ātman is the most complete state of Knowledge ; because, when the world becomes Brahmified (*brahmarūpa*), that is, One in form, one has reached the climax of the process of knowledge which is described in the Gītā by the words "*avibhaktaṁ vibhakteṣu*" —unifying that which is diverse—and it is not possible to get

---

the state attained by self-absorption (*samādhi*) is true and natural. But, I have mentioned this here, because the existence of a state of non-dual feeling (*abheda-bhāva*) can be proved by the evidence of this artificial state of mind.

any further knowledge about anything. In the same way, when one has experienced this immortal Element which is beyond Name and Form, one automatically escapes the cycle of birth and death, since birth and death is included in the category of Name and Form, and such a man has gone beyond Name and Form (Gī. 8. 21). Therefore, Tukārāma has referred to this state as "the death of death" (Gā. 3580); and Yājñavalkya has, for the same reason, referred to this state as the limit or climax of immortality. This is indeed the 'state of being released from birth' (*jīvan-muktāvasthā*). It is stated in the Pātañjala Yoga-Sūtras, and also in other books, that in this state of mind, a man acquires superhuman powers like levitation etc. (Pātañjala Sū. 3. 16–55); and, it is on this account that some persons take to Yoga practices. But, as has been stated by the author of the Yoga-Vāsiṣṭha, the power of levitation etc. is neither an ideal, nor any part of the state of a Brahman-engrossed (*brahma-niṣṭha*), and the man who is a Birth-released (*jīvanmukta*) makes no attempt to acquire these powers, which very often are not to be seen in him (Yo. 5. 89). Therefore, not only are these powers not referred to in the Yoga-Vāsiṣṭha, but one does not come across them anywhere even in the Gītā. Vasiṣṭha has clearly said to Rāma, that these wonderful powers are only tricks of Māyā, and are not the science of the Brahman. They may be true; I do not insist that they cannot be true, but in any case, they undoubtedly do not form part of the *brahma-vidyā* (science of the Brahman). Therefore, the Brahma-Vidyā science says that whether these powers are acquired or not, a man should pay no attention to them, nor entertain any hope or desire about them, but should exert himself only in such efforts as will be sufficient to enable him to reach the ultimate beatific Brahmified state, in which he feels that there is only one Ātman in all created beings. Realisation of the Brahman is the purest state of Ātman; it is neither magic nor Māyic wonders; and therefore, not only is the worth of the science of the Brahman not increased by such wonders, but they cannot be any proof of the worth of that science. Birds, or in these days even aeronauts, fly in the sky; but, on that account no one considers them as knowers of the Brahman. Nay, people, who have acquired the powers of levitation may, like Aghoraghaṇṭa in the *Mālatī-Mādhava*, be cruel and treacherous persons.

The indescribable experience of the beatitude of realising the identity of the Brahman and the Ātman cannot be fully related by one person to another; because, in doing so, one has to use the Dualistic phraseology of 'I' and 'You', and one's entire experience of non-duality cannot be described in this Dualistic phraseology. Therefore, the descriptions of this ultimate state which are to be found in the Upaniṣads must also be considered incomplete or unimportant; and if these descriptions are unimportant, then the purely Dualistic descriptions, which are found given in the Upaniṣads for explaining the creation or the formation of the universe, must also be considered unimportant. For instance, the descriptions of the creation of the visible universe to be found in the Upaniṣads, that the qualityful Puruṣa, named Hiraṇyagarbha, or the various perceptible objects in the world like *āpa* (water) etc. gradually came into existence out of the pure, permanent, all-pervading and immutable Ātman-formed Brahman; or that the Parameśvara first created these Names and Forms, and then entered them (Tai. 2. 6; Chān. 6. 7. 3; Bṛ. 1. 4. 7) etc., cannot be correct from the point of view of Non-Dualism; because, if the qualityless Parameśvara, realisable only by Knowledge, pervades everything, it is scientifically without foundation to say that one created the other. But, as the Dualistic phraseology is the only possible medium for explaining the formation of the universe to ordinary persons, the above mentioned descriptions of the perceptible universe, or of Names and Forms, have been given in the Upaniṣads. Nevertheless, even in these descriptions the substratum of Non-Dualism is, in many places, kept intact, and it is made quite clear that though the Dualistic phraseology has been used in the descriptions, Non-Dualism is the true doctrine. Just as, though we now definitely know that it is not the Sun which revolves, we still speak of the rising or the setting of the Sun, so also, although it was definitely known that one and only one Parabrahman, in the form of the Ātman, pervades everything in all directions and without division, and that It is immutable, yet, we come across expressions like "the perceptible universe was created out of the Parabrahman" in the Upaniṣads; and in the same way, also in the Gītā, although the Blessed Lord has said: "My true form is imperishable and unborn" (Gī. 7. 25), yet, He at the same time says, "I create the whole world" (Gī. 4. 6). But some scholars, neglecting the meaning underlying these descriptions, and looking upon them as literally true and important, lay down the proposition that the Upaniṣads support the Dvaita (Dualistic) or Viśiṣṭādvaita (Qualified Monistic) theory. They say that if one believes that there is only one qualityless Brahman which pervades everything, one cannot explain how the mutable, perishable, and qualityful objects came into existence out of this immutable Brahman; because, although one may describe the Name-d and Form-ed universe as 'Māyā', yet, in as much as it is logically impossible for the qualityful Māyā to come into existence out of the qualityless Brahman, the theory of Non-Dualism falls to the ground. Rather than that, it would be more proper (i) to accept as eternal a qualityful but perceptible form of the Name-d and Form-ed perceptible universe like Prakṛti, as is done in Sāṁkhya philosophy, and (ii) to imagine that at the innermost core of this Prakṛti, there is another permanent element in the shape of the Parabrahman (Bṛ. 3. 7), just as there is steam in an iron engine, and (iii) to believe that these two Elements form a Unity like the grains in a pomegranate. But, in my opinion, it is not proper to ascribe this meaning to the Upaniṣads. It is true that the Upaniṣads contain descriptions which are sometimes Dualistic, and at other times purely Non-Dualistic, and that we have to reconcile them with each other. But, we cannot reconcile the various statements in the Upaniṣads with each other by accepting the Dualistic point of view, as satisfactorily as can be done by accepting the Non-dualistic point of view, and saying that when the qualityless Brahman is taking up a qualityful form an illusory Dualistic state seems, only to that extent, to have come into existence. For instance, the words in the phrase '*tat tvam asi*' can never be satisfactorily explained from the Dualistic point of view. It is not that Dualists did not realise this difficulty. But these Dualists have analysed that phrase by saying that '*tat tvam*' means '*tasya tvam*', that is, "Thou art OF That, which is something different from thee; thou art not That Itself"; and they have, in this way, somehow or other explained away this very important canon, and satisfied themselves. But those persons who understand even a little of Sanskrit, and whose minds are not perverted as a result of obstinacy, will at once see that this forced meaning is not correct. In the Kaivalyopaniṣad (Kai. 1. 16), the terms '*tat*' and '*tvam*' have been interchanged by analysing the phrase '*tat tvam asi*' as "*sa tvameva tvameva tat*" (i. e., "It is thou, thou art It"), and this canon has been proved to be in support of Non-Dualism. What more shall I say? Unless one excises away the major portion of the Upaniṣads, or intentionally closes one's eyes to them, it is impossible to show that there is any other import in the Upaniṣad science except a Non-Dualistic import. But, as these arguments are endless, I shall not further discuss the matter here. Those, who are in favour of any opinion other than the Non-Dualistic theory, are perfectly welcome to accept it. I do not think that anything except a Non-Dualistic import could have been intended to be conveyed by those noble souls, who, after describing their self-experience in unmistakable terms by saying: "*neha nānāsti kiṁcana*" (Bṛ. 4. 4. 19; Kaṭha. 4. 11), i. e., "there is no diversity of any kind in this world", and that whatever there is, is fundamentally "*ekamevādvitīyam*" (Chān. 6. 2. 2), i. e., "one only, without a second", have gone further and said: "*mṛtyoḥ sa mṛtyum āpnoti ya iha nāneva paśyati*", that is, "he who sees diversity in this world, falls into the cycle of birth and death". But, though there is room for doubt whether all the Upaniṣads convey one and the same import, since there are different Upaniṣads of the different branches of the Vedas, one does not experience the same difficulty in the case of the Gītā. As the Gītā is a single work, it is clear that it expounds one kind of Vedānta; and, when one considers what that Vedānta is, one has to interpret the Gītā as expounding the Non-Dualistic doctrine that the only Reality is "That which remains over after all created things are destroyed" (Gī. 8. 20), and Which pervades on all sides all the material bodies (*piṇḍa*) as It pervades the

Cosmos (*brahmāṇḍa*), (Gi. 13. 31). Nay, the principle of identifying everything with oneself (*ātmaupamya*), which has been mentioned in the Gītā, cannot be fully explained by any aspect of Vedānta other than a Non-Dualistic aspect. I do not mean to suggest that all the various philosophical speculations or doctrines, which were expounded at the time of Śrī Śaṁkarācārya, or after him, in support of the Non-Dualistic theory, have been accepted *in toto* in the Gītā. The Gītā was in existence before the Dualistic, Non-Dualistic and the Qualified-Monistic doctrines had been formulated; and I also accept the position that the Gītā cannot, on that account, contain any doctrinal arguments belonging to any particular sect. But this does not prevent one from saying that the Vedānta expounded in the Gītā is generally of the Non-Dualistic kind supported by the Śāṁkara school (the school of Śrī Śaṁkarācārya), and not Dualistic. But, although, from the point of view of philosophy, there is some common ground between the Gītā and the Śāṁkara school, yet, from the point of view of mode of life, the Gītā gives higher importance to the doctrine of Action (Karma-Yoga) than to the doctrine of Renunciation of Action (Karma-Saṁnyāsa) which is supported by Śaṁkarācārya. But, this subject-matter will be considered later on. What I am dealing with at present is the question of philosophy, and all that I have to say here is that this philosophy is of the same kind in the Gītā as in the Śāṁkara school, that is, it is Non-Dualistic; and that is the reason why the Śāṁkarabhāṣya on the Gītā is considered more valuable than the other doctrinal commentaries.

When one has thus come to the conclusion that there remains behind only one immutable and qualityless Element after all Names and Forms are eliminated, from the point of view of Knowledge, and that one has, on that account, to accept Non-Dualism after full and minute consideration, it becomes necessary to explain how the variegated perceptible qualityful universe came into existence out of one qualityless and imperceptible Element, from the point of view of Non-Dualistic Vedānta. It has been stated before that the Sāṁkhyas have got over this difficulty by looking upon Matter with its three constituents (that is, qualityful Matter) as eternal and independent, in the same way, as the qualityless Spirit. But, if in this way one looks upon qualityful Matter as independent, the fundamental Elements of the world become two, and the theory of Non-Dualism, which has been unconditionally accepted as correct for the various reasons mentioned above, comes into question; and if one does not look upon qualityful Matter as independent, it becomes impossible to explain how the variegated qualityful universe came into existence out of one fundamental qualityless substance; because, the theory that it is not possible for the Qualityful to come into existence out of the Qualityless, that is to say, for something to come into existence out of something which does not exist—according to *satkāryavāda**— has also been accepted by Non-Dualists. In short, there is a difficulty on either hand. Then, how are we to get over this dilemma? One must find out some way for explaining how the Qualityful came into existence out of the Qualityless without giving the go-bye to Non-Dualism, and that way seems to be closed to us by the theory of *satkāryavāda*. True, the position is a difficult one. Nay; according to some, this is the principal difficulty in the way of accepting Non-Dualism, and, on that account, they accept Dualism. But the Non-Dualists have, by their intelligence, found out a skilful and unquestionable way for getting over this difficult position. They say that the theory of *satkāryavāda* or of the *guṇa-pariṇāmavāda*† applies only when the cause and the product are both of the same kind or class; and on that account, even Non-Dualists will accept that the Real and Qualityless Brahman cannot give birth to a Real and Qualityful Māyā; but, this admission is effective only when both the substances are Real (*satya*). Where one substance is Real, and the other one is only a reflection of it, *satkāryavāda* does not apply. The Sāṁkhyas consider Prakṛti as an independent Real substance, in the same way as the Puruṣa. Therefore, they cannot, having regard to the theory of *satkāryavāda*, account for the outcome of a qualityful Prakṛti from a qualityless Puruṣa. But as the Non-Dualistic Vedānta holds that though

* See p. 210 above.—Translator. † See p. 234 above.—Trans.

Māyā may be eternal, it is neither Real nor independent, but is, as stated in the Gītā, a 'folly' (*moha*), an 'ignorance' (*ajñāna*), or an 'illusion (*māyā*) seen by the organs', the objection based on *satkāryavāda*, does not in the least affect the Non-Dualistic doctrine. If a son is born to a father, we can say that he is the result of the *guṇa-pariṇāma* of the father; but when there is only one individual, namely, the father, and he is seen appearing sometimes in the guise of an infant, and sometimes of a young man, and sometimes of an old man, there does not exist, as we readily realise, the relation of cause and product, or of *guṇa-pariṇāma* between the man and his various disguises. In the same way, when we have come to the conclusion that there is only one Sun, we say that the reflection of that Sun seen in water is a kind of illusion, and that there is not another Sun which has come into existence by *guṇa-pariṇāma;* and astronomy tells us that when once the true form of a planet has been defined by means of a telescope, that form of it which we see by the naked eyes, is only an appearance resulting from the weakness of our eyes and the immense distance of the planet from us. From this, it becomes clear that a particular thing cannot be looked upon as an independent, real, and existing thing, merely on account of the fact that it is actually perceptible to our eyes and other organs. Then, why should we not make use of the same argument in the philosophy of the Absolute Self, and say that the qualityless Parabrahman which has been defined by the telescope of the knowledgeful (spiritual) eyes is the only thing which is Real, and that the Names and Forms, which are visible to the knowledgeless natural eyes, is not the product or result of, or something which has come out of, this Parabrahman, but is purely a deceptive and illusory appearance due to the incapacity of our organs? The objection that the Qualityful cannot come into existence out of the Qualityless can itself not be made here; because, the two substances do not belong to the same category, and whereas the one is Real, the other is merely an appearance; and it is common experience, that, though there may be fundamentally one Real substance, the appearances of that same substance change according to the faulty vision, or the ignorance, or the

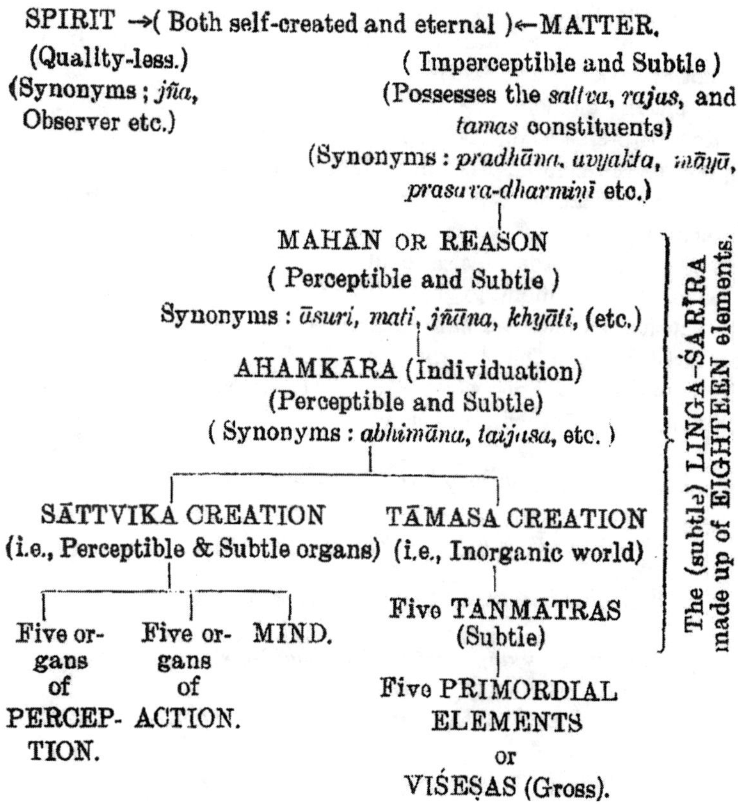

> By mixing black and white I we get the grey colour I
> By mixing black and yellow I we get the green colour II
> (9. 6. 40)

blindness of the person who sees. Take, for instance, the two qualities, namely, the words which can be heard by the ears, or the colours which can be seen by the eyes. Natural sciences have by minutely analysing the word or sound, which can be heard by the ears, clearly proved that 'sound' is nothing but waves or vibrations of the air. In the same way, it has now been determined by minute researches that the red, yellow, blue and other colours, which are visible to the eyes, are the evolutes of one fundamental sunlight, and that this sunlight itself is a kind of motion or vibration. If, although 'motion' or vibration is fundamentally one, the ears recognise it as 'sound' and the eyes as 'colour', then, the same argument being applied in a more comprehensive way to all the various organs, it follows that (i) the different human senses attribute (i. e., make an *adhyāropa* of) the different qualities of sound, colour, etc., which (qualities) are embodied in Name and Form, to one and the same Fundamental Substance, and thereby various appearances come into being; that (ii) it is not necessary for these appearances, qualities, or Names and Forms to exist in the Fundamental Substance; and that (iii) the coming into existence of all Names and Forms can thus be logically explained without the help of the doctrine of *satkāryavāda*. And in order to establish this proposition, Vedānta philosophy gives the various illustrations of a string being taken for a serpent, or a shell being taken for silver, or one thing being seen as two things by poking the finger under the eyeball, or the same substance being seen to be of different colours by the use of spectacles of different colours. It is true that a man will always perceive the various Names and Forms or qualities in the world, in as much as he can never get rid of his organs. But, this relative appearance of the world, which is seen by the eyes of the organised human being, cannot be said to be the fundamental, that is, the non-relative and eternal form of the world. If human beings come to have fewer or more organs than they have at present, they may not see the universe in the same way as they now see it; and, if this is true, then, on being asked to explain the eternal and real nature of the Element which is at the root of the world, without reference to the organs of the person who sees, one has to answer by saying that the Fundamental Element is qualityless, and our seeing it as qualityful is the result of the nature of our organs, and not the quality of the Fundamental Substance. Such questions do not arise in the Material sciences, because, in those sciences only such things are to be examined as are perceptible to the organs. But, from the fact that a man or his organs come to an end, we cannot conclude that the Parameśvara also comes to an end; nor can we conclude from the fact that a man sees Him as being of a particular kind, that His Real, non-relative form, which is uncircumscribed by Time, is what the man sees. Therefore, in that philosophy of the Absolute Self in which one has to determine the fundamental form of the Reality which is at the root of the universe, one must give up the relative and dependent vision of the human organs, and one has ultimately to consider the matter purely by his spiritual vision, that is to say, as far as possible, by Reason only; and when that is done, all the qualities which are perceptible to the organs automatically drop off; and one sees that the real form of the Brahman is beyond the reach of the organs, that is, qualityless; and that that form is a super-excellent form. But who is going to describe that which is qualityless and how?. Therefore, the Non-Dualist Vedānta has laid down the proposition that the ultimate, that is to say, the non-relative and eternal form of the Parabrahman is not only qualityless but indescribable, and that, man sees a qualityful appearance, in this qualityless form, by reason of his organs. But, here again a question arises as to how the organs have acquired the power of changing the Qualityless into the Qualityful. The reply of the Non-Dualist Vedānta to this is: as human knowledge stops at this stage, one has either to say that this must be called the ignorance of the organs, and that their seeing the appearance of the qualityful universe in the qualityless Parabrahman is due to that ignorance; or, one has to content oneself with drawing the definite inference that the visible universe (Prakṛti) is only a 'divine illusion' of the qualityless Parameśvara, since the organs themselves are part of the creation of the Parameśvara (Gī. 7. 14). My readers will understand from this the import of the statements in the Gītā (Gī. 7. 14, 24, 25) that though the *a-prabuddha*, that is, those who see merely by the physical organs, see the Parameśvara to be perceptible and qualityful, yet, His real and excellent form is qualityless; and that Realising that form by spiritual vision is the climax of Knowledge. But though, in this way, one arrives at the conclusion that the Parameśvara is fundamentally qualityless, and that the human organs see in Him the variegated appearance of the qualityful universe, yet, it becomes necessary to precisely explain in what meaning the word 'qualityless' has to be taken in this proposition. It is true that though our organs attribute the qualities of sound, colour etc., to vibrations of air, or mistake a shell for silver, the vibrations of air do not possess the quality of sound or colour, nor does the shell possess the quality of silver; but, from the fact that the Fundamental Substance does not contain the particular attributed qualities, one cannot draw the necessary conclusion that It will not possess other qualities. Because, as we actually see, though the shell does not possess the quality of silver, yet, it possesses some qualities other than those of silver. This, therefore, gives rise to the following difficulty, namely, though one admits that the fundamental Brahman does not possess the qualities which are ascribed to it by one's organs as a result of one's ignorance, how can one be sure that the Parabrahman does not possess other qualities; and if it possesses other qualities, how is it qualityless? But, if one considers the matter a little minutely, it will be seen that even assuming the fundamental Brahman to possess qualities other than those ascribed to it by the organs, how are we going to find them out? The qualities which a man perceives are perceived by him through the medium of his organs; and those qualities, which are not perceptible to the organs, cannot be known. In short, even if the Parabrahman possesses some qualities other than those which are ascribed to it by our organs, it is not possible for us to know them; and saying that the Parabrahman does possess qualities is illogical, if it is impossible for us to know those qualities. Therefore, Vedāntists understand the word '*guṇa*' as meaning 'qualities which are knowable by human beings', and formulate the proposition that the Brahman is 'qualityless' in this sense. Non-dualistic Vedānta does not say that the fundamental Parabrahman cannot possess qualities or powers which are beyond the imagination of human beings, and no one, as a matter of fact, can say that. Nay, even the Vedāntists say that the ignorance of the organs or Māyā, which was mentioned above, must be an unimaginable power of that fundamental Parabrahman.

The three-constituented Māyā or Prakṛti is not some independent substance; but, what happens is that the human organs, as a result of ignorance, ascribe (make an *adhyāropa* of) a qualityful appearance to one homogeneous, and qualityless Brahman. This theory is known as 'VIVARTA-VĀDA'. The explanation given by the Non-Dualistic Vedāntists as to how the variegated qualityful universe first came to be seen, if the qualityless Brahman was the only Fundamental Substance, is as follows:—The Kāṇāda Nyāya philosophy propounds the doctrine that innumerable atoms are the fundamental cause of the universe, and the followers of Nyāya philosophy consider these atoms to be Real. They have, therefore, come to the conclusion, that the various objects in the world begin to come into existence when these innumerable atoms begin to coalesce. As according to this theory, the universe starts to come into existence when the union between the atoms *commences* to take place, it is called 'Ārambha-vāda' (the Theory of Commencement). But Sāṁkhya philosophy does not accept this Nyāya theory of innumerable atoms, and says that the Fundamental Root of the Gross world is 'one, homogeneous, real, and three-constituented Prakṛti'; and they say that the perceptible world comes into existence as a result of the unfurling or *pariṇāma* of the constituents of this three-constituented Prakṛti. This doctrine is known as the 'Guṇa-pariṇāma-vāda' (Theory of the Development of Constituents), because, it maintains that the entire perceptible universe is the result of the unfurling of the constituents of one fundamental qualityful Prakṛti. But both these theories are negatived by the Non-Dualistic Vedāntists. As atoms are innumerable, they cannot be the Root of the world according to Non-Dualism; and the Dualistic theory, that though Prakṛti is one, it is different from Puruṣa and independent, is also inconsistent with Non-Dualism; but, when in this way, both these theories are negatived, it becomes necessary to explain how the qualityful universe came into existence out of one qualityless Brahman; because, according to the *satkāryavāda*, the Qualityful cannot come into existence out of the Qualityless. To this, the reply of the Vedāntists is, that the doctrine of *satkāryavāda* applies only where both the Cause and the Product are Real substances; where the fundamental substance is one, and only its forms or appearances are changed, this theory does not apply; because, as is common experience, seeing various appearances of one and the same thing is not a quality of that thing, and these various appearances can come into existence as a result of the difference in the vision of the persons who see. * When this theory is applied to the qualityless Brahman and the qualityful universe, one has to say that the Brahman is qualityless, and that an appearance of qualityfulness comes into existence in it, as a result of the nature of the human organs. This is known as the 'Vivarta-vāda.' According to Vivarta-vāda, there is believed to be only one, fundamental, Real substance, and it is said that numerous, unreal or constantly changing Appearances are ascribed to it; and in the Guṇa-pariṇāma-vāda, two Real susbtances are taken for granted from the very commencement, and it is said that the Guṇas (constituents) of one of these two become unfurled, and that all other things in the universe which are possessed of various qualities come into existence in consequence. The impression of the existence of a serpent, where, as a matter of fact, there is only a string, is the Vivarta-vāda; and, fibres being formed into a rope, or curds out of milk, is the Guṇa-pariṇāma-vāda. Therefore, in the book called *Vedāntasāra*, these two theories are described and differentiated between in the following words:—

yas tāttviko 'nyathābhāvaḥ pariṇāma udīritaḥ ।
atāttviko 'nyathābhāvo vivartaḥ sa udīritaḥ ॥ (Ve. Sā. 21).

* To explain this meaning in English, we have to say: Appearances are the results of subjective conditio n, viz., the senses of the observer, and not of the Thing-in-itself.

that is, "when from one fundamental substance, another substance of a different nature comes into existence essentially, that is, really, that is called (*guṇa-*) *pariṇāma;* but when instead of this, the fundamental substance looks something different (*atāttvika*), it is said to be *vivarta*". The Ārambha-vāda is the theory of the Nyāya school, the Guṇa-pariṇāma-vāda is the theory of the Sāṁkhya school, and the Vivarta-vāda is the theory of the Non-Dualist Vedānta school. The Non-Dualist Vedāntists do not look upon the two qualityful substances, atoms and Prakṛti, as different from or independent of the qualityless Brahman; but by their doing so, the objection that the Qualityful cannot spring out of the Qualityless arises on account of *satkārya-vāda*; and in order to get rid of that objection, the Vivarta-vāda has come into existence. But, the conclusion drawn by some, that, on that account the Vedāntists will not at any time or cannot accept the Guṇa-pariṇāma-vāda is wrong. The principal object of the Vivarta-vāda is to show that (i) the objection of the Sāṁkhyas, or of other Dualists against Non-Dualism, namely, that the qualityful Prakṛti or Māyā cannot spring out of the qualityless Brahman, is not impossible to answer, and that (ii) it is possible for our organs to see innumerable Māyic (illusory) appearances in one qualityless Brahman. When this object has been achieved, that is to say, when it has been proved by Vivarta-vāda, that it is possible to see the Appearance of the three-constituented qualityful Prakṛti in one qualityless Parabrahman, Vedānta philosophy has no objection to accept that the further development of that Prakṛti has taken place according to the Guṇa-pariṇāma-vāda. The chief doctrine of Non-Dualistic Vedānta is that the fundamental Prakṛti is an Appearance, or an Illusion, and that it is not Real. But once this first Appearance of Prakṛti begins to be seen, Non-Dualist Vedāntists have no objection to accept that the appearances, which are subsequently evolved from this one original Appearance, are not-independent; and to accept that the qualities of one appearance spring out of the qualities of another appearance, and that, in this way, appearances possessing various qualities have come into existence. Therefore, although the Blessed Lord has said in the Gītā that

"Prakṛti is nothing but My Māyā" (Gī. 7. 14; 4. 6), the Gītā itself also says that this Prakṛti, which has become imbued with or inhabited by the Parameśvara (Gī. 9. 10), is further developed according to the rule "*guṇā guṇeṣu vartante*" (Gī. 3. 28; 14. 23). From this it will be clear, that when once the appearance of Māyā has taken place in the fundamentally qualityless Brahman according to Vivarta-vāda, the principle of *guṇotkarṣa* (Development of Constituents) has been accepted even by the Gītā for explaining this Māyic appearance, that is, this further development of Prakṛti. It is not that because you say that the entire visible world is a Māyic appearance, therefore, there cannot be some such rule like *guṇotkarṣa* which controls the changes in form which take place in this Appearance. Vedāntists do not wish to deny that the further development of this Māyic appearance is bound by rules. All that they say is that these rules are also Māyic, like the fundamental Prakṛti, and that the Parameśvara is the Over-Lord of all these Māyic rules, and is beyond them, and that it is by His power that some sort of permanence or regularity has come into these rules. It is not possible for the qualityful, that is, perishable Prakṛti, which is in the form of an Appearance, to lay down rules which are not circumscribed by Time.

From the foregoing discussion, my readers will understand the nature and the mutual relationship between the Jīva (personal self) and the Parameśvara (the Absolute Īśvara), or according to Vedāntic terminology, between Māyā (that is, the universe which has been brought into existence by Māyā), the Ātman, and the Parabrahman. From the point of view of the philosophy of the Highest Self, all the things in the universe are divided into two classes, namely, 'Names and Forms, and the Eternal Element' (*nitya-tattva*) clothed in those Names and Forms. Out of these, 'Names and Forms' are known as the qualityful Māyā or Prakṛti. But when you eliminate the Names and Forms, the Eternal Element (*nitya-dravya*) which remains, must be qualityless; because, no quality can exist without the support of a Name and Form. This eternal and imperceptible Element is the Parabrahman; and the weak organs of human beings see the qualityful

Māyā as a growth out of this qualityless Parabrahman. This Māyā is not a Real substance, and it is only the Parabrahman which is Real, that is, uncircumscribed by Time, and never-changing. These are the doctrines which relate to the nature of the Names and Forms of the visible universe and the Parabrahman clothed by them. Now, when the human being is viewed from the same point of view, it is seen that the human body and organs are substances defined by Name and Form, like other substances in the visible world, that is to say, that they fall into the category of the non-permanent Māyā; and that the Ātman, which is clothed by this Body and organs, falls into the category of the eternal Parabrahman; or, that the Brahman and the Ātman are one and the same. My readers must have now noticed the difference between these Non-Dualistic doctrines, which do not look upon the external world as an independent substance in this sense, and the Buddhistic doctrines. Buddhists, who believe in the Vijñāna-vāda, say that the external world does not exist at all, and that Jñāna (Knowledge) alone is Real; and Vedāntists look upon only the ever-changing Names and Forms of the external universe as unreal, and say that under these Names and Forms, as also in the human body, there is, in both cases, one and the same Ātman-formed Substance; and that this homogeneous Ātman-Element is the ultimate Reality. In the same way, Sāṁkhya philosophy has accepted the synthesis of the diversity of created things by the law of "*avibhaktaṁ vibhakteṣu*," only so far as it applies to Gross Matter; but, as the Vedāntists have got over this difficulty of the *satkāryavāda*, and established the doctrine that "whatever is in the Body, is also in the Cosmos," the innumerable Puruṣas and the Prakṛti of Sāṁkhya philosophy have, in Vedānta philosophy, been comprised in one Paramātman by the principle of Non-Dualism (*advaita*) or Non-Division (*avibhāga*). The purely Materialistic philosopher Haeckel was, it is true, a Non-Dualist. But he includes even Consciousness (*caitanya*) in Gross Matter, and Vedānta philosophy does not give pre-eminence to the Gross, but proves that the immortal and independent Thought-Formed (*cidrūpi*) Parabrahman, which is uncircumscribed by Time or Space, is the Fundamental Root of the world : this is the most important difference between the Non-Dualism of of the philosophy of the Absolute Self and the Gross-Non-Dualism (*jaḍādvaita*) of Haeckel. The same doctrines of Non-dualistic Vedānta have been mentioned in the Gītā; and an ancient poet has summarised the Non-Dualistic Vedānta philosophy very concisely as follows :—

ślokārdhena pravakṣyāmi yad uktaṁ granthakoṭibhiḥ ।
brahma satyaṁ jagan mithyā jīvo brahmaiva nāparaḥ ॥

that is, "I will explain in half a stanza the summary of a million books—(1) the Brahman is Real, (2) the world (*jagat*) that is, all the Names and Forms in the world, are *mithyā*, or perishable, and (3) the Ātman of a man and the Brahman are fundamentally ONE and the same, and not two." If anybody does not appreciate the word '*mithyā*' in this stanza, he is quite welcome to read the third section of the stanza as '*brahmāmṛtaṁ jagat satyam*', consistently with the Bṛhadāraṇyakopaniṣad; thereby, the purport does not change at all as has been stated before. Nevertheless, many Vedāntists enter into a fruitless discussion as to whether the invisible but eternal Fundamental Element of the visible world, in the shape of the Brahman, should be called *sat* (*satya*) or *asat* (*asatya*=*anṛta*). I shall, therefore, explain here concisely what the underlying principle in this discussion, is. This discussion has come into existence because the word *sat* or *satya* has two different meanings; and if one first carefully considers in what meaning the word *sat* has been used by any particular person, no confusion will arise; because, everybody accepts the distinction that though the Brahman is invisible, it is Real; and that though the Name-d and Form-ed Cosmos is visible, yet, it is ever-changing. The ordinary meaning of the word *sat* or *satya* is: (1) that which is, at the moment, actually visible to the eyes, that is to say, perceptible (whether this visible appearance of it, does or does not change to-morrow); and the other meaning of that word is: (2) that of which the nature always remains the same, and never changes, notwithstanding that it is invisible to the eyes, i. e., imperceptible. Those who accept the first meaning say, that the Name-d and Form-ed world which is visible to the eyes is *satya* (visible) and that the Parabrahman is just the opposite, that is, it is not visible to the eyes and therefore, *asat* or *asatya* (invisible). For instance, in the Taittirīyopaniṣad, the visible world has been called '*sat*', and that which is beyond the visible world, has been called '*tyat*' (THAT, that is, which is beyond) or '*anṛta*' (invisible to the eyes); and the Brahman is described by saying that that substance which was in existence at the commencement of the world has become two-fold as follows:—"*sacca tyaccābhavat* I *niruktaṁ cāniruktaṁ ca* I *nilayanaṁ cānilayanaṁ ca* I *vijñānaṁ cāvijñānaṁ ca* I *satyaṁ cānṛtaṁ ca* I" (Tai. 2. 6), that is: "It became "*sat* (visible to the eyes) and That (which is beyond); describable and indescribable; dependent and independent; known and unknown (unknowable); and real (visible) and invisible". But though the Brahman has in this way been described as '*anṛta*', the word *anṛta* does not mean false or unreal; but later on, in the Taittirīyopaniṣad itself, it is stated that "this *anṛta* (invisible) Brahman is the '*pratiṣṭhā*' (support) of the world, that it does not depend on anything else, and that he who has realised this need not fear anything". From this it is clear, that though there is a difference in words, there is no difference in the intended meaning. In the same way, it is ultimately said that "*asadvā idam agra āsit*", that is, "this world was *asat* (Brahman) in the beginning"; and, as stated in the Ṛg-Veda (10. 129. 4), the *sat*, that is, the Name-d and Form-ed perceptible world, is said to have subsequently grown out of it (Tai. 2. 7). From this, it becomes quite clear that the word '*asat*' has been used here only in the meaning of *avyakta*, that is, not visible to the eyes; and in the Vedānta-Sūtras, Bādarāyaṇācārya has interpreted those words in the same meaning (Ve. Sū. 2. 1. 17). But, those who interpret the word '*sat*' or '*satya*, as meaning existing permanently, or ever-lasting, though not visible to the eyes (which is the second of the two meanings mentioned above), give to the invisible but immutable Parabrahman the name *sat* or *satya* and call the Name-d and Form-ed Māyā, *asat* or *asatya*, i. e., perishable. For instance, there is a description in the Chāndogya that: "*sadeva saumyedam agra āsīt katham asataḥ sajjāyeta*", that is, "O my son! this world was

43—44

originally *sat* (Brahman); how can '*sat*', that is, that which exists, come into existence out of something which is *asat*, that is, which never was in existence?" (Chān. 6. 2. 1, 2). But in this Chāndogyopaniṣad itself, the Parabrahman has in one place been called '*asat*' in the sense of *avyakta*, that is, imperceptible (Chān. 3. 19. 1). * This confusing method by which the same Parabrahman was at different times and in different meanings given the mutually contradictory names of once '*sat*' and at another time '*asat*'—which was a method promoting verbal warfare, though the intended import was the same—gradually wore out; and ultimately, the one terminology of calling the Brahman *sat* or *satya*, i. e., eternally lasting, and the visible world *asat* or perishable, has become fixed. In the Bhagavadgītā, this ultimate terminology has been accepted and in the second chapter, the Parabrahman has been described as *sat* and imperishable, and Names and Forms are described as *asat*, that is, perishable, in those meanings of those words (Gī. 2. 16-18); and the same is the doctrine of the Vedānta-Sūtras. Nevertheless, the old terminology of the Taittirīyopaniṣad of referring to the visible world as '*sat*' and to the Parabrahman as '*asat*' or as '*tyat*' (THAT = that which is beyond) has not been totally exterminated; and what the original meaning of the description of the Brahman in the Gītā (Gī. 17. 23) as 'OṀ-Tat-Sat' must have been, can very clearly be seen by reference to the old terminology. 'OṀ' is a Vedic prayer in the form of a mystic word, and it has been explained in various ways in the Upaniṣads (Pra. 5; Mān. 8-12; Chān. 1. 1.). '*tat*' means 'THAT', that is, the indescribable Element which is far beyond the visible world, and '*sat*' is the visible world which can be seen by the eyes; and this canon means that these three together constitute the Brahman. And it is with this import that the

* Even among the English writers on Metaphysics, there is a difference of opinion as to whether the word *real*, i. e., *sat* should be applied to the appearance of the world (Māyā) or to the *vastu-tattva* (Brahman). Kant looks upon the Appearance as *sat* (real) and calls the *vastu-tattva*, imperishable. But, Haeckel, Green and others call the Appearance, *asat* (unreal), and the *vastu-tattva*, *sat* (real).

Blessed Lord has said in the Gītā (Gī. 9. 19) that "*sad asaccāham arjuna*", that is, "*sat* is the Parabrahman and *asat* is the visible world, and I am both". Still, in as much as the Gītā propounds the Karma-Yoga, it has been explained at the end of the seventeenth chapter that by taking the word '*sat*' in the canon, OṀ-Tat-Sat, as meaning Action, which is good from the point of view of respectability, or which has been done with a good intention, or of which the result is good, and by taking the word '*tat*' as meaning, Action, which is beyond the above-mentioned Action, that is, which has been performed by giving up the desire for fruit, as and when occasion arises to use that canon, the doctrine of Karma-Yoga can be fully supported on the basis of this description of the Brahman. As that which has been referred to as '*sat*' in the canon, is nothing else but the visible world, that is to say, Karma (See the next chapter), this interpretation of the definition of the Brahman in terms of Karma, easily arises out of the original interpretation. There are to be found in the Upaniṣads other descriptions of the Brahman than '*oṁ-tat-sat*', '*neti neti*', '*saccidānanda*' and '*satyasya satyam*'; but as they are not necessary for understanding the meaning of the Gītā, I have not given them here.

When the mutual relationship between the Cosmos (*jagat*), the personal Self (*jīva*) and the Parameśvara (Paramātman) have been explained in this way, it becomes quite clear in what sense one has to take the word '*aṁśa*' used by the Blessed Lord in the phrases "the Jīva is an '*aṁśa*' of Myself" (Gī. 15. 7), and "I have pervaded the whole of this world by one '*aṁśa*'" (Gī. 10. 42) in the Bhagavadgītā, and also used by Bādarāyaṇācārya in the Vedānta-Sūtras (Ve. Sū. 2. 3. 43; 4. 4. 19), or the word '*pāda*' used in the Puruṣa-Sūkta in the line "*pādo 'sya viśvā bhūtāni tripād asyāmṛtaṁ divi*"—'the *jagadātman* (the Cosmic-Self) Which has pervaded the moveable and the immoveable, and yet remained over ten fingers'. Although the Parameśvara or the Paramātman is all-pervading, yet, as It is unorganised, homogeneous, and devoid of Name and Form, that is to say, uncuttable (*acchedya*) and immutable (*avikārya*), it is impossible to break It up into individual pieces (Gī. 2. 25). Therefore, in order to distinguish between this homogeneous Parabrahman which pervades everything on all sides, and the Ātman within the body of a man, one has to say in common parlance that the '*śārīra-ātman*' (the Ātman within the body) is an '*aṁśa*' (part) of the Parabrahman. Yet, the word '*aṁśa*' or 'part' has not to be taken in the meaning of 'an independent piece which has been cut out', or 'one of the grains taken out of the numerous grains in a pomegranate'; and it must be taken in its elementary meaning to indicate that the Ātman is a part of the Parabrahman in the same way as ether (*ākāśa*) in the house or in an earthenware pot (*maṭhākāśa, ghaṭākāśa*) are parts of an all-pervading ether (See Amṛtabindūpaniṣad 13). The Sāṁkhya Prakṛti, and the homogeneous element accepted by the Materialistic Gross-Non-Dualism of Haeckel, are in the same way qualityful, that is, limited, parts of the Real qualityless Parameśvara. Nay, whatever perceptible or imperceptible fundamental element is arrived at according to the Materialistic sciences, (then may it be how much soever comprehensive like ether), it is only a Name and Form broken in upon by Time and Space, that is to say, it is perishable and limited. It is true that it has occupied the Parabrahman to the extent of its capacity, but instead of the Parabrahman being thereby in any way limited, It has fully pervaded and saturated the former and one cannot gauge to what extent It remains over. Although the words '*daśāṁgula*' (ten fingers), or '*tripāda*' (three steps) have been used in the Puruṣa-Sūkta in order to indicate to what extent the Parameśvara has gone beyond the visible universe, yet, they are to be taken as meaning '*ananta*' (endless); because, strictly speaking, Space and Time, weights and measures, and even numbers are only kinds of Names and Forms; and it has been shown above that the Parabrahman is beyond all these Names and Forms. Therefore, the Parabrahman has been described in the Upaniṣads as, that Element which swallows up or absorbs '*kāla*' (Time), which '*kāla*' has swallowed up everything (Mai. 6. 15); and the same is the purport conveyed by the descriptions to be found in the Gītā and in the Upaniṣads of the habitation of the Parameśvara, such as, "*na tad bhāsayate sūryo na śaśāṁko na pāvakaḥ*", that is, "there is no such luminary object like the Sun or the Moon or Fire for illuminating the seat of the Parameśvara, who is self-illumined" (Gī. 15. 6; Kaṭha. 5. 15; Śve. 6. 14). The Sun, the Moon, the stars, etc., are Name-d and Form-ed perishable objects. That self-illumined Knowledge-filled Brahman which is "*jyotiṣāṁ jyotiḥ*" (Gī. 13. 17; Bṛ. 4. 4. 16)—that is, "brilliance of brilliance"—extends endlessly beyond all of them; and it is stated in the Upaniṣads that not only does It not depend on any other luminary objects, but whatever light is possessed by the Sun, the Moon etc., is obtained by them from this self-illumined Brahman (Muṇ. 2. 2. 10). Take the most subtle or the most distant object, which is made perceptible to the organs by instruments invented by Material sciences; it is but the world defined by Name and Form, which is circumscribed by the limitations of Time and Space. As the true Parameśvara is in them, and yet different from and more comprehensive than all of them, and also homogeneous and uncircumscribed by the bonds of Names and Forms, that is to say, as He is independent, it is not possible for the devices or instruments of Material sciences, which consider merely Names and Forms, to find out the '*amṛta-tattva*' (imperishable Element) which is the Root of the world, though they might become a thousand times more subtle or comprehensive than they are at present. That imperishable, immutable and undying element must ultimately be found out by the Path of Knowledge shown in the philosophy of the Absolute Self.

From the exposition of the principal doctrines of the philosophy of the Absolute Self and their concise scientific explanation given so far, it will be clear why all the perceptible Name-d and Form-ed appearances of the Parameśvara are Māyic or perishable, why His imperceptible form is superior to them, why His qualityless form, that is, the form undefined by Name and Form, is still superior, and why it is stated in the Gītā that the qualityless form seems qualityful as a result of ignorance. But this work of setting out these doctrines in words can be easily done by anyone who has acquired a little knowledge like me; there is nothing much in that. In order that these doctrines should be impressed on the mind, engraved on the heart and ingrained in one's flesh and bone after they have been understood, and that one should thereby fully realise that there is only one Parabrahman which saturates all living things; and in order that by reason of such feeling, one should acquire an immutable mental frame which will enable one to behave with equability towards everybody in times of misfortune, it is necessary to have the continual additional help of impressions acquired during numerous births, control of the organs, persevering practice, meditation, and worship. Therefore, the summary of all the above doctrines, and the highest doctrine of the philosophy of the Ābsolute Self is: only that man may be said to have become fully saturated with the knowledge of the Brahman in whose every action the principle, "there is only one Ātman in all created things", has become naturally and clearly visible, even in times of distress; and such a man alone gets Release (Gī. 5. 18-20; 6. 21, 22). The 'earthenware pot' of that man in whom such behaviour is not to be seen is to that extent imperfectly or insufficiently 'baked', in the fire of the Knowledge of the Brahman. This is the difference between real saints and mere Vedāntists; and, therefore, in describing Knowledge, it is stated in the Gītā that true Knowledge may be said to have been acquired, when noble emotions like "humility (*amānitva*), peacefulness (*śānti*), self-control (*ātmanigraha*), equability of mind (*samabuddhi*)" are awakened, whereby the total purification of the mind is continually expressed in conduct, instead of saying that 'Knowledge is the understanding by Reason of what is at the root of the external world' (Gī. 13. 7-11). That man whose Discerning Reason has become devoted to the Self, that is, has become steady in the contemplation on the Self and Non-Self, and who has Realised the identity of the Ātman with all created beings, must, undoubtedly, also possess a Desiring Reason which is pure. But, as there is no other external measure except a man's conduct for finding out the state of his Reason, the words '*jñāna*' (Knowledge) or '*samabuddhi*' (equable mind) are usually made to include the pure Discerning Reason, the pure Desiring Reason, and pure Conduct; this thing must be borne in mind, especially in these days of bookish knowledge. There may be many who can give long dry discourses on the Brahman, and also others who hearing those discourses will nod their heads in appreciation and say 'Hear, hear', or, like courtiers in a drama, say, "Let us hear the same thing again" (Gī. 2. 29; Ka. 2. 7); but, as stated above, that man who has become internally and externally pure, that is, equable in mind, is the true devotee of the Ātman, and he alone attains Release, and not mere learned men who may be how well-read or intelligent soever. It has been plainly stated in the Upaniṣads that: "*nāyam ātmā pravacanena labhyo na medhayā na bahunā śrutena*" (Ka 2. 22; Mun 3. 2. 3.), (that is, "this Ātman is not reached by giving discourses, nor by intelligence, nor by great learning"—Trans.), and the Saint Tukārāma has also said:—"you have become a Pandit (i.e., learned man), you interpret the Purāṇas । but you do not know who you are ॥" (Gā. 2599). See how narrow our minds are! The words 'attains Release' easily come out of our mouths, as if Release is something different from the Ātman. There would be difference between the Observer and the visible world, before the Knowledge has been acquired that the Brahman and the Ātman are identical; but, our Vedāntists have come to the conclusion that when one has fully Realised the identity of the Brahman and the Ātman, the Ātman is merged into the Brahman, and the *brahmajñānī* (one who has Realised the Brahman) acquires the form of Brahman wherever he is; and this Metaphysical state is known as the '*brahmanirvāṇa* Release,' which is not given by anybody to anybody, and which does not come from anywhere, and for obtaining which it is not necessary to leave this world and to go to another world. Whenever and wherever the complete Realisation of the Ātman comes, Release is obtained at that very moment and at that place; because, Release is the fundamental pure state of the Ātman, and is not some independent thing or place. There is a stanza in the Śiva-Gītā that:—

mokṣasya na hi vāso 'sti na grāmāntaram eva vā ।
ajñānahṛdayagranthināśo mokṣa iti smṛtaḥ ॥

(Śiva. 13. 32)

that is, "Release is not in a particular place, nor has one to go to some other town or country in order to obtain it: the destruction of the knot of Ignorance (*ajñāna*) round our hearts is known as Release". And this final conclusion which arises out of the philosophy of the Absolute Self has been described in the words, "*abhito brahmanirvāṇaṁ vartate viditātmanām*" (Gī. 5. 26), i. e., "those, who have fully Realised the Ātman, attain Release in the form of *brahmanirvāṇa* wherever they may be", or, "*yaḥ sadā mukta eva saḥ*" (Gī. 5. 28) in the Bhagavadgītā, as also in the canons, "*brahma veda brahmaiva bhavati*", i. e., "he who has Realised the Brahman has become Brahman" (Muṇ. 3. 2. 9) etc. in the Upaniṣads. Therefore, this state of perfection of the human Ātman from the point of view of Knowledge is known as the '*brahmabhūta*' (Gī. 18. 54), or 'the Brāhmī state' (Gī. 2. 72); and the descriptions to be found elsewhere in the Bhagavadgītā of the '*sthitaprajña*' (steady-in-mind), (Gī. 2. 55–72), '*bhaktimān*' (devotee), (Gī. 12. 13–20) or '*triguṇātīta*' (beyond the three constituents), (Gī. 14. 22–27) are of this state. From the term, '*triguṇātīta*', one is not to draw the conclusion that the Gītā looks upon Prakṛti and the Puruṣa as independent, and the isolation (*kaivalya*) of the Puruṣa as Release, as is done by the Sāṁkhyas; but, according to the Gītā, the Brāhmī state described in the philosophy of the Absolute Self by the words, '*ahaṁ brahmāsmi*', i. e., "I am the Brahman" (Bṛ. 1. 4. 10), is obtained sometimes by the Path of Devotion, sometimes by the Pātañjala Yoga practice of the Control of the Mind, and sometimes by the path of the Discernment of Constituents (*guṇāguṇa-vivecana*) described in Sāṁkhya philosophy. As the philosophy of the Absolute Self, out of these paths, is a purely rational philosophy, Devotion has been mentioned in the Gītā as the easiest means for an ordinary person for acquiring the Knowledge of the form of the Parameśvara; and, I have later on, in the thirteenth chapter, fully considered this matter. Whatever may be the means employed, this much is beyond doubt, that attaining the Knowledge of the true Parameśvara, that is, Realising the identity of the Brahman and the Ātman, and that there is only one Ātman in all created beings, and behaving accordingly, is the climax of Spiritual Knowledge (*adhyātma-jñāna*); and that those who have reached this state are indeed blessed and perfect; because, as has been stated above, as organic pleasure is the same in the case of men as of animals, the purpose of a human birth or the manhood of man is fully satisfied only by the acquisition of Knowledge. Continually observing this Equability of Mind towards all created beings in the performance of all bodily, vocal, or mental Actions is known as the '*nityamuktāvasthā*' (state of perpetual Release), '*pūrṇa-yoga*' (perfect Yoga), or '*siddhāvasthā*' (the state of a perfect being). The saint Jñāneśvara, in commenting on the description of the Devotee in the twelvth chapter of the Gītā (Gī. 12. 18) says:

Oh, Pārtha, that man in whom ।
there is no trace of differentiation ।
Who, both friend and foe । looks upon as alike ॥
Lighting his own house ।
and leaving the house of another in darkness ।
Is a thing which he does not do, O, Pāṇḍava ।
he is like a light ॥
To the one who deals the blow to cut ।
and to the one who planted it ।
It (the tree) gives both shelter ।
he is like the tree ॥

(Jñā. 12. 197–99).

And earlier in the same chapter, in commenting on the 13th stanza of the twelvth chapter of the Gītā, he says:

Supporting the best । rejecting the worst ।
Is a thing which he does not do ।
he is like the earth ॥
Activating the body of a king ।
and refusing to activate the body of a poor man ।
Is a thing which the Prāṇa (Vital Force) does not do ।
so is he; he is kind ॥
Slaking the thirst of a cow ।
and becoming a poison to kill a tiger ।
Is a thing which water does not do ।
he is like the water ॥

Towards all created beings ।
he is friendly, looking upon all as one ।
He is kind to all ।
with a sense of equability ॥
He does not know the word 'I' ।
he does not say of anything that it is 'mine'
Experience of pain and happiness ।
for him there is none
(Jñā. 12. 145–149).

And Jñāneśvara has thus, by giving numerous illustrations, and in very sweet and attractive language, described in Marathi the equability of the Brahmified man; and we may safely say, that this description contains a summary of the description of the Brāhmī state given in four different places in the Gītā. This is what is to be ultimately acquired by Spiritual Knowledge.

My readers will have understood from what has been stated above, how the tradition of Spiritual Knowledge, which is the root of the science of Release, has come to us in an unbroken line from the Upaniṣads right upto Tukārāma. But, in order to impress on my readers that this knowledge had come into existence in our country even before the date of the Upaniṣads, that is to say, already in very very ancient times, and that the ideas in the Upaniṣads have gradually grown from those times, I shall give here, before concluding, a well-known hymn (*sūkta*) from the Ṛg-Veda, which is the foundation even of the Spiritual Knowledge in the Upaniṣads, together with its Marathi translation. Not only do we not come across in the scriptures of any religion, critical philosophical ideas, as to what the unknowable Fundamental Element of the Cosmos must have been, and how this variegated visible universe sprang from it, which are as comprehensive, independent and root-touching as those in this hymn, but no one has yet come across any text replete with such Spiritual Knowledge, which is equal to it in point of antiquity. Therefore, many wonder-struck Western scholars have translated this hymn into their various languages, looking upon it as important, from the point of view of religious history, for showing how the natural tendency of the human mind runs beyond the Name-d and Form-ed universe to reach the permanent and unimaginable Brahman-Energy which is beyond it. This hymn is the 129th hymn in the tenth *maṇḍula* of the Ṛg-Veda, and is known as the 'Nāsadīya-Sūkta', having regard to its commencing words. And this Sūkta has been adopted in the Taittirīya Brāhmaṇa (2. 8. 9), and the description given in the Nārāyaṇīya or the Bhāgavata religion in the Mahābhārata as to how the universe was first created by the desire of the Blessed Lord has been based on this hymn (Ma. Bhā. Śān. 342. 8). According to the general index (*sarvānukramaṇikā*), the Ṛṣi of this hymn is Parameṣṭhi Prajāpati, its deity is the Paramātman, and it consists of seven stanzas (*ṛcā*) in the *triṣṭup* metre, each stanza containing four lines of eleven words each. As the words, *sat* and *asat*, have a double meaning, the difference of opinion among the writers of the Upaniṣads, as regards describing the Fundamental Element of the world as '*sat*', which has been referred to earlier in this chapter, is also to be found in the Ṛg-Veda. For instance, this Fundamental Cause of the world is in some places described by saying "*ekaṁ sad viprā bahudhā vadanti*" (Ṛg. 1. 164. 46), or "*ekaṁ santaṁ bahudhā kalpayanti*" (Ṛg. 10. 114. 5)—that is, "It, being one and *sat* (i. e. lasting for ever), has been given different names by people"; whereas in other places, it has been described by saying: "*devānāṁ pūrvye yuge 'sataḥ sad ajāyata*" (Ṛg. 10. 72. 7), that is, "the *sat*, that is, the perceptible universe, came into existence out of the *asat*, that is, the Imperceptible, even before the gods had come into existence." In addition to this, there are other descriptions all differing from each other in the Ṛg-Veda itself as to how the entire universe came into being out of one visible Element, e. g., :—in the beginning of the world, there was the Golden Embryo (*hiraṇya-garbha)*, of which both death and immortality are shadows, and It later on created the entire world (Ṛg. 10. 121. 1, 2); or, that a Virāṭa-formed Puruṣa existed at first, and from him the entire world was created by means of a sacrifice (Ṛg. 10. 90): or, that there was *āpa* (water) at first, and in that water Prajāpati came into existence (Ṛg. 10. 72. 6; 10. 82. 6); or, that *ṛta* and *satya* first came into existence, and afterwards, darkness; and after that, water (*samudra*), the year etc. came into existence (Ṛg. 10. 190. 1). These Fundamental Elements mentioned in the Ṛg-Veda have been later on referred to as follows:—(1) in the Taittirīya Brāhmaṇa, water has been referred to as the Fundamental Element as: "*āpo vā idam agre salilam āsīt*" (Tai. Brā. 1. 1. 3. 5), i. e., "all this was liquid water in the beginning"; (2) in the Taittirīyopaniṣad, *asat* has been mentioned as the Fundamental Element, as: "*asad vā idam agra āsīt*" (Tai. 2.7), i. e., "all this was *asat* in the beginning"; (3) in the Chāndogyopaniṣad, *sat* has been mentioned as the Fundamental Element, as: "*sad eva saumyedam agra āsīt*" (Chān. 6. 2), i. e., "all this was *sat* in the beginning"; or, (4) ether is said to be such Element, as: "*ākāśaḥ parāyaṇam*" (Chān. 1. 9), i. e., "ether was the root of everything"; (5) in the Bṛhadāraṇyaka, death (*mṛtyu*) is mentioned as the Fundamental Element, as: "*naiveha kiṁcanāgra āsīn mṛtyunaivedam āvṛtam āsīt*" (Bṛ. 1. 2. 1), i. e., "in the beginning, there was nothing whatsoever; everything was covered by death"; and (6) in the Maitryūpaniṣad, darkness (*tamas*) has been mentioned as the Fundamental Element, as: "*tamo vā idam agra āsīd ekam*" (Mai. 5. 2), i. e., "this entire universe was in the beginning *tamas* (*tamoguṇi*, darkness)", and *sattva* and *rajas* afterwards came into existence out of it. In the same way, the Manu-Smṛti contains the following description of the commencement of the universe, consistent with these descriptions in the Vedas:—

āsīd idaṁ tamobhūtam aprajñātam alakṣaṇam ।
apratarkyam avijñeyam prasuptam iva sarvataḥ ॥

that is, "all this was first covered up by darkness (*tamas*), and it was undiscernible and as if in a sleeping state, so that it would be impossible to differentiate between one thing and another; thereafter, the imperceptible Paramātman entered it and first created water" (Manu. 1. 5—8). Such and other different descriptions about the Fundamental Substance existing at the commencement of the universe must have been in vogue even at the time of the Nāsadīya-Sūkta; and the question as to which of these Fundamental Substances, was the really fundamental one, must also then have arisen. Therefore, the Ṛṣi of that hymn gives the following explanation, in order to explain what the truth (*bīja*) about the whole thing was in the following words:

nāsadāsīn no sad āsīt tadānīm
nāsīd rajo no vyomā paro yat ।
kim āvarīvaḥ kuha kasya śarma-
nnambhaḥ kim āsīd gahanaṁ gabhīram ॥ 1 ॥

that is: (1) "then, that is, in the beginning, there was neither *asat*, nor *sat*, nor the firmament (*antarikṣa*), nor the ether (*ākāśa*) beyond it. (In this state) who (can be said to have) covered (whom)? Where? For whose benefit? Was there (even) unfathomable and deep water ?"*

na mṛtyur āsīd amṛtaṁ na tarhi
na rātryā anha āsīt praketaḥ ।
ānīd avātaṁ svadhayā tad ekaṁ
tasmād dhānyan na paraḥ kiṁcanāsa ॥ 2 ॥

that is: (2) "then, death, that is, the perishable, visible, mortal universe was not existing; and, therefore, there was not (the distinction of) also (another) *amṛta*, i. e., imperishable, eternal substance. (Similarly) there was no means (= *praketa*) for finding out the difference between day and night. (Whatever there was) That solitary thing was breathing, that is, throbbing by *svadhā*, that is, by its own power, without there being any air. Except or beyond that, there was nothing."

tama āsīt tamasā gūdham agre
'praketaṁ salilaṁ sarvamā idam ।
tucchenābhvapihitaṁ yad āsīt
tapasas tan mahinā 'jāyataikam ॥ 3 ॥

that is: (3) "though there was (said to be) darkness in the beginning; or that all this was water enveloped in darkness devoid of any differentiation; (or) that *ābhu*, that is, the all-pervading Brahman was (from the beginning) covered by *tuccha*, that is, by illusory Māyā; yet, that came into existence

* First *ṛcā* :—I have given the above meaning, analysing the words '*kim āsīd*' in the fourth line as "*āsīt kim*"; and the purport of it is, "water did not exist then" (Tai. Brā. 2. 2. 9).

as a result of austerity (subsequently, by transformation), from the fundamentally one Brahman" *

kāmas tad agre samavartatādhi
manaso retaḥ prathamaṁ yad āsīt ।
sato bandhum asati niravindan
hṛdi pratīṣyā kavayo manīṣā ॥ 4 ॥

that is: (4) "the semen, that is, the seed of the Mind (of This) which first came into existence, became Kāma (that is, the desire or the power to create the world). (This is) the (first) relation between *sat*, that is, the perishable visible world, and

* Third *ṛcā*:—Some commentators consider the first three lines of this stanza as independent, and interpret it by saying that in the beginning of the universe, there was "darkness, or water covered by darkness, or *ābhu* (void) covered by *tuccha*". But, according to me that interpretation is not correct. Because if in the first two stanzas there is a clear statement that nothing whatsoever existed in the beginning, it is not possible that it should be stated in this *ṛcā* that there was in the beginning either darkness or water—which is something quite the opposite. Besides, according to this interpretation, the word *yat* in the third part of the stanza has to be considered meaningless; therefore, it becomes necessary to refer the word '*yat*', in the third part of the stanza, to the word '*tat*' in the fourth part, and to interpret the stanza as has been done by me above. This *ṛcā* has been included in this hymn as an answer to those persons who maintained that there were in the beginning substances like water etc.; and what the Ṛṣi intended to say was that there were no fundamental substances like darkness, water etc., as was said by these people, but that, all that was the further development of one and the same Brahman. As the two words '*tuccha*' and '*ābhu*' are mutually opposite, the word *ābhu* means opposite of *tuccha*, that is to say, big or powerful, and the same meaning has been given to it by Sāyaṇācārya in the other two places where that word occurs in the Ṛg-Veda (Ṛg. 10. 27. 1, 4) In the *Pañcadaśī* (Chitra. 129, 130). the word *tuccha* has been interpreted as meaning Māyā (See Nṛsiṁ. Utta 9). Therefore, *ābhu* has not to be interpreted as meaning 'void' but as Parabrahman. The word *āḥ* (*a*+*as*) in the phrase '*sarvam āḥ idam*' is the past tense form of the root '*as*', and it means '*āsīt*', that is, 'was'.

the *asat*, that is, the fundamental Parabrahman, as has been ascertained by scients by means of their Reason, by meditating in their minds".

> *tiraścīno vitato raśmireṣām*
> *adhaḥ svid āsid upari svid āsīt* ।
> *retodhā āsan mahimāna āsan*
> *svadhā avastāt prayatiḥ parastāt* ॥ 5 ॥

that is: (5) "(this) *raśmi*, that is, shred or ray, fell transversely (between) them; and if you say it was below, it was also above; (some of these) became *retodhā*, that is, productive of seed, and (growing) became bigger. Their self-prowess (*svaśakti*) pervaded on one side, and *prayati*, that is, development (pervaded everything) on the other side".

> *ko addhā veda ka iha pra vocat*
> *kuta ājātā kuta iyaṁ visṛṣṭiḥ* ।
> *arvāg devā asya visarjanenā-*
> *tha ko veda yata ābabhūva* ॥ 6 ॥

that is: (6) "who is there who can in greater (than this) detail (*pra*), explain how came the *visarga*, that is, the development (of the *sat*) and from whom it came? Who knows this definitely? Even the gods came after the *visarga* of this (visible *sat* universe). Then who is to know from where it came?"

> *iyaṁ visṛṣṭir yat ābabhūva*
> *yadi vā dadhe yadi vā na dadhe* ।
> *yo asyādhyakṣaḥ parame vyoman*
> *so aṅga veda yadi vā na veda* ॥ 7 ॥

that is: (7) "The *adhyakṣa* (Hiraṇyagarbha) of this universe, inhabiting the highest (*parama*) firmament, may know the place from where the development of this *sat* came about, or, from where it was created, or was not created; or, even the Hiraṇyagarbha may not be knowing it ! (Who is in a position to say that ?)".

The sum and substance of Vedānta philosophy is, that one should not remain enmeshed in the various Name-d and Form-ed, mutable and perishable Appearances which are perceptible to the eyes or the other organs, but should recognise by means of Knowledge that THERE IS SOME, ONE AND IMMORTAL ELEMENT, which is beyond them; and, the fact that the Reason of the Ṛṣi who composed this hymn unerringly grasped the crux of the whole matter at the first attempt, clearly shows the keenness of his introspection!. Instead of entering into a discussion with persons, who raised the questions, whether That, which existed in the beginning of the universe and before the various things in the world came into existence, was *sat* or *asat*, death or immortality, ether or water, light or darkness etc., this Ṛṣi speeds beyond all of them, and says that *sat* and *asat*, mortal and immortal light and darkness, the covering and the covered, the giver of happiness and the feeler of happiness, are mutually dependent opposites, which came into existence after the visible world was created; and he asks, who was there to cover whom before these opposite couples in the world came into existence, that is to say, when there was no such difference as this one and that one. The Ṛṣi of this hymn, therefore, says, to start with, that it is not proper to describe the Fundamental, homogeneous, Substance as *sat* or *asat*, ether or water, light or darkness, death or immortality, or by such other mutually dependent expressions; he says, that whatever there was, was stranger than all these things; that It was one and one alone, and was throbbing in all directions by its inexhaustible energy; and that there was nothing else which was a mate to it or which covered it. The root word '*an*' in the verb '*ānīt*' in the second *rcā* means to breathe or to throb; and the word '*prāṇa*' is derived from that root. But who can say that That, which was neither *sat* nor *asat*, was breathing like a living being? and where was the air to breathe? Therefore, the words *avātaṁ* (that is, without air) and *svadhayā* (by its own prowess) have been added to the word '*ānīt*', and the idea that the Fundamental Element of the world was not Gross Matter, which (idea) pertains to the stage of Non-Dualism, has been very skilfully described in the language of Dualism by saying that "that ONE substance was breathing or throbbing by Its own prowess without air, that is, without depending on air!"; and the apparent contradiction in terms, which is involved in this, is the result of the insufficiency of Dualistic terminology. The descriptions of the Parabrahman to be found in the Upaniṣads, such as, "*neti, neti*", or "*ekamevādvitīyam*" or "*sve mahimni pratiṣṭhitaḥ*" (Chān. 7. 24. 1), that is, "that which subsists by Itself alone, by Its own prowess, that is, without depending on anyone else", are mere repetitions of this idea. It is clear that that indescribable Element, which has been referred to in this hymn as throbbing in all directions at the commencement of the entire universe, will survive when the entire visible universe is destroyed. Therefore, this same Parabrahman has been described in the Gītā with a slight amplification, in the words: "Which is not destroyed though all other things are destroyed" (Gī. 8. 20); and it is stated later on (Gī. 13. 12) by clear reference to this hymn that " It is neither *sat* nor *asat*". But, if there was nothing in the beginning except the qualityless Brahman, a difficulty arises as to how to dispose of such descriptions as, " there were in the beginning, water, darkness, or the couple of *ābhu* and *tuccha* ", which are to be found even in the Vedas. Therefore, this Ṛṣi says in the third *ṛcā*, that the descriptions, which we come across, to the effect that in the beginning of the universe there was darkness, or water clothed in darkness, or, that *ābhu* (Brahman) and the Māyā (*tuccha*) which covered It, existed from the very beginning, are descriptions of the ONE and sole, fundamental Parabrahman, after It had developed into a diversified expansion by the prowess of Its austere meditation, and not of Its fundamental state. The word '*tapa*' in this *ṛcā* is intended to describe the wonderful Spiritual power of the fundamental Brahman, and the same thing is described in the fourth *ṛcā*. (See Muṇ. 1. 1. 9). It need not be said that that Fundamental Substance, the result of the prowess of Which is this entire universe, according to the saying: *etāvān asya mahimā 'to jyāyāṁś ca pūruṣaḥ*" (Ṛg. 10. 90. 3), is beyond such universe and superior to and different from everything. But, though this Ṛṣi had, in this way, at a stroke cast off all Dualistic couples like, the object to be seen and the observer, the enjoyer and the enjoyed, the clother and the clothed, darkness and light, mortal and immortal etc., and come to the conclusion that there was fundamentally only one unmixed wonderful Parabrahman in the form of Consciousness (i. e., *cidrūpī*), yet, when he was faced with the problem of having to explain how the diverse, perishable, qualityful,

Name-d and Form-ed universe, consisting of the couples of water etc. or the three-constituented Prakṛti from which it (the universe) sprang, had come into existence out of this ONE and sole, indescribable, and qualityless Element, he had to take shelter under the Dualistic terminology of Mind, Desire, *asat*, *sat* etc., and he ultimately frankly admits that this question is beyond the grasp of human Reason. In the fourth *ṛcā*, the fundamental Brahman has been referred to as *asat*; but that word cannot be interpreted as meaning 'nothing'; because, already in the second *ṛcā*, there is a clear statement that 'It is'. Not only in this hymn, but in the Ṛg-Veda and the Vājasaneyi Saṁhitā, moot questions have been asked, making use of the language of ordinary parlance, by comparing the visible world with a sacrifice (*yajña*), and asking from where the ingredients such as, clarified butter, dried sticks etc. necessary for performing the *yajña* were initially brought (Ṛg. 10. 130. 3); or, by taking the illustration of a house, and asking the question as to from where the timber (fundamental Prakṛti) for constructing this imposing edifice of ether and the earth, which is actually visible to the eyes, out of one Fundamental qualityless Substance, was brought; such as, "*kiṁ svid vanaṁ ka u sa vṛkṣa āsa yato dyāvāpṛthivī niṣṭatakṣuḥ* (Ṛg. 10. 31. 7; 10. 81. 4; Vāja. Saṁ. 17. 20). These questions cannot be answered further than by saying what has been said in the fourth and fifth stanzas of this hymn, that is to say, by saying that the Kāma-formed Element of creating the universe, somehow or other came into existence in the Mind of that indescribable ONE and sole Parabrahman, and that the entire development of *sat*, that is, the imposing edifice of ether and earth, came into existence as a result of its branches spreading out above and below, and in all directions, like the threads in a piece of cloth or the rays of sunshine. (Vāja. Saṁ. 33. 74). And, therefore, the meaning conveyed in this hymn has been adopted in the Upaniṣads in the words: "*so 'kāmayata* । *bahu syām prajāyeyeti* ।" (Tai 2. 6; Chān. 6. 2. 3), that is, "that Parabrahman acquired the Desire of becoming multifarious" (See Bṛ. 1. 1. 4); and even in the Atharva-Veda, there is a statement that 'Kāma' (Desire) came first into existence out of the Fundamental Substance at the root of the visible world (Atharva. 9. 2. 19). But, the wonder about this hymn is, that instead of becoming a slave to Reason like the Sāṁkhyas, and imagining the existence of another self-created and independent element like Fundamental Matter, because the question of the creation of the Qualityful from the Qualityless, or of the *asat* from the *sat*, or of the *dvaṁdva* (subject to doubles) from the *nirdvaṁdva* (beyond doubles), or of the *saṅga* (attached) from the *asaṅga* (unattached), is beyond the grasp of human intelligence, this Ṛṣi frankly says: "Say that you do not understand that which you do not understand; but on that account, it is not proper to give to the Illusion in the form of the visible world, the same value as the indescribable Brahman, which has been definitely ascertained by means of an absolutely purified Mind and as a self-experience. Besides, one must also realise that even if one considers the three-constituented Prakṛti as a second independent substance, one still cannot answer the question as to how Reason *(mahān)* or Individuation first entered that substance, in order that the universe should be created; and if this difficulty cannot be overcome, where is the point in looking upon Prakṛti as independent? All that one need say is, that it is impossible to understand how Prakṛti or *sat* came into existence out of the fundamental Brahman. For that, it is not necessary to look upon Prakṛti as independent. It is not possible even for gods to find out how *sat* came into existence; much less, then, for human intelligence; because, as even the gods came into existence after the visible world, how can they know anything about it? (Gī. 10. 2). But, some one may here raise the following doubt: it is stated in the Ṛg.-Veda itself that the Hiraṇyagarbha is prior in point of time and superior even to the gods, that He alone was in the beginning "*bhūtasya jātaḥ patireka āsīt*" (Ṛg. 10. 121. 1), that is, "the '*pati*', or 'king', or '*adhyakṣa*, of the entire universe"; then, how can He not be knowing this Thing?; and, if it is possible for Him to have known it, how can you say that It is unknowable? Therefore, the Ṛṣi gives, in the beginning, a formal answer to that question by saying: "Yes, He may be knowing the answer to it"; but, immediately thereafter, this Ṛṣi, who seeks by his Reason to fathom the knowledge of even Brahmadeva, ultimately and in a state of doubt says: "Or, He may even not be knowing it! Who can say?; because, as He also falls within the category of *sat*, how can this '*adhyakṣa*' or king of the universe, who lives in what is in fact ether (*ākāśa*), though you may call it '*parama*', have a definite knowledge about something which existed before *sat* or *asat*, ether or water, came into existence?" But, although he does not know how this ONE, *asat*, that is, imperceptible, and qualityless Substance came into contact with the variegated Name-d and Form-ed *sat*, that is, Prakṛti, yet, he does not swerve from his Non-Dualistic conviction that this fundamental Brahman is ONE and only ONE!. This is an excellent example of how the human mind fearlessly roams about like a lion in the impregnable forests of unimaginable things, on the strength of its *sāttvika* devotion and its pure inspiration, and defines, to whatever extent it can, the unimaginable things existing in that forest; and it is really a matter of great surprise that this hymn is to be found in the Ṛg-Veda. The subject-matter of this hymn has been very minutely examined in our country, and also by Kant and other philosophers in the Western countries, by considering the Brāhmaṇas, the Upaniṣads, and the later treatises on Vedānta philosophy (Taitti. Brā. 2. 8. 9). But, nobody has so far gone beyond giving to the opposite party convincing arguments like the Vivartavāda for making firmer, clearer, or logically more unquestionable those very doctrines which inspired the pure mind of this Ṛṣi, as appearing in this hymn; and we need not entertain any hopes that anybody will do so.

The chapter on the philosophy of the Absolute Self, (*adhyātma*) is now over. Before I go further, I will, following the usual practice of the '*kesari*' (lion), and look back on the subject-matter or road which I have so far traversed; because, unless such a lion-look has been given, there is a risk of the link between this subject-matter and the next being lost, and of one's going astray. In the beginning of this book, after introducing my readers to the subject-matter, I have concisely explained to them the nature of Karma jijñāsā (Desire for Action), and shown to them in the third chapter, that the science of Karma-Yoga (Proper Action) is the subject-matter of exposition in the Gītā. Then, after having proved in the fourth, fifth and sixth chapters, by considering the question of happiness and unhappiness, that the Materialistic exposition of this subject-matter is one-sided and insufficient, and that its Intuitional exposition is lame, I have, before entering into the Metaphysical exposition of Karma-Yoga, and already in the sixth chapter, dealt with the question of the Body and the Ātman in order to determine what the Ātman is; and having in the seventh and eighth chapters dealt with the subject-matter of the Mutable and the Immutable according to the Dualistic Sāṁkhya philosophy, I have in this chapter explained what the nature of the Ātman is, and in what way ONE, sole, immortal and qualityless Ātman-Element saturates fully and eternally both the Body and the Cosmos; and I have finally drawn the conclusion that the Yoga of acquiring an equable frame of Mind, which believes that there is only one Ātman in all created beings, and keeping that frame of Mind perpetually alive, is the climax of Self-Knowledge (*ātmajñāna*) and of Self-Happiness (*ātmānanda*); and that the highest humanness of man, that is, the fulfilment of the purpose of human birth, or the highest ideal of a human being, consists in bringing one's mind to this pure Self-Devoted (*ātma-niṣṭha*) state. Having, in this way, determined what the highest Metaphysical ideal of mankind is, the question as to the basis on which one has to perform all the various Actions in this world, or, as to what is the nature of that Pure Reason with which those Actions are to be performed, which is the principal question in the science of Karma-Yoga, is *ipso facto* solved. Because, as need not be told, all these Actions must be performed in such a way as will not be ultimately inconsistent with, but will foster, that equable frame of mind, which looks upon the Brahman as identical with the Ātman. This Metaphysical philosophy of Karma-Yoga has been explained to Arjuna in the Bhagavadgītā. But, the justification of the Karma-Yoga is not thereby finished. Some persons say that in as much as the Actions to be performed in this Name-d and Form-ed world are inconsistent with Self-Knowledge, a scient must give them up. And, if that were so, all the activities in the world would become unperformable, and consequently, the science of what ought to be done and what ought not to be done would also become meaningless! Therefore, in order to determine this question, the Karma-Yoga science must also deal with such important questions as: what are the rules relating to Action, aud what are the effects of Action, or why this Action or Karma must be performed, although the Mind may have become purified; and, therefore, these questions have also been dealt with in the Bhagavadgītā. As people following the Path of Renunciation attach no importance to these questions, they usually begin to close their shop as soon as the subject-matter of Vedānta or of Devotion in the Bhagavadgītā has been dealt with. But, doing so, amounts, in my opinion, to sadly neglecting the most important doctrine enunciated in the Gītā; and, therefore, I shall, in their respective order, explain what answers have been given in the Bhagavadgītā to these various questions.

CHAPTER X.

THE EFFECT OF KARMA AND FREEDOM OF WILL.

(KARMA-VIPĀKA AND ĀTMA-SVĀTAṀTRYA).

karmaṇā badhyate jantur vidyayā tu pramucyate । *

Mahābhārata, Śānti. 240. 7.

Although the proposition that, whatever there is in the world, is the Parabrahman, and that there is nothing else besides the Parabrahman, is true in effect, yet, when one passes through the sieve of Spiritual Knowledge the various objects in the visible world, which are perceived by the human organs, one has to divide everything into two factors, namely, (i) the daily changing, that is, non-permanent Name-d and Form-ed Appearance of those objects, which is actually visible to the organs, and (ii) the invisible but permanent Paramātman-Element, which is clothed in these Names and Forms. It is true that these two factors cannot be placed before the eyes individually, in the same way as a substance is analysed and its components separated from each other in Chemistry. But, from the point of view of Knowledge, these two factors have to be separated from each other, and for convenience of scientific treatment, they are respectively called 'Brahman' and 'Māyā', or the 'BRAHMAN-WORLD' and the 'MĀYĀ-WORLD'. Nevertheless, as the Brahman is fundamentally Eternal and Real, the word 'world' is suffixed to it merely for rhyme. The word 'Brahman-*world*' is not to be understood as indicating that the Brahman was *created* by somebody. I have considered, in the last chapter, what the pure form of the Ātman and the highest ideal of mankind are, by searching with spiritual eyes, the Brahman-world out of these two worlds, which is not limited by Names and Forms like Time and Space, and is eternal, permanent, imperishable, immortal, and independent, and which, remaining at the core of the visible world, is the foundation of it; and strictly speaking, the pure philosophy of the Absolute Self ends at that point. But, although the human Ātman belongs

* "A living being is bound by Karma, and it is released by Knowledge".

fundamentally to the Brahman-world, yet, like other things in the visible world, it is covered by bodily organs in the shape of Names and Forms, and these Names and Forms in the shape of the bodily organs are perishable. Therefore, every human being is naturally desirous of knowing how it is possible to escape from these Names and Forms, and to attain immortality; and, in order to consider what mode of life has to be adopted for satisfying that desire, which subject belongs to the science of Karma-Yoga, we must now enter the Dualistic territory of the non-permanent MĀYĀ-WORLD which is bound by the laws of Karma (Action). If there is fundamentally only one permanent and independent Ātman, both in the Body and in the Cosmos, the questions which necessarily arise, are, what are the difficulties which are experienced by the Ātman in the body, in Realising the Ātman in the Cosmos, and how those difficulties can be overcome; and, in order to solve these questions, it becomes necessary to expound what Names and Forms are; because, as all objects fall into the two classes of the Ātman or Parabrahman, and the Name-d and Form-ed covering on It, nothing else now remains for consideration except the Name-d and Form-ed covering. As this Name-d and Form-ed covering is dense in some cases and thin in other cases, the objects in the visible world fall, according to Vedānta, into the two classes of *sacetana* (Activated) and *acetana* (Non-Activated), and even the Activated are again sub-divided into animals, birds, men, gods, *gandharvas*, and demons etc. There is no place where the Brahman in the shape of Ātman does not exist. It is in the stone, and It is in the human being. But, as there is a difference according to whether a light is put into an iron box, or in a lantern with more or less clean glasses, though it may be one and the same light, so also, although the Ātman-Element is everywhere the same, the different divisions of Activated and Non-Activated arise, as a result of the difference in density of the clothing of Names and Forms in each case. Nay, that is the reason why, even among the Activated, the power of acquiring Knowledge is not the same in the case of men and beasts. It is true that the Ātman is the same everywhere; yet, as it is fundamentally qualityless and apathetic, it cannot by itself do anything, without some Name-d and Form-ed means like the Mind, Reason etc.; and, as these means are not fully available to the Ātman except in the human birth, such birth is considered to be the most superior of all. When the Ātman has got this human birth, this its Name-d and Form-ed clothing falls into the two divisions of Gross and Subtle. According to Vedānta, this gross clothing is the embodiment of the mixture of blood and semen; and whereas, muscles, bones, and nerves grow from the semen, skin, flesh, hair etc. grow from the *śoṇita*, that is, from the blood; and all this is referred to as the '*annamaya-kośa*' (covering made up of food). When we pass this covering and go further inside, we come across Life in the shape of breath, that is, the '*prāṇamaya-kośa*'; the Mind, that is, the *manomaya-kośa;* Reason, that is, the *jñānamaya-kośa*; and ultimately, the *ānandamaya-kośa.* The Ātman is beyond all these; and therefore, in the Taittirīyopaniṣad, Varuṇa has acquainted Bhṛgu with the various forms of the Ātman by describing to him the various envelopes (*kośa*) rising from the *annamaya-kośa* to the *ānandamaya-kośa* (Tai. 2. 1-5; 3. 2-6). Vedāntists refer to these envelopes (*kośa*), except the Gross Body, such as the Prāṇa-covering etc., together with the subtle organs and the five Fine Elements (Tanmātras) as the '*liṅga*' or the '*sūkṣma śarīra*' (the Subtle Body). But, instead of explaining the fact of the Ātman taking births in various species of life *(yoni)* by imagining the existence of diverse 'Bhāvas' of the Reason (See p. 261 above—Trans.) as is done by the Sāṁkhyas, they say that that is the result of Karma-Vipāka, or the fruit of Action. It has been clearly stated in the Gītā, the Upaniṣads, and the Vedānta-Sūtras, that this Karma clings to the support of the Subtle Body, and when the Ātman leaves the Gross Body, this Karma accompanies the Ātman, embodied in the Subtle Body, and compels it to take birth after birth. Therefore, in considering the difficulty which stands in the way of the embodied Ātman attaining the Parabrahman, or obtaining Release, after escaping the cycle of birth and death in the shape of Names and Forms, one has to consider both Karma and the Subtle Body. Out of these, the Subtle Body has been dealt with before, both from the point of view of the Sāṁkhya philosophy, as of Vedānta; and, therefore, I shall not repeat the same subject-matter here. In this chapter, I have considered only the nature of that Karma or Action, whereby the Ātman falls into the cycle of birth and death instead of Realising the Brahman, and also how a man has to live in this world in order that the Ātman should escape that cycle and acquire immortality. Those qualities of Time and Space embodied in Name and Form, as a result of which the fundamental, non-perceptible, and qualityless Parabrahman existing at the commencement of the world, appears in the form of the visible world, are known in Vedānta philosophy as 'Māyā' (Gī. 7. 24, 25), and that also includes Karma (Bṛ. 1. 6. 1). Nay, we may even say that 'Māyā' and 'Karma' are synonymous; because, unless some Karma or Action has been performed, it is not possible for the Imperceptible to become Perceptible, or for the Qualityless to become Qualityful. Therefore, the Blessed Lord has, after first saying "I take birth in Prakṛti by my Māyā" (Gī. 4. 6), defined Karma later on in the eighth chapter of the Gītā itself, as: "the Action, whereby the variegated Cosmos, such as, the five primordial elements etc. comes into existence out of the imperishable Parabrahman is known as 'Karma' (Gī. 8. 3). Karma has been here used in the comprehensive meaning of Activity or Action–whether it is performed by a human being or by the other objects in the world, or it is the activity comprised in the Cosmos itself coming into existence. But, whatever Action is taken, its result always is that one Name and Form is changed, and another comes into existence in its place; because, the Fundamental Substance, which is covered by this Name and Form, never changes and always remains the same. For instance, by the Action of weaving, the name 'thread' disappears, and the same substance gets instead the name of 'cloth'; and by the Action of a potter, the name 'pot' takes the place of the name 'earth'. Therefore, in defining Māyā, Karma or Action is sometimes not mentioned at all, and only Name and Form are included in Māyā. Yet, when one has to consider Karma by itself, one has to say that the form of Karma is the same as the form of Māyā. Therefore, it is more convenient to make it clear in the very beginning that Māyā, Names and

Forms, and Karma are fundamentally the same in nature. One can, it is true, make the subtle distinction that MĀYĀ is the common word, and its Appearance has the specific name of Names and Forms, and its Activity, the specific name of KARMA. But, as ordinarily it is not necessary to make this distinction, these three words are very often used synonymously. This clothing (or this *upādhi* i. e., superimposed covering) of perishable Māyā on one part of the Parabrahman, which is visible to the eyes, has been described in Sāṁkhya philosophy as the three-constituented Prakṛti. Sāṁkhya philosophers look upon Puruṣa and Prakṛti as two self-created, independent and eternal Elements. But, as Māyā, Names and Forms, or Karma change constantly, it would be logically incorrect to look upon them as of the same standard as the permanent and immutable Parabrahman; because, as the two ideas, 'permanent' and 'non-permanent', are contrary to each other, both of them cannot become applicable at the same time. Therefore, Vedāntists have come to the conclusion that Perishable Prakṛti or Māyā, in the shape of Karma, is not independent, but that the Appearance of a qualityful Māyā is seen in the one, permanent, all-pervading, and qualityless Parabrahman by the feeble human organs. But, it is not enough to say, that Māyā is not independent, and that one only sees this Appearance in the qualityless Parabrahman. Although, according to Vivartavāda, if not according to the Guṇapariṇāma-vāda, it is possible to see this Appearance of qualityful Names and Forms, that is, of Māyā in the qualityless and eternal Brahman, yet, we are faced with the further question, namely, when, in what order, and why, did this qualityful Appearance, which is seen by human organs, appear in the qualityless Parabrahman? or, to say the same thing in ordinary language, when, and why, did the eternal and thought-formed Parameśvara create the Name-d and Form-ed, perishable, and gross universe? But, as this subject is unknowable, not only to human beings, but even to gods, and to the Vedas, as stated in the Nāsadīya-Sūkta in the Ṛg-Veda (Ṛg. 10. 129; Tai. Brā. 2. 8. 9) one cannot answer that question better than by saying: "this is an unknowable pastime (*līlā*) of the qualityless Parabrahman, which has been realised by

Knowledge." (Ve. Sū. 2. 1. 33). One has to take it for granted that ever since the commencement of things, Name-d and Form-ed perishable Karma, or qualityful Māyā, has been seen side by side with the qualityless Brahman. Therefore, Karma embodied in Māyā has been called eternal in the Vedānta-Sūtras (Ve. Sū. 2. 1. 35-37), and even in the Bhagavadgītā, the Blessed Lord has, after saying that Prakṛti is not independent, but "is My Māyā" (Gī. 7. 14), said further on that this Prakṛti, that is, Māyā, and Puruṣa are both 'eternal' (Gī. 13. 19). In the same way, in describing Māyā, Śaṁkarācārya has said in this Bhāṣya or commentary, that "*sarvajñeśvarasyā 'tmabhūte ivā 'vidyākalpite nāmarūpe tattvānyatvābhyām anirvacanīye saṁsāraprapañcabījabhūte sarvajñasyeśvarasya 'māyā' 'śaktiḥ' 'prakṛtir' iti ca śrutismṛtyor abhilapyete*" (Ve. Sū. Śāṁ. Bhā. 2. 1. 14.), i. e., "the Names and Forms imagined to exist in the fundamental Brahman as a result of the ignorance (of the organs), which are supposed to be of the nature of the Ātman of the All-Scient Parameśvara, but of which, it is not possible to say whether they are different or not-different (*tattvānyatva*) from the Parameśvara, since they are Gross, and which are the root of the (visible) expansion of gross world, are, in the Śruti and Smṛti texts, called the '*māyā*', '*śakti*' or '*prakṛti*' of the all-knowing Parameśvara"; and "as the subsequent universe seems to have come into existence from the Parameśvara on account of His Māyā, this Māyā, though perishable, is essential and extremely useful for the creation of the visible universe, and it is seen to have been given the names of '*avyakta*', '*ākāśa*' and '*akṣara*' in the Upaniṣads" (Ve. Sū. Śāṁ. Bhā. 1. 4. 3). The Sāṁkhyas look upon the Elements, Knowledge-formed (*cinmaya*) Spirit, and inactive (*acetana*) Māyā (Prakṛti) as independent and eternal; but, it will be seen from the above, that, though Vedāntists admit the eternity of Māyā from one point of view, they do not accept the position that Māyā is self-created and independent; and on that account, in describing the Māyā embodied in worldly life by comparing it to a tree, the Gītā says, "*na rūpam asyeha tathopalabhyate nānto na cādir na ca saṁpratiṣṭhā*" (Gī. 15. 3), i. e., "the FORM, END, BEGINNING, root, or habitation of this tree of worldly life (*saṁsāra vṛkṣa*) cannot be found". In the same way, the descriptions which are come across in the third chapter, such as, "*karma brahmodbhavaṁ viddhi*" (Gī. 3. 15), i. e., "Karma was created out of the Brahman"; or, "*yajñaḥ karmasamudbhavaḥ*" (Gī. 3. 14), i. e., "even the Yajña springs out of Karma"; or, "*sahayajñāḥ prajāḥ sṛṣṭvā*" (Gī. 3. 10), i. e., "the Brahmadeva created *prajā* (*sṛṣṭi*) and *yajña* (Karma) at the same time", mean that, "Karma, or Yajña in the form of Karma, and the *sṛṣṭi*, that is, *prajā* (the creation) all came into existence at the same time". Then whether you say that this *sṛṣṭi* came into existence out of Brahmadeva himself, or, in the words of the Mīmāṁsā school, that it was created by Brahmadeva from the eternal Vedic words, the meaning is the same (Ma. Bhā. Śān. 231; Manu. 1. 21). In short, Karma is the activity which is to be seen in the fundamental qualityless Brahman, at the time when the visible world began to be created. This activity is known as the Name-d and Form-ed Māyā, and the activities of the Sun, the Moon, and all the other objects in the world have gradually come into existence from this fundamental Karma (Bṛ. 3. 8. 9). Scients have determined by means of their Reason that this Karma or Māyā, performed at the time of the creation of the universe, which is the foundation of all the activities in the world, is some unknowable pastime (*līlā*) of the Brahman, and not something independent of the Brahman. * But, as the scients cannot go further, it is not possible for them to ascertain 'when' this wonder, or these Names and Forms, or this Karma embodied in Māyā first came into existence. Therefore, when it is necessary to consider only this Karma-world (*karma sṛṣṭi*), it is usual in the Vedānta science (Ve. Sū. 2. 1. 35) to refer to this dependent, perishable Māyā and, at the same time, the Karma which is appurtenant to it, as 'eternal' (*anādi*). It must be borne in mind that the word '*anādi*' in this place does not mean fundamentally 'without beginning' (*nirārambha*) and independent, like the

* "What belongs to mere appearance is necessarily subordinated by reason to the nature of the Thing-in-itself" Kant's *Metaphysics of Morals* (Abbot's trans. in Kant's *Theory of Ethics*. p. 81). [In one edition, this page is shown as 18–Trans.]

Parameśvara, as is maintained by the Sāṁkhyas, but '*durjñeyārambha*' that is, "something, the beginning of which cannot be known".

But, although we are not in a position to say definitely when and why the Knowledge-formed Brahman first began to take up the Appearance of the visible world, yet, the rules by which the further activities of this Karma in the shape of Māyā go on, are fixed; and many of those rules can be determined by us. The order in which the various Name-d and Form-ed objects in the world came into existence out of the fundamental Prakṛti, that is, out of eternal Karma in the shape of Māyā, has been described by me according to the Sāṁkhya philosophy in the eighth chapter of this book; and I have, in the same place, mentioned the doctrines of modern Material sciences for comparison. It is true that Vedānta does not look upon Prakṛti as self-created like the Parabrahman; but, as the further development of Prakṛti, according to Sāṁkhya philosophy, is acceptable to Vedānta, I will not repeat that subject-matter here. Yet, in the order of the creation of the universe from fundamental Prakṛti in the shape of Karma, which has been described above, I have nowhere considered the ordinary rules according to which man has to suffer the results of Karma (Action). It is, therefore, necessary to consider those rules now. This is known as 'KARMA-VIPĀKA'. (effect of Karma). The first of the rules relating to Karma-Vipāka is that once the Karma is started, its activity or expansion continues without a break: and, though the day and night of Brahmadeva may be over and the universe destroyed, yet, this Karma survives in the form of a seed; and, when the universe begins to come into existence again, fresh sprouts grow out of that seed of Karma. It is stated in the Mahābhārata that:

yeṣāṁ ye yāni karmāṇi prāk sṛṣṭyāṁ pratipedire |
tāny eva pratipadyante sṛjyamānāḥ punaḥ punaḥ ||

(Ma. Bhā. Śān. 231, 48, 49; Gī. 8. 18 and 19).

that is, "those very Actions which have been committed by any being in the previous world, find him again and again (whether he may will it or no)". Not only is it that "*gahanā karmaṇo gatiḥ*" (Gī. 4. 17)—"the effects of Karma are unfathomable"—

but, even the persistence of Karma is very difficult to get rid of. Nobody has got rid of Karma. The wind blows by Karma. The Sun and the Moon move on account of Karma; and Brahmadeva, Viṣṇu Śaṅkar, and other qualityful gods also are all tied up in Karma. All the more so, Indra and others. Qualityful (*saguṇa*) means, defined by Name and Form; and being defined by Name and Form means Karma, or the result of Karma. In as much as it is not possible to say how Karma, in the shape of Māyā, first came into existence, it is also not possible to say when man first got involved in the cycle of Karma. But, once he has got into that cycle, however he may have got into it, he cannot later on, that is, after his Name-d and Form-ed body has been destroyed, escape taking up different Forms in this world as a result of his Actions. Because, as Material scientists have now definitely established, the energy of Karma is never destroyed, and that energy which appears to-day under one Name and Form, reappears under another Name and Form when the former Name and Form has been destroyed;* and, if he cannot escape taking up other Names and Forms after one Name and Form has been destroyed, one cannot definitely say that these various subsequent Names and Forms will be lifeless, and that it is not possible for them to be something different. This recurrence of Names and Forms is known as the cycle of births and deaths, or *saṁsāra*, according to the Philosophy of the Absolute Self; and that Energy, which is the foundation

* It is not that this idea of re-incarnation has been accepted only in the Hindu religion or by theists. Although the Buddhists do not believe in the Ātman, yet, they have wholly adopted the theory of re-incarnation into their religion; and, even in the twentieth century, the inveterately atheistic German philosopher Nietzsche, who pronounced that 'God is dead', has accepted the theory of re-incarnation. He has said that he was *inspired* with the idea or explanation that: as the perpetually recurring transformations of the energy of Karma are limited, and Time is eternal, a Name and Form which has once been created, must occur again; and, therefore, the cycle of Karma is established even from the point of view of the Material sciences. (Nietzsche's *Eternal Recurrence*, Complete works, Engl. Trans. Vol. XVI. pp. 235–256).

of these Names and Forms, is synthetically called Brahman, and distributively, Jīvātman. It is stated in the Mahābhārata and in the Manu-Smṛti, that, strictly speaking, this Ātman neither comes to birth nor dies; that it is eternal, that is, perpetual; but that, as it is involved in the cycle of Karma, one cannot escape taking up another Name and Form, when one Name and Form has been destroyed; one has to suffer to-morrow for what one does to-day, and day after to-morrow, for what one does to-morrow; nay, one has to suffer in the next birth for what one does in this birth, and in this way the cycle of the universe is continually going on; and that the results of these Actions have to be borne not only by ourselves, but even by the sons, grand-sons, and great-grand-sons, who come to birth out of our Name-d and Form-ed body (Manu. 4. 173; Ma. Bhā. Ā. 80. 3). Bhīṣma says to Yudhiṣṭhira in the Śāntiparva that:-

pāpaṁ karma kṛtaṁ kiṁcid yadi tasmin na dṛśyate ।
nṛpate tasya putreṣu pautreṣv api ca naptṛṣu ॥

(Śān. 129. 21.)

that is: "O King, although a particular man may not be seen to suffer the results of his evil actions, yet, his sons, grandsons and great-grandsons have to suffer them"; and we actually see that some incurable diseases recur hereditarily. In the same way, the fact of one person being born a beggar, and another person being born in the family of a king, has also to be explained by the theory of Karma; and, according to some, this is the proof of the correctness of the theory of Karma. Once this cycle of Karma is started, the Parameśvara Himself does not interfere with it. Seeing that the entire universe is going on by the will of the Parameśvara, who other than the Parameśvara can be the giver of the fruit of our Actions (Ve. Sū. 3. 2. 38; Kau. 3. 8)? And, for this reason, the Blessed Lord has said, "*labhate ca tataḥ kāmān mayaiva vihitān hi tān*" (Gī. 7. 22), i. e., "the desired result, which is prescribed by Me, is acquired by man". Vedānta, therefore, comes to the ultimate doctrine that though the act of prescribing the result of an Action belongs to the Parameśvara, yet, in as much as these results are fixed according to a man's good or bad Actions, that is, according to the worth of his Action, Non-action, or Bad action, the Parameśvara is, strictly speaking, apathetic in this matter; and that, therefore, if there is the distinction of good or bad among men, the Parameśvara does not, on that account, become liable to the blame of partiality (*vaiṣamya*) or cruelty (*nairghṛṇya*), (Ve. Sū. 2. 1. 34); and with reference to this position, it is stated in the Gītā that: "*samo 'haṁ sarva-bhūteṣu*" (Gī. 9. 29), i. e., "I am equal towards all", or,

nādatte kasyacit pāpaṁ na caiva sukṛtaṁ vibhuḥ ॥

(Gī. 5. 14, 15)

that is: "the Parameśvara does not accept either the sin or the meritorious Action of anybody; the cycle of the inherent effects of Karma or Māyā is continually going on; each created being has to suffer happiness or unhappiness according to its own Actions". In short, although it is not possible for human reason to explain when Karma was first started in the world by the desire of the Parameśvara, or when man first came within the clutches of Karma, yet, in as much as the further consequences or fruits of Karma are found to result according to the laws of Karma, human reason can come to the definite conclusion, that every living being has been caught in the prison of eternal Karma in the shape of Names and Forms, from the very commencement of the world. This is what is meant by the quotation given at the commencement of this chapter, namely, "*karmaṇā badhyate jantuḥ*"

The words '*saṁsāra*', '*prakṛti*', '*māyā*', 'visible world', or 'rules or laws of creation' (*sṛṣṭi*) mean the same thing as 'the eternal course of Karma'; because, the laws of creation are the laws which govern the changes which take place in Names and Forms; and, from this point of view, all Material sciences come under the denomination of Māyā defined by Names and Forms. The rules or limitations of this Māyā are hard and comprehensive; and therefore, even a pure Materialist like Haeckel, who was of the opinion that there is no Fundamental Element which is at the root of or beyond the visible world, has laid down the proposition that a man must go where the cycle of creation drags him. According to this philosopher, the feeling which every man has, that he should obtain a release from his perishable Name-d and Form-ed Appearance, or that he will obtain immortality by doing a particular thing, is a mere illusion. Not only are the Ātman or the Paramātman not independent, and not only is immortality a humbug, but, no human being in this world is a free agent to do any particular act. As whatever act a man does to-day is the result of what has been done before by him or by his ancestors, it is also never dependent on his will, whether or not to do a particular thing. For example, a desire to steal nice things belonging to others comes into existence in the hearts of particular persons against their will, as a result of previous Actions or hereditary impressions; and they are inspired to steal that particular thing. In short, these Materialists are of the opinion that the principle mentioned in the Gītā, namely, "*anicchan api vārṣṇeya balād iva niyojitaḥ*" (Gī. 3. 36), i. e., "a man commits sin, although he might not desire to do it", applies in all places in the same way, that there are no exceptions to it, and that there is no way of escaping it. From this point of view, a desire which a man gets to-day is the result of his Action of yesterday, and the desire he had yesterday was the result of his action of day before yesterday; a man can never do anything by his independent volition, as this chain of causes is endless; whatever happens is the result of former actions or of destiny, because people give the name Destiny to pre-destined Karma; and, if a man is, in this way, not free to do or not to do a particular Action, it becomes futile to say that he should improve his conduct in a particular way, or that he should, in a particular manner, realise the identity of the Brahman and the Ātman and purify his intelligence. Like a log which has fallen in the stream of a river, one must without demur go wherever Māyā, Prakṛti, the laws of Creation, or the Stream of Karma drags him, whether that is progress or regress. In reply to this, some other evolutionist Materialists say that in as much as the form of Prakṛti is not steady, and Names and Forms continually change, man should watch and find out by what rules of creation these changes take place, and bring about such a change in the external creation as will be beneficial to him; and we see in actual life, that by following this logic, man utilises fire or electricity for his own benefit. Similarly, it is our experience that human nature can to some extent be altered by effort. But, the question in hand is not whether or not there can be a change in the formation of the universe or in human nature, nor whether or not man should effect such a change; and we have, at the moment, to determine whether or not a man is in a position to control or to yield to the inspiration or desire which he has to bring about such a change. And if, from the point of view of Materialistic philosophy, the fulfilment or non-fulfilment of this desire is pre-destined by the laws of Prakṛti, or of Karma, or of the Creation, according to the principle '*buddhiḥ karmānusāriṇī*', then it follows, according to this philosophy, that a man is not free or independent to do or not to do a particular Action. This doctrine is known by the name '*vāsanāsvātaṁtrya*' (Freedom of Desire), or '*icchāsvātaṁtrya*' (Freedom of Will), or '*pravṛttisvātaṁtrya*' (Freedom of Inclination). And if one considers the matter purely from the point of view of the Effects of Karma (*karma-vipāka*) or of the purely Materialistic philosophy, one has to come to the conclusion that no man has got any kind of freedom of inclination or freedom of will, and that every man is circumscribed in all directions like the unbreakable iron ring fixed on the wheel of a cart. But, if one takes the evidence of his own Conscience in this matter, it will be seen that although one may not possess the power of making the Sun rise in the West, yet, we believe that doing or not doing, after careful consideration, whatever one intends to do by his own hands, or, where there is one course which is sinful and another which is meritorious, or one course which is righteous and another which is unrighteous, choosing the good or the bad course out of the two, is a thing which is subject to the control of a man's desire. We have now to see whether this belief is right or wrong. If one says that this belief is wrong, then those who commit thefts or murders are judged to be wrong-doers on the basis of this belief, and are punished accordingly; and, if one says that it is correct, then the Theory of Karma, or the Theory of Karma-Vipāka or the laws of the visible creation fall to the ground. As in the Material sciences, one has to consider only the actions of gross substances, this question does not arise there. But, it acquires importance in the science of Karma-Yoga, which deals with the duty and the non-duty of those who have acquired Knowledge, and it has to be answered; because, if it is definitely proved that there is no freedom of inclination for man, then the science of right or wrong (*vidhiniṣedha-śāstra*), which shows how to purify the mind, or explains whether a particular thing should be done or should not be done, or whether a particular thing is righteous or unrighteous, automatically loses need of consideration (Ve. Sū. 2. 3. 33);* and the height of manhood will consist in remaining in the eternal bondage of Mahāmāyā or Prakṛti, whether personally or as a result of heredity. Or, where is there any manhood left at all? Manhood will have to be considered if a person is in a position to control anything at all. What can there be except imprisonment and serfdom where a man has not the smallest authority or will? Like the bullocks tied to a plough, every one will have to toil under the authority of Prakṛti, and as our poet Shankara says, "the shackles of the inherent qualities of substances" must be perpetually kept by oneself on his feet! The attention of all scholars has been fixed on the question of the Freedom of Will, as a result of Karma-Vāda (Theory of Karma) or Daiva-Vāda (Theory of Destiny) in our country, and of the Theory of Providence in the Christian religion in former years, and of the Theory of the Laws of Nature propounded by Materialistic philosophers in modern times; and any amount of discussion has taken place, and is still taking place on this question. But as it is impossible to deal with the whole of that matter here, I am in this chapter dealing only with what the idea of the Bhagavadgitā and of Vedānta philosophy on that question is.

* This portion of the Vedānta-Sūtras is called the '*jīvakartṛtvādhikaraṇa*', and the first of these Sūtras is '*kartā śāstrārthavatvāt*,' that is to say, 'in order that the science of right or wrong should have any significance, the Jīva (Personal Self) must be considered as a doer'. When one considers the Sūtra of Pāṇini (Pā. 1. 4. 54) that:—"*svatamtraḥ kartā*" (i.e., the doer is independent), the word '*kartā*' conveys the impression of Freedom of Self; and it will be seen that this *adhikaraṇa* deals with that question.

It is true that the course of Karma is eternal, and that even the Parameśvara does not interfere with the course or cycle of Karma which has once been started. But according to our philosophers, the doctrine of Adhyātma (Philosophy of the Absolute Self), that the visible world is not purely Karma or merely Names and Forms, that there is some imperishable independent Ātman-formed Brahman-world which is clothed by these Names and Forms, and that the Ātman within the human body is a particle of that permanent and independent Parabrahman, shows the path for getting out of this seemingly unconquerable difficulty. But, before explaining this path, it is necessary to complete the description of the process of the Effects of Karma, which has remained incomplete. It is not that the rule that one has to suffer according to what one does, applies only to a particular individual. A family, a community, a nation, or even the whole universe cannot escape suffering the consequences of their Actions in the same way as an individual cannot do so; and in as much as every human being is born in some family, some community, or some country, it has to some extent to suffer on account of the Actions not only of itself, but also of the community or society, such as, the family etc. to which it belongs. But, as one has to refer ordinarily only to the Actions of a particular individual, the divisions of Karma, in the Theory of the Effects of Karma, have been made primarily by reference to a single individual. For instance, Manu has divided the evil actions of a man into bodily (*kāyika*), vocal (*vācika*) and mental (*mānasika*); and of these, prostitution, murder, and theft are called bodily Actions; the four Actions, namely, speaking what is painful, speaking an untruth, speaking what is derogatory, and speaking what is incoherent, are called vocal Actions; and the three Actions, namely, desiring the wealth of another, desiring the evil of another, and false insistence, are said to be mental Actions; and having in this way classified evil Actions or sins into ten kinds (Manu. 12.5-7; Ma. Bhā. Anu. 13.), their effects are next enumerated. Yet, this differentiation is not final; because, later on, in this very chapter, Karma has again been divided into *sāttvika*, *rājasa*, and *tāmasa*; and the characteristics of these three kinds of qualities *(guṇa)*, or of Karma, which have been given there are primarily the same as those given in the Bhagavadgītā (Gī. 14. 11-15; 18. 23-25; Manu. 12. 31-34). But, the division of Karma which one commonly comes across in the subject of the Effect of Actions is different from both these divisions; and according to that division, Karma is divided into '*saṁcita*' (Accumulated), '*prārabdha*' (Commenced), and '*kriyamāṇa*' (Being-suffered). Whatever Action has been performed by a man upto date, whether he has performed it in this birth or in the previous births, is his '*saṁcita*', i. e., 'Accumulated' Karma. This *saṁcita* is also known as '*adṛṣṭa*' (invisible), or, in the terminology of the Mīmāṁsā school, '*apūrva*' (strange). The reason for this terminology is, that any particular Action is visible only during that particular time when it is being performed; and when that time has gone, it does not any more remain in its actual form, but all that remains is its subtle, that is, invisible, or *apūrva*, that is, strange effects (Ve. Sū. Śāṁ. Bhā. 3. 2. 39, 40). Whatever may be said, the words '*saṁcita*', '*adṛṣṭa*', or '*apūrva*' undoubtedly mean the 'accumulation' of the effects of all the various Actions performed upto the moment of performing the last Action. It is not possible to suffer the effects of all these Accumulated Actions at the same time; because, the consequences of these Accumulated Actions can produce either good or bad, that is, mutually contrary effects. For instance, some Accumulated Actions lead to heaven, whereas others lead to hell; and, the results of all of them cannot possibly be enjoyed at one and the same time, but have to be enjoyed one after the other; and therefore, those out of the '*saṁcita*' (Accumulated) Actions, of which the results are first begun to be suffered are known as '*prārabdha*' (Commenced Actions), or 'that *saṁcita*, which has started'. In the Marathi language, the word '*prārabdha*' is very often used synonymously with '*saṁcita*'; but it will be seen that this meaning is not correct, and that scientifically speaking, '*prārabdha*' is only a sub-division of '*saṁcita*', which is the total aggregate of Actions. *prārabdha* is not the whole of *saṁcita*, but that portion of *saṁcita*, the effects (kārya) of which, one has begun to suffer for; and, therefore, '*prārabdha*' is also called '*ārabdha-kārya*

(Commenced Action). In addition to Commenced and Accumulated Action, a third division of Karma is ordinarily made, namely, the '*kriyamāṇa*'. '*kriyamāṇa*' is a derivative participle indicating the present tense, and means 'that Action which is now going on, or which we are now performing'. But, whatever we are now doing is the result of the Commenced Karma, that is to say, of that portion of Accumulated Karma which we have commenced to suffer for. Therefore, I do not see any reason for making the third division, '*kriyamaṇa*' (Being-suffered). It is true that one can differentiate between Commenced and Being-suffered Karma by saying that the Commenced Karma is the cause and the Being-suffered is its effect *(phala)*, that is to say, its product *(kārya)*. But, this distinction is of no use in the process of suffering the results of Actions. Some word is necessary to indicate those Actions, out of the Accumulated Karma, which one has not yet commenced to suffer for, that is to say, which remain over after the Commenced is deducted from the Accumulated. Therefore, in the Vedānta Sūtras (Ve. Sū. 4. 1. 15), Commenced Karma is known as '*prārabdha-kārya*', and all the Actions which are not '*prārabdha*' are known as '*anārabdha-kārya*' (Actions, which one has not yet begun to suffer for). In my opinion, it is scientifically more accurate to divide Accumulated Action *(saṁcita-kārya)* into *prārabdha-kārya* and *anārabdha-kārya* in this way; and therefore, instead of understanding the word '*kriyamāṇa* (Being-suffered) as a derivative participle indicating the present tense, we can look upon it as indicating the future tense on the strength of the Sūtra of Pāṇini: "*vartamāna sāmipye vartamānavadvā*" (Pā. 3. 3. 131), and interpret it as meaning "that, which is to be suffered for, soon in the future"; in this way, *kriyamāṇa* will mean *anārabdha-kārya*, and the words *prārabdha* (Commenced) and *kriyamāṇa* (To-be-Suffered) will respectively be synonymous with *ārabdha-kārya* (Commenced Karma) and *anārabdha-kārya* (Uncommenced Karma) of the Vedānta-Sūtras. But now-a-days, at any rate, no one interprets the word '*kriyamāṇa*' in that way; and *kriyamāṇa* is interpreted as meaning the Actions which are now being suffered for. But, if it is taken in that meaning, not only has one to call the result of *prārabdha* by the name *kriyamāṇa*, but the interpretation becomes further subject to the serious objection, that none of the words '*saṁcita*', '*prārabdha*' or '*kriyamāṇa*' can be used for showing the *anārabdha-kārya*. On the other hand, it is also not proper to disregard the ordinary meaning of the word '*kriyamāṇa*'. Therefore, instead of accepting the commonly accepted divisions of Karma in the *saṁcita*. *prārabdha*, and *kriyamāṇa*, in discussing the process of suffering the results of Actions, I divide Karma into *ārabdha-kārya* (Commenced Karma) and *anārabdha-kārya* (Uncommenced Karma); and that is also scientifically more convenient. The action of 'suffering' is divided, according to the tense, into 'that which has been suffered' (past), 'that which is now being suffered' (present), and 'that which has still to be suffered' (future). But, in the science of the Effects of Karma, Karma cannot be divided into three divisions in this way. Because, that portion of Accumulated Karma (*saṁcita*), which is suffered for after having become Commenced Karma (*prārabdha*), produces results which go again to swell the ranks of Accumulated Karma (*saṁcita*): and, therefore, in considering the question of the suffering for Actions, it is not necessary to divide *saṁcita* further than into *prārabdha*, which means that which one has begun to suffer for, and *anārabdha*, which means that which one has not yet begun to suffer for. When the effects of all Actions have, in this way, been classified into a two-fold division, the science of the effects of Karma now tells us about the suffering of those effects, that Accumulated Karma is all that has to be suffered for. Out of this, those Actions, the suffering of the effects of which has resulted in one's acquiring the present birth, that is to say, that portion of Accumulated Karma which has become Commenced Karma, cannot be escaped suffering for—"*prārabdhakarmaṇām bhogād eva kṣayaḥ*". In the same way as an arrow, which has left one's hands, cannot come back, but must go on upto its destination, or, as once the wheel of the potter starts to revolve, it will go on revolving until the force of the revolution has been exhausted, so also does *prārabdha*, that is, that Karma for the results of which one has begun to suffer, go on. Whatever has been started, must come to an end; there is no escape from it. But, the same is not the case with the Karma, which is *anārabdha-kārya.* One can totally annihilate all this kind of Karma by means of Knowledge. As a result of this important difference between the Commenced Karma *(prārabdha kārya)* and Uncommenced Karma *(anārabdha kārya)*, the scient has got to patiently wait for a natural death, even after having acquired Knowledge, that is to say, until the Karma, which has started with his body coming to birth, comes to an end. If instead of doing so, he puts an end to his life, then, although he may have destroyed his *anārabdha* Karma by means of Knowledge, yet, he will have to take another birth for suffering the effects of that *prārabdha-karma,* which made him take the former birth, and the suffering of which has remained incomplete as a result of his perversity in putting an end to his life; and both the Vedānta and the Sāṁkhya philosophy have drawn the conclusion that on that account he will necessarily not attain Release (Ve. Sū. 4. 1. 13–15 and Sāṁ. Kā. 67). Besides, committing suicide in defiance of these natural laws will be another Karma, which will have been started, and it will be necessary to take another birth to suffer the consequences of that Karma. From this, it will be clear, that from the point of view of the doctrine of Karma, even suicide is a madness.

I have now mentioned the divisions of Karma from the point of view of suffering the Effects of Karma. I shall now consider in what way, that is, by what device one can escape the bonds of Karma. The first of these devices is that prescribed by the supporters of the Karma-Vāda (Doctrine of Karma). '*anārabdha-kārya*' has been defined by me above as those Accumulated Actions, for which one has to suffer in the future—whether they can be suffered for in this life or it is necessary to take other births to suffer them. But, disregarding this meaning, some followers of the Mīmāṁsā school have found out a way, easy in their opinion, for obtaining Release. As has been stated before in the third chapter, Karma is divided by the Mīmāṁsā school into *nitya* (daily), *naimittika* (occasional), *kāmya* (desire-prompted), and *niṣiddha* (forbidden). Out of these, if one fails to perform the daily Actions like *saṁdhyā* (worship at twilight) etc., one incurs sin; and the occasional Actions have to be performed whenever the occasion arises. Therefore, according to the Mīmāṁsā school, both these kinds of Actions have to be performed. That leaves the *kāmya* and the *niṣiddha* Actions. Out of these, one incurs sin by performing the *niṣiddha* (forbidden) Actions, and, therefore, they should not be performed; and as, by performing the *kāmya* (desire-prompted) Actions, one has to take birth after birth to suffer their effects, they too should not be performed. When a man, in this way, mentally balances the effects of Actions, and gives up some Actions and performs others according to the prescribed rites, he must automatically obtain Release; because, the *prārabdha-karma* is exhausted by its being suffered for in this life; and by performing the daily and the occasional Actions and eschewing the forbidden ones in this life, one escapes perdition; and by giving up desire-prompted Actions, there does also not remain the necessity of enjoying heavenly happiness. When the suffering in this world and in hell and in heaven has thus been exhausted, no other state is possible for the Ātman except Release. This doctrine is known as '*karma-mukti*' or '*naiṣkarmya-siddhi*' (salvation by abstinence from Action). The state in which in spite of performing an Action, one is in the same position as if one did not perform it, that is to say, in which the doer does not suffer the bondage of the sin or the merit of the Action, is known as the '*naiṣkarmya*' state. But, Vedānta philosophy has proved that, one does not fully succeed in *naiṣkarmya* by this device of the Mīmāṁsā school (Ve. Sū. Śāṁ. Bhā. 4. 3. 14); and for the same reason, the Gītā says: "*naiṣkarmya* does not result from abstinence from Actions, nor does one obtain Release by giving up Action" (Gī. 3. 4). In the first place, it is impossible to eschew all the forbidden Actions, and Ethics itself says that by making a *naimittika* (occasional) *prāyaścitta* (self-imposed penance), one does not entirely get rid of the sin of having performed that forbidden Action. Yet, even taking it for granted that such a thing is possible, the statement of the Mīmāṁsā school that by suffering for the '*prārabdha*' Karma, and performing the various performable Actions in the manner mentioned above in this life, or by not performing them, one exhausts accumulation of *saṁcita* Karma, is itself not correct; because, if the results of two accumulated Actions are contrary to each other, e. g., if the effect of one is heavenly happiness, and that of the other, the tortures of hell, then, as it is not possible to suffer both at the same time and at the same place, it is impossible to exhaust the suffering for the effects of the entire '*saṁcita*' Karma by the '*prārabdha*' which has been started in this life, and by the Actions which have to be performed in this life. It is stated in the Parāśaragītā in the Bhārata that,.

kadācit sukṛtaṁ tāta kūṭastham iva tiṣṭhati ı
majjamānasya saṁsāre yāvad duḥkhād vimucyate ıı

(Ma. Bhā. Śān. 290. 17)

that is, "sometimes, the meritorious Actions previously performed by a man wait (to give him their beneficial effects) until he has escaped from the pain of this worldly life"; and the same argument applies to the Accumulated sins. Thus, suffering the effects of Accumulated Karma is not exhausted in one life, and some portion of the Accumulated Karma, always remains over as *anārabdha-kārya* (Uncommenced Karma); and, even if all Actions in this life are performed in the manner mentioned above, one still does not escape having to take another birth for suffering the Uncommenced Karma which is part of the Accumulated Karma. Therefore, Vedānta philosophy has come to the conclusion, that this seemingly easy device of the Mīmāṁsā school for obtaining Release, is false and misleading. No Upaniṣad has mentioned this way of escaping the bondage of Karma. This device has been erected merely on the foundation of inference, and this inference does not stand the test till the end. In short, expecting to escape the bondage of Karma merely by performing Karma, is as foolish as expecting a blind man to save another blind man by showing him the right way. Well; if one does not accept this device of the Mīmāṁsā school, and sits idle without performing any Action, expecting thereby to escape the bondage of Karma, that too is not possible; because, not only does the suffering for the Uncommenced Karma remain in balance, but the idea of giving up Karma, as also the act of sitting idle are both *tāmasa* Actions in themselves, and one cannot escape having to take another birth in order to suffer the effects of these *tānusa* Actions, simultaneously with suffering for those of the Uncommenced portion of one's Accumulated Karma (See Gī. 18. 7 and 8). Besides, so long as this body is alive, breathing, sleeping, sitting and such other Actions continue; and, therefore, the position of giving up all Actions also becomes untenable; and it has been stated in various places in the Gitā, that no one can even for a single moment escape Karma in this world (See Gī. 3. 5; 18. 11).

When it has thus been proved, that whether the Action be good or bad, man must always be ready to suffer the effect of it by taking some birth or other; that Karma is eternal and that even the Parameśvara does not interfere with its unbreakable continuity; that it is impossible to give up all Actions; and that one cannot escape the bondage of Karma by performing some Actions and not performing others as advised by the Mīmāṁsā school, the next question which crops up is:— how can one satisfy the natural desire of a human being to escape the cycle of Karma in the shape of perishable Names and Forms, and to go and be merged into the immortal and imperishable Element, which is at the root of that cycle. In the Vedas as also in the Smṛti texts, many devices, such as, sacrifices etc. have been prescribed for obtaining benefit in the life after death. But, from the point of view of the philosophy of Release, all these are of a lower order; because, even if one attains heaven by performing meritorious acts like sacrifices etc., yet, when the benefit of that meritorious Action is over, one does not escape having to come back again to the land of Action (*karmabhūmi*) sometime or other, though it may be after the expiry of a very long period of time (Ma. Bhā. Vana. 259 and 260; Gī. 8. 25 and 9.20) In short, it is quite clear that this is not the correct path for being merged into the immortal substance and finally and permanently escaping from the troublesome cycle of births and deaths by escaping the clutches of Karma. According to the philosophy of the Absolute Self, Jñāna (knowledge) is the only way to permanently escape this troublesome cycle, that is to say, to obtain Release. 'Jñāna' does not mean the knowledge of the ordinary things of life *(vyavahāra-jñāna)*, or the knowledge of the creation defined by Names and Forms, but the Realisation of the identity of the Brahman and the Ātman. This is also known as 'Vidyā', and the word '*vidyā*' which has been used in the line "*karmaṇā badhyate jantuḥ vidyayā tu pramucyate*", i. e., "a man is tied by *karma* and released by *vidyā*", which has been quoted in the beginning of this chapter, means 'Jñāna' (Knowledge). In the Bhagavadgītā the Blessed Lord says to Arjuna :—

jñānāgniḥ sarvakarmāṇi bhasmasāt kurute 'rjuna ।

(Gī. 4. 37).

that is, "all Karma is reduced to ashes in the fire of Knowledge" ; and also in the Mahābhārata, it has been stated in two places, that :

bījāny agny upadagdhāni na rohanti yathā punaḥ ।
jñānadagdhais tathā kleśair nātmā saṁpadyate punaḥ ॥

(Ma. Bhā. Vana. 199. 106, 107 : Śān. 211. 17).

that is, "in the same way as a seed, which has been burnt, will not take root, so also when the suffering (of Karma) has been burnt by Jñāna, it does not have to be suffered for again by the Ātman." In the Upaniṣads also, there are several phrases which mention the great worth of Jñāna, as follows :—"*ya evaṁ vedāhaṁ brahmāsmīti sa idaṁ sarvaṁ bhavati*" (Bṛ. 1. 4. 10), i. e., "he who realises that he is the Brahman, becomes immortal Brahman" ; or, in the same way as water does not adhere to the lotus leaf, so also is that person who has acquired the Knowledge of the Brahman not defiled by Karma (Chān. 4. 14. 3) ; or, one who realises the Brahman obtains salvation (Tai. 2. 1); or, he, who has Realised that everything is saturated by the Ātman, is not at any time affected by sin (Bṛ. 4. 4. 23); or "*jñātvā devaṁ mucyate sarvapāśaiḥ*" (Śve. 5. 13; 6. 13), i. e., "a man escapes from all bonds after he has acquired the knowledge of the Parameśvara "; or "*kṣīyante cāsya karmāṇi tasmin dṛṣṭe parāvare*" (Muṇ. 2. 2. 8), i. e., "when one has Realised the Parabrahman, all his Karma is destroyed"; or, "*vidyayāmṛtam aśnute*" (Īśā. 11 ; Maitryu. 7. 9), i. e., "by *vidyā* (Knowledge), immortality is attained"; or "*tameva viditvāti mṛtyum eti nānyaḥ panthāḥ vidyate 'yanāya*" (Śve. 3. 8), i. e., "by Realising the Parameśvara, one acquires immortality ; there is no other path for attaining

Release." And if we consider the matter scientifically, we become more convinced of the same conclusion. Because, although whatever there is in the visible world is an embodiment of Karma, yet, in as much as that is a pastime of the Parabrahman which is the foundation of the entire universe, no Karma can affect the Parabrahman ; and, the Parabrahman though responsible for the doing of all things yet remains unaffected. As has been stated in the beginning of this chapter, all the objects in this world are divided into the two classes, Karma (Māyā) and Brahman, according to the philosophy of the Absolute Self. The only thing which he, who wishes to escape from one of these classes, that is, from Karma, can do, is to go into the other class, namely, into the Brahman; because, there being two fundamental classes of all things, there is no third state, which is free from Karma other than the Brahman-state. But, in order to achieve this Brahman-state, it is necessary to first properly understand what it is; otherwise, one will go to do one thing and actually do another thing. It will be like "*vināyakaṁ prakurvāṇo racayāmāsa vānaram*", i. e., "I wanted to make an image of Gaṇapti, but (not succeeding in it) I have made an image of a monkey." Therefore, it follows logically from the philosophy of the Absolute Self, that the true means of escaping from the bonds of Karma is to acquire a true knowledge of the form of Brahman, that is to say, of the identity of the Brahman and the Ātman, and of the unattachedness of the Brahman. The same meaning is conveyed by the statement of the Blessed Lord in the Gītā that: "he who realises that Karma does not affect Me, because I am not attached to it, becomes free from the bonds of Karma" (Gī. 4. 14 and 13. 23). But, it must not be forgotten that the word 'Jñāna' in this place does not mean merely bookish knowledge, or the mere mental process, as has been stated in the very beginning of the Śāṁkarabhāṣya on the Vedānta-Sūtras. 'Jñāna' means 'the state of becoming *brahmi-bhūta* (merged in the Brahman), or the Brāhmi-state, which a man acquires after having acquired Spiritual Knowledge and conquered his organs.' The whole of this meaning is intended in each place. The same definition of Jñāna according to the philosophy of the Absolute Self has been mentioned at the end of the last chapter; and even in the Mahābhārata (Śān. 320. 30), Janaka has said to Sulabhā that:– "*jñānena kurute yatnaṁ yatnena prāpyate mahat*", i. e., "when a man has acquired Jñāna, which means Jñāna in the form of mental activity, he is inspired to effort; and by this path of effort, he ultimately reaches the Mahat-Element (Parameśvara)". The philosophy of the Absolute Self cannot tell one anything more than what path has to be followed, and where one has to go, in order to attain Release. When philosophy has told one these things, it is for everybody by his own efforts to remove all the thorns or obstacles which there may be in the path prescribed by it, and to clear up the road, and ultimately attain the ideal by that road. But, even this effort may be made in different ways, such as, the Pātañjala-Yoga, Meditation on the Absolute Self, Devotion, or Renunciation of the fruit of Effort etc. (Gī. 12. 8–12); and on that account, a man is very often confused. Therefore, the Gītā after first mentioning the Desireless Karma-Yoga as the most important of these means, has also described in the sixth chapter the various devices of *yama* (restraint)—*niyama* (religious observance)—*āsana* (pose)—*prāṇāyāma* (control of breath)—*pratyāhāra* (withdrawing the organs from the objects of sense)—*dhāraṇā* (keeping the mind collected)—*dhyāna* (meditation)—*samādhi* (mental absorption into the object of meditation) etc. which are appurtenant to it; and from the seventh chapter onwards, it is stated how this Realisation of the Parameśvara is acquired, while observing the Karma-Yoga, by means of meditation on the Absolute Self or by the easier Path of Devotion (Gī. 18. 56).

Though it is thus established beyond doubt that Abstention from Action is not the way for escaping the bonds of Karma; that ultimate Release is attained only by keeping the Mind pure, by Realising the identity of the Brahman and the Ātman, and by behaving like the Parameśvara; and that the idea of giving up Action is an illusion, because, no one can escape Karma, yet, the fundamental question, whether it is within the control of man to make that effort which has to be made in order to acquire the Knowledge necessary for making this course of Action successful, or whether he must go wherever Name-d and Form-ed Prakṛti will drag him, still remains unsolved. The Blessed Lord Himself has said; "*prakṛtiṁ yānti bhūtāni nigrahaḥ kiṁ kariṣyati*" (Gī. 3. 33), i. e., "what will determination do ?; every living being is bound to act according to its inherent tendencies"; and that, "*mithyaiṣa vyavasāyas te prakṛtis tvām niyokṣyati*", i. e., "your efforts and determination are useless; your Prakṛti (inherent tendencies) will drag you even where you do not want to go" (Gī. 18. 59 and 2.60) ; and even Manu has stated that "*balavān indriyagrāmo vidvāṁsam api karṣati*" (Manu. 2. 215), i. e., "the organs are too much even for scients"; and the sum and substance of the process of Causality (*karma-vipāka-prakriya*) is the same; because, once one admits that all the desires in the mind of a man are the result of previous Karma, one has to come to the conclusion that man has to move perpetually from one Karma to another Karma in the cycle of Destiny. Nay; one may even say that the inspiration to escape Karma, and Karma itself, are mutually antagonistic. And, if this is true, then one falls into the impossible position (*āpatti*) than no man is free to acquire Jñāna (Knowledge). To this the answer of the philosophy of the Absolute Self is that, in as much as the Element which is the support of the Name-d and Form-ed visible world also circulates in the gross human body in the form of an Ātman, the Actions of a human being are to be considered from the point of view both of the Body and of the Ātman. Out of these, in as much as the Ātman-formed Brahman is fundamentally one, and only one, it can never be dependent; because, in order that one should be dependent on another, the distinction of 'one' and 'another' must remain. In the present place, that 'another' is Nam-ed and Form-ed Karma. But Karma is non-permanent, and is essentially the pastime (*līlā*) of the Parabrahman ; and, therefore, although it acts as a covering over one part of the Parabrahman, it can undoubtedly never enslave the Parabrahman ; besides, as I have already stated before, that Ātman which synthesises all the activities in the world of Karma, and gives rise to one's knowledge of the creation, must be different from the Karma-world, that is to say, it must belong to the Brahman-world. It, therefore, follows that the

Parabrahman and the embodied Ātman (*śārira-ātman*), which is fundamentally a part of the Parabrahman, are both fundamentally independent, that is to say, that they are both outside the province which is subject to the control of Prakṛti. Out of these two, the Paramātman is eternal and all-pervading, and is always in the pure and released state; and that is all the knowledge which human intelligence can get of it. But, as the Jīvātman (personal Ātman), which is a part of the Paramātman (Supreme Ātman), is caught inside the cage of the Body and Reason and the other organs, though fundamentally it is in a pure and released form, and qualityless, and a non-doer, the inspiration which it gives to the human mind, can be actually perceived by us by personal experience. Although there is no force in free vapour, yet, when it is enclosed in a vessel, it begins to exert a pressure on that vessel. In the same way, when the Gross Body burdened by previous Karma, and the organs, enclose the Jīva (personal Ātman), which is a particle of the Supreme Ātman (Gī. 15. 7), the bodily organs acquire the desire and inclination to do those Actions which can liberate it (the Jīva) from this enclosure, (or, which are favourable to Release); and, that is what is known in ordinary parlance as, 'the independent tendencies of the Ātman'. The reason for my saying in 'ordinary parlance' is that, in its pure released state, or, 'from the philosophical aspect of it', the Ātman is desireless and a non-doer *(akartā)*, and all the activity is of Prakṛti (Gī. 13. 29 and Ve. Sū. Śāṁ. Bhā. 2. 3. 40). But, Vedāntins do not with the Sāṁkhyas say that this Prakṛti, of its own accord, performs Actions which favour Release; because, if one says so, it follows that gross Prakṛti can blindly release even those who have no Knowledge. And, we cannot also say that, that Ātman which is fundamentally a non-doer, will, of itself, that is to say, without any provocation, and by inherent tendencies, become a doer. Therefore, Vedānta explains the independence of the Ātman by saying, that although the Ātman is fundamentally a non-doer, yet, on account of the provocation of the enclosure of the body, it, to that extent, becomes apparently a provocator or inspirer; and, when by reason of some cause or other, the Ātman acquires this foreign power of provocation, this provocation is distinct from the laws of Karma and independent. 'Independent' (when applied to the Ātman) does not mean 'non-provocative'; and the Ātman in its fundamental, pure state is also not a doer. But, instead of everytime giving this lengthy explanation, it is usual to speak of this as the independent tendency, or the inspiration, of the Ātman. This inspiration which is received by the organs through the Ātman as a result of its being enclosed in an enclosure, and the inspiration which is received by the organs as a result of their contact with the objects in the external world, are two entirely different things. Eat, drink, and make merry are the inspirations of the organs; and the inspiration of the Ātman tells us to perform actions which are favourable to Release. The first kind of inspiration belongs purely to the external world, that is, to the Karma-world; whereas the second inspiration, namely, that of the Ātman pertains to the Brahman-world; and as these two kinds of inspiration are at the outset mutually contradictory, the greater part of a man's life is spent in the mutual warfare between them. Out of these, when a man does not accept the inspiration from the Karma-world in matters of doubt (Bhāg. 11. 10. 4), but begins to act according to the independent inspiration of the Ātman—and that is, what is understood by true *ātma-jñāna* (Spiritual Knowledge), or *ātma-niṣṭhā* (devotion to the Ātman)—all the Actions which he performs are naturally favourable to Release; and, ultimately

viśuddhadharmā śuddhena buddhena ca sa buddhimān ।
vimalātmā ca bhavati sametya vimalātmanā ।
svatantraś ca svatantreṇa svatantratvam avāpnute ॥

that is:—"the fundamentally INDEPENDENT embodied Ātman becomes merged in the permanent, pure, knowledgeful *(buddha)*, untarnished, and INDEPENDENT Supreme Ātman" (Ma. Bhā. Śān. 308. 27–30). This is what is meant by the statement above that Release is obtained by knowledge. But, on the other hand, when the inherent tendencies of the gross body and organs inspired by Prakṛti, that is to say, the inspirations from the Karma-world become predominant, a man goes to perdition. It is with reference to this independent power of the enclosed embodied Ātman to force the body and the organs to perform Actions favourable to Release, and in that way, to obtain Release by the Realisation of the identity of the Brahman and the Ātman, that the Blessed Lord has explained to Arjuna the principle of the independence of the Ātman or of self-dependence, in the following words :—

uddhared ātmanā 'tmānam nātmānam avasādayet ।
ātmaiva hy ātmano bandhur ātmaiva ripur ātmanaḥ ॥

(Gī. 6.5)

that is, "man must obtain his Release himself; he should not allow himself to be discouraged by anything; because (each one) one is one's own brother (benefactor), as also one's own enemy (destroyer)". And, it is with the same idea that the Yoga-Vāsiṣṭha has deprecated Destiny, and with great detail extolled the eminence of manhood (Yo. 2. sarga. 4-8). When a man acts in this way, realising the principle that there is only one Ātman in all created things, his conduct is described as *sadācaraṇa* (meritorious Action), or Action favourable to Release; and, as it is the independent nature of the Jīvātman to inspire the body and the organs towards Action of this kind, the conscience of the evil-doer always bears testimony in favour of meritorious Action; and, therefore, even evil-doers repent of their evil deeds. Intuitionists refer to this matter as the independent inspiration of a deity in the form of Conscience, but considering the matter from the scientific point of view, Reason cannot possibly escape the bonds of Karma, as it is an evolute of Gross Matter; and it is clear, that this inspiration must come from the Ātman which is outside the Karma-world. In the same way, the expression 'Freedom of Will' used by Western scholars is not correct from the point of view of Vedānta philosophy; because, as Desire or Will is an inherent tendency of the Mind, and as Reason, and along with Reason, the Mind, are, as stated in the eighth chapter, also the un-self-intelligible evolutes of Gross Matter in the shape of Karma, it (the Mind) cannot by itself escape the bondage of Karma. Therefore, Vedānta philosophy has laid down that true independence is not of the Mind, nor of the Reason, but of the Ātman. It is not necessary for anybody to give this independence to the Ātman, nor can anyone deprive the Ātman of it. When the particle of the independent Supreme Ātman gets caught within an enclosure, it, of itself, and independently, gives an inspiration to the Mind and to the Reason in manner mentioned above. If any one disregards these inspirations of the internal organs (*antaḥkaraṇa*), we must with the Saint Tukārāma say :

> Who has thereby lost anything ? ।
> one has oneself done harm to oneself ॥
>
> (Gā. 4448)

The same principle has been referred to in the Gītā in the words "*na hinasty ātman ātmānam*", i. e., "he who does not ruin himself, obtains the highest salvation"; and the same principle has again been clearly repeated in the Dāsabodha (Gī. 13. 28 ; Dāsa. 17. 7. 7–10). The fact that a man naturally feels that he can do a particular thing independently, notwithstanding that he is tied down hand and foot by the laws of an apprently inpregnable Karma-world, cannot be explained in any way as satisfactorily as by concluding, as stated above, that the Brahman-world is different from the Gross Material world. Therefore, that man who does not accept as correct the science of the Absolute Self, must either accept the position of the eternal slavery of mankind in this matter, or he must give up the question of the independence of inherent tendencies as unsolveable. I have explained the independence of inherent tendencies, or Freedom of Will, on the basis of the proposition of Non-Dualistic Vedānta, that the Jīvātman (personal Ātman) and the Paramātman (Supreme Ātman) are fundamentally uniform (Ve. Sū. Śāṁ. Bhā. 2. 40). But for those who do not accept this Non-Dualistic doctrine, or when Dualism has to be accepted in order to justify the Path of Devotion, it is said that this power of the Jīvātman is not its own power, but is received by it from the Parameśvara. But, in any case, it is always said that in order to acquire this power, the Jīvātman must first make the necessary effort, having regard to the principle enunciated in the Ṛg-Veda, that "*na ṛte śrāntasya sakhyāya devāḥ*" (Ṛg. 4. 33. 11), i. e., "the gods do not help any one except the man who makes effort, until he is tired"; and the principle of personal effort, and inferentially the principle of the Freedom of the Ātman, is left intact (Ve. Sū. 2. 3. 41, 42; Gī. 10. 5 and 10). Nay, the Buddhists do not accept the theory of the Ātman, or of the Parabrahman; but though they do not accept the theory of the Realisation of the Brahman or of the Ātman, their religious treatises contain the advice that "*attanā (ātmanā) codayattānam*", i. e., "one must put oneself into the right path"; and in support of that doctrine, it is said that:

attā (ātmā) hi attano nātho attā hi attano gati ।
tasmā sañjamaya 'ttāṇaṁ assaṁ (aśvaṁ) bhaddaṁ va vāṇijo ॥
(Dhammapada, 380).

that is, "one is the owner of oneself, and there is no other redeemer for oneself except one's Ātman; therefore, just as a merchant keeps under proper control his good horse, so must one keep oneself under proper control"; and the importance and the existence of the freedom of the Ātman is there shown in the same way as in the Gītā. (See, Mahāparinibbāṇa-sutta, 2. 33-35). The French Materialist Comte must also be included in this class; because, although he does not accept the theory of the Absolute Self. yet, he has, as a matter of personal experience, that is to say, without any logical justification accepted the fact that every person can by his own efforts improve his conduct and his circumstances.

Although, it has in this way been proved that (i) the Realisation of the identity of the Brahman and the Ātman is the most successful method for escaping the bonds of Karma, and acquiring the metaphysically perfect state of Realising that there is only one Ātman in all created beings, and that (ii) it is within the control of everybody to acquire that Realisation, yet, we must also remember the second fact, that even this independent Ātman cannot get rid of this mill-stone of Prakṛti round its neck in a moment. As, though an artisan is very skilful himself, he cannot do anything without implements, and he has to spend sometime in repairing the implements, if they are not in proper condition, so also is the case with the personal Self. It is true that the personal Self is free to give to the organs the inspiration to acquire Knowledge; yet, scientifically, it is fundamentally qualityless and isolated, or, as stated above in the seventh chapter, it has eyes, but is lame (Maitryu. 3. 2, 3; Gī. 13. 20); and therefore, it does not possess the implements which are necessary (e. g., the wheel, to a potter, etc.) for doing a particular Action according to a particular inspiration. The Body, the Reason, and the other organs are evolutes of Matter. Therefore, the personal Self has got to bring about its own Release, through the medium of the bodily organs etc., which it has got according to its Commenced Action (*prārabdha-karma*). As the Reason is the most important organ among the bodily organs, the personal Self (Jīvātman) has to first inspire the Reason, if it has to get anything done by any of the organs. But, having regard to one's inherent tendencies, which depend on previous Action, it is not certain that this Reason will always be pure and *sāttvika*. And therefore, in order that this Reason should be released from the meshes of three-constituented Matter, and become introspective-*sāttvika*, and Self-devoted (*ātmaniṣṭha*), that is, such as will listen to the dictates inspired by the Self, and decide to perform only such Actions as are beneficial to the Self, one has to practise Renunciation (*vairāgya*) for a considerable length of time. Even then, hunger, thirst, and other corporeal needs and those Accumulated (*sañcita*) Actions, for the consequences of which one has begun to suffer, do not in any case leave one till death. Therefore, although the Ātman is free to give to the corporeal organs the inspiration to perform Actions favourable to Release, yet, as all the subsequent Actions have to be performed through Matter, as a result of the superimposition of a corporeal body on the Ātman, it (the Ātman) is, to that extent, dependent, like a carpenter, a potter, or other artisans; and, it has first to purify its implements, namely, the corporeal organs etc., and to keep them under its control (Ve. Sū. 2. 3. 40). This thing cannot be achieved at once, and has to be acquired gradually and courageously; otherwise, the organs will positively rear up on their haunches like a frightened horse. Therefore, the Blessed Lord has said that Reason needs the help of courage (*dhṛti*) for acquiring control over the organs (Gī. 6. 25); and later on in the eighteenth chapter, *dhṛti* has, in the same way as Reason, been divided into the *sāttvika*, *rājasa* and *tāmasa* classes (Gī. 18.

33-35). Out of these, one has to discard the *rājasa* and *tāmasa* stages, and to control the organs in order to make one's Reason *sāttvika*. Therefore, the place, method of sitting, and the food, proper for the performance of this Yoga in the form of practising control over the organs, have been described in the sixth chapter of the Gītā. And, it is further stated in the Gītā that when practice has been performed in this way "*śanaiḥ, śanaiḥ*" (Gī. 6. 25), i. e., gradually, the Mind *(citta)* becomes steady, and the organs come under one's control; and thereafter, after the lapse of a considerable length of time (not at once), one realises the identity of the Brahman and the Ātman; and by the acquisition of Knowledge, the bondage of Karma is broken: "*ātmavantaṁ na karmāṇi nibadhnanti dhanañjaya*", i. e., "such a person who has realised the Ātman, cannot be bound by Karma (Gī. 4. 38-41). But, because the Blessed Lord has prescribed the practice of Yoga in solitude (Gī. 6. 10), one must not understand the import of the Gītā as being that one should give up all the activities in the world, and spend one's life in the practice of Yoga. Just as a merchant starts business with what little capital he has, and gradually acquires vast wealth by such business, so also is the case of the practice of Karma-Yoga prescribed in the Gītā. This Karma-Yoga has got to be started by exercising as much control over the organs as is possible, and thereby, gradually, more and more of control over the organs is acquired. At the same time, it is also not proper to always sit in a gossiping place; because, thereby the habit of concentration, which has been acquired by the Mind, is likely to weaken. Therefore, when one is continually practising Karma-Yoga, it is necessary to spend sometime every day or at intervals in solitude (Gī. 13. 10). But, the Blessed Lord nowhere says, that for that purpose one should give up one's ordinary activities in life. On the other hand, this control of the organs has been prescribed in order that one should be able to perform one's activities in life with a desireless frame of mind, and the advice of the Gītā is, that while control of the organs is being practised, one must simultaneously, continually, and according to one's own abilities, practise the desireless Karma-Yoga, and not wait till one has acquired complete control over the organs.

According to the Maitryupaniṣad and the Mahābhārata, one can acquire equability of Reason within six months, if one is intelligent and determined (Maitryu. 6. 28; Ma. Bhā. Śān. 239. 32; Aśva. Anugītā. 19.66). But, a doubt is likely to be raised here, that this *sāttvika*, equable, and Self-devoted frame of the Mind, which has been described by the Blessed Lord, may not be acquired by some, as a result of their inherent nature, even in six years, to say nothing of six months; and that, if this practice remains incomplete, not only will perfection or Release not be reached in this life, but the practice will have to be started from its very commencement in the next birth; and, if the practice in this next birth also remains incomplete, as in in the previous births, such a person will never acquire perfection. And, on that account, it is also likely to be believed that one must learn to acquire the non-subjective and non-objective mental absorption (*nirvikalpa-samādhi**) by practising the Pātañjala Yoga before starting the practice of the Karma-Yoga. Arjuna was beset by this very doubt, and he has in the sixth chapter of the Gītā (Gī. 6. 37-39) asked Śrī Kṛṣṇa, what a man should do in these circumstances. To this question, the Blessed Lord has replied that, as the Ātman is immortal, the impressions received by it in this life through the Subtle Body, whatever they may be, are not destroyed; and that such a '*yogabhraṣṭa*' (apostate from Yoga), that is, one who has abandoned the Karma-Yoga without having completely acquired it, starts his efforts in the next birth from the point where he has left off in this birth; and that, in this way, gradually "*anekajanmasaṁsiddhas tato yāti parāṁ gatim*" (Gī. 6. 45), i. e., "he ultimately acquires perfection after many births, and obtains Release". The statement in the second chapter that "*svalpam apy asya dharmasya trāyate mahato bhayāt*" (Gī. 2. 40), i. e., "even a little practice of this method, that is, of the Karma-Yoga, redeems a person from great danger", is with reference to this proposition. In short, although the

---

* '*nirvikalpa-samādhi*' is defined in Apte's Sanskrit dictionary as: "an exclusive contemplation upon the one entity without the distinction and separate consciousness of the Knower, the Known and the Knowing, and without even self-consciousness (Apte, 3rd Edition, 1924)—Translator.

Ātman of a person is fundamentally independent, yet, as a result of the impure inherent nature of the Body, which a person has acquired as a result of his previous Actions, it is not possible for him to acquire complete Release in one life. But on that account, "*nātmānam avamanyeta pūrvābhir asamṛddhibhiḥ*" (Manu. 4. 137), i. e. "no one should despair, nor should one waste one's whole life in practising the Pātañjala-Yoga, that is, the mere gymnastic exercise of the organs, by a foolish insistence that one will acquire complete Release in one life". The Blessed Lord has said in the Gītā, that there is no haste where the Ātman is concerned; that, one should acquire as much Yogic strength as can possibly be acquired in this life, and start the practice of Karma-Yoga; that thereby, the Mind gradually becomes more and more *sāttvika*, and pure; that, not only this small practice of the Karma-Yoga, but even the mere desire to practise it, will forcibly push forward a man as if he had been put into a grinding mill, and ultimately cause the complete merger of the Ātman into the Brahman, if not to-day, to-morrow, and in the next birth, if not in this birth; that, therefore, even the smallest practice of the Karma-Yoga, or even the desire to practice it, is never wasted; and that this is the most important characteristic feature of the Karma-Yoga (See my Commentary on Gī. 6. 15.). One must not restrict one's attention to this life, and give up courage, but should continue one's practice of performing desireless Action, independently, courageously, and according to one's own abilities. This bondage of Matter which one considers to be indissoluble in this life or to-day, as a result of pre-destination (*prāktana-saṁskāra*) will become gradually and automatically loose, by the gradually increasing practice of Karma-Yoga; and when this goes on for some time, "*bahūnāṁ janmanām ante jñānavān māṁ prapadyate*" (Gī. 7. 19),—sometime or other, as a result of the complete acquisition of Knowledge, the bondage of or the dependence on Matter is broken, and the Ātman at last acquires its fundamental or perfect qualityless free state, or Release. What is impossible for a man? The well-known proverb, 'if a man performs the proper duties of manhood, he will become the same as the Nārāyaṇa', is only a repetition of this proposition of Vedānta; and, it is on this very account that the writer of the Yoga-Vāsiṣṭha has, in the chapter dealing with those who desire Release (*mumukṣu*), praised the worth of Effort, and laid down the firm proposition, that by Effort everything is ultimately achieved (Yo. 2. 4. 10-18).

Although it has in this way been definitely proved, that the personal Self is fundamentally free to make the effort of acquiring Knowledge, and that by ceaseless effort based on self-dependence, it, sometime or other, escapes from the clutches of pre-destined *(prāktana)* Karma, yet, it remains to give some further explanation as to what is meant by the annihilation of Karma *(karma-kṣaya)*, and when it takes place. '*karma-kṣaya*' means the total, that is, the balanceless release from the bonds of Karma. But, as has been stated before, though a man may have acquired Knowledge, yet, in as much as he does not escape Karma (Action) in the form of drinking, eating, sleeping, sitting, etc. so long as his body lives, and, in as much as his Commenced *(prārabdha)* Karma is not annihilated otherwise than by suffering, he cannot determine to destroy his body by suicide. Therefore, although all the Karma done before the acquisition of Knowledge is annihilated by the acquisition of Knowledge, yet, the scient has to perform some Karma or other, so long as he is alive, even after the acquisition of Knowledge. Then, how is he to be released from this Karma?; and, if there is no such release, there is no annihilation of the previous Karma, nor is there any Release *(mokṣa)* later on. The answer of Vedānta philosophy to this doubt is, that although Karma, in the shape of Names and Forms, does not at any time leave the Name-d and Form-ed body of a scient, yet, in as much as the Ātman is competent to adopt or reject such Karma, a man can, by conquering his organs and destroying the Attachment, which exists in the case of every living being towards the Karma, so to say, kill the sting of Karma, though he may be performing it. Karma is inherently blind, lifeless *(acetana)*, and dead. It does not by itself either catch hold of or leave anybody; inherently, it is neither good nor bad. But, a man, by allowing his Self to get entangled in this Karma, gives it the character of good or bad, beneficial or malefic, by his Attachment *(āsakti)*. Therefore, when this Attachment in the shape of a feeling of mine-ness *(mamatva)* comes to an end, the bondage of Karma may be said to be broken; then let that Karma remain or not remain. On the basis of this proposition, it is stated in the Gītā in several places that: true abstention from Action (*naiṣkarmya*) consists in this, and not in the abandonment of Action (Gī. 3. 4); your jurisdiction extends to the performance of Action, you cannot control getting or not getting the fruit of the Action (Gī. 2. 47); "*karmendriyaiḥ karmayogam asaktaḥ*" (Gī. 3. 7), i. e., "let the organs of Action perform their various Actions without entertaining any hope for the fruit"; *tyaktvā karmaphalāsaṅgam*" (Gī. 4. 20), i. e., "having given up the fruit of Action"; *sarvabhūtātmabhūtātmā kurvann api na lipyate*" (Gī. 5. 7), i. e.: "that man, whose mind has become equable towards all created things, is not bound by Actions, though he may perform them"; "*sarvakarmaphalatyāgaṁ kuru*" (Gī. 12. 11), i. e., "give up the fruit of all Actions"; "*kāryam ity eva yat karma niyataṁ kriyate*" (Gī. 18. 9), i. e., "those who perform whatever Action befalls them, looking upon it as a duty, are *sāttvika*"; "*cetasā sarva-karmāṇi mayi saṁnyasya*" (Gī. 18. 57), i. e., "dedicate all Actions to Me when you act". The question whether or not the scient should perform all Actions which arise in life, is an independent question; and the doctrine of the Gītā on that point will be considered in the next chapter. We have, for the present, to consider only what is the real meaning of the *dictum* that all Karma is reduced to ashes by Jñāna; and from the quotations from the Gītā which have been given above, the opinion of the Gītā on this question becomes quite clear. We apply this logical argument everywhere in ordinary life. For instance, if a person unintentionally gives a push to another person, we do not call him a rowdy; and, even under the criminal law, death caused by mere accident is not looked upon as murder. If fire burns a house, or a deluge washes away a field, does one consider the fire or the rain as criminals ? If one considers only Action by itself, there will be found in every act some or other fault, defect, or evil, from the point of view of the human being; because, "*sarvārambhā hi doṣeṇa dhūmenāgnir ivāvṛtāḥ*" (Gī. 18. 48), i. e., "just as fire is enveloped in smoke, so also is all Action (*ārambha*) enveloped in some fault or other". But the fault which the Gītā advises one to give up, is not this fault. The Gītā has laid down that the evil or virtue, which we ascribe to any particular Action of a man, does not lie in the Action itself, but depends on the frame of mind of the man who does it; and, from this point of view, eliminating the evilness from an Action, means the doer of the Action keeping his Reason or Mind pure (Gī. 2. 49-51); and, even in the Upaniṣads, importance is attached to the Reason of the person who performs the Action, as follows:

mana eva manuṣyāṇāṁ kāraṇaṁ bandhamokṣayoḥ ।
bandhāya viṣayāsaṅgi mokṣe nirviṣayaṁ smṛtam ॥

(Maitryu. 6. 34 ; Amṛtabindu. 2)

that is: "the mind of a man is the only (*eva*) cause for his being bound (by Karma) or being Released; when the mind is enslaved by objects of pleasure, it is bound; and when it goes beyond those objects (becomes *nirviṣaya*), that is, when it becomes desireless (*niṣkāma*), or unattached (*niḥsaṅga*), that is Release". The Bhagavadgītā has principally stated in what way one can acquire this equability of the mind by the Realisation of the identity of the Brahman and the Ātman; and when this state of mind has been acquired, Action is totally destroyed, notwithstanding that it is performed. Karma is not destroyed by becoming homeless (*niragni*), that is, by Renunciation (*saṁnyāsa*), and by giving up sacrificial ritual to fire etc; nor by remaining Actionless (*akriya*), that is, by remaining idle without performing any Action whatsoever (Gī. 6. 1). Whether a man desires it or no, the wheel of Matter will go on; and, therefore, man must also move round and round with it (Gī. 3. 33; 18. 60). But, that man, who does not dance as a dependent on Matter like an ignorant person, but keeps his mind steady and pure by control of the organs and performs all Action, which befalls him in the ordinary course of life, as a duty merely, and calmly, and without allowing his mind to become attached, is the true emotionless (*virakta*) man, the true Steady-in-Mind (*sthitaprajña*), and one, who may be said to be truly merged in the Brahman (Gī. 3. 7; 4. 21; 5. 7–9; 18. 11.). A scient may perhaps renounce the world, and give up the Action of ordinary life, and go and sit in a forest; but it is wrong to imagine that by his having, in this way, abandoned the duties of ordinary life, he has annihilated them (Gī. 3. 4). One must bear in mind the principle that whether he performs Actions or not, the annihilation of his Karma is the result of his having attained equability of mind, and not of his having abandoned, or of his not performing, Action. For explaining the true nature of the annihilation of Karma, the illustration given in the Upaniṣads and in the Gītā (Chān. 4. 14. 3; Gī. 5. 10), that the scient, that is, one who performs Actions by dedicating them to the Brahman, or without Attachment, is not touched by Karma, in the same way as water being on the leaf of the lotus flower does not adhere to it, is more appropriate, than the illustration that Karma is burnt by Knowledge, in the same way as fuel is burnt by fire. Karma is essentially never burnt, nor is it at all necessary to burn it. If Karma is Name and Form, and if Name and Form means the visible world, then how is this visible world to be burnt up?; and, assuming for the sake of argument that it is burnt, then, according to the theory of Satkārya-vāda, the utmost that can happen, is that its Name and Form will be changed. As Name-d and Form-ed Karma or Māyā changes eternally, man cannot totally destroy this Name-d and Form-ed Karma, however much of a Self-knower he may become, though he may, as he wills, bring about a change in the Name and Form; and such a thing can be done only by the Parameśvara (Ve. Sū. 4. 4. 17). But, the seed of goodness or evilness, which did not exist inherently in this gross Karma, and which a man instills into it by his feeling of mine-ness, can be destroyed by him; and what has to be burnt up by him, is this seed. That man alone who has burnt this seed of mine-ness in his ordinary activities, by maintaining an equable frame of mind towards all created things, is the Blessed, the Accomplished (*kṛtakṛtya*), and the Released; and his Karma is said to have been burnt by the fire of Knowledge, though he may be performing all Actions (Gī. 4. 19; 18. 56). In as much as the being burnt up of Karma in this way is entirely dependent on the Mind being free from objects of pleasure, and on the Realisation of the identity of the Brahman and the Ātman, no time is lost in such Realisation performing its function of destroying Karma, in the same way as fire begins to exercise its function of burning, the moment it comes into existence. The moment Realisation comes, Karma is immediately destroyed. Nevertheless, the moment of death is considered to be more important than all other times in this matter, because death is the last moment in a man's life; and, though the Uncommenced Accumulated Karma may have been destroyed by previous Realisation, yet the Commenced *(prārabdha)* Karma is not destroyed. Therefore, if this Realisation of the Brahman does not continue till the end, the good or bad Actions which may have been performed in the meantime as a result of Commenced Karma, will become desireful *(sakāma)*, and one will not be able to escape having to take a fresh birth to suffer their consequences. It is true that that man who has become really Released from birth *(jīvanmukta)* is not subject to this fear. But, when one is considering this subject-matter scientifically, one has also to consider the possibility that the Knowledge of the Brahman, which has been acquired before death, may not continue till the end. Therefore, philosophers consider the exact moment of death as of greater importance than the time before death; and they say that the Realisation of the identity of the Brahman and the Ātman must necessarily take place at that moment, that is, at the moment of death; and that otherwise Release is not possible. On the basis of this theory the Gītā, on the authority of the Upaniṣads, states that: "by remembering Me at the moment of death, and Realising that there is no other than I, the man is Released" (Gī. 8. 5). According to this proposition it follows that, any man, who has spent the whole of his life in evil deeds, will become Released by Realising the Parameśvara at the moment of death, which, according to some, is not correct; but, if one considers the matter carefully, it will be seen that there is nothing wrong in it. The man who has spent the whole of his life in evil deeds cannot acquire purity of mind, and Realise the Brahman at the moment of death. As in all other matters, it is necessary to acquire the habit of devoting the Mind to the Brahman; and, it will be very difficult, nay impossible, for the man who has not even once in his lifetime Realised the identity of the Brahman and the Ātman, to get that experience suddenly at the moment of death. Therefore, the second important teaching of the Gītā in this matter is, that everyone should continually carry on the practice of abstracting his mind from the objects of pleasure, so that there is no difficulty in that state of mind being present at the moment of death, and the man being thereby ultimately Released (Gī. 8. 6,7 and 2. 72). But, for critically examining this philosophical doctrine, let us suppose that someone, as a result of the impressions of previous lives, Realises the Parameśvara suddenly only at the moment of death. No doubt, the case of such a man will be perhaps one in a hundred thousand, nay, one in a million; but, we have to disregard the fact that such a case is difficult to come across, and to consider for the present what will happen if such a case actually takes place. As Realisation has come to such a man, though only at the moment of death, the Uncommenced Karma of such a man is destroyed, and the Commenced Karma comes to an end at the moment of death by its having been suffered for in this life. Therefore, such a man has no Karma left which has to be suffered for; and, it then necessarily follows, that he becomes free from all Karma, that is, from the cycle of life (*saṁsāra*). This proposition has been expounded in the Gītā in the stanza: "*api cet sudurācāro bhajate mām ananyabhāk*", i. e., "even a great evil-doer will be released, if he worships the Parameśvara with the idea that there is no one else to worship"; and it has been accepted even by the other religions of the world. It may be borne in mind that the word '*ananyabhāva*' signifies the state of mind of a person, whose mind is fully merged in the Parameśvara, and the person who simply utters the words "Rāma, Rāma" by the mouth, while his mind is engaged somewhere else, is not meant. In short the importance of the Realisation of the Parameśvara is such that the moment it comes, all the Uncommenced Accumulated Karma is destroyed at a stroke. Whenever this state of Mind comes, it is welcome; but our philosophers have concluded that it is essential that such a state should continue in existence at the moment of death, or, if one has not acquired that Realisation before death, that one should acquire it at least at the moment of death; otherwise, some desire or other will remain in balance at that moment, and re-birth will not be averted; and if re-birth is not averted, Release *(mokṣa)* also becomes impossible.

We have so far dealt with the questions, what the bondage of Karma is; what is meant by the destruction of Karma; and how that is brought about, and when. Now, I will shortly consider the state in which those persons who have not escaped the bondage of Karma, and destroyed the consequences of Karma find themselves after death, according to the Vedic religion, and close this chapter. This question has been dealt with at great length in the Upaniṣads (See Chān. 4. 15; 5. 10; Bṛ 6. 2. 2. 16; Kau. 1. 2. 3). And all these Upaniṣads have been harmonised in the third *pāda* of the fourth chapter of the Vedānta-Sūtras. But, it is not necessary to go into the whole of that discussion here, and we have only to consider the two courses which are mentioned in the Bhagavadgītā (Gī. 8. 23–27). The Vedic religion is divided into two well-known divisions, Karma-Kāṇḍa and Jñāna-Kāṇḍa. The original meaning of the Karma-Kāṇḍa out of these, is the worship of the Sun, Fire, Indra, Varuṇa, Rudra and other Vedic deities by sacrificial ritual, and obtaining children and grand-children, and cows, horses, or other wealth in this life, and a happy state after death by the grace of those deities. As at the present day, this sacrificial ritual of the Śrutis has more or less ceased to exist, people devote themselves to the worship of God, and to the meritorious Actions, like charity etc., enjoined by the Śāstras, in order to achieve this object. But, it is clear from the Ṛg-Veda that in ancient times, people used to worship these deities by sacrificial ritual not only for personal benefit, but also for the benefit of the community; because, the Sūktas in the Ṛg-Veda are full of praise of the deities Indra etc., whose favour had to be acquired for these purposes; and everywhere we come across prayers like "O God! give us children and wealth"; "make us live a hundred years"; "do not kill us, or our children or our warriors, or our cattle".* As these ritualistic practices

*** These prayers are to be come across in many places but instead of mentioning all of them, I will only mention the prayer which is**

are common to the three Vedas, this course of worship was known in ancient times as '*trayī dharma*'; and there is a detailed description in the Brāhmaṇas as to the way in which they are to be performed. But, as the ritual prescribed for these various sacrifices was different in the different Brāhmaṇas, doubts arose as to which one was correct. Therefore, Jaimini has made a collection of explanatory rules for bringing about harmony between these mutually contradictory ritualistic directions. The rules laid down by Jaimini are known as 'Mīmāṁsā-Sūtras' or the 'Pūrva-Mīmāṁsā'; and, therefore, the ancient Karma-kāṇḍa came later on to acquire the name of the 'Mīmāṁsaka-mārga'; and, as that name is still in vogue, I have made use of it on various occasions in this book. But, it must be remembered that though the word '*mīmāṁsā*' came into vogue only in later times, this Karma-mārga of sacrificial ritual has been current from very ancient times. The word '*mīmāṁsā*' occurs nowhere in the Gītā, and that is why we find in it the words '*trayī dharma*" (Gī. 9. 20-21), or, '*trayī-vidyā*' instead. Āraṇyakas and Upaniṣads are Vedic treatises later in point of time than the Brāhmaṇas, which describe the sacrificial ritual laid down by the Śrutis. As these treatises maintain that sacrificial ritual is inferior, and that the Knowledge of the Brahman is superior, the religion described in these later works is known as 'Jñāna-kāṇḍa'. Yet, as the different Upaniṣads contain different ideas, it was also necessary to harmonise them. This has been done by Bādarāyaṇācārya in his Vedānta-Sūtras, which are also known as the Brahma-Sūtras, or the Śārīra-Sūtras or the Uttara-Mīmāṁsā. In this way, the Pūrva-Mīmāṁsā and the Uttara-Mīmāṁsā are at present the two treatises which deal with the Karma-kāṇḍa and the Jñāna-kāṇḍa respectively. Strictly speaking, both these works fundamentally discuss the meanings of Vedic expressions, that is to say, of the Mīmāṁsā; yet, it is usual to refer to the followers of the Karma-kāṇḍa as 'Mīmāṁsakas', and to the followers of the Jñāna-kāṇḍa as 'Vedāntins'. The followers of the Karma-kāṇḍa, that is to say, the Mīmāṁsakas say that the observance

come across in every day worship, namely, "*mā nastoke tanaye mā na āyu mā no goṣu mā no aśveṣu ririṣaḥ | virān mā no rudra bhāmito vadhīr haviṣmantaḥ sadamittvā havāmahe* || (Ṛg. 1. 114. 8) of the four months, and of the sacrificial ritual, such as, the Jyotiṣṭoma-yajña, etc. are the important doctrines of the Śruti religion; and that according to the Vedas, he alone will acquire Release who performs that Karma. Whoever he may be, he must not give up this sacrificial Karma; and if he does so, he must be taken to have abandoned the Śruti religion; because, the Vedic sacrificial ritual was created at the same time as the Universe, and the virtuous circle of men performing it and pleasing the deities, and the deities in return producing rain and the other things needed by men, has been going on from times immemorial. At present, we do not attach much importance to these ideas, because the Śruti religion of sacrificial ritual is not now in vogue. But, as the state of things was different at the time of the Gītā, the importance of this circle of sacrifice has been described as above in the Bhagavadgītā (Gī. 3. 16–25). Nevertheless, it becomes clear from the Gītā, that as a result of the Knowledge conveyed in the Upaniṣads, this Karma ritual had even then acquired an inferior place from the point of view of Release (2. 41–46); and this inferiority has increased later on by the growth of the doctrine of non-sacrifice (*ahiṁsā*). It is clearly mentioned in the Bhāgavata religion, that although sacrificial ritual is prescribed by the Vedas, the appurtenant slaughter of animals is not a proper thing, and that the ritual should be performed by offering only grain (Ma. Bhā. Śān. 336. 10 and 337). On that account, (and also to some extent, because the Jains later on raised the same kind of objection), the ritual prescribed by the Śrutis has at present reached such a state, that persons who keep burning a perpetual fire as prescribed by the Śrutis (that is, *agnihotris*) are rarely to be come across even in sacred places like Benares, and one hears that somebody has performed an animal sacrifice like the Jyotiṣṭoma, only sometimes in 20 or 25 years. Yet, as the Śruti religion is the root of all Vedic religion, the respect felt for it still continues, and the Sūtras of Jaimini have become authoritative as a science explaining its meaning. But, although the Śruti ritual has in this way fallen into the back-ground, the other ritual mentioned in Smṛtis like the Manu-Smṛti etc.—which is known as the five principal sacrificial rites (*pañca mahāyajña*)—is still in vogue; and the same argument is applied to them as to the cycle of sacrificial ritual prescribed by the Śrutis mentioned above. For instance, Manu and other Smṛti writers have mentioned five daily sacrificial rites to be performed at home, which do not entail the slaughter of animals, namely, the study of the Vedas as a *brahma-yajña*, oblations to the ancestors as a *pitṛ-yajña*, oblations into the fire as a *deva-yajña*, offering of food as *bali* as a *bhūta-yajña*, and entertaining guests as a *manuṣya-yajña;* and the ritual prescribed for a man in the state of a householder is, that he should partake of food after he has in this way satisfied respectively the Ṛṣis, the ancestors, the deities, the spirits of the departed, and men, by these five sacrifices. (Manu. 3. 68–123). The food which remains over after the performance of these sacrifices is known as '*amṛta*', and the food which remains over after everybody has eaten is known as '*vighasa*' (Manu. 3. 285). The '*amṛta*' and the '*vighasa*' is the proper and beneficial food for the householder; and it is stated not only in the Manu-Smṛti, but also in the Ṛg-Veda and in the Gītā, that if a person does not follow this precept, but eats food only by himself, he eats '*agha*' or sin, and he is to be known as '*aghāśī*' (Ṛg. 10. 117. 6; Manu. 3. 118; Gī. 3. 13). Besides, these five principal sacrifices, the Upaniṣads and the Smṛtis also consider other acts which are productive of public benefit, such as, charity, truth, kindness, and non-slaughter as proper for the householder (Tai. 1. 11); and, in these texts we find the clear statement : "*prajātantuṁ mā vyavacchetsīḥ*", i. e., "enlarge thy family, and perpetuate thy generation." All these Actions are looked upon as a kind of sacrifice, and the Taittirīya-Saṁhitā explains the reason for performing them by saying that a Brahmin comes to birth with three kinds of indebtedness, namely, to the Ṛṣis, to the deities, and to his ancestors. Of these, the indebtedness to the Ṛṣis must be satisfied by the study of the Vedas; the indebtedness to the deities, by sacrifice; and the indebtedness to the ancestors, by procreation; otherwise, there is no Release for him (Tai. Saṁ. 6. 3. 10. 5).*

* The statement in the Taittirīya Saṁhitā is as follows :

"*jāyamāno vai brāhmaṇas tribhir ṛṇavā jāyate brahmacaryeṇa ṛṣibhyo yajñena devebhyaḥ prajayā pitṛbhyaḥ eṣa vā anṛṇo yaḥ putrī yajvā brahmacārī vāsīti.* "

There is a story in the Ādiparva of the Mahābhārata that Jaratkāru did not follow this precept but started austere religious practices before marrying; that, as a result of his having thus destroyed his possible children, he saw his ancestors named Yāyāvara dangling in the air; and that, in performance of their injunctions, he later on married. (Ma. Bhā. Ā. 13). It is not that all this Karma or sacrifice is to be performed only by Brahmins; and as even women and Śudras are competent to perform all other Karma, except the Vedic sacrificial ritual, all the Karma performed according to the classification of the four castes made by the writers of the Smṛtis—e. g., warfare by Kṣatriyas etc.—is also a YAJÑA (sacrifice); and the word YAJÑA has been used in this comprehensive meaning in these texts. Manu has said that whatever is proper for anyone, is his religious austerity (TAPA), (11. 236); and it is stated in the Mahābhārata that:

ārambhayajñāḥ kṣatrāś ca haviryajñā viśaḥ smṛtāḥ ।
paricārayajñāḥ śūdrāś ca japayajñā dvijātayaḥ ॥

(Ma. Bhā. Śān. 237. 12)

that is "*ārambha* (industry), *havi* (corn etc), service, and prayer are the four Yajñas, which are proper for the Kṣatriyas, the Vaiśyas, the Śūdras, and the Brahmins respectively. In short, as Brahmadeva has created all the human beings in the world and with great propriety prescribed for them their various duties (Karma) in life (Ma. Bhā. Anu. 48. 3; and Gī. 3. 10 and 4. 32), all the Karmas enjoined by the Śāstras for the four classes, are Yajñas in a way; and if all these Yajñas or Śāstra-enjoined Karma, or trades, or duties are not kept going by everybody according to his own status, the entire community will suffer, and will ultimately run the risk of being destroyed. It, therefore, follows that Yajñas, in this comprehensive meaning, are always necessary for public benefit.

Here a question arises as follows:—as this course of life, in which predominance is given to Yajñas, and which is proper for the householder according to the Vedas and according to the arrangement of the four castes made by the Smṛtis, is nothing but the performance of Karma, will a man, who performs this household Karma properly in the manner prescribed by the Śāstras, that is, morally, and according to Śāstric injunction, thereby escape the cycle of birth and death? And if he escapes that cycle, then where is the importance of Jñāna? The Jñāna-kāṇḍa and the Upaniṣads clearly say that unless a man realises the identity of the Brahman and the Ātman, and acquires apathy towards Karma, he will not escape the cycle of birth and death, or from the Name-d and Form-ed Māyā or Illusion; and if one considers the religion laid down by the Śrutis and the Smṛtis, it will be seen that Karma predominates the life of everybody, which (life) is nothing but a Yajña in its comprehensive meaning. Besides, it is clearly stated in the Vedas themselves, that no Karma performed for the sake of Yajña, creates bondage, and that heaven is attained only by the performance of Yajñas. Even if the question of heaven is kept aside, Brahmadeva himself has laid down the rule that rain does not fall unless Indra and other deities are kept satisfied, and the deities are not satisfied except by the performance of a Yajña. Then, what escape is there for anybody, unless he performs Yajñas or Karma? The chain of creation has been described by Manu, and in the Mahābhārata, the Upaniṣads, and even in the Gītā as follows:–

agnau prāstāhutiḥ samyag ādityam upatiṣṭhate ı
ādityāj jāyate vṛṣṭir vṛṣṭer annaṁ tataḥ prajāḥ ıı

that is, "when the material sacrified in the Yajña reaches the Sun through the medium of the fire, the Sun causes rain, rain causes food, and the food causes living beings" (Manu. 3. 76; Ma. Bhā. Śān. 262. 11; Maitryu. 6. 37; and Gī. 3. 14). And if these Yajñas are to be performed by Karma, how will it do to give up Karma? If the Karma in the shape of Yajñas is given up, the wheel of the world will come to a stop, and nobody will have anything to eat. The answer of the Bhāgavata doctrine and of the Gītā science to this objection is, that they do not ask anybody to give up the sacrificial ritual (Yajña) prescribed by the Vedas, or any other Karma in the shape of Yajña prescribed by the Smṛtis or performed in ordinary life; that they accept the argument that if this cycle of Yajñas, which has been going on from times immemorial is stopped, the world will become desolate; and that, therefore, they also lay down the proposition that nobody should give up Yajñas which entail Karma (Ma. Bhā. Śān. 340; Gī. 3. 16.). Nevertheless, it has been clearly stated in the Jñāna-kāṇḍa, that is, in the Upaniṣads themselves, that unless Karma is destroyed by Jñāna and Renunciation, there can be no Release: and therefore, they harmonise both these propositions and come to the conclusion that all Actions or Karma must be performed, giving up the desire for the fruit or reward, and desirelessly or with an apathetic frame of mind (Gī. 17-19). If one performs the sacrifices, such as, the Jyotiṣṭoma etc., prescribed by the Vedas, with a frame of mind which entertains the hope of heaven, one will undoubtedly reach heaven; because, what is laid down in the Vedas cannot be false; yet, in as much as heaven is not permanent, the Upaniṣads themselves say that:

prāpyāntaṁ karmaṇas tasya yat kiṁceha karotyayam ।
*tasmāl lokāt punarety asmai lokāya karmaṇe** ॥

that is, "when the fruit of meritorious Action in the shape of sacrifices etc. performed in this life, is exhausted by enjoyment in heaven, the orthodox performer of the Yajña has to come back once more from heaven to this Karma-world or earth." (Bṛ. 4. 4. 6; Ve. Sū. 3. 1. 8: Ma. Bhā. Vana. 260. 39); and even the way of coming down from heaven is described in the Chāndogyopaniṣad (5. 10. 3-9). The following slightly derogatory statements in the Bhagavadgītā, namely, "*kāmātmānaḥ svargaparāḥ*" (Gī. 2. 43), (i. e., "desire-filled persons running after heaven"—Trans.). or "*traiguṇyaviṣayā vedāḥ*" (Gī. 2. 45), (i. e., "the Vedas, which deal with matters relating to the three constituents"—Trans.), have been made with reference to these orthodox persons; and it is again clearly stated in the ninth chapter that: "*gatāgataṁ kāmakāmā labhante*" (Gī. 9. 21), i. e., "such persons have to move backwards and forwards between the heaven and this world". This moving backwards and forwards cannot be escaped otherwise than by the acquisition of Knowledge; and unless these transi-

* In reading the second part of this stanza, '*punaretyasmai*' should be broken up as '*punareti*' and '*asmai*', so that the requisite number of letters will not be found wanting. One has to do this very often in reading Vedic treatises.

tions are over, the Ātman does not get true bliss, perfection, or Release. Therefore, the summary of the advice given in the Gītā to everybody is, that one should perform not only the sacrificial ritual etc., but also all other acts prescribed for the four different castes, realising the identity of the Brahman and the Ātman, and with equability of mind, and unattachedly, so that one will keep going the cycle of Karma and at the same time be Released (Gī. 18. 5, 6.). It is not that a Yajña or sacrifice is performed merely by uttering the word "*idaṁ amuka devatāyai na mama*" (i. e., "this is for such and such a deity and not for me"—Trans.) with reference to some deity, and offering sesamum, rice, or animals into the sacrificial fire. It is more meritorious to offer up animal tendencies like, Desire, Anger etc., which are in everybody's body, by way of sacrifice into the fire of mental control in the shape of an equable frame of mind, than to slaughter the animals themselves (Gī. 4 33); and it is in support of this proposition, that the Blessed Lord has said both in the Gītā and in the Nārāyaṇīya-Dharma that; "from among the sacrifices, I am the sacrifice in the shape of prayer", that is, the highest form of sacrifice (Gī. 10. 25; Ma. Bhā. Śān. 3. 37.); and the Manu-Smṛti says, that by continual prayer a Brahmin attains Release, whether he does anything else or not (Manu. 2. 87). The most important element in a Yajña is the giving up of the idea of mine-ness (*mamatva*) with reference to the object thrown into the sacrificial fire, by uttering the words: '*na mama*' (i. e., 'this is not for me'), at the time of the throwing; and the same is the underlying import of charity etc. Charitable gifts stand on the same footing as sacrificial Yajñas. In short, one may say that doing a particular Karma, in which there is no selfish purpose, with a pure frame of mind, is a Yajña in itself. When one accepts this definition of a Yajña, all acts done with a selfless and desireless frame of mind become a great Yajña in a comprehensive meaning, and the doctrine of the Mīmāṁsā school that no act performed for the purpose of a Yajña becomes a source of bondage, which has reference to sacrifice of wealth, applies to all desireless actions. And as, in performing these actions, the desire of fruit has also been given up, the man has not to move like a shuttle between heaven and earth, and he ultimately acquires the blissful state of Release, though he may be performing all that Karma (Gī. 3. 9). In short, although *saṁsāra* (life) entails the performance of Karma or Yajña, the performers fall into two divisions, namely, those who go through life (*saṁsāra*) in the manner prescribed by the Śāstras, but with the desire of reward (the orthodox ritualists), and those who go through life with a desireless frame of mind, and merely as a duty (the scients). And the doctrine of the Gītā is, that persons falling in the first of these divisions, that is to say, the pure orthodox ritualists, obtain non-permanent fruit in the shape of heaven etc., whereas the others, that is, the Jñānins who perform all Actions by Jñāna or with a desireless frame of mind, obtain permanent reward in the shape of Release. The Gītā nowhere asks us to give up Karma for the sake of Release. On the other hand, it is clearly stated in the commencement of the eighteenth chapter that the word '*tyāga*'=giving up, has been used everywhere in the Gītā as meaning not the Renunciation of Action, but the Renunciation of the reward of Action.

As the fruits of Action which are obtained by the orthodox ritualists and by the scients following the Karma-Yoga, are in this way different, those persons have to go to different spheres by different paths after their death; and these paths are respectively known as '*pitṛyāṇa*' and '*devayāna*' (Śān. 17. 15, 16); and these two paths are described in the eighth chapter of the Gītā on the basis of the Upaniṣads. The man who has acquired Knowledge—and he must have acquired this Knowledge at least at the moment of death—(Gī. 2. 72) goes and reaches the sphere of the Brahman, after his body has fallen and has been burnt in fire, through that fire, passing through the flames, daylight, the bright half of the month and the six months of the *uttarāyaṇa*; and as he attains Release there, he does not take birth again and come back to this mortal world; but, that man, who has been a mere orthodox performer of ritual and has not acquired Knowledge, reaches the sphere of the Moon, through the smoke of the same fire, and through night, and the dark half of the month, and the six months of the *dakṣiṇāyana*; and when he has enjoyed the reward of all the meritorious Actions, which he has performed, he again returns to this world. This is the difference between the two paths (Gī. 8. 23-27). As the Upaniṣads use the word '*arciḥ*' (flame) instead of '*jyotiḥ*' (flame), the first path is also called '*arcirādi*', and the second path is called '*dhūmrādi*'. When one bears in mind the terminology that our *uttarāyaṇa* (period during which the Sun is seen moving towards the North) is the day of the deities living on the North Pole, and our *dakṣiṇāyana* (when the Sun is seen moving towards the South) is their night, it becomes quite clear that the first out of these two paths, namely, '*arcirādi*' (*jyotirādi*) is lighted from beginning to end, and that the other one or the *dhūmrādi* is one of darkness throughout. In as much as Jñāna (Knowledge) is an embodiment of light, and the Parabrahman is "*jyotiṣām jyotiḥ*" (Gī. 13. 17), i. e., "the brilliance of all brilliance", it is only proper that the path taken by the scients (Jñānins) after death should be lighted; and the adjectives '*śukla*' (white) and '*kṛṣṇa*' (black) used in the Gītā with reference to these two paths, mean that they are respectively lighted and dark. The Gītā does not mention the stages subsequent to the *uttarāyaṇa*; but the Nirukta of Yāska contains a description of the spheres of the Gods, the Sun, the lightning, and the mental Puruṣa, which come after the *uttarāyaṇa* (Nirukta 14. 9); and the descriptions of the *devayāna* given in the various Upaniṣads are harmonised in the Vedānta-Sūtras in which all the subsequent stages after the *uttarāyaṇa*, namely, the year (*saṁvatsara*), the spheres of the air, the Sun, the Moon, lightning, Varuṇa, Indra, Prajāpati, and ultimately, the sphere of the Brahman are described (Bṛ. 5. 10; 6. 2. 15; Chān. 5. 10; Kauṣī. 1. 3.; Ve. Sū. 4. 3. 1-6).

I have thus far given the description of the various stages in the *devayāna* and the *pitṛyāṇa* paths; but as the stages of the day, the bright half of the month, and the *uttarāyaṇa* among them commonly denote Time, the questions which next arise are whether the *devayāna* and the *pitṛyāṇa* have or at any time had or had not, any reference to Time. Although the words, day, night, bright half of the month etc. denote Time, yet, the other stages which are mentioned, namely, fire, flame, sphere of air, sphere of lightning etc. do not denote Time; and if one believes that a scient reaches different spheres after death according as he dies during the day or during the night, the importance of Jñāna also comes to an end. Therefore, in the Vedānta-Sūtras, the words, fire, day, *uttarāyaṇa* etc. are not understood as denoting Time, but are interpreted as referring to the deities embodied in those ideas; and it is stated that these deities take the Ātmans of the ritualists or of Jñānins to the sphere of Moon, or the sphere of Brahman, by different paths (Ve. Sū. 4. 2. 19-21; 4. 3. 4). But, there is a doubt as to whether or not this opinion is acceptable to the Gītā; because, not only does the Gītā not mention the subsequent stages of the *uttarāyaṇa*, which do not denote Time, but the Blessed Lord has Himself made a definite reference to Time in mentioning the two paths, in the words "I shall mention to you that TIME, dying at which TIME the Karma-Yogin returns or does not return" (Gī. 8. 23); and, there is a statement in the Mahābhārata, that when Bhīṣma was lying on the bed of arrows, he was waiting for the *uttarāyaṇa* that is, for the time when the Sun begins to move towards the North, for giving up his life (Bhī. 120; Anu. 167). From this, it is clear that at some date in the past, the day, the bright half of the month, or the *uttarāyaṇa* were looked upon as proper times for dying. Even in the Ṛg-Veda, where the *devayāna* and the *pitṛyāṇa* are described (Ṛg. 10. 88, 15; and Bṛ. 6. 2. 15), a meaning denoting Time is intended. For this and many other reasons, I have come to the conclusion that when the Vedic Ṛṣis were living near the Meru or the North Pole, that is to say, near the place in the Northern hemisphere, where the Sun is continually visible above the horizon for six months, the lighted period of the *uttarāyaṇa*, lasting for six months, must have come to be considered an appropriate time for dying; and, I have made a detailed exposition of this theory in another work of mine. But, whatever the reason may be, there is no doubt that this belief is a very ancient one, and this belief has become merged, at least indirectly if not directly, in the belief in the two paths of the *devayāna* or the *pitṛyāṇa*; nay, according to me, one can trace the idea of these two paths to this belief. Otherwise, there is no explanation for the fact that two words having distinct meanings, namely, *kāla* (Time), (Gī. 8. 23) in one place and '*gati*' (goal), or '*sṛti*' (path), (Gī. 8. 26 and 27) in another place, have been used in the Bhagavadgītā with reference to the *devayāna* and the *pitṛyāṇa*. In the Śāṁkarabhāṣya on the Vedānta-Sūtras, it is stated that the Time-denoting meaning of the words *devayāna* and *pitṛyāṇa* is the one described in the Smṛtis, which is applicable only to the Karma-Yoga, and that the true Brahmajñānin reaches the sphere of Brahman through the lighted path described in the Śrutis which is governed by deities; and in this way, the 'Time-denoting' and the 'deity-denoting' meanings have been disposed of (Ve. Sū. Śāṁ. Bhā. 4. 2. 18-21). But in my opinion, if one considers the original Vedānta-Sūtras themselves, the meaning given by Bādarāyaṇācārya of the word '*devayāna*' as deity-denoting, by taking the words *uttarāyaṇa* etc. as referring to deities, and not to Time, must have been the one in general acceptance; and it is not proper to believe that the path mentioned in the Gītā is an independent path different from this path of *devayāna* mentioned in the Upaniṣads. But, there is no necessity to go into such deep waters here; because, although there is a difference of opinion on the question whether the words, day, night, *uttarāyaṇa* etc. in the *devayāna* and *pitṛyāṇa* were, from the historical point of view, originally Time-denoting or not, yet, there is no doubt that this Time-denoting meaning ultimately dropped out, and that these two words *devayāna* and *pitṛyāṇa* have ultimately come to commonly and definitely mean, that whenever a man may die, and without any reference to the time when he dies, the Jñānin reaches the other world by the lighted path according to his Karma, and the orthodox ritualist reaches it by the dark paths. Therefore, whether one considers the words 'day' and '*uttarāyaṇa*' as indicative of deities as Bādarāyāṇācārya says, or one considers them figuratively as the rising stages of the lighted path, the proposition that the ordinary meaning of those words in those contexts is indicative of the path followed, is not affected.

But, whether it is the *devayāna* or the *pitṛyāṇa*, these paths are obtained only by those who perform the Karma recommended by the Śāstras, that is, righteous Karma; because, it is quite clear that though the *pitṛyāṇa* path is of a lower order than the *devayāna* path, yet, as it takes a person to the sphere of the Moon, which is a kind of heaven, he must have performed some righteous Action or other, prescribed by Śāstras, in this life in order to have deserved experiencing the happiness of that sphere (Gī. 9. 20-21). It is, therefore, clearly stated in the Upaniṣads that those persons who do not perform in this life even a little of the righteous Karma prescribed by the Śāstras, but are steeped in the performance of Actions which are '*kapūya*', i. e., sinful, cannot obtain either of these paths, and immediately after death, they either take birth in the '*tiryak*' species, that is, in the species of birds, beasts etc., or repeatedly go to the sphere of Yama, that is, to hell. This is known as the 'Third' path (Chān. 5. 10. 8; Katha. 2. 6. 7); and it is stated even in the Bhagavadgītā that purely demonian (*āsuri*) or sinful persons attain this low state (Gī. 16. 19-21; 9. 12; Ve. Sū. 3. 1. 12, 13; Nirukta 14. 9).

I have so far explained the manner in which a human being reaches three different states after his death, having regard to his Karma, according to the ancient tradition of the Vedic religion. It is true that Release is attained only by the *devayāna* path out of these three; yet, this Release is attained only ultimately, after rising step by step through the various stages of the *arcirādi* (*pitṛyāṇa*) path. This path has also the other names of *krama-mukti*' (gradual Release); and. in as much as ultimate Release is attained by going to the sphere of the Brahman after the fall of the body, that is, after death, it is also called '*videha-mukti*' (bodyless Release); but the pure philosophy of the Absolute Self asks why it should be necessary for the man, in whose mind the Realisation of the identity of the Brahman and the Ātman is continually present, to go anywhere else to reach the Brahman, or to wait for death. The Knowledge of the Brahman which is acquired by the worship of symbols like the Sun etc. taken for worship, that is to say, by the worship of the qualityful Brahman, is, in the beginning, a little incomplete; because, thereby the mind conceives the ideas of the sphere of the Sun, or of the sphere of the Brahman, and there is a risk of these ideas remaining fixed in the mind, to a greater or less extent, even at the moment of death. It is, therefore, proper to say that in order to remove this defect and attain Release, such persons must go by the *devayāna* path (Ve. Sū. 4. 3. 15); because, it is a firm doctrine of the philosophy of the Absolute Self that every man reaches after death a '*gati*' (goal) which is consistent with the desire or '*kratu*' present in his mind at the moment of death (Chān. 3. 14. 1). But, the man, in whose mind there does not exist the Dualistic differentiation between the Brahman and his own Ātman resulting from the worship of a qualityful Brahman, or for any other reason (Tai. 2. 7), has evidently not to go anywhere else for attaining the Brahman, in as much as he is perpetually Brahman-natured. It is for this reason that Yājñavalkya has told Janaka in the Bṛhadāraṇyaka (Bṛ. 4. 4. 6) that the vital airs (*prāṇa*) of the man who has become totally desireless, as a result of the pure Realisation of the Brahman, do not go anywhere else—"*na tasya prāṇā utkrāmanti brahmaiva san brahmāpyeti*";—and that such a person is always full of the Brahman and merged in the Brahman; and there are statements both in the Bṛhadāraṇyaka and the Kaṭha Upaniṣads that such a person "*ATRA brahma samaśnute*" (Kaṭha. 6. 14), i. e., "Realises the Brahman HERE"; and on the authority of these Śrutis, it is stated in the Śivagītā, that it is not necessary to leave one's place in order to obtain Release. The Brahman is not such a thing that it can be said to be in a particular place, and not to be in a particular place (Chān. 7. 25; Muṇ. 2. 2. 11). Then, where is the necessity for the person who has acquired complete Realisation to go to the sphere of the Sun through the *uttarāyaṇa*, by these gradual steps, in order to attain the Brahman? "*brahma veda brahmaiva bhavati*" (Muṇ. 3, 2. 9). i. e., "that man who has realised the Brahman, has become the Brahman in this world", that is, wherever he is; because, in order that it should be necessary for somebody to go to another place, the distinction between the one place, and the other place, which depends on Time or Space, must have remained; and these differences cannot exist in the final, that is to say, the Non-Dual and Supreme Realisation of the Brahman. Therefore, why should that man, whose permanent mental state is: "*yasya sarvam ātmaivā 'bhūt*" (Bṛ. 2. 4. 14) or, "*sarvaṁ khalv idaṁ brahma*" (Chān 3. 14. 1), or "*ahaṁ brahmāsmi*" (Bṛ. 1, 4. 10), i. e., "I myself am the Brahman", go to another place for attaining the Brahman? He is always Brahmified (*brahma-bhūta*). As stated at the end of the last chapter, there are descriptions in the Gitā itself, of such supreme scients, in such words as follows:—"*abhito brahma nirvāṇaṁ vartate viditātmanām*" (Gī. 5. 26),—since the man, who has given up the Dualistic feeling and Realises the nature of the Ātman, has not to go anywhere else for attaining Release, though he may have to wait for death in order to exhaust his Commenced Karma, the reward of Release in the shape *brahma nirvāṇa* is always in front of him; or, "*ihaiva tair jitaḥ sargo yeṣāṁ sāmye sthitaṁ manaḥ*" (Gī. 5. 19), i. e., "those men, in whose minds the equality of all created beings in the form of the identity of the Brahman and the Ātman is fixed, have conquered both life and death in this world (without having to depend on the *devayāna* path)"; or, "*bhūtapṛthagbhāvam ekastham anupaśyati*", i. e., "that man for whom the diversity in the various created things has disappeared, and who has begun to see them unified *(ekastham)*, that is, as of the same nature as the Parameśvara, has "*brahma saṁpadyate*", i. e., 'gone and joined the Brahman' " (Gī. 13. 30). In the same way, the meaning of the words "who knows essentially" in the sentence "the Karma-Yogin WHO KNOWS ESSENTIALLY the *devayāna* and *pitṛyāṇa* paths, is not confused" which has been quoted above, seems to be "who has Realised the ultimate form of the Brahman" (Bhāg. 7. 15. 56). This is the complete Brahmified *(brahma-bhūta)* state, or the most supreme Brāhmī-state, and Śrīmat Śaṁkarācārya has stated in his Śārīraka-bhāṣya (Ve. Sū. 4. 3. 14), that this is the most Supreme or the most complete state of the Realisation of the Absolute Self. Nay, in order to acquire this state, a man must be said to have become the Parameśvara in a way; and, it need not be said further, that persons who have thus become Brahmified may be said to have gone beyond the rules of what should be done and what should not be done in the world of Actions; because, as the Realisation of the Brahman is always awake in the case of these people, whatever they do is always inspired by a pure and desireless frame of mind, that is to say, is always free from sin or merit. As it is not necessary to go somewhere else or to die, in order to attain the Brahman after this state has been reached, such a Steady-in-Mind devotee of the Brahman (*(sthitaprajña brahmaniṣṭha)* is known as '*jīvan-mukta*' (birth-released), (See Yo. 3. 9). Though Buddhists do not admit the existence of the Ātman or of the Brahman, yet, they have accepted the position that this desireless state of a *jīvan-mukta* is the ultimate ideal of man; and they have accepted this doctrine with nominal verbal differences in their religious treatises (see the Appendices). Many persons say that as this ultimate self-less state is naturally antagonistic to the ordinary Actions of life, the man, who has reached this state, automatically escapes Karma and becomes an ascetic *(saṁnyāsin)*. But, as will be seen from the exposition in the next chapter, this position is not accepted by the Gītā; and the doctrine of the Gītā is that it is more proper for the Birth-released man to go on performing all Actions, till he dies, desirelessly, and for the public benefit, as is done by the Parameśvara himself. This doctrine of the Gītā has also been accepted in the Yoga-vāsiṣṭha (Yo. 6. U. 199).

CHAPTER XI.

RENUNCIATION AND KARMA-YOGA.

(SAMNYĀSA AND KARMA-YOGA).

saṁnyāsaḥ karmayogaś ca niḥśreyasakarāvubhau ।
tayos tu karmasaṁnyāsāt karmayogo viśiṣyate ॥ *

Gītā. 5. 2.

I have, in the last chapter, considered in detail the position that there is only one way, in which one can escape the toils of eternal Karma, by Realising by personal experience the Parabrahman, which exists homogeneously in all created things; as also the questions whether man is or is not free to Realise that immortal Brahman, and how he should perform the transient affairs or Actions in the Māyā-world in order to obtain that Realisation; and I drew the conclusions, that bondage is not the characteristic feature of Action, but of the Mind; and that, therefore, by performing these Actions with a pure, that is, with a disinterested frame of mind, after having by means of mental control gradually reduced the Attachment which one has for the result of the fruit of Action, the Realisation of the Ātman, in the shape of an equable frame of mind, gradually saturates the corporeal organs, and complete Release is ultimately obtained. In this way, I have answered the question as to what is required to be done as being the means for acquiring the highest of ideals in the shape of Release, or the perfect state

* "Renunciation (*saṁnyāsa*) and Energism (*karma-yoga*) are both *niḥśreyasakara*, i. e., productive of Release; but out of the two, Adherence to Action (*karma-yoga*) is superior to the Renunciation of Action (*karma-saṁnyāsa*)". The meaning, in which the word '*saṁnyāsa*' used in the first line is to be taken, becomes clear from the phrase '*karma saṁnyāsa*' used in the second line. These questions and answers from the Gītā are found adopted at the beginning of the fourth chapter of the Gaṇeśagītā, and there, the present verse has been given with a slight verbal difference as, "*kriyāyogo viyogaś cāpy ubhau mokṣasya sādhane* । *tayor madhye kriyāyogas tyāgāt tasya viśiṣyate* ॥".

according to the philosophy of the Absolute Self. We have now to consider the most important question, whether after having thus broken the bondage of Karma and fully Realised the Brahman, as a result of the purification of his Mind arising from his having acted in this way, that is, from his having performed Desireless Actions according to his own capacity and status, a scient or Steady-in-Mind (*sthitaprajña*) should subsequently, that is, when being in the state of a Perfect (*siddha*), continue performing Action, or, looking upon himself as one who has performed all that was to be performed, because he has acquired all that was to be acquired, consider all Actions in the world of Illusion as useless and inconsistent with Knowledge, and totally give them up; because, logically speaking, in such a situation, both the positions of totally abandoning Action (*karma-saṁnyāsa*), and performing those Actions upto death with a desireless frame of mind (*karma-yoga*), are possible; and, as it is more convenient to chalk out one's course of action consistently with that mode of life which is the better of the two, from the very beginning, that is to say, while one is training onself (*sādhanāvasthā*), no Metaphysical exposition on Action and Non-Action becomes complete, unless one comparatively considers both these modes of life. It would not have been sufficient to say to Arjuna that after the Realisation of the Brahman, it is just the same whether one performs or does not perform Action (Gī. 3. 18) on the ground that a man, whose Reason has become equable towards all created beings as a result of Knowledge, is not affected by the merit or demerit of any Action (Gī. 4. 20, 21), since Reason is superior to Action in all the affairs of life. The definite injunction of the Blessed Lord to Arjuna was: "Fight"! (*yudhyasva!*), (Gī. 2. 18); and it would be necessary to adduce some cogent reasons in support of this firm advice rather than placing before him the indecisive advice that it was just the same whether he fought or did not fight after he had acquired Realisation. Nay, the doctrine of the Gītā has come into existence only in order to explain why a wise man must perform a particular act, notwithstanding that he sees before his eyes the terrible consequences of it; and this is indeed the most important feature of the Gītā. If it is true that a man is bound by Action, whereas, he gets salvation by Knowledge, why should the person, who has acquired Knowledge, at all perform Action? Though the doctrines, that destruction of Karma (*karma-kṣaya*) does not mean Abadonment of Action, that Action is annihilated by its being performed after one has given up the hope for the Fruit of the Action, and that it is not possible to give up every kind of Action etc., are true, yet, it does not thereby conclusively follow, that one should not give up as much of Action as one can; and logically thinking, such a conclusion does arise. Because, as has been stated in the Gītā, in the same way as it is no more necessary to go to a well for water, when water is to be found in all directions, so also has a scient no more to depend on Action for anything, after he has acquired that Knowledge, which can be acquired by the performance of Action (Gī. 2. 46). Therefore, Arjuna has said to Śrī Kṛṣṇa in the commencement of the third chapter as follows: if in Your opinion the desireless or equable frame of mind is superior to Action, I shall make my Reason pure like that of a Sthitaprajña; why do You compel me to perform a terrible act like war"? (Gī. 3. 1). In reply to this question, the Blessed Lord has said that no one can escape Action etc., and in that way justified the doctrine of Action. But, if philosophy has prescribed the two paths of Sāṁkhya (Renunciation) and Energism (Karma-Yoga), it follows naturally that after the acquisition of Knowledge, a man may follow whichever path he considers better. Therefore, in the commencement of the fifth chapter, Arjuna has again said to the Blessed Lord that He should not mix up the two courses of life, but should explain to him (Arjuna) in a definite way which of the two was superior (Gī. 5. 1); if, after the acquisition of Knowledge, it was just the same whether Action was performed or not performed, he would perform Action or not perform it as he liked; but, if performing Action was the better course of the two, the Blessed Lord should tell him the reason why that was so, so that, he would act according to His directions. This question of Arjuna is not something new. In the Yoga-Vāsiṣṭha (5. 56. 6), Rāma has asked the same question to Vasiṣṭha, and in the Gaṇeśagītā (4. 1) the king named Vareṇya has asked the same question to Gaṇeśa; and it even appears from the works of Aristotle that this question had been raised in very ancient times in Europe in Greece, where philosophical ideas first originated. This same question has been raised at the end of the book on Ethics written by this well-known Greek philosopher (10. 7 and 8); and he has, in the first instance, expressed his opinion that true happiness consists in a scient spending his life in the quiet contemplation on philosophy instead of in the ups and downs of life *(saṁsāra)* or of political activity. Yet, in the book written by him subsequently on Politics (7. 2. and 3), Aristotle himself says :—some philosophers are engrossed in thoughts of philosophy and others in political activities; and if one considers which of these two modes of life is better, one must say that both the paths are to a certain extent proper; nevertheless, it would be wrong to say that Non-Action is better than Action, * because, happiness is nothing but Action; and one may safely say that the acquisition of true nobility consists to a considerable extent of Action founded on Knowledge and the principles of Ethics. From the fact that Aristotle has made two different statements in two different places, the importance of the clear statement in the Gitā that "*karma jyāyo hy akarmaṇaḥ*" (Gī. 3. 8)—ACTION IS SUPERIOR TO NON-ACTION—becomes clear to the reader. Augustus Comte, a well-known French philosopher of the last century says in his book on Material Philosophy that :—"it is misleading to say that it is better to spend one's life in the contemplation of philosophy; and the philosopher, who adopts such a course of life, and abandons the doing of whatever public welfare it is possible for him to do, must be said to misuse the material which is at his disposal". On the other hand, the German philosopher Schopenhauer has maintained that in as much as all the activities of the world, nay, even keeping alive itself, is painful, the true duty of every human being in this world is to learn philosophy and to destroy all this Action as early as possible. Comte died in 1857 A. D. and Schopenhauer in 1860

* "And it is equally a *mistake to place inactivity above action,* for happiness is activity, and the actions of the just and the wise are the realisation of much that is noble". (See Aristotle's *Politics* trans. by Jowett. Vol. I. p. 212. The italics are ours).

A. D. The school of Schopenhauer has been continued in Germany by Hartmann. It need not be said that the English philosophers Spencer, Mill, and others are of the same opinion as Comte. But the modern Materialistic philosopher Nietzsche has gone beyond all these philosophers, and he has in his works so severely criticised those who are for giving up Action, that according to him, it is not possible to refer to the supporters of Renunciation (*karma-saṁnyāsa*) by any milder terms than 'fools of fools'. *

Just as in Europe there have been two schools of thought from the time of Aristotle upto the present day, so also, have there been two modes of life according to the Vedic religion in India from ancient times upto the present day (Ma. Bhā. Śān. 349. 72). Out of these two, one course is known as the Saṁnyāsa-Mārga or Sāṁkhya-niṣṭhā or merely SĀMKHYA or Jñāna-niṣṭhā (because, it consists of being continually steeped in Knowledge); and the other path is known as the Karma-Yoga or shortly YOGA or Karma-niṣṭhā. I have already in the third chapter clearly explained that the words Sāṁkhya and Yoga do not respectively indicate the Kāpila-sāṁkhya and the Pātañjala-yoga. But, in as much as, the word '*saṁnyāsa*' is also rather ambiguous, it is necessary to explain its meaning here more fully. The word '*saṁnyāsa*' does not in this place mean 'not marrying', or 'giving up wife and children and wearing saffron-coloured robes', in case

* Sully has in his book *Pessimism* given the names 'Optimism' and 'Pessimism' respectively to Karma-Yoga and Karma-Tyāga (Sāṁkhya or Renunciation). But, in my opinion, these names are not correct. 'Pessimism' implies the meaning of 'whiner' or 'despondent'. But those persons who give up wordly life, looking upon it as transient, are joyful; and though they give up such life, they do so joyfully. Therefore, it is not correct, according to me, to refer to them as 'Pessimists'. Rather than that, it would be more proper to refer to Karma-Yoga in English as 'Energism', and to the Sāṁkhya or the Saṁnyāsa path as 'Quietism'. As Knowledge of the Brahman is common to both these paths according to the Vedic religion, happiness or peace is the same according to both; we do not make the difference that one path leads to happiness and the other to unhappiness, or that one is hopeful and the other hopeless.

one has married, or 'merely adopting the fourth stage of life'. Because, though Bhīṣma was a celibate, he was taking part in politics till the moment of his death; and Śrīmat Śaṁkarācārya, after passing to the fourth state straight from the first state of celibacy, or in the Mahārāṣtra, Śrī Samartha Rāmadāsa, remaining a celibate mendicant for life, have brought about the salvation of the world by spreading Knowledge. The crucial point in the present place is whether after having acquired Knowledge, a man should take part in all the activities of the world as duties and for public welfare, or should entirely give them up, looking upon them as illusory. He who takes part in these activities is the Karma-Yogin, whether he has married or has not married, and whether he wears white clothes or saffron-coloured clothes. Nay, for performing these activities, it is sometimes more convenient to remain unmarried or to wear saffron-coloured robes, or to go and live outside the town; because, by doing so, there is no obstruction in the way of applying one's whole time and energy to public welfare, as it does not entail the worry of maintaining a family. Though such persons may be ascetics according to the dress which they wear, yet, essentially they are Karma-Yogins; but on the other hand, such persons as look upon all worldly activities as useless, and abandon them and sit quiet, may be said to be ascetics, whether they have entered the fourth state of life or not. In short, the Gītā does not attach importance to white clothing or saffron-coloured clothing or to marriage or celibacy, but considers only whether the scient takes or does not take part in worldly activities, in differentiating between Renunciation and Energism. All other things are of no importance, at any rate according to the religion of the Gītā. The words '*karma-saṁnyāsa*' or '*karma-tyāga*' would be more appropriate and unambiguous in the present place than '*saṁnyāsa*' (Renunciation) or '*caturthāśrama*' (the fourth state). But, as it is more usual to use the single word '*saṁnyāsa*' rather than the two words mentioned above, I have here explained the technical meaning of that word. Those, who consider worldly activities as fruitless, give up worldly life; and, entering the forests, take to the fourth state of life, according to the Smṛti religion; and, therefore, this path of Abandonment of Action is called 'Saṁnyāsa'. But, the important factor in that procedure is the Abandonment of Action, and not the saffron-coloured robes.

Though it is thus usual either to continue the performance of Action (Karma-Yoga) or to abandon Action (Karma-Saṁnyāsa), after the complete acquisition of Knowledge, doctrine-supporting commentators on the Gītā have in this place raised the question whether both these paths are equally independent and in a position to give Release, or whether the Karma-Yoga is the preliminary or first step, and one has ultimately to abandon Action, and renounce the world in order to attain Release. It is seen that these two courses of life have been mentioned as independent paths in the second and third chapters of the Gītā. But those commentators, in whose opinion it is impossible to attain Release unless a man renounces the world and abandons the ordinary activities of life,—and who have started commenting on the Gītā with the preconceived notion that that must be the doctrine propounded by the Gītā—pronounce the sum and the substance of the Gītā to be that: "Karma-Yoga, is not an independent path of obtaining Release; that one must, in the beginning, perform Actions in order to purify the mind, but ultimately go in for Renunciation; and that Renunciation is the paramount and the ultimate cult." But if this meaning is adopted, then the importance of the word '*dvividhā*' (two-fold) in the statement of the Blessed Lord that the Sāṁkhya (Saṁnyāsa) and Yoga (Karma-Yoga) are two kinds of cults in this world (Gī. 3. 3), is lost. The word 'Karma-Yoga' can be interpreted in three different ways: (1) according to the first interpretation, Release is obtained by performing the Karma laid down by the Śrutis and the Smṛtis, or the duties of the four castes, such as sacrifice etc. But this interpretation of the Mīmāṁsā school is not acceptable to the Gītā (2. 45); (2) the second meaning is, that Action should be performed, but only for the purification of the Mind, in as much as the performance of Action (Karma-Yoga) is essential for the purification of the Mind. According to this interpretation, Karma-Yoga becomes the anterior part or the preliminary preparation for the Renunciation (Saṁnyāsa) state. But this is not the Karma-Yoga mentioned in the Gītā. (3) The important question in the Gītā is, whether or not a scient, who has Realised in what the benefit of his Self lies, should go on performing till death the worldly Actions, prescribed for the caste to which he belongs, such as, fighting etc.; and the Karma-Yoga described in the Gītā is, that even a scient, who has acquired Knowledge, must perform the Actions prescribed for the four castes with a distinterested frame of mind (Gī. 3.35); and it can never be a preliminary preparation for Renunciation; because, in this path, a man can never abandon Action, and the only question is of obtaining Release. But, the Gītā clearly says that in as much as Knowledge has already been acquired by the man, Desireless Action does not become a source of bondage; and that the Release which can be obtained by Renunciation, can also be obtained by this Karma-Yoga (Gī. 5. 5.) Therefore, the words: "*loke smin dvividhā niṣṭhā*" in the Gītā (Gī. 3. 3) must be interpreted as indicating that the path of Karma-Yoga taught by the Gītā is not a preparation for Renunciation, but that both these paths are equally good (*tulyabala*), from the point of view of Release, after Realisation has come (Gī. 8. 2). That is why the Blessed Lord has distinguished between these two paths in the latter half of the stanza (Gī. 3. 3) by saying: "*jñānayogena sāṁkhyānāṁ karma-yogena yoginām*" (i. e. "the path for Release followed by Sāṁkhyas is the Jñāna-Yoga, and that followed by Yogins is the Karma-Yoga"–Trans.); and the two words '*anye*' (the one) and '*apare*' (the other) in the line "*anye sāṁkhyena yogena karma-yogena cāpare*" in the thirteenth chapter, do not become appropriate unless these two paths are considered independent (Gī. 13. 24). Besides, if one considers the history given in the Mahābhārata of the Nārāyaṇīya doctrine, from which the Activistic path (Yoga) has been adopted into the Gītā, the same proposition is confirmed. The origin of these two paths has been described in the Mahābhārata by saying that after the Blessed Lord had, in the beginning of the world, directed Hiraṇyagarbha, that is, Brahmadeva, to create the world, the seven mind-born sons, Marīci and others, came into existence from him; and these seven sons adopted YOGA, that is the Activistic (*pravṛtti*) path of Action for properly carrying out the work of creation;

whereas, his other seven mind-born sons, namely, Sanatkumāra, Kapila, and others took up the SĀMKHYA, that is, the Path of Renunciation (*nivṛtti*) from birth; and later on, it is clearly stated that, from the point of view of Release, both these paths are equally useful (*tulyabala*), that is to say, they are different from each other and independent, and individually capable of bringing about the attainment to one and the same Parameśvara in the form of the Vāsudeva (Ma. Bhā. Śān. 348. 74; 349. 63-73). In the same way, a distinction has been made between Hiraṇyagarbha as the founder of the Activistic Path and Kapila as the founder as the Saṁkhya Path, and it is nowhere stated that Hiraṇyagarbha later on gave up the performance of Action. On the other hand, it is stated that the Blessed Lord created the cycle of Yajñas in the shape of Karma, in order to keep going without a hitch all the activities of the creation, and directed Hiraṇyagarbha, as also the other gods, to keep this cycle continually moving. (Ma. Bhā. Śān. 340. 44-75 and 339. 66, 67). From this, it is established beyond doubt that Sāṁkhya and Yoga are two essentially independent modes of life. It will thus be seen that the attempt of some commentators on the Gītā to make out that the Karma-Yoga is inferior, is the result of a traditionary insistence; and that the statement occurring every now and then in these commentaries that the Karma-Yoga is merely a medium for the acquisition of Knowledge, or for Renunciation, is something, which these commentators say of their own accord, and which is not borne out by the Gītā. In my opinion, this is the greatest fault of those commentators on the Gītā who support the Path of Renunciation; and unless this doctrine-supporting point of view of the commentators is given up, the true and mystic import of the Gītā can never be realised.

It is not enough to say that Karma-Saṁnyāsa and Karma-Yoga are individually equally productive of Release, and that one is not the preliminary part of the other; because, if both these paths are equally productive of Release, it follows that one may adopt whichever path he likes; and then, instead of arriving at the conclusion that he must fight, Arjuna would have the choice of the two paths of fighting, or renouncing the world instead of fighting, after he had acquired Knowledge by the advice of the Blessed Lord. Therefore, Arjuna has asked the natural and straight question, namely, "tell me in a definite way which of these two paths is more proper" (Gī. 5. 11), so that it would be easy for him to act according to that path. Arjuna having asked this question in the beginning of the fifth chapter, the Blessed Lord has immediately in the next verse given a clear answer to it, namely, "though the Path of Renunciation, and the Path of Karma-Yoga are both equally productive of Release (*niḥśreyasa*), yet, out of these two paths THE WORTH OR IMPORTANCE OF KARMA-YOGA IS GREATER (*viśiṣyate*)", (Gī. 5. 2); and I have designedly quoted this stanza at the beginning of this chapter. It is not that these are the only words in the Gītā which support the superiority of Karma-Yoga. There are several other statements in the Gītā which contain that advice to Arjuna, such as,:—"*tasmād yogāya yujyasva*" (Gī. 2. 50), i. e., "therefore, adopt the Karma-Yoga"; or, "*mā te saṁgo 'stv akarmaṇi*" (Gī. 2. 47), i. e., "do not insist on not performing Actions"; or,

yastv indriyāṇi manasā niyamyārabhate 'rjuna ।
karmendriyaiḥ karma-yogam asaktaḥ sa viśiṣyate ॥
(Gī. 3.7.)

that is, instead of abandoning Action, "controlling the organs by the Mind, and using the organs of Action for performing Actions with a desireless frame of mind is *VIŚEṢA* (more IMPORTANT), (*viśiṣyate*)"; because, in any case, "*karma jyāyo hy akarmaṇaḥ*", i. e., "Action is SUPERIOR (*śreṣṭha*) to Inaction" (Gī. 3. 8); "therefore, go on performing Actions" (Gī. 4. 15); or, "*yogamātiṣṭhottiṣṭha*" (Gī. 4. 2), i. e., "accept the Path of (Karma-)Yoga and stand up to fight"; or "*(yogi) jñānibhyo 'pi mato 'dhikaḥ*", i.e., "the merit of the (Karma-) Yogin is more *(adhikaḥ)* than that of the Jñāna-mārgin (of Saṁnyāsa)"; or, "*tasmād yogī bhavārjuna*" (Gī. 4. 6), i. e., "therefore, O Arjuna, become a (Karma-) Yogin"; or, "*mām anusmara yudhya ca*" (Gī. 8. 7), i.e., "think of me and fight" etc. etc.; and in that advice the clear words '*JYĀYAḤ*', '*ADHIKAḤ*', '*VIŚIṢYATE*' have been used in order to show that the merit of Karma-Yoga is higher than that of Renunciation or Non-Action. And even in the summing up in the 18th chapter, the Blessed Lord has again said (Gī. 18. 6, 7) that, "it is my DEFINITE and BETTER opinion that it is not proper to abandon those Actions which have been prescribed, and that one must always perform Actions without being attached to them". From this, it is established beyond doubt, that according to the Gītā, Karma-Yoga is superior to Renunciation.

But how will this doctrine of the Gīta be appreciated by these commentators, whose doctrinal opinion is that Renunciation or Devotion is the ultimate and most superior duty, and that Karma is merely a means for the purification of the Mind, and not the principal ideal or duty? It is not that they had not seen that the Gītā has clearly given a higher importance to Karma-Yoga than to Renunciation; but, if they accepted this opinion as correct, their doctrines would become inferior; and, therefore, these doctrine-supporting commentators have experienced considerable difficulty in disposing of the question put by Arjuna, and the answer given to it by the Blessed Lord, in the beginning of the fifth chapter, though they are both clear, logical, and unambiguous. Their first difficulty has been that the question as to which one out of the two paths, namely, Action or Inaction, is superior, does not arise, unless both these paths are considered independent; because, if, as these commentators say, Karma-Yoga is only a preliminary preparation for Jñāna or Knowledge, it naturally follows that the preliminary part is inferior, and that Jñāna or Saṁnyāsa is superior; and then, there would remain no room for Arjuna to ask the question he asked; but, if it is admitted that the question was a proper one, it becomes necessary to admit that these two paths are independent; and, if that admission is made, the position that the Path of Renunciation supported by them is the only path which leads to Release, becomes untenable! Therefore, they have first passed judgment that the question asked by Arjuna was itself not proper; and they have made up their minds to say the same thing about the reply of the Blessed Lord! But, even after this struggle, the clear answer given by the Blessed Lord to Arjuna that: "the merit or superiority of the Karma-Yoga is GREATER (*viśeṣa*)", (Gī. 5. 2), cannot be satisfactorily explained; and, therefore, these commentators have gone to the length of laying down, on their own hook, and contrary to the anterior and posterior context, that the statement "*karm-yogo viśiṣyate*", i. e., "the superiority of Karma-Yoga is greater," is a fallow praise of the Karma-Yoga, or merely an *artha-vāda* (See. p. 31 above—Trans.); and that, even according to the Blessed Lord, the Path of Renunciation is better; and they have, in this way attempted to satisfy themselves (Gī. Śāṁ. Bhā. 5. 2; 6. 1, 2; 18. 11). Not only in the Śāṁkarabhāṣya, but also in the Rāmānujabhāṣya has this stanza been interpreted as being a mere praise of the Karma-Yoga and an *obiter dicta (artha-vāda)*, (Gī. Rā. Bhā. 5. 1); because, although Rāmānujācārya was not a Non-Dualist, yet, as in his opinion Devotion was the principal ideal, Karma-Yoga became merely a means for Devotion based on Knowledge (Gī. Rā. Bhā; 3. 1). My readers will see how the meaning in the original is stretched and mutilated, where the original work and the commentators support different doctrines, and the commentators begin to comment on the original in the firm belief that the doctrine supported by them is borne out by the original. Were not Śrī Kṛṣṇa or Śrī Vyāsa in a position to clearly say to Arjuna in plain Sanskrit: "O Arjuna, your question is improper"? But as, instead of doing so, it has been stated in numerous places that "Karma-Yoga is superior", one has to say that the doctrine-supporting interpretation, which has been put on the stanza by these commentators, is incorrect; and if one refers to the previous and the subsequent context, this inference is fortified. Because, it is stated in various places in the Gītā, that the scient does not abandon Action, but performs all Actions with a disinterested frame of mind after attaining Realisation. (Gī. 2. 64; 3. 19; 3. 25; 18. 9). Śrīmat Śaṁkarācārya has, in his Śāṁkarabhāṣya, in the beginning raised the question whether Release is obtained by means of Knowledge, or by the combination of Knowledge and Action; and he has expounded the import of the Gītā as being that Release is obtained by Knowledge alone, by the destruction of Karma resulting from Knowledge, and that Karma is not necessary for Realisation; and, he has from this drawn the subsequent inference, that the Blessed Lord must be considered to have accepted the position in the Gītā, that even according to the Gītā, Karma becomes meaningless when once the Mind has been purified, as Karma is not necessary for obtaining Release; and that as Karma is inherently binding or inconsistent with Knowledge, a scient must give up (Action after acquiring Knowledge. That school of thought which says that even after having acquired Knowledge, a man must perform Action, is known as the Knowledge-Action (*jñāna-karma-samuccaya*) school, and the above-mentioned argument of Śrī Śaṁkarācārya is the principal argument against it. The same argument has been accepted even by Madhvācārya (Gī. Mā. Bhā. 3. 31). But from my point of view, this argument is neither satisfactory nor unanswerable; because (1) although Desire-prompted (*kāmya*) Actions are binding and contra-indicated for Knowledge, the same reasoning does not apply to Desireless (*niṣkāma*) Actions; and (2) although Action may not be necessary for obtaining Release after having acquired Knowledge, that does not negative the proposition that a scient must, for other cogent reasons, perform Desireless Action, though he has obtained Realisation. It is not that Karma has come into existence only for the purpose of purifying the Mind of those who desire Release, nor that that is the sole object of Karma. Therefore, one may say, that a scient has to perform the various activities in the world of Karma, which are appropriate for him according to his status in life, for other reasons than the obtaining of Release. I have in this chapter, later on, considered in detail, what these reasons are. For the moment, I will only say that the doctrine of the Gītā was expounded for the sole purpose of explaining these reasons to Arjuna, who was desirous of becoming an ascetic; and one cannot draw the inference that the Gītā supports the Path of Renunciation, by arguing that after the purification of the Mind, performance of Action is not necessary for obtaining Release. It is true that the followers of Śaṁkarācārya hold that after the acquisition of Knowledge, one must renounce the world and give up Action; but on that account it does not follow, that the same is the teaching of the Gītā, or that one has to interpret the Gītā in a manner consistent with the doctrines laid down by Śaṁkarācārya or some other doctrinaire, after first taking it for granted that the doctrine expounded by Śaṁkarācārya or such other doctrinaire, is the only true doctrine. It has been definitely laid down in the Gītā that even after the acquisition of of Knowledge, it is better to perform Action than to renounce the world; then you may call it a different school of thought or give it some other name. Still, it must be borne in mind that, although according to the Gītā, Energism (Karma-Yoga) is in this way stated to be superior, the Gītā does not maintain like other schools, which cannot endure a different philosophy, that the Path of Renunciation is altogether objectionable; and nowhere in the Gītā has any disrespect being shown for that path. On the other hand, the Blessed Lord has clearly stated that both the Path of Renunciation and the Path of Energism or Action (Karma-Yoga) equally lead to Release, that is to say, that they are both of the same value from the point of view of Release; and later on, the Blessed Lord has stated that "*ekaṁ sāṁkhyaṁ ca yogaṁ ca yaḥ paśyati sa paśyati*" (Gī. 5. 5), i. e., "that man who has realised that both these paths are of equal value, has realised the true principle", as also that even in the 'Karma-Yoga,' one has to make a 'Renunciation' of the hope for the fruit of Action—"*na hy asaṁnyasta saṁkalpo yogī bhavati kaś ca na*" (Gī. 6. 2), (i. e., "unless a man performs a *saṁnyāsa (tyāga)* of the *saṁkalpa*, that is, of the hope of reward, born of a desireful mind, he does not become a (Karma-) Yogin"—Trans.) and He has in this way skilfully harmonised as far as possible these two paths. But, though from the point of view of Release, the two paths of either abandoning Karma or continuing to perform Karma after acquiring Knowledge (and not before) may be of the same value, yet, from the point of view of worldly affairs, the most superior mode of life is to keep the Renunciation in the Mind itself, and to go on performing lifelong the Action which is beneficial to the world, through the medium of the bodily organs; because, the Blessed Lord has definitely said that in such a mode of life, both Renunciation and Action find a place; and Arjuna has, according to this advice, become ready to fight. This is really the difference between the scient (*jñānin*) and the ignorant (*ajñānin*). If one considers only the *śārira-karma*, that is, the Actions which are to be performed by the organs, these are the same in both the cases; but the ignorant person performs them with an attached Reason, and the scient, with an unattached Reason (Gī. 3. 25). This doctrine of the Gītā has been expounded by the dramatist Bhāsa in one of his dramas in the following words:-

prājñasya mūrkhasya ca kāryayoge ।
samatvam abhyeti tanur na buddhiḥ ॥

(Avimāra 5. 5).

that is, "when Actions are performed by the wise man, or the fool, the Body is the same, but the Mind is different".

Some sundry supporters of the Path of Renunciation go further and say in this matter that: "it is true that the Gītā advises Arjuna to perform Actions; but, this advice was given by the Blessed Lord, bearing in mind the fact that Arjuna had still not acquired Knowledge, and was fit only for performing Actions for purifying the Mind. The path of *karma-tyāga* (Abandonment of Action) is the proper course in the state of a *siddha* (Perfect,), even according to the Blessed Lord". But, this means that the Blessed Lord feared that if He had told Arjuna that he was ignorant, he (Arjuna) would have insisted on acquiring complete Knowledge, as was done by Naciketa in the Kaṭhopaniṣad; and then He (the Blessed Lord) would have to initiate Arjuna into the complete Knowledge, and when this complete Knowledge had been imparted, he (Arjuna) would give up war-fare and become an ascetic, and upset His (the Blessed Lord's) plans about the war; and that, the Blessed Lord expounded the Gītā to his most beloved devotee, in order to deceive him. In my opinion, one cannot do better than give up all argument with persons, who, in order to be able to support their own doctrine, stoop so low as to suggest that the Blessed Lord was guilty of such a mean action as to deceive His own beloved disciple. But in order that ordinary people should not be taken in by this deceptive argument, I say that Śrī Kṛṣṇa had not to be afraid of anyone, if He had wanted to say Arjuna in clear terms: "you are ignorant, and therefore, you must go on performing Actions"; and if after that, Arjuna had become rebellious, the Blessed Lord was quite capable of keeping him in ignorance, and making him fight according to his inherent tendencies (*prakṛti-dharma*), (Gī. 18. 59 and 61); but instead of doing so, He has over and over again explained to Arjuna the meaning of '*jñāna*' and '*vijñāna*' (Gī. 7. 2; 9. 1; 10. 1; 13. 2; 14. 1), and at the end of the fifteenth chapter, He has said to Arjuna: "by understanding this science, a man becomes a scient, and a perfect being (Gī. 15. 23); and having in this way made of Arjuna a complete scient, the Blessed Lord has made him fight of his own free will (Gī. 18. 63). From this, it becomes abundantly clear that the best mode of life for a scient according to the Blessed Lord, is to continue to perform Action desirelessly, even after having acquired Knowledge. Besides, even if Arjuna is, for the sake of argument, looked upon as ignorant, one cannot say that Janaka and other ancient Karma-Yogins, as also the Blessed Lord Himself, whose illustrations have been given by the Blessed Lord in support of His doctrine, were all ignorant. Therefore, one has to say that this fallow argument, based on a doctrinal insistence, is totally improper and objectionable, and that the Gītā has expounded nothing but the doctrine of Action combined with Knowledge.

It has become necessary for me to go in for this introduction, in order to show that the two paths of Abandonment of Action (Sāṁkhya) and Energism (Karma-Yoga) were in vogue from times immemorial, not only in our country, but in other countries; and to show how and why doctrine-supporting commentators have perversely dealt with the the two important doctrines of the Gītā on this subject, namely that, (1) these two paths are independent, that is, not inter-dependent, from the point of view of Release; and are of equal value; and that one is not a part of the other; and that, (2) out of these two, Karma-Yoga is the superior path, though these doctrines are quite clear by themselves. I will now consider the subject-matter of the present chapter, namely, the reasons which have been given in the Gītā for proving that even in the state of Perfection, the path of Karma-Yoga, that is, of performing Actions till death with a desireless frame of mind, is more meritorious than Abandonment of Action. Some of these matters have been explained by me in the chapter on

Happiness and Unhappiness (*sukha-duḥkha-viveka*) above ; but, as the argument in that chapter was restricted to the question of happiness and unhappiness, it was not possible for me to fully deal with this subject-matter there. I have, therefore, started this independent chapter here. I have explained in the last chapter that the Vedic religion is divided into the Karma-kāṇḍa and Jñāna-kāṇḍa, and shown what the difference between the two, is. Out of them, there are directions in the Karma-kāṇḍa, that is, in the Śruti texts, such as, the Brāhmaṇas, and partly also in the Upaniṣad texts, that every man, be he a Brahmin or a Kṣatriya, must maintain a sacred fire, and perform the '*jyotiṣṭoma*' and other sacrificial ritual according to his own status; and there also clear statements that it is the duty of every one to marry and increase his generation. See for instance, the statements: "*etad vai jarāmaryaṁ satraṁ yad agnihotram*", i. e., "this sacrifice in the shape of the sacrificial fire (*agnihotra*) must be kept alive till death" (Śa. Brā. 12. 4. 1. 1); or "*prajātantuṁ mā vyavatchhetsīḥ*". i. e. "do not break the thread of thy generation" (Tai. U. 1. 11. 1); or "*īśāvāsyam idaṁ sarvam*", i. e., "whatever is in this world, should be located into the Parameśvara, that is to say, one should realise that it is of the Parameśvara and not of oneself"; and, with this desireless frame of mind,

kurvan neveha karmāṇi jijīviṣec chataṁ samāḥ ।
evaṁ tvayi nānyatheto 'sti na karma lipyate nare ॥

(Īśā. 1 and 2)

that is, "one should entertain the desire of living upto a hundred years, which is the limit of the life of man, whilst performing Actions ; and when Actions are performed '*evam*', that is, with that *īśāvāsya* (god-dedicating) frame of mind, they will not have a binding force *(lepa)* on you (on any human being), and there is no other way for escaping (that *lepa* or bondage)". But, when one leaves the Karma-kāṇḍa and moves on to the Jñāna-kāṇḍa, one also comes across contradictory statements in the same Vedic treatises, such as, "*brahmavidāpnoti param*" (Tai. 2. 1. 1), i. e., "Release is obtained by Knowledge of the Brahman" ; or, "*nānyaḥ panthā vidyate 'yanāya*" (Śve. 3. 8), i. e., "there is no other path, except Knowledge, for obtaining

Release"; or "*pūrve vidvāṁsaḥ prajāṁ na kāmayante । kiṁ prajayā kariṣyāmo yeṣāṁ no 'yam ātmā 'yaṁ loka iti te ha sma putraiṣaṇāyāś ca vittaiṣaṇāyāś ca lokaiṣaṇāyāś ca vyutthāyātha bhikṣācaryaṁ caranti*" (Bṛ. 4. 4. 22 and 3. 5. 1), i. e., "the scients of yore did not have any desire for children; they used to say: 'as we see that the whole world is nothing but our Ātman, why should we have any (other) generation ?' and, without entertaining the '*eṣaṇā*', that is, desire, for wealth, children, heaven, and the other spheres, such scients used to renounce those things, and roam about the world at will begging for alms"; or, "such persons, who have thus become ascetics, attain Release (Muṇ. 1. 2. 11); or, ultimately "*yad ahar eva virajet tad ahar eva pravrajet*" (Jābā. 4), i. e., "on such day as your mind becomes apathetic, on that day you should renounce the world". As the directions of the Vedas are in this way two-fold (Ma. Bhā. Śān. 240-6), it becomes necessary to see whether there is some other means of deciding which of the two paths, namely, Activism *(pravṛtti)* or Renunciation *(nivṛtti)*, Karma-Yoga or Sāṁkhya, is superior. The question could have been decided by considering the '*ācāra*', that is, the conduct, usage, or custom of well-behaved persons *(śiṣṭa)*; but, in this matter, even the conduct of such persons is seen to be two-fold. It is clear from history that Śuka, Yājñavalkya, and others had taken to the Path of Renunciation, whereas Janaka, Śrī Kṛṣṇa, Jaigīṣavya and other scients had adopted the Path of Action. Therefore, Bādarāyaṇācārya has said in the argument in the demonstrated conclusion (*siddhānta-pakṣa*), that both these paths are '*tulyaṁ tu darśanam*', that is, of equal value from the point of view of conduct (Ve. Sū. 3. 4. 9); and there is even a Smṛti text that:-

vivekī sarvadā muktaḥ kurvato nāsti kartṛtā ।
alepavādam āśritya śrīkṛṣṇajanakau yathā ॥

that is, "that person who has acquired complete Knowledge of the Brahman, is always a non-doer (*akartā*), isolated (*alipta*), and eternally released like Śrī Kṛṣṇa and Janaka". *

* Ānandagiri has taken this statement as being from the Smṛtis in his commentary on the Śaṁkarābhāṣya on the Kaṭhopaniṣad (Kaṭha. 2. 19). I have not found where the original is.

In the same way, in the Bhagavadgītā, after mentioning the tradition of the Karma-Yoga from Manu to Ikṣvāku etc. it is stated that: "*evaṁ jñātvā kṛtaṁ karma pūrvair api mumukṣubhiḥ*" (Gī. 4. 15), i. e., "knowing this, scients like Janaka and others performed Action, in ancient times"; and in the Yogavāsiṣṭha and the Bhāgavata, there have been given other illustrations besides that of Janaka (Yo. 5. 75; Bhāga. 2. 8. 43–45). If some one doubts whether Janaka and others had acquired complete Knowledge of the Brahman, I say that it is clearly stated in the Yogavāsiṣṭha that all these persons were '*jīvanmukta*' (birth-released); and, not only in the Yogavāsiṣṭha, but also in the Mahābhārata, Vyāsa is stated to have sent his son Śuka ultimately to Janaka in order to get complete Knowledge of the science of Release (Ma. Bhā. Śān. 325, and Yo. 2. 1). So also, even in the Upaniṣads, there are traditions that the king Aśvapati Kaikeya had taught the Knowledge of the Brahman to the Ṛṣi Uddālaka, and that Ajātaśatru, the king of Kāśi, had taught it to Gārgya Bālāki (Bṛ. 2. 1). Yet, there is nowhere any statement that either Aśvapati or Janaka had given up their kingdom, and had taken to Renunciation in the form of the Abandonment of Action. On the other hand, in the conversation between Janaka and Sulabhā, he (Janaka) first describes to her his own state by saying, "I am attachmentless, that is, I am ruling without being attached; and if one of my hands is annointed with sandal-wood paste, and the other hand cut off, the pain and the pleasure of both, would be the same" etc.; and then goes on to say:—

mokṣe hi trividhā niṣṭhā dṛṣṭvā 'nyair mokṣavittamaiḥ ।
jñānaṁ lokottaraṁ yac ca sarvatyāgaś ca karmaṇām ।
jñānaniṣṭhāṁ vadanty eke mokṣaśāstravido janāḥ ।
karmaniṣṭhāṁ tayaivānye yatayaḥ sūkṣmadarśinaḥ ॥
prahāyobhayam apy evaṁ jñānaṁ karma ca kevalam ।
tṛtīyeyaṁ samākhyātā niṣṭhā tena mahātmanā ॥

(Ma. Bhā. Śān. 320. 38-40).

that is, "those who know the science of Release have prescribed three different systems: (1) acquiring '*jñāna*', and abandoning all Action; that is known by the experts in the science of Release as 'Jñāna-niṣṭhā; (2) in the same way, other subtle philosophers mention a Karma-niṣṭhā; but besides the pure Jñāna-niṣṭhā and the pure Karma-niṣṭhā, this (3) third Niṣṭhā or path, (that is, the path of performing Action after having destroyed Attachment by means of Knowledge) has been mentioned to me by that sage (Pañcaśikha)". The word '*niṣṭhā*' means 'that course of leading one's life by which ultimate Release is obtained'; and even in the Sāṁkarabhāṣya on the Gītā, the word '*niṣṭhā*' has been interpreted as meaning '*anuṣṭheyatātparyam*', that is, the '*tatparatā*' (being engrossed) in that which is '*anuṣṭheya*' (to be performed in life). Out of these paths of living one's life, Jaimini and other followers of the Mīmāṁsā school have not given any importance to Knowledge, but have maintained that Release is obtained solely by performing sacrificial ritual :—

ijānā bahubhiḥ yajñaiḥ brāhmaṇā veda-pāragāḥ ı
śāstrāṇi cet pramāṇaṁ syuḥ prāptās te paramāṁ gatim ıı

(Jai. Sū. 5. 2. 23)

because, if one believes the contrary, the injunctions of the Śāstras, that is, of the Vedas, will become futile. (See the Sābara-bhāṣya on Jai. Sū. 5. 2. 23); and the writers of the Upaniṣads, as also Bādarāyaṇācārya have treated all sacrificial ritual as inferior, and laid down the doctrine that Release is obtained by Knowledge, and that it cannot be obtained by anything other than Knowledge (Ve. Sū. 3. 4. 1, 2). But Janaka says that Pañcaśikha (being himself a follower of Sāṁkhya philosophy) had taught a third system *(niṣṭhā)* distinct from both these systems, namely, of performing Actions, being free from Attachment. It becomes clear from the words "distinct from both these *niṣṭhā*" that this third system is not a part of either of the two systems, but is a totally independent one. This third system of Janaka has been ultimately mentioned even in the Vedānta-Sūtras (Ve. Sū. 3. 4. 32-35); and even in the Bhagavadgītā, it is this third system of Janaka—with the addition of Devotion—which has been mentioned. But the doctrine of the Gītā is, that the path of the Mīmāṁsā school, that is, of Karma without Jñāna, does not lead to Release, but only to heaven (Gī. 2. 42–44; 9. 21); and, that path which does not produce Release can also not be called a '*niṣṭhā*'; because, the definition of '*niṣṭhā*' as a path which ultimately leads to Release is accepted by everybody. Therefore, although in referring in a general way to the various schools of thought, Janaka has referred to three systems, yet, the pure Karma-mārga of the Mīmāṁsā school, which excludes Knowledge, has been omitted from the class of '*niṣṭhā*', and the other remaining two have been described in the beginning of the third chapter of the Gītā (Gī. 3. 3). These are the system of Pure Knowledge (Sāṁkhya), and the system of Knowledge combined with Desireless Action (Yoga); and, in support of the second out of these two systems, (namely, of the third system according to Janaka), the historical illustration of Janaka has been mentioned as: "*karmaṇaiva hi saṁsiddhim āsthitā janakādayaḥ*" (Gī. 3. 20), i. e., "Janaka and others obtained Release only by performing Action in this way". Even if we do not take into account the case of Janaka and other Kṣatriya kings, Vyāsa procreated the two *kṣetraja* sons, Dhṛtarāṣṭra and Pāṇḍu, in order to keep unbroken the ruling line of Vicitravīrya; and he wrote the Mahābhārata by three years' continuous labour in order to redeem the world; and it is well-known that in the Kaliyuga, Śrī Śaṁkarācārya, who was a protagonist of the Saṁnyāsa school based on the Smṛtis, re-established the Hindu religion by his super-human intelligence and industry. Nay, the world itself came into existence when Brahmadeva was ready to perform Action; and, as I have stated above, there is a statement in the description of the Nārāyaṇīya doctrine in the Mahābhārata, that Marīci and the other six mind-born sons came into existence out of Brahmadeva, and stuck to the Activistic path till death, without taking to asceticism, in order to keep alive the course of Action, whereas the other seven mind-born sons of Brahmadeva, namely, Sanatkumāra and others, were from birth free from Desire, and followers of the Path of Renunciation (Ma. Bhā. Śān. 339 and 340). The explanation as to why those who had realised the Brahman, and even Brahmadeva himself, adopted this Activistic path (*pravṛtti-mārga*) of performing Action, has been given in the Vedānta-Sūtras in the following words: "*yāvad adhikāram avasthitırādhikāriṇām*" (Ve Sū. 3. 3. 32), i. e., "until that which has been prescribed for a particular person by the Parameśvara has been completely performed, he does not escape the performance of Action". This explanation will be considered later on. Whatever the explanation may be, this much becomes clear, namely, that the two Paths of Action *(pravṛtti)*, and Inaction *(nivṛtti)*, were followed by scients from the very commencement of the world; and therefore, it is clear that one cannot decide as to which of the two is the better path merely from the conduct of scients.

But, the next argument of Asceticists is that, although one cannot, merely from the consideration of conduct, decide whether Inaction is better than Action, since the traditional conduct is in this way two-fold, yet, as it is clear that there is no Release until one has broken the bondage of Karma, it follows that it is more beneficial to discard the ties of desire-creating Karma, or Action, as early as possible after the acquisition of Knowledge. In the Śukānuśāsana chapter of the Mahābhārata—this chapter is also known as 'Śukānupraśṇa'—the Path of Renunciation has been advocated; and there, to the following question made by Śuka to Vyāsa, namely,

yad idaṁ vedavacanaṁ kuru karma tyajeti ca ।
kāṁ diśaṁ vidyayā yānti kāṁ ca gacchanti karmaṇā ॥
(Śān. 240. 1)

that is, "the Vedas enjoin the performance of Action, as also the Abandonment of Action; therefore, tell me what results are obtained by '*vidyā*', that is, by Knowledge without Action, or by Action alone", Vyāsa in replying has said:

karmaṇā badhyate jantur vidyayā tu pramucyate ।
tasmāt karma na kurvanti yatayaḥ pāradarśinaḥ ॥
(Śān. 240. 7)

that is, "by Karma, the created being is bound, and by Knowledge he is released; therefore, the through-seeing Yatins or ascetics, do not perform Action". I have already fully dealt with the first part of this stanza in the last chapter. There is not the slightest dispute about the proposition: "*karmaṇā badhyate jantur vidyayā tu pramucyate*". And I have shown in that chapter that if one considers what is meant by the words "*karmaṇā badhyate*", one sees that, gross or lifeless Karma by itself does not either bind or release anybody; that, man is bound by Karma as a result of his Hope for Fruit, or by his own Attachment; and that, when this Attachment has been got rid of, a man stands Released, notwithstanding that he may be performing Action by his external organs. With this idea in mind, Śrī Rāmacandra says to Lakṣmaṇa in the Adhyātma-Rāmāyaṇa, that:

pravāhapatitaḥ kāryaṁ kurvann api na lipyate ।
bāhye sarvatra kartṛtvam āvahann api rāghava ॥

that is, "the man who has fallen in the stream of *saṁsāra* (worldly life), which is the embodiment of Action, remains untouched, though he may externally perform all sorts of duties". When one considers this doctrine of the philosophy of the Absolute Self, one sees that it is no more necessary to abandon Action on the ground that it is productive of unhappiness, and that it is enough if one makes one's mind pure and equable, and gives up the hope of reward. In short, though there may be an opposition between Knowledge and Desireful Action, no kind of opposition can exist between Knowledge and Desireless Action. Therefore, in the Anugītā, instead of the phrase "*tasmāt karma na kurvanti*", i. e., "therefore Actions are not performed", it is stated that:

tasmāt karmasu niḥsnehā ye kecit pāradarśinaḥ ॥

(Aśva. 51. 33.)

that is: "therefore, through-seeing scients are not attached to Action"; and before that sentence, there is a clear defence and advocacy of the Karma-Yoga in the following words, namely,

kurvate ye tu karmāṇi śraddadhānā vipaścitaḥ ।
anāśiryogasaṁyuktās te dhīrāḥ sādhudarśinaḥ ॥

(Aśva. 50. 6,7)

that is, "those scients, who, having faith, adopt the (Karma-) Yoga path and perform Actions without entertaining desire, are *sādhudarśin*". In the same way, in the advice given by

Śaunaka to Yudhiṣṭhira in the Vanaparva, there has been added to the following first part of the stanza,

yad idaṁ vedavacanaṁ kuru karma tyajeti ca ।

the following latter part, namely,

tasmād dharmān imān sarvān nābhimānāt samācaret ॥

(Vana. 2. 73).

that is, "though the Vedas enjoin both the performance of and the abandonment of Action, one should perform all one's duties (Karma) without entertaining the pride (of being the doer)"; and in the Śukānupraśna also, Vyāsa has in two places clearly said to Śuka that:—

eṣā pūrvatarā vṛttir brāhmaṇasya vidhīyate ।
jñānavān eva karmāṇi kurvan sarvatra sidhyati ॥

(Ma. Bhā. Śān. 237. 1; 234. 29.)

that is, "obtaining Release by acquiring Knowledge and also performing Actions, is the most ancient (*pūrvatara*) method of Brahmins". It is clear that Karma combined with Jñāna, and after the acquisition of Jñāna, is intended by the words *jñānavān eva.* When one considers dispassionately these statements which support either side of the question, it becomes clear that the argument "*karmaṇā badhyate jantuḥ*", does not yield the only inference "*tasmāt karma na kurvanti*", i. e., "therefore, Actions are not performed", which supports Abandonment of Action, but also the equally important inference "*tasmāt karmasu niḥsnehāḥ*", i. e., "therefore, one does not become attached to Karma"—which is in support of Desireless Action. It is also not that I alone draw this two-fold inference of my own accord, but even Vyāsa himself has clearly expressed this meaning in the following verse from the Śukānupraśna, namely,

dvāv imāv atha panthānau yasmin vedāḥ pratiṣṭhitāḥ ।
pravṛttilakṣaṇo dharmaḥ nivṛttiś ca vibhāṣitaḥ ॥ *

(Ma, Bhā. Śān. 240. 6).

* There are the following other readings of this part of the second line of the stanza, namely, '*nivṛttiś ca subhāṣitaḥ*' and

that is, "such are the two modes of life, both of which are equally supported by the Vedas,—the one is the Activistic path, and the other is of Inaction, that is, of Renunciation". So also, as I have mentioned before, is it stated in the Nārāyaṇīya doctrine that these two paths have existed independently from the commencement of the world. But, as both these paths have been mentioned independently, as occasion arose, in the Mahābhārata, we find in one and the same Mahābhārata statements, which support the Path of Inaction, side by side with statements, which support the Path of Activism; and in the commentaries on the Gītā, which support the Path of Renunciation, the statements supporting the Path of Inaction have been referred to as the only important ones, as though there could be no other path, or as if any other path which might be possible, was either inferior, or only a preparatory step of the Path of Renunciation. But, this kind of argument is only doctrinal; and on that account, though the meaning of the Gītā is clear and plain in itself, it has now-a-days become unintelligible to many. The stanza "*dvāv imāv atha panthānau*" etc., is of the same importance as the stanza "*loke 'smin dvividhā niṣṭhā*" (Gī. 3. 3) in the Gītā; that is to say, one can clearly see the intention to refer in this place to two modes of life which are of equal value. But some persons, closing their eyes to this plain meaning, and to the previous and subsequent context, attempt to maintain that this verse indicates only one path and not two paths.

Though the Vedic religion thus falls into these two independent paths of Karma-Saṁnyāsa (Sāṁkhya) and Desireless Action (Yoga), yet, as the Gītā does not look upon them as equally good alternatives, but is of the firm opinion that 'the Karma-Yoga is superior to the Path of Renunciation', it further says, in support of the superiority of Karma-Yoga, that it will be impossible for us to abandon Karma, so long as the world in which we live, as also our very existence in it for even a single moment, is itself Karma; and if one has to live in this world, that is to say, in this land of Action, how

nivṛttiś ca vibhāvitaḥ'. Whichever reading is taken, the words "*dvāv imāu*" appear in the beginning in each reading; and from this, it is clear that these two paths are independent.

can one escape Action? We see ourselves that thirst, hunger, and other desires do not leave us so long as our body lives (Gī. 5. 8, 9); and if the Path of Renunciation gives us the liberty of performing a disgraceful Action like begging for satisfying those desires, what prevents us from performing all other worldly Actions, prescribed by the Śāstras, with a desireless frame of mind? If a person wishes to give up the performance of these other Actions, fearing that he will lose the happiness of the Brahman, or forget his Non-Dualistic Realisation of the identity of the Brahman and the Ātman, by becoming bound up in the bonds of Karma, his mental control must be looked upon as still imperfect; and all Abandonment of Action made when the mental control is not perfect, is, according to the Gītā, the result of ignorance (*moha*) and is a *tāmasa* or futile act (Gī. 18. 7; 3. 6). Not only is this so, but it naturally follows that in order to perfect such imperfect mental control by means of the purification of the mind, such a man must continue to perform the Karma prescribed by the Śrutis or Smṛtis for a householder, such as, sacrificial ritual, charity etc., which promotes the desireless frame of mind. In short, such an Abandonment of Action is never meritorious. Well; if you say that the man's mind is unaffected by objects of pleasure and is under his control, then why should he be afraid of Karma, or, why should he take up the futile attitude of not-performing Action? Just as an umbrella made for protecting against rain, can be tested only in the rain, so also, or, by the comprehensive test of Kālidāsa:-

vikārahetau sati vikriyante ।
yeṣāṁ na cetāṁsi ta eva dhīrāḥ ॥

(Kumāra. 1. 59)

that is: "that man, whose mind does not fall a prey to mental confusion, when the objects which create the emotions are in front of the eyes, may truely be said to be brave", is the control of the mind really tested by means of Karma; and the fact as to whether or not the mind has become perfect is ascertained not only by others, but also by the doer of the Actions himself. It, therefore, follows, even on this basis, that those Actions which befall one according to the injunctions of the Śāstras, that is to say, those Actions which befall one in the stream of life, must be performed (Gī. 18. 6). If one says, "I am not afraid that the acquired purification of my mind will be affected by the performance of Action, because, my mind is under proper control; but I do not wish to waste my time in the performance of Action, and thereby unnecessarily tire my body, if it is not necessary to do so for obtaining Release", such an abandonment of Action, which is due to the contemptible fear of troubling the body, becomes a '*rājasa*' abandonment, and the fruit or good result to be obtained by Abandonment of Action, is not obtained by the man who abandons Action in this way (Gī. 18. 8). Then, why is Action to be abandoned at all ? If some one says that it is not proper for the Self, which pertains to the permanent world of the Brahman, to take part in Action, which pertains to the Māyā-world and is non-permanent, even such an objection is not proper; because, if the Paramātman Itself is covered by Māyā, where is the objection for a man to be clothed in Māyā in the same way ? Just as there are the two divisions of the world, namely, the Brahman-world and the Māyā-world, so also are there the two divisions of the Self and of the corporeal organs in the case of a human being. Out of these, couple the Self with the Brahman, merge the Self in the Brahman, and, keeping your mind unattached in this way, by realising the identity of the Brahman and the Ātman, perform all the activities in the Māyā-world by the Māyic corporeal organs; that is all. When one behaves in this way, not only will there be no obstruction to one's obtaining Release, but further, the proper portions will be joined together, and one will not incur the blame of not having shown proper respect to, or having disjointed, any portion of the creation; and one will obtain the merit of having performed one's duty both in the Māyā-world and in the Brahman-world—this world and the next. This is the theory which has been supported in the Īśāvāsyopaniṣad (Īśā. 11). But, these statements from the Śrutis will be considered in detail later on. For the time being, I will only say that the statement in the Gītā, that the scients, who realise the identity of the Brahman and the Ātman, perform all activities in the illusory world merely by their body or merely by their organs (Gī. 4. 21 ; 5. 12), means the same thing; and the propositions in the Gītā (Gī. 18. 9), that "the true *sāttvika* Abandonment of Action consists in performing Actions with an unattached frame of mind, without entertaining the hope of reward, and merely as a duty", and that "the non-performance of Action is not the true abandonment of Action", have been made to bring out this idea. Though Karma belongs to the Māyā-world, the Parameśvara has created it for some unintelligible reason; and, it is not within the power of any human being to stop it; it is within the power only of the Parameśvara to do so; and there is no doubt that the performance of Actions merely by the body, keeping the Reason unattached, does not prevent a person from obtaining Release. Then, where is the objection to performing the Actions prescribed by the Śāstras through the medium solely of the organs and being renounced in Mind? It is said in the Gītā that, "*na hi kaścit kṣaṇam api jātu tiṣṭhaty akarmakṛt*" (Gī. 3. 5; 18. 11), i. e., "in this world, no one can for a single moment remain without performing Action"; and, in the Anugītā, that "*naiṣkarmyaṁ na ca loke 'smin muhūrtam api labhyate*" (Aśva. 20. 7), i. e., "in this world, there is no escape from Karma (for anybody) even for a single moment". Not only men, but even the Sun and the Moon are continually performing Action! Nay; as it is definite that Karma is nothing but the creation, and that the creation is nothing but Karma, we ourselves see that the activities of the world, that is to say, Karma, does not rest for a moment. The Blessed Lord has said in the Bhagavadgītā (Gī. 3. 8) that, "if one gives up Action, it will be impossible to get food to eat, and Draupadī has said to Yudhiṣṭhira in the Mahābhārata that "*akarmaṇāṁ vai bhūtānāṁ vṛttiḥ syān na hi kācana*" (Vana. 32. 8), i. e., "living beings cannot exist without performing Action"; and accordingly, even Śrī Samartha Rāmadāsa Svāmī says in the Dāsabodha, after having referred to the Knowledge of the Brahman, that: "if one tries to reach the highest goal, giving up the activities of life । one will not get even food to eat" । (Dā. 12. 1. 3). And, if one considers the life of the Blessed Lord Himself, He is seen to be performing the Action of helping saints and destroying villains in this illusory world from Yuga to Yuga.

by taking up various incarnations (Gī. 4. 8. and Ma. Bhā. Śān. 339. 103); and the Blessed Lord has Himself said in the Gītā, that if He did not perform these Actions, the world would become desolate and be destroyed (Gī. 3. 24). If the Blessed Lord Himself is, in this way, performing Actions for the maintenance of the world, it clearly follows that there is no sense in saying that the performance of Action after the acquisition of Knowledge is useless. Therefore, the Blessed Lord advises everybody in the name of Arjuna, according to the rule, "*yaḥ kriyāvān sa paṇḍitaḥ*" (Ma. Bhā. Vana. 312. 108), i. e. "that man is the truly learned man, who is a doer", that since nobody in this world can escape Karma, one must perform all the duties which befall one according to one's own status in life, giving up the desire for fruit, that is, with one's mind in a state of renunciation, in order that one should not be affected by Karma; and that this is the only and the best way (Yoga) which is possible for man. Matter (*prakṛti*) will always go on performing its activities; but when one gives up the egotistical idea that he is the performer of the Action, one is Released (Gī. 3. 27; 13. 29; 14. 19; 18. 16). Not only is the non-performance of Action, or Renunciation in the shape of the Abandonment of Action (as prescribed by the Sāṁkhyas), not necessary to obtain Release, but it is never possible to entirely abandon Action in this world of Action.

To this, some persons raise a further objection, that though it may not be necessary to abandon Action for breaking the bondage of Karma, and it may be enough to merely give up the desire for the fruit of Karma, yet, when the mind has become desialess as a result of the acquisition of Knowledge, and all desires have been destroyed, there remains nothing which will provoke one to perform Action; and therefore, if not as a result of the fear of unnecessarily taxing the body, at least as a result of the destruction of Desire, Karma comes to an end of itself. The highest goal of a man in this world is the obtaining of Release; and, as the man who has obtained such Release by means of Knowledge has no more any '*eṣaṇā*' (desire) for children, wealth, or heaven (Bṛ. 3. 5. 1 and 4. 4. 22), it is the natural, inherent and ultimate result of such Jñāna, that Karma should leave such a person, although he may not wish to give it up. That is why it is stated in the Uttaragītā that:

jñānāmṛtena tṛptasya kṛtakṛtyasya yoginaḥ ।
na cāsti kiṁcit kartavyam asti cen na sa tattvavit ॥

(Uttara. 1. 23).

that is, "for that man who has become Accomplished (*kṛtakṛtya*), as a result of having drunk the nectar of Knowledge, no further duty remains; and if any further duty remains, that man is not a real '*tattvavit*', i. e., Jñānin".* And if this is looked upon as a fault in a Jñānin, that is wrong. As a matter of fact, Śrī Śaṁkarācārya has said that this is an ornament of the person who has acquired the Knowledge of the Brahman—"*alaṁkāro hy ayam asmākaṁ yad brahmātmāvagatau satyāṁ sarvakartavyatāhāniḥ*" (Ve. Sū. Śāṁ. Bhā. 1. 1. 4). So also, are there such statements in the Gītā as, "*tasya kāryaṁ na vidyate*" (Gī. 3. 17), i. e., "for the Jñānin, nothing remains to be done"; or, "for him, there is no necessity of the Vedic Karma-ritual" (Gī. 2. 46); or, "*yogārūḍhasya tasyaiva śamaḥ kāraṇam ucyate*" (Gī. 6. 3), i. e., "when once a man has become steeped in the Yoga, abandonment (*śama*) becomes necessary (*kāraṇa*) for him"; and such adjectives as "*sarvārambhaparityāgī*" (Gī. 12. 16), i. e., "one who has given up all activities" and "*aniketaḥ*" (Gī. 12. 19), i. e., "one who has no home" etc. have been used in the Gītā with reference to a Jñānin. Some persons, therefore, think that the Bhagavadgītā accepts the position that Karma leaves a man of its own accord, after the acquisition of Knowledge. But, in my opinion, these meanings ascribed to these words and sentences in the Gītā, as also the arguments mentioned above, are not correct. I will, therefore, set out here in short what I have to say to the contrary.

As I have already shown above in the chapter on Happiness and Unhappiness, the Gītā does not accept the position, that when a man has acquired Knowledge, all his wishes or desires

* The idea that this verse is from the Śrutis is not correct. It does not appear in the Śāṁkara-bhāṣya on the Vedānta-Sūtras; but it has been taken by Śaṁkarācārya in his Bhāṣya on the Sanatsujātīya, and it is there stated to be from the Liṅga-purāṇa. It is clearly not in support of Karma-Yoga, but of the Saṁnyāsa-mārga. There are similar statements in Buddhistic works (See the Appendix).

must necessarily have come to an end. There is no unhappiness in merely having a desire or a wish, and the true root of unhappiness is the Attachment, which is part of the Desire. Therefore, the doctrine of the Gītā is, that instead of killing desires of all kinds, one should only give up the Attachment to the objects of desire, and go on performing all Actions. It is not that when this Attachment is given up, activity must also be simultaneously given up. Nay, it is impossible that activity should come to an end, though Desire may have come to an end; and we see that whether there is Desire or not, everyday Actions like breathing etc. continue. But why go so far? Remaining alive, even for a single moment, is an Action by itself; and though a man may have acquired perfect Knowledge, this living does not come to an end by his desire or by the destruction of his desires. It is a matter of everybody's experience, that no Jñānin commits suicide because he has acquired Knowledge; and that is why the Gītā says that "*na hi kaścit kṣaṇam api jātu tiṣṭhaty akarmakṛt*" (Gī. 3. 5), i. e., "no one, whoever he is, can remain without performing Action". The first doctrine of the Karma-Yoga in the Gītā is, that in this world of Action, Action is something which befalls every one naturally, and that it is not only a part of the stream of life, but also inevitable, and not dependent on the desire of man. When it has thus been proved that there is no mutual and permanent relationship between Desire and Action, the statement, that Karma must come to an end simultaneously with the destruction of desire, falls to the ground of itself; and then the question naturally arises as to in what way the scient (Jñānin) should perform those Actions, which befall him even after the destruction of Desire. The reply to this question is given in the third chapter of the Gītā (See Gī. 3. 17–19, and my commentary on it). The Gītā accepts the position that there remains no duty for the Jñānin, after the acquisition of Knowledge, as of his own. But it goes further and says that no man, whoever he may be, escapes Action. The two propositions that the Jñānin (scient) is free from duty and that he does not escape Karma, appear to some persons mutually contradictory. But the same is not the case with the Gītā. It harmonises them by saying that in as much as Karma is unavoidable, the scient must perform it even after the acquisition of Knowledge; but, in as much as a Jñānin has no more any duty for his own Self, it now becomes necessary for him to perform all his duties desirelessly. In short, the word '*tasya*' (that is, 'for the Jñānin') in the line "*tasya kāryaṁ na vidyate*", in the seventeenth stanza of the third chapter is more important than the words "*kāryaṁ na vidyate*"; and the sum and substance of the stanza is, that as there is nothing more to be got by a Jñānin 'as for himself', he must thereafter, that is, after the acquisition of Knowledge, perform his duties desirelessly; and the same purport has been conveyed to Arjuna by the words, "*tasmād asaktaḥ satataṁ kāryaṁ karma samācara*" (Gī. 3. 19), i. e., "therefore, go on performing whatever duties have befallen you, according to the injunction of the Śāstras, without becoming attached to the Karma, and do not give up the Karma", by using the cause-denoting word '*tasmāt*' in the beginning of the stanza. When this relation of data and conclusion between the seventeenth and the nineteenth verses of the third chapter, as also the entire context of the chapter, is taken into account, it will be seen that it is not correct to take the words "*tasya kāryaṁ na vidyate*" as an independent proposition, as is done by the supporters of the Path of Renunciation. The best proof of this position are the following illustrations. In support of the proposition that one has to perform all the duties which befall one as a result of the injunctions of the Śāstras, even after the acquisition of Knowledge, though no duty for one's own benefit remains, the Blessed Lord says immediately afterwards that:-

na me pārthā 'sti kartavyaṁ triṣu lokeṣu kiṁcana |
nānavāptam avāptavyaṁ varta eva ca karmaṇi ||

(Gī. 3. 22).

that is: "O Pārtha, there is not (remaining) for Me any duty which is Mine in this three-fold universe, nor is there (in Me any desire to obtain) anything which has not been obtained by Me; see that I am also nevertheless performing Karma". The words, "*na me kartavyam asti*", i. e., "for me, no duty has remained" in this stanza have been said with reference to the words, "*tasya kāryaṁ na vidyate*", i. e., "for him, there remains no duty", in the former stanza (Gī. 3. 17); and, therefore, it is quite clear that these four or five stanzas bear out the proposition that, "though no duty may have remained as a result of the acquisition of Knowledge, yet, and even for that very reason, one must perform all the duties prescribed by the Sāstras, with an unattached frame of mind". Otherwise, His own illustration given by the Blessed Lord for emphasising the doctrine enunciated in the stanza, "*tasya kāryaṁ na vidyate* etc"., becomes totally out of place; and the impossible position of the enunciated doctrine being different from the illustration given, will arise. In order to get over this impossible position, the commentators, who follow the Renunciation school, interpret the word '*tasmāt*', in the sentence "*tasmād asaktaḥ satataṁ kāryaṁ karma samācara*", in quite a different way. According to them, the main doctrine of the Bhagavadgītā is that the scient must give up Action. But Arjuna was not a scient; therefore—' *tasmāt* '—the Blessed Lord has enjoined him to perform Karma. But, as I have already explained above, the argument that Arjuna was still ignorant, after having heard the Gītā, is incorrect. Besides, even though the meaning of the word '*tasmāt*' may be thus stretched, the illustration about Himself given by the Blessed Lord, in support of the main proposition, by the words "*na me pārthā 'sti kartavyaṁ* etc.", i. e., "I am performing Action, although no duty is left for Me for My own benefit", cannot be properly explained in the same way. Therefore, the word '*tasya*' in the sentence "*tasya kāryaṁ na vidyate*" must be considered important instead of the words "*kāryaṁ na vidyate*"; and when that is done, the sentence '*tasmād asaktaḥ satataṁ kāryaṁ karma samācara*" must be interpreted as meaning: "you are a scient; and, therefore, it is true that there is no Karma left for you for your own personal benefit; but, for the very reason that such Karma is not necessary for your own benefit, do whatever duties befall you according to the Śāstras, with the feeling 'this is not for me', that is, with a desireless frame of mind". In short, according to the Gītā, the idea 'this is not for me' does not become a reason for not performing Karma, and we have to draw the inference, that as Action is unavoidable, therefore, this unavoidable Action, which has been prescribed by the Śāstras, must be performed with a self-sacrificing frame of mind; and, considering the matter from the point of view of consistency, the same meaning has to be adopted. This is the great and important difference between Renunciation of Action (Karma-Saṁnyāsa) and Energism (Karma-Yoga). Those who follow the Renunciation school say: "nothing has remained for you to do; therefore, do nothing"; and the Gītā says: "nothing has remained for you to do, for your own benefit; and, therefore, do henceforth whatever you have to do, giving up selfish desires, and with an unattached frame of mind". Why should two such different inferences arise from one and the same sentence? The only reply to this is, that as the Gītā considers Karma as unavoidable, the conclusion, 'therefore, give up Action', cannot at all arise according to the philosophy of the Gītā. Therefore, the Gītā has drawn the conclusion that Action should be performed, giving up selfish desires, from the data 'it is not for your benefit.' The argument adopted by Vasiṣṭha in the Yoga-Vāsiṣṭha, after he had preached the Knowledge of the Brahman to Rāma, for inducing him to perform Desireless Action is the same; and the above-mentioned doctrine of the Bhagavadgītā has been adopted literally at the end of the Yoga-Vāsiṣṭha (See Yo. 6. U. 199 and 216. 14; and my commentary on the translation of Gī. 3. 19). The teaching of the Gītā has been adopted in the Buddhistic religion in the sacred books of the Mahāyāna sect, in the same way as it has been adopted in the Yoga-Vāsiṣṭha. But, I have not dealt with that matter here, as it will be straying from the subject, and I have considered it later in the Appendix.

When a man has got the Knowledge of the Ātman, the individualistic language of 'I' and 'mine' does not remain (Gī. 18. 16 and 26); and therefore, the Jñānin is said to be '*nir-mama*'. '*nir-mama*' means, one who does not say, 'mine', 'mine' (*mama*); and Jñāneśvara Mahārāja has conveyed the same idea in describing the Jñānin in the following stanza (*oṁvīṁ*):

He does not know the word 'I' ।

he does not say of anything that it is 'mine' ।

Experience of pain and happiness ı
for him there is none ıı

(Jñā. 12. 149. See p. 346 above).

But, it must not be forgotten that although the feeling of 'I' or 'mine' may be got rid of, as a result of the Knowledge of the Brahman, their place is taken by the words 'the world' and 'for the world'—or speaking in the language of Devotion, by the words 'the Parameśvara', and 'of the Parameśvara'. Every ordinary human being in the world carries out all his activities with the feeling of 'mine', or, 'for my benefit'. But, as that man who has become a scient, has lost his 'mine-ness' (*mamatva*), he begins to perform all the activities in the world created by the Īśvara with the feeling (the mine-less, i. e., *nirmama* feeling) that they are of the Parameśvara, and that the Parameśvara has created him for performing them: this is the difference between the Jñānin and the Ajñānin (Gī. 3. 27, 28). When one takes into account this doctrine of the Gītā, the plain meaning of the words, "'*śama*' becomes a '*kāraṇa*' to the person who has become steeped in Yoga", becomes apparent (See. Gī. 6. 3 and my commentary on it). Some commentators on the Gītā interpret this stanza as meaning that, the man, who has become steeped in Yoga, should thereafter take to '*śama*' that is, '*śānti*', and do nothing else. But this meaning is not correct. '*śama*' means 'peace of mind'; and instead of describing that '*śama*' as the ultimate 'result' (*kārya*), it is said in this stanza that this '*śama*' or '*śānti*' is the 'cause' (*kāraṇa*) of something else—"*śamaḥ kāraṇam ucyate*". Therefore, '*śama*' must be considered as a '*kāraṇa*' (cause), and we must see what the '*kārya*' (result) of it is. If one considers the previous and subsequent context, it becomes clear that that result (*kārya*) is 'Karma'; and then this stanza has to be interpreted as meaning, that the Yogin should make his mind peaceful, and perform all his further activities by means of that *śama* or *śānti* (peace); and one cannot interpret it, as has been done by the commentators, as meaning that 'the Yogin (*yogārūḍha*) should give up Karma'. In the same way, the words "*sarvārambha-parityāgi*" and "*aniketaḥ*" must be interpreted as indicating the Abandonment of the Hope of Fruit, rather than the Abandonment of the Action itself, as has been shown by me in my commentary attached to the translations of the verses in the various places. The second illustration given by the Blessed Lord in addition to His own, for proving the proposition that the Jñānin must perform all the various duties prescribed for the four castes, giving up the Hope for Fruit, and according to the Śāstras, is that of Janaka. Janaka was a Karma-yogin of a very high order. He had become unselfish to such a great extent that he is said to have uttered the words: "*mithilāyāṁ pradīptāyāṁ na me dahyati kiṁcana*" (Śān. 275. 4 and 219. 50), i. e., "I will not feel it at all, even if the capital of my kingdom is burnt"; and in explaining why he was still carrying on the activities of ruling, though he had no selfish interest or advantage or disadvantage of his left, Janaka himself says:--

devebhyaś ca pitṛbhyaś ca bhūtebhyo 'tithibhiḥ saha ।
ity arthaṁ sarva evaite samāraṁbhā bhavanti vai ॥
(Ma. Bhā. Aśva. 32. 24)

that is, "all these activities are going on for the benefit of the gods, of the ancestors, of all created beings *(bhūta)*, and of my guests, and not for myself". It need not be said that if noble souls like Janaka and Śrī Kṛṣṇa do not come forward for the benefit of the world, when no duty of any kind is left for their own benefit, or when they have no desire to obtain any particular thing for themselves, this world will become desolate—"*utsīdeyur ime lokāḥ*" (Gī. 3. 24).

Some people say that there is not much of a difference between the doctrine of the Gītā that the desire for the fruit must be given up, and that it is not necessary to give up desires of all kinds, and the doctrine of the Destruction of Desire; because, as there is no stimulus left towards Action, whether it is Desire which is destroyed, or the hope for the fruit which is destroyed, the ultimate result of Karma being given up, follows in either case. But, this objection is based on ignorance, that is to say, it is raised because the true meaning of the words 'hope for fruit' (*phalāśā*) has not been understood. Giving up the hope for fruit, does not mean giving up all kinds of Desire, or entertaining the desire that nobody should get the fruit of one's Action, or that if somebody gets it, he should not enjoy it. As has been stated by me above in the fifth chapter, the words '*phalāśā*', '*saṅga*' or '*kāma*' have been used in the Gītā to indicate the ATTACHMENT (*āsakti*) or INSISTENCE (*āgraha*) that, 'I am doing this particular Action in order that the fruit of it must accrue to ME'. But, though one does not entertain the AMBITION, or the INSISTENCE, or the vain Attachment, that the fruit should be obtained, it does not follow that the desire, and also the enthusiasm, to do a particular thing which has fallen on one's shoulders, as a duty, should also disappear with this insistence. It is true that those persons, who do not see anything in this world except their own benefit, and who are continually steeped in performing Actions merely by the ambition of reaping some fruit or other, will not believe that it is possible to perform Actions, giving up the hope for fruit. But, the same is not the case with those persons, whose mind has become equable, and is in a state of Renunciation as a result of Knowledge. In the first place, the belief that the fruit which one obtains for a particular Action, is the fruit of that Action, is itself wrong. If there is not the assistance of the liquidity of water, or of the heat of fire, it will not be possible for man to cook anything, in spite of all his efforts; and the possessing or not possessing of these qualities by fire etc. is not something, which is within the control of man, or subject to his efforts. Therefore, a man has to make all his various efforts, after having first acquired the knowledge of these self-existent activities in the world of Action, and of the way in which these various activities will become helpful to his own efforts. Therefore, whatever fruit is obtained by a man by his own Action, is not actually the fruit of his Action, but must be said to be the fruit of the union of his Action with the self-existent forces existing in the world of Action, which are promotive of his efforts. But, it very often happens that a man has not acquired a complete knowledge of all these various natural activities, the promotiveness of which is, in this way, necessary to make his efforts successful; and in some cases, it is impossible for him to acquire this knowledge. This is known as DESTINY. If the assistance of natural activities, which are not within our control and which may not even be known to us, is thus necessary in order that success should crown our efforts, believing that 'I will do a particular thing purely by my own efforts' is naturally an extremely foolish belief (Gī. 18. 14–16); because, in as much as the fruit to be obtained by the co-operation between the known and the unknown activities of the natural world of Action and the efforts of man, is the result of the laws of Action (Karma), there will not be the slightest difference, so far as the success of the effort goes, whether one entertains the desire for fruit, or does not entertain it; and there is only the chance of one's hope for the fruit causing one unhappiness. Nevertheless, the activities of Nature do not of their own accord bring about that thing which a man wants. As it is necessary to add salt to the flour, in order to make the bread palatable, so also is it necessary to add some human effort, more or less, to these self-existent activities of the Natural world of Action, in order that they should become beneficial to man. Therefore, those persons, who are scients and discriminators, do not entertain any Attachment or ambition about the fruit of their Action, and perform the small or big portion of Śāstra-enjoined Action which is destined for them, consistently with their authority, in the eternal course of Karma (*pravāha-patita),* in order to carry on the activities of the world; and they rely on the co-operation (*saṅyoga*) between Action (Karma) and Destiny (Dharma), so far as the question of the success of the effort goes; or, speaking in the language of Devotion, they rely on the desire of the Parameśvara, so far as that matter goes. This is what is implied in the advice: "Your authority extends only to the performance of Action; obtaining the result is not a matter which you can control" (Gī. 2. 47), given by the Blessed Lord to Arjuna. When one goes on performing Action, without entertaining any hope for the fruit, one does not have any reason for feeling unhappy about the fruitlessness of the Action, if for any reason it becomes fruitless, as one has performed the duty of doing the Action, which is the only thing within one's control. For instance, the science of Medicine tells us, that unless the thread of life (that is, the inherent strength of the vital elements in the body) is strong, a patient never gets well merely by medicines; and, as the strength of this thread is the result of many pre-destined or hereditary causes, that is a matter which is outside the control of the doctor, and it is even impossible for him to definitely calculate the quantity of that strength. Yet, we actually see, that considering it his duty to give medicine to his patients, a doctor medicates thousands of patients in this way, to the extent of his abilities, and purely with the intention of doing good to others. When a doctor has thus disinterestedly performed his duty of giving medicine, not only does he not become despondent, if a particular patient is not cured, but he even draws up with a peaceful mind the statistics, that a particular percentage of patients is cured by a particular medicine. But, when the son of that same doctor falls ill, and he has to give medicine to him, he forgets the fact that there is such a thing as 'the thread of life,' and becoming confused by the selfish Hope of Fruit, in the shape of the idea that 'my son must get well', he calls in another doctor to treat his son, or at any rate for consultation. This simple illustration will explain what is meant by the selfish Attachment to the Result of Action, and how it is possible to perform some Action merely as a duty, even when there is no hope as regards the result. It is true that in order that the Hope for result may thus be destoryed, the mind has to be imbued with Renunciation, by means of Knowledge. But, just as when one is asked to take away the colour (characteristic) from a piece of cloth, it does not become necessary to destroy the cloth, so also, when it is said that one should not entertain Desire, Attachment, or Love in the matter of Action, it does not follow that Action itself should be given up. If it were to become impossible to perform Action as a result of Renunciation, that would be a different matter. But, not only is it possible to perform Action, in spite of Renunciation, but also, as we ourselves see, nobody can at any time escape Karma. Therefore, the true principle of leading one's life, from the point of view of Ethics, and from the point of view of Release, is that the scient should, after acquisition of Knowledge, perform those very Actions, which are performed by the ignorant with a Hope for Result, but looking upon advantage or disadvantage, happiness or unhappiness as one and the same (Gi. 2. 38); and courageously and enthusiastically, but with a pure Reason, that is, being renounced or indifferent in the matter of the fruit (Gī. 18. 26); and with a peaceful mind, according to his own authority, and purely as a matter of duty (Gī. 6. 3). This is the course of Action, which has been adopted by numerous Steady-in-minds (*sthitaprajña*), by devotees of the Blessed Lord, by persons who have acquired the highest knowledge, nay, even by the Blessed Lord Himself; and the highest goal of man consists in this Path of Energism (Karma-Yoga); and the Bhagavadgītā proclaims in unquestionable terms that ultimate Release results from this 'Yoga' on account of the worship of and meditation on the Parameśvara which it entails (Gī. 18. 46). If in spite of this, some one intentionally misunderstands the matter, we must look upon him as unfortunate. Spencer did not accept the Metaphysical point of view. Yet, he has in his book called the *Study of Sociology* come to the conclusion, that since, even from the Materialistic point of view, it is not possible for a man to cause anything to happen at once in this world, and human efforts are fruitful, fruitless, or more or less fruitful in proportion to the way in which the hundreds of other causative things, which are necessary for it to happen, have happened previously, the wise man must go on performing his duties peacefully and enthusiastically, without entertaining any Desire for Result of Action, though the ordinary man is induced to perform the Action only by desire for the fruit—which is the same as what the Gītā says. *

Even if it is thus proved that the scient must, so long as life lasts, desirelessly perform all the duties, which befall him in the course of life, having given up the Hope for Result, the

* "thus admitting that for the *fanatic*, some *wild anticipation* is needful as a stimulus; and recognising the usefulness of his delusion as adapted to his particular nature and his particular function, the *man of higher type* must be content with greatly *moderated expectations*, while he perseveres with undiminished efforts. He has to see how comparatively little can be done, and yet to find it worth while to do that little: so uniting philanthropic energy with philosophic calm"—Spencer's *Study of Sociology*, 8th Ed. p. 403. (The italics are ours). If, in this sentence, one substitutes

subject matter of Karma-Yoga is not exhausted unless it is explained why, and for what purpose, these Actions at all come into existence. And, therefore, the last and the most important direction of the Blessed Lord to Arjuna in support of the doctrine of Karma-Yoga is that: "*lokasaṁgraham evā 'pi saṁpaśyan kartum arhasi*" (Gī. 3. 20), i. e., "even having regard to public benefit (*lokasaṁgraha*), you must perform these Actions". Public benefit does not mean 'making societies of men' or 'making a farce of performing Action like other people, though one has the right to abandon Action, in order that ignorant people should not give up Action, and in order to please them'; because, the object of the Gītā is not that people should remain ignorant, or that scients should make a farce of performing Action only in order to keep them ignorant. Far from any hypocrisy being advised, when Arjuna was not satisfied by arguments which would have been conclusive for ordinary people, such as, "people will sing YOUR disgrace" (Gī. 2. 34) etc., the Blessed Lord goes on to give more weighty and philosophically more powerful arguments. Therefore, the word '*saṁgraha*', which has been defined in dictionaries to mean 'protecting,' 'keeping', 'regulating' etc., has in this place to be taken in all those meanings according to the context; and when that is done '*lokasaṁgraha*' (public benefit) means "binding men together, and protecting, maintaining and regulating them in such a way that they might acquire that strength which results from mutual co-operation, thereby putting them on the path of acquiring merit while maintaining their good condition." The words 'welfare of a nation' have been used in the same sense in the Manu-Smṛti (7. 144) and the word '*lokasaṁgraha*' has been defined in the

the words 'maddened by the qualities of Matter' (Gī. 3. 29), or, 'befooled by Individuation (*ahaṁkāra*)' (Gī. 3. 27), or, the word 'fool' used by the dramatist Bhāsa (see p. 430 above—Trans.) for the word 'fanatic', and one substitutes the word '*vidvān*' (scient) (Gī. 3.25) for the words '*man of higher type*', and the words 'indifference towards the fruit of Action,' or 'abandonment of the fruit of Action', for the words '*greatly moderated expectations*', one may almost say that Spencer has copied the doctrine of the Gītā.

Sāṁkarabhāṣya as meaning "*lokasyonmārgapravṛttinivāraṇam*" (i. e., "weaning men from the tendency to take to the path of wrong"); and from this it will be clear, that my interpretation of that word as meaning "making wise, those persons who behave recklessly as a result of ignorance, and keeping them together in a happy state, and putting them on the path of self-amelioration" is neither strange nor without authority. The word '*saṁgraha*' has been explained in this way. I must now make it clear that the word '*loka*' in '*lokasaṁgraha*' does not indicate only mankind. It is true that the word '*loka-saṁgraha*' ordinarily means 'the benefit of human beings', as man is superior to the other created beings in the world. Yet, in as much as the Blessed Lord also desires that the *bhūrloka*, *satyaloka*, *pitṛloka*, *devaloka*, and the several other *loka* or worlds, which have been created by Him, should also be properly maintained and go on in a proper way, I must say that the word '*lokasaṁgraha*' has, in this place, the comprehensive meaning that the activities of all these various spheres should go on properly in the same way as those of mankind, (*lokasaṁgraha=lokānāṁ saṁgrahaḥ*, i. e., the maintenance of various worlds). The description given above by Janaka of the way in which he performed his duties refers to the sphere of gods and the sphere of ancestors; and it is stated in the description of the cycle of Yajñas (sacrificial ritual), which has been given in the third chapter of the Bhagavadgītā, and in the Nārāyaṇīyopākhyāna of the Mahābhārata, that Brahmadeva has created the Yajña in order that the sphere of humans, as also the sphere of gods, should be maintained (Gī. 3. 10-12). From this, it becomes clear that the word '*lokasaṁgraha*' has been used in the Bhagavadgītā to mean the maintenance, not only of human beings, but that the human and all the other spheres, such as of the gods etc., should be maintained, and that they should become mutually beneficial. This authority or right of the Blessed Lord of performing *loka-saṁgraha* by maintaining the entire universe in this way, is acquired by a man when he becomes a Jñānin as a result of the acquisition of Knowledge. Whatever is considered proper by a Jñānin, is also considered proper by other people, and they behave accordingly (Gī. 3. 21); because, ordinary people believe that it is the right of Jñānins (scients) to consider with a peaceful and equable mind, in what way the maintenance and uplift of the entire world can best be carried on, and to lay down the rules of Ethics accordingly; and such a belief is not ill-founded. Nay, one may even say that ordinary people put faith in Jñānins in this matter, because they themselves do not understand these things correctly. It is for expressing the same idea that Bhīṣma has said to Yudhiṣṭhira in the Śāntiparva that:–

lokasaṁgrahasaṁyuktaṁ vidhātrā vihitaṁ purā ।
sūkṣmadharmārthaniyataṁ satāṁ caritam uttamam ॥
(Ma. Bhā. Śān. 258. 25)

that is, "Brahmadeva himself has created the most excellent lives of saints in order to explain which path of duty should be adopted on critical occasions, as being universally beneficial". It, therefore, follows that *lokasaṁgraha* does not mean some humbug or other, or, a trick for keeping people in ignorance, but means one of the important duties created by Brahmadeva for saints; because, the world is likely to be destroyed if Action based on Knowledge disappears from the world. The same purport is conveyed by the following words of the Blessed Lord, namely, "if I do not perform this Action, all these '*loka*' that is, spheres, will be destroyed" (3. 24). The scients are the eyes of the world; and if they give up their duties, the world will become blind, and cannot but be destroyed. It is the scients who have to make people wise and ameliorate their condition. But, such a thing cannot be done by mere oral directions, that is, by mere advice; because, as we always see it in the world, if some one merely preaches the Knowledge of the Brahman to those people, who are not in the habit of behaving righteously, and whose minds are not purified, they misapply the knowledge, saying, "what is yours is mine, and what is mine is also mine". Besides, it is usual for people to test the correctness of the advice given by a particular person by reference to his own behaviour. Therefore, if the scient does not perform Action himself, that becomes an excuse for ordinary people to become idle. This is what is meant by '*buddhi-bheda*' (difference of vision); and in order that such a difference of vision should not arise, and that people should become really desireless, and should be alive to their duties, it is the duty (not the hypocrisy) of scients to remain in worldly life and to give a living lesson to ordinary people of moral behaviour (*sadācaraṇa)*, that is, of living their lives desirelessly, by showing them their own behaviour. Therefore, the Gītā says that a scient never acquires the right to give up Action, and that it is necessary for him to perform the various duties which have been enjoined for the four castes, for promoting universal benefit, if not for their own benefit. But, as the followers of the school of Renunciation are of opinion that the Jñānin need not perform the activities enjoined on the various castes, with a desireless frame of mind, or need not even perform them at all, the commentators belonging to this school of thought, have made a mess of the doctrine of the Gītā that a scient must go on performing Actions for universal benefit; and they seem to be prepared to indirectly, if not directly, suggest that the Blessed Lord has Himself given only hypocritical advice! But, it becomes clear from the previous and subsequent context that this forceless interpretation of the word '*lokasaṁgraha*' used in the Gītā, is not correct. The Gītā does not in the first place admit the position that the Jñānin has got a right to give up Action; and *lokasaṁgraha* is the most important reason out of the various reasons adduced in the Gītā for the Jñānin not doing so. It is, therefore, absolutely unjust to first take it for granted that a Jñānin can give up Action and then to interpret the word *lokasaṁgraha* as meaning something hypocritical. Man has not come into this world merely for his own benefit. It is true that ordinary people are engrossed in selfish activities as a result of ignorance. But, if a man, to whom the whole world has become identified with himself as "*sarvabhūtastham ātmānaṁ sarvabhūtāni cātmani*", i. e., "I am in all created beings, and all created beings are in me", says: "Release has been attained by ME, now why should I care if everybody else is unhappy?", he will be degrading his own Knowledge by his own mouth. Is the Ātman of a scient something which is independent or individual? So long as his Ātman was covered by the cloak of ignorance, the difference between 'I' and 'the world' existed; but after the acquisition of Knowledge, the Ātman of the world becomes his own Ātman; and therefore, Vasiṣṭha has said to Rāma in the Yoga-Vāsiṣṭha that:–

yāval lokaparāmarśo nirūḍho nāsti yoginaḥ ।
tāvad rūḍhasamādhitvaṁ na bhavaty eva nirmalam ॥

(Yo. 6. Pū. 128. 97)

that is, "so long as the duty of looking after other people (that is of *lokasaṁgraha)* remains to howsoever small an extent, it cannot be said that the state of the person, who has attained Yoga, has become free from blame". For such a man to become engrossed in the happiness of meditation, is to some extent like attending only to his own selfish needs. The chief fault in the argument of the supporters of the school of Renunciation, is that they disregard this factor. It is not possible to come across any one who is more a Jñānin, more desireless, or more fully a Yogin, than the Blessed Lord. But if even the Blessed Lord Himself takes incarnations from time to time for universal benefit, e. g., for "the protection of saints, the destruction of villains, and the re-establishment of religion (*dharma)*", (Gī. 4. 8), it would be totally improper for a Jñānin to give up universal welfare, and say: "that Parameśvara who has created all these various spheres, will maintain them in any way He likes; that is no part of my duty"; because, after the acquisition of Knowledge, the difference of 'Parameśvara', 'I' and 'the world' does not remain; and if such a difference remains, then such a man is not a Jñānin: he is a hypocrite. If a Jñānin becomes uniform with the Parameśvara as a result of Jñāna, how will he escape the necessity of performing that Action which is performed by the Parameśvara, in the same way as it is performed by the Parameśvara, that is, desirelessly (Gī. 3. 22 and 4. 14 and 15)? Besides, whatever the Parameśvara has to do, has to be done by Him through the medium of scients. Therefore, active noble sentiments, full of sympathy towards all created beings, must arise in the mind of the man who has had the direct Realisation of the form of the Parameśvara in the shape of the feeling that 'there is only one Ātman in all created beings'; and the trend of his mind must naturally be towards universal welfare. The Saint Tukārāma has with that intention described the characteristic features of a saint by the following words:—

> Of them who are unhappy and in distress ।
> he who says that they are his ।
> That man should be recognised as a saint ।
> know that God is in such a man ।
>
> (Gā. 960. 1–2)

Or,

> He who spends his energies in doing good to others ।
> has realised the true state of the Ātman ।
>
> (Gā. 4562).

And he has described Saints, that is, those noble souls who have Realised the Parameśvara by means of Devotion in the following terms :–

> The incarnations of saints are for the public welfare ।
> they labour their own bodies for the benefit of others ॥
>
> (Gā. 929).

And Bhartṛhari has said that,, "*svārtho yasya parārtha eva sa pumān ekaḥ satām agraṇīḥ*", i. e., "that man with whom the interests of others have become identical with his own, is really the highest of saints". Were not Manu and other law-makers, Jñānins? But, instead of exaggerating the worth of the illusion in the shape of the pain of Desire, and destroying all natural instincts, such as, of doing good to others etc. along with Desire, they have laid down the Śāstric bonds, such as the arrangement of the four castes etc., for the universal benefit (*lokasaṁgraha*). The laws which prescribe learning for the Brahmins; warfare, for the Kṣatriyas; agriculture, protection of cattle, and business for the Vaiśyas; and service for the Śūdras and which have been enjoined by the Śāstras consistently with the characteristic qualities of the different castes, have not been made for the benefit of every individual. It is stated in the Manu-Smṛti, that the division of vocations among the four castes, has been made for universal benefit, bearing in mind the fact that in the interests of the protection of society, some persons must for a considerable length of time study warfare and be ready for war, and that others have got to meet the other needs of society by attending to agriculture, business, education, and other matters; and even the Gītā supports the same division (Manu. 1. 87; Gī. 4. 13; 18. 41). I have stated above that if any of these four castes ceases to perform its duties, then to that extent, society will be incapacitated, and even runs the risk of being destroyed. Nevertheless, it is not that this vocational division is uniform everywhere. The arrangements which have been suggested for the maintenance of society by the ancient Greek Philosopher Plato in his book on this subject, and by the modern French Philosopher Comte in his book called *Natural Philosophy*, though similar to the arrangement of the four castes, are yet, to some extent, different from the arrangement of four castes mentioned in the Vedic religion, as will be seen by any one reading those books. Many questions have arisen on this point, such as, which arrangement of society is the best of these all; or, whether this goodness of arrangement is relative; and whether there can be a change in it by reference to change of times; and, the welfare of society (*lokasaṁgraha*) has become a very important science at the present day in Western countries. But, as my present object is only to elucidate the import of the Gītā, it is not necessary for me to consider those questions here. It cannot be doubted that at the time of the Gītā, the arrangement of the four castes was rigidly enforced, and that it had originally been given effect to for the welfare of society. Therefore, I have to mention here emphatically, that *lokasaṁgraha* according to the Gītā means, giving to other people a living example of how one can perform desirelessly all the various activities, which are allotted to one, according to the arrangement of the four castes. Scients are not only the eyes, but also the preceptors of society. Therefore, in order to effect *lokasaṁgraha* as mentioned above, it becomes necessary for them to engage in such activities, as will prevent the disruption of the self-maintaining and self-uplifting capacity of society, and will allow it to grow, after they have in the first place weeded out whatever they might find faulty in the prevalent social arrangements, having regard to the changed times and places, as was done by Śvetaketu. In order to effect universal welfare in this way, Janaka continued to rule till the end of his life instead of renouncing the world, and Manu consented to become the first king; and it is for this reason that there is frequent advice in the Gītā to Arjuna to engage in the warfare, which was the law for him in accordance with the arrangement of the four castes, by the use of such expressions as the following:- "*svadharmam api cāvekṣya na vikaṁpitum arhasi*" (Gī. 2. 31), i. e. "it is not proper that you should bemoan having to perform that duty which is your lot according to your caste"; or, "*svabhāva-niyataṁ karma kurvan nāpnoti kilbiṣam*" (Gī. 18. 47), i. e., "by doing that duty which has been enjoined on you by the arrangement of the four castes, having regard to characteristic natures, you will not incur any sin". No one says that one should not, to the best of one's capacity, acquire the Knowledge of the Parameśvara. Nay, it is the doctrine also of the Gītā that it is the highest duty of every human being in this world to acquire this Knowledge. But, as the benefit of one's own Ātman also includes exerting oneself to the fullest extent of one's abilities, for the benefit of the all-pervading Ātman, the Gītā goes further and says that the Realisation of the identity of the Brahman and the Ātman ultimately resolves itself into bringing about *lokasaṁgraha*. Nevertheless, from the fact that a particular person has acquired Knowledge of the Brahman, it does not follow that he, on that account, becomes capable of personally taking part in all the various vocations in the world. Both Bhīṣma and Vyāsa were great Jñānins, and great devotees of the Blessed Lord. But no one says that Vyāsa could have carried out the work of warfare as well as Bhīṣma; and even if one considers the gods, one does not find that the work of destroying the world has been entrusted to Viṣṇu instead of Śaṅkara. The state of being birth-released (*jīvan-mukta*) is the last stage of the mind's freedom from objects of pleasure, and of an equable and pure Reason, and of Metaphysical excellence; it is not a test of excellence in Material vocations. Therefore, the Gītā has again preached twice in the same chapter that the Jñānin must, after acquisition of Knowledge, continue to perform that business or duty for the universal welfare, which is consistent with his caste, and which he had been performing during the whole of his life consistently with the arrangment of the four castes, which has been based on inherent qualities, because, it is likely that he will be an adept in that business alone; and that if he takes to any other business, there is a chance of harm being done to society (Gī. 3. 35; 18. 47). This diverse capacity, which exists within every person, consistently with the god-given inherent natural characteristics, is known as '*adhikāra*' (qualification or authority); and it has been stated in the Vedānta-Sūtras, that "*yāvad adhikāram avasthitir ādhikāriṇām*" (Ve. Sū. 3. 3. 32), i. e., "even if a man has acquired the knowledge of the Brahman, he must go on performing those duties, which are his lot according to his qualification (*adhikāra*), so long as he lives, for the welfare of society". Some say that this injunction of the Vedānta-Sūtras applies only to persons, who are really men of high authority; and if one considers the illustrations given in the commentaries on these Sūtras, in support of the Sūtra, it is seen that they are of Vyāsa and other persons holding high authority. But, the original Sūtra makes no mention of the greatness or the smallness of authority. Therefore, the word '*adhikāra*' must be taken to mean high or low qualification of every kind; and if one considers minutely and independently what this qualification is, and how it is acquired, it is seen that in as much as the Parameśvara created man simultaneously with society, and society simultaneously with man, every human being, as a result of the arrangement of four castes, or of any other social arrangement consistent with the division of inherent qualities, acquires, by birth, the high or low qualification of maintaining and uplifting society, according to his or her own powers, and proportionately with whatever intellectual capacity, authoritative capacity, financial capacity, or physical capacity is naturally possessed by him, or can be acquired by him having regard to his status in life. Just as extremely small wheels are necessary along with large wheels in order that any machine should work properly, so also is it necessary that the authority of common-place persons should be exercised properly and fully in the same way as the authority of superior persons like Vyāsa and others, in order that the immense and ponderous activity or mechanism of the Cosmos should continue to work in a properly regulated manner. Because, if potters do not manufacture pots or weavers do not weave clothes, the maintenance of society (*lokasaṁgraha*) cannot be satisfactorily carried out, even if the king protects society properly; or, if the most insignificant pointsman or cabinman in a railway administration does not properly perform his duty, it will not be possible for the railway train to rush along with safety and with the speed of wind, both during the day and during the night, as it now does. Therefore, it follows from the above argument advanced by the writer of the Vedānta-Sūtras, that even an ordinary person, and not only superior persons like Vyāsa and others—whether such ordinary person is a king or is a poor man—must not, after acquisition of Knowledge, fail to exercise the large or small authority of carrying out public welfare, which has properly befallen him; but should, so long as life lasts, execute that authority desirelessly, and as a matter of duty, to the fullest extent of his powers and his intelligence, and as far as circumstances will permit. It is not proper for him to say that if he does not do it, somebody else will; because, in that case, not only does one man fall short in the performance of the total work of society, and thereby society lose its aggregate power, but, as another person cannot do that particular work as well as a Jñānin, the general welfare of society suffers to that extent. Besides, as has been mentioned above, the mental frame of other people is also disturbed by the example of Abandonment of Action by a Jñānin. It is true that the followers of the Saṁnyāsa school sometimes say that when one's own Ātman has obtained Release, by the Mind having been purified as a result of Karma, one should be satisfied with that; and without caring if the whole world goes to dogs, one should neither perform *lokasaṁgraha*, nor cause it to be performed—"*lokasaṁgrahadharmaṁ ca naiva kuryān na kārayet*" (Ma. Bhā. Aśva. Anugītā. 46. 39). But, it becomes quite clear from the justification which they advance about the life of Vyāsa and others, or from the advice

59—60

given by Vasiṣṭha or Pancaśikha to Rāma or Janaka to go on performing their duties of maintaining and uplifting society according to their authority till death, that the doctrine of the Saṁnyāsa school is one-sided, and is not a scientific verity which will stand firm at all times. Therefore, it must be said that one should not pay attention to this one-sided advice, and that the only path which is excellent and is consistent with the Śāstras is to continue Action beneficial to society, so long as life lasts, even after having acquired Realisation, and with due regard to one's own qualification, following the illustration of the Blessed Lord Himself. Nevertheless, this *lokasaṁgraha* must not be performed, entertaining any Hope for Fruit (*phalāśa*); because, if one entertains the Hope for Fruit, though it may be about *lokasaṁgraha*, one cannot but suffer unhappiness, if that hope is frustrated. Therefore, a man should not entertain the proud or desireful thought that 'I shall bring about *lokasaṁgraha*', and a man has to bring about *lokasaṁgraha* merely as a duty. It is for the same reason that the Gītā has used the rather longish phraseology of: "*lokasaṁgraham evāpi saṁpaśyan*", i. e., "you must perform Action, keeping in sight (*saṁpaśyan*) public welfare" (Gī. 3. 20), instead of saying that '*lokasaṁgrahārtha*' means, "for obtaining fruit in the shape of public welfare". It is true that *lokasaṁgraha* is an important duty; but it must not be forgotten that the advice given by the Blessed Lord to Arjuna in the previous verse (Gī. 3. 19) that all acts should be performed being free from Attachment, applies equally to *lokasaṁgraha*.

If it is proved by logical argument that the opposition between Jñāna and Karma is an opposition between Jñāna and Desireful Karma, that there is no opposition between Jñāna and Desireless Karma from the Metaphysical point of view, and that as Karma is unavoidable, and is also essential from the point of view of *lokasaṁgraha*, even a Jñānin must, so long as life lasts, continue to perform the duties of the four castes, according to his qualification, and without Attachment; and if the Gītā says the same thing, a doubt naturally arises as to what becomes of the Saṁnyāsa (ascetic) state, out of the four states of life, which have been described in the Smṛti texts of the

Vedic religion. In the Manu-Smṛti and other Smṛtis, the four states (*āśrama*), namely, celibacy, householdership, living in the woods, and asceticism have been mentioned; and it is there stated that after the Mind has been gradually purified by carrying out the duties of education (*adhyayana*), sacrificial ritual, charitable gifts etc. which befall a person according to the arrangement of the four castes, as prescribed by the Śāstras, in the first three states of life, a man should in the end literally give up all Action and renounce the world, and attain Release (See Manu. 6. 1 and 33-37). From this it follows, that according to all the writers of the Smṛtis, though sacrificial ritual and charitable gifts etc. are proper to the state of a householder, yet, their only purpose is the purification of the Mind, that is to say, to bring one to the stage of Realising that there is only one Ātman in all created beings, by the gradual elimination of one's Attachment to objects of pleasure, and of one's self-serving Reason, which (elimination) results in the gradual increase of the desire to do good to others; and that once this mental state has been acquired, one must in the end literally abandon all Action and take to the fourth state of Saṁnyāsa (Asceticism) in order to obtain Release. This is the Path of Saṁnyāsa which was established by Śrī Śaṁkarācārya in the present Kali-yuga, and Kālidāsa, who followed the teaching of the Smṛtis, has described the powerful kings of the Solar Dynasty (*sūryavaṁśi*), in the beginning of the *Raghuvaṁśa* as follows:—

śaiśave 'bhyastavidyānāṁ yauvane viṣayaiṣiṇām ı

vārdhake munivṛttīnāṁ yogenānte tanutyajām ıı

(Raghu. 1. 8.)

that is, "they were such as performed *abhyāsa* (*brahmacarya*) as children, took up the worldly life entailing the enjoyment of the objects of pleasure in their youth (*gṛhasthāśrama*), they lived in the woods during old age, or led the life of a *muni* and ultimately took their Ātman into the Brahman according to the rules of the Saṁnyāsa state, by practising the Pātañjala-

Yoga and gave up their lives. Similarly, it is stated in the Śukānupraśna in the Mahābhārata that:–

catuṣpadī hi niḥśreṇī brahmaṇyeṣā pratiṣṭhitā ।
etām āruhya niḥśreṇīṁ brahmaloke mahīyate ॥
(Śān. 241. 15).

that is, "this ladder with four steps (in the shape of the four stages) ultimately leads to the state of the Brahman. When in this way, a man goes up this ladder from one state into the next higher state, he ultimately acquires greatness in the sphere of the Brahman". And after that, the following order has been described, namely:–

kaṣāyaṁ pācayitvāśu śreṇisthāneṣu ca triṣu ।
pravrajec ca paraṁ sthānaṁ pārivrājyam anuttamam ॥
(Śān. 244. 3).

that is, "a man should, in the three steps of this ladder, destroy as early as possible his *kilbiṣa*, that is, his faults in the shape of selfish tendencies, or Attachment to objects of pleasure, and should then renounce the world; *pārivrājya*, that is, Saṁnyāsa is the most excellent state of all". This same course of going from one state to another state of life has also been mentioned in the Manu-Smṛti (Manu. 6. 4). But Manu had fully realised the fact that if in this way there was an inordinate increase in the desire of people to take up the fourth state, the activity in the world would be destroyed, and society would ultimately be lamed. Therefore, after having definitely enjoined the performance of all activities which are necessary to be performed in the previous states of a householder, and which consisted of acts of valour or of universal welfare, Manu has laid down the clear limit in the following words, namely:

gṛhasthastu yadā paśyed valīpalitam ātmanaḥ ।
apatyasyaiva cāpatyaṁ tad araṇyaṁ samāśrayet ॥
(Manu. 6. 2).

that is, "when his body has become covered with wrinkles, and he has seen his own grand-children, the householder should become a denizen of the woods, and should take Saṁnyāsa". The Manu-Smṛti gives the following reason why this limit has to be followed, namely: in coming to birth, every man brings on his back the three debts (duties) to the Ṛṣis, to his ancestors, and to the deities. Therefore, until a man has discharged all these three obligations, that is, to the Ṛṣis, by the study of Vedas; to the ancestors, by the procreation of off-spring; and to the deities, by the performance of sacrificial ritual, he is not in a position to give up worldly life and take Saṁnyāsa; and if he does so, he will go to perdition as a result of his not having discharged the indebtedness which he has acquired as a result of his birth. (See, Manu. 6. 35-37; and the canon (*mantra*) from the Tai. Saṁ. quoted in the last chapter). According to ancient Hindu Law, a man's children, and even his grand-children, had to discharge the debts of their ancestors, without pleading the law of limitation; and they used to consider it a great misfortune to have to die without having discharged the debts due to others. When this fact is brought to mind, my readers will clearly understand what the intention of our law-givers was, in referring to the above-mentioned important social duties, as 'debts'. Kālidāsa has said in the *Raghuvaṁśa* that all the kings belonging to the Solar Dynasty (*sūryavaṁśi*) led their lives according to the rules laid down by the Smṛtis, and that they used to leave the state of the householder after (not before) installing their sons on the throne, after the sons had grown up and become capable of ruling (Raghu. 7. 68). And there is statement in the Bhāgavata (Bhāg. 6. 5. 35-42), that because Nārada advised the sons of Dakṣa Prajāpati named Haryaśva and also again his several other sons named Śabalāśva to take to the Path of Saṁnyāsa before they had married, and made Saṁnyāsins of them, Dakṣa-Prajāpati reprimanded Nārada for this his unlawful and objectionable behaviour, and laid a curse on him. From this, the original idea of this arrangement of the four states appears to have been, that when a man has lived his worldly life according to the injunctions of the Śāstras, and his children have become more capable than him, he should not interfere with their enthusiasm yielding to the interfering tendency of old age; but should become imbued solely with the idea of acquiring Release; and should of his own accord and voluntarily give up worldly life. The same idea is conveyed in the advice given by Vidura to Dhṛtarāṣṭra in the Viduranīti in the following words:-

utpādya putrān anṛṇāṁśca kṛtvā
vṛttiṁ ca tebhyo 'nuvidhāya kāṁcit ।
sthāne kumārīḥ pratipādya sarvā
araṇyasaṁstho 'tha munir bubhūṣet ॥

(Ma. Bhā. U. 36. 39)

that is, "after a man has begotten sons in the state of a householder, and left no debts to be discharged by them, and made some arrangements for their maintenance, and after having got all his daughters properly married, he should become a denizen of the woods and satisfy his desire of renouncing the world"; and the idea of ordinary people about worldly life in this country is more or less consistent with the dictates of Vidura. Nevertheless, as it was believed that giving up worldly life and taking to Saṁnyāsa was the highest ideal of manhood, the beneficial direction of the three previous stages of life laid down by the writers of the Smṛtis for the successful carrying out of the ordinary affairs of the world, gradually lost importance; and people came to the stage of saying, that if a man had at birth, or in comparatively young age, acquired Knowledge, it was not wrong for him to renounce the world at once without waiting to go through the other three stages— "*brahmacaryād eva pravrajet gṛhād vā vanād vā*" (Jābā. 4). For the same reason, Kapila has given the following advice to Syūmaraśmi in the Gokāpilīya catechism in the Mahābhārata, namely:-

śarīrapaktiḥ karmāṇi jñānaṁ tu paramā gatiḥ ।
kaṣāye karmabhiḥ pakve rasajñāne ca tiṣṭhati ॥*

(Śān. 269 38)

* This verse has been adopted in the Śāṁkarabhāṣya on the Vedānta-Sūtras, and there it runs as follows:—

kaṣāyapaktiḥ karmāṇi jñānaṁ tu paramā gatiḥ ।
kaṣāye karmabhiḥ pakve tato jñānaṁ pravartate ॥

(Ve. Sū. Śāṁ. Bhā. 3. 4. 26)

I have quoted the verse here as I found it in the Mahābhārata.

that is, "the object of Karma is to eliminate the disease in the body in the shape of Attachment to objects of pleasure, and Jñāna is the highest and the ultimate goal; when the disease in the shape of ignorance, or the *kaṣāya,* in the body is eliminated, as the result of Karma, desire for the Knowledge of the essence (*rasa*) is created". In the same way, it is stated in the chapter on Release (*mokṣa*) in the Piṅgalagītā, that "*nairāśyaṁ paramaṁ sukhaṁ*", i. e., despair is the highest happiness" or, "*yo 'sau prāṇāntiko rogas tāṁ tṛṣṇāṁ tyajataḥ sukham*", i. e., "until the fatal disease, in the shape of Desire, has left the body, there can be no happiness" (Śān. 174. 65 and 58). And in addition to the statements in the Jābāla and Bṛhadāraṇyaka Upaniṣads, there are also statements in the Kaivalya and Nārāyaṇ-opaniṣads that "*na karmaṇā na prajayā dhanena tyāgenaike amṛtatvam ānaśuḥ*", i. e., "not by Karma, nor by progeny, or money, but by *tyāga* (Renunciation), is Release attained by some" (Kai. 1. 2; Nārā. U. 12. 3. 3 and 78). If the doctrine of the Gītā is that even a Jñānin must go on performing Action till the end, I must explain how these statements have to be disposed of. The same doubt arose in the mind of Arjuna, and he has in the beginning of the eighteenth chapter asked the Blessed Lord:—"then, explain to me what Renunciation (*saṁnyāsa*) and Abandonment (*tyāga*) respectively are". But before considering the reply given by the Blessed Lord to this question, it is necessary to consider here shortly another equally important Vedic Path of Action, which has been mentioned in the Smṛti texts in addition to this Path of Renunciation.

This path of four steps, namely, celibacy, householdership, living in the woods, and asceticism is known as the '*Smārta*' path, that is, 'the path prescribed by the writers of the Smṛtis'. This arrangement of the four states has been made by the writers of the Smṛtis, consistently with the growth in a man's age, in order to mutually harmonise the contradictory statements in the Vedas, which enjoin the Performance of Action, as also the Abandonment of Action; and if the literal Abandonment of Action is considered the highest ideal, it would not be incorrect to consider the path of four steps laid down by the writers of the Smṛtis for leading one's life, as the means or the preliminary preparation for reaching that ideal. It is true that if one accepts these rising steps of leading one's life, the activity of the world will not come to an end, and the Karma laid down by the Vedas, can be harmonised with the Knowledge expounded in the Upaniṣads. Yet, in as much as the state of the householder is the state which provides the other three states with food (Manu. 6. 89), the importance of the state of a householder has ultimately been frankly acknowledged in the Manu-Smṛti, and even in the Mahābhārata in the following stanza:

yathā mūlaram āśritya sarve jīvanti jantavaḥ ।

evaṁ gārhasthyam āśritya vartanta itarāśramāḥ ॥

(Śān. 268. 6)

that is, "as all living beings (*jantavaḥ*) live by the support of of the mother (earth), so also do the other three states live on the support of the state of a householder" (See Śān. 268. 6; and Manu. 3. 77). And Manu has referred to the other three states of life as rivers, and to the state of the householder as the sea (Manu. 6. 90; Ma Bhā. Śān. 295. 39). If the importance of the state of a householder is thus unquestionable, where is the sense of the advice that one must sometime give up the state of the householder, and make a Renunciation of Action (*karma-saṁnyāsa*)? Is it impossible to perform the duties of the state of a householder even after the acquisition of Knowledge? No; then, where is the sense of saying that a Jñānin should go out of worldly life? The perfect Jñānins who lead their lives desirelessly, are certainly more capable and fit for performing universal welfare, than ordinary people who entertain some selfishness or other in their hearts. Therefore, if a Jñānin is given permission to leave worldly life, just when his capacity has become perfect as a result of Knowledge, that society, for the benefit of which the arrangement of the four castes has been made, will suffer serious loss. The case would be different if some persons left society and went to live in the forest for want of physical strength; and that must have been the idea of Manu in relegating Renunciation (*saṁnyāsa*) to old age. But, as has been stated above, this beneficial limit was not observed. Therefore, although the writers of the Smṛtis had created the rising ladder of the four states, in order to harmonise the two-fold order of the Vedas, viz., to perform Action, and to give up Action, the Blessed Lord, who was undoubtedly as competent, or even more competent that the writers of the Smṛtis, to harmonise these dictates of the Vedas, has Himself revived, and fully supported, in the form of the Bhāgavata religion, the Path which combines Karma with Jñāna, and which was followed by Janaka and others in ancient times. The difference between the two is, that in the Bhāgavata doctrine, reliance is not placed only on Metaphysical ideas, but the additional easy remedy of Devotion to Vāsudeva has been added. But, a detailed discussion of this matter will be made later on in the thirteenth chapter. Although the Bhāgavata religion is Devotional, yet, as it has adopted the important principle enunciated in the Path prescribed by Janaka, namely, that after the acquisition of the Knowledge of the Parameśvara, a Jñānin should not take to Saṁnyāsa in the shape of Abandonment of Action, but should go on desirelessly performing all his activities till death for universal welfare, giving up the Hope for Fruit of Action (*phalāśa*), both paths are identical from the point of view of Karma, that is to say, they both embody the union of Jñāna with Karma, or are Activistic. As the first protagonists of this Activistic religion were the two Ṛṣis, Nara and Nārāyaṇa, who were living incarnations of the Parabrahman, the ancient name of this religion is the 'Nārāyaṇīya Religion'. Though, both these Ṛṣis had acquired the highest Knowledge, they advised people to perform Action desirelessly, and did so themselves (Ma. Bhā. U. 48. 21); and therefore, this religion has been described in the Mahābhārata by saying: "*pravṛttilakṣaṇaś caiva dharmo nārāyaṇātmakaḥ*" (Ma. Bhā. Śān. 347. 81), or, "*pravṛttilakṣaṇaṁ dharmaṁ ṛṣir nārāyaṇo 'bravīt*"—the religion propounded by the Ṛṣi Nārāyaṇa was lifelong Activistic (Ma. Bhā. Śān. 217. 2). This religion is the Sātvata or Bhāgavata religion, and it has been clearly stated in the Bhāgavata, that the form of this Sātvata or original Bhāgavata religion was '*naiṣkarmya-lakṣaṇa*', that is, desirelessly Activistic (See Bhāg. 1. 3. 8 and 11. 4. 6). This Activistic path was also known as 'Yoga', as is clear from the line "*pravṛttilakṣaṇo yogaḥ jñānaṁ saṁnyāsalakṣaṇam*" in the Anugītā (Ma. Bhā. Aśva. 43. 25); and, that is why the religion propounded in the Gītā by Śrī Kṛṣṇa, who was the incarnation of Nārāyaṇa, to Arjuna, who was the incarnation of Nara, has been called 'Yoga' in the Gītā itself. Some persons now-a-days believe that the Bhāgavata and the Smārta paths originally came into existence as a result of a difference between the objects of worship; but according to me, this belief is wrong; because, although the objects of worship in these two paths may be different, yet the Metaphysical Knowledge contained in both is the same; and when the Metaphysical foundation of both was the same, it is not likely that these ancient Jñānins, who were steeped in this Supreme Knowledge, would have kept up differences between themselves, merely on account of a difference in the objects of worship. For this reason, it is stated both in the Bhagavadgītā (9. 14) and in the Śivagītā (12. 4) that whatever is worshipped, the worship ultimately reaches one and the same Parameśvara; and these two deities have been described in the Nārāyaṇīya doctrine in the Mahābhārata as being identical, by saying that Nārāyaṇa is the same as Rudra, that the worshippers of Nārāyaṇa were the worshippers of Rudra, and the enemies of Nārāyaṇa, the enemies of Rudra (Ma. Bhā. Śān. 341. 20-26 and 342. 129). I do not say that the difference between Śaivism and Vaiṣṇavism did not exist in ancient times. What I mean to say is that the original reason for the difference between the Smārta and Bhāgavata paths, was not the difference in the objects of worship, namely, Śiva and Viṣṇu; and that these two paths must have first come into existence as a result of a difference of opinion on an important point, namely, whether Asceticism or Activism should be followed after the acquisition of Knowledge. After a considerable lapse of time, when this Activistic path or Karma-Yoga of the original Bhāgavata religion ceased to exist, and it got its present form of the pure worship of Viṣṇu, that is to say, a more or less Non-Activistic form, and on that account, people began to fight with each other merely on the ground that the deity of one was Śiva, whereas the deity of the other was Viṣṇu, the words 'Smārta' and 'Bhāgavata' became respectively synonymous with 'Śaiva' and 'Vaiṣṇava'; and ultimately the Vedānta of these present-day followers of the Bhāgavata religion (Dualism or Qualified Monism), and their astrology, that is to say, the observance of the eleventh day of the month, as also the way of applying the sandal-wood paste on the forehead, became different from the Smārta way. But, it becomes quite clear from the word 'Smārta' that these differences were not real, that is, original. As the Bhāgavata religion was promulgated by the Blessed Lord Himself, there is no wonder that the object of worship in it should be the Blessed Lord Śrī Kṛṣṇa or Viṣṇu. But, as the root-meaning of the word 'Smārta' is 'prescribed by the Smṛtis', the deity worshipped according to the Smārta path need not be Śiva; because, it is nowhere stated in the works of Manu or other ancient Smṛti texts, that Śiva is the only deity which should be worshipped. On the other hand, Viṣṇu has been mentioned more often, and in some places Gaṇapati and other deities are also mentioned. Besides, as both the deities Śiva and Viṣṇu are Vedic, that is, as both have been mentioned in the Vedas, it is not proper to refer to only one of them as 'Smārta'. Besides, Śrī Śaṁkarācārya is looked upon as a protagonist of the Smārta religion; yet, Śāradā (goddess of learning—Trans.) is the deity worshipped in the Śāṁkara monasteries; and wherever there has been occasion in the Śāṁkarabhāṣya to refer to the worship of an idol, the Ācārya has referred, not to the Śiva-liṅga, but to the Śāligrāma that is, the image of Śrī Viṣṇu (Ve. Sū. Śāṁ. Bhā. 1. 2. 7; 1. 3. 14 and 4. 1. 3; Chān. Śāṁ. Bhā. 8. 1. 1). There is also a tradition that the worship of the Pañcāyatana (group of five deities) was first started by Śaṁkarācārya. Therefore, it follows that according to the original meaning of these words, people disregarded whether a person worshipped Śiva or Viṣṇu, and considered those as SMĀRTA, whose ultimate ideal was to first go through worldly life in youth as prescribed by the Śāstras, and consistently with the arrangement of the four states laid down systematically and in detail in the Smṛti texts, and to take Saṁnyāsa, or the fourth state, by giving up Action altogether in old age; and considered those as BHĀGAVATA, who believed that all the

Actions appropriate to the state of a householder should be performed desirelessly till death, according to the advice of the Blessed Lord, simultaneously with the acquisition of Knowledge and with the possession of a passionate devotion to the Blessed Lord; and in these meanings, these two words are respectively synonymous with Sāṁkhya and Yoga or Saṁnyāsa and Karma-Yoga. Saṁnyāsa subsequently ceased to exist as a state of life, whether as a result of the incarnations taken by the Blessed Lord, or because the importance of the state of a householder, which included Spiritual Knowledge, began to be realised; and it has been included among the Kali-varjya, that is, those things which are prohibited in the Kali-yuga according to the Śāstras.* But, later on the protagonists of the Buddhist and the Jain religions accepted the opinions of the Kāpila-Sāṁkhya school, and brought into prominence the doctrine that Release is impossible unless a man takes Saṁnyāsa, and gives up worldly life. It is well-known in history that Buddha himself gave up his kingdom and his wife and children and entered the Saṁnyāsa state in youth. Although Śrī Śaṁkarācārya refuted the Jain and Buddhistic doctrines, yet the path of Asceticism, which was principally put into vogue by the Jains and Buddhists, was allowed to remain by the Ācārya as being the Saṁnyāsa prescribed by the Śrutis and the Smṛtis; and he has, therefore, interpreted the Gītā as supporting the Saṁnyāsa path. But, really speaking the Gītā is not a work which supports the Smārta path; and although the earlier portions of it refer to the Sāṁkhya or the Saṁnyāsa path, the later portions, which contain the conclusion, support the Activistic or Bhāgavata religion, as

* See the chapter of Kali-varjya in the third part (*pariccheda*) of the *Nirṇaya-Sindhu*. Here, the Smṛti texts, "*agnihotraṁ gavālaṁbhaṁ saṁnyāsaṁ palapaitṛkam* | *devarāc ca sutotpattiḥ kalau pañca vivarjayet*" ||, and "*saṁnyāsaś ca na kartavyo brāhmaṇena vijānatā*", etc., are mentioned. The first of these two texts means that *agnihotra*, (perpetual sacred fire), slaughter of cows, Saṁnyāsa, partaking of meat at the time of the performance of the *śrāddha* (ancestor-worship), and *niyoga* (procreating off-spring from the wife of another –Trans.), these five are prohibited in the Kaliyuga. The prohibition against Saṁnyāsa, out of these, was removed by Śaṁkarācārya.

has been mentioned by me already in the first chapter to have been stated by the author of the Mahābhārata itself. As both these paths are Vedic, it is possible to harmonise them with each other to a considerable extent, if not wholly. But harmonising them in this way, is one thing, and saying that the Gītā supports only the Path of Renunciation, and that the references in it to the Path of Energism as being productive of Release, are merely praise, is quite a different thing. As a result of difference in taste, one man may prefer the Smārta religion to the Bhāgavata religion; or he may consider as more convincing the reasons which are commonly given in support of the Abandonment of Action. I will not deny that possibility. For instance, no one has any doubt that Śrī Śaṁkarācārya favoured the Smārta or Saṁnyāsa path and looked upon all other paths as based on ignorance. But, on that account, one cannot conclude that that was the purport of the Gītā. If you do not accept the doctrines laid down by the Gītā, do not follow them. But, it is not proper on that account to interpret the statement, "there are, in this world, two independent Niṣṭhās or paths leading to Release for living one's life," made in the commencement of the Gītā, as meaning that: "the Saṁnyāsa path is the only true and superior path". These two paths, which have been described in the Gītā, have been current in the Vedic religion, independently of each other, even from before the days of Janaka and Yājñavalkya; and we see that persons like Janaka, on whom the duty of the maintenance and uplift of society had befallen, as a result of their status as Kṣatriyas, or hereditarily, or as a result of their own prowess, continued their activities desirelessly, even after the acquisition of Knowledge; and were spending their lives in bringing about the benefit of the world. Bearing in mind this status of certain persons in society, the Mahābhārata contains two such distinct statements, according to difference in status, as, "*sukhaṁ jīvanti munayo bhaikṣyavṛttiṁ samāśritāḥ*", i. e., "ascetics living in the woods, joyfully accept the status of beggars" (Śān. 178. 11), and "*daṇḍa eva hi rājendra kṣatradharmo na muṇḍanam*", i. e., "it is the duty of the Kṣatriyas to maintain and uplift people by punishment, and not to shave off the hair on their heads" (Śān. 23. 46). But, from this, one must not conclude that Karma-Yoga was the proper duty only for the Kṣatriyas, who were responsible for the maintenance of society. The true meaning of the above statement from the science of Karma-Yoga is, that every man must, after the acquisition of Knowledge, go on performing those duties, which are his according to his qualification *(adhikāra)*; and it is on this account, that it is stated in the Bhārata that, "*eṣā pūrvatarā vṛttir brāhmaṇasya vidhīyate*" (Śān. 237), i. e., "even the Brahmins used, in ancient times, to continue Yajñas and Yāgas, according to their qualification, after the acquisition of Knowledge"; and in the Manu-Smṛti, the Vedic Karma-Yoga has been considered more proper for all classes than the Saṁnyāsa path (Manu. 6. 86-96). It is also nowhere stated that the Bhāgavata religion exists only for the Ksatriyas; but on the other hand, it has been praised by saying that it is accessible even to women, Śūdras etc. (Gī. 9. 32); and there are also definite stories in the Mahābhārata that this religion was followed by the Tulādhāra, or a merchant, and Vyādha, or a hunter, and that these taught it to the Brahmins (Śān. 261; Vana. 215); and the illustrations, which are given in the books on the Bhāgavata religion, of prominent persons who followed the Desireless Karma-Yoga are not only of Kṣatriyas like Janaka and Śrī Kṛṣṇa, but also of learned Brahmins like Vasiṣṭha, Jaigīṣavya, Vyāsa and others.

Although the Gītā supports only the Energistic Path, it must not be forgotten that it does not look upon the path of performing Action without Knowledge as leading to Release. There are also two paths of performing Knowledge-less Actions. The one is of performing Actions hypocritically (with *daṁbha*), or with an ungodly (*āsurī*) frame of mind; and the other, is of performing them with religious faith (*śraddhā*). Out of these, the path of hypocrisy, or the *āsurī* path, was considered objectionable and productive of perdition, not only by the Gītā, but also by the writers of the Mīmāṁsā; and even in the Ṛg-Veda, religious faith has been extolled in many places (Ṛg. 10. 151; 9. 113. 2 and 2. 12. 5). But, the Mīmāṁsā school says, with regard to those who perform Karma without Knowledge, but putting faith in the Śāstras, that if a man performs ritual throughout life merely with religious faith, and relying on the Śāstras, he will ultimately attain Release, though he may not have had a true Realisation of the form of the Parameśvara. I have stated in the last chapter that this path of the Mīmāṁsā school has been current from very ancient times in the shape of the Karma-kāṇḍa. Jaimini says that it is nowhere stated either in the Veda-Saṁhitās or in the Brāhmaṇas that the Path of Saṁnyāsa was essential; and that, on the other hand there are clear statements in the Vedas, that Release is attained by remaining in the state of a householder (Ve. Sū. 3. 4. 17-20); and this statement of his is not without foundation. Because, this ancient path of of the Karma-kāṇḍa came to be first looked upon as inferior only in the Upaniṣads. Although the Upaniṣads are Vedic, yet, they are later in point of time than the Saṁhitās and the Brāhmaṇas, as is clear from the method of dealing with the subject-matter adopted in them. It is not that people had not acquired the Knowledge of the Parameśvara before that date. But the opinion that a man should apathetically abandon Action, after the acquisition of Knowledge, in order to attain Release, first began to be acted upon only at the time of the Upaniṣads; and thereafter, the Karma-kāṇḍa described in the Saṁhitās and in the Brāhmaṇas came to be looked upon as inferior. Before that date, Karma was considered superior. When the Path of Saṁnyāsa, that is, of Knowledge coupled with apathy towards the world, thus became preponderant in the time of the Upaniṣads, Jñānins naturally began to neglect ritualistic sacrifices, as also the religious injunctions prescribed for the four castes; and the idea that universal welfare (*lokasaṁgraha*) was a duty, began to lose ground. It is true that the writers of the Smṛtis have stated in their works, that the sacrificial Karma enjoined in the Śrutis, and the duties proper for the four castes enjoined in the Smṛtis must be performed during the state of a householder; and they have in that way praised that state. But, as even according to the writers of the Smṛtis, indifference towards the world, or the state of Asceticism, was excellent, it was not possible that the inferiority placed on the Karma-kāṇḍa by the Upaniṣads, should be reduced by the arrangement of the four stages of life enjoined in the Smṛtis. In this state of things the Gītā has come forward to harmonise the Jñāna-kāṇḍa with the Karma-kāṇḍa, without deprecating either, by tacking on both of them to Devotion. The Gītā accepts the doctrines of the writers of the Upaniṣads that there is no Release without Jñāna, and that by sacrificial ritualistic Karma, one can at most attain heaven (Muṇḍa. 1. 2. 10; Gī. 2. 41-45). But, it is also a doctrine of the Gītā, that in order that the affairs of the world should go on, the wheel of Yajñas, or of Karma, must be kept going on; and that it is foolish to give up Karma at any time; and therefore, the Gītā advises that instead of performing the sacrificial ritual and other acts prescribed by the Śrutis, or the worldly activity enjoined by the arrangement of the four castes, merely with religious faith and ignorantly, one should perform them with a frame of mind which combines Spiritual Knowledge with indifference towards the world and merely as a duty, so that the Karma which is performed will not obstruct Release, and at the same time, the circle of the Yajñas will not be disrupted. It need not be said that this skill of the Gītā of harmonising the Jñāna-kāṇḍa with the Karma-kāṇḍa (that is, Saṁnyāsa and Karma) is better than what the writers of the Smṛtis have done; because, by the path prescribed in the Gītā, the benefit of the collective Ātman, which pervades the creation is achieved without at the same time in any way prejudicing the benefit of the individual Ātman. The Mīmāṁsā school says that as Karma is eternal, and is enjoined by the Vedas, one must perform it although one may not have acquired Knowledge; many (but not all) writers of the Upaniṣads treat Karma as inferior, and say that it must be given up by cultivating indifference towards the world; or, at any rate, one may safely say, that they are inclined to do so; and the writers of the Smṛtis harmonise these two opinions by differentiating between youth and old age, and relying on the arrangement of the four states, and by saying that Actions should be performed in the three previous states of life, and that after the Mind has been purified by the performance of Actions, one should in old age give up Action and renounce the world. But the path prescribed by the Gītā is different from all these three paths. Though there is an opposition between Jñāna and Desire-prompted Action, there is no opposition between Jñāna and Desireless Action; therefore, the Gītā asks you to perform all Actions desirelessly, and never to give them up. If these four doctrines are compared with each other, it will be seen that all accept the position that Karma is necessary before Knowledge is acquired. But, the Upaniṣads and the Gītā say that Actions performed in that state and merely with religious faith do not yield any fruit except heaven. As to whether Karma should or should not be performed after this, that is, after the acquisition of Knowledge, there is a difference of opinion even among the writers of the Upaniṣads. Some of the Upaniṣads say, that the man who has become fit for Release after all desire has been destroyed in his heart as a result of Knowledge, need not perform Desire-prompted Actions, which lead only to heaven; and, other Upaniṣads, such as, Īśāvāsya etc., insist that all these Actions must nevertheless be kept going on in order that the activities of the world should go on. It is quite clear that the Gītā accepts the second one out of these two paths prescribed by the Upaniṣads (Gī. 5. 2). But, though it may be said that the Jñānin, who has become fit for Release, should go on desirelessly performing all Actions for universal welfare, a doubt naturally arises here as to why he should perform such Karma like sacrificial ritual, which leads only to heaven. Therefore, this doubt has been raised in the beginning of the eighteenth chapter, and the Blessed Lord has given His clear decision, that in as much as, "sacrificial ritual, charity, austerity" etc., always have the effect of purifying the Mind, and of making the Mind more and more desireless, "these actions also" (*etāny api*) should be performed by the Jñānin desirelessly, continually, and without Attachment, for social welfare (Gī. 18. 6.). When all acts are desirelessly performed in this way, that is, with the intention of dedicating them to the Parameśvara, that amounts to the performance of a stupendous Yajña in the wide sense of the term; and then, the Karma performed for the sake of this Yajña does not become a source of bondage (Gī. 4. 23). Not only that; but as all these Actions have been performed desirelessly, they do not produce the bondage-creating result in the shape of the attainment of heaven, which springs from sacrificial ritual, and do not stand in the way of Release. In short, although the Karma-kāṇḍa of the Mīmāṁsā school has been kept intact in the Gītā, yet, it has been kept intact in such a way, that it definitely leads to Release instead of making a person journey to and from heaven, since all Actions have to be performed desirelessly. It must be borne in mind that this is the important difference between the Karma-mārga prescribed by the Mīmāṁsā school and the Karma-Yoga prescribed by the Gītā; and that both are not the same.

I have, thus, explained that the Bhagavadgītā has advocated the Activistic Bhāgavata religion or the Karma-Yoga, as also what the difference is, between this Karma-Yoga and the Karma-kāṇḍa of the Mīmāṁsā school. I shall now consider the difference in principles between the Karma-Yoga of the Gītā and the arrangement of the four states made by the writers of the Smṛtis on the authority of the Jñāna-kāṇḍa. This difference is very subtle; and strictly speaking, there is no need to enter into a fruitless discussion about this matter. Both accept the position that every one must perform the duties proper to the first two states of life for the purification of the Mind. The only point of difference is whether after the acquisition of Knowledge, one should continue performing Action or renounce the world. Here, some are likely to think that as such Jñānins are necessarily few and far between, it is not necessary to trouble much about whether these few persons perform or do not perform Action. But this position is not correct; because, as the conduct of the Jñānins is considered exemplary by other people, and also as every man directs his behaviour from the very beginning according to what his ultimate end is, the question 'what the Jñānin should do' is a very important question from the general point of view. It is true that the Smṛti texts say that a Jñānin should finally renounce the world. But, as has been stated above, there are exceptions even to this rule according to the directions of the Smṛtis. For instance, in the Bṛhadāraṇyakopaniṣad, Yājña-valkya has given a considerable amount of advice about the Knowledge of the Brahman to Janaka; but, he has nowhere said to Janaka: "you now give up ruling and renounce the world". It is stated there, on the contrary, that those Jñānins who give up worldly life after the acquisition of Knowledge, do so because they do not like (*na kāmayante)* worldly life (Bṛ. 4. 4. 22). From this, the opinion of the Bṛhadāraṇyakopaniṣad seems clearly to be that taking or not taking Saṁnyāsa, after the acquisition of Knowledge, is a matter purely within the discretion of everybody; and that there is no permanent relationship between the Knowledge of the Brahman and Saṁnyāsa; and this statement in the Bṛhadāraṇyakopaniṣad has been explained in the same way in the Vedānta-Sūtras (Ve. Sū. 3. 4. 15). Śaṁkarācārya has definitely laid down that it is not possible to attain Release unless Action is abandoned after the acquisition of Knowledge; and he has attempted to show in his Bhāṣya that all the Upaniṣads are in favour of that proposition. Nevertheless, even Śrī Śaṁkarācārya has admitted that there is no objection to one's performing Actions till death, according to one's own qualification in life, even after the acquisition of Knowledge, as was done by Janaka and others. (See Ve. Sū. Śāṁ. Bhā. 3. 3. 32; and Gī. Śāṁ. Bhā. 2. 11 and 3. 20). From this it is clear that even the school of Saṁnyāsa or the Smṛtis do not look upon the performance of Action, after the acquisition of Knowledge, as objectionable; and that this school of thought allows some Jñānins to perform Actions according to their own qualifications, though as exceptions. The Gītā widens the scope of this exception and says that every Jñānin must go on performing the duties enjoined on the four castes, even after the acquisition of Knowledge, as a matter of duty, and for universal welfare. It, therefore, follows that though the religion of the Gītā is more comprehensive, the principle established by it is faultless, even from the point of view of the Saṁnyāsa school; and if one reads the Vedānta-Sūtras independently, he will notice that even in them, the Karma-Yoga combined with Knowledge has been considered acceptable as being a kind of Saṁnyāsa. (Ve. Sū. 3. 4. 26; 3. 4. 32-35).* Nevertheless, it is necessary to show

* This portion of the Vedānta-Sūtras has been interpreted in a slightly different way in the Śāṁkarabhāṣya. But, according to me, the words "*vihitatvāc cāśramakarmāpi*" (3. 4. 32) mean: "there is no objection to the Jñānin doing the various acts prescribed for

what becomes of the fourth state or Saṁnyāsa in the shape of Abandonment of Action, which has been prescribed in the Smṛti texts, if Karma has to be performed lifelong, though desirelessly. Arjuna was thinking that the Blessed Lord would sometime or other say to him that it was not possible to attain Release unless sometime or other Saṁyāsa in the shape of Abandonment of Action was taken; and that, he would then get a chance of giving up fighting on the authority of something the Blessed Lord had Himself said. But, when Arjuna saw that the Blessed Lord did not even touch the question of Saṁnyāsa by Abandonment of Action till the end of the seventeenth chapter, and that He over and over again advised the Abandonment of the Fruit of Action, he, in the commencement of the eighteenth chapter, has at last said to the Blessed Lord: "then, tell me the difference between Saṁnyāsa (Renunciation) and Tyāga (Abandonment)". In replying to this question of Arjuna, the Blessed Lord says: "O Arjuna, if you think that the path of Karma-Yoga which I have described so far, does not include Saṁnyāsa, you are wrong. Karma-Yogins divide all Actions into '*kāmya*', that is, Actions performed with an Attached frame of mind, and '*niṣkāma*', that is, Actions performed without Attachment. (These two are referred to as '*pravṛtta*' and '*nivṛtta*' Action respectively in the Manu-Smṛti 12. 89). Out of these, the Karma-Yogin totally gives up all Actions which fall into the category of Desireful Actions, that is to say, he makes a 'Saṁnyāsa' (Renunciation) of them. That leaves the *niṣkāma* (Desireless) or the *nivṛtta* Actions. It is true that the Karma-Yogin performs these Desireless (*niṣkāma*) Actions; but in performing them he has made a 'Tyāga' (Abandonment) of the Hope for Fruit. In short, how does one escape Saṁnyāsa or Tyāga, even in the Path of Karma-Yoga? Whereas the followers of the Smṛtis literally renounce Karma, the Yogins in the Path of Karma-Yoga renounce instead, the Hope for the Fruit of

---

the various states, because they are proper (*vihita*)". In short, according to me, the Vedānta-Sūtras have accepted both the positions of the Jñānin performing Actions, and also not performing them.

Action. But, in either case, Saṁnyāsa is a common factor" (See my commentary on Gī. 18. 1-6). Nay, that man who has started performing all Actions desirelessly and with the idea of dedicating them to the Parameśvara, must be said to be an 'eternal ascetic' (*'nitya-saṁnyāsin'*), though he may be a householder (Gī. 5. 3). This is the principal doctrine of the Bhāgavata religion; and it is this doctrine which has been preached by Nārada to Yudhiṣṭhira in the Bhāgavata-Purāṇa after he had first explained to him the duties of the four states of life. As has been stated by Vaman Pandit in his commentary on the Gītā, that is, in the *Yathārtha Dīpikā* (18. 2), it is not that there is no Saṁnyāsa unless a man "shaves off his hair, and throws away the sacred thread"; or, takes a staff in his hand and goes about begging; or, gives up all Action and goes and lives in the forest. Renunciation (*saṁnyāsa)* and indifference towards the world (*vairāgya)* are properties of the Mind; they are not the properties of the staff, or of the hair on the head, or of the sacred thread. If one says that they are the properties of the staff etc. and not of the Mind or of Knowledge, then even the man who holds the handle of the royal umbrella or of any umbrella, must get the same Release as is obtained by a Saṁnyāsin. It is stated in the conversation between Janaka and Sulabhā, that:

tridaṇḍādiṣu yady asti mokṣo jñānena kasyacit ।
chatrādiṣu kathaṁ na syāt tulyahetau parigrahe ॥

(Śān. 320. 42).

Because, in either case taking the staff in the hand is a common factor. In short, the control of the body, of the speech, and of the mind is the true *'tridaṇḍa'*, (three-fold staff), (Manu. 12. 10); and the true Saṁnyāsa is the Renunciation of the Desire-prompted frame of Mind (Gī. 18. 2); and as one cannot escape that Saṁnyāsa in the Bhāgavata religion (Gī. 6. 2), so also can one not escape the Action of keeping the mind steady or of eating etc. in Sāṁkhya philosophy. Then, where is the sense of making childish objections that the Path of Karma-Yoga does not include Saṁnyāsa in the shape of Abandonment of Action, and is, therefore, contrary to the injunctions of the Smṛtis or unacceptable; and fighting about white clothes or saffron-coloured robes? The Blessed Lord has candidly and without bias said that:

ekaṁ sāṁkhyaṁ ca yogaṁ ca yaḥ paśyati sa paśyati ।

(Gī. 5. 5.)

that is, "that man is truly wise who has realised that Sāṁkhya and (Karma-) Yoga are not two from the point of view of Release, but are one and the same"; and it is stated even in the Bhārata that, "*sāṁkhyayogena tulyo hi dharma ekānta-sevitaḥ*" (Śān. 348. 74), that is, "the Ekāntika or Bhāgavata religion is equal in merit to the Sāṁkhya religion". In short, in as much as true indifference to the world *(vairāgya)* or 'eternal renunciation' *(nitya-saṁnyāsa)*, (5. 3), consists in merging all selfish interests in universal interests, and in desirelessly performing all duties which befall one in worldly life according to one's own qualifications, so long as life lasts, for the welfare of all created beings, and purely as duties, those who follow the Path of Karma-Yoga never literally abandon Karma and beg. But, though there may be this seeming difference in outward action, the essential principles of Renuciation *(saṁnyāsa)* and Abandonment *(tyāga)* continue in the Path of Karma-Yoga; and therefore, the Gītā lays down the ultimate doctrine that there is no opposition between the Desireless Karma-Yoga and the arrangement of states of life according to the Smṛti texts.

From what has been stated above, it might be thought by some that an attempt has been made in the Gītā to harmonise the Karma-Yoga with the Path of Renunciation, because, the Path of Renunciation prescribed by the Smṛtis was an ancient religion; and that the Path of Karma-Yoga was a later creation. But, anybody will see that such is not the case, if the matter is considered from the historical point of view. I have already stated before that the most ancient form of the Vedic religion consisted of the Karma-kāṇḍa. By the Knowledge imparted in the Upaniṣads, the Karma-kāṇḍa gradually became inferior, and Saṁnyāsa in the shape of Abandonment of Action gradually came into vogue. This was the second step in the growth of the tree of the Vedic religion. But even in those times, philosophers like Janaka and others used to harmonise the Karma-kāṇḍa with the Knowledge propounded in the Upaniṣads, and to go on desirelessly performing Actions till death. Therefore, this second stage of the tree of Vedic religion must be said to fall into two classes; the one was the class to which Janaka and others belonged, and the other was the class to which Yājñavalkya and others belonged. The arrangement of stages of life made in the Smṛtis was the third step. But, this third step was also two-fold like the second step. It is true that the Smṛti texts praise the worth of the fourth state of life entailing the Abandonment of Action; but at the same time, the Karma-Yoga, which included Knowledge and which was followed by Janaka and others, has also been mentioned by the Smṛti texts as an alternative for the Saṁnyāsa state. For instance, take the Manu-Smṛti, which is the foundation of all the Smṛti texts. It is stated in the sixth chapter of this Smṛti, that a man should gradually rise from the state of the celibate to the states of the house-holder and of the denizen of the woods, and should ultimately take up the fourth state, which entailed the Abandonment of Action. But, when this description of the fourth state, that is, of the religion of ascetics (Yatins) is over, Manu, after saying by way of introduction that: "I have so far described the religion of Yatins, that is, of Saṁnyāsins; I will now explain the Karma-Yoga of the Vedic Saṁnyāsins", and explaining how the state of the householder is superior to the other states, goes on to describe the Karma-Yoga to be followed in the desireless state of the householder, as an alternative for the Saṁnyāsa state or for the religion of Yatins (Manu. 6. 86-96); and later on in the twelvth chapter, this religion has been described as the "Vedic Karma-Yoga", and it is stated that this path is as *niḥśreyasakara*, that is, as productive of Release as the fourth state (Manu. 12. 86-90). The doctrine of Manu also finds a place in the Yājñavalkya-Smṛti. In the third chapter of this Smṛti, after the description of the religion of Yatins is over, the conjunction 'or' (*athavā*) is used, and then it is stated that even the householder, who is a devotee of Knowledge, and who speaks the truth, attains Release (without taking Saṁnyāsa), (See Yājña. 3. 204 and 205). In the same way, Yāska has stated in his *Nirukta*, that the ascetics, who abandon Action, as also the Karma-Yogins, who perform Action though they have acquired Knowledge, go to the next life by the *devayāna* path (Ni. 14. 9). Another authority in support of this proposition, besides Yāska, is of the writers of the Dharma-Sūtras. These Dharma-Sūtras are in prose and scholars believe them to be earlier in point of time than the Smṛti texts, which are written in verse. We are not concerned at the moment with considering whether this opinion is correct or not. Whether it is correct or incorrect, the only important thing we have to consider in the present chapter is that the importance of the state of a householder or of the Karma-Yoga has, in these works, been stated to be more than has been done in the statements quoted above from the Manu and the Yājñavalkya Smṛtis. Manu and Yājña-valkya have referred to the Karma-Yoga as an alternative for the fourth state; but Baudhāyana and Āpastaṁba have not done so; and they have clearly stated that the state of the house-holder is the most important state, and that immortality is subsequently attained in that state only. In the Baudhāyana Dharma-Sūtras, after referring to the statement "*jāyamāno vai brāhmaṇas tribhir ṛṇavā jāyate*"—that is, "every Brahmin in coming to birth brings with himself the burden of three debts" etc. found in the Taittirīya-Saṁhitā, it is stated that the man who takes shelter into the state of a householder, which entails the performance of sacrificial ritual etc., in order to discharge these debts, attains the sphere of the Brahman; and that those who attach importance to the state of celibacy, or of Saṁnyāsa, are ruined (Bau. 2. 6. 11. 33 and 34); and there is a similar statement also in the Āpastaṁba Sūtras (Āpa. 2. 9. 24. 8). It is not that the fourth state of Saṁnyāsa has not been described in these two Dharma-Sūtras; but, even after describing that state, the importance of the state of the householder has been stated to be greater. From this fact, and especially from the fact that the adjective 'Vedic' has been applied to the Karma-Yoga in the Manu-Smṛti, the following two things become absolutely clear, namely, (i) that even in the times of the Manu-Smṛti, the state of the householder, which entailed the

Desireless Karma-Yoga, was considered more ancient than the Path of Renunciation by Abandonment of Action; and that (ii) from the point of view of Release, it was considered as meritorious as the fourth state. As the leaning of the commentators on the Gītā was towards Saṁyāsa, or towards Devotion coupled with Abandonment of Action, the above statements from the Smṛtis are not found referred to in their commentaries; but, though they have disregarded those statements, the ancientness of the Karma-Yoga is not thereby in any way diminished. Nay, one may even without objection say that as this path of Karma-Yoga was the more ancient one, the writers of the Smṛtis had to accept it as an alternative for the Path of Renunciation. This is the Vedic Karma-Yoga. This was practised by Janaka and others before the times of Śrī Kṛṣṇa. But, as the Blessed Lord added the creed of Devotion to that Path, and gave it further circulation, His religion came to be known as the 'Bhāgavata Doctrine'. I shall later on consider historically how this Karma-Yoga again came to be looked upon as inferior, and the Path of Renunciation acquired greater importance, although the Bhagavadgītā had in this way declared Karma-Yoga to be superior to Renunciation. All that I have to say for the present is that the Karma-Yoga is not later in point of time than the Path prescribed by the Smṛtis, and that it has been in vogue from the ancient Vedic times.

My readers will now appreciate the inner reason for the words "*iti śrīmad bhagavadgītāsu upaniṣatsu brahmavidyāyāṁ yogaśāstre*", used at the end of each chapter of the Gītā. The Upaniṣad which has been sung by the Blessed Lord contains the Brahmavidyā like all other Upaniṣads. But, these words mean that it does not contain only the Brahmavidyā, and that the principal object of the Bhagavadgītā was to support only the Yoga or the Karma-Yoga, out of the two paths of Sāṁkhya and Yoga (the Vedāntic Saṁnyāsa, and the Vedāntic Karma-Yoga), which are included in the Brahmavidyā. Nay, one may even without objection say that the Bhagavadgītopaniṣad is the most important treatise on the science of Karma-Yoga; because, although the Karma-Yoga has been in vogue from the times of the Vedas, yet, except for some few references like "*kurvann eveha karmāṇi*" (Īśā. 2), or "*ārabhya karmāṇi guṇānvitāni*" (Śve. 6. 4), or, "simultaneously with the Vidyā, ritual, such as, *svādhyāya* etc., should be performed" (Tai. 1. 9) there is nowhere any detailed explanation of the Karma-Yoga in any of the Upaniṣads. The Bhagavadgītā is the principal authoritative treatise on that subject; and it is also proper from the point of view of poetic literature that that Bhārata, which describes the lives of the great heroes in the Bhārata-land should also explain the theory of the Karma-Yoga in its relation to Metaphysics. This also now clearly explains why the Bhagavadgītā was included in the Prasthānatrayī. Although the Upaniṣads are fundamental, yet, as they have been written by various Ṛṣis, the ideas contained in them are diverse, and in some places apparently mutually contradictory. It was, therefore, necessary to include the Upaniṣads in the Prasthānatrayī, along with the Vedānta-Sūtras, which attempted to harmonise them. If the Gītā did not contain anything more than the Upaniṣads and the Vedānta-Sūtras, there would be no point in including the Gītā in the Prasthānatrayī. But, the trend of the Upaniṣads is principally towards the Path of Renunciation, and they support chiefly the Jñāna-mārga (Path of Knowledge); and when one says that the Bhagavadgītā supports the Karma-Yoga based on Devotion simultaneously with Knowledge, the distinction of the Bhagavadgītā becomes clear, and at the same time the appropriateness of the three parts of the Prasthānatrayī also becomes clear. Because, if the authoritative treatises on the Vedic religion had not dealt with both the Vedic paths of Jñāna and Karma (Sāṁkhya and Yoga), the Prasthānatrayī would to that extent have remained incomplete. Some people think, that as the Upaniṣads are ordinarily in support of Saṁnyāsa, there will arise a mutual opposition between the three parts of the Prasthānatrayī, if the Gītā is explained as being in support of Action; and the authoritativeness of the three parts will be endangered. Such a doubt would be appropriate if the Sāṁkhya or Saṁnyāsa was the only true Vedic Path to Release; but, I have shown above, that in some Upaniṣads at any rate, such as the Īśāvāsya and others, the Karma-Yoga has been specifically mentioned. Therefore, if one lays down the proposition, as has been done in the Gītā, that the Vedic Religion is not to be looked upon as a one-handed man, that is, as being only in support of Saṁnyāsa; and that although it has only one head, namely, Brahmavidyā, yet, Sāṁkhya and Karma-Yoga, which, from the point of view of Release, are of equal value, are its right hand and left hand respectively, there remains no opposition between the Gītā and the Upaniṣads. Nay, as the Upaniṣads support the one path, and the Gītā the other path, these two parts of the Prasthānatrayī are seen to be mutually co-operative like two hands, instead of being mutually antagonistic. In the same way, the Gītā does not acquire the subordinate position of merely repeating what has already been said, which it would acquire if it is said to be supporting only what the Upaniṣads have maintained. As the doctrine-supporting commentators on the Gītā have neglected this question, I have shortly set out in the following table in two columns, opposite each other, the principal reasons which the supporters of the two independent paths of Sāṁkhya and Yoga adduce in support of their respective doctrines, in order that the similarity and the difference between the two should be easily ascertained. This tabular statement will also clearly show the important differences between the arrangement of the states of life according to the Smṛtis and the original Bhāgavata religion:—

After acquisition of the
BRAHMAVIDYĀ or the KNOWLEDGE of
the ĀTMAN

KARMA-SAṀNYĀSA (Sāṁkhya)	KARMA-YOGA (Yoga)
1. Release is obtained only by Knowledge of the Ātman, and not by Karma. The happiness of heaven, obtained by credulously performing sacrificial ritual, is inconstant.	1. Release is obtained only by Knowledge of the Ātman, and not by Karma. The happiness of heaven, obtained by credulously performing sacrificial ritual is inconstant.

2. In order to acquire the Knowledge of the Ātman, the Mind must be made steady, desireless, apathetic, and equable by means of the control of the organs.	2. In order to acquire the Knowledge of the Ātman, the Mind must be made steady, desireless, apathetic and equable by means of the control of the organs.
3. Therefore, break the bonds of the objects of pleasure, which please the organs, and be free.	3. Therefore, do not give up the objects which please the organs; but maintain your association with them apathetically, that is desirelessly, and test the control you have over the organs. Desirelessness does not mean inactivity.
4. Action, which is productive of Desire, is causative of pain and bondage.	4. If you consider in what unhappiness and bondage lies, you will see that lifeless *(acetana)* Karma does not bind or leave anybody; and that the cause of bondage and unhappiness is the Desire or the hope of reward existing in the Mind of the doer.
5. Therefore, though Action has to be performed until the mind is purified, it must ultimately be given up.	5. Therefore, even after the purification of the Mind, perform all Action courageously and enthusiastically, giving up the Hope for Fruit. One cannot give up Karma, even if one wishes to give it up. Karma is the Creation; and it has no rest.
6. As Karma performed in connection with sacrificial ritual does not create bondage, there is no objection to its being performed	6. All Actions which are performed with a desireless frame of mind or with the idea of dedicating them to the Brahman are a great

during the state of a householder.	'Yajña' (sacrifice). Therefore, all duties, which are appropriate to one's own status in life should be performed desirelessly, as pure duties; and these should be performed continually.
7. As the natural needs of the Body cannot be escaped from, it is not improper to beg, for earning one's livelihood, after having taken Saṁnyāsa.	7. Begging for earning one's subsistence is also Karma, and that too, 'disgraceful'. If this Karma is to be performed, why not perform all other Actions desirelessly ? Besides, if the state of a householder is done away with, who is going to give you food?
8. After Acquisition of Knowledge, no duty remains to you for your own benefit; and there is no necessity to act for universal welfare.	8. After Acquisition of Knowledge, although no duty remains to you for your own benefit, yet, you cannot escape Karma. Therefore, whatever duties are enjoined by the Śāstras should be performed with a selfless (*nirmama*) frame of mind, saying: 'I do not want it,' and with an eye to universal welfare. No one can escape *lokasaṁgraha* (universal welfare). For instance, see the life of the Blessed Lord Himself.
9. Nevertheless, persons of high authority may, till death, carry on their duties, after Acquisition of Knowledge, as was done by Janaka and	9. According to the arrangement of the four castes, which is based on the divisions of the qualities (*guṇa-vibhāga*), every one acquire

and others, but only as exceptions.	by birth great or small authority; and this authority, which is acquired according to one's own state in life (*dharma*) must be exercised, till death, desirelessly and without exception; because, this cycle of activities has been created by the Parameśvara for the maintenance of the world.
10. But in any case, Saṁnyāsa in the shape of abandonment of Action is the best. The duties of the three other states are the means, or the preparatory stages, for the purification of the Mind; and there is an inherent oppsosition between Jñāna and Karma. Therefore, acquire purification of the Mind as early as possible in the earlier stages of life, and after having acquired Knowledge, take ultimately to Saṁnyāsa in the shape of Abandonment of the Action. If you have acquired purification of the Mind with birth or in young age, there is no necessity of performing the duties pertaining to the state of a householder. The true state of Saṁnyāsa cosists in the literal Abandonment of Action.	10. It is true that by performing the Actions pertaining to worldly life in the manner enjoined by the Śāstras, one acquires the purification of the Mind. But, purification of the Mind is not the only use of Karma. Karma is necessary in order that the activities of the world should go on. In the same way, though there is an opposition between Jñāna and Desire-prompted Action, there is none between Jñāna and Desireless Action; and therefore, after the purification of the Mind, continue the Actions prescribed for the various castes, abandoning the hope of the Fruit of Action, and desirelessly, till death, for the benefit of the world. This is the true Saṁnyāsa; it is neither possible nor proper, to literally abandon Karma (Action) at any time.
11. Even after Abandonment of Action, you must observe the rules of *śama*, *dama*, etc.	11. After Acquisition of Knowledge, take Saṁnyāsa in the shape of Abandonment of the Fruit of Action, and observe all the rules arising

	as a result of Self-identification (*ātmaupamya*), except *śama, dama* etc.; and perform by means of this *śama* or peaceful frame of mind, all the duties enjoined by the Śāstras, till death, for the purpose of universal welfare. Do not give up Desireless Action.
12. This path is eternal, and has the support of the Śrutis as also of the Smṛtis.	12. This path is eternal, and has the support of the Śrutis as also of the Smṛtis.
13. This path was adopted by Śuka, Yājñavalkya, and others.	13. Vyāsa, Vasiṣṭha, Jaigīsavya, and others, as also Janaka, Śrī Kṛṣṇa and others followed this path.

ULTIMATE RELEASE.

(*mokṣa*)

Both these paths or Niṣṭhās are based on the Knowledge of the Brahman, and as the desirelessness or peacefulness of the Mind is a common factor in both, both the paths ultimately lead to Release (Gī. 5. 5.). The important difference between the two is that in the one case Karma (Action) is abandoned after Jñāna (Knowledge), and in the other, Desire-prompted (*kāmya*) Action is abandoned, and Desireless Action is continued.

These two paths of abandoning Action and not abandoning Action have both been adopted and followed by Jñānins after the Acquisition of Knowledge. But Action can be abandoned or performed even when Knowledge has not been acquired. It is, therefore, also necessary to shortly consider here this Action or Abandonment of Action, which is based, not on Knowledge, but on Ignorance. That is why three varieties of Abandonment of Action have been mentioned in the eighteenth chapter of the Gītā. Some persons abandon Action for fear of physical labour, though they have not acquired Knowledge. This is described in the Gītā as a '*rājasa tyāga*' (Gī. 18. 8). In the same way, many persons perform sacrificial ritual only with religious faith (*śraddhā*), though they have not acquired Knowledge. But the Gītā says this path of performing Action leads only to heaven and not to Release (Gī. 9. 20). As the performance of sacrificial ritual prescribed by the Śrutis is not now in vogue, some persons think that the doctrine of the Gītā relating to the pure Karma-mārga supported by the Mīmāṁsā school, is not of much use in these days. But, such a belief is not correct; because, although the sacrificial ritual enjoined by the Śrutis has gone out of vogue, the ritual prescribed by the Smṛtis, in the shape of the duties enjoined on the four castes, is still in existence. Therefore, the dictum of the Gītā with reference to people who perform Desire-prompted Actions like sacrificial ritual, with religious faith, though ignorantly, also applies in the present day to people who perform the duties enjoined on the four castes, with religious faith, though without Knowledge. If one visualises the activities of the world, it will be seen that the majority of persons in society perform their various duties, keeping religious faith in the Śāstras, and according to the accepted moral code. But such persons have not fully acquired the Knowledge of the Parameśvara. Therefore, these credulous persons, who perform sacrificial Karma, are in the same position as those who make calculations by mental arithmetic without understanding the reasons for that calculation given in Mathematics. As these persons perform the ritual in manner enjoined by the Śāstras and with religious faith, it is performed correctly, and will be productive of merit (*puṇya*) or of heaven. But, as the doctrine of the Śāstras themselves is that Release cannot be obtained except by Knowledge, such persons cannot possibly obtain any result more valuable than heaven. Therefore, those persons who wish to obtain that immortality which is beyond the happiness of heaven—and this is, indeed, the true highest ideal of man—should, in the beginning, as a means, and later on, that is, in the state of perfection, for the purpose of universal welfare, (which means, so long as life exists), accept the path of performing Action desirelessly, with a frame of mind chastened by Knowledge, and with the Realisation that, 'in all created beings there is only one Ātman'.

Of all the paths of leading one's life, this path is the best. In the tabular statement above, I have called this path, Karma-Yoga, on the authority of the Gītā; and it is usually referred to by some writers as the Path of Action (*karma-mārga)*, or the Activistic Path (*pravṛtti-mārga*). But the words Karma-mārga or Pravṛtti-mārga ordinarily also connote the heaven-producing path of performing Action, with religious faith, but without Knowledge. It, therefore, becomes necessary to use two distinct words in order to make clear the difference between the Knowledge-less but Faith-full Karma, and the Desireless Karma performed with Knowledge; and for this reason, the Manu-Smṛti, as also the Bhāgavata, call Knowledge-less Karma, '*pravṛtta-karma*', and Desireless Karma based on Knowledge, '*nivṛtta-karma*' (Manu. 12. 89; Bhāg. 7. 15. 47). But even these words are, in my opinion, not as unambiguous as they ought to be; because, the word '*nivṛtti*' is ordinarily used as meaning 'recoiling (becoming *parāvṛtta*) from Karma'. In order that such a doubt should not remain, the word '*karma*' is added after the word '*nivṛtta*', and when that is done, the adjective '*nivṛtta*' does not mean 'abstaining from Karma'; and we get the interpretation '*nivṛtta-karma*'='Desireless Action'. But whatever is done, so long as the word '*nivṛtta*' is used, the idea of the Abandonment of Action inevitably enters the mind. Therefore, in my opinion, it is better to call the path of performing Desireless Action, after the acquisition of Knowledge, by the name 'Karma-Yoga' instead of calling it '*nivṛtti*' or '*nivṛtta-karma*'; because, when the word 'Yoga' is tacked on after the word 'Karma', it naturally means "the device of performing Action without obstructing Release," and Karma based on ignorance is also naturally eliminated. Nevertheless, if one wishes to refer to this path as '*Karma-mārga*' or '*Pravṛtti-mārga*', without forgetting that the Karma-Yoga of the Gītā is based on Knowledge, there is no objection to the same being done; and in some places, I myself have used the same words for indicating the Karma-Yoga of the Gītā for diversity of language. I have in the following tabular statement shown the opinion of the Gītā as to the two paths of Abandonment of Action and Performance of Action, which are based respectively on Knowledge and Ignorance.

WAY OF LEADING LIFE	GRADE	ULTIMATE SPHERE		
1. Performing Actions only for one's own happiness, egotistically, with an ungodly (*āsurī*) frame of mind, or hypocritically, or being prompted by avarice—(Gī. 16. 16)—the ĀSURA, or UNGODLY path.	LOWEST	HELL		
1. Although the Knowledge of the form of the Parameśvara by the Realisation that there is only one Ātman in all created beings has not been acquired, performing all Desire-prompted Actions with faith, and according to moral principles, and consistently with the injunctions of the Śāstras, or the Vedas (Gī. 2. 41-44 and 9. 20)—PURE KARMA, or TRAYĪ—DHARMA or MĪMĀMSAKA-MĀRGA.	MEDIUM (Best, according to the Mīmāṁsā school)	HEAVEN (Release, according to the Mīmāṁsakas)	The three paths (*niṣṭhā*) described by Janaka	
1. After the Acquisition of the Knowledge of the Parameśvara, by the desireless performance of the duties enjoined by the Śāstras, giving up all Action, and finding happiness only in Jñāna (Gī. 5. 2)—PURE JÑĀNA or the SĀMKHYA or the SMĀRTA-MĀRGA.	SUPERIOR	RELEASE (*mokṣa*)		The two paths (*niṣṭhā*) of the Gītā
1. Performing life-long Desireless Actions, in the beginning, for the purification of the Mind, and afterwards, that is, after having thereby acquired the Knowledge of the Parameśvara, for universal welfare (*lokasaṁgraha*), in the same way as was done by the Blessed Lord (Gī. 5. 2)—the KNOWLEDGE-ACTION path or KARMA-YOGA, or the BHĀGAVATA-MĀRGA.	BEST OF ALL	RELEASE (*mokṣa*)		

In short, although Action (Karma) is not necessary for obtaining Release, yet, the Gītā has declared the path of desirelessly and continuously performing Action as the best path of all, for other co-existent reasons, namely, because it is, in the first place, unavoidable, and secondly because, it is essential for the maintenance of the world. Or, the ultimate doctrine of the Gītā is that the union of Action and Spiritual Knowledge is the best, and that mere Action or mere Spiritual Knowledge is each one-sided, according to the statement of Manu that: "*kṛta buddhiṣu kartāraḥ kartṛṣu brahmavādinaḥ*" (Manu. 1. 97).

Really speaking this chapter ought to end here. But, it is necessary to say something here about the quotations given above in various places for showing that the doctrine laid down by the Gītā has the authority of the Śrutis and the Smṛtis; because, many persons have come to the conclusion that all the Upaniṣads support Renunciation (*saṁnyāsa or nivṛtti*) by reading the doctrine-supporting commentaries on the Upaniṣads. I do not say that the Path of Renunciation is not supported by the Upaniṣads at all. It is stated in the Bṛhadāraṇyakopaniṣad (4. 4. 22), that after they have Realised that the Parabrahman is the only Reality, "some Jñānins do not any more entertain in their hearts the desire for children (*putraiṣaṇā*), or the desire for wealth (*vittaiṣaṇā*), or the desire for higher worlds (*lokaiṣaṇā*), and saying: 'what have we to do with children? the whole world is our Self (Ātman)', they go about the world contentedly, and earn their livelihood by begging". But it is nowhere stated in the Bṛhadāraṇyaka that all persons who have Realised the Brahman should follow this path. Nay, there is a statement in this very Upaniṣad that that king Janaka, to whom this advice was given, had reached the highest peak of the Knowledge of the Brahman, and had become immortal. But, it is nowhere stated that he had, like Yājñavalkya, given up the world and taken Saṁnyāsa. Therefore, it becomes quite clear that the Bṛhadāraṇyakopaniṣad accepted both the Desireless Karma-Yoga of Janaka and the Path of Abandonment of Action followed by Yājñavalkya as alternative paths; and the author of the Vedānta-Sūtras has come to the same conclusion (Ve.- Sū. 3. 4. 15). The

Kaṭhopaniṣad has gone even further than this, and, as I have stated before in the fifth chapter, it says, according to me, that the Desireless Karma-Yoga is the only proper path of life. The same conclusion is arrived at in the Chāndogyopaniṣad (8. 15. 1), and there is a clear statement in it at the end, that "the Jñānin who first finishes his course of education at the hands of his preceptor, and thereafter lives in his family and follows the rules of Ethics and morality, goes to the sphere of the Brahman and does not return"; and sentences from the Taittirīya and the Śvetāśvatara Upaniṣads having the same purport have been quoted by me above (Tai. 1. 9 and Śve. 6. 4). Besides, we do not see it stated in the Upaniṣads, that those who have advised the Knowledge of the Brahman to others, or their disciples who had acquired the Knowledge of the Brahman, adopted Renunciation in the shape of Abandonment of Action, except one or two like Yājñavalkya. On the other hand, they seem to have been householders, from the descriptions which have been given of them. One cannot, therefore, look upon all the Upaniṣads as supporting Saṁnyāsa, and has to say that some of them mention the alternative paths of Saṁnyāsa and Karma-Yoga, whereas others support the union of Jñāna and Karma (*jñāna-karma-samuccaya)*. But, the doctrine-supporting commentaries on the Upaniṣads do not show these differences, and they usually say that all the Upaniṣads support only one Path—and that too principally the Saṁnyāsa Path. In short, these doctrine-supporting commentators have dealt with both the Gītā and the Upaniṣads in the same way; that is to say, these commentators have had to stretch and mutilate some hymns in the Upaniṣads, as has been done by them in the matter of some of the stanzas in the Gītā. Take, for example, the case of Īśāvāsyopaniṣad. Though this Upaniṣad is short, that is, consisting only of eighteen stanzas, it is considered to be of greater importance than the other Upaniṣads; because, this Upaniṣad has been mentioned in the Vājasaneyī Saṁhita, whereas the other Upaniṣads have been mentioned in the Āraṇyakas; and it is generally accepted that the Brāhmaṇas are of lesser importance than the Saṁhitās, and the Āraṇyakas of lesser importance than the Brāhmaṇas. This Īśāvāsyopaniṣad is from top to bottom in support of the harmonising of Jñāna and Karma. It is stated in the very first hymn (*mantra*) of this Upaniṣad that, "whatever existed in the world must be considered as '*Īśāvāsya*', that is, located in the Parameśvara; and in the second hymn, there is a clear statement that, "one should desire to live for a hundred years while performing Action desirelessly". This statement from the Īśāvāsya has been quoted as an authority for the harmonising of Jñāna and Karma, wherever there was occasion to deal with the Karma-Yoga in the Vedānta-Sūtras, as also in other places. But, the Īśāvāsya Upaniṣad does not rest there. In order to support the statement made in the second stanza, it subsequently starts the exposition of '*avidyā*', that is, Karma, and '*vidyā*', that is, Jñāna; and in the ninth stanza, it is stated that "persons who devote thmselves only to *avidyā* or Karma enter darkness, and those who are steeped merely in *vidyā* or the Knowledge of the Brahman enter a still darker darkness". Having in this way shown the inferiority of pure *avidyā* (Karma), and pure *vidyā* (Jñāna), this Upaniṣad explains in the eleventh stanza the necessity of the union of '*vidyā*' and '*avidyā*' in the following words:-

vidyāṁ cā 'vidyāṁ ca yas tad vedobhayaṁ saha ।
avidyayā mṛtyuṁ tīrtvā vidyayā 'mṛtam aśnute ॥

Īśā. 11.

The plain and clear meaning of this stanza is: "that man, who understands both *vidyā* (Jñāna) and *avidyā* (Karma) at the same time, goes (easily) through the affairs of the '*mṛtyu*' that is, of the perishable illusory world, by means of *avidyā* that is, Karma; and attains immortality by means of *vidyā*, that is, of the Realisation of the Brahman"; and the same idea is repeated in the three succeeding stanzas (Īśā. 12-14), in which *vidyā* is referred to as '*saṁbhūti*', that is, the original cause of the world, and *avidyā*, which is different from that *vidyā*, as '*asaṁbhūti*' or '*vināśa*'. From this, it becomes quite clear that the Īśāvāsyopaniṣad is in favour of the simultaneous possession (*ubhayaṁ saha*) of *vidyā* and *avidyā*. In the above stanza, the words '*mṛtyu* and '*amṛta*' are mutual opposites, just like '*vidyā*' and '*avidyā*'. Out of them, *amṛta* quite clearly means the imperishable Brahman, and it follows that *mṛtyu*, which is the opposite of it, means the perishable *mṛtyu-loka* (mortal world) or the life in this world; and both these words have been used in the same sense in the Nāsadīya-Sūkta of the Ṛg-veda (Ṛg. 10. 129. 2). When one interprets the eleventh stanza of the Īśāvāsyopaniṣad, which has been quoted above, taking these clear meanings of the words *vidyā* etc., that is, taking *vidyā* as meaning Jñāna, *avidyā* as meaning Karma, *amṛta* as meaning the Brahman, and *mṛtyu* as meaning the mortal world, it will be clearly seen that the simultaneous possession (*ekakālīna-samuccaya*) of *vidyā* and *avidyā* is mentioned in the first line of this stanza: the separate results of both are mentioned in the second part of the stanza, in order to further emphasise that statement. Both these results are considered desirable by the Īśāvāsyopaniṣad, and the simultaneous possession of Jñāna and Karma has been advocated in this Upaniṣad. Carrying on properly the affairs of the mortal world, or going through those affairs successfully is called '*loka-saṁgraha*' in the Gītā. It is true that obtaining Release is the duty of every man; yet, as it is also essential that he should simultaneously bring about universal welfare (*loka-saṁgraha*), the Gītā has laid down the doctrine that the Jñānin should not give up this Karma, which is productive of universal welfare; and the same doctrine has been propounded in the line, "*avidyayā mṛtyuṁ tīrtvā vidyayā 'mṛtam aśnute*" mentioned above, with only a verbal difference. In short, it will be seen that not only is the Gītā consistent with the Upaniṣads, but that the proposition definitely propounded by the Īśāvāsyopaniṣad has been accepted *in toto* in the Gītā. The Śatapatha-Brāhmaṇa is a part of that very Vājasaneyī Saṁhitā, of which the Īśāvāsyopaniṣad is a part; and the Bṛhadāraṇyakopaniṣad is to be found in the Āraṇyakas of the Śatapatha-Brāhmaṇa; and this ninth hymn (*mantra*) of the Īśāvāsyopaniṣad, namely, "persons who are steeped in pure Knowledge (*vidyā*), that is, in the Realisation of the Brahman, enter a still greater darkness" has been literally adopted in it (Bṛ. 4. 4. 10). This Bṛhadāraṇyakopaniṣad contains the story of the King Janaka, and the illustration of that Janaka has been taken by the Blessed Lord in support of the theory of Karma-Yoga (Gī. 3. 20). This establishes all the more firmly, the relation between the Īśāvāsyopaniṣad and the Karma-Yoga of the Bhagavadgītā referred to by me above.

But those commentators whose sectarian doctrine is that there is only one path mentioned in each and every Upaniṣad for obtaining Release, and that too the Path of Indifference (*vairāgya)* or Saṁnyāsa (Renunciation), and that the Upaniṣads cannot prescribe two paths, are driven to somehow or other put a stretched and different meaning on this clear sacred hymn (*mantra*) in the Īśāvāsyopaniṣad; otherwise, these hymns negative their doctrines; and that is a thing they do not want. Therefore, in commenting on the eleventh hymn in the Śāṁkarabhāṣya, the word '*vidyā*' is not taken to mean Jñāna (Knowledge), but *upāsanā* (worship). It is not that the word '*vidyā*' does not mean '*upāsanā*' (worship). In the phrases *Śāṇḍilya-vidyā*' etc. '*vidyā*' means '*upāsanā*'. But, that is not the principal meaning of that word. It is not that Śrī Śaṁkarācārya did not or could not have realised this fact. Nay, it is impossible that he did not realise it; because, there are statements in the other Upaniṣads, such as, "*vidyayā vindate 'mṛtam*" (Kena. 2. 12); or "*prāṇasyādhyātmaṁ vijñāyāmṛtam aśnute*" (Praśna. 3. 12); and in the seventh *prapāṭhaka* of the Maitryupaniṣad, the hymn "*vidyāṁ cā 'vidyāṁ ca*" etc., being the eleventh hymn of the Īśāvāsyopaniṣad, has been taken literally; and immediately before it, the hymn in Kaṭha. 2. 4, and after it, the hymn in Kaṭha. 2. 5 are to be found; that is to say, these three hymns are to be found in the same place one after the other, and the central hymn is from the Īśāvāsyopaniṣad; and each of the three verses contains the word '*vidyā*'. From this it follows, that according to the Maitryupaniṣad, the word '*vidyā*' in the Īśāvāsyopaniṣad must be taken to mean the same thing as in the Kaṭhopaniṣad, that is to say, Jñāna. But, in the Śāṁkarabhāṣya on the Īśāvāsya, it is stated that: if the words '*vidyā*' and '*amṛta*' in the eleventh hymn of the Īśāvāsyopaniṣad are taken in their ordinary meaning of '*vidyā*'=Knowledge of the Self, and *amṛta*=*mokṣa*, one will have to say that the union of Jñāna (*vidyā*) and Karma (*avidyā*) has been prescribed by this Upaniṣad; but, in as much as such a combination is logically incorrect, the words '*vidyā*' and '*amṛta*' must be taken in their respective inferior meanings of 'worship of a deity' and 'sphere of the deities' respectively. In short, in order that this hymn in the Īśāvāsya should not falsify the principal doctrine of the Śāṁkara school that: "after the Acquisition of Knowledge, one must not perform Actions; because, the combination of Jñāna and Karma can never be logical", the eleventh hymn of the Īśāvāsya has been interpreted, as mentioned above, in the Śāṁkarabhāṣya, by taking the inferior meaning of the word '*vidyā*', with the clear intention of harmonising all the statements in the Śrutis with the doctrine of the Śāṁkara school; and from the point of view of the justification of a doctrine, this mis-interpretation was not only important but necessary. But those, who do not accept the fundamental proposition that all the Upaniṣads must support only one particular line of thought, and that the Śrutis cannot prescribe two different modes of life, have no occasion to pervert the meanings of the words '*vidyā*' and '*amṛta*' in the above hymn. Although one accepts the principle that the Parabrahman is '*ekamevādvitīyam*' (one, and one only), it does not follow that there cannot be more than one path of Realising that Parabrahman. As it is possible to have two stair-cases for going to the same floor, or two roads for going to the same place, so also can there be two methods or Niṣṭhās for acquiring Release; and it has, therefore, been clearly stated in the Bhagavadgītā that "*loke 'smin dvividhā niṣṭhā*". When it is once admitted that it is possible to have two Niṣṭhās (paths of Release), it does not become impossible that some Upaniṣads should describe the Jñāna-niṣṭhā, and others describe the Jñāna-Karma-combined Niṣṭhā. Necessarily, there does not remain any occasion to pervert the clear, natural, and unequivocal meaning of the words used in the Īśāvāsyopaniṣad on the ground that they are inconsistent with the Jñāna-niṣṭhā. There is another reason for saying that Śrīmat Śaṁkarācārya aimed rather at insisting on a homogeneity in the Upaniṣads on the question of the Saṁnyāsa-niṣṭhā than at accepting the clear meaning of the hymn. In the Śāṁkarabhāṣya on the Taittirīya Upaniṣad (Tai. 2. 11), only the portion "*avidyayā mṛtyuṁ tīrtvā vidyayā 'mṛtam aśnute*", out of the hymn in the Īśāvāsya, has been given; and there has been joined to it a statement from the Manu-Smṛti (Manu. 12. 104) that "*tapasā kalmaṣaṁ hanti vidyayā 'mṛtam aśnute*", and the word '*vidyā*' in both these lines has been taken by Śaṁkarācārya in only one meaning, namely, Brahma-jñāna, which is the original and primary meaning. But, here the Ācārya says that the word '*tīrtvā*'='swimming over' implies that the action of swimming through the mortal sphere (*mṛtyu-loka*) is first completed, and afterwards (not simultaneously) the action of obtaining immortality by *vidyā* follows; but I need not point out that such an interpretation is inconsistent with the words "*ubhayaṁ saha*" in the first half of the hymn, and it seems that this meaning must have been left out in the Śāṁkarabhāṣya on the Īśāvāsya, possibly for this reason. Whatever may be the case, this clearly shows why a different explanation of the eleventh hymn of the Īśāvāsya was given in the Śāṁkarabhāṣya on it. This reason is merely a desire to support a doctrine, and those who do not accept the doctrinal vision of commentators, may not accept this explanation. I am certainly willing that, as far as possible, one should avoid having to give up an interpretation adopted by a superman like Śrīmat Śaṁkarācārya. But, such a position is bound to arise when one gives up the doctrinal vision; and, therefore, even other commentators have, before me, interpreted the hymns in the Īśāvāsyopaniṣad in a way different from that adopted in the Śāṁkarabhāṣya, that is to say, in the same way as has been done by me. For instance, in the commentary by Uvaṭācārya on the Vājasaneyi-Saṁhitā, and necessarily on the Īśāvāsyopaniṣad, it is stated in expounding the canon, '*vidyāṁ cā 'vidyāṁ ca*' that "*vidyā* means the Knowledge of the Ātman, and *avidyā* means Karma, and immortality or Release is obtained by the combination of both"; and Anantācārya has in his commentary on this Upaniṣad accepted this interpretation, which combines Knowledge and Action; and he has ultimately clearly said that the doctrine expounded in this hymn is the same as that underlying the statement in the Gītā, that: "*yat sāṁkhyaiḥ prāpyate sthānaṁ tad yogair api gamyate*" (Gī. 5. 5); and that the words '*sāṁkhya*' and '*yoga*' in this stanza in the Gītā respectively connote 'Jñāna' and 'Karma'. *In the same way, Aparārkadeva has

* All these commentaries on the Īśāvāsyopaniṣad have been given in the edition of the Īśāvāsyopaniṣad printed in the Ānandashram Press at Poona; and the commentary of Aparārka on the

given the eleventh hymn of the Īśāvāsya in his commentary on the Yājñavalkya-Smṛti (Yā. 3. 57 and 205), and interpreted it as supporting the combination of Jñāna and Karma, as was done by Anantācārya. From this it will be clear to my readers, that I have not been the first person to interpret this hymn from the Īśāvāsyopaniṣad in a way different from that in which it has been interpreted in the Śāṁkarabhāṣya.

So far we have considered the hymn in the Īśāvāsyopaniṣad itself. Let us now consider shortly the statement "*tapasā kalmaṣaṁ hanti vidyayā 'mṛtam aśnute*" from the Manu-Smṛti which has been quoted in the Śāṁkarabhāṣya. This is the 104th stanza of the twelvth chapter of the Manu-Smṛti, and that chapter deals with the Vedic Karma-Yoga, as will be seen from Manu. 12. 86. In the course of the disquisition on the Karma-Yoga, Manu says,

tapo vidyā ca viprasya niḥśreyasakaraṁ param I
tapasā kalmaṣaṁ hanti vidyayā 'mṛtam aśnute II

that is:—"*tapa* and (*ca*) *vidyā*, these (that is, necessarily both) are producers of excellent Release to the Brahmin"; and having stated this in the first part of the stanza, he, in order to show the use of both these things, says in the second part of the stanza: "by *tapa* (religious austerity) all sin is annihilated, and by *vidyā*, one obtains *amṛta*, that is, Release". From this, it is quite clear that Manu had, in this place, implied the combination of Jñāna and Karma, and that he had in this stanza adopted the doctrine enunciated in the eleventh hymn in the Īśāvāsya Upaniṣad. This meaning is further emphasised by the statements in the Hārīta Smṛti. This Hārīta-Smṛti is available independently, and is also included in the Nṛsiṁha-

Yājñavalkya-Smṛti has also been separatety printed in the Anandashram Press. The translation of the Īśāvāsyopaniṣad included in the translations of the Upaniṣads made by Prof. Max Müller is not according to the Śāṁkarabhāṣya, and he has stated his reasons for doing so at the end of his translation (*Sacred Books of the East Series* Vol. I, p. 314-320). The commentary of Anantācārya had not come to the hands of Prof. Max. Müller; and he also does not seem to have understood why different meanings are given for the same words in different places in the Śāṁkarabhāṣya.

Purāṇa (Nṛ. Pu. 57–61). The Nṛsiṁha Purāṇa (61. 9–11) and the Hārīta-Smṛti (7. 9–11) contain the following stanzas regarding the combination of Knowledge (Jñāna) and Action (Karma):–

yathāśvā rathahīnāś ca rathāś cāśvair vinā yathā ।
evaṁ tapaś ca vidyā ca ubhāv api tapasvinaḥ ॥

yathānnaṁ madhusaṁyuktaṁ madhu cānnena saṁyutam ।
evaṁ tapaś ca vidyā ca saṁyuktaṁ bheṣajaṁ mahat ॥

dvābhyām eva hi pakṣābhyāṁ yathā vai pakṣiṇāṁ gatiḥ ।
tathaiva jñānakarmabhyāṁ prāpyate brahma śāśvatam ॥

that is, "In the same way, as horses without a chariot, or a chariot without horses (are of no use), the same is the case with the *tapa* of the *tapasvin*, and *vidyā*. In the same way, as *anna* (food) mixed with *madhu* (honey), and honey mixed with food become a potent medicine, so also do '*tapa*' and '*vidyā*', when combined. In the same way as birds acquire motion by means of two wings, so also is the immutable Brahman acquired as a result of the combination of Jñāna and Karma". These statements in the Hārīta-Smṛti are also to be found in the second chapter of the Vṛddhātreya-Smṛti. From these statements, and especially from the illustrations which have been given in them, one clearly understands in what way the statements of the Manu-Smṛti are to be interpreted. I have stated before that Manu includes all the Karma (ritual or Action) enjoined for the four castes in the word '*tapa*' (Manu. 11. 236); and it will now be seen that the observance of *tapa* and *svādhyāya-pravacana* which has been prescribed in the Taittirīyopaniṣad (Tai. 1. 9), has been prescribed accepting the position of the combination of Jñāna and Karma. The same is the summary of the whole of the Yoga-Vāsiṣṭha; because, in the beginning of this book, Sutīkṣṇa has asked whether Release is obtained by Jñāna alone, or by Karma alone, or by the combination of both; and in replying to that question, after first stating that, "just as the movement of birds in the sky is made by two wings, so also is Release obtained by the combination of Jñāna and Karma, and perfection is not attained by only one of them", by taking the illustration of the wings of the birds from the Hārīta-Smṛti, the Yoga-Vāsiṣṭha has been written in order to prove that proposition in detail (Yo. 1. 1. 6-9). Similarly, in the book itself, Vasiṣṭha has again and again given to Rāma the advice that, "perform all your activities in life, keeping your mind pure like a *jīvan-mukta*" (Yo. 5. 17. 18-26); or "as it is not possible to give up Action (Karma) so long as life lasts (Yo. 6. U. 2. 42), perform the duty of protecting and maintaining that kingdom which has fallen on your shoulders by virtue of your caste" (Yo. 5. 5. 54 and 6, U. 213. 50); and the summing up of the work, as also what Śrī Rāmacandra did afterwards, is consistent with that advice. But, as the commentators on the Yoga-Vāsiṣṭha, belonged to the Saṁnyāsa school, they have passed a judgment on their own book, that Jñāna and Karma are not '*yugapat*', that is, 'proper at the same time,' although the illustration of the two wings of a bird is perfectly clear in itself. But, this interpretation is a stretched, unintelligible, and doctrinal interpretation, as will be seen by any one who reads the original work by itself, without the commentary. There is a well-known treatise in the Madras Presidency known as *Gurujñāna-vāsiṣṭha-Tattvasārāyaṇa*, which is subdivided into three parts, namely, Jñāna-kāṇḍa, Upāsanā-kāṇḍa and Karma-kāṇḍa. I have stated before that this work is not as old as it is made out to be. But, although, it might not be ancient, yet, as it accepts the position of the combination of Jñāna and Karma, it is necessary to mention it in this place. As the Vedānta in this work is Non-Dualistic, and as it lays a special emphasis on Desireless Action, the doctrine supported by it may safely be said to be different from the doctrine supported by Śrī Śaṁkarācārya, and independent. This doctrine is known on the Madras side as 'Anubhavādvaita'; and really speaking this is only an imitation of the Karma-Yoga in the Gītā. Yet, it is stated in it, that this conclusion is arrived at by all the 108 Upaniṣads, instead of supporting it on the authority of the Gītā; and besides, it also includes two new Gītās, namely the Rāma-gītā and the Sūrya-gītā. This book will correct the impression some persons have, that accepting the Monistic (*advita*) theory amounts to an acceptance of the Abandonment of Action; and it will now be clear from the authorities given above, that the statement that the Desireless Karma-Yoga is supported only by the Saṁhitās, the Brāhmaṇas, the Upaniṣads, the Dharma-Sūtras, the Manu and Yājñavalkya-Smṛtis, the Mahābhārata, the Bhagavadgītā, the Yoga-Vāsiṣṭha, and lastly by the Tattvasārāyaṇa, but is not acceptable to the Śrutis and the Smṛtis, and that the Śrutis and the Smṛtis support only the Path of Renunciation, is without any foundation whatsoever.

I have so far proved that in order to carry on the activities of the mortal world or for universal welfare, the simultaneous combination of Desireless Action, according to one's own qualification, with Release-giving Knowledge, is necessary according to the Gītā: or, as has been stated by the Maratha Poet Śivadina-kesarī: "that man who has attained the highest ideal, attending also to his worldly activities। such a man is good indeed, he is good indeed॥"; that this Path of Karma-Yoga has been in vogue from ancient times, and was accepted by Janaka and others; and that it is also known as the Bhāgavata religion, because, it was extended further and revived by the Blessed Lord. It is now necessary, from the point of view of general welfare (*loka-saṁgraha*), to deal with the question of how the scients, who follow this path, carry on their worldly activities simultaneously with the acquisition of the highest ideal of man. But, as the present chapter has been lengthened out to a considerable extent, I shall deal with this subject in the next chapter.

CHAPTER XII.

THE STATE AND THE ACTIVITIES OF THE SIDDHA (PERFECT).

(SIDDHĀVASTHĀ AND SIDDHA-VYAVAHĀRA)

sarveṣāṁ yaḥ suhṛn nityaṁ sarveṣāṁ ca hite rataḥ ।
karmaṇā manasā vācā sa dharmaṁ veda jājale ॥ *

Mahābhārata, Śānti. 261. 9.

That school of thought according to which nothing remains to be done by way of duty after a man has acquired the Knowledge of the Brahman and his mind has become extremely equable and desireless, and according to which a Jñānin should, on that account, give up entirely the painful and insipid activities of a transient worldly life with an apathetic frame of mind, can never think that the Karma-Yoga, or the mode of life appropriate to the state of a householder, is a science which deserves consideration. They admit that before a man takes Saṁnyāsa, his Mind must have been purified and Knowledge acquired: and they, therefore, admit that one must lead one's worldly life in a way which will purify the Mind and make it *sāttvika*. But, if one believes that leading the worldly life till death is foolish, and considers it to be the highest duty of everyone in this life to renounce the world (take Saṁnyāsa) as early as possible, Karma-Yoga has no independent importance; and the scholars, who belong to the School of Renunciation, do not trouble to deal with the question of the doable and the not-doable in the state of a householder, beyond, concisely and when occasion arises, considering how one should lead one's worldly life, and advising that one should go up the ladder of the four states of life (*āśrama*) described by Manu and other philosophers and reach as quickly as possible the last step of that ladder, namely, of Saṁnyāsa. That is why Śrīmat Śaṁkarācārya, who was the principal protagonist of the Path of Renunciation in the Kaliyuga, has in his commentary on the Gītā

* "That man, who, by his actions, by his mind, and by his speech is continually engrossed in the welfare of others, and who is always a friend of others, he alone, O Jājali, may be said to have understood what Morality (*dharma*) is".

either belittled the statements in the Gītā advising Energism, or considered them to be merely laudatory, and drawn the ultimate conclusion of the Gītā that the whole of it has supported the doctrine of the Abandonment of Action (*karma-saṁnyāsa*); or why other commentators have, consistently with their own doctrines, stated the import of the Gītā to be that the Blessed Lord advised Arjuna on the battle-field to follow only the renunciatory paths of Release, namely, the path of pure Devotion, or the Pātañjala-Yoga. There is no doubt that the Knowledge of the Absolute Self included in the Path of Renunciation is faultless; and that the equability of Reason, or the desireless state of mind produced by it, is acceptable to and admitted by the Gītā. Nevertheless, the opinion of the Saṁnyāsa school, that one must entirely abandon Action in order to obtain Release is not acceptable to the Gītā; and I have shown in detail in the last chapter that the most important doctrine laid down by the Gītā is, that the Jñānin must, even after the acquisition of Knowledge, perform all the activities of life, with the help of the feeling of indifference to the world and the equability of mind, which results from the Realisation of the Brahman. When it is admitted that (i) the deletion of Knowledge-full (*jñāna-yukta*) Action from the world will result in the world becoming blind and being destroyed; and that (ii) even Jñānins must desirelessly perform all the duties of worldly life, and so give to ordinary people a living example of a good and pure life, since it is the desire of the Blessed Lord that the world should not be so destroyed and that its activities should go on without a hitch; and that (iii) this path is the most excellent and acceptable of all, it becomes necessary to consider in what way such a Jñānin performs the activities of his worldly life; because, as the life of such a Jñānin is nothing but an example set by him to other people, the consideration of that example automatically discloses to us the device sought by us for making a true discrimination between morality (*dharma*) and immorality (*adharma*), between the doable (*kārya*) and the non-doable (*akārya*) and between the duty (*kartavya*) and the non-duty (*akartavya*). This is the important difference between the Path of Renunciation and the Path of Karma-Yoga. That man whose Pure Reason (*vyavasāyātmikā buddhiḥ*) has become capable of realising the identity, that "there is only one Ātman in all created things", on account of its having become steady by means of mental control, must also possess a Desire (*vāsanā*) which is pure. And when his Practical Reason (*vāsanātmikā buddhiḥ*) has in this way become pure, equable, mine-less (*nirmama*) and sinless, it is impossible that he should commit any sin or any Action obstructive of Release; because, (i) whatever Action is prompted by a pure desire, is bound to be pure, seeing that in the usual order of things, there is first a desire, and that such desire is followed by appropriate action; and (ii) whatever is pure, is promotive of Release. We have, therefore, in this way found such a preceptor as will give to us a visible reply, in the form of his own life, to the difficult question of the discrimination between what should be done and what should not be done (*karmākarma-vicikitsā*), or, between what is a duty and what is not a duty (*kāryākārya-vyavasthiti*), (Tai. 1. 11. 4: Gī. 3. 21). Such a preceptor was standing in life before Arjuna in the form of Śrī Kṛṣṇa: and this preceptor has, after clearing the doubt in the mind of Arjuna that a Jñānin must abandon such Action as warfare etc. because it created bondage, given to Arjuna clear advice as to the device by which one can lead his life in this world, without committing sin and consistently with the science of the Absolute Self (*adhyātma*), and induced him to fight. But, it is not possible for every one to get such preceptors; and one also ought not to entirely depend on the external activities of such saints, as has been mentioned by me towards the end of the third chapter, when I was considering the proverb "*mahājano yena gataḥ sa panthāḥ*" (i. e., "follow the path which has been followed by the great"). It is, therefore, necessary to minutely examine the course of life of those Jñānins, who are examples to the whole world, and to consider what the true fundamental element in that course of life is. This subject is known as the Science of Karma-Yoga; and the state and the actions of the Jñānins mentioned above, is the foundation of this science. If all men in this world become Knowers of the Ātman and Karma-yogins in this way, there would be no necessity of a Science of

Karma-Yoga. It is stated in one place in the Nārāyaṇiya religion, that:-

ekāntino hi puruṣā durlabhā bahavo nṛpa ।
yady ekāntibhir ākīrṇaṁ jagat syāt kurunandana ॥
ahiṁsakāir ātmavidbhiḥ sarvabhūtahite rataiḥ ।
bhavet kṛtayugaprāptiḥ āśīḥkarmavivarjitā ॥

(Śān. 348. 62, 63).

that is, "it is difficult to find many persons who fully and completely follow the Bhāgavata doctrine, which is 'Ekāntika', that is, Activistic. If this world is filled with Self-knowing harmless Jñānins, following the Ekānta doctrine, who continually tax themselves for general welfare, all '*āśīḥ-karma*', that is, desire-prompted or selfish Action, will disappear from this world, and the Kṛta-yuga will come again!"; because, as all persons will be Jñānins in such a state of things, no one will cause harm to no one. Not only that, but every one will always keep before his own mind in what the general welfare lies, and regulate his conduct accordingly, with a pure and desireless frame of mind. It is the opinion of our philosophers that such a state of society existed at some very ancient date, and that it will recur again (Ma. Bhā. Śān. 59. 14); but Western scholars say on the authority of modern history, that though such a state of things never existed before, it is possible that such a state of things may come into existence, sometime or other in the future, as a result of the advancement of mankind. However, as I am not now concerned with history, I may without being contradicted say, that according to both opinions, every person in this state, which is supposed to be the highest or the most perfect state of society, will be fully a Jñānin, and every Action of his is bound to be pure, beneficial, and moral, or the pinnacle of dutifulness. The well-known English biologist Spencer has expressed this opinion at the end of his work on Ethics; and he says that the same doctrine had been formerly laid down by the ancient Greek philosophers. * For example,

* See Spencer's *Data of Ethics*, Chap. XV, pp. 215–218. Spencer has called this 'Absolute Ethics'.

the Greek philosopher Plato says in his work that, that Action which appears to be proper to the philosopher, mut be beneficial or just; that ordinary persons do not understand these principles of Ethics; and that they must, therefore, look upon the decisions of philosophers as authoritative. Another Greek philosopher named Aristotle says in his book on Ethics (3. 4) that the decision given by a Jñānin is always correct, because, he has understood the true principle; and this decision or conduct of a Jñānin is exemplary for others. A third Greek philosopher, named Epicurus, in describing such an exemplary and highly cultivated Jñānin, says that he is "peaceful, equable, and probably always joyful like the Parameśvara; and that there is not the slightest harm done by him to other people, or by other people to him". * My readers will realise how similar this description is to the description given in the Bhagavadgītā of the Steady-in Mind (*sthitaprajña*), of the one who is beyond the three constituents (*triguṇātīta*), or of the highest Devotee (*parama-bhakta*), or the Brahman-merged (*brahma-bhūta*). In the Bhagavadgītā, the characteristics of the Sthitaprajña have been mentioned in three or four places in the following words, namely: "*yasmān nodvijate loko lokān nodvijate ca yaḥ*" (Gī. 12. 15), i. e., "one, of whom people do not get tired, and who is not tired of people"; or, who is always cheerful, and always free from the doubles of joy and sorrow, fear and dislike, happiness and unhappiness, and is always content with himself ("*ātmany evātmanā tuṣṭaḥ*", Gī. 2. 55); or, one whose Reason is not moved by the three constituents ("*guṇair yo na vicālyate*", Gī. 14. 23); or, one for whom praise or adverse criticism, honour or dishonour is just the same, and who, realising the identity of one Ātman in all created things (Gī. 18. 54), does his duty with an equable frame of mind, without Attachment,

* Epicurus held the virtuous state to be a "tranquil, undisturbed, innocuous, non-competitive fruition, which approached most nearly to the perfect happiness of the Gods", who "neither suffered vexation in themselves, nor caused vexation to others". Spencer's *Data of Ethics* p. 278; Bain's *Mental and Moral Science*, Ed. 1875, p. 530. Such a person is known as the 'Ideal Wise Man'.

courageously, and enthusiastically; or, is "*samaloṣṭāśma-kāñcana*" (Gī. 14. 24), (i. e., one who looks upon earth, stone, and gold as the same—Trans.); and this state is known as the State of the Perfect *(siddhāvasthā)*, or the Brāhmī state. The Yoga-Vāsiṣtha and other works refer to this state as the state of being free from re-birth *(jīvanmuktāvasthā)*. As this state is extremely difficult of accomplishment, the German philosopher Kant says that the description given by Greek philosophers of such a state, is not of the state of any living being; but that they have personified the 'Pure Desire', which is the root of all Ethics, in order to impress the elements of pure morality on the minds of people; and have created this picture of a super-Jñānin and moral person out of their own imagination. But, our philosophers say that such a state of things is not an imaginary state, and that it can be accomplished by man in this life by mental control and effort; and we have seen actual examples of such persons in our country. Nevertheless, such a thing is not a matter of ordinary occurrence, and there is possibly only one among thousands who makes any effort in this direction; and it is clearly stated in the Gītā that only one, out of the thousand who make an effort in this direction, ultimately attains this beatific ideal state, at the end of innumerable lives (Gī. 7. 3).

However difficult of accomplishment this state of a Sthitaprajña *(sthitaprajñāvasthā)* or this state of being free from re-birth *(jīvan-muktāvasthā)* may be, it follows from the description of such a man, which has been given above, that the man, who has once accomplished this ultimate state, does not need to be taught any laws about what should be done or should not be done, i.e., of Ethics; because, as the purest, the most equable and the most sinless frame of mind is the essence of morality, laying down laws of Ethics for such a Sthitaprajña would be as unreasonable as imagining that the Sun is surrounded by darkness, and holding up a torch for it. There may be a doubt as to whether or not a particular person has reached this highest of states. But, when once it has been established by whatever means that a particular person has reached this state, no proposition is possible, except the

Metaphysical proposition mentioned above, regarding the merit or de-merit of his actions. Just as regal authority is vested in one independent person or collection of persons, and as, according to some Western jurists, the ruler is not governed by any laws, though the ruled are so governed, so also are the Sthitaprajñas vested with authority in the kingdom of Ethics. No Desire exists in their minds; and, therefore, they are not induced to perform Action by any motive, except the fact that it is a duty enjoined by the Śāstras; and therefore, the words sin or meritorious action, morality or immorality, can never be applied to the conduct of such persons, who are filled by a stainless and pure desire. They have gone beyond the bounds of sin and merit. Śaṁkarācārya has said that:

nistraiguṇye pathi vicaratāṁ ko vidhiḥ ko niṣedhaḥ ।

that is, "laws dictating what is proper and what improper do not apply to persons who have gone beyond the three constituents"; and Buddhistic writers have said that: "just as the purest diamond does not require to be polished, so are the actions of that person who has reached the state of Absolution (*nirvāṇa*) not required to be limited by rules of conduct" (Milindapraśna 4. 5. 7). This is the import of the statement made by Indra to Pratardana in the Kauṣītakyupaniṣad (Kauṣī. 3. 1), that the Self-knower (*ātmajñānin*) is "untouched by the sins of matricide, patricide, or infanticide"; or of the statement in the Gītā (Gī 18. 17), that "a man who has totally lost the feeling of individuation (*ahaṁkāra*) is untouched by sin or merit, even if he kills others (See Pañcadaśī 14. 16 and 17); and the same principle has been repeated in the Buddhistic work called '*Dhammapada*' (See Dhammapada, stanzas 294 and 295). * Nay, according to me, the statement of St. Paul,

* The statement from the Kauṣītakyupaniṣad is: "*yo māṁ vijānīyān nāsya kenacit karmaṇā loko mīyate na matṛvadhena na pitṛvadhena na steyena na bhrūṇahatyayā* ।"; and the stanzas in the Dhammapada are as follows:-

mātaraṁ pitaraṁ hantvā rājāno dve ca khattiye ।
raṭhṭhaṁ sānucaraṁ hantvā anīgho yāti brāhmaṇo ॥ (294)
mātaraṁ pitaraṁ hantvā rājāno dve ca sotthiye ।
veyyagdha pañcamaṁ hantvā anīgho yāti brāhmaṇo ॥ (295)

the disciple of the Lord Christ, in the New Testament of the Bible that: "all things are lawful for me" (1. Cori. 6. 12; Romans 8. 2), or the statement of St. John that: "it is not possible that any sin is committed by those who have become the sons (perfect disciples) of the Lord" (John. 1. 3. 9) conveys the same import. Those who have got into the habit of arriving at a decision about morality by merely considering the external Action, without attaching proper importance to mental purity, may consider this doctrine as strange; and some people perversely interpret 'not bound by rules of right or wrong' as meaning 'one who commits any wrong he likes,' and distort the doctrine mentioned above by me as meaning "the Sthitaprajña is at liberty to commit any sin he likes". But, just as the fact that a blind man does not see a pillar, is not the fault of the pillar, so does the fact of these objectors, who have become blind because they support a particular doctrine, not clearly understanding the meaning of the doctrine mentioned above, not become a fault of the doctrine. Even the Gītā accepts the position that the purity of anybody's mind has first to be tested by his external

---

(that is, (294) "in killing a mother or a father, or two kings of a warrior race, or destroying a whole kingdom with its inhabitants, a Brahmin (still) remains sinless"; (295) "in killing a mother, a father, two Brahmin kings, and an eminent man, to make up five, a Brahmin (still) remains sinless"—Trans.)

This idea in the Dhammapada has evidently been borrowed from the Kauṣitakyupaniṣad. But the Buddhistic writers do not take those words in their literal meaning of matricide or patricide, and have understood mother (*mātā*) as meaning thirst (*tṛṣṇā*), and father (*pitā*) as meaning self-respect (*abhimāna*). But, in my opinion, these writers have adopted these figurative meanings only because they have not properly understood the principle of Ethics conveyed in this verse. In the Kauṣītakyupaniṣad, before the verse "*matṛvadhena pitṛvadhena*" etc., it is stated by Indra that: "even if I kill Vṛtra, a Brahmin, I do not thereby commit any sin"; and it is quite clear from this, that actual murder was referred to. The commentary of Max Müller on this verse in his English translation on the Dhammapada (S. B. E., Volume X, pp. 70 and 71) is, according to me, due to misunderstanding.

actions; and the Metaphysical science does not wish to apply the abovementioned doctine to those imperfect persons, the purity of whose mind remains to be tested, even a little, by that test. But the case is different with the man who has reached the state of perfection, and whose mind has undoubtedly become entirely merged in the Brahman and infinitely desireless; and although some Action of his might appear improper from the ordinary point of view, yet, as it is admitted that his mind is perfectly pure and equable, it follows that such Action, however it appears to the ordinary observer, must be essentially sinless; or, it must have been committed for some ethically correct reason, and is not likely to be founded on avarice or immorality like the actions of ordinary people. The same is the reason why Abraham in the Bible was not guilty of the sin of attempting infanticide, though he was about to kill his son; or, why Buddha did not incur the sin of murder, when his father-in-law died as a result of his curse; or, why Paraśurāma was not guilty of matricide though he killed his own mother. And the advice given in the Gītā to Arjuna by the Blessed Lord that, "if your mind is pure and stainless, you will not be guilty of the sin of having killed your ancestor or your preceptor, though you may happen to kill Bhīṣma and Droṇa in warfare, according to the duty of the Kṣatriyas, and without having any hope of any benefit to be derived thereby; because, in such circumstances, you have become merely an instrument for carrying into effect the desire of the Parameśvara" (Gī. 11. 33), is based on the same principle. We see in ordinary life that if a millionaire snatches away money from a beggar, the millionaire is not called a thief, but it is believed that the beggar has committed some wrong, and that on that account the millionaire has punished him. This argument applies still more appropriately, or more fully, to the conduct of the Sthitaprajña, the *arhata*, or the devotee of the Blessed Lord; because, the Reason of the millionaire may on occasion falter, but it is a settled fact that such emotions cannot touch the Reason of the Sthitaprajña. As the Parameśvara, the Creator of the universe, is untouched by sin or merit, notwithstanding that He performs all Actions, so also is the state of these saints, who have become merged in the Brahman, always holy and sinless. It may even be said that laws of conduct are framed on the basis of the Actions performed by such persons on previous occasions, of their own free will; and on that account, these saints become the fathers of those laws of behaviour, and are never the slaves of them. Such illustrations are come across not only in the Vedic religion, but also in the Buddhistic and Christian religions; and this principle was accepted even by the ancient Greek philosophers; and in the present age, Kant * has in his book on the science of Ethics proved this by conclusive reasons. When it has thus been proved what the unpollutable original spring or the stainless model of all rules of Morality is, such persons as want to scrutinise the fundamental principles of Ethics, or of the doctrine of Energism (*karma-yoga*) must minutely examine the lives of such holy and stainless saints. That is why Arjuna has asked Śrī Kṛṣṇa the following questions in the Bhagavadgītā, namely;— "*sthitadhīḥ kiṁ prabhāṣeta kim āsīta vrajeta kim*" (Gī. 2. 54), i. e., "how does the Sthitaprajña speak, sit, move about?"; or, in the fourteenth chapter, "*kair liṅgais trīnguṇān etān atīto bhavati prabho, kimācāraḥ*" (Gī. 14. 21), i. e., "how does a man go beyond the three constituents, (become a *triguṇātīta*), what is his behaviour, and how is such a man to be recognised?" As an assayer tests the golden ornament, which has been taken to him for examination, by comparing it with a sample piece of hundred carat gold in his possession, so also is the behaviour of the Sthitaprajña a test for deciding

* "A perfectly good will would therefore be equally subject to objective laws (viz., laws of good), but could not be conceived as *obliged* thereby to act lawfully, because of itself from its subjective constitution, it can only be determined by the conception of good. Therefore *no imperatives* hold for the Divine will, or in general for a *holy* will; *ought* is here out of place, because the volition is already of itself necessarily in unison with the law". Kant's *Metaphysic of Morals*, p. 31. (Abbot's trans. in Kant's *Theory of Ethics*, 6th Ed). Nietzsche does not accept any Metaphysical basis; yet, in the description of a superman given by him in his books, he has said that such a person is beyond good and evil, and one of his books is entitled *Beyond Good and Evil*.

between the duty and the non-duty, the just and the unjust; and the implied meaning of these questions is that the Blessed Lord should explain to Arjuna what that test was. Some persons say that the descriptions which have been given by the Blessed Lord of the state of the Sthitaprajña or of the Triguṇātīta, in reply to this question, are of Jñānins following the Path of Renunciation, and not the Karma-Yoga; because, it is with reference to such persons that the adjective '*nirāśrayaḥ*' (i. e., homeless—Trans.), (Gī. 4. 20) has been used in the Gītā; and in the twelvth chapter, where the description of the Sthitaprajña devotees of the Blessed Lord is being given, the words "*sarvārambhaparityāgī*" (i. e., "one who has abandoned all *ārambha* or commencement of Action—Trans.), (Gī. 12. 16), and "*aniketaḥ*" (i. e., "one who has no abode"—Trans.), (Gī. 12. 19), have been used clearly. But the words '*nirāśrayaḥ*' or '*aniketaḥ*' do not mean 'one who does not remain in a home, but roams about in a forest', and they must be taken as synonymous with "*anāśritaḥ karmaphalam*" (i. e., "not taking shelter in the Fruit of the Action"—Trans.), (Gī. 6. 1), that is to say, as meaning 'one who does not take shelter in the Fruit of Action', or, 'one, the home of whose mind, is not in that Fruit', as will be clearly seen from my commentaries on the translations of those respective verses. Besides, it is stated in the description itself of the Sthitaprajña, that "he moves about among the objects of pleasure, keeping control over his organs", that is, he performs Actions desirelessly (Gī. 2. 64); and, in the stanza which contains the word '*nirāśrayaḥ*' occurs also the description, "*karmaṇy abhipravṛtto'pi naiva kiṁcit karoti saḥ*", that is, "he is free from and untouched by all Actions, though he performs them". The same argument must be applied to the use of the word '*aniketaḥ*' in the twelvth chapter; because, in that chapter, after having praised the abandonment of the Fruit of Action (not the Abandonment of Action), the Blessed Lord has gone on to describe the characteristics of His devotees, in order to explain what peace (*śānti*) is obtained by performing Action after abandoning the Hope for Fruit (*phalāśā*); and in the same way, a description has been given in the eighteenth chapter, of a person who has been merged in the Brahman, in order to explain how peace is obtained by performing Actions without being attached to the Fruit of Action (Gī. 18. 50). It, therefore, becomes necessary to come to the conclusion that these descriptions are not of persons who follow the Path of Renunciation, but of Karma-yogins. It is not that, the Knowledge of the Brahman, the peace of mind, the Self-identification *(ātmaupamya)*, or the Desirelessness of Mind, of the Karma-yogin Sthitaprajña, is different from those of the Saṁnyāsin-Sthitaprajña. As both are perfect Knowers of the Brahman, the mental frame and the peace of mind are the same in either case; but the one is merely engrossed in Peace *(śānti)*, and does not care for anything else; whereas, the other is continually bringing into use his peace of mind and his Self-identification in his activities of ordinary life, as occasion arises. This is the important difference between the two from the point of view of Karma. Therefore, that Sthitaprajña, whose personal conduct has to be taken as an example for determining what is right and what is wrong in ordinary life, must be one who performs Action, and not one who has abandoned Action or is a beggar *(bhikṣu)*. The sum and substance of the advice given to Arjuna in the Gītā is, "it is not necessary to give up Action, nor can you give it up; but, Realise the identity of the Brahman and the Ātman and keep your pure Reason *(vyavasāyātmikā buddhi)* equable like that of a Karma-yogin, so that your Practical Reason (*vāsanātmikā buddhi*) will thereby also become pure, mine-less, and saintly, and you will not be caught in the bondage of Karma"; and that is why in explaining to Jājali the principle of Ethics embodied in the stanza quoted at the beginning of this chapter, namely, "that man who, by his Actions and by his speech, is continually engrossed in the welfare of others, and who is always a friend of others, may alone be said to have understood what morality (*dharma*) is", Tulādhāra has mentioned Karma, side by side with Speech and Mind, and even before mentioning them.

It is not necessary to explain principles of Ethics in detail to that man, whose mind has become equable towards all created things, like that of a Karma-yogin Sthitaprajña or a Jīvanmukta, and all whose selfish interests have been merged in the interests of others. He may be said to have become self-enlightened or a '*buddha*'. As Arjuna had reached that stage, it was not necessary to give him any advice beyond stating: "make your mind equable and steady, and instead of falling in the futile mistake of giving up Action, make your mind similar to that of the Sthitaprajña, and perform all Action which has befallen you according to your status in life." Yet, as this Yoga in the shape of equability of mind, cannot, as has been stated above, be attained by every one in one life, the life of a Sthitaprajña must be a little more minutely examined and explained for the benefit of ordinary people. But, in making this disquisition, one must also bear in mind that the Sthitaprajña, whom we are going to consider, is not a man living in a society which has reached the perfect state of the Kṛta-yuga, but is one who has to live in a society in this Kali-yuga, in which almost all people are steeped in their own selfish interests. Because, however great and complete the Knowledge of a man may be, and whatever the state of equability of Mind which he has reached, it will not do if he adopts the practice of harmlessness, kindness, peacefulness, forgiveness etc., which are permanent virtues of the highest order, in dealing with persons whose minds are impure, and who are caught within the toils of Desire, Anger etc. * It need not be said that the rules of Right and Wrong, applicable to a society in which the majority is of avaricious persons, must be at least somewhat different from the rules of Right and Wrong and of Absolute

* "In the second place, ideal conduct such as ethical theory is concerned with, is not possible for the ideal man in the midst of men otherwise constituted. An absolutely just or perfectly sympathetic person could not live and act according to his nature in a tribe of cannibals. Among people who are treacherous and utterly without scruple, entire truthfulness and openness must bring ruin". Spencer's *Data of Ethics*, Chap. XV, p 280. Spencer has called this 'Relative Ethics'; and he says that: "On the evolution-hypothesis, the two (Absolute and Relative Ethics) presuppose one another; and only when they co-exist, can there exist that ideal conduct which Absolute Ethics has to formulate, and which Relative Ethics has to take as the standard by which to estimate divergencies from right, or degrees of wrong".

Ethics applicable to a society in which every person is a Sthitaprajña; otherwise, saints will have to leave this world, and evil-doers will be the rulers everywhere. This does not mean that saints must give up their equable frame of mind; but there are kinds and kinds of equability of mind. It is stated in the Gītā that the hearts of saints are equal towards "*brāhmaṇe gavi hastini*" (Gī. 5. 18), i. e., "Brahmins, cows, and elephants". But if, on that account, some one feeds a Brahmin with the grass which has been brought for the cow or feeds the cow with the food which has been cooked for the Brahmin, shall we call him a wise man? If persons following the School of Renunciation do not attach any importance to this question, the same cannot be done by people who follow the Karma-Yoga. The Sthitaprajña lives his life in this world, taking into account what the nature of Right and Wrong was in the perfect state of the Kṛta-yuga, and deciding what changes are necessary in those rules, in this world of selfish persons, having regard to the difference of Time and Place; and it will be clear from what has been stated in the second chapter above, that this is the most difficult question in Karma-Yoga. Saints perform their duties in this life apathetically, and only for the benefit of such selfish people, instead of getting angry with them, or allowing their own equability of mind to change on account of their avaricious tendencies. Bearing this principle in mind, Śrī Samartha Rāmadāsa has, after having in the first part of the Dāsabodha dealt with the Knowledge of the Brahman, started in the eleventh chapter a description of the activities performed by such Sthitaprajñas or saints for social welfare, with indifference to the world, or desirelessly, and with the intention of instilling wisdom into such people (Dāsa. 11. 1; 12. 8-10; 15. 2); and he has stated later on in the eighteenth chapter, that one should thoroughly understand and grasp the traditions, stories, stratagems, devices, circumstances, intentness of pursuit, inferences, cleverness, diplomacy, forbearance, acuteness, generosity, Metaphysical Knowledge, devotion, aloofness, indifference to the world, daringness, assiduity, determination, firmness, equability, discrimination, and numerous other qualities of such Jñānins (Dāsa. 18. 2). But as such disinterested persons have to deal with avaricious persons, the ultimate advice of Śrī Samartha is:–

> Meet boldness with boldness ı impertinence by impertinence ı villainy by villainy ı must be met ıı
>
> (Dāsa. 19. 9. 30)

In short, when a man descends from the state of perfection to ordinary life, it is undoubtedly necessary to make some changes in the rules of Right or Wrong which apply to the highest state.

To this position, Materialistic philosophers raise the following objection, namely: if, when one descends from the perfect state into ordinary society, one has to deal with many things with discrimination, and modify Absolute Ethics to a certain extent, where is the permanence of Ethical principles, and what becomes of the axiom "*dharmo nityaḥ*", i. e., "Morality is immutable," which has been enunciated by Vyāsa in the Bhārata-Sāvitrī? They say that the immutability of Ethics from the point of view of Metaphysics is purely imaginary, and that those are the only true rules of Ethics, which come into existence consistently with the state of society at particular periods of time, on the basis of the principle of the 'greatest good of the greatest number'. But, this argument is not correct. Just as the scientific definition of a straight line or of a perfect circle does not become faulty or purposeless, because no one can draw a straight line without breadth or a faultless circumference of a circle as defined in Geometry, so also is the case with simple and pure rules of Ethics. Besides, unless one has determined the absolutely pure form of anything, it is not possible to bring about improvements in the various imperfect forms of it which we come across in life, or to ascertain the relative worth of the various forms after careful consideration; and that is why the assayer first decides what is pure hundred carat gold. Persons who live only according to the times, and without taking into account the absolute form of Ethical principles, will be in the same position as sailors on a ship, who guide the rudder on the boundless ocean, considering only the waves and the wind, and without taking into account the compass, which shows the cardinal directions, or the Polar star. Therefore, even considering everything from the Materialistic point of view, it is necessary to first fix some principle of Ethics, which is unchangeable and permanent like the Polar star; and once this necessity has been admitted, the entire Materialistic argument falls to the ground. Because, as all enjoyment of objects of pleasure which causes pain or happiness falls into the Name-d and Form-ed, and therefore, the non-permanent or perishable category of illusory objects, no principle of Ethics based on such enjoyment, that is, on merely external effects, can be permanent. Such Ethical principles must go on changing as the ideas of the material, external, pain and happiness on which they are based, change. Therefore, if one has to escape from this perpetually changing state of Ethics, one must not take into account the enjoyment of objects of pleasure in this illusory world, but must stand on the sole Metaphysical foundation of the principle, "there is only one Ātman in all created things"; because, as has been stated before in the ninth chapter, there is nothing in this world which is permanent except the Ātman; and the same is the meaning conveyed by the statement of Vyāsa: "*dharmo nityaḥ sukhaduḥkhe tv anitye*", i. e., "the rules of Ethics or of pure behaviour are immutable, and happiness and unhappiness are transient and mutable". It is true that in a society which is full of cruel and avaricious persons, it is not possible to fully observe the immutable Ethical laws of harmlessness, truth, etc.; but one cannot blame these Ethical laws for that. Just as one cannot, from the fact that the shade of an object cast by the Sun's rays is flat on a flat surface, but is undulating on an undulating surface, draw the inference that the shade must be originally undulating, so can one not, from the fact that one does not come across the purest form of Ethics in a society of unprincipled persons, draw the inference that the imperfect state of Ethics which we come accross in an imperfect society is the principal or the original form of Ethics. The fault here is not of Ethics, but of the society; therefore, those who are wise, do not quarrel with pure and permanent laws of Ethics, but apply their efforts towards elevating society, so as to bring it to the ultimate highest state. Although our philosophers have mentioned some exceptions to the permanent laws of Ethics in dealing with avaricious persons in society, as being unavoidable, they also mention penances for acting according to such exceptions; and this will also clearly explain the difference pointed out by me in previous chapters in explaining to my readers that Western Materialistic Ethical science bare-facedly supports and propounds these exceptions as laws, and by confusion of thought, looks upon the principles of discrimination between external results, which are useful only for fixing these exceptions, as the true laws of Ethics.

I have thus explained that the true foundation of Ethics is the frame of mind and the mode of life of the Sthitaprajña Jñānin (the Steady-in-Mind scient); and why, although the laws of Ethics to be deduced from the same are permanent and immutable in themselves, they have got to be varied in an imperfect state of society; and, how and why the immutability of fundamental laws of Ethics is not affected, though these laws may be varied in that way. I shall now consider the question first mentioned by me, namely, what is the hidden significance or fundamental principle underlying the behaviour of a Sthitaprajña Jñānin in an imperfect society. I have stated before in the fourth chapter that this question can be considered in two ways: the one way is to consider the state of mind of the doer as the principal factor; and the other way is to consider his external mode of life. If one considers the matter only from the second point of view, it will be seen that all the activities of the Sthitaprajña are *prima facie* for the benefit of the world. It is stated in two places in the Gītā that, saints who have acquired the highest Knowledge, are "engrossed in bringing about the welfare of all created things", that is, they are "*sarvabhūtahiteratāḥ*" (Gī. 5. 25 and 12. 4); and the same statement also appears in various places in the Mahābhārata. I have stated above that the laws of harmlessness etc., which are followed by Sthitaprajña Jñānins, are in fact '*dharma*', or the model of pure behaviour. In explaining the necessity of these rules of harmlessness etc., and in describing the nature of these laws of Ethics *(dharma)*, the Mahābhārata contains various statements explaining their external usefulness, such as:—"*ahiṁsā satyavacanaṁ sarvabhūtahitaṁ param*" (Vana. 206. 73), i. e., "non-violence and truthfulness are laws of Ethics, beneficial to everybody"; or, "*dhāraṇād dharmam ity āhuḥ*" (Śān. 109. 12), i. e., "it is called *dharma*, because it maintains the world"; or, "*dharmaṁ hi śreya ity āhuḥ*" (Anu. 105. 14), i. e., "that is *dharma*, which is beneficial"; or, "*prabhavārthāya bhūtānāṁ dharmapravacanaṁ kṛtam*" (Śān. 109. 10), i. e., "laws of Ethics have been made for the amelioration of society"; or, "*lokayātrārtham evehaṁ dharmasya niyamaḥ kṛtaḥ* । *ubhayatra sukhodarkaḥ*" (Śān. 258. 4), i. e., "laws of Ethics have been made in order that the activities of society should go on, and that benefit should be acquired in this life and the next". In the same way, it is stated that, when there is a doubt between what is right and what is wrong, the Jñānin—

lokayātrā ca draṣṭavyā dharmaś cātmahitāni ca ।

(Anu. 37. 16; Vana. 206. 90)

that is, "should discriminate between external factors like the usual activities of men, laws of Ethics, and one's own benefit", and decide what is to be done; and the king Śibi has, in the Vanaparva, followed the same principle for discriminating between right and wrong (Vana. 131. 11 and 12). From these statements, it will be clearly seen that the 'external guiding factor' of the mode of life of a Sthitaprajña, is the advancement of society; and if this is accepted as correct, the next question which faces us is: why do Metaphysicians not accept the Materialistic Ethical law of 'the greatest happiness or, (using the word 'happiness' in a more extensive meaning), benefit, or advantage of the greatest number'? I have shown above in the fourth chapter that the one great drawback of the principle of the 'greatest happiness of the greatest number' is, that it does not provide for either, the happiness or amelioration resulting from Self-Realisation, or the happiness in the next world. But this drawback can to a great extent be removed by taking the word 'happiness' in a comprehensive meaning; and the Metaphysical argument given above in support of the immutability of Ethical laws, will, therefore, not appear of importance to many. It is, therefore, necessary to again give a further elucidation of the important difference between the Metaphysical and the Materialistic aspect of Ethics.

The question whether a particular act is ethically proper or improper can be considered in two ways: (1) by considering merely its external result, that is to say, its visible effect on the world; and (2) by considering the Reason or the Desire of the doer. The first method of consideration is known as the MATERIALISTIC (*ādhibhautika*) method. In the second method, there are again two sub-divisions, each of which has a different name. I have in the previous chapters referred to the doctrines that (i) in order that one's Action should be pure, one's Practical Reason has got to be pure, and that (ii) in order that one's Practical Reason should be pure, one's Pure Reason, that is, the reasoning faculty, which discriminates between what ought to be done and what ought not to be done, has got to be steady, equable, and pure. According to these doctrines, one has to see whether the Practical Reason which prompted a particular action was or was not pure, in order to determine whether the Action is pure; and when one wishes to consider whether the Practical Reason was or was not pure, one has necessarily to see whether the Deciding Reason was or was not pure. In short, whether the Reason or the Desire of the doer was or was not pure, has ultimately to be judged by considering the purity or the impurity of the Deciding Reason (Gī. 2. 41). When this Deciding Reason is considered to be an independent deity, embodying the power of discrimination between Right and Wrong (*sadasadvivecana-śakti*), that method of consideration is called the INTUITIONIST (*ādhidaivika*) method; but if one believes that this power is not an independent deity, but is an eternal organ of the Ātman, and on that account, one looks upon the Ātman, instead of the Reason, as the principal factor and determines the pureness of Desire on that basis, that method of determining principles of Ethics is known as the METAPHYSICAL (*ādhyātmika*) method. Our philosophers say that this Metaphysical method is the best of all these methods; and although the well-known German philosopher Kant has not clearly enunciated the doctrine of the identity of the Brahman and the Ātman, he has commenced his disquisition of the principles of

Ethics, with a consideration of Pure Reason, that is, in a way; from the Metaphysical point of view; and he has clearly stated there his reasons for doing so. * Green is of the same opinion: but these matters cannot be dealt with in detail in a small book like this. I have, in the fourth chapter above, explained by giving a few illustrations why, in finally deciding questions of Ethics, one has to pay more special attention to the pureness of the Reason of the doer, than to the external result of his Actions; and this subject-matter will be further considered in the fifteenth chapter when I will compare the Western and the Eastern ethical laws. For the time being, I will only say that, in as much as it is necessary that there should be a desire to perform any particular Action before it is actually performed, the consideration of the propriety or the impropriety of such Action, depends entirely on the consideration of the purity or the impurity of the Reason. If the Reason is sinful, the Action will be sinful; but, from the fact that the external Action is bad, one cannot draw the conclusion that the Reason also must be bad; because, that act may have been performed by mistake, or as a result of a misunderstanding, or as a result of ignorance; and in these cases it cannot be said to be ethically sinful. The Ethical principle of 'the greatest happiness of the greatest number' can apply only to the external results of Actions; and as no one has so far invented any external means for definitely measuring the external results of such Actions in the shape of pain or happiness, it is not certain that this test of Morality will always give us a correct result. In the same way, however wise a man may be, if his Reason is not pure, it is not certain that he will on every occasion behave in a morally correct way. And the position will be much worse if his own selfish interests are in any way affected in that matter; because, "*svārthe sarve vimuhyanti ye 'pi dharmavido janāḥ*" (Ma. Bhā. Vi. 51. 4), i. e., "all are blinded by selfish interests, even if they are well-versed in Morality"—Trans.). In short, however much a man may be a Jñānin, or well-versed in Morality, or wise, if his

* See Kant's *Theory of Ethics* trans. by Abbott, 6th Ed., especially *Metaphysics of Morals* therein.

Reason has not become equable towards all created beings, it is not certain that his Actions will always be pure or morally faultless. Therefore, our philosophers have decided definitely that in dealing with ethical problems, one must consider principally the Reason of the doer, rather than the external results of his Actions; and that equability of Reason is the true principle underlying an ethically correct mode of life. And the Blessed Lord has given to Arjuna the following advice on the same principle in the Bhagavadgītā:

dūreṇa hy avaraṁ karma buddhiyogād dhanañjaya ।
buddhau śaraṇam anviccha kṛpaṇāḥ phalahetavaḥ ॥ *
(Gī. 2. 49).

Some say that the word '*buddhi*' in this stanza is to be understood as meaning 'Jñāna' (Knowledge), and that a higher place has been given to Jñāna, as between Jñāna and Karma. But, according to me, this interpretation is incorrect. Even in the Śāṁkarabhāṣya on this stanza, the word '*buddhi-yoga*' has been interpreted as meaning '*samatva-buddhi-yoga*' (the Yoga of equability of Reason); and further, this stanza occurs in that part of the Gītā which deals with the Karma-Yoga. Therefore, this stanza must be interpreted with reference to Karma only; and such an interpretation is also naturally arrived at. Those who perform Actions fall into the two categories of (i) those who keep an eye merely on the fruit—for example, on the question, how many persons will be benefited thereby, and to what extent; and (ii) those who keep their Reason equable and desireless, and remain unconcerned as to the Fruit of the Action, which (fruit) results from the combination of Action *(karma)* and Destiny (*dharma*). Out of these, this stanza has treated the '*phalahetavaḥ*', that is, 'those who perform Action, keeping an eye on the result of the Action', as *kṛpaṇa*,

* The literal meaning of this verse is :—O Dhanañjaya! (pure) Action is very much inferior to the Yoga of the (equable) Reason; (therefore), rely on (the equable) Reason. Those (persons), who perform Actions keeping an eye to the Fruit of Action, are '*kṛpaṇa*', that is, of an inferior order".

that is, of a lower order from the ethical point of view; and those who perform Action with an equable Reason as superior. That is what is meant by the statement in the first two parts of the stanza, namely, "*dureṇa hy avaraṁ karma buddhiyogād dhanañjaya*", i.e., "O Dhanañjaya, Action alone is very much inferior to the Yoga of the equable Reason"; and that is the answer given by the Blessed Lord to the question of Arjuna "How shall I kill Bhiṣma, Droṇa and others?" The implied meaning of this is, that one has to consider not merely the Action of dying or of killing, but the motive with which that Action has been performed; and therefore, the advice has been given in the third part of the stanza that: "Rely on your Reason (*buddhi*), that is, on the equable Reason (*sama-buddhi*)"; and later on, in the summing up in the eighteenth chapter, the Blessed Lord has again said: "Perform all your Actions, relying on the Yoga of the equable Reason". That the Gītā looks upon the consideration of the Action itself as inferior, and of the motive which inspires the particular Action as superior, will be apparent from another stanza in the Gītā. In the eighteenth chapter, Karma has been classified into *sāttvika*, *rājasa*, and *tāmasa*. If the Gītā had intended to consider only the result of the Action, the Blessed Lord would have said that those Actions, which produce the greatest good of the greatest number, are *sāttvika*; but, instead of doing so, it is stated in the eighteenth chapter that, "that Action is the most excellent, which has been performed desirelessly, that is, after abandoning the Hope for the Fruit of the Action" (Gī. 18. 23). Therefore, the Gītā, in discriminating between the doable and the not-doable, attaches a higher importance to the desireless, equable, and unattached Reason of the doer, than to the external result of the Action; and if the same test is applied to the conduct of the Sthitaprajña, it follows that the true principle involved in the mode of life of a Sthitaprajña is the equable Reason with which he behaves towards his equals and his subordinates; and that the welfare of all created beings resulting from such a mode of life is the external or concomitant result of that equability of Reason. In the same way, it is improbable that the man whose Reason has reached the perfectly equable state, will perform Action with the sole idea of giving merely

Material happiness to other people. It is true that he will not cause harm to others. But, that cannot be considered to be his principal ideal; and all the activities of a Sthitaprajña are directed towards more and more purifying the minds of all the persons forming a society, and thereby enabling such persons to ultimately reach the Metaphysically perfect state he himself has reached. This is the highest and the most *sāttvika* duty of mankind. We look upon all efforts directed merely towards the increase of the Material happiness of human beings as inferior or *rājasa*.

To the doctrine of the Gītā that in order to decide between the doable and the not-doable, one has to attach a higher importance to the pureness of the motive of the doer than to the result of the Action, the following mischievous objection has been raised, namely, if one does not take into account the result of the Action, but merely considers the pureness of the motive, it will follow that a person with a pure Reason can commit any crime he likes; and that he will then be at liberty to perform all sorts of crimes! This objection has not been imagined by me, but I have as a matter of fact seen objections of this kind, which have been advanced agaist the Gītā religion by some Christian missionaries.* But, I do not feel the slightest compunction in characterising these allegations or objections as totally foolish and perverse. Nay, I may even go so far as to say that these missionaries have become as incapable of even understanding the Metaphysical perfection of the Sthitaprajña described in the Vedic religion on account of an over-weening admiration for their own religion, or of some other nefarious or evil emotions, as a black-as-ebony Negro from Africa is unfit for or incapable of appreciating the principles of Ethics accepted in civilised countries. Kant, the well-known German philosopher of the nineteenth century, has stated in several places in his book on Ethics, that one must consider only the Reason of the doer, rather than the external result

* One missionary from Calcutta has made this statement; and the reply given to it by Mr. Brooks appears at the end of his treatise *Kurukṣetra* (Kurukṣetra, Vyāsāśrama, Adyar, Madras, pp. 48-52).

of his Action, in deciding questions of Ethics.* But, I have nowhere come across any such objection having been raised to that statement of Kant. Then how can such an objection apply to the principle of Ethics enunciated by the Gītā? When the Reason has become equable towards all created beings, charity becomes a matter of inherent nature; and therefore, it is as impossible that a person who has acquired this highest Knowledge, and is possessed of the purest Reason, should commit sin, as that nectar should cause death. When the Gītā says that one should not consider the external result of the Action, that does not mean that one is at liberty to do what one likes. The Gītā says: though a person can hypocritically or with a selfish motive, appear to be charitable, he cannot hypocritically possess that equability of Reason and stability, which can arise only by Realising that there is but one Ātman in all created beings; therefore, in considering the propriety or the impropriety of any Action, one has to give due consideration to the Reason of the doer, instead of considering only the external results of his Action. To express the matter in short, the doctrine of the Gītā is that Morality does not consist of Material Action only, but that it wholly depends on the Reason of the doer; and the Gītā says later on (Gī. 18. 25), that if a man, not realising the true principle underlying this doctrine, starts doing whatever he likes, he must be said to be *tāmasa* or a devil. Once the mind has become equable, it is not necessary to give the man any further advice about the propriety or the impropriety of Actions. Bearing this principle in mind, Saint Tukārāma has

---

* "The second proposition is: That an action done from duty derives its moral worth, *not from the purpose* which is to be attained by it, but from the maxim by which it is determined". The moral worth of action "cannot lie anywhere but in the *principle of the will*, without regard to the ends which can be attained by action". Kant's *Metaphysic of Morals* (trans.by Abbott in Kant's *Theory of Ethics*, p. 16. The italics are the author's and not our own). And again, "When the question is of moral worth, it is not with the actions which we see that we are concerned, but with those inward principles of them which we do not see". p. 24. *Ibid.*

preached to Shivaji Maharaja the sole doctrine of Karma-Yoga, same as the Bhagavadgītā, in the *abhaṅga*:-

"This has only one merit-producing meaning ।
there is only one Ātman, that is, God in all created beings ॥"

(Tu. Gā. 4428. 9).

But, although the essential basis of proper conduct (*sadācaraṇa*) is the equable Reason, I must repeat here that, one cannot from that fact draw the inference that the man who performs Action, must wait for performing Action until his Reason has reached that stage. It is the highest ideal of everybody to make his mind like that of a Sthitaprajña. But it is stated already in the commencement of the Gītā, that because this is the highest ideal, one need not wait for performing Action until that ideal has been reached; that one should in the meantime perform all Actions with as much unselfishness as possible, so that thereby the Reason will become purer and purer, and the highest state of perfection will ultimately be reached; and that one must not waste time by insisting on not performing any Action until the perfect state of the Reason has been reached (Gī. 2. 40).

A further objection is raised by many that, although it has in this way been proved (i) that the ethical principle of '*sarva-bhūta-hita*' or of 'the greatest good of the greatest number' is a one-sided and superficial (*śākhāgrāhi*) principle, as it applies, only to external Actions, and (ii) that the 'equability of Reason' according to which 'there is only one Ātman in all created beings' is a thing which goes to the root of the matter (is *mūlagrāhi*), and must, therefore, be considered as of higher importance in determining questions of Morality, yet, one does not thereby get a clear idea as to how one should behave in ordinary life. These objections have suggested themselves to the objectors principally by seeing the worldly behaviour of Sthitaprajñas, who follow the Path of Renunciation. But anybody will see after a little thought, that they cannot apply to the mode of life of the Karma-yogin Sthitaprajña. Nay; we may even say that no ethical principle can more satisfactorily justify worldly morality, than the principle of considering that there is only one Ātman in all created beings, or of Self-identification (*ātmaupamya*). For example, let us take the doctrine of charity, which has been given an important place in all countries and according to all codes of Ethics. This doctrine can be justified by no Materialistic principle, as satisfactorily as by the Metaphysical principle that 'the Ātman of the other man is the same as my Ātman'. The utmost that Materialistic philosophy can tell us is, that philanthropy is an inherent quality which gradually grows, according to the Theory of Evolution (*utkrānti-vāda*). But not only is the immutability of the principle of philanthropy not established by that philosophy, but, as has been shown by me before in the fourth chapter, when a man is faced with a conflict between his own interests and the interests of others, the 'enlightened selfish', who would like to sit on two stools, thereby get a chance of justifying their own attitude. But even to this, an objection is raised by some, that it is no use proving the immutability of the principle of philanthropy. If every one tries to serve the interests of others believing that there is only one Ātman in all created beings, who is going to look after his interests; and if in this way, his own interests are not looked after, how will he be in a position to do good to others? But these objections are neither new, nor unconquerable. The Blessed Lord has answered this very question in the Bhagavadgītā on the basis of the Path of Devotion, by saying; "*teṣāṁ nityābhiyuktānāṁ yogakṣemaṁ vahāmy aham*" (Gī. 9. 22), (i. e., "I look after the maintenance and welfare of those persons, who are permanently steeped in Yoga"—Trans.); and the same conclusion follows on the Metaphysical basis. That man, who is inspired with the desire of achieving the benefit of others, has not necessarily to give up food and drink; but he must believe that he is maintaining and keeping alive his own body for the benefit of others. Janaka has said (Ma. Bhā. Aśva. 32) that the organs will remain under one's control, only if one's Reason is in that state, and the doctrine of the Mīmāṁsā school that, 'that man is said to be *amṛtāśī*, who eats the food which has remained over after the performance of the sacrificial offering', is based on the same idea (Gī. 4. 31). Because, as the

Yajña is, from their point of view, an Action for the maintenance and conduct of the world, they have come to the conclusion, that one maintains oneself and should maintain oneself, while performing that act of public benefit; and that, it is not proper to put an end to the cycle of Yajñas for one's own selfish interest. Even according to the ordinary worldly outlook, one sees the appropriateness of the statement made by Śrī Samartha Rāmadāsa in the *Dāsabodha* that:

> That man is continually achieving the good of others ।
> That man is always wanted by everybody ।
> Then what can he need । in this world ? ॥
>
> (Dāsa. 19. 4. 10).

In short, it never happens that the man, who toils for public welfare, is found to suffer for want of being maintained. A man must only become ready to achieve the good of others with a desireless frame of Reason. When once the idea, that all persons are in him and that he is in all persons, has been fixed in a person's mind, the question whether self-interest is distinct from the interest of others, does not arise at all. The above-mentioned foolish doubts arise only in the minds of those persons who start to achieve 'the greatest good of the greatest number', with the Materialistic dual feeling that 'I' am different from 'others'. But, the man who starts to achieve the good of others with the Monistic idea that "*sarvaṁ khalv idaṁ brahma*" (i. e., "all this which exists is the Brahman"—Trans.), is never assailed by any such doubts. This important difference between the Metaphysical principle of achieving the welfare of all created beings, on the basis that there is only one Ātman in all created beings, and the Materialistic principle of general welfare, arising from a discrimination between the duality of self-interest and other's-interest, or from the consideration of the good of the multitude, has got to be carefully borne in mind. Saints do not achieve public welfare with the idea of achieving public welfare. Just as giving light is the inherent quality of the Sun, so does achieving the good of others become the inherent quality of these saints, as a result of the complete realisation of the unity of the Ātman in all created things; and when this has become the inherent quality of a saint, then, just as the Sun in giving light to others also gives light to itself, so also is the maintenance of such a saint achieved automatically by the activities directed by him towards the interests of others. When this inherent tendency of doing good to others is coupled with an unattached Reason, saints, who have realised the identity of the Ātman and the Brahman, continue their beneficent activities, without caring for the opposition they come across, and without trying to discriminate between whether it is better to suffer adversity or to give up public welfare; and if occasion arises, they are even ready to and indifferent about sacrificing their own lives. But, those who distinguish between self-interest and other's-interest, and begin to discriminate between what is right and what is wrong by seeing which way the scale turns when they weigh self-interest against other's-interest, can never experience a desire for public welfare, which is as intense as that of such saints. Therefore, although the principle of the benefit of all created beings in acceptable to the Gītā, it does not justify that principle by the consideration of the greatest external good of the greatest number, but looks upon the consideration of whether the numbers are large or small, or the consideration of the large or small quantity of happiness, as short-sighted and irrelevant; and it justifies the equability of Reason, which is the root of pure conduct, on the basis of the eternal Realisation of the Brahman which is propounded by Metaphysical philosophy.

From this it will be seen how a logically correct justification of one's making efforts for the benefit of others or of universal welfare, or of charity, can be arrived at from the point of view of Metaphysics. I will now consider the fundamental principles, which have been enunciated in our Śāstras for guiding the behaviour of one person towards another in society, from the point of view of equability of Reason. The principle that "*yatra vā asya sarvam ātmaivābhūt*" (Bṛ. 2. 4. 14), i. e., "the man for whom everything has been merged in the Self (Ātman)", behaves towards others with a perfectly equable mind, has been enunciated in the Īśāvāsya

(Īśā. 6) and Kaivalya (Kai. 1. 10) Upaniṣads, in addition to the Bṛhadāraṇyaka, as also in the Manu-Smṛti (Manu. 12. 91 and 125); and this same principle has been literally enunciated in the sixth chapter of the Gītā, in the words "*sarvabhūtastham ātmānaṁ sarvabhūtāni cātmani*" (Gī. 6. 29), (i. e., "he sees himself in all created things, and all created things in himself"—Trans.). The Self-identifying (*ātmaupamya*) outlook is only another form of this principle of believing in the unity of Ātman in all created things, or of the equability of Reason. Because, if I am in all created things, and all created things are in me, it naturally follows that I must behave towards all created things, in the same way as I would behave towards myself; and, therefore, the Blessed Lord has told Arjuna, that that man must be looked upon as the most excellent Karma-yogin Sthitaprajña, who "behaves towards all others with equability, that is, with the feeling that his Ātman is the same as the Ātman of others"; and he has advised Arjuna to act accordingly (Gī. 6. 30-32). As Arjuna was duly initiated, it was not necessary to further labour this principle in the Gītā. But, Vyāsa has very clearly shown the deep and comprehensive meaning embodied in this principle, by enunciating it in numerous places in the Mahābhārata, which has been written in order to teach Religion and Morality to ordinary people (Ma. Bhā. Śān. 238. 21; 261. 36). For example, in the conversation between Bṛhaspati and Yudhiṣṭhira in the Mahābhārata, this same principle of identifying one's Ātman with others, which has been succinctly mentioned in the Upaniṣads and in the Gītā, has at first been mentioned in the following words:-

ātmopamas tu bhūteṣu yo vai bhavati pūruṣaḥ ।
nyastadaṇḍo jitakrodhaḥ sa pretya sukham edhate ॥

(Ma. Bhā. Anu. 113. 6)

that is, "that man, who looks upon others in the same way as he looks upon himself, and who has conquered anger, obtains happiness in the next world"; and then, without completing there the description of how one person should behave towards others, the Mahābhārata goes on to say :–

na tat parasya saṁdadhyāt pratikūlaṁ yad ātmanaḥ ।
eṣa saṁkṣepato dharmaḥ kāmād anyaḥ pravartate ॥

(Ma. Bhā. Anu. 113. 8)

that is, "one should not behave towards others in a way which one considers adverse or painful to oneself; this is the essence of all religion and morality, and all other activities are based on selfish interests"; and it lastly says :–

pratyākhyāne ca dāne ca sukhaduḥkhe priyāpriye ।
ātmaupamyena puruṣaḥ pramāṇam adhigacchati ॥
yathāparaḥ prakramate pareṣu tathā pare prakramante 'parasmin ।
tathaiva teṣūpamā jīvaloke yathā dharmo nipuṇenopadiṣṭaḥ ॥

(Anu. 113. 9 and 10).

that is, " in the matter of pain and happiness, the palatable or the unpalatable, charity or opposition, each man should decide as to what should be done to others, by considering what his own feelings in the matter would be. Others behave towards one, as one behaves towards others; therefore, wise persons have stated, by taking that illustration, that *dharma* means behaving in the world, by placing oneself in the position of others". The line "*na tat parasya saṁdadhyāt pratikūlaṁ yad ātmanaḥ*", (i.e., "one should not behave towards others, in a way which one considers adverse or painful to oneself"— Trans.) has also appeared in the Viduranīti (Udyo. 38. 72) ; and later on, in the Śānti-parva, Vidura has explained the same principle again to Yudhiṣṭhira (Śān. 167. 9). But, "do not cause pain to others, because that which is painful to yourself is also painful to others", is only one part of the doctrine of Self-identification; and some people are likely to be assailed by the doubt that, we cannot deduce from this doctrine the definite inference that : " as that which is pleasant to yourself will also be pleasant to others, therefore, behave in such a way that pleasure will be caused to others". Therefore, Bhiṣma in explaining the nature of *dharma* (Morality) to Yudhiṣṭhira has gone further and clearly indicated both the aspects of this law in the following words :-

yad anyair vihitaṁ necched ātmanaḥ karma pūruṣaḥ ।
na tat pareṣu kurvīta jānann apriyam ātmanaḥ ॥

jīvitaṁ yaḥ svayaṁ cecchet kathaṁ so 'nyaṁ praghātayet ।
yad yad ātmani ceccheta tat parasyāpi cintayet ॥

(Śān. 258. 19, 21)

that is, " one should not behave towards others in that way in which one, by considering one's own happiness, desires that others should not behave towards one. How can that man, who desires to live himself, kill others? One should always desire that others should also get what one oneself wants". And in mentioning the same rule in another place, Vidura has, without using the adjectives '*anukūla*' (favourable) and '*pratikūla*' (unfavourable), laid down a general rule, with reference to every kind of behaviour, in the words :-

tasmād dharmapradhānena bhavitavyaṁ yat ātmanā ।
tathā ca sarvabhūteṣu vartitavyaṁ yathātmani ॥

(Śān. 167. 9)

that is, "control your organs, and behave righteously; and behave towards all created beings, as if they are yourself", because, as Vyāsa says in the Śukānupraśna,

yāvān ātmani vedātmā tāvān ātmā parātmani ।
ya evaṁ satataṁ veda so 'mṛtatvāya kalpate ॥

(Ma. Bhā. Śān. 238. 22)

that is, "there is in the bodies of others, just as much of Ātman as there is in one's own body. That man who continually realises this principle, comes to attain Release". Buddha did not accept the existence of the Ātman; at any rate, he has clearly stated that one should not unnecessarily bother about the consideration of the Ātman. Nevertheless, in teaching how Buddhist mendicants should behave towards others, even Buddha has preached the doctrine of Self-identification *(ātmaupamya)* in the following words:—

yathā ahaṁ tathā ete yathā ete tathā ahaṁ ।
attānaṁ (ātmānaṁ) upamaṁ katvā (kṛtvā) na haneyya na ghātaye ॥

(Suttanipāta, Nālakasutta, 27)

that is, "as I am, so are they; as they are, so am I; taking (thus) an illustration from oneself, one should not kill or cause (the) death (of anybody)". Even in another Pali treatise called *Dhammapada*, the second part of the above stanza has appeared twice verbatim; and immediately thereafter, the stanzas occurring both in the Manu-Smṛti (5.45) and Mahābhārata (Anu. 113. 5) have been repeated in the Pali language in the following words:—

sukhakāmāni bhūtāni yo daṇḍena vihiṁsati ।
attano sukhamesāno (icchan) pecya so na labhate sukham ॥

(Dhammapada. 131)

that is, "that man, who for his own *(attano)* benefit, kills with a rod other persons, who also desire happiness (like himself), does not obtain any happiness after death" *(pecya = pretya)*. As we see that the principle of Self-identification is recognised in Buddhistic works, although they do not admit of the existence of the Ātman, it becomes quite clear that these ideas have been taken by Buddhist writers from Vedic texts. But this matter will be further considered later on. The above quotations will clearly show that even from ancient times, we Indians have believed that that man, whose state of mind is "*sarvabhūtastham ātmānaṁ sarvabhūtāni cātmani*" (i. e., "all created things are in me, and I am in all created things"—Trans.), always conducts himself in life by identifying others with himself; and that that is the important principle underlying such conduct. Any one will admit that this principle or canon *(sūtra)* of Self-identification used in deciding how to behave with other persons in society, is more logical, faultless, unambiguous, comprehensive, and easy than the Materialistic doctrine of the 'greatest good of the greatest number'; and is such as will easily be grasped by even the most ignorant of persons. * This fundamental principle or mystic import of the philosophy of Right and Wrong *(eṣa saṁkṣepato dharmaḥ)* is justified in a more satisfactory way from the Metaphysical point of view than from the Materialistic point of view, which takes into account only the external effects of Actions; and therefore, the works of Western philosophers, who consider the question of Karma-Yoga merely from the Materialistic point of view, do not give a prominent place to this important doctrine of the philosophy of Right and Wrong. Nay, they attempt to explain the bond of society on merely external principles like the 'greatest happiness of the greatest number' etc., without taking into consideration this canon (*sūtra*) of the principle of Self-identification. But, it will be seen that this easy ethical principle of Self-identification has been given the highest place not only in the Upanisads, the Manu-Smṛti, the Gītā, the other chapters of the Mahābhārata, and the Buddhistic religion, but also in other countries and in other religions. The commandment "Thou shalt love thy neighbour as thyself" (Levi. 19. 15; Matthew, 22. 39), to be found in Christian and Jewish religious texts, is nothing but this rule in another form. Christians look upon this as a golden rule, that is to say, as a rule as valuable as gold; but their religion does not explain it by the principle of the unity of the Ātman. The advice of Christ that, "And as ye would that men should do to you, do ye also to them likewise" (Matthew 7. 12; Luke 6. 31) is only a part of the *sūtra* of Self-identification; and the Greek philosopher Aristotle has literally enunciated this same principle of behaviour for men. Aristotle lived about 300 years before Christ, but the Chinese philosopher Khūn-Phū-Tse (corrupted in English into 'Confucius') lived 200 years before

* The word '*sūtra*' is defined as "*alpākṣaram asaṁdigdhaṁ sāravad viśvatomukham | astobham anavadyaṁ ca sūtraṁ sūtravido viduḥ*". Those various meaningless letters which are added in a *mantra* for the purpose of convenience of recitation, without adding to the meaning, are called '*stobhākṣara*' (complementary words). There are no such meaningless words in a *sūtra*, and therefore, the adjective '*astobhaṁ*' has been used in the definition above.

Aristotle, and he has enunciated the above rule of Self-identification by a single word according to the practice of the Chinese language. But, this principle was enunciated in our country, long before Confucius, in the Upaniṣads (Īśa. 6; Kena. 13); and later on in the Bhārata, and the Gītā; and also in the works of Maratha saints by such words as: "like unto oneself I one should consider others" II (Dāsa. 12. 10. 22): and there is also a proverb in Marathi which means, 'one should judge the world by one's own standard'. Not only is this so, but it has been Metaphysically explained by our ancient philosophers. When one realises that (i) religions other than the Vedic religion have not logically justified this generally accepted canon, though they have mentioned it, and (ii) that this canon cannot be logically justified in any way except by the Metaphysical principle of the identification of the Brahman with the Ātman, one will clearly see the importance of the Metaphysical Ethics preached in the Gītā, or the Karma-Yoga.

This easy principle of 'Self-identification', (*ātmaupamya*) which regulates the mutual behaviour of persons living in a society, is so comprehensive, so easy to understand, and so universally accepted, that when once one lays down the rule: "Realise the identity of the Ātman in all created beings, and behave towards others with an equable frame of mind, as if they are yourself", it is no more necessary to lay down such individual commandments as: be kind to others; help others as much as possible; bring about their welfare; put them on the path of advancement; love them; do not get tired of them; do not hurt their feelings; behave towards them with justice and equality; do not deceive any one; do not deprive any one of his wealth or of his life; do not tell any one an untruth; bear always in mind the idea of bringing about the greatest good of the greatest number; behave towards all, looking upon them as the children of one and the same father, and as if they were your brothers etc. Everybody soever naturally understands in what his happiness or unhappiness lies; and, as a result of the family system, he realises the truth of the rule that he must love his wife and children in the same way as he loves himself, according to the doctrines, "*ātmā vai putranāmāsi*" (i. e., "your son is the same as yourself"—Trans.), or "*ardhaṁ bhāryā śarīrasya*" (i. e "your wife is half of your body"—Trans.). But, the ultimate and most comprehensive interpretation of the canon of Self-identification is, that the highest idea of manhood and the most complete fructification of the arrangement of the four states of life consists in: (i) realising that family life is but the first lesson in the science of Self-identification, and (ii) instead of being continually engrossed in the family, making one's Self-identifying Reason more and more comprehensive, by substituting one's friends, one's relations, or those born in the same *gotra* (clan) as oneself, or the inhabitants of one's own village, or the members of one's own community, or one's co-religionists, and ultimately all human beings, or all created beings, in the place of one's family, thereby realising that that Ātman, which is within oneself is also within all created beings; and that one should regulate one's conduct accordingly. And, it then naturally follows that the sacrificial ritual etc., or Karma, which enhances one's capacity to achieve this ideal state, is a purifier of the Mind, and a moral act, that is, such a duty as ought to be performed in the state of a householder. Because, as I have already explained before, the true meaning of the word '*citta-śuddhi*' (purification of the Mind) is the total elimination of selfishness, and the Realisation of the identity of the Brahman and the Ātman; and the writers of the Smṛtis have enjoined the performance of the various duties pertaining to the state of a householder only for that purpose. The same is the deep meaning underlying the advice given by Yājñavalkya to Maitreyī in the words '*ātmā vā are draṣṭavyaḥ*' ('see first who the Ātman is'—Trans.). The philosophy of Karma-Yoga, which has been based on the foundation of the Knowledge of the Supreme Self, advises every one not to limit the extent of the Ātman by saying "*ātmā vai putranāmāsi*"; and says that one should realise the inherent comprehensiveness of the Ātman by feeling that, "*loko vai ayam ātmā*". (i. e., "your Ātman is the whole universe"—Trans.), and that every one should regulate one's activities, believing that "*udāracaritānāṁ tu vasudhaiva kuṭuṁbakam*". i. e., "the whole universe is the family of noble-minded persons". And I am confident that, in this matter, our philosophy of Karma-Yoga will not only be not inferior to any other ancient philosophy of Karma-Yoga, but will even embrace all such philosophies like the Parameśvara, Who has embraced everything and has remained over to the extent of of 'ten fingers'.

But, even to this position an objection is raised by some that: when a man has by this Self-identification acquired the comprehensive Vedāntic vision of "*vasudhaiva kuṭuṁbakam*" (i. e., 'the universe is the family'—Trans.), not only will virtues like pride of one's country, or of one's family or clan, or of one's religion etc., as a result of which some nations have now been fully advanced, be totally destroyed, but even if some one comes to kill us or to harm us, it will become our duty not to kill him in return with a harmful intent, having regard to the words of the Gītā: "*nirvairaḥ sarvabhūteṣu*" (Gī. 11. 55) (i. e., non-inimical towards all created beings—Trans.), (See Dhammapada, 338); and as a result of evil-doers being unchecked, good persons will run the risk of being the victims of evil deeds; and, as a result of the preponderance of evil-doers, the entire society or even a country will be destroyed. It is clearly stated in the Mahābhārata itself that "*na pāpe pratipāpaḥ syāt sādhur eva sadā bhavet*" (Ma. Bhā. Vana. 206. 44), i. e., "do not become an evil-doer in dealing with evil-doers, but behave towards them like a saint"; because, "enmity is never done away with by enmity or by evil-doing"—"*na cāpi vairaṁ vaireṇa keśava vyupaśāmyati*"; that, on the other hand, the man whom we defeat, being inherently evil-minded, becomes more evil-minded as a result of the defeat, and is only waiting for the chance of revenging himself again—"*jayo vairaṁ prasṛjati*"; and that, therefore, it is proper to circumvent evil-doers by peace (Ma. Bhā. Udyo. 71. 59 and 63). And these very stanzas in the Bhārata have been copied in the Buddhistic treatises (See Dhammapada, 5 and 201; Mahāvagga, 10. 2 and 3); and even Christ has repeated the same principle by saying: "Love your enemies" (Matthew, 5. 44), and, "but whosoever shall smite thee on thy right cheek, turn to him the other also" (Matthew, 5. 39), or "And unto him that smiteth thee on the one cheek, offer also the other" (Luke, 6. 29). The same was the advice of the Chinese philosopher Lā-O-Tse, who lived before Christ, and there are even stories of this having been done by Ekanātha Maharaj and others from among our Maratha saints. I have not the slightest intention of belittling the sacred importance of these examples, which show the highest development of the principle of forgiveness or peace. There is no doubt that the religion of Forgiveness will, just like the religion of Truth, always remain permanent and without exception in the ultimate or the most perfect state of society. Nay, we even see in the imperfect condition of our present society, that results are achieved on various occasions by peace, which cannot be achieved by anger. When, in trying to find out what warriors had come forward to help Duryodhana, Arjuna saw venerable persons like ancestors and preceptors among them, he realised that in order to circumvent the evil-doings of Duryodhana, he would have to perform not only Action, but also the difficult action of killing by his weapons those preceptors who had sold themselves for money (Gī. 2. 5); and he began to say, that according to the rule, "*na pāpe pratipāpaḥ syāt*", it was not proper for him to become an evil-doer because Duryodhana had become an evil-doer; and that "even if they kill me, it is proper for me to sit quiet with a 'non-inimical' mind" (Gī. 1. 46). The religion of the Gītā has been propounded solely for solving this doubt of Arjuna; and on that account, we do not anywhere come across an exposition of this subject, similar to the exposition made in the Gītā. For instance, both the Christian and the Buddhistic religions adopt the principle of Non-Enmity, as is done by the Vedic religion; but it is nowhere clearly stated either in the Buddhistic or in the Christian religious treatises,—or at any rate not in so many words—that it is not possible for the conduct of a person, who gives up all Energistic Action and renounces the world, disregarding universal welfare and even self-preservation, to be in all respects the same as the conduct of the Karma-yogin, who, notwithstanding that his Reason has become non-inimical and unattached, takes part in all Energistic activities with that same non-inimical, and unattached Reason. On the other hand, Western moralists find it very difficult to harmonise properly the advice of Non-Enmity given by Christ with worldly morality,* and Nietzsche, a modern German philosopher, has fearlessly stated his opinion in his works, that the ethical principle of Non-Enmity is a slavish and destructive principle, and that the Christian religion, which gives a high place to that principle, has emasculated Europe. But, if one considers our religious treatises, one sees that the idea, that the two ethical and religious courses of Renunciation and Energism are to be distinguished from each other in this matter, was accepted by and was well-known not only to the Gītā but even to Manu. Because, Manu has prescribed the rule, "*krudhyantaṁ na pratikrudhyet*", i. e., "do not become angry in return towards one who has become angry towards you" (Manu. 6. 48), only for Saṁnyāsins, and not for the householder or in regal science. I have shown above in the fifth chapter, that the method adopted by our commentators of mixing up the mutually contradictory doctrines pertaining to the two paths of Renunciation and Karma-Yoga, without taking into account what dictum applies to which path, and how it is to be used, gives rise to a confusion regarding the true doctrine of Karma-Yoga. When one gives up this confusing method adopted by the commentators on the Gītā, one can clearly understand in what sense the word Non-Enmity (*nirvaira*) is understood by the followers of the Bhāgavata religion or Karma-yogins. Because, even Prahlāda, that highest of the devotees of the Blessed Lord, has himself said that, "*tasmān nityaṁ kṣamā tāta paṇḍitair apavāditā*" (Ma. Bhā. Vana. 28. 8), i. e., "therefore, my friend, wise men have everywhere mentioned exceptions to the principle of forgiveness", in order to show how the Karma-yogin householder should behave on these occasions. It is true that the ordinary rule of the doctrine of Self-identification is, that one should not cause harm to others by doing such Actions as, if done to oneself, would be harmful; yet the Mahābhārata has made it clear, that this rule should not be followed in a society, where there do not exist persons who follow the other religious principle, namely, "others should not cause harm

* See Paulsen's *System of Ethics*, Book III, Chap. X (Eng. Trans.) and Nietzsche's *Anti-Christ*.

to us", which is a corollary from this first principle. The word 'equability' is bound up with two individuals, that is, it is relative. Therefore, just as the principle of Non-Violence is not violated by killing an evil-doer, so also is the principle of Self-identification or of Non-Enmity, which is observed by saints, in no way affected by giving condign punishment to evil-doers. On the other hand, they acquire the merit of protecting others by having opposed the injustice of evil-doers. That Parameśvara, than Whom nobody's Reason can be more equable, Himself takes incarnations from time to time for protecting saints and destroying evil-doers, and thereby brings about universal welfare (*lokasaṁgraha*), (Gī. 4. 7 and 8); then how can the case of ordinary persons be different? To say that the distinction between those who are deserving and those who are undeserving, or between what is proper and what improper, disappears, as a result of one's vision having become equable in such a way that he says: '*vasudhaiva kuṭuṁbakam*' (i. e., "the whole world is my family"—Trans.) or of one's giving up the Hope for Fruit of Action, is a confusion of thought. The doctrine of the Gītā is that mine-ness (*mamatva*) is the predominant factor in the Hope for Fruit; and that unless that feeling is given up, one cannot escape the bondage of sin or merit. But, though I may have no object to achieve for myself, I nevertheless commit the sin of helping evil-doers or undeserving persons, and of harming deserving saints and even society itself to that extent, if I allow some one to take that which he ought not to get. Just as, though a multi-millionaire like Kubera goes to purchase vegetables in the market, he does not pay a lakh of rupees for a bundle of coriander leaves, so also does the man, who has reached the state of perfection, not forget the discrimination as to what is good for whom. It is true that his Reason has become equable. But, 'equability' does not mean giving to a man the grass, which is fit for a cow, and to a cow, the food which is proper for a man; and with the same intention, the Blessed Lord has said in the Gītā that that *sāttvika* charity which is to be made as *dātavya*, that is, because it is a duty to give, must be given, considering "*deśe kāle ca pātre ca*", that is, considering the propriety of the place, the time, and the deservingness of the person (Gī. 17. 20). In describing this equable state of mind of saints, Jñāneśvara has compared them to the earth. The earth is also known as "*sarvasahā*" (i. e., one who bears everything—Trans.). But, if this bearer-of-everything earth is given a kick, it proves its 'equability' by giving to the kicker an equally strong counter-kick. This clearly shows how one can make a non-inimical (*nirvaira*) resistance, even when there is no enmity in the heart; and that is why it is stated in the chapter on Causality of Action above (Effect of Karma) that the Blessed Lord remains free from the blame of partiality (*vaiṣamya*), cruelty (*nairghṛṇya*) etc., notwithstanding that He deals with people as: "*ye yathā māṁ prapadyante tāṁs tathaiva bhajāmy aham*" (Gī. 4. 11), i. e., "I give to them reward in the same manner and to the same extent as they worship me". In the same way, in ordinary life and according to law, no one calls the Judge, who directs the execution of a criminal, the enemy of the criminal. According to Metaphysics, when a man's Reason has become desireless and has reached the state of equability, he does not of his own accord do harm to anybody; and if somebody is harmed as a result of something which he does, that harm is the result of the Karma of such other person; or in other words, the desireless Sthitaprajña does not, by the act which he performs in these circumstances—even if it appears as terrible as matricide, or the murder of a preceptor—incur the bondage or the taint of the good or evil effects of the act. (Gī. 4. 14; 9. 28; and 18. 17). The rules of self-defence included in criminal law are based on the same principle. There is a tradition about Manu that when he was requested by people to become a king, he at first said: "I do not wish to become a king for punishing persons who commit sins, and to thereby incur sin"; but when in return, "*tam abruvan prajāḥ mā bhīḥ kartṛneno gamiṣyati* (Ma. Bhā. Śān. 67. 23), that is, "people said to him: 'do not be afraid, the sinner will incur the sin, and you will acquire the merit of having protected the people", and, when on top of it, they further gave him a promise that: "we will give to you by way of taxes that amount which will have to be expended for the protection of the people", he consented to become a king. In short, the natural laws of a reaction being equal in intensity and effect to the action, which is seen in the lifeless world, is translated into the principle of 'measure for measure' in the living world. Those ordinary persons whose Mind has not reached the state of equability, add their feeling of mineness (*mamatva*) to this law of Cause and Effect, and making the counterblow stronger than the blow, take their revenge for the blow; or if the other person is weak, they are ready to take advantage of some trifling or imaginary affront, and rob him to their own advantage, under pretext of retaliation. But, if a man, whose Mind has become free from the feelings of revenge, enmity, or pride, or free from the desire of robbing the weak as a result of anger, avarice, or hatred, or free from the desire of obstinately making an exhibition of one's greatness, authority, or power, which inhabits the minds of ordinary people, merely turns back a stone which has been thrown at him, that does not disturb the peacefulness, non-inimicality, and equability of his Mind; and it is on the other hand his duty, from the point of view of universal welfare, to take such retaliatory action, for the purpose of preventing the predominance of wrong-doers and the consequent persecution of the weak in the world (Gī. 3. 25); and the summary of the entire teaching of the Gītā is that: even the most horrible warfare which may be carried on in these circumstances, with an equable state of mind, is righteous and meritorious. It is not that the Karma-yogin Sthitaprajña disregards the religious doctrines of behaving non-inimically towards everybody, not doing evil to evil-doers, or not getting angry with those who are angry with one. But, instead of accepting the doctrine of the School of Renunciation that 'Non-inimicality' (*nirvaira*) means inactivity or non-retaliation, the philosophy of Karma-Yoga says, that '*nirvaira*' means merely giving up '*vaira*' or 'the desire to do evil'; and that in as much as nobody can escape Karma, one should perform as much Karma as is possible and necessary for retaliation or for social welfare, without entertaining an evil desire, and as a matter of duty, and apathetically, and without Attachment (Gī. 3. 19); and therefore, instead of using the word '*nirvaira*' by itself, the

Blessed Lord has placed the important adjective '*matkarmakṛt*' before it, in the stanza:

matkarmakṛt matparamo madbhaktaḥ saṅgavarjitaḥ ।
nirvairaḥ sarvabhūteṣu yaḥ sa mām eti pāṇḍava ॥
(Gī. 11. 55)

which (word '*matkarmakṛt*') means 'one who performs Action for Me, that is, for the Parameśvara, and with the idea of dedicating it to the Parameśvara'; and the Blessed Lord has thus interlocked non-inimicality with Desireless Action, from the point of view of Devotion. And it has been stated in the Sāṁkarabhāṣya and also in other commentaries that this stanza contains the essential summary of the doctrine of the Gītā. It is nowhere stated in the Gītā that one should give up all kind of Action, in order to make one's mind non-inimical (*nirvaira*), or after it has become non-inimical. When a man in this way performs that amount of Action which is necessary for retaliation non-inimically and with the idea of dedicating it to the Parameśvara, he commits no sin whatsoever; but what is more, when the work of retaliation is over, the desire to wish the good of the person whom he has punished, by Self-identification, does not leave his mind. For example, when Bibhīṣaṇa was unwilling to attend to the obsequial ceremonies of Rāvaṇa, after the sinless and non-inimical Rāmacandra had killed him (Rāvaṇa) in war, on account of his (Rāvaṇa's) evil doings, Śrī Rāmacandra has said to Bibhīṣaṇa:—

maraṇāntāni vairāṇi nivṛttaṁ naḥ prayojanam ।
kriyatām asya saṁskāro mamāpyeṣa yathā tava ॥
(Valmiki Rā. 6. 109. 25)

that is; "the enmity (in the mind of Rāvaṇa) has come to an end with his death. My duty (of punishing evil-doers) has come to an end; now he is my (brother), just as he was your (brother); therefore, consecrate him into the fire". This principle mentioned in the Rāmāyaṇa has also in one place been mentioned in the Bhāgavata (Bhāg. 8. 19. 13); and the same principle is conveyed by the traditions in the Purāṇas that the Blessed Lord had afterwards benevolently given an excellent state to those very evil-doers whom He Himself had killed. Śrī Samartha has used the words "meet impertinence by impertinence" (see p. 524 above—Trans.) on the basis of the same principle; and in the Mahābhārata, Bhīṣma has, on the same principle, said to Paraśurāma:—

yo yathā vartate yasmin tasminn evaṁ pravartayan ।
nādharmaṁ samavāpnoti na cāśreyaś ca vindati ॥

(Ma. Bhā. Udyo. 179.30)

that is, "there is no breach of religion (immorality) in behaving towards another person in the same way as he behaves towards you; nor does one's benefit thereby suffer"; and further on in Satyānṛtādhyāya of the Śāntiparva, the same advice has again been given to Yudhiṣṭhira in the following words:—

yasmin yathā vartate yo manuṣyaḥ
tasmiṁs tathā vartitavyaṁ sa dharmaḥ ।
māyācāro māyayā bādhitavyaḥ
sādhvācāraḥ sādhunā pratyupeyaḥ ॥

(Ma. Bhā. Śān. 109. 29 and Udyo. 36. 7)

that is, "Religion and Morality consist in behaving towards others in the same way as they behave towards us; one must behave deceitfully towards deceitful persons, and in a saintly way towards saintly persons". So also in the Ṛg-veda, Indra has not been found fault with for his deceitfulness, but has on the other hand, been praised in the following words: "*tvaṁ māyābhir anavadya māyinaṁ......vṛtraṁ ardayaḥ* ।" (Ṛg. 10. 147. 2; 1. 80. 7), i. e., "O, sinless Indra! you have by deceit killed Vṛtra, who was himself deceitful"; and the poet Bhāravi has in his drama *Kirātārjunīyam* repeated in the following words the principle enunciated in the Ṛg-veda:

vrajanti te mūḍhadhiyaḥ parābhavam ।
bhavanti māyāviṣu ye na māyinaḥ ॥

(Kirā. 1. 30)

that is, "those, who do not become deceitful in dealing with deceitful persons, are themselves destroyed". But in this place it must also be borne in mind that if it is possible to offer retaliation to an evil-doer by a saintly act, such saintly act should in the first instance be attempted; because, from the fact that the other man has become an evil-doer, it does not follow that one should also become an evil-doer with him, nor does it follow that others should cut their noses because some one has cut his own nose; nay, there is even no Morality in that. This is the true meaning of the canon "*na pāpe pratipāpaḥ syāt*" (i. e., "do not become an evil-doer towards an evil-doer"—Trans.); and for the same reason, Vidura, after having first mentioned to Dhṛtarāṣṭra in the Viduranīti, the ethical principle that, "*na tat parasya saṁdadhyāt pratikūlaṁ yad ātmanaḥ*", i. e., "one should not behave towards others in a way which is undesirable from one's point of view", immediately afterwards says:—

akrodhena jayet krodhaṁ asādhuṁ sādhunā jayet ।
jayet kadaryaṁ dānena jayet satyena cānṛtam ॥

(Ma. Bhā. Udyo. 38. 73, 74)

that is, "the anger (of others) should be conquered, by one's peacefulness; evil-doers should be conquered by saintliness; the miser should be conquered by gifts; and falsehood should be conquered by truth". This stanza has been copied word for word in the Buddhistic treatise on Morality in the Pali language, known as the *Dhammapada*, in the following stanza:—

akkodhena jine kodhaṁ asādhuṁ sādhunā jine ।
jine kadariyaṁ dānena saccen ālikavādinam ॥

(Dhammapada, 223)

and, in the Śāntiparva of the Mahābhārata, Bhīṣma, in counselling Yudhiṣṭhira, has praised this ethical principle in the following terms:—

karma caitad asādhūnāṁ asādhu sādhunā jayet ।
dharmeṇa nidhanaṁ śreyo na jayaḥ pāpakarmaṇā ॥

(Ma. Bhā. Śān. 95. 16)

that is, "the *asādhu*, that is, 'evil' actions of evil-doers (*asādhūnām*) should be counteracted by saintly actions; because, even if death follows as a result of righteousness or Morality, that is better than the victory which follows from a sinful action". But, if the evilness of evil-doers is not circumvented by such saintly actions, or, if the counsel of peacefulness or propriety is not acceptable to such evil-doers, then according to the principle "*kantakenaiva kantakam* (i. e., "take out a thorn by a thorn"—Trans.), it becomes necessary to take out by a needle, that is, by an iron thorn, if not by an ordinary thorn, that thorn which will not come out by the application of poultices (Dāsa. 19.9. 12-31); because, under any circumstances, punishing evil-doers in the interests of general welfare, as was done by the Blessed Lord, is the first duty of saints from the point of view of Ethics. In enunciating the proposition "evilness should be conquered by saintliness", the fact that the conquest of or the protection from evil is the primary duty of a saint, is first taken for granted; and the first step to be taken for attaining that result is mentioned. But, it is nowhere stated by our moral philosophers, that if protection against evil-doers cannot be obtained by saintliness, one should not give 'measure for measure', and protect oneself, but should allow oneself to become a victim of the evil-doings of villains; and it must be borne in mind that, that man who has come forward to cut the throats of others by his own evil-doings, has no more any ethical right to expect that others should behave towards him like saints. Nay, it is clearly stated in our religious treatises, that when a saint is thus compelled to perform some unsaintly Action, the responsibility of such unsaintly Action does not fall on the pure-minded saint, but that the evil-doer must be held responsible for it, as it is the result of his evil doings (Manu. 8. 19 and 351); and the punishment, which was meted out by the Blessed Buddha himself to Devadatta, has been justified in Buddhistic treatises on the same principle (Milinda-Pra. 4. 1. 30-34). In the world of lifeless things, action and re-action always take place regularly and without a hitch. It is true that as the activities of a man are subject to his desires, and also, as the ethical knowledge necessary for deciding when to use the *trailokya-cintāmaṇi-mātrā* (infallible remedy) in dealing with evil-doers, is very subtle, even a meritorious person is at times in doubt as to whether that which he would like to do is right or wrong, moral or immoral—"*kiṁ karma kim akarmeti kavayopy atra mohitāḥ*" (Gī. 4. 16), (i. e., " what should be done and what should not be done is a question which puzzles even learned persons"—Trans.). On these occasions, the right thing to do is to take as authoritative the decision which is arrived at by the pure mind of a saint, who has reached the highest state of complete equability of Reason, instead of depending on the wisdom of wise persons, who are always more or less subject to selfish desires, or merely on one's own powers of reasoning and discrimination; because, as arguments and counter-arguments wax in direct ratio with the power of inferential logic, these difficult questions are never truly or satisfactorily solved by mere wisdom, and without the help of pure Reason; and one has to seek the shelter and protection of a pure and desireless preceptor to arrive at such a solution. The Reason of those law-givers, who are universally respected, has become pure in this way; and, therefore, the Blessed Lord has said to Arjuna in the Bhagavadgītā that:—"*tasmāc chāstraṁ pramāṇaṁ te kāryā-kāryaṁ-vyavasthitau*" (Gī. 16. 24), i. e., "in discriminating between what should be done and what should not be done, you must look to the authority of the religious and moral treatises". At the same time, it must not be forgotten, that saintly law-givers like Śvetaketu, who come later in point of time, acquire the authority of effecting changes even in these religious principles.

The prevalent misconception regarding the conduct in life of non-inimical and peaceful saints is due to the fact that the Path of Karma-Yoga is now practically extinct, and the Path of Renunciation, which considers all worldly life as discardable, is on all hands being looked upon as superior. The Gītā neither advises nor intends that when one becomes non-inimical, one should also become non-retaliatory. To that man who does not care for universal welfare, it is just the same whether or not evil-doers predominate in the world, and whether or not he continues to live. But, the philosophy of

Karma-Yoga teaches us that though the Karma-yogins, who have reached the most perfect state, behave non-inimically towards all created beings, recognising the identity of the Ātman in all, they never fail to do that duty which has befallen them according to their own status in life, after discriminating between who is worthy and who unworthy, with a frame of mind, which is unattached; and that any Action which is performed in this manner, does not in the least prejudicially affect the equability of Reason of the doer. When this principle of the Karma-Yoga in the Gītā has been accepted, one can properly account for and justify the pride of one's family, the pride of one's country, or other similar duties on the basis of that principle. Although the ultimate doctrine of this philosophy is that, that is to be called Religion which leads to the benefit of the entire human race, nay of all living beings, yet, as pride of one's family, pride of one's religion, and pride of one's country are the ascending steps which lead to that highest of all states, they never become unnecessary. Just as the worship of the qualityful (*saguṇa*) Brahman is necessary in order to attain to the qualityless (*nirguṇa*) Brahman, so also is the ladder of pride of one's family, pride of one's community, pride of one's religion, pride of one's country etc. necessary in order to acquire the feeling of "*vasudhaiva kuṭuṁbakam*" (i. e., "the whole universe is the family"—Trans.); and as every generation of society climbs up this ladder, it is always necessary to keep this ladder intact. In the same way, if persons around one, or the other countries around one's country, are on a lower rung of this ladder, it is not possible for a man to say that he will always remain alone on a higher rung of the ladder; because, as has been stated above, those persons who are on the higher steps of that ladder, have occasionally to follow the principle of 'measure for measure', in order to counteract the injustice of those who are on the lower steps. There is no doubt that the state of every human being in the world, will improve gradually and reach the stage when every one realises the identity of the Ātman in every created being. At any rate, it is not improper to entertain the hope of creating such a frame of mind in every human being. But, it naturally follows that so long as every one has not reached this ultimate state of development of the Ātman, saints must, having regard to the state of other countries or other societies, preach the creed of pride of one's country etc., which will for the time being be beneficial to their own societies. Besides, another thing, which must also be borne in mind is that, as it is not possible to do away with the lower floors of a building, when the higher floors are built; or, as the pick-axe does not cease to be necessary, because one has got a sword in one's hand; or, as fire does not cease to become necessary, because one has also got the Sun, so also does patriotism, or the pride of one's family, not become unnecessary, although one has reached the topmost stage of the welfare of all created things. Because, considering the matter from the point of view of the reform of society, that specific function, which is performed by the pride of one's family, cannot be got merely out of pride of one's country, and the specific function, which is performed by the pride of one's country, is not achieved by the Realisation of the identity of the Ātman in all created beings. In short, even in the highest state of society, patriotism and pride of one's family and other creeds are always necessary to the same extent as Equability of Reason. But, as one nation is prepared to cause any amount of harm to another nation for its own benefit, on the basis that the pride of one's own country is the only and the highest ideal, such a state of things is not possible if the benefit of all created beings is looked upon as such ideal. If there is a conflict between the pride of one's family, the pride of one's country, and ultimately the benefit of the entire human kind, then, according to the important and special preaching of that Ethics, which is replete with Equability of Reason, duties of a lower order should be sacrificed for duties of a higher order. When Vidura was advising Dhṛtarāṣṭra, that rather than not give a share of the kingdom to the Pāṇḍavas, at the desire of Duryodhana, and thereby run the risk of the whole clan being destroyed in the resulting war, he (Dhṛtarāṣṭra) should give up the single individual Duryodhana, though Duryodhana was his son, if he was obstinate, he (Vidura) in support of that position has said:

tyajed ekaṁ kulasyārthe grāmasyārthe kulaṁ tyajet ।
grāmaṁ janapadasyārthe ātmārthe pṛthivīṁ tyajet ॥
(Ma. Bhā. Ādi. 115. 36; Sabhā. 61. 11)

that is, "for protecting a family, one person may be abandoned; for protecting a town, a family may be abandoned; for the protection of society, a town may be abandoned; and for the protection of the Ātman, even the earth may be abandoned". The principle mentioned above is borne out by the first three parts of this stanza, and the fourth part of the stanza enunciates the principle of the protection of the Ātman. As the word 'Ātman' is a common pronoun, this doctrine of Self-protection applies to a united society, community, country, or empire, in the same way as it applies to an individual; and when one considers the rising gradation of one man for a family, a family for a town, a town for a country, etc., one sees clearly that the word 'Ātman' must be considered to carry a higher value than all the other things. Nevertheless, some selfish persons, or persons unacquainted with ethical principles, sometimes interpret this part of the stanza in quite a perverse way, that is to say, as importing merely selfishness; it is, therefore, necessary to mention here that this principle of the protection of the Ātman is not the same as the principle of selfishness. Because, these moral philosophers who have declared the path advocated by the self-worshipper Cārvāka as devilish (See, Gī. chap. 16) cannot preach to any one the destruction of the universe for one's own selfish interests. The word '*arthe*' in the above stanza does not indicate merely a selfish interest, but must be interpreted as meaning 'for defending oneself against a calamity, if it has come'; and the same meaning is to be found in dictionaries. There is a world of difference between selfishness and protection of the Self (Ātman). Causing the detriment of others, being inspired by the desire of enjoying objects of pleasure, or by avarice, and for one's own benefit is selfishness. This is inhuman and forbidden, and it is stated in the first three parts of the above stanza, that one must always consider the benefit of the multitude, rather than of an individual. Yet, as there is one and the same Ātman in all created things, everyone has an inherent natural right of being happy in this world; and no single individual or society in the world can ever ethically acquire the right to cause the detriment of another individual or society by disregarding this universal, important, and natural right, merely because the one is more than the other in numbers, or in strength, or because the one has a larger number of means than the other for conquering the other. If, therefore, some one seeks to justify the selfish conduct of a society, which is bigger in numbers than another society, on the ground that the benefit of a larger multitude, is of higher importance than the benefit of an individual or of a smaller multitude, such a method of reasoning must be looked upon as demonical (*rākṣasī*). Therefore, the fourth part of the stanza says, that if other people behave unjustly in this way, then the inherent ethical right of everybody of protecting himself, is of higher importance than the benefit of a larger multitude; nay, of even the whole world; and this has been mentioned along with the matter explained in the first three parts of the stanza, as an important exception to the principle enunciated in them. Further, it must also be realised, that one can bring about universal welfare only if one lives; therefore, even considering the matter from the point of view of universal benefit, one has to say with Viśvāmitra that "*jīvan dharmam avāpnuyāt*", i. e., "one can think of Morality, only if one remains alive"; or, with Kālidāsa that, "*śarīram ādyaṁ khalu dharmasādhanam*" (Kumā. 5. 33), i. e., "the body is the fundamental means of bringing about Morality"; or, with Manu, that, "*ātmānaṁ satataṁ rakṣet*", i. e., "one should always protect oneself". But although this right of self-protection thus becomes higher than the benefit of the world, yet, as has been mentioned above in the second chapter, saints are, of their own will, willing on several occasions to sacrifice their lives for their family, or country, or religion, or for the good of others; and the same principle has been enunciated in the three parts of the above stanza. As on these occasions, the man of his own free will sacrifices his important right of self-protection, the ethical value of such an act is considered higher than that of all other acts. Yet, it becomes quite clear from the story of Dhṛtarāṣṭra mentioned above, that mere learning or logic is not sufficient to rightly determine whether such an occasion has arisen, and that in order to arrive at a correct decision on that matter, the inner consciousness (*antaḥkaraṇa*) of the person, who wishes to decide, must first have become pure and equable. It is not that Dhṛtarāṣṭra was so feeble-minded as not to understand the advice which was given by Vidura. But, as has been stated in the Mahābhārata itself, his Reason could not become equable as a result of his love for his son. Just as Kubera is never in need for a lakh of rupees, so the man whose Mind has become equable, experiences no dearth of the feeling of the identity of the Ātman in the members of a family, or a country, or in co-religionists, or any other inferior orders of identities. All these identities are included in the identity of the Brahman and the Ātman; and saints carry on the maintenance and welfare of the world by preaching to different persons either their duty to their country, or their duty to their family, or other narrow religions, or the comprehensive religion of universal welfare, as may be meritorious for a particular person on a particular occasion, according to the state of his Reason, or for his own protection. It is true that in the present state of the human race, patriotism has become the highest religion; and even civilised countries utilise their learning, skill, and money, in contemplating on and preparing for the destruction of as large a number of persons in as short a time as possible, from a neighbouring inimical country, as soon as the occasion arises. But Spencer, Comte, and other philosophers have distinctly maintained in their works, that one cannot, on that account, look upon that as the highest ethical ideal of the human race; and I do not understand how that objection, which has not been raised to the doctrine preached by them, can become effective as against the doctrine of the identity of the Ātman in all created beings, which arises from our Metaphysical philosophy. As, when the child is young, one has to make its clothes as will fit its body—or perhaps slightly bigger, because it is growing—so also is the case with the Realisation of identity of the Ātman in all created beings. Be it a society or an individual, if the ideal placed before it, in the shape of the identity of the Ātman in all created beings, is consistent with the spiritual qualification of that individual or society, or at most a little advanced, it will be beneficial to it; but if one asks that society or individual to achieve some thing, how excellent soever, which is more than it can accomplish, it will never be benefited by it. That is why the worship of the Parabrahman has been prescribed in the Upaniṣads by rising gradations, though in fact the Parabrahman is not circumscribed by any grades; and though a warrior class is not necessary in a society in which every one has reached the state of a Sthitaprajña, yet, our religion has included that caste in the arrangement of the four castes, having regard to the contemporary state of other societies in the world, and on the basis of the principle "*ātmānaṁ satataṁ rakṣet*" (i.e., "protect yourself at all timse"—Trans.); and even in that highest and ideal state of society which has been mentioned in his works by the Greek philosopher Plato, the highest importance has been given to the class which becomes proficient in warfare by constant practice, because that class occupies the position of protectors of society. This will clearly show that though philosophers are always immersed in the contemplation of the highest and purest of ideas, they never fail to take into account the then prevailing imperfect state of society.

When all things have been considered in this way, it becomes clear that the true duty of scients is (i) to keep their own Reason free from objects of pleasure, peaceful, non-inimical, and equable, by Realising the identity of the Brahman and the Ātman; and (ii) without getting disgusted with ordinary ignorant people, because they themselves have attained this high state of mind, and without perverting the Reason of such ordinary people, by themselves abandoning worldly duties and accepting the state of Abandonment of Action (*karma-saṁnyāsa*), to preach to people whatever is proper for them, having regard to prevailing conditions, and to place before their eyes the living example of a model moral life, in the shape of their own desireless adherence to duty; and (iii) in that way to place all on the path of betterment, as gradually and peacefully as possible, but at the same time enthusiastically. This is what is done by the Blessed Lord by taking various incarnations from time to time; and the sum and substance of the entire philosophy of the Gītā is, that scients should follow the same example, and should at all times continue to do their duty in this world desirelessly, and to the best of their abilities, and with a pure mind, and without an eye to the Fruit; that they should be willing to lay down their lives, if necessary, while they are doing so (Gī. 3. 35); and that they must not under any circumstances fail in their duty. This is what is known as universal welfare (*lokasaṁgraha*); and this is the true Karma-Yoga. It was only when the Blessed Lord had explained to Arjuna this wisdom about what should be done and what should not be done, on the basis of Vedānta, simultaneously with explaining Vedānta to him, that Arjuna, who at first was on the point of giving up warfare and taking up the life of a mendicant, was later on ready to participate in the terrible war—not only because the Blessed Lord asked him to do so, but voluntarily. This principle of the equable Reason of the Sthitaprajña (Steady-in-Mind), which had been preached to Arjuna, being the fundamental basis of the philosophy of Karma-Yoga, I have in this chapter taken that as a hypothesis, and after having explained how the highest principles of Ethics are justified and explained on the basis of that principle, I have afterwards shortly stated the prominent parts of the philosophy of Karma-Yoga, such as: how people should behave towards each other in society from the point of view of Self-Identification; what modifications become necessary in the principles of Absolute Ethics, as a result of the law of 'measure for measure', or as a result of the worthiness or unworthiness of the person one has to deal with; as also how saints living in morally imperfect societies have to follow principles of morality, which are exceptions to the general principles etc. If the same method of argument is applied to the questions of justice, charity, philanthropy, kindness, non-violence, truth, not-stealing and other eternal principles, and if even a separate treatise is written on each of these subjects, in order to show what modifications will have to be made in the case of each of them, as occasion arises, consistently with the present morally imperfect state of society, they will not be exhausted; and that is also not the principal object of the Bhagavadgītā. I have, in the second chapter of this book, touched on the questions of how a conflict arises between Non-Violence and Truth, or Truth and Self-Protection, or Self-Protection and Peacefulness etc., and how, on that account, there arises at times a doubt as to what should be done and what should not be done. It is clear, that on such occasions, saints make a careful discrimination between 'ethical principles,' 'ordinary worldly affairs,' 'self-interest', 'benefit of all created things' etc., and then arrive at a decision as to what should be done and what should not be done; and this fact has been definitely stated by the *śyena* bird to king Śibi in the Mahābhārata; and the English writer Sidgwick has, in his Book on Ethics, propounded the same principle in great detail, and by giving many examples; but the inference drawn from this fact by several Western philosophers, that the accurate balancing of self-interest and other's-interest, is the only basis for determining ethical laws, has never been accepted by our philosophers; because, according to our philosophers, this discrimination is very often so subtle and so '*anaikāntika*', that is, so productive of so many conclusions, that unless the Equability of realising that 'the other man is the same as myself', has been thoroughly impressed on one's mind, it is impossible to arrive at an invariably correct discrimination between what should be done and what should not be done, merely by inferential reasoning; and if one does so, it will be a case of 'the pea-hen tries to dance because the the peacock dances'. This is the main drawback in the arguments of Western Utilitarians like Mill and others. If because an eagle, swooping down, takes a lamb in its claws high up in the air, a crow also attempts to do so, he is sure to come to grief; therefore, the Gītā says, that it is not sufficient to place reliance merely on the outward devices adopted by saints; and that one must depend on the principle of an equable Reason, which is always alive in their hearts; and that Equability of Reason is the true root of the philosophy of Karma-Yoga. Some modern Materialistic philosophers maintain that SELF-INTEREST is the basic foundation of Ethics; whereas others give that place to

PHILANTHROPY, that is, 'the greatest good of the greatest number'. But I have shown above in the fourth chapter, that these principles, which touch merely the external results of Action, do not meet all situations; and that one has necessarily to consider to what extent the Reason of the doer is pure. It is true that the discrimination between the outward effects of Action, is a sign of wisdom and far-sightedness. But, far-sightedness is not synonymous with Ethics; and, therefore, our philosophers have come to the conclusion that the true basis of Proper Action does not lie in the mere mercenary process of discriminating between different external Actions; and that the HIGHEST IDEAL *(paramārtha)* in the shape of Equability of Reason, is the fundamental basis of Ethics; and one comes to the same conclusion if one properly considers what the most perfect state of the Personal Self *(jīvātman)*, is ; because, though many persons are adepts in the art of robbing each other by avarice, nobody says that this cleverness, or the futile Knowledge of the Brahman, consisting of knowing in what 'the greatest good of the greatest number' lies, is the highest ideal of everyone in this world. That man alone is the highest of men, whose Reason is pure. Nay; one may even say that the man, who, without having a stainless, non-inimical, and pure mind, is only engrossed in the calculating discrimination between outward Actions, runs the risk of becoming a hypocrite (See Gī. 3. 6). If one accepts Equability of Reason as the basis of the philosophy of Karma-Yoga, this objection does not arise. It is true that by taking Equability of Reason as the fundamental basis, one has to consult saints for determining between morality and immorality, in circumstances of exceptional difficulty; but there is no help for that. Just as when a man is down with a very serious illness, its diagnosis or treatment is impossible without the help of a clever doctor, so also will it be futile for an ordinary person to proudly imagine that he will be able to arrive at a faultless decision between morality and immorality, without the help of saints, and merely on the basis of the principle of 'the greatest good of the greatest number', when there is a difficult and doubtful situation. One must always increase Equability of Reason by constant practice; and when the minds of all the human beings in the world gradually reach the state of perfect Equability in this way, the Kṛtayuga will start, and the highest ideal or the most perfect state of the human race will be reached by everyone. The philosophy of the Duty and Non-Duty has been evolved for this purpose; and, therefore, the edifice of that philosophy must also be based on the foundation of Equability of Reason. But, even if one does not go so deep as that, but only considers Ethics from the point of view of the test of public opinion, the theory of Equability of Reason expounded in the Gītā, is seen to be more valuable and more consistent with fundamental principles, than the Western Materialistic or Intuitionist philosophies, as will be apparent from the comparative examination of these different principles made by me later on in the fifteenth chapter. But, before coming to that subject, I shall deal with one important part of the explanation of the import of the Gītā, which still remains to be dealt with.

CHAPTER XIII.

THE PATH OF DEVOTION.

(BHAKTI-MĀRGA).

sarva dharmān parityajya mām ekaṁ śaraṇaṁ vraja ।
ahaṁ tvā sarvapāpebhyo mokṣayiṣyāmi mā śucaḥ ॥ *

(Gī. 18. 66).

I have so far dealt, from the Metaphysical point of view, with the question of how the Desireless Realisation of the identity of the Ātman in all created beings, which is instilled into the body, is the foundation of the Karma-Yoga and of Release; and of how this pure Reason is acquired by Realising the identity of the Ātman and the Brahman; and why every one must, so long as life lasts, perform the duties, which have befallen him according to his status in life, with his pure Reason. But, the subject-matter preached in the Bhagavadgītā is not thereby exhausted; because, although there is no doubt that the Realisation of the identity of the Brahman and the Ātman is the only true Reality and the ideal, and that "there is nothing in the world which is equally holy" (Gī. 4. 38), yet, in as much as the consideration of that subject-matter, which has been made so far, as also the path or manner of acquiring that Equability of Reason, is wholly dependent on the Reason itself, ordinary persons feel a doubt as to how one can acquire that keenness of Intelligence by which that path or manner can be fully realised, and whether if somebody's Reason is not so keen, that man must be considered as lost; and such a doubt is certainly not ill-founded. They say: if even the greatest of Jñānins have to say '*neti, neti*' (i. e., 'It is not this, It is not that'—Trans.) in describing that your immortal highest Brahman (Parabrahman), which is clothed in the perishable Name-d and Form-ed Māyā, how are ordinary persons like us to understand it? Therefore, why should any one be found fault with

---

* "Give up all kinds of religions (*dharma*), that is, means of attaining the Parameśvara, and surrender yourself to Me alone. I shall redeem you from all sins, do not be afraid". See the explanation of the meaning of this stanza at the end of this chapter.

if he asks to be shown some easy path or manner, by following which this deep knowledge of the Brahman can come within the periphery of his limited receptiveness? It is stated in the Gītā and in the Kaṭhopaniṣad that though there are many who, being struck by astonishment, describe their experience of the Ātman (that is, of the Brahman), and though there are others who listen to that description, yet, no one understands that Ātman (Gī. 2. 29; Kaṭha. 2. 7); and there is even a very instructive story about this in one place in the Śruti texts. In this story, there is a description that when Bāṣkali asked Bāhva the question: " My lord, explain to me, please, what the Brahman is", Bāhva would not give any answer. Though Bāṣkali repeated that question, Bāhva was still silent. When this had happened three or four times, Bāhva said to Bāṣkali: "I have been all this while giving an answer to your question, and yet you do not understand it. What more can I do? The form of the Brahman cannot be described in any way, and therefore, remaining quiet and not giving any description of it, is the truest description of the Brahman. Have you now understood it?" (Ve. Sū. Śāṁ. Bhā. 3. 2. 17). In short, how is a man possessing only an ordinary Reason to realise this indescribable, unimaginable Parabrahman, which is absolutely different from the visible world (*dṛśyasṛṣṭi-vilakṣaṇa*), and which can be described only by keeping quiet, which can be seen only after the eyes have ceased to see, and which can be Realised only after one has ceased to Realise? (Kena. 2. 11); and how is a man to thereby acquire the state of Equability and afterwards attain Release? If there is no means except a keen intelligence for realising by personal experience and in all its bearings, the form of the Parameśvara described by the words "there is only one Ātman in all created beings", and for thereby attaining the highest excellence, then, millions of people in the world must give up the hope of attaining the Brahman, and sit quiet; because, highly intelligent people are necessarily always few. If one says that it will be enough to place reliance on what these scients say, we come across numerous differences of opinion even among the scients. Besides, if one says that it is enough to merely place such reliance, it necessarily follows that the path of 'faith' or 'belief' is open for acquiring this recondite Knowledge, in addition to the path of Reason; and really speaking, it will be seen that Knowledge does not become complete or even fruitful without Religious Faith (*śraddhā*). That all Knowledge is acquired merely by Intelligence, and that no other mental faculties are necessary for that purpose is an idle belief of certain philosophers, whose minds have become crude as a result of life-long contact with sciences based on inferential reasoning. For instance, let us take the proposition that, ' to-morrow morning the Sun will rise again '. We think that the knowledge contained in this proposition is absolutely immutable. Why? Because, we and our ancestors have seen this occurrence going on uninterruptedly so long. But, if one considers the matter deeply enough, it will be seen that the fact that one and one's ancestors have so far seen the Sun rising daily can never become a reason for the Sun to rise to-morrow, that the Sun does not rise every day in order that one should see it rise, nor because one sees it rise; and that the reasons for the Sun to rise are quite different. And if the fact that you see the Sun rise every day, cannot be a reason for the Sun to rise to-morrow, what guarantee is there that the Sun will rise to-morrow? After a particular occurrence has been observed to take place in the case of a particular thing for a GREAT LENGTH of TIME, concluding that that occurrence will continue in future PERMANENTLY is a kind of Faith; and although we may give it the high sounding name of 'inference', yet, it must be borne in mind that this inference is not an inference based on a consideration of Cause and Effect, and arrived at by the Intelligence, but is fundamentally based on Faith. The inference drawn by us that because Rāmā finds sugar sweet, Somā will also find it sweet, is, as a matter of fact, fundamentally of the same nature; because, though it is true that our Intelligence actually experiences the knowledge that sugar is sweet, yet, when we go beyond that, and say that all persons find sugar sweet, we have to combine Faith with Intelligence. In the same way, it need not be told that in order to understand the principle of Geometry, that it is possible to have two straight lines which will never touch each other, however far they may be extended, one has to go beyond the bounds of all personal experience, with the help of Faith. Besides, all the activities of the world go on with the help of inherent mental faculties like Faith, Love etc., and Intelligence does nothing beyond controlling these mental faculties. I have explained above in the chapter on the Body and the Ātman, that when once the good or bad nature of any particular thing has been ascertained by the Intelligence, the further execution of that decision has to be carried out with the help of the Mind or of the mental faculties. Therefore, in order to perfect the knowledge which has been acquired by Intelligence, and in order that that knowledge should be translated by means of the Intelligence into behaviour and action, such knowledge has always to rely on Faith, Kindness, Affection, Love of Duty, and other inherent mental tendencies; and that knowledge which does not rely on the help of these mental tendencies after they have been awakened and purified, must be looked upon as bare, incomplete, perversely inferential, and barren or immature. Just as the bullet in a gun cannot be fired without the help of gunpowder, so also can the knowledge acquired merely by Intelligence not redeem any one without the help of mental qualities like Love, Faith, etc.; and this principle was fully known to our ancient Ṛsis. For example, it is stated in the Chāndogya that in order to prove to Śvetaketu that the imperceptible and subtle Parabrahman is the fundamental cause of the visible world, his father asked him to bring the fruit of a banian tree (*vaṭa-vṛkṣa*), and to see what was inside. When Śvetaketu had cut open that fruit and seen inside, he said: "there are innumerable minute seeds or grains inside." When his father again said to him: "take one of those seeds, and tell me what is inside it", Śvetaketu replied: "I see nothing inside the seed". To that his father replied: "O my son, this tremendous banian tree (*vaṭa-vṛkṣa*) has sprung from that nothing which you see inside"; and his father has ultimately said to him, "*śraddhasva*", i. e., "put faith in this", that is, "do not merely keep this idea in your Mind, and say 'yes' to my face, but go beyond it; in short, let this principle be impressed on your heart, and let it be translated into your actions" (Chān. 6. 12). If Faith is ultimately necessary in order to obtain the definite knowledge that the Sun is going to rise to-morrow morning, then it undoubtedly follows that after having gone by the cart-road of Intelligence as far as possible for completely Realising the eternal, unending, all-causing, all-knowing, independent, and vital Principle, Which is the root of the entire universe, one has to go further, at least to some extent, by the foot-path of Faith and Affection. That woman whom a man looks upon as venerable and worshipful, because she is his mother, is looked upon by others as an ordinary woman, or according to the scientific camouflage of words of Logicians, she is "*garbhadhāraṇaprasavādi strītva-sāmānyāvacchedakāvacchinnavyaktiviśeṣaḥ*". From this simple example, one can easily understand the difference brought about by pouring the Knowledge acquired by mere inference, into the mould of Faith and Affection; and for this very reason, it is stated in the Gītā that "the most excellent Karma-Yogin from among all, is the one who has Faith" (Gī 6. 47); and, as has been stated above, there is also a theorem of the Philosophy of the Absolute Self that, "*acintyāḥ khalu ye bhāvāḥ na tāṁs tarkeṇa cintayet*", i. e., "the form of those objects which, being beyond the organs, cannot be imagined, should not be determined merely by the help of inference".

If the only difficulty were that the qualityless Parabrahman is difficult to Realise for ordinary persons, then, that difficulty could be overcome by Faith or confidence, though there might be a difference of opinion among the intelligent persons; because, in that case we could judge for ourselves which of these intelligent persons was more reliable, and put faith in his statements (Gī. 13. 25). In logic, this course is known as '*āpta-vacana-pramāṇa*' (i. e., "belief in the statements of a credible person"—Trans.). '*āpta*' means a reliable person. If we look at the affairs of the world, we see that hundreds of persons carry on their activities, relying on the statements of trustworthy persons. There will be very few persons who will be in a position to explain scientifically why two into five is equal to ten and not seven, or why when a second figure one is placed after the first figure one, we get eleven, and not two. Nevertheless, the affairs of the world are going on in the belief by Faith that these statements are true. We will come across very few persons who will have an actual personal knowledge of the fact whether the height of the Himalayas is five miles or ten miles ; yet, if some one asks us what the height of the Himalayas is, the figure of "23000 feet", learnt by heart by us in school from books on Geography at once escapes from our lips! Then, if some one says to us : 'describe the nature of the Brahman', what is the objection to our saying : 'it is qualityless'? Although the ordinary man in the street may not have sufficient intelligence to investigate into whether or not it is really qualityless, and to discuss the pros and cons, yet, Faith is not such a quality that it is possessed only by persons of the highest intelligence. Even the most ignorant man has no dearth of faith, and if he carries on all his numerous affairs with the help of Faith, there is not the slightest difficulty in the way of his believing by Faith that the Brahman is qualityless. Even if one considers the history of the doctrine of Release, it will be seen that even before Jñānins had come to the conclusion that the Brahman is qualityless, after having analysed its nature and form, man had by Faith come to the conclusion that there was, at the bottom of the created universe, some Principle far different from and stranger than the perishable and mutable things in the world, Which was eternal, immortal, independent, omnipotent, omniscient, and all-pervasive ; and he had been worshipping it in some form or other. It is true that he could not at that time explain or justify this Knowledge ; but even in the Material sciences, the rule is that the experience comes first, and the explanation or justification of it comes afterwards. For instance, before Bhāskarācārya discovered the principle of gravity of the earth, and ultimately Newton discovered the principle of gravity of the entire universe, the fact that the fruit from a tree falls down to the earth, was known to every one from times immemorial. The same argument applies to Metaphysics. It is true that the purpose of Intelligence is to analyse the Knowledge which has been acquired by Faith, and to give an explanation of it ; but though a proper explanation of that Realisation is not forthcoming, it cannot, on that account, be said that the Knowledge which has been acquired by Faith is a mere illusion.

If it were enough merely to believe that the Brahman is qualityless, there is no doubt that that could be done merely by Faith as stated above (Gī. 13. 25). But, as has been stated at the end of the ninth chapter, the bare Realisation that the Brahman is qualityless, is not enough to enable a person to reach his highest ideal in this world, namely, the Brāhmī state or the state of the Siddha (Perfect). That Knowledge must be made to permeate the heart and the bodily organs by means of intense practice and continual habit, and the Realisation of the identity of the Brahman and the Ātman must become an inherent nature, by means of constant behaviour consistent with that idea; and the only way for achieving that result is to imbibe the nature and form of the Parameśvara by Love, and to make one's mind uniform with the Parameśvara. This measure or method has been in vogue in our country from times immemorial, and it is known as Worship (*upāsanā*) or Devotion (*bhakti*). The Śāṇḍilya-Sūtra defines 'Bhakti' as: "*sā (bhaktiḥ) parānuraktir Īśvare*", i.e., '*bhakti*' is the '*para*,' that is, the most intense love towards the Īśvara" (Śāṇ. Sū. 2). '*para*' does not mean only 'most intense'; but it must also be purposeless (*nirhetuka*), that is, it must not be for this or that purpose, but unselfish and immutable. It is stated in the Bhāgavata-Purāṇa that it must be "*ahetukya-vyavahitā yā bhaktiḥ puruṣottame*" (Ma. Bhā. 3. 29. 12); because, when the Devotion is purposeful (*sahetuka*), and the man says: "O, God! give me a particular thing," it, to some extent, acquires a mercenary appearance like the Desireful Vedic sacrificial ritual. When Devotion thus becomes mercenary or *rājasa*, one does not thereby acquire purification of the Mind; and if the purification of the Mind is not complete, Metaphysical excellence or the obtaining of Release is to that extent prejudiced. As the principle of total desirelessness, which is part of the philosophy of the Highest Self (*adhyātma-śāstra*), thus also finds a place in the Path of Devotion, the Gītā has divided the devotees of the Blessed Lord into four classes, and has stated that the Devotee, who worships the Parameśvara, '*arthārthi*', that is, 'with some particular motive', is of a lower order, and the Jñānin, who like Nārada and others, worships the Blessed Lord merely as a matter of duty, like other desireless

Actions, though he has Realised the Parameśvara and has, therefore, nothing more to obtain (Gī. 3. 18) is the most excellent of all (Gī. 7. 16-18). This Devotion is of nine kinds according to the Bhāgavata-Purāṇa as follows :—

śravaṇaṁ kīrtanaṁ viṣṇoḥ smaraṇaṁ pādasevanam ı
arcanaṁ vandanaṁ dāsyaṁ sakhyaṁ ātmanivedanam ıı
(Bhāg. 7. 5. 23).

(that is: "listening to the praise of Viṣṇu, praising Him, thinking of Him, serving at His feet, worshipping Him, bowing down before Him, being His slave, loving Him, and dedicating oneself to Him "—Trans.); and in the Bhakti-Sūtra by Nārada, it is divided into eleven classes. But, as all these kinds of Devotion have been described in detail in the Dāsabodha and other Marathi books, I will not further discuss them here. Whatever may be the nature of the Devotion, it is clear that the ordinary purpose of Devotion, namely, of cultivating an intense and Desireless love for the Parameśvara, and forming one's mental tendencies accordingly, must be carried out by every man with the help of his Mind; because, as has been explained by me above in the sixth chapter, the internal organ of Intelligence does nothing beyond deciding between what is good or bad, righteous or unrighteous, and performable or unperformable; and all the other mental functions have to be carried out by the Mind itself. Therefore, we now arrive at the Dual division, (i) the Mind, and (ii) the object of worship, that is to say, the object which is to be loved; but that most excellent form of the Brahman, which has been advocated in the Upaniṣads, is beyond the organs, imperceptible, eternal, qualityless, and '*ekamevādvitīyam*' (i. e., 'one alone, without a second'—Trans.); and therefore, one cannot start one's worship with the Brahman. Because, when one Realises this excellent form of the Brahman, the Mind does not any more remain a separate entity, and, as has been stated before in the chapter on the Philosophy of the Absolute Self, the worshipper and the worshipped, or the Knower (*jñātā*) and the Knowable (*jñeya*) both become uniform. The qualityless Brahman is the ultimate goal, it is not the means to be employed for reaching the goal;

and unless the mind acquires, by some means or other, the capacity of becoming unified with the qualityless Brahman, one cannot personally get a vision of this excellent form of the Brahman. Therefore, the Form of the Brahman which has to be taken for the Devotion or Worship to be performed, as a means of Realising the Brahman, is of the second order, that is to say, it is the qualityful *(saguṇa)* form, which can be Realised by the Mind, on account of the difference between the worshipper and the worshipped; and therefore, wherever the worship of the Brahman has been prescribed in the Upaniṣads, the Brahman to be worshipped has been described as qualityful, notwithstanding that it is imperceptible. For example, although that Brahman, of which the worship has been prescribed in the Śāṇḍilya-Vidyā, is imperceptible, that is, formless, yet, it is stated in the Chāndogyopaniṣad, that it must possess existence *(satya-saṁkalpa)*, and also all such faculties as smelling *(gandha)*, tasting *(rasa)*, and acting *(karma)*, which are perceptible to the Mind (Chān. 3. 14). Although the Brahman to be worshipped is in this case qualityful, yet, it is imperceptible *(avyakta)*, that is, formless *(nirākāra)*. But, the natural formation of the human Mind is such that man finds it extremely difficult, or almost impossible, to love or to make his mind uniform, by meditation and concentration, with an object from even among the qualityful objects, which is imperceptible, that is, which, having no definite form, smell, etc., is, on that account, not cognisable by the organs. Because, as the Mind is naturally restless, it cannot understand on what to concentrate itself, unless it has before itself, by way of support, some steady object, which is perceptible to the organs. If this mental act of concentration is found difficult even by Jñānins, how much more so then by ordinary people? Therefore, just as in teaching Geometry one has to draw on a slate or on a board, by way of sample, a small portion of a line, in order to impress on the Mind the nature of a straight line, which, though in itself eternal, endless, and breadthless, that is to say, imperceptible, is yet qualityful, because it possesses the quality of length, so also, ordinary people at least have got to keep before the mind, some perceptible object, which has a '*pratyakṣa*' (visible) Name and Form, in order that they should acquire affection for and make their minds uniform with the Parameśvara, Who is the cause of everything, omnipotent, and omniscient, that is to say, qualityful, but who is yet formless, that is to say, imperceptible (*avyakta*). * Nay, unless some perceptible thing has been seen, the human mind cannot conceive the idea of the Imperceptible. For instance, it is only after one has seen by one's own eyes the perceptible colours red, green etc., that the common and imperceptible idea of 'colour' comes into existence in the human mind, and not otherwise. You may call this the natural quality or the defect of the human mind. Whatever may be the case, so long as the embodied human being cannot get rid of this mental quality, there is no other way except to descend from the Qualityless into the Qualityful, and into the Perceptible Qualityful rather than the Imperceptible Qualityful, for purposes of Worship (*upāsanā*) or Devotion (*bhakti*). Therefore, the path of worshipping the Perceptible, has been in vogue since times immemorial, and ultimately in Upaniṣads like the Rāma-tāpanīya and others, the worship of the perceptible form of the Brahman, in the shape of human beings, is mentioned; and in the Bhagavadgītā also, this doctrine has been reiterated in the following logical form :—

kleśo 'dhikataras teṣāṁ avyaktāsaktacetasām ı
avyaktā hi gatir duḥkhaṁ dehavadbhir avāpyate ıı

(Gī. 12. 5).

that is, "that man who wishes to concentrate his Mind (Citta) on the Imperceptible (*avyakta*), suffers much ; because, to the

* In this matter, the following stanza is mentioned as being from the Yoga-Vāsiṣṭha :

akṣarāvagamalabdhaye yathā sthūlavartula-
dṛṣatparigrahaḥ ı
śuddhabuddhaparilabdhaye tathā dāru-
mṛṇmayaśilāmayārcanam ıı

that is, "as pieces of stone are arranged (before a child), in order to acquaint it with letters, so are idols of wood, or earth, or stone taken, in order to acquire knowledge of the pure and knowledgeful Parabrahman ". This stanza, however, is not to be found in the Yoga-Vāsiṣṭha.

human being, clothed in a body and organs, it is inherently difficult to reach this state of the Imperceptible". This path of 'visible experience' is known as the "Path of Devotion". When once the form of the Parabrahman has been defined by means of the Intelligence, concentrating the mind on Its imperceptible form by means of thought, will be possible for an intelligent person; not that it is impossible; but in as much as this act of attaching the 'Mind' on the Imperceptible, has to be accomplished by the help of Faith or Affection, one does not escape the necessity of Faith and Affection in this path. Therefore, from the philosophical point of view, even the worship of the *saccidānanda* Brahman (the Brahman which is eternal, conscious, and joyful), must be included in the Path of Devotion, which is founded on Love. Nevertheless, as the form of the Brahman, which is taken for purposes of meditation in this path, is essentially imperceptible, and is accessible only to the Reason, that is, only to Jñāna, and is the most important factor, it is usual not to refer to this path as the Path of Devotion, but as Contemplation of the Absolute Self (*adhyātma-vicāra*), the Worship of the Imperceptible (*avyaktopāsanā*) or simply Worship (*upasānā*), or the PATH OF KNOWLEDGE; and although the Brahman which is worshipped is required to be qualityful, yet, if one takes a perceptible, instead of an imperceptible form, and especially a human form for worship, that makes it the PATH OF DEVOTION. But, it will be clearly seen, that (i) though the paths may be two, yet since one attains the same Parameśvara, and ultimately acquires Equability of Reason by either path, these two paths are eternal stair-cases for rising to the same floor, which are used by different persons according to their respective qualifications; and that (ii) the ideals do not become different because the paths are different. Out of these, the first step of the one staircase is Intelligence, whereas the first step of the other staircase is Faith and Love; and whichever path is followed, the man acquires the same kind of Realisation of the same Parameśvara, and attains the same Release. Therefore, the doctrine that, "there is no salvation unless it is based on actually experienced Knowledge", is common to both the paths. Then, where is the sense of entering into the futile discussion as to whether the Path of Knowledge is superior or the Path of Devotion is superior? Though these two paths are at first different having regard to the qualification of the man, they are ultimately of the same value in effect, and are both called 'Adhyātma' (the Philosophy of the Absolute Self) in the Gītā (Gī. 11. 1). But although Knowledge and Devotion are of the same value as means (*sādhana*), yet, there is this important difference between the two, that whereas Devotion can never become a Niṣṭhā, Knowledge can become a Niṣṭhā, that is, the highest stage in the State of Perfection (*siddhāvasthā*). It is true that one can get the same Knowledge of the Parameśvara by means of Devotion, as by means of the Contemplation of the Absolute Self, or the Worship of the Imperceptible (Gī. 18. 55); but if, after having acquired this Knowledge, the man gives up worldly life and remains steeped in the Knowledge, the Gītā calls him a 'Jñāna-niṣṭha' and not a 'Bhakti-niṣṭha.' As the process of Devotion is based on the duality of the worshipper and the worshipped, no Devotion or any other kind of worship survives in the ultimate state of the merger of the Ātman into Brahman. The ultimate resolution of Devotion is into Knowledge; Devotion is a means for acquiring Knowledge, it is not a goal in itself. In short, Knowledge becomes a means, as meaning the worship of the Imperceptible; whereas, it becomes a Niṣṭhā, that is, an ultimate state, as meaning the direct Realisation of the identity of the Brahman and the Ātman; and when it is necessary to make this difference clear, the two words 'Jñāna-mārga' and 'Jñāna-niṣṭhā' are not used synonymously, but the word 'Jñāna-mārga' is used to indicate the worship of the Imperceptible in its preparatory stages, and the word 'Jñāna-niṣṭhā' is used to indicate the State of Perfection (*siddhāvasthā*), which consists of giving up all Action after Acquisition of Knowledge, and becoming engrossed in Knowledge. That is to say, Jñāna once becomes a means (Jñāna-mārga), in the sense of the Worship of the Imperceptible (*avyaktopāsanā*), or the Meditation on the Absolute Self (*adhyātma-vicāra*); and it becomes a Niṣṭhā, that is to say, the ultimate state of Abandonment of Action, in the sense of a Direct Realisation (*aparokṣānubhava*); and the same is the case with Karma. That Karma (Action) which has to be initially performed according to the limits laid down by the Śāstras for the purification of the Mind is a means (*sādhana*). By this Karma, the Mind becomes purified and Knowledge and Peace are ultimately acquired; but when, instead of remaining steeped in this Knowledge, the man continues to perform Desireless Action peacefully, so long as life lasts, this Desireless Action combined with Knowledge is a Karma which becomes a Niṣṭhā (Gī. 3. 3). But, the same is not the case with Devotion. Devotion is only a path, that is to say, it is a means of acquiring Knowledge; it is not a Niṣṭhā. Therefore, in the beginning of the Gītā, only the two Niṣṭhās of Jñāna (Sāṁkhya) and Yoga (Karma) have been dealt with; and in mentioning the various means, ways, ritual, or paths of acquiring the Karma-Yoga-Niṣṭhā, out of the two (Gī. 7. 1), the Gītā has described the two sister paths of the Worship of the Imperceptible (Jñāna-mārga) and the Worship of the Perceptible (Bhakti-mārga), which have been in vogue from times immemorial, and states that the Worship of the Imperceptible out of the two is fraught with difficulty, whereas the Worship of the Perceptible, or Devotion, is a path which is easier, that is, is such as can be followed by every body; or as Tukārāma has said: "if you want to reach the Parameśvara । then this is the easier path ॥" (Gā. 3002). The ancient Upaniṣads deal with the Jñāna-mārga (the Path of Knowledge) and the Śāṇḍilya-Sūtra and other Sūtras or the Bhāgavata, and other works, praise the Path of Devotion; but no ancient religious treatise is seen to have differentiated between the Jñāna-mārga and the Bhakti-mārga as two paths, according to the qualification of the person, and to have ultimately harmonised both of them with the Path of Desireless Action, as has been impartially done in the Gītā.

If one considers, as mentioned above, what should be done by man, who is embodied in a Body and organs, in order to acquire the true and self-experienced Knowledge of the form of the Īśvara, to the effect that there is only one Parameśvara in all created beings, one comes to the conclusions that, (i) although the eternal, inexpressible, and unimaginable form of the Parameśvara, which can be described only by the words "It is not this, It is not this" ('*neti, neti*'), is the most superior form, yet, as it is QUALITYLESS, UNKNOWABLE, AND IMPERCEPTIBLE, the Dualistic difference of the worshipper and the worshipped does not remain any more when it has been Realised; that, (ii) therefore, worship (*upāsanā*) cannot start with that form; that, (iii) that form is something which is to be reached, and not the means of reaching it; and that, (iv) worship (*upāsanā*) is a means for acquiring the Non-Dualistic state of becoming uniform with that form. Therefore, that object which has to be taken for this worship, has necessarily to be a qualityful object. The all-knowing, omnipotent, all-pervading, and uncircumscribed form of the Brahman is such a form, that is, a QUALITYFUL form. But, as such a form is ACCESSIBLE ONLY TO THE INTELLIGENCE, AND IMPERCEPTIBLE, that is, not perceptible to the organs, it is a difficult form for purposes of worship. Therefore, in all religions, man is seen to naturally adopt for purposes of 'Devotion', in preference to both these forms, that sympathetic and easily accessible QUALITYFUL, LOVE-EARNED, PERCEPTIBLE, and VISIBLE Parameśvara, Who, notwithstanding that He is the unimaginable, omnipresent, all-pervading, and all-powerful Self of the whole world, will yet speak with us, love us, place us on the path of righteousness, and lead us to a happy state; Whom we can call our own; Who will be sympathetic towards our pain and happiness, and forgive our sins; with reference to Whom we can establish the direct relation that He is ours, and we are His; Who will protect us like a father; Who will be a mother to us; or Who will be "*gatir bhartā prabhuḥ sākṣī nivāsaḥ śaraṇaṁ suhṛt*" (Gī. 9. 17 and 18), i. e., "our goal, our maintainer, our owner, our companion, our home of protection and rest, our ultimate support and hope, our friend and our protector"; and Whom we can, on that account, realise by love and caressingly; and Who is truthful, endowed with all glory, the ocean of kindness, the lover of His devotees, the holy of holies, the height of magnanimity, the height of kindness, the most revered, the height of beauty, and the home of all qualities. These two last kinds of the form of the fundamentally unimaginable and 'one only, without a second'

Parabrahman, which are visible to man by means of the mental spectacles of Love, Devotion, etc., are, in Vedānta philosophy, given the technical name of 'Īśvara.' If the Parameśvara is all-pervading, why has Pāṇḍuraṅga or Viṭhobā a diminutive form ? To this question, the answer given by Tukārāma is:-

Tukā says that although the Hari is
all-pervading and only one ।
He has become small for purposes of Devotion ॥
(Gā. 38. 7);

and the same doctrine has been expounded in the Vedānta-Sūtras (1. 2. 7). Even the Upaniṣads, in describing the worship of the Brahman, do not mention only, Life, Mind, and other qualityful, but purely imperceptible things, but they at the same time mention the worship of qualityful, perceptible objects like the Sun (*āditya*) or the food, etc. (Tai. 3.26; Chān. 7); and in the Śvetāśvataropaniṣad, after describing the 'Īśvara' as: "*māyāṁ tu prakṛtiṁ vidyāt māyinaṁ tu maheśvaram*" (Śve. 4. 10), that is, "Māyā is the name given to Matter (*prakṛti*), and the Lord of this Māyā is the highest Īśvara (*maheśvara*)", the qualityful Īśvara is further described as: "*jñātvā devaṁ mucyate sarvapāśaiḥ*", that is, "by knowing this god (*deva*), one becomes free from all bonds" (Sve. 4. 16)—which is more or less the same as in the Gītā. The Name-d and Form-ed object necessary for purposes of worship as the symbol, sign, incarnation, particle, or representation of the worshipped Parabrahman, is known in Vedānta philosophy as a '*pratīka*'. The etymological meaning of '*pratīka*', is *prati*+*ika*, that is, 'one, who is turned, towards (*prati*) ourselves'; and that side or portion of any particular object, which first becomes perceptible to us, and whereby we subsequently obtain a knowledge of it, is called '*pratīka*'. According to this meaning, any perceptible side, part, or particular incarnation of the all-pervading Parameśvara can become a '*pratīka*' for acquiring His Knowledge. For instance, in the conversation between the Brahmin and the Vyādha (hunter), the Vyādha, after explaining the Knowledge of the Absolute Self to the Brahmin, says in the end: "*pratyakṣaṁ mama yo dharmas taṁ ca paśya dvijottama*" (Vana. 213. 3), i. e., "O most excellent among Brahmins, now see my visible religion"; and he then takes the Brahmin to his aged parents and says, "these are my 'visible deities', and serving them with all my heart and soul, as if they are the Parameśvara, is my 'visible' (*pratyakṣa*) religion"; and even in the Gītā, the Blessed Lord has, before mentioning the worship of His perceptible form, said with the same object, that this Path of Devotion is:

rājavidyā rājaguhyaṁ pavitram idam uttamam ।
pratyakṣāvagamaṁ dharmyaṁ susukhaṁ kartum avyayam ॥

(Gī. 9. 2),

that is, "the most superior among all Vidyās and all mysticisms, (*rāja-vidyā* and *rāja-guhya*), excellent, sacred, literally VISIBLE, consistent with Religion, easily observable, and inexhaustible". The two compound words '*rāja-vidyā*' and '*rāja-guhya*' are analysed as: '*vidyānāṁ rājā*' (sovereign of all cults) and '*guhyānāṁ rājā*' (the sovereign among all mysticisms); and in forming the compound, the word '*rāja*' is placed first according to the rules of Sanskrit grammar. But instead of this, some people analyse the word '*rāja-vidyā*' as '*rājñāṁ vidyā*' (the cult of kings), and say that, when in ancient times Ṛṣis (ascetics) used to explain the Brahma-Vidyā to kings, as stated in the Yoga-Vāsiṣṭha (Yo. 2. 11. 16-18), this Brahma-Vidyā or Knowledge of the Absolute Self came to acquire the names of '*rāja-vidyā*' and '*rāja-guhya*'; and that therefore, the Gītā must be taken to have used these two words in the same meaning, that is, as meaning not Devotion, but the Knowledge of the Absolute Self. As the path mentioned in the Gītā was traditionally followed by kings, such as, Manu, Ikṣvāku etc., (Gī. 4.1), one cannot definitely say that the words '*rāja-vidyā*' and '*rāja-guhya*' have not been used in the Gītā in the meaning of 'the cult of kings' or the 'mysticism of kings', that is to say, the cult or the mysticism, which was accepted by kings (*rāja-mānya*). But, if these meanings are accepted, it has still to be borne in mind that they have not been used in the present context with reference to the Path of Knowledge; because this chapter of the Gītā in which this stanza appears is, on the whole, in support of the Path of Devotion (See Gī. 9. 22-31); and although the Brahman to be reached may be the same, yet, in as much as it is clearly stated in the Gītā itself (Gī. 12. 5), that the Jñāna-mārga to be followed as a means, in the philosophy of the Absolute Self, is 'accessible only to the Intelligence' (*buddhigamya*), and therefore 'imperceptible' (*avyakta*) and 'difficult' (*duḥkha-kāraka*), it is not likely that the Blessed Lord can now refer to that same path as '*pratyakṣāvagamaṁ*', that is, 'perceptible', and '*kartuṁ susukham*' (easy to follow). It, therefore, follows, on the ground of consistency in the subject-matter of the chapter, as also on the ground of the appropriateness of the words '*pratyakṣāvagamaṁ*' and '*kartuṁ susukham*', which can apply wholly and on all fours to the Path of Devotion, that the word '*rāja-vidyā*' in this context indicates only the Path of Devotion. The word '*vidyā*' does not indicate only 'the Knowledge of the Brahman'; and it has been used in the Upaniṣads to indicate 'the means or paths by which that Knowledge can be acquired', e. g., Śāṇḍilya-Vidyā, Prāṇa-Vidyā, Hārda-Vidyā, etc.; and all such various Vidyās, or paths, which have been mentioned in the Upaniṣads, have been considered in the third section of the third chapter of the Vedānta-Sūtras. It also appears from the Upaniṣads, that these Vidyās were kept secret, and that in ancient times they used to be taught to no one except one's disciples. Therefore, whatever the Vidyā was, it was bound to be mystic (*guhya*). But, although these various mystic Vidyās or paths, which were a means for the Acquisition of the Brahman, were many, yet, among all of these means, the Vidyā in the shape of the Path of Devotion mentioned in the Gītā, was the highest ('*guhyānāṁ vidyānāṁ ca rājā*', i. e., the king of mysticisms and Vidyās—Trans.); because, this path is not '*avyakta*' (imperceptible) like the Vidyā in the Jñāna-mārga, but is actually visible to the eyes, and, on that account, easy to follow. This is how I read that stanza. If the Gītā had supported only the Path of Knowledge, which is accessible only to the Intelligence, it is doubtful whether all the sects of the Vedic Religion would have clung to this treatise, as has been done by them during the last hundreds of years. The sweetness, affectionateness, and charm, which permeates the Gītā is due to its having propounded the Path of Devotion. The Blessed Lord Śrī Kṛṣṇa, who was the living incarnation of the Parameśvara, was, in the first place, the person who sung the Gītā; and further, instead of preaching the barren Knowledge of the unknowable Parabrahman, the Blessed Lord has given advice in the Gītā to Arjuna in different places like: "every thing is invested in ME" (7. 7); "all this is MY Māyā" (7. 14); "there is nothing which is different from ME" (7. 7); "to ME friends and enemies are alike" (9. 29); "I have created this universe" (9. 4); and ultimately, "I am the root of the Brahman and of Release" (14. 27); or "I am the Puruṣottama" (15. 18); and therefore, "give up all other religions and worship only ME, I will redeem you from all sins, do not be afraid" (18. 66) which is advice, which refers in the first person to His qualityful and perceptible form. On this account, the hearer gets the feeling that he is actually standing before a living, equal-visioned, extremely affectionate, and most reverential Puruṣottama; and his Niṣṭhā becomes fixed on the Knowledge of the Ātman. But this is not all; for, instead of dividing the chapters severally between Jñāna on the one hand, and Devotion on the other, Jñāna is amalgamated with Devotion, and Devotion is amalgamated with Jñāna, so that there is no mutual conflict between Knowledge and Devotion, or between Intelligence and Love; and one experiences the sweetness of the Knowledge of the Parameśvara, while at the same time acquiring that Knowledge; and the feeling of Self-Identification with all living beings being aroused in the Mind, it acquires the most wonderful peace and the bliss of content. The Karma-Yoga is further tacked on to this, like adding sugar to milk; then, what is the wonder that our philosophers have laid down the proposition that the Knowledge expounded in the Gītā is, as is said in the Īśāvāsyopaniṣad, beneficial both in '*mṛtyu*' and '*amṛta*', that is, both in this world and the next?

From what has been stated above, my readers will have understood what is meant by the Path of Devotion, what is the similarity and the dissimilarity between the Path of Knowledge and the Path of Devotion, why the Path of Devotion is called the royal path (the royal Vidyā) or the easy ladder, and also why, the Path of Devotion has not been referred to as an independent Niṣṭhā in the Gītā. But, it is now necessary to point out a position of danger, which exists in this easy, long-standing, and visible path of acquiring Knowledge; otherwise, there is a chance that an unwary wayfarer along the road may fall into that pit. This pit-fall has been clearly defined in the Bhagavadgītā, and that is the important point of difference between the Vedic Path of Devotion and other paths of Devotion. Although it is generally accepted that, in order that the human Mind should become attached to the Parabrahman, and that a man should acquire an equable Reason by means of the purification of the Mind, there must be some qualityful and perceptible object as a symbol (*pratīka*) of the Parabrahman in front of the Devotee, and that otherwise, the Mind cannot become steady, yet, as will be clear from history, there are grave disputes about what that symbol should be. From the Metaphysical point of view, there is no place in the world where the Parameśvara does not exsist; and even in the Bhagavadgītā, after Arjuna had asked Śrī Kṛṣṇa the following question, namely, "tell me which various objects I should meditate on, as being Your Manifestations" (Gī. 10. 18), the Blessed Lord has, in the tenth chapter, mentioned the Mind out of all organs, the Himalayas out of all immoveables, the Yajña by way of repetition of prayers out of all Yajñas, Vāsuki among the serpents, Prahlāda among the demons, Aryamā among the ancestors, Citraratha among the Gandharvas, the pipal-tree out of all trees, the eagle among the birds, Bhṛgu out of the great Ṛṣis, the letter 'A' out of all letters, and Viṣṇu out of all the various Suns, as being the numerous forms of Himself, which fill the moveable and the immoveable world on all sides; and He has ultimately said :-

yad yad vibhūtimat sattvaṁ śrīmad ūrjitam eva vā ।
tat tad evāvagaccha tvaṁ mama tejoṁśasaṁbhavam ॥

(Gī. 10. 41).

that is, "O, Arjuna understand that all things which are possessed of excellence, wealth, or prowess, are created from a part of My effulgence; what more shall I say? I have pervaded the whole of this universe by only a part of Myself"; and He has given to Arjuna an actual experience of this proposition, by showing to him His Cosmic Form in the next chapter. If all the things or qualities to be seen in the world are only forms or symbols of the Parameśvara, how can one say that the Blessed Lord is in one of them and not in another; and who is going to say it? It becomes logically necessary to say that He is near and yet afar; existent and yet non-existent, also beyond both; the eagle, as also the serpent; the death, as also the one who dies; the one who creates obstacles, and the one who removes them; the one who creates fear, and one who removes it; the terrible and yet the not-terrible; the pleasant and yet the unpleasant; the one who causes the rain, and the one who prevents rain from falling (Gī. 9. 19 and 10. 32); and Tukārāma Buvā, a devotee of the Blessed Lord, has with the same import said:–

> Tukā says whatever name you give ।
> such name is proper for this Viṭhṭhala ॥
> (Tu. Gā. 3065.4).

If everything in this world is in the same way in part a form of the Parameśvara, why should not such persons as cannot at a stroke grasp this all-pervasive form of the Parameśvara, take for worship, in the beginning, any one of these numerous things, as a means or a symbol for Realising this imperceptible and pure form? Some may worship the Mind, others may perform the Yajña of wealth, others again the Yajña of prayer, some may worship the eagle, others may worship only the Sacred symbol 'OM', some may worship Viṣṇu and others Śiva, some may worship Gaṇapati, and others Bhavānī, some again may look upon their parents as the Parameśvara and serve them, whereas others might choose for worship a form which is much more comprehensive, such as the Virāṭa form made up of all created beings. One may prescribe the worship of the Sun, whereas others may say that Śrī Kṛṣṇa or Śrī Rāmacandra is better than the Sun. But, as the idea that all these Forms are fundamentally one and the same, has been lost sight of, as a result of Ignorance or Delusion, or as it is not to be found at all in some religions, a false arrogance sometimes arises as to the relative merits of these objects of worship, and matters come to physical violence. If one for the moment keeps out of consideration the mutual conflicts between the Vedic, Buddhistic, Jain, Christian, or Mahomedan religions, the history of Europe shows us that matters had come to the point of the worshippers of one and the same qualityful and perceptible Christ, murdering each other, as a result of difference in ritualistic practices; and quarrels are even now going on among the worshippers of the Qualityful, on the ground that the deity worshipped by one is better than the deity worshipped by another, because the former is Formless, and the latter has a Form. Unless one explains whether there is a way for bringing these quarrels arising in the Path of Devotion to a close, and if so, which that way is, the Path of devotion does not become free from danger; and we shall, therefore, consider what the reply of the Gītā to that question is. I need not say that in the present state of India, it is of special importance to give a proper answer to this question.

The methods of contemplating in the first place, or placing before one's eyes as a symbol, the form of any one of the numerous qualityful Manifestations of the Parameśvara, in order to acquire Equability of Reason by steadying the Mind, have been described in the ancient Upaniṣads; and ultimately in the later Upaniṣads like the Rāma-Tāpanī, or the Gītā, the unlimited and concentrated worship of a human-formed, qualityful Parameśvara has been considered as the principal means of reaching the Parameśvara. But, although the worship of Vāsudeva has been given an important position in the Gītā, in so far as it is a means to an end, yet, considering the matter from the Metaphysical point of view, it has been stated in the Vedānta-Sūtras (Ve. Sū. 4. 1. 4), as also further on in the Gītā itself, that a symbol *(pratika)* is only a kind of means, and that the true all-pervading and permanent Parameśvara cannot be limited to any one of these symbols. What more shall I say? Whatever qualityful, that is, Name-d and Form-ed perceptible object is taken, it is nothing but Māyā, and he who wishes to see the true Parameśvara, must ultimately extend his vision beyond such qualityful forms. It is clear that no manifestation, out of the many manifestations of the Parameśvara, can be more comprehensive than the Cosmic Form which was shown by the Blessed Lord to Arjuna; yet, after this same Cosmic Form had been shown by the Blessed Lord to Nārada, He has said, "this form which you see is not My true form, this is only a Māyā; and in order to see My real form, you must go beyond this Māyā" (see Nārāyaṇīyadharma, Śān. 339. 44); and even in the Gītā, the Blessed Lord has clearly given to Arjuna the advice that :–

avyaktaṁ vyaktimāpannaṁ manyante mām abuddhayaḥ ।
paraṁ bhāvam ajānanto mamāvyayam auuttamam ॥

(Gī. 7. 24),

that is, "although I am imperceptible, ignorant people call Me perceptible, or endowed with a human form (Gī. 9. 11); but that is not My true form; My imperceptible form is My true form". Also, although the Upaniṣads prescribe the Mind, the Speech, the Sun, Ether, and numerous other perceptible and imperceptible symbols of the Brahman for purposes of worship, yet, it is ultimately clearly stated, that that which is accessible to the eyes, or the speech, or the ears, is not the true Brahman, but :

yan manasā na manute yenā 'hur mano matam ।
tad eva brahma tvaṁ viddhi nedaṁ yad idam upāsate ॥

(Kena. 1. 5-8),

that is "That, which cannot be meditated on by the Mind, but on the contrary, the power of meditation of Which includes the Mind, is the true Brahman; that which is worshipped (as a '*pratika*', i.e., symbol) is not the (true) Brahman"; and the same meaning is conveyed by the canon (*sūtra*) "*neti, neti*". Take the Mind, or Ether (*ākāśa*), or according to the path of the worship of the Perceptible, take the Śālagrāma, or the Śivaliṅga, or the tangible form of Śrī Kṛṣṇa, or of some Saint, or take a temple which contains a stone or a metal idol of a god, or a musjid or a temple which contains no idol; all these are mere means for steadying the Mind, that is, for fixing the Mind on the Parameśvara, like the go-carts of little children. However much these symbols, taken by different persons according to their own liking or according to their respective spiritual qualifications, may be loved by them, like the go-carts of children, which are simple or coloured, or of sandal-wood, or to which a tambourine or a jingling bell is attached, yet, one must realise that the true Parameśvara is 'not in these symbols'—'*na pratīke na hi saḥ*' (Ve. Sū. 4. 1. 4)–but is beyond them; and for the same reason, is the proposition laid down in the Bhagavadgītā that: "those ignorant persons, who do not understand My Māyā, do not Realise Me" (Gī. 7. 13-15). The power of redemption which is contained in the Path of Devotion is not a power possessed by some living or lifeless image, or by a building of brick and mortar; but that belief, which every worshipper for his own convenience holds with reference to such image, to the effect that it is the Īśvara, is the thing which really redeems. Let the symbol be of stone, or of metal, or of anything else, it can never be worth more than what it really is. Whatever may be your faith with reference to the symbol, it is the fruit of your Devotion, which the Parameśvara—not the symbol—gives you. Then, where is the sense of fighting that the symbol chosen by oneself is better than the one chosen by another? If your faith is not pure, then, however good the symbol may be, what is the use of it? If the whole day you are engaged in deceiving others, then, it will be impossible for you to attain the Parameśvara, notwithstanding that you go to worship an idol in a temple, or go for worship in some temple which does not contain any image, and whether every morning and evening, or on feast days. Śrī Samartha has described persons who go into temples for listening to sermons (*purāṇa*) in the following terms:–

Sensual persons go to the temple for listening to the sermons ।
but their eyes are fixed on the ladies who are present ।
At the same time, those who have come with the intention of stealing ।
steal your shoes and go away ॥ *

(Dāsa. 18. 10. 26).

If idols of deities or temples had any redeeming power in themselves, then even such sensual persons or thieves must attain Release. Some people believe that Devotion to the

* It is usual in India to leave one's shoes outside the temple when one enters it for worship, and that is how the shoes are stolen—Translator.

Parameśvara is only for the purposes of Release; but those persons who wish to obtain some Material or selfish object, must devote themselves to the worship of different deities; and it is said in the Gītā itself that such persons run after these deities, with such selfish motives (Gī. 7. 20). But the Gītā itself says later on, that the idea that these deities, of their own accord, give you the reward of the worship is philosophically incorrect (Gī. 7. 21). It is a definite doctrine of the Philosophy of the Absolute Self, that whichever deities you worship with whatever desire in your heart, giving the fruit of that worship is not in the hands of that deity, but of the all-pervading Parameśvara (Ve. Sū. 3. 2. 38-41); and the same doctrine has been accepted by the Gītā (Gī. 7. 22). But, though the Parameśvara Who gives the reward may, in this way, be One, yet, as He gives a different reward to each one according to his good or evil intentions (Ve. Sū. 2. 1. 34–37), the results of the worship of different symbols or deities are seen to be different from each other; and it is with this import in mind, that the Blessed Lord has said in one place:

śraddhāmayo 'yaṁ puruṣo yo yacchraddhaḥ sa eva saḥ ।

(Gī. 17. 3; Maitryu. 4. 6),

that is, "man is governed by Faith; whatever may be the symbol which is taken, as his Faith, so does the man become"; and in another place:–

yānti devavratā devān pitṛn yānti pitṛvratāḥ ।
bhūtāni yānti bhūtejyā yānti madyājino 'pi mām ॥

(Gī. 9. 25).

that is, "those who worship deities, reach the sphere of the deities; those who worship ancestors, the sphere of ancestors; those who worship the departed, reach that of the dead; and those who worship Me, reach Me"; or again in a third place :–

ye yathā māṁ prapadyante tāṁs tathaiva bhajāmy ahaṁ ॥

(Gī. 4. 11).

that is, "in that way, in which people are devoted to Me, in the same way, am I devoted to them". The Śālagrāma is only a stone. If you entertain the faith with reference to it that it is Viṣṇu, you will reach the sphere of Viṣṇu; if you worship the same symbol believing that it is some past being like a Yakṣa, or a demon, etc., you will reach the spheres of past beings like a Yakṣa or a demon, etc. All our philosophers have accepted the doctrine that the fruit is of your Faith, and not of the symbol; and the same is the reason for the ordinary practice of instilling life into an image (making a *prāṇa-pratiṣṭhā*) before taking the image for worship. That deity, which is believed to inhabit any particular image, in worshipping that image, is the deity of which a *prāṇa-pratiṣṭhā* is made in that image. No one worships any image without believing that it is inhabited by the Parameśvara, that is, merely believing that it is earth, or stone, or metal, having some particular form; and if any one worships it in that way, then, the man will undoubtedly reach the state of the earth, or the stone, or the metal, according to the above-mentioned doctrine enunciated by the Gītā. When in this way a difference has been made between the symbol, and the Faith with which that symbol is worshipped, no reason remains for quarrelling about the symbol, whatever that symbol may be; because, the idea that the symbol is the god or Parameśvara, no more remains. That omnipresent Parameśvara, Who gives the reward for all Actions, looks only to the Faith of the devotees. Therefore, Tukārāma has said that the 'Parameśvara takes into account only the Faith', and not the symbol which is worshipped. Those persons who have realised this principle of the Path of Devotion, do not obstinately insist that "that form of the Īśvara or the symbol which I worship, is the only true symbol, and that other symbols are false"; but he has the charitable feeling, that whatever may be the symbol which is taken, all those who worship the Parameśvara through that symbol, reach one and the same Parameśvara; and then he realises the truth of the statement of the Blessed Lord that:—

ye 'py anyadevatābhaktāḥ yajante śraddhayānvitāḥ ı
te 'pi mām eva kaunteya yajanty avidhipūrvakam ıı

(Gī. 9. 23),

that is, "although the ritual, or the external routine, or the means employed, may not be such as have been enjoined by the Śāstras, yet, those who worship a deity with Faith (that is, believing that the pure Parameśvara is in that deity) worship (indirectly) only Me". The same meaning has been conveyed in the Bhāgavata, with a slight verbal difference (Bhāg. 10. Pū. 40. 8-10); and in the Śivagītā the above stanza has been taken word for word (Śiva. 12. 4); and the same is the meaning of the statement in the Vedas that: "*ekaṁ sad viprā bahudhā vadanti*" (that is, "the one Reality is given various names by learned people"—Trans.), (Rg. 1. 164. 46). From this it becomes clear, that this principle has been in vogue in the Vedic Religion from very ancient times; and the fact that in modern times, the fault of intolerance of other religions was not to be found in a man of prowess like Śrī Śivājī Mahārāja, who was a believer in the Vedic Religion, even when he was at the height of his power, is due to this principle. That men should not realise the true principle that the Īśvara is all-pervading, omnipresent, omniscient, omnipotent, and possibly even beyond all that, that is to say, unimaginable; that they should entertain a false pride about a Name and Form, and insist that the particular perceptible form which was taken up by the Parameśvara at a particular time, or in any particular place, by being born from particular parents, in any particular caste, with a particular Name and Form, is the only true form of the Parameśvara; and that they should, on that account, come to the stage of cutting each other's throats with a sword, is a proof of the most regrettable stupidity of men. It is true that the Path of Devotion mentioned in the Gītā is called a '*rāja-vidyā*'. But, if one considers in which country there have been first born any religious preachers who have irradicated false begotisms in the Path of Devotion (i) by preaching, that: "My visible form is only a Māyā, if you wish to see My true Form, transcend that Māyā and go beyond", as was done by the Blessed Lord, or (ii) by Realising the unity of all religions by means of the *sāttvika* knowledge-full vision of "*avibhaktaṁ vibhakteṣu*" (i. e., "the unity in the division"—Trans.); or, if one considers which country contains the largest number of followers of their opinion, I must say that the first place has to be given to this our India. When this philosopher's stone of a '*rāja-vidyā*' and of a '*rāja-guhya*' is in our hands, it is certainly a matter of great misfortune that some of us should put on our eyes the spectacles of ignorance, and say that that philosopher's stone is nothing but a flint!

It is thus true, that whatever symbol is taken, the result got by following the Path of Devotion is the result of the belief with which we invest that symbol, and not of the symbol; and that, therefore, it is useless to go on fighting about the symbol itself. But, now a doubt arises that that pure form of the Parmeśvara with which the symbol has to be invested, can very often not be readily imagined by many people, on account of their inherent nature or their ignorance. Then, how is it possible for such persons to place absolute faith in the symbol and attain the Parameśvara? It is not enough to say that in the Path of Devotion, the work of Knowledge is done by Faith, and that one should imagine the pure form of the Parameśvara by confidence or by Religious Faith, and invest the symbol with that belief; because, although holding a particular belief is a characteristic feature of the Mind, that is, of Faith, yet, one cannot do without supporting that Faith by Intelligence, since, Faith and Love, like all other mental qualities, are by themselves to a certain extent blind, and they, by themselves, cannot understand to which object one should pin one's faith, and which not, or what one should love and what not. This question must be solved by everybody by his own Intelligence; because, there is no other organ except the Intelligence which can discriminate; and, therefore, though the Intelligence of a particular person might not be very keen, yet, it must be capable of, at any rate, determining on what things to pin his faith; otherwise, this blind Faith and this blind Love will both be deceived and fall into a pit-fall. On the contrary, if one exercises only his Intelligence without Faith, there is no saying what turn it will perversely take; for, the keener the Intelligence, the wilder will be its run. Besides, as has been stated by me already in the beginning of this chapter, mere Knowledge acquired by Intelligence is not capable of doing anything useful, unless it is supplemented by mental processes like Faith etc.; and therefore, Faith and Knowledge or Mind and Reason have always to be linked together. But, in as much as the Mind and the Reason are both manifestations of the three-

-constituented Matter, each of them can from birth naturally fall into the three classes, *sāttvika*, *rājasa*, and *tāmasa*; and though the combination of the Mind and the Reason be permanent, the natures, beliefs, and Actions of different persons will differ in the proportion in which these will be more or less pure. If the Reason itself is from birth impure or *rājasa* or *tāmasa*, then, as the decision made by it as to a particular thing being good or bad will be wrong, blind Faith, though it may be *sāttvika* or pure, will notwithstanding be misguided; and, if the Faith is itself impure from birth, then, the fact that the Reason is *sāttvika* is useless; because, in these circumstances, the Faith will not listen to the dictates of the Reason. But, ordinarily the Mind and the Reason are not individually impure; and if the Reason of a man is inherently impure, his Mind, that is, his Faith, is also more or less impure; and in these circumstances, this impure Reason more and more confuses the inherently impure Faith. We find in ordinary life that in these circumstances, however much of advice may be given to a person about the pure form of the Parameśvara, such advice is not fully impressed on his Mind; or very often—and specially if the Faith and the Reason are both initially immature and weak—the man takes a perverse view of that advice itself. For instance, when Christian Missionaries begin to preach to the ebony-black Abyssinian in Africa about the Christian religion, he cannot by any means get a true idea of the Father in Heaven or of the Christian religion; and it has been observed that whatever is said to him, is imbibed by him in an incongruous meaning, according to his immature Reason; and, therefore, as an English writer * has said, one must bring such persons to the state of a modern man, in order that they should be in a position to understand reformed religion. Although the preceptor may be the same, there is a difference

* "And the only way, I suppose, in which beings of so low an order of development (e. g., an Australian savage or a Bushman) could be raised to a civilised level of feeling and thought, would be by cultivation continued through several generations; they would have to undergo a gradual process of humanisation before they could attain to the capacity of civilisation". Dr. Maudsley's *Body and Mind*. Ed. 1873, p. 57.

between disciple and disciple; and Bhavabhūti means the same thing when he says that though the Sun may be one and the same, its light can cause fire by passing through a prism, but does not have the same effect on a clod of earth (U. Rāma. 2. 4); and it would appear that it was principally for this Reason, that Śūdras and other ignorant classes were in ancient times looked upon as unfit for listening to the Vedas. * This subject-matter has been dealt with in the eighteenth chapter of the Gītā, and there, after stating that Reason is inherently of the three kinds, *sāttvika*, *rājasa* and *tāmasa*, (18. 30-32), just as Faith is of those three kinds (17. 2), the Blessed Lord has stated that in as much as the Faith of different persons is in this way different from birth according to their respective bodily natures (17. 3), *sāttvika* persons naturally put faith in deities, *rājasa* persons in Yakṣas and demons, and *tāmasa* persons put faith in ghosts and dead beings and spirits (Gī. 17. 4-6). But, if the fact of a man having a pure and impure Faith depends in this way on his inherent nature, a question naturally arises as to whether or not this Faith will gradually get better, and sometime or other reach the absolutely pure, that is to say, the *sāttvika* state after Devotion has, in the first instance, been practised according to one's own qualification. The above difficulty in the Path of Devotion is of the same nature as the difficulty which arises in the subject of Cause and Effect, namely, whether or not a man is free to acquire Knowledge; and the reply to both is the same. That is why after having advised Arjuna in the beginning that "*mayyeva mana ādhatsva*" (Gī. 12. 8), i. e., "concentrate your mind on My pure form", the Blessed Lord has later on explained the different paths of fixing the form of the Parameśvara in one's mind in the following words: "if you cannot concentrate your mind on Me, then practise doing so, that is, make a continual effort of doing so; and if you cannot perform that practice, then perform for My sake such Actions as will have the effect of purifying the Mind; and if you cannot do even that, then abandon the Fruit of Action, and thereby attain to Me" (Gī. 12. 9-11; Bhāga. 11. 11. 21-25). If the inherent bodily

* See Max Muller's *Three Lectures on the Vedānta Philosophy* pp. 72-73.

nature or *prakṛti* is *tāmasa*, the attempt of concentrating one's mind on the pure form of the Parameśvara, will not become successful at once or in one life. But as in the Karma-Yoga, so also in the Path of Devotion, nothing is wasted; and the Blessed Lord has given an assurance to everyone that:—

> *bahūnāṁ janmanām ante jñānavān māṁ prapadyate* ।
> *vāsudevaḥ sarvam iti sa mahātmā sudurlabhaḥ* ॥
>
> (Gī. 7. 19).

that is, "once a man has started on the Path of Devotion, then in the next birth, if not in this birth, he will acquire the true Knowledge of the form of the Parameśvara, to the effect that 'everything is pervaded by Vāsudeva'; and by the Acquisition of such Knowledge, he will ultimately attain Release". In the sixth chapter also, the Blessed Lord has said with reference to those who practise the Karma-Yoga that "*anekajanma-saṁsiddhas tato yāti parāṁ gatim*" (6. 45)—(i. e., "acquiring success, after many births, he reaches the most superior state"—Trans.); and the same rule applies to the Path of Devotion. One should start by imagining as pure a form as it is possible for one to imagine, having regard to one's bodily nature, of that deity which one wishes to invest in the symbol. For sometime, the Parameśvara (not the idol), gives you the reward of this conviction (7. 22); but later on, there does not remain the necessity of any other means of purifying the mind, and this continued Devotion to the Parameśvara, which is kept going according to one's spiritual qualification, results in this Faith being purified; and gradually the Realisation of the Parameśvara also goes on increasing, and ultimately the Mind acquires the belief that "*vāsudevaḥ sarvaṁ*" (i. e. "Vāsudeva is everything"—Trans.); and there no more remains any difference between the worshipper and the worshipped, and the Self ultimately becomes merged in the pure joy of the Brahman. All that is required is that the man should not give up his efforts; in short, the doctrine of the Gītā is, that in the same way as, the moment the man acquires the desire of practising the Karma-Yoga he is drawn towards complete perfection, as though he had been put into a grinding-mill (Gī. 6. 44), so also, in the Path of Devotion, when once the Devotee has consigned himself to the Parameśvara, the Blessed Lord Himself gradually increases his Niṣṭhā, and makes him ultimately fully realise His own form (Gī. 7. 21; 10. 10); and that by this Knowledge (not by barren or blind Faith) the Devotee of the Blessed Lord ultimately attains Release. This state, which is ultimately acquired by gradually rising in the Path of Devotion, being the same as the ultimate state acquired by the Path of Knowledge, the description which is given in the twelvth chapter of the Gītā of the ultimate state of the Devotee, is absolutely the same as the description given, in the second chapter, of the Sthitaprajña, as will be noticed by anybody who reads those descriptions. It follows from this, that though the Path of Knowledge and the Path of Devotion are different from each other in the beginning, and though some follow the one path, and others follow the other path according to their own qualifications, yet, both these paths ultimately come together, and the Devotee acquires the same state as is acquired by the Jñānin. The difference between these two paths is that in the Path of Knowledge, Knowledge is acquired from the very beginning by Reason; whereas, in the Path of Devotion, that same Knowledge is acquired by means of Faith. But, the Blessed Lord says that this initial difference disappears later on, and—

śraddhāvān labhate jñānaṁ tat paraḥ saṁyatendriyaḥ ।
jñānaṁ labdhvā parāṁ śāntiṁ acireṇādhigacchati ॥
(Gī. 4. 39).

that is, "if the man who is filled with Devotion pursues Knowledge by controlling the organs, he gets the practical personal experience of the Knowledge of the identity of the Ātman and the Brahman, and he soon thereafter acquires complete Peace by means of such Knowledge"; or—

bhaktyā māṁ abhijānāti yāvān yaś cāsmi tatvataḥ ।
tato māṁ tatvato jñātvā viśate tad anantaram ॥
(Gī. 18. 55).

that is, "by means of Devotion, one acquires the philosophical knowledge of who 'I', the Parameśvara, am, and how much I am; and after this Knowledge has been acquired (not before), the Devotee comes to be merged in Me" (See Gī. 11. 54). * There is no third way except these two ways for acquring the fullest knowledge of the Parameśvara. Therefore, that man who does not possess in himself either Intelligence or Devotion, may, as has been stated further on in the Gītā itself, be considered as totally lost: "*ajñaś cāśraddadhānaś ca saṁśayātmā vinaśyati*" (Gī. 4. 40).

To the doctrine that, by Faith and Devotion a man ultimately acquires a complete Realisation of the identity of the Brahman and the Ātman, some logicians have raised an objection to the following effect, namely: if the Path of Devotion starts with the Duality that the worshipper is different from the worshipped, how will the person ultimately realise the Non-Dualistic Knowledge of the identity of the Ātman and the Brahman? But this doubt is based on confusion of thought. If all that these objectors want to say, is that when once the Knowledge of that identity has been acquired, Devotion will, to that extent, come to an end, there is nothing wrong in that position; because, even Metaphysics accepts the position that when the trinity of the worshipper, the worshipped, and the worship, is at an end, that which we ordinarily call Devotion comes to an end. But, if this objection means that the Path of Devotion, which is based on Duality, can never lead to Non-Dualistic Knowledge, then this objection will be proved to be groundless, not only by logic, but also by the experience of well-known Devotees of the Blessed Lord There is no objection, from the point of view of logic, to the position that the feeling of difference gradually disappears, as the Devotion towards the Parameśvara becomes more and more steady in the heart of the Devotee; because, even in the Brahman-world, there is no difficulty in the way of globules

* An attempt has been made in the Śāṇḍilya-Sūtra to show that Devotion is not a means of acquiring Knowledge, by emphasising the word '*abhi*' in this stanza, and to show that it is an independent goal to be acquired by itself (Sū. 15). But this meaning is a distorted meaning, like other doctrine-supporting interpretations; and is not a correct and straight-forward interpretation.

of mercury becoming unified later on, though they appear as separate entities in the beginning; and we see ourselves personally that the process of unification, in other matters also, starts with diversity; and it is a well-known illustration. that a worm becomes a hornet by continually contemplating on a hornet. But, the actual experience of saints is a more convincing answer to this objection than mere logic; and among all these, I consider the practical experience of that king among Devotees, the saint Tukārāma, as of the utmost importance. No one need be told that the Knowledge of the Absolute Self (*adhyātma*), which had been acquired by the saint Tukārāma, had not been acquired by him by reading treatises like the Upaniṣads. Nevertheless, in his Gāthā, about 300 to 350 *abhaṅga* stanzas are devoted to the description of the state of Non-Duality; and in those stanzas, the doctrine of "*vāsudevaḥ sarvaṁ*" (Gī. 7.19), (i. e., "Vasudeva is everything"—Trans.), or, as stated by Yājñavalkya in the Bṛhadāraṇyakopaniṣad, "*sarvam ātmaivābhūt*" (i. e., everything has become identified with the Self"—Trans.), has been propounded, as being based on personal experience. For instance:—

As every part of jaggery is sweet ।
so has God come to be everywhere ।
Now whom shall I worship । God is inside as also outside ॥
The film on the water । is not separate from the water ।
Just as gold gets a name by being made into an ornament ।
Tukā says, so are we ॥

(Gāthā. 3627)

The two first lines have been quoted by me in the chapter on the Philosophy of the Absolute Self (see p. 318 above—Trans.); and I have shown there the complete similarity between the meaning conveyed by them and the Knowledge of the identity of the Brahman and the Ātman expounded in the Upaniṣads. When the saint Tukārāma himself describes in this way the supreme state which is reached by the Devotee, as a matter of his own personal experience, it is strange that argumentative people should dare to make such foolish assertions as: "it is not possible to acquire the Knowledge of Non-Dualism by the Path of Devotion", or, "one can attain Release by putting blind faith in the Parameśvara; Knowledge is not necessary for that purpose".

Not only do the propositions that, 'the ultimate ideal in the Path of Devotion and in the Path of Knowledge is the same' and that 'one ultimately attains Release by the experienced Realisation of the Parameśvara', remain unchanged in both these Paths, but all the other doctrines, which have been mentioned either in the chapter on the Absolute Self, or in the chapter on Cause and Effect, have been left untouched in the Path of Devotion mentioned in the Gītā. For example, some persons maintain that according to the Bhāgavata religion, the universe was created in the following four-stepped way, namely, that Jīva in the form of the Saṁkarṣaṇa first came into being out of the Parameśvara in the form of Vāsudeva; Pradyumna, that is, the Mind, sprang from Saṁkarṣaṇa; and Aniruddha, that is, Individuation, sprang from Pradyumna, thus making a '*caturvyūha*' (i. e., four steps—Trans.); whereas, there are others who believe that the true '*vyūha*' of the creation was of only three, or two, out of these four steps, or of Vāsudeva alone. It has been proved in the Vedānta-Sūtras on the authority of the Upaniṣads, that these ideas about the coming into existence of the Personal Self (*jīva*) are not correct, and that from the Metaphysical point of view, the Personal Self is an eternal portion of an eternal Parameśvara (Ve. Sū. 2. 3. 17; and 2. 2. 42-45). Therefore, the Bhagavadgītā has not accepted this idea of a four-stepped (*caturvyūha*) evolution as pertaining to the pure Path of Devotion, and has accepted the above-mentioned doctrine of the writers of the Vedānta-Sūtras with reference to the Personal Self (Gī. 2. 24; 8. 20; 13. 22; and 15. 7). In short, although the principles of the worship of Vāsudeva and of Karma-Yoga have been adopted into the Gītā from the Bhāgavata religion, yet, it can be clearly seen that the Gītā has not countenanced any blind or foolish ideas about the form of the Personal Self in the shape of the Ātman (*kṣetrajña*) and of the Paramātman, which are inconsistent with the Philosophy of the Absolute Self. But, it must not be forgotten that, though the Gītā is so strong on establishing a complete harmony between Devotion and the Philosophy of the Absolute Self, or between Faith and Knowledge, yet, it becomes necessary to make minor verbal changes in the doctrines of the Philosophy of the Absolute Self in adopting them into the Path of Devotion; and that, that has been done in the Gītā. Some persons seem to have conceived the misunderstanding that as a result of these verbal differences between the Path of Knowledge and the Path of Devotion, there is a mutual conflict between the various doctrines, which are enunciated in the Gītā, once from the point of view of Devotion, and again from the point of view of Knowledge; and that there are inconsistencies, to that extent, in the Gītā. But, I am of opinion that these conflicts are not substantial, and that these doubts arise as a result of the doubters not having clearly understood the harmony which has been brought about by our philosophers between the Philosophy of the Absolute Self and Devotion. It is, therefore, necessary to deal in some detail with that matter here. As it is a doctrine of the Philosophy of the Absolute Self, that there is only Ātman in the Body and in the Cosmos, which (Ātman) has become clothed in a Name and Form, we say from the Metaphysical point of view that "*sarvabhūtastham ātmānaṁ sarvabhūtāni cātmani* (Gī. 6. 29), i. e., "that Ātman which is in Me, is also in all other created beings", or again, "*idaṁ sarvam ātmaiva*," i. e., "all this is the Ātman"; and the saint Tukārāma has with the same idea said: "Tukā says, whatever I come across । I think that it is myself" ॥ (Gā. 4444. 4). But, in the Path of Devotion, the imperceptible Paramātman takes up the form of the perceptible Parameśvara; and therefore, we find in the chapter on Devotion in the Gītā, the following propositions, instead of the above-mentioned propositions, namely, such propositions as "*yo māṁ paśyati sarvatra sarvaṁ ca mayi paśyati*" (Gī. 6. 29), i. e., "I (the Blessed Lord) am in all created beings, and all created beings are in Me"; or, "*vāsudevaḥ sarvam iti*" (Gī. 7. 19), i. e., "Whatever is, is full of Vāsudeva;" or, "*sarvabhutāny aśeṣeṇa drakṣasy ātmany atho mayi*" (Gī. 4. 35.), i. e., "When you have acquired Knowledge, you will see all created beings in Me, as also in yourself"; and for the same reason, the Devotee of the Blessed Lord has been described as follows in the Bhāgavata-Purāṇa:-

> *sarvabhūteṣu yaḥ paśyed bhagavadbhāvam ātmanaḥ* ।
> *bhūtāni bhagavaty ātmany eṣa bhāgavatottamaḥ* ॥
>
> (Bhāg. 11. 2. 45; and 3. 24. 46),

that is, "that Devotee, who does not entertain in his mind any such differentiation that I am something different, the Blessed Lord is something different, and all other people are something different, but who keeps in his mind the belief, with reference to all created beings, that he and the Blessed Lord are one and the same, and who believes that all created beings subsist in the Blessed Lord as also in himself, is the most excellent amongst the Devotees of the Blessed Lord". Nevertheless, it will be seen that the only change which has been made is, that we have substituted the words 'the perceptible Parameśvara' for the words 'the imperceptible Paramātman' from the Philosophy of the Absolute Self. As the Paramātman in the Philosophy of the Absolute Self is imperceptible, the fact that the entire universe is pervaded by the Ātman, has been proved in that philosophy by means of logic; but as the Path of Devotion is based on personal experience, the Blessed Lord has now described the numerous perceptible manifestations of the Parameśvara, and He has, by endowing Arjuna with supernatural sight, now given him a visible proof of the fact that the entire universe is pervaded by the Parameśvara, (pervaded by the Ātman), (Gī. chapters X and XI). In the Philosophy of the Absolute Self, He has stated that Karma is destroyed by Knowledge; but, as it is a doctrine of the Path of Devotion, that there is nothing else in the world except the qualityful Parameśvara, and that He is Himself Knowledge as also Action, the Knower as also the Doer, and the One who causes Action as also the one who gives the Fruit of Action, there is now made no differentiation between different Actions (*karma*) such as, '*saṁcita*', '*prārabdha*', '*kriyamāṇa*' etc.; and it is stated that the One Who gives the desire to perform the Action, as also the Fruit, and the One Who destroys the bondage of the Action, is the Parameśvara alone. For instance, the saint Tukārāma, imagining himself in solitude with the Parameśvara, lovingly but fearlessly asks Him:

> O. Pāṇḍuraṅga, listen to what I say ।
> I have to say something to You in solitude ।
> If I can be redeemed by my '*saṁcita*' ।
> then what is the use of You ? ॥
>
> (Gāthā, 499);

and he conveys the same meaning in another place in the following words, namely,

> Neither '*prārabdha*,' nor '*kriyamāṇa*, ।
> nor '*saṁcita*' exists for the Devotee ।
> If he sees that the Parameśvara alone has become everything ।
> and has pervaded everything in and out ॥
>
> (Gāthā, 1023);

and it has been stated by the Blessed Lord even in the Bhagavadgītā that "*īśvaraḥ sarvabhūtānāṁ hṛddeśe 'rjuna tiṣṭhati*" (18. 61), i. e., "the Blessed Lord Himself has His abode in the heart of all persons, and makes them do all Actions mechanically". It has been proved in the chapter on Cause and Effect, that the Ātman is absolutely free to acquire Knowledge; but instead of that, there now occur statements in the chapter on Devotion, to the effect that the Reason itself is guided by the Parameśvara, such as, "*tasya tasyācalāṁ śraddhāṁ tām eva vidadhāmy aham*" (Gī. 7. 21), (i. e., "Whatever form of deity any Devotee may desire to worship with Devotion, I steady his devotion thereon"—Trans.) or "*dadāmi buddhiyogaṁ taṁ yena mām upayānti te*" (Gī. 10. 10), (i. e., "to them, I give the Yoga of the (equable) Reason, to enable them to come and reach me"—Trans.);. and in as much as all the Action, which is performed in the universe, is carried on by the authority of the Parameśvara, it is stated in the Philosophy of Devotion, that the wind blows out of dread of His anger, and that the Sun and the Moon rotate as a result of His strength (Kaṭha. 6. 3, Bṛ. 3. 8. 9); nay, that even the leaf of a tree does not move unless He desires it; and on that account, we come across statements in the Philosophy of Devotion, that man is only a tool which is put forward (Gī. 11. 33); and that the Parame-

-śvara inhabits his heart, and makes him mechanically perform all his various actions like a machine. Tukārāma Buvā says:-

> The created being is only a nominal doer ।
> his life is wasted in saying 'this is mine', 'this is mine' ॥
>
> (Gā. 2310. 4).

In order to carry on properly the various activities of the world and to maintain its beneficial condition, it is necessary that everybody must continue performing Action; and the summary of the advice given above is, that instead of performing these Actions with the feeling that they are 'mine', as is done by ignorant people, the Jñānin should perform all Actions till death with the idea of dedicating them to the Brahman, consistently with the principle enunciated in the Īśāvasyopaniṣad; and the same advice has been preached to Arjuna by the Blessed Lord in the following words:—

> *yat karoṣi yad aśnāsi yaj juhoṣi dadāsi yat* ।
> *yat tapasyasi kaunteya tat kuruṣva mad arpaṇam* ॥
>
> (Gī. 9, 27)

that is, "whatever you do, or eat, or offer by way of sacrifice, or give, or perform by way of austerity, dedicate all that to Me," so that you will not be caught in the bondage of the Karma. This very stanza from the Bhagavadgītā has been taken into the Śiva-gītā; and the same meaning has been conveyed in the following stanza in the Bhāgavata:—

> *kāyena vācā manasendriyair vā*
> *buddhyātmanā vā 'nusṛtasvabhāvāt* ।
> *karoti yad yat sakalaṁ parasmai*
> *nārāyaṇāyeti samarpayet tat* ॥
>
> (Bhāg. 11. 2. 26).

that is, "all that we do, as a result of the inspiration of the Body or Speech, or Mind, or of the organs, or of the Intelligence, or of the Ātman, or according to our inherent nature, should be dedicated by us to the highest of the highest (*parātpara*) Nārāyaṇa". In short, that which is known as the combination of Knowledge and Action, or the Abandonment of the Hope of Fruit, or as Action performed with the idea of dedicating it to the Brahman (Gī. 4. 24; 5.10; 12. 12) in the Philosophy of the Absolute Self, is now known as "Action performed with the idea of dedicating it to Śrī Kṛṣṇa". At the root of the fact that persons who follow the Path of Devotion utter the words 'Govinda', 'Govinda' each time they partake of food, is the idea of dedicating everything to Śrī Kṛṣṇa. The Jñānin Janaka said that all his activities were carried on by him desirelessly, for public welfare; and the Devotees of the Blessed Lord perform even the Action of partaking of food or drink, with the sole idea of dedicating it to Śrī Kṛṣṇa. The prevalent practice of uttering the words, '*idaṁ kṛṣṇārpaṇam astu*" (i. e. "this is dedicated to Śrī Kṛṣṇa" —Trans.) uttered at the end of feasts given to Brahmins, or other religious performances, or of making an oblation of water with the words, "*harir dātā harir bhoktā*" (i. e., "the Blessed Lord is the Giver, the Blessed Lord is the Enjoyer" —Trans.) owes its origin to the above stanza from the Bhagavadgītā. It is true that the same thing has now happened to these utterances, as happens when the ear-ornaments disappear and the holes in the ear, which held those ornaments, remain; and the officiating priest now utters these words like a parrot, without understanding the true deep import conveyed by them; and the person who gives the feast, performs the physical exercise of making an oblation of water, like a deaf person; but, if we go to the root of the matter, this is nothing but a way of performing all Actions, after having given up the Hope of Fruit; and if one makes fun of this practice, the practice does not come into disrepute, but the person who makes fun, only makes an exhibition of his own ignorance. If every one performs all his Actions in this life—and even the Action of remaining alive—with the idea of dedicating them to Śrī Kṛṣṇa, and abandoning the Hope of Fruit, where is the room for a sinful desire, and how can any person perform any sinful Action? And also, where is the necessity of separately giving the advice that one should perform Action for the benefit of others, or even sacrifice one's life for the benefit of others? As both one's self, and every one else, has been included in the Parameśvara, and as the Parameśvara is included in one's self and every one else, both one's-interest and other's-interest are merged in the highest goal in the shape of the dedication to Śrī Kṛṣṇa; and then, the following words of the saint Tukārāma, namely, "the incarnations of saints are for the benefit of the world । they labour their own bodies by philanthropy", applies everywhere. I have proved logically in the last chapter, that there is no difficulty about the personal maintenance of that person, who performs all Actions with the idea of dedicating them to Śrī Kṛṣṇa; and it is with the same purport that the Blessed Lord has now conveyed the assurance in the Philosophy of Devotion in the Gītā that: "*teṣāṁ nityābhiyuktānāṁ yogakṣemaṁ vahāmy aham*" (Gī. 9 22), (i. e., "I look after the maintenance and welfare of those persons who are continually steeped in the Yoga"—Trans.) It is, therefore, not necessary to mention specifically that the highest of the Devotees of the Blessed Lord have to gradually raise Devotees of the lower orders to higher stages, without upsetting their devotion, and according to their respective competence, in the same way as the Jñānins, who have reached the highest state, must place ordinary persons on the Path of Righteousness, without upsetting their Intelligence (making a '*buddhi-bheda*'). (Gī. 3. 26). In short, all the doctrines which have been propounded in the Philosophy of the Absolute Self, or in the Philosophy of Cause and Effect, have in this way been left untouched in the Philosophy of Devotion, with only verbal differences; and it will be seen, that this method of harmonising Knowledge with Devotion, had come into vogue in India in very ancient times.

But, if a totally different meaning results from a verbal change, such a verbal change is not made; because, under any circumstances, the meaning of the words is the most important factor. For instance, if we make a verbal change in the doctrine from the Philosophy of Cause and Effect that everybody must personally make an effort for the Acquisition of Knowledge, and for thereby bringing about his own Release, and say, that even this Action is to be performed by the Parameśvara, the ignorant will become idle. Therefore, the doctrine "*ātmaiva hy ātmano bandhuḥ ātmaiva ripur ātmanaḥ*" (Gī. 6. 5.) i. e., "one is one's own friend and also one's own enemy", is also enunciated in the Philosophy of Devotion as it is, that is to say, without any verbal alteration. I have quoted above the stanza of Tukārāma, "Who has thereby lost anything? । one has oneself done harm to oneself" (Gā. 4448), (See p. 388 above—Trans). But the saint Tukārāma has in a still more explicit way said:

> "There is not with God, the bundle of Release ।
> that He can come and give it to you, as an object by itself ।
> One must conquer one's organs and liberate one's mind ।
> from the objects of pleasure ॥
>
> (Gā. 4297).

I have quoted above in the tenth chapter a similar stanza from the Upaniṣads, namely, '*mana eva manuṣyāṇāṁ kāraṇaṁ bandha-mokṣayoḥ*," (i. e., "the Mind alone is the reason for the Bondage, or the Release of man"—Trans). It is true that the Parameśvara is the performer of, and the One who causes to be performed, all the various makes and breaks in the world; yet, the doctrine of the Philosophy of Cause and Effect, that He gives a reward to every human being according to his own deeds, which has been formulated in order that He should not remain open to the charge of cruelty or partiality, has, for the same reason, been adopted without any verbal alteration in the Philosophy of Devotion. In the same way, although the Īśvara is looked upon as perceptible for purposes of worship, yet, the doctrine of the Philosophy of the Absolute Self, that 'whatever is perceptible, is only Māyā, and that the true Parameśvara is beyond that Māyā', is not given up in the Philosophy of Devotion; and I have stated above that the form of the Jīva, according to the Vedānta-Sūtras, has been retained unchanged in the Gītā for the same reason. This skill of our Vedic religion of harmonising the natural inclination of the human mind towards the Visible or the Perceptible, with the recondite doctrines of philosophy, is not to be seen in the Philosophy of Devotion of any other people, in any other country. When these people once attach themselves to some qualityful form of the Parameśvara, and thus come into the sphere of the Perceptible, they remain entangled in that sphere; and, not being able to see anything else besides that form, a vain glory about their own qualityful symbol, takes hold of their minds; and when this happens, they wrongly begin to differentiate between Philosophy on the one hand, and the Path of Devotion on the other hand. But, as the dawn of philosophy had taken place in our country from extremely ancient times, there is seen no conflict between Devotion and Spiritual Knowledge in the religion of the Gītā; and, whereas the Vedic Path of Knowledge is chastened by Devotion, the Vedic Path of Devotion is likewise chastened by Knowledge; and therefore, whichever Path is taken by man, he ultimately attains the same excellent state. The importance of this harmony between imperceptible Knowledge and perceptible Devotion, was not fully appreciated by the philosophers pertaining to the religion which adhered merely to the perceptible Christ; and it is not a matter of surprise, that from their one-sided and philosophically short-sighted point of view, there should appear to them an inconsistency in the philosophy of the Gītā. But, the most surprising part of it all is, that instead of appreciating this valuable quality of our Vedic religion, some imitative persons among us have come forward to find fault with that very religion! This is an excellent example of the saying in the *Māghakāvya* that:

athavā 'bhiniviṣṭabuddhiṣu | vrajati vyarthakatāṁ subhāṣitam ||,

i. e., "when once the Mind is engrossed by a false idea, even that which is true, is not appreciated by it" (Māghakāvya 16. 43).

The importance, which is attached to the fourth stage of life in the Path of Renunciation mentioned in the Smṛtis, is not attached to it in the Philosophy of Devotion, or in the Bhāgavata religion. It is true that the religious arrangement of the four castes and the four stages of life, is also mentioned in the Bhāgavata religion; but, as the principal emphasis of that religion is on Devotion, that man whose Devotion is the most intense, is the best of all, according to the Bhāgavata religion, whether he is a householder, or a denizen of the woods or a Saṁnyāsin; and that religion does not attach much importance to these modes of life (Bhāg. 11. 18. 13, 14). The state of a Saṁnyāsin is a very important part of the religion of the Smṛtis, but not of the Bhāgavata religion. Nevertheless, there is no rule that those who follow the Bhāgavata religion should never become Saṁnyāsins; and it is stated in the Gītā itself that Asceticism and Energism (Karma-Yoga) are both of equal value, from the point of view of Release. It is not impossible to come across people following the Path of Devotion, who have given up all their worldly activities, and become indifferent to the world, without having actually taken up the state of a Saṁnyāsin. Nay, we even come across such persons from early times; but I have clearly shown above in the eleventh chapter, that such persons did not carry any weight at that time; and that in the Bhagavadgītā, Energism (Karma-Yoga) has been considered superior to Abandonment of Action (Karma-Tyāga). This importance of the philosophy of Karma-Yoga gradually lost ground as time went, and in modern times it is the common belief of even persons following the Bhāgavata religion, that the Devotee of the Blessed Lord is a person who pays no attention to worldly affairs, but is steeped in Devotion, with total indifference to the world. It is, therefore, necessary to again explain here at some length what the chief doctrine and the true advice of the Gītā on this matter is, from the point of view of Devotion. The Brahman, according to the Philosophy of Devotion or the Bhāgavata religion, is the qualityful Bhagavān (Blessed Lord) Himself. If this Blessed Lord Himself carries on the activities of the world, and maintains the world by taking up various incarnations for the protection of saints and the punishment of evil-doers, it need not be said that the Devotees of the Blessed Lord must themselves follow the same example for the benefit of the world. Śrī Hanumān was the greatest devotee of Śrī Rāmacandra; but he did not give up the task of punishing evil-doers like Rāvaṇa and others by his own prowess. Even Bhīṣma is considered to be one of the greatest of the devotees of the Blessed Lord, but though he was himself a celibate throughout life he still carried on the work of protecting his kingdom and those on his side, according to his own status in life, so long as he was alive. It is true that when a man has Realised the Parameśvara by means of Devotion, he has no more anything left to acquire for his own benefit; but the Path of Devotion, which is founded on Love, does not eradicate noble sentiments like kindness, generosity, love of duty, etc.; and these emotions become on the contrary extremely purified; and then, instead of falling into the logical dilemma of whether to perform Action or not to perform Action, the Devotees of the Blessed Lord necessarily and naturally acquire a tendency, which promotes universal welfare and according to which, "the incarnations of saints are for the welfare of the world । they labour their own bodies by philanthropy ॥" (Gā. 929. 3); because, they acquire a non-differentiating frame of mind, as described above in the eleventh chapter, according to which:

He who takes to his bosom । such as are helpless ॥
And he who shows to his male and female servants ।
the same kindness which he shows to his son ॥

(Gā. 960).

If one says that it is the Parameśvara Who creates the world and carries on all the activities in it, it becomes clear that the arrangements of the four castes, which exist in order to satisfactorily carry on the activities of that creation, have come into existence by His will; and even in the Gītā, the Blessed Lord has clearly said that: "*cāturvarṇyaṁ mayā sṛṣṭaṁ guṇakarmavibhāgaśaḥ*" (Gī. 4. 13), (i. e., "I myself have created the four castes, according to the divisions of the qualities and of Karma" —Trans.). In short, it is the desire of the Parameśvara that every one should perform his social duties according to his own qualifications, and thereby bring about universal welfare *(lokasaṁgraha)*; and it then logically follows that the Parameśvara causes a human being to be born in order to make him a tool for getting performed by his hands, a particular portion of these worldly activities, which are going on by His will; and if a man does not perform that duty which the Parameśvara has intended that he should perform, he incurs the sin of not having carried out the behests of the Parameśvara Himself. If a man entertains the egotistical idea that "these Actions are Mine or that I perform them for my self-interest", then he will have to suffer the good or evil consequences of those Actions. But the Gītā says, that when a man performs those Actions merely as duties, and with the idea of dedicating them to the Parameśvara, in the belief that He is causing to be performed those Actions, which He intends to perform, by making him the man a tool for performing them (Gī. 11. 33), there is nothing wrong or improper about them; and, on the contrary, carrying out one's own duties in this way amounts to a kind of *sāttvika* worship of the Parameśvara Who lives in all created beings. The Blessed Lord has explained, by way of summary, the full sum and substance of His advice in the following words: "the Parameśvara remains in the hearts of all created beings, and makes them dance about like mechanical toys; therefore, the ideas that 'I give up a particular Action' or that 'I perform it' are both false; give up the Hope of Fruit, and continue performing all Actions with the idea of dedicating them to Śrī Kṛṣṇa; even if you determine that you will not perform those Actions, you will be forced to perform them as a result of your inherent nature (*prakṛti-dharma*); therefore, you must merge all selfish interests in the Blessed Lord, and perform all Actions which have befallen you, according to your status in life, for universal welfare, with an eye to the highest ideal (*paramārtha*), and with perfect indifference to the world; I am doing the same thing; see My example, and act accordingly". As there is no conflict between Jñāna and Desireless Karma, so also does there arise no conflict between Devotion, and Actions performed with the idea of dedicating them to Kṛṣṇa. Saint Tukārāma, the king of Devotees in the Maharashtra, has explained his merger into the form of the Parameśvara, Who is "*aṇoraṇiyān mahato mahīyān*" (Kaṭha. 2. 20; Gī. 8. 9), i. e., "smaller than the atom, and bigger than the biggest', as a result of Devotion; and he has clearly said that he was living in the world only for the purpose of doing good to others, in the following *abhaṅga* stanzas :-

I (Tukā) am more minute than the minutest atom ।
 I am as big as the firmament ।
I have annihilated by swallowing that body ।
 which is only a form of the Cosmic Illusion ॥
I have gone beyond the trinity ।

a light has been lighted in this Body ı
Tukā says that: "now ı I survive only for philanthropy"ıı
(Gā. 3587).

He has nowhere stated that there is no more anything left for him to do, as is said by those who follow the Path of Saṁnyāsa; in the same way, the opinion of the saint Tukārāma on this matter becomes quite clear from the following other *abhaṅga* stanzas, namely,

Taking up the beggar's bowl ı
fie on such a disgraceful life ! ı
Such persons will by Nārāyaṇa ı be always abandoned ıı
(Gā. 2595)

or,

The Real-worshipper (*satyavādi*) performs all the activities of worldly life ı
in the same way as the lotus remains in the water, untouched by the water ı
He who is philanthropical, he who is kindly towards all created beings ı
he is in the state of being merged in the Ātman ı
(Gā. 3780. 2. 3).

But, although the saint Tukārāma was a householder, his inclination was towards Abandonment of Action; and therefore, if one wants a full explanation of the doctrine of the Gītā, or of the characteristic of the Bhāgavata religion, namely, 'intense Devotion combined with Desireless Action, performed with the idea of dedicating it to the Parameśvara', he must turn to the work *Dāsabodha*, written by Śrī Samartha Rāmadāsa Svāmi, who was the 'venerable preceptor' to whom saint Tukārāma himself directed Śivāji Mahārāja to 'surrender himself'. He (Rāmadāsa) has said, that ordinary people should learn to perform their own Actions, by seeing how the Siddhas, who have become perfect by realising the pure form of the Parameśvara, keep performing their own Actions, desirelessly, according to their own qualifications, and in order to "make many persons wise" (Dāsa. 19. 10. 14); and after repeating several times that "unless a man does something, nothing happens" (Dāsa. 19. 10. 25; 12. 9. 6; 18. 7. 3), he has said as follows in the last dixaine, in order to establish a complete harmony between the power of Karma and the redeeming power of Devotion:

Strength lies in activity । the strength will be his who is active ।
But in such a man there must be । the seat of the Blessed Lord ॥

(Dāsa. 20. 4. 26)

The same meaning is conveyed by the words: "*mām anusmara yudhya ca*" (Gī. 8. 7), i. e., "always remember me and fight"; or, by the statement at the end of the sixth chapter that, "even among the Karma-yogins, the Devotee is the most excellent"; and, there is also a statement in the eighteenth chapter that:

yataḥ pravṛttir bhūtānāṁ yena sarvam idam tatam ।
svakarmaṇā tam abhyarcya siddhiṁ vindati mānavaḥ ॥

(Gī. 18. 46)

that is, "man attains perfection (*siddhi*) by worshipping by Desireless Actions, proper to his status in life (and not by flowers, or by words merely) that Parameśvara, Who has created the whole of this world". Nay; the meaning of this stanza and even of the entire Gītā is that by performing Actions desirelessly, according to one's own status in life, a man performs a sort of worship, devotion, or prayer of that Virāṭa-formed Parameśvara. Who is inside all created beings. When the Gītā asks a person to perform the worship of the Parameśvara by Actions proper to his status in life, it is not to be understood as saying that the nine kinds of Devotion, such as, "*śravaṇaṁ kīrtanaṁ viṣṇoḥ*", (i. e., "saying or hearing the praise of the Lord Viṣṇu"—Trans.) are not acceptable to it. But the Gītā says, that (i) it is not proper to abandon Action as being inferior, and to remain steeped only in this nine-fold form of Devotion; (ii) that one must perform all the various Actions, which have befallen one, according to the injunctions of the Śāstras, and that (iii) "these Actions should not be performed, as pertaining to oneself, but with the idea of the Parameśvara in the Mind, and with a mine-less (*nirmama*) frame of mind, believing that they are the Actions of the Parameśvara, and for the benefit of the world created by Him; so that, the Karma is not wasted, but on the other hand, these Actions amount to the service or worship of, or the Devotion to the Parameśvara; and instead of one's acquiring the sin or merit of the Action, one attains a blissful state". Those commentators on the Gītā, who follow the Path of Devotion, disregard this doctrine; and in their works, they explain the purport of the Gītā to be, that Karma or Action is inferior and Devotion is paramount. But, this summary drawn by commentators pertaining to the School of Devotion, is as one-sided as that drawn by the followers of the School of Renunciation. The Path of Devotion mentioned in the Gītā is based on Action, and the most important principle in it is, that the worship of the Parameśvara is made not only by speech or by flowers, but also by Desireless Actions, pertinent to one's own status in life; and that such a worship must necessarily be performed by everybody. And, as this principle of Devotion *cum* Action has not been enunciated anywhere else in the same way as in the Gītā, this must be considered to be the characteristic of the Philosophy of Devotion mentioned in the Gītā.

Although in this way, I have established a complete consonance between the Path of Knowledge and the Path of Devotion from the point of view of Karma-Yoga, yet, I must, before concluding, clearly mention the one important factor which is to be found in the Philosophy of Devotion in addition to those found in the Philosophy of Knowledge. As the Path of Knowledge is based entirely on Intelligence, it becomes difficult to follow for ordinary persons of poor intelligence; and, as has been stated above, it is easy for everybody to follow the Path of Devotion, as it is based on Faith, and is accessible by love, and visible. But, there is another difficulty in the Path of Knowledge besides its being difficult to follow. If one considers the Mīmāṁsā of Jaimini, or the Upaniṣads, or the Vedānta-Sūtras, they are full of discussions about sacrificial ritual prescribed by the Śrutis, or about the Parabrahman in the form of "*neti, neti*" (i. e., "It is not this, It is not that"—Trans.), which are based on Abandonment of Action; and they have ultimately laid down that the right of performing sacrificial ritual prescribed by the Śrutis as a means of acquiring heaven, as also of reciting the Vedas and the Upaniṣads, which was necessary for obtaining Release, belonged only to the three upper classes (Ve. Sū.

1. 3. 34–38). How the women belonging to these three classes, or the ordinary men and women engaged in agriculture, and other occupations, for the benefit of society, according to the arrangement of the four castes, are to obtain Release, is a question which has not been considered in these books. Well; if one says that women and Śūdras can never attain Release because the Vedas are thus inaccessible to them, then, there are statements in the Upaniṣads that Gārgī and other women obtained Perfection by acquiring Knowledge; and there are statements in the Purāṇas that Vidura and other Śūdras did likewise (Ve. Sū. 3. 4. 36–39). Therefore, one cannot lay down the proposition, that it is only the men folk belonging to the three upper classes, who obtain Release: and if one accepts the position that even women and Sūdras can obtain Release, then, one must explain by what means they can obtain Knowledge. Bādarāyaṇācārya mentions the means: "*viśeṣānu-grahaś ca*" (Ve. Sū. 3. 4. 38), i. e., "the special favour of the Parameśvara"; and it is stated in the Bhāgavata (Bhāg. 1. 4. 25) that this means, in the shape of Devotion *cum* Action, has been mentioned as a special favour *(viśeṣānugraha)*, "in the Bhārata and naturally also in the Gītā, because the Śrutis cannot be heard by women, Śūdras, or nominal Brahmins (of the Kali-yuga)". Although the Knowledge which is acquired by this path, and the Knowledge of the Brahman mentioned in the Upaniṣads, are one and the same, yet, the difference between men and women or between Brahmins, Kṣatriyas, Vaiśyas, and Śūdras does not any more remain in this path, and the special quality of this path has been mentioned in the Gītā in the following stanza:—

mām hi pārtha vyapāśritya ye 'pi syuḥ pāpayonayaḥ ।
striyo vaiśyās tathā śūdrās te 'pi yānti parām gatim ॥

(Gī. 9. 32)

that is, "O, Partha, by taking shelter in Me, women, Vaiśyas and Śūdras and other lower classes, in which birth has been taken as a result of sin, attain the highest perfection"; and this same stanza has appeared again in the Anugītā in the Mahābhārata (Ma. Bhā. Aśva. 19. 61); and, it is stated in the conversation between the Brahmin and the hunter *(vyādha)* in the Vanaparva, that the flesh-selling hunter has explained how

Release can be obtained by acting according to one's own duties desirelessly; and the same explanation has been given in the Śānti-parva by Tulādhāra, who was a merchant, to the Brahmin ascetic Jājali (Ma. Bhā. Vana. 206-214; Śān. 260-263). From this it follows that, that man whose Reason has become equable towards all, is the highest of men, whether he is a carpenter, or a merchant, or a butcher, by profession. It is clear that, according to the Blessed Lord, the spiritual worth of a man does not depend on the profession followed by him, or on the caste to which he belongs, but entirely on the purity of his conscience. When in this way, the gateway of Release has been opened to all people in society, there arises in the hearts of all such persons, a strange self-consciousness, of which the nature can be gauged from the history of the Bhāgavata religion in Maharashtra. To the Parameśvara, women, or the lowest of mixed tribes, or Brahmins are the same. "The Parameśvara craves (only) for your Faith". He does not care for symbols, or for the black or white colour of the skin, nor does He care for the difference between men and women, or castes like the Brahmins or the Cāṇḍālas (tribes born of the mixture of Brahmins and Śūdras). The saint Tukārāma says that:—

> Brahmins, Kṣatriyas, Vaiśyas, and Śūdras ।
> and the Cāṇḍālas, all have the right ।
> As also children, women, men, । and even prostitutes ॥
> Tukā says that he has । found by experience ।
> That even others, who are devout ।
> experience happiness by their good fortune ॥
> (Gā. 2382. 5, 6)

Nay; it is a doctrine of the Gītā, that "however sinful a man may be, if he surrenders himself to the Blessed Lord, wholly and solely, even at the moment of his death, the Parameśvara does not cast him off" (Gī. 9. 30; and 8. 5–8). Seeing the word 'prostitutes' in the above stanza, some learned persons, who parade their purity, might feel offended; but it must be said that such persons do not understand the true principle of Religion. This doctrine has been adopted not only in the Hindu religion, but also in the Buddhist religion (Milinda-Praśṇa 3. 7. 2); and there are stories in Buddhistic religious treatises, that Buddha initiated a prostitute by name Āmrapālī, as also a thief by name Agulīmāla; and there is a statement even in the Christian scriptures that because one of the two thieves, who were crucified at the same time as the Lord Christ, surrendered himself to the Lord at the moment of his death, he was saved by the Christ on that account (Luke. 23. 42 and 43); and the Lord Christ has Himself said in one place that even prostitutes, who put faith in His religion would obtain salvation (Matthew. 21. 31; Luke. 7. 50). And I have shown above in the tenth chapter that the same conclusion is arrived at even from the point of view of the Philosophy of the Absolute Self (*adhyātma*). But, although this religious doctrine is logically unquestionable, yet, a man, the whole of whose life has been spent in doing evil actions, will, in all probability, not get the inspiration of surrendering himself wholly and solely to the Blessed Lord at the moment of his death; and then nothing more results beyond mechanically opening the mouth in the throes of death to utter the letter 'Rā', and then closing it for ever by uttering the next letter 'ma'. Therefore, the definite assurance of the Blessed Lord to everybody is that, if a man throughout his life, and not only at the moment of death, keeps the thought of the Blessed Lord continually in his mind, and performs all Actions pertaining to his status in life, solely with the idea of dedicating them to Him, then, whatever may be the caste to which he belongs, he is as good as Released, notwithstanding that he has been performing Actions (Gī. 9. 26–28 and 30–34).

When one considers and takes into account the sense of Equality appearing in the Philosophy of Devotion taught by the Gītā, and its capacity to enable all equally, to easily grasp the Knowledge of the identity of the Brahman and the Ātman mentioned in the Upaniṣads, without sacrificing the ordinary activities of worldly life, and without establishing any difference between the four castes or the four stages of life, or the communities, or even between men and women, one understands the true import of the summing up of the Religion of the Gītā made by the Blessed Lord in the last chapter of the Gītā, by way of a definite assurance, in the following terms:

"give up all other religions (*dharma*), and surrender yourself solely to Me; I shall redeem you from all sins, do not be afraid". The word '*dharma*' has here been used in the comprehensive meaning that, all the practical paths or means, which have been shown for acquiring the highest excellence of the Self, in the shape of reaching the Parameśvara, by remaining free from sin, while following the ordinary activities of life, are '*dharma*' (duty). In the Anugītā, in the conversation between the preceptor and the disciple, the Ṛṣis are said to have questioned Brahmadeva as to which of the various paths, such as, Non-Violence, Veracity, Penances, Spiritual Knowledge, Sacrificial ritual, Charity, Karma, Renunciation etc., mentioned by different people, was the most correct one (Aśva. 49); and even in the Śānti-parva, a question has been asked in the Uncchа-vṛtyupākhyāna as to which of the various paths, such as, the duties enjoined on the householder, or on the denizens of the woods, or on kings, or the service of one's parents, or death on a battle-field for the Kṣatriya, or religious contemplation for the Brahmin, etc., was the most acceptable path, as all these had been mentioned in the Śāstras as the means of acquiring heaven. These various paths of *dharma* or Dharmas may appear to be mutually inconsistent; but, in as much as the ultimate ideal of 'equality of affection towards all created beings' is reached by means of the concentration of the Mind by Faith, arising from one's taking to any one of these paths, the writers of the Śāstras consider all these practical paths as of equal value. Nevertheless, as there is a likelihood of the Mind becoming confused as a result of its being caught in the various paths of the worship of different symbols, the final and definite assurance of the Blessed Lord, not only to Arjuna, but to everybody in the name of Arjuna, is that, one should give up all the various paths of Purification of the Mind, and should "surrender yourself solely to ME; I shall redeem you from all sins, do not be afraid". Even the Saint Tukārāma makes his ultimate prayer to God, which entails the annihilation of diverse kinds of *dharma*, in the following words:—

Burn that knowledge, burn that wisdom ।
may my Faith remain on the feet of the Viṭhṭhala ॥

Burn those religious practices, burn that contemplation ।
may my Mind remain fixed on the feet of the Viṭhṭhala ॥
(Gā. 3464)

This is the pinnacle of definite advice, or of prayer.

'Devotion' is the last sweet mouthful out of the golden dish of Śrīmad Bhagavadgītā. We have taken this mouthful of Love; now let us take the final sip of water (*āposṇī*) * and prepare to rise from the feast.

---

* This is a religious practice followed by Brahmins in India, who take a final sip of water, known as '*āposṇī*', from the hollow of palm, uttering a *mantra* (sacred words), just before finishing the dinner and rising—Trans.

END OF VOLUME I

TEXT OF BHAGAVADGITA

नासतो विद्यते भावो नाभावो विद्यते सतः । उभयोरपि दृष्टोऽन्तस्त्वनयोस्तत्त्वदर्शिभिः ॥१६॥ अविनाशि तु तद्विद्धि येन सर्वमिदं ततम् । विनाशमव्ययस्यास्य न कश्चित्कर्तुमर्हति ॥१७॥ अन्तवन्त इमे देहा नित्यस्योक्ताः शरीरिणः । अनाशिनोऽप्रमेयस्य तस्माद्युध्यस्व भारत ॥१८॥ य एनं वेत्ति हन्तारं यश्चैनं मन्यते हतम् । उभौ तौ न विजानीतो नायं हन्ति न हन्यते ॥१९॥ न जायते म्रियते वा कदाचिन्नायं भूत्वा भविता वा न भूयः । अजो नित्यः शाश्वतोऽयं पुराणो न हन्यते हन्यमाने शरीरे ॥२०॥ वेदाविनाशिनं नित्यं य एनमजमव्ययम् । कथं स पुरुषः पार्थ कं घातयति हन्ति कम् ॥२१॥ वासांसि जीर्णानि यथा विहाय नवानि गृह्णाति नरोऽपराणि । तथा शरीराणि विहाय जीर्णान्यन्यानि संयाति नवानि देही ॥२२॥ नैनं छिन्दन्ति शस्त्राणि नैनं दहति पावकः । न चैनं क्लेदयन्त्यापो न शोषयति मारुतः ॥२३॥ अच्छेद्योऽयमदाह्योऽयमक्लेद्योऽशोष्य एव च । नित्यः सर्वगतः स्थाणुरचलोऽयं सनातनः ॥२४॥ अव्यक्तोऽयमचिन्त्योऽयमविकार्योऽयमुच्यते । तस्मादेवं विदित्वैनं नानुशोचितुमर्हसि ॥२५॥ अथ चैनं नित्यजातं नित्यं वा मन्यसे मृतम् । तथापि त्वं महाबाहो नैवं शोचितुमर्हसि ॥२६॥ जातस्य हि ध्रुवो मृत्युर्ध्रुवं जन्म मृतस्य च । तस्मादपरिहार्येऽर्थे न त्वं शोचितुमर्हसि ॥२७॥ अव्यक्तादीनि भूतानि व्यक्तमध्यानि भारत । अव्यक्तनिधनान्येव तत्र का परिदेवना ॥२८॥ आश्चर्यवत्पश्यति कश्चिदेनमाश्चर्यवद्वदति तथैव चान्यः । आश्चर्यवच्चैनमन्यः शृणोति श्रुत्वाप्येनं वेद न चैव कश्चित् ॥२९॥ देही नित्यमवध्योऽयं देहे सर्वस्य भारत । तस्मात्सर्वाणि भूतानि न त्वं शोचितुमर्हसि ॥३०॥ स्वधर्ममपि चावेक्ष्य न विकम्पितुमर्हसि । धर्म्याद्धि युद्धाच्छ्रेयोऽन्यत्क्षत्रियस्य न विद्यते ॥३१॥ यदृच्छया चोपपन्नं स्वर्गद्वारमपावृतम् । सुखिनः क्षत्रियाः पार्थ लभन्ते युद्धमीदृशम् ॥३२॥ अथ चेत्त्वमिमं धर्म्यं संग्रामं न करिष्यसि । ततः स्वधर्मं कीर्तिं च हित्वा पापमवाप्स्यसि ॥३३॥ अकीर्तिं चापि भूतानि कथयिष्यन्ति तेऽव्ययाम् । संभावितस्य चाकीर्तिर्मरणादतिरिच्यते ॥३४॥ भयाद्रणादुपरतं मंस्यन्ते त्वां महारथाः । येषां च त्वं बहुमतो भूत्वा यास्यसि लाघवम् ॥३५॥ अवाच्यवादांश्च बहून्वदिष्यन्ति तवाहिताः । निन्दन्तस्तव सामर्थ्यं ततो दुःखतरं नु किम् ॥३६॥ हतो वा प्राप्स्यसि स्वर्गं जित्वा वा भोक्ष्यसे महीम् । तस्मादुत्तिष्ठ कौन्तेय युद्धाय कृतनिश्चयः ॥३७॥ सुखदुःखे समे कृत्वा लाभालाभौ जयाजयौ । ततो युद्धाय युज्यस्व नैवं पापमवाप्स्यसि ॥३८॥ एषा तेऽभिहिता सांख्ये बुद्धिर्योगे त्विमां शृणु । बुद्ध्या युक्तो यया पार्थ कर्मबन्धं प्रहास्यसि ॥३९॥ नेहाभिक्रमनाशोऽस्ति प्रत्यवायो न विद्यते । स्वल्पमप्यस्य धर्मस्य त्रायते महतो भयात् ॥४०॥ व्यवसायात्मिका बुद्धिरेकेह कुरुनन्दन । बहुशाखा ह्यनन्ताश्च बुद्धयोऽव्यवसायिनाम् ॥४१॥ यामिमां पुष्पितां वाचं प्रवदन्त्यविपश्चितः । वेदवादरताः पार्थ नान्यदस्तीति वादिनः ॥४२॥ कामात्मानः स्वर्गपरा जन्मकर्मफलप्रदाम् । क्रियाविशेषबहुलां भोगैश्वर्यगतिं प्रति ॥४३॥ भोगैश्वर्यप्रसक्तानां तयापहृतचेतसाम् । व्यवसायात्मिका बुद्धिः समाधौ न विधीयते ॥४४॥ त्रैगुण्यविषया वेदा निस्त्रैगुण्यो भवार्जुन । निर्द्वन्द्वो नित्यसत्त्वस्थो निर्योगक्षेम आत्मवान् ॥४५॥ यावानर्थ उदपाने सर्वतः संप्लुतोदके । तावान्सर्वेषु वेदेषु ब्राह्मणस्य विजानतः ॥४६॥ कर्मण्येवाधिकारस्ते मा फलेषु कदाचन । मा कर्मफलहेतुर्भूर्मा ते सङ्गोऽस्त्वकर्मणि ॥४७॥ योगस्थः कुरु कर्माणि सङ्गं त्यक्त्वा धनंजय । सिद्ध्यसिद्ध्योः समो भूत्वा समत्वं योग उच्यते ॥४८॥ दूरेण ह्यवरं कर्म बुद्धियोगाद्धनंजय । बुद्धौ शरणमन्विच्छ कृपणाः फलहेतवः ॥४९॥ बुद्धियुक्तो जहातीह उभे सुकृतदुष्कृते । तस्माद्योगाय युज्यस्व योगः कर्मसु कौशलम् ॥५०॥ कर्मजं बुद्धियुक्ता हि फलं त्यक्त्वा मनीषिणः । जन्मबन्धविनिर्मुक्ताः पदं गच्छन्त्यनामयम् ॥५१॥ यदा ते मोहकलिलं बुद्धिर्व्यतितरिष्यति । तदा गन्तासि निर्वेदं श्रोतव्यस्य श्रुतस्य च ॥५२॥ श्रुतिविप्रतिपन्ना ते यदा स्थास्यति निश्चला । समाधावचला बुद्धिस्तदा योगमवाप्स्यसि ॥५३॥

अर्जुन उवाच ॥ स्थितप्रज्ञस्य का भाषा समाधिस्थस्य केशव । स्थितधीः किं प्रभाषेत किमासीत व्रजेत किम् ॥५४॥

श्रीभगवानुवाच ॥ प्रजहाति यदा कामान्सर्वान्पार्थ मनोगतान् । आत्मन्येवात्मना तुष्टः स्थितप्रज्ञस्तदोच्यते ॥५५॥ दुःखेष्वनुद्विग्नमनाः सुखेषु विगतस्पृहः । वीतरागभयक्रोधः स्थितधीर्मुनिरुच्यते ॥५६॥ यः सर्वत्रानभिस्नेहस्तत्तत्प्राप्य शुभाशुभम् । नाभिनन्दति न द्वेष्टि तस्य प्रज्ञा प्रतिष्ठिता ॥५७॥ यदा संहरते चायं कूर्मोऽङ्गानीव सर्वशः । इन्द्रियाणीन्द्रियार्थेभ्यस्तस्य प्रज्ञा प्रतिष्ठिता ॥५८॥ विषया विनिवर्तन्ते निराहारस्य देहिनः । रसवर्जं रसोऽप्यस्य परं दृष्ट्वा निवर्तते ॥५९॥ यततो ह्यपि कौन्तेय पुरुषस्य विपश्चितः । इन्द्रियाणि प्रमाथीनि हरन्ति प्रसभं मनः ॥६०॥ तानि सर्वाणि संयम्य युक्त आसीत मत्परः । वशे हि यस्येन्द्रियाणि तस्य प्रज्ञा प्रतिष्ठिता ॥६१॥ ध्यायतो विषयान्पुंसः सङ्गस्तेषूपजायते । सङ्गात्संजायते कामः कामात्क्रोधोऽभिजायते ॥६२॥ क्रोधाद्भवति संमोहः संमोहात्स्मृतिविभ्रमः । स्मृतिभ्रंशाद्बुद्धिनाशो बुद्धिनाशात्प्रणश्यति ॥६३॥ रागद्वेषवियुक्तैस्तु विषयानिन्द्रियैश्चरन् । आत्मवश्यैर्विधेयात्मा प्रसादमधिगच्छति ॥६४॥ प्रसादे सर्वदुःखानां हानिरस्योपजायते । प्रसन्नचेतसो ह्याशु बुद्धिः पर्यवतिष्ठते ॥६५॥ नास्ति बुद्धिरयुक्तस्य न चायुक्तस्य भावना । न चाभावयतः शान्तिरशान्तस्य कुतः सुखम् ॥६६॥ इन्द्रियाणां हि चरतां यन्मनोऽनुविधीयते । तदस्य हरति प्रज्ञां वायुर्नावमिवाम्भसि ॥६७॥ तस्माद्यस्य महाबाहो निगृहीतानि सर्वशः । इन्द्रियाणीन्द्रियार्थेभ्यस्तस्य प्रज्ञा प्रतिष्ठिता ॥६८॥ या निशा सर्वभूतानां तस्यां जागर्ति संयमी । यस्यां जाग्रति भूतानि सा निशा पश्यतो मुनेः ॥६९॥ आपूर्यमाणमचलप्रतिष्ठं समुद्रमापः प्रविशन्ति यद्वत् । तद्वत्कामा यं प्रविशन्ति सर्वे स शान्तिमाप्नोति न कामकामी ॥७०॥ विहाय कामान्यः सर्वान्पुमांश्चरति निःस्पृहः । निर्ममो निरहंकारः स शान्तिमधिगच्छति ॥७१॥ एषा ब्राह्मी स्थितिः पार्थ नैनां प्राप्य विमुह्यति । स्थित्वास्यामन्तकालेऽपि ब्रह्मनिर्वाणमृच्छति ॥७२॥ इति सांख्ययोगो नाम द्वितीयोऽध्यायः ॥२॥

अर्जुन उवाच ॥ ज्यायसी चेत्कर्मणस्ते मता बुद्धिर्जनार्दन । तत्किं कर्मणि घोरे मां नियोजयसि केशव ॥१॥ व्यामिश्रेणेव वाक्येन बुद्धिं मोहयसीव मे । तदेकं वद निश्चित्य येन श्रेयोऽहमाप्नुयाम् ॥२॥

श्रीभगवानुवाच ॥ लोकेऽस्मिन्द्विविधा निष्ठा पुरा प्रोक्ता मयानघ । ज्ञानयोगेन सांख्यानां कर्मयोगेन योगिनाम् ॥३॥ न कर्मणामनारम्भान्नैष्कर्म्यं पुरुषोऽश्नुते । न च संन्यसनादेव सिद्धिं समधिगच्छति ॥४॥ न हि कश्चित्क्षणमपि जातु तिष्ठत्यकर्मकृत् । कार्यते ह्यवशः कर्म सर्वः प्रकृतिजैर्गुणैः ॥५॥ कर्मेन्द्रियाणि संयम्य य आस्ते मनसा स्मरन् । इन्द्रियार्थान्विमूढात्मा मिथ्याचारः स उच्यते ॥६॥ यस्त्विन्द्रियाणि मनसा नियम्यारभतेऽर्जुन । कर्मेन्द्रियैः कर्मयोगमसक्तः स विशिष्यते ॥७॥ नियतं कुरु कर्म त्वं कर्म ज्यायो ह्यकर्मणः । शरीरयात्रापि च ते न प्रसिद्ध्येदकर्मणः ॥८॥ यज्ञार्थात्कर्मणोऽन्यत्र लोकोऽयं कर्मबन्धनः । तदर्थं कर्म कौन्तेय मुक्तसङ्गः समाचर ॥९॥ सहयज्ञाः प्रजाः सृष्ट्वा पुरोवाच प्रजापतिः । अनेन प्रसविष्यध्वमेष वोऽस्त्विष्टकामधुक् ॥१०॥ देवान्भावयतानेन ते देवा भावयन्तु वः । परस्परं भावयन्तः श्रेयः परमवाप्स्यथ ॥११॥ इष्टान्भोगान्हि वो देवा दास्यन्ते यज्ञभाविताः । तैर्दत्तानप्रदायैभ्यो यो भुङ्क्ते स्तेन एव सः ॥१२॥ यज्ञशिष्टाशिनः सन्तो मुच्यन्ते सर्वकिल्बिषैः । भुञ्जते ते त्वघं पापा ये पचन्त्यात्मकारणात् ॥१३॥ अन्नाद्भवन्ति भूतानि पर्जन्यादन्नसंभवः । यज्ञाद्भवति पर्जन्यो यज्ञः कर्मसमुद्भवः ॥१४॥ कर्म ब्रह्मोद्भवं विद्धि ब्रह्माक्षरसमुद्भवम् । तस्मात्सर्वगतं ब्रह्म नित्यं यज्ञे प्रतिष्ठितम् ॥१५॥ एवं प्रवर्तितं चक्रं नानुवर्तयतीह यः । अघायुरिन्द्रियारामो मोघं पार्थ स जीवति ॥१६॥ यस्त्वात्मरतिरेव स्यादात्मतृप्तश्च मानवः । आत्मन्येव च संतुष्टस्तस्य कार्यं न विद्यते ॥१७॥ नैव तस्य कृतेनार्थो नाकृतेनेह कश्चन । न चास्य सर्वभूतेषु कश्चिदर्थव्यपाश्रयः ॥१८॥ तस्मादसक्तः सततं कार्यं कर्म समाचर । असक्तो ह्याचरन्कर्म परमाप्नोति पूरुषः ॥१९॥ कर्मणैव हि संसिद्धिमास्थिता जनकादयः । लोकसंग्रहमेवापि संपश्यन्कर्तुमर्हसि ॥२०॥ यद्यदाचरति श्रेष्ठस्तत्तदेवेतरो जनः । स यत्प्रमाणं कुरुते लोकस्तदनुवर्तते ॥२१॥ न मे पार्थास्ति कर्तव्यं त्रिषु लोकेषु किंचन । नानवाप्तमवाप्तव्यं वर्त एव च कर्मणि ॥२२॥ यदि ह्यहं न वर्तेयं जातु कर्मण्यतन्द्रितः । मम वर्त्मानुवर्तन्ते मनुष्याः पार्थ सर्वशः ॥२३॥ उत्सीदेयुरिमे लोका न कुर्यां कर्म चेदहम् । संकरस्य च कर्ता स्यामुपहन्यामिमाः प्रजाः ॥२४॥ सक्ताः कर्मण्यविद्वांसो यथा कुर्वन्ति भारत । कुर्याद्विद्वांस्तथासक्तश्चिकीर्षुर्लोकसंग्रहम् ॥२५॥ न बुद्धिभेदं जनयेदज्ञानां कर्मसङ्गिनाम् । जोषयेत्सर्वकर्माणि विद्वान्युक्तः समाचरन् ॥२६॥ प्रकृतेः क्रियमाणानि गुणैः कर्माणि सर्वशः । अहंकारविमूढात्मा कर्ताहमिति मन्यते ॥२७॥ तत्त्ववित्तु महाबाहो गुणकर्मविभागयोः । गुणा गुणेषु वर्तन्त इति मत्वा न सज्जते ॥२८॥ प्रकृतेर्गुणसंमूढाः सज्जन्ते गुणकर्मसु । तानकृत्स्नविदो मन्दान्कृत्स्नविन्न विचालयेत् ॥२९॥ मयि सर्वाणि कर्माणि संन्यस्याध्यात्मचेतसा । निराशीर्निर्ममो भूत्वा युध्यस्व विगतज्वरः ॥३०॥ ये मे मतमिदं नित्यमनुतिष्ठन्ति मानवाः । श्रद्धावन्तोऽनसूयन्तो मुच्यन्ते तेऽपि कर्मभिः ॥३१॥ ये त्वेतदभ्यसूयन्तो नानुतिष्ठन्ति मे मतम् । सर्वज्ञानविमूढांस्तान्विद्धि नष्टानचेतसः ॥३२॥ सदृशं चेष्टते स्वस्याः प्रकृतेर्ज्ञानवानपि । प्रकृतिं यान्ति भूतानि निग्रहः किं करिष्यति ॥३३॥ इन्द्रियस्येन्द्रियस्यार्थे रागद्वेषौ व्यवस्थितौ । तयोर्न वशमागच्छेत्तौ ह्यस्य परिपन्थिनौ ॥३४॥ श्रेयान्स्वधर्मो विगुणः परधर्मात्स्वनुष्ठितात् । स्वधर्मे निधनं श्रेयः परधर्मो भयावहः ॥३५॥

अर्जुन उवाच ॥ अथ केन प्रयुक्तोऽयं पापं चरति पूरुषः । अनिच्छन्नपि वार्ष्णेय बलादिव नियोजितः ॥३६॥

श्रीभगवानुवाच ॥ काम एष क्रोध एष रजोगुणसमुद्भवः । महाशनो महापाप्मा विद्ध्येनमिह वैरिणम् ॥३७॥ धूमेनाव्रियते वह्निर्यथादर्शो मलेन च । यथोल्बेनावृतो गर्भस्तथा तेनेदमावृतम् ॥३८॥ आवृतं ज्ञानमेतेन ज्ञानिनो नित्यवैरिणा । कामरूपेण कौन्तेय दुष्पूरेणानलेन च ॥३९॥ इन्द्रियाणि मनो बुद्धिरस्याधिष्ठानमुच्यते । एतैर्विमोहयत्येष ज्ञानमावृत्य देहिनम् ॥४०॥ तस्मात्त्वमिन्द्रियाण्यादौ नियम्य भरतर्षभ । पाप्मानं प्रजहि ह्येनं ज्ञानविज्ञाननाशनम् ॥४१॥ इन्द्रियाणि पराण्याहुरिन्द्रियेभ्यः परं मनः । मनसस्तु परा बुद्धिर्यो बुद्धेः परतस्तु सः ॥४२॥ एवं बुद्धेः परं बुद्ध्वा संस्तभ्यात्मानमात्मना । जहि शत्रुं महाबाहो कामरूपं दुरासदम् ॥४३॥ इति श्रीमद्भगवद्गीता० कर्मयोगो नाम तृतीयोऽध्यायः ॥३॥

श्रीभगवानुवाच ॥ इमं विवस्वते योगं प्रोक्तवानहमव्ययम् । विवस्वान्मनवे प्राह मनुरिक्ष्वाकवेऽब्रवीत् ॥१॥ एवं परंपराप्राप्तमिमं राजर्षयो विदुः । स कालेनेह महता योगो नष्टः परंतप ॥२॥ स एवायं मया तेऽद्य योगः प्रोक्तः पुरातनः । भक्तोऽसि मे सखा चेति रहस्यं ह्येतदुत्तमम् ॥३॥

अर्जुन उवाच ॥ अपरं भवतो जन्म परं जन्म विवस्वतः । कथमेतद्विजानीयां त्वमादौ प्रोक्तवानिति ॥४॥

श्रीभगवानुवाच ॥ बहूनि मे व्यतीतानि जन्मानि तव चार्जुन । तान्यहं वेद सर्वाणि न त्वं वेत्थ परंतप ॥५॥ अजोऽपि सन्नव्ययात्मा भूतानामीश्वरोऽपि सन् । प्रकृतिं स्वामधिष्ठाय संभवाम्यात्ममायया ॥६॥ यदा यदा हि धर्मस्य ग्लानिर्भवति भारत । अभ्युत्थानमधर्मस्य तदात्मानं सृजाम्यहम् ॥७॥ परित्राणाय साधूनां विनाशाय च दुष्कृताम् । धर्मसंस्थापनार्थाय संभवामि युगे युगे ॥८॥ जन्म कर्म च मे दिव्यमेवं यो वेत्ति तत्त्वतः । त्यक्त्वा देहं पुनर्जन्म नैति मामेति सोऽर्जुन ॥९॥ वीतरागभयक्रोधा मन्मया मामुपाश्रिताः । बहवो ज्ञानतपसा पूता मद्भावमागताः ॥१०॥ ये यथा मां प्रपद्यन्ते तांस्तथैव भजाम्यहम् । मम वर्त्मानुवर्तन्ते मनुष्याः पार्थ सर्वशः ॥११॥ काङ्क्षन्तः कर्मणां सिद्धिं यजन्त इह देवताः । क्षिप्रं हि मानुषे लोके सिद्धिर्भवति कर्मजा ॥१२॥ चातुर्वर्ण्यं मया सृष्टं गुणकर्मविभागशः । तस्य कर्तारमपि मां विद्ध्यकर्तारमव्ययम् ॥१३॥ न मां कर्माणि लिम्पन्ति न मे कर्मफले स्पृहा । इति मां योऽभिजानाति कर्मभिर्न स बध्यते ॥१४॥ एवं ज्ञात्वा कृतं कर्म पूर्वैरपि मुमुक्षुभिः । कुरु कर्मैव तस्मात्त्वं पूर्वैः पूर्वतरं कृतम् ॥१५॥ किं कर्म किमकर्मेति कवयोऽप्यत्र मोहिताः । तत्ते कर्म प्रवक्ष्यामि यज्ज्ञात्वा मोक्ष्यसेऽशुभात् ॥१६॥ कर्मणो ह्यपि बोद्धव्यं बोद्धव्यं च विकर्मणः । अकर्मणश्च बोद्धव्यं गहना कर्मणो गतिः ॥१७॥ कर्मण्यकर्म यः पश्येदकर्मणि च कर्म यः । स बुद्धिमान्मनुष्येषु स युक्तः कृत्स्नकर्मकृत् ॥१८॥ यस्य सर्वे समारम्भाः कामसंकल्पवर्जिताः । ज्ञानाग्निदग्धकर्माणं तमाहुः पण्डितं बुधाः ॥१९॥ त्यक्त्वा कर्मफलासङ्गं नित्यतृप्तो निराश्रयः । कर्मण्यभिप्रवृत्तोऽपि नैव किंचित्करोति सः ॥२०॥ निराशीर्यतचित्तात्मा त्यक्तसर्वपरिग्रहः । शारीरं केवलं कर्म कुर्वन्नाप्नोति किल्बिषम् ॥२१॥ यदृच्छालाभसंतुष्टो द्वन्द्वातीतो विमत्सरः । समः सिद्धावसिद्धौ च कृत्वापि न निबध्यते ॥२२॥ गतसङ्गस्य मुक्तस्य ज्ञानावस्थितचेतसः । यज्ञायाचरतः कर्म समग्रं प्रविलीयते ॥२३॥ ब्रह्मार्पणं ब्रह्म हविर्ब्रह्माग्नौ ब्रह्मणा हुतम् । ब्रह्मैव तेन गन्तव्यं ब्रह्मकर्मसमाधिना ॥२४॥ दैवमेवापरे यज्ञं योगिनः पर्युपासते । ब्रह्माग्नावपरे यज्ञं यज्ञेनैवोपजुह्वति ॥२५॥ श्रोत्रादीनीन्द्रियाण्यन्ये संयमाग्निषु जुह्वति । शब्दादीन्विषयानन्य इन्द्रियाग्निषु जुह्वति ॥२६॥ सर्वाणीन्द्रियकर्माणि प्राणकर्माणि चापरे । आत्मसंयमयोगाग्नौ जुह्वति ज्ञानदीपिते ॥२७॥ द्रव्ययज्ञास्तपोयज्ञा योगयज्ञास्तथापरे । स्वाध्यायज्ञानयज्ञाश्च यतयः संशितव्रताः ॥२८॥ अपाने जुह्वति प्राणं प्राणेऽपानं तथापरे । प्राणापानगती रुद्ध्वा प्राणायामपरायणाः ॥२९॥ अपरे नियताहाराः प्राणान्प्राणेषु जुह्वति । सर्वेऽप्येते यज्ञविदो यज्ञक्षपितकल्मषाः ॥३०॥ यज्ञशिष्टामृतभुजो यान्ति ब्रह्म सनातनम् । नायं लोकोऽस्त्ययज्ञस्य

स्य कुतोऽन्यः कुरुसत्तम ॥३१॥ एवं बहुविधा यज्ञा वितता ब्रह्मणो मुखे । कर्मजान्विद्धि तान्सर्वानेवं ज्ञात्वा विमोक्ष्यसे ॥३२॥ श्रेयान्द्रव्यमयाद्यज्ञाज्ज्ञानयज्ञः परंतप । सर्वं कर्माखिलं पार्थ ज्ञाने परिसमाप्यते ॥३३॥ तद्विद्धि प्रणिपातेन परिप्रश्नेन सेवया । उपदेक्ष्यन्ति ते ज्ञानं ज्ञानिनस्तत्त्वदर्शिनः ॥३४॥ यज्ज्ञात्वा न पुनर्मोहमेवं यास्यसि पाण्डव । येन भूतान्यशेषेण द्रक्ष्यस्यात्मन्यथो मयि ॥३५॥ अपि चेदसि पापेभ्यः सर्वेभ्यः पापकृत्तमः । सर्वं ज्ञानप्लवेनैव वृजिनं संतरिष्यसि ॥३६॥ यथैधांसि समिद्धोऽग्निर्भस्मसात्कुरुतेऽर्जुन । ज्ञानाग्निः सर्वकर्माणि भस्मसात्कुरुते तथा ॥३७॥ न हि ज्ञानेन सदृशं पवित्रमिह विद्यते । तत्स्वयं योगसंसिद्धः कालेनात्मनि विन्दति ॥३८॥ श्रद्धावाँल्लभते ज्ञानं तत्परः संयतेन्द्रियः । ज्ञानं लब्ध्वा परां शान्तिमचिरेणाधिगच्छति ॥३९॥ अज्ञश्चाश्रद्दधानश्च संशयात्मा विनश्यति । नायं लोकोऽस्ति न परो न सुखं संशयात्मनः ॥४०॥ योगसंन्यस्तकर्माणं ज्ञानसंछिन्नसंशयम् । आत्मवन्तं न कर्माणि निबध्नन्ति धनंजय ॥४१॥ तस्मादज्ञानसंभूतं हृत्स्थं ज्ञानासिनात्मनः । छित्त्वैनं संशयं योगमातिष्ठोत्तिष्ठ भारत ॥४२॥ इति० कर्मब्रह्मार्पणयोगो नाम चतुर्थोऽध्यायः ४

अर्जुन उवाच ॥ संन्यासं कर्मणां कृष्ण पुनर्योगं च शंससि । यच्छ्रेय एतयोरेकं तन्मे ब्रूहि सुनिश्चितम् ॥१॥ श्रीभगवानुवाच ॥ संन्यासः कर्मयोगश्च निःश्रेयसकरावुभौ । तयोस्तु कर्मसंन्यासात्कर्मयोगो विशिष्यते ॥२॥ ज्ञेयः स नित्यसंन्यासी यो न द्वेष्टि न काङ्क्षति । निर्द्वन्द्वो हि महाबाहो सुखं बन्धात्प्रमुच्यते ॥३॥ सांख्ययोगौ पृथग्बालाः प्रवदन्ति न पण्डिताः । एकमप्यास्थितः सम्यगुभयोर्विन्दते फलम् ॥४॥ यत्सांख्यैः प्राप्यते स्थानं तद्योगैरपि गम्यते । एकं सांख्यं च योगं च यः पश्यति स पश्यति ॥५॥ संन्यासस्तु महाबाहो दुःखमाप्तुमयोगतः । योगयुक्तो मुनिर्ब्रह्म नचिरेणाधिगच्छति ॥६॥ योगयुक्तो विशुद्धात्मा विजितात्मा जितेन्द्रियः । सर्वभूतात्मभूतात्मा कुर्वन्नपि न लिप्यते ॥७॥ नैव किंचित्करोमीति युक्तो मन्येत तत्त्ववित् । पश्यञ्शृण्वन्स्पृशञ्जिघ्रन्नश्नन्गच्छन्स्वपञ्श्वसन् ॥८॥ प्रलपन्विसृजन्गृह्णन्नुन्मिषन्निमिषन्नपि । इन्द्रियाणीन्द्रियार्थेषु वर्तन्त इति धारयन् ॥९॥ ब्रह्मण्याधाय कर्माणि सङ्गं त्यक्त्वा करोति यः । लिप्यते न स पापेन पद्मपत्रमिवाम्भसा ॥१०॥ कायेन मनसा बुद्ध्या केवलैरिन्द्रियैरपि । योगिनः कर्म कुर्वन्ति सङ्गं त्यक्त्वात्मशुद्धये ॥११॥ युक्तः कर्मफलं त्यक्त्वा शान्तिमाप्नोति नैष्ठिकीम् । अयुक्तः कामकारेण फले सक्तो निबध्यते ॥१२॥ सर्वकर्माणि मनसा संन्यस्यास्ते सुखं वशी । नवद्वारे पुरे देही नैव कुर्वन्न कारयन् ॥१३॥ न कर्तृत्वं न कर्माणि लोकस्य सृजति प्रभुः । न कर्मफलसंयोगं स्वभावस्तु प्रवर्तते ॥१४॥ नादत्ते कस्यचित्पापं न चैव सुकृतं विभुः । अज्ञानेनावृतं ज्ञानं तेन मुह्यन्ति जन्तवः ॥१५॥ ज्ञानेन तु तदज्ञानं येषां नाशितमात्मनः । तेषामादित्यवज्ज्ञानं प्रकाशयति तत्परम् ॥१६॥ तद्बुद्धयस्तदात्मानस्तन्निष्ठास्तत्परायणाः । गच्छन्त्यपुनरावृत्तिं ज्ञाननिर्धूतकल्मषाः ॥१७॥ विद्याविनयसंपन्ने ब्राह्मणे गवि हस्तिनि । शुनि चैव श्वपाके च पण्डिताः समदर्शिनः ॥१८॥ इहैव तैर्जितः सर्गो येषां साम्ये स्थितं मनः । निर्दोषं हि समं ब्रह्म तस्माद्ब्रह्मणि ते स्थिताः ॥१९॥ न प्रहृष्येत्प्रियं प्राप्य नोद्विजेत्प्राप्य चाप्रियम् । स्थिरबुद्धिरसंमूढो ब्रह्मविद्ब्रह्मणि स्थितः ॥२०॥ बाह्यस्पर्शेष्वसक्तात्मा विन्दत्यात्मनि यत्सुखम् । स ब्रह्मयोगयुक्तात्मा सुखमक्षयमश्नुते ॥२१॥ ये हि संस्पर्शजा भोगा दुःखयोनय एव ते । आद्यन्तवन्तः कौन्तेय न तेषु रमते बुधः ॥२२॥ शक्नोतीहैव यः सोढुं प्राक्शरीरविमोक्षणात् । कामक्रोधोद्भवं वेगं स युक्तः स सुखी नरः ॥२३॥ योऽन्तःसुखोऽन्तरारामस्तथान्तर्ज्योतिरेव यः । स योगी ब्रह्मनिर्वाणं ब्रह्मभूतोऽधिगच्छति ॥२४॥ लभन्ते ब्रह्मनिर्वाणमृषयः क्षीणकल्मषाः । छिन्नद्वैधा यतात्मानः सर्वभूतहिते रताः ॥२५॥ कामक्रोधवियुक्तानां यतीनां यतचेतसाम् । अभितो ब्रह्मनिर्वाणं वर्तते विदितात्मनाम् ॥२६॥ स्पर्शान्कृत्वा बहिर्बाह्यांश्चक्षुश्चैवान्तरे भ्रुवोः । प्राणापानौ समौ कृत्वा नासाभ्यन्तरचारिणौ ॥२७॥ यतेन्द्रियमनोबुद्धिर्मुनिर्मोक्षपरायणः । विगतेच्छाभयक्रोधो यः सदा मुक्त एव सः ॥२८॥ भोक्तारं यज्ञतपसां सर्वलोकमहेश्वरम् । सुहृदं सर्वभूतानां ज्ञात्वा मां शान्तिमृच्छति ॥२९॥ इति श्रीमद्भगवद्गीता० संन्यासयोगो नाम पंचमोऽध्यायः ॥५॥

श्रीभगवानुवाच ॥ अनाश्रितः कर्मफलं कार्यं कर्म करोति यः । स संन्यासी च योगी च न निरग्निर्न चाक्रियः ॥१॥ यं संन्यासमिति प्राहुर्योगं तं विद्धि पाण्डव । न ह्यसंन्यस्तसंकल्पो योगी भवति कश्चन ॥२॥ आरुरुक्षोर्मुनेर्योगं कर्म कारणमुच्यते । योगारूढस्य तस्यैव शमः कारणमुच्यते ॥३॥ यदा हि नेन्द्रियार्थेषु न कर्मस्वनुषज्जते । सर्वसंकल्पसंन्यासी योगारूढस्तदोच्यते ॥४॥ उद्धरेदात्मनात्मानं नात्मानमवसादयेत् । आत्मैव ह्यात्मनो बन्धुरात्मैव रिपुरात्मनः ॥५॥ बन्धुरात्मात्मनस्तस्य येनात्मैवात्मना जितः । अनात्मनस्तु शत्रुत्वे वर्तेतात्मैव शत्रुवत् ॥६॥ जितात्मनः प्रशान्तस्य परमात्मा समाहितः । शीतोष्णसुखदुःखेषु तथा मानापमानयोः ॥७॥ ज्ञानविज्ञानतृप्तात्मा कूटस्थो विजितेन्द्रियः । युक्त इत्युच्यते योगी समलोष्टाश्मकाञ्चनः ॥८॥ सुहृन्मित्रार्युदासीनमध्यस्थद्वेष्यबन्धुषु । साधुष्वपि च पापेषु समबुद्धिर्विशिष्यते ॥९॥ योगी युञ्जीत सततमात्मानं रहसि स्थितः । एकाकी यतचित्तात्मा निराशीरपरिग्रहः ॥१०॥ शुचौ देशे प्रतिष्ठाप्य स्थिरमासनमात्मनः । नात्युच्छ्रितं नातिनीचं चैलाजिनकुशोत्तरम् ॥११॥ तत्रैकाग्रं मनः कृत्वा यतचित्तेन्द्रियक्रियः । उपविश्यासने युञ्ज्याद्योगमात्मविशुद्धये ॥१२॥ समं कायशिरोग्रीवं धारयन्नचलं स्थिरः । संप्रेक्ष्य नासिकाग्रं स्वं दिशश्चानवलोकयन् ॥१३॥ प्रशान्तात्मा विगतभीर्ब्रह्मचारिव्रते स्थितः । मनः संयम्य मच्चित्तो युक्त आसीत मत्परः ॥१४॥ युञ्जन्नेवं सदात्मानं योगी नियतमानसः । शान्तिं निर्वाणपरमां मत्संस्थामधिगच्छति ॥१५॥ नात्यश्नतस्तु योगोऽस्ति न चैकान्तमनश्नतः । न चातिस्वप्नशीलस्य जाग्रतो नैव चार्जुन ॥१६॥ युक्ताहारविहारस्य युक्तचेष्टस्य कर्मसु । युक्तस्वप्नावबोधस्य योगो भवति दुःखहा ॥१७॥ यदा विनियतं चित्तमात्मन्येवावतिष्ठते । निःस्पृहः सर्वकामेभ्यो युक्त इत्युच्यते तदा ॥१८॥ यथा दीपो निवातस्थो नेङ्गते सोपमा स्मृता । योगिनो यतचित्तस्य युञ्जतो योगमात्मनः ॥१९॥ यत्रोपरमते चित्तं निरुद्धं योगसेवया । यत्र चैवात्मनात्मानं पश्यन्नात्मनि तुष्यति ॥२०॥ सुखमात्यन्तिकं यत्तद्बुद्धिग्राह्यमतीन्द्रियम् । वेत्ति यत्र न चैवायं स्थितश्चलति तत्त्वतः ॥२१॥ यं लब्ध्वा चापरं लाभं मन्यते नाधिकं ततः । यस्मिन्स्थितो न दुःखेन गुरुणापि विचाल्यते ॥२२॥ तं विद्याद्दुःखसंयोगवियोगं योगसंज्ञितम् । स निश्चयेन योक्तव्यो योगोऽनिर्विण्णचेतसा ॥२३॥ संकल्पप्रभवान्कामांस्त्यक्त्वा सर्वानशेषतः । मनसैवेन्द्रियग्रामं विनियम्य समन्ततः ॥२४॥ शनैः शनैरुपरमेद्बुद्ध्या धृतिगृहीतया । आत्मसंस्थं मनः कृत्वा न किंचिदपि चिन्तयेत् ॥२५॥ यतो यतो निश्चरति मनश्चञ्चलमस्थिरम् । ततस्ततो नियम्यैतदात्मन्येव वशं नयेत् ॥२६॥ प्रशान्तमनसं ह्येनं योगिनं सुखमुत्तमम् । उपैति शान्तरजसं ब्रह्मभूतमकल्मषम् ॥२७॥ युञ्जन्नेवं सदात्मानं योगी विगतकल्मषः । सुखेन ब्रह्मसंस्पर्शमत्यन्तं सुखमश्नुते ॥२८॥ सर्वभूतस्थमात्मानं सर्वभूतानि चात्मनि । ईक्षते योगयुक्तात्मा सर्वत्र समदर्शनः ॥२९॥ यो मां पश्यति सर्वत्र सर्वं च मयि पश्यति । तस्याहं न प्रणश्यामि स च मे न प्रणश्यति ॥३०॥ सर्वभूतस्थितं यो मां भजत्येकत्वमास्थितः । सर्वथा वर्तमानोऽपि स योगी मयि वर्तते ॥३१॥ आत्मौपम्येन सर्वत्र समं पश्यति योऽर्जुन । सुखं वा यदि वा दुःखं स योगी परमो मतः ॥३२॥ अर्जुन उवाच ॥ योऽयं योगस्त्वया प्रोक्तः साम्येन मधुसूदन । एतस्याहं न पश्यामि चञ्चलत्वात्स्थितिं स्थिराम् ॥३३॥ चञ्चलं हि मनः कृष्ण प्रमाथि बलवद्दृढम् । तस्याहं निग्रहं मन्ये वायोरिव सुदुष्करम् ॥३४॥ श्रीभगवानुवाच ॥ असंशयं महाबाहो मनो दुर्निग्रहं चलम् । अभ्यासेन तु कौन्तेय वैराग्येण च गृह्यते ॥३५॥ असंयतात्मना योगो दुष्प्राप इति मे मतिः । वश्यात्मना तु यतता शक्योऽवाप्तुमुपायतः ॥३६॥ अर्जुन उवाच ॥ अयतिः श्रद्धयोपेतो योगाच्चलितमानसः । अप्राप्य योगसंसिद्धिं कां गतिं कृष्ण गच्छति ॥३७॥ कच्चिन्नोभयविभ्रष्टश्छिन्नाभ्रमिव नश्यति । अप्रतिष्ठो महाबाहो विमूढो ब्रह्मणः पथि ॥३८॥ एतन्मे संशयं कृष्ण छेत्तुमर्हस्यशेषतः । त्वदन्यः संशयस्यास्य छेत्ता न ह्युपपद्यते ॥३९॥ श्रीभगवानुवाच ॥ पार्थ नैवेह नामुत्र विनाशस्तस्य विद्यते । न हि कल्याणकृत्कश्चिद्दुर्गतिं तात गच्छति ॥४०॥ प्राप्य पुण्यकृतांल्लोकानुषित्वा शाश्वतीः समाः । शुचीनां श्रीमतां गेहे योगभ्रष्टोऽभिजायते ॥४१॥ अथवा योगिनामेव कुले भवति धीमताम् । एतद्धि दुर्लभतरं लोके जन्म यदीदृशम् ॥४२॥ तत्र तं बुद्धिसंयोगं लभते पौर्वदेहिकम् । यतते च ततो भूयः संसिद्धौ कुरुनन्दन ॥४३॥ पूर्वाभ्यासेन तेनैव ह्रियते ह्यवशोऽपि सः । जिज्ञासुरपि योगस्य शब्दब्रह्मातिवर्तते ॥४४॥ प्रयत्नाद्यतमानस्तु योगी संशुद्धकिल्बिषः । अनेकजन्मसंसिद्धस्ततो याति परां गतिम् ॥४५॥ तपस्विभ्योऽधिको योगी ज्ञानिभ्योऽपि मतोऽधिकः । कर्मिभ्यश्चाधिको योगी तस्माद्योगी भवार्जुन ॥४६॥ योगिनामपि सर्वेषां मद्गतेनान्तरात्मना । श्रद्धावान्भजते यो मां स मे युक्ततमो मतः ॥४७॥ इति श्रीमद्भगवद्गीता० आत्मसंयमयोगो नाम षष्ठोऽध्यायः ॥६॥

श्रीभगवानुवाच ॥ मय्यासक्तमनाः पार्थ योगं युञ्जन्मदाश्रयः । असंशयं समग्रं मां यथा ज्ञास्यसि तच्छृणु ॥१॥ ज्ञानं तेऽहं सविज्ञानमिदं वक्ष्याम्यशेषतः । यज्ज्ञात्वा नेह भूयोऽन्यज्ज्ञातव्यमवशिष्यते ॥२॥ मनुष्याणां सहस्रेषु कश्चिद्यतति सिद्धये । यततामपि सिद्धानां कश्चिन्मां वेत्ति तत्त्वतः ॥३॥ भूमिरापोऽनलो वायुः खं मनो बुद्धिरेव च । अहंकार इतीयं मे भिन्ना प्रकृतिरष्टधा ॥४॥ अपरेयमितस्त्वन्यां प्रकृतिं विद्धि मे पराम् । जीवभूतां महाबाहो ययेदं धार्यते जगत् ॥५॥ एतद्योनीनि भूतानि सर्वाणीत्युपधारय । अहं कृत्स्नस्य जगतः प्रभवः प्रलयस्तथा ॥६॥ मत्तः परतरं नान्यत्किंचिदस्ति धनंजय । मयि सर्वमिदं प्रोतं सूत्रे मणिगणा इव ॥७॥ रसोऽहमप्सु कौन्तेय प्रभास्मि शशिसूर्ययोः । प्रणवः सर्ववेदेषु शब्दः खे पौरुषं नृषु ॥८॥ पुण्यो गन्धः पृथिव्यां च तेजश्चास्मि विभावसौ । जीवनं सर्वभूतेषु तपश्चास्मि तपस्विषु ॥९॥ बीजं मां सर्वभूतानां विद्धि पार्थ सनातनम् । बुद्धिर्बुद्धिमतामस्मि तेजस्तेजस्विनामहम् ॥१०॥ बलं बलवतां चाहं कामरागविवर्जितम् । धर्माविरुद्धो भूतेषु कामोऽस्मि भरतर्षभ ॥११॥ ये चैव सात्त्विका भावा राजसास्तामसाश्च ये । मत्त एवेति तान्विद्धि न त्वहं तेषु ते मयि ॥१२॥ त्रिभिर्गुणमयैर्भावैरेभिः सर्वमिदं जगत् । मोहितं नाभिजानाति मामेभ्यः परमव्ययम् ॥१३॥ दैवी ह्येषा गुणमयी मम माया दुरत्यया । मामेव ये प्रपद्यन्ते मायामेतां तरन्ति ते ॥१४॥ न मां दुष्कृतिनो मूढाः प्रपद्यन्ते नराधमाः । माययापहृतज्ञाना आसुरं भावमाश्रिताः ॥१५॥ चतुर्विधा भजन्ते मां जनाः सुकृतिनोऽर्जुन । आर्तो जिज्ञासुरर्थार्थी ज्ञानी च भरतर्षभ ॥१६॥ तेषां ज्ञानी नित्ययुक्त एकभक्तिर्विशिष्यते । प्रियो हि ज्ञानिनोऽत्यर्थमहं स च मम प्रियः ॥१७॥ उदाराः सर्व एवैते ज्ञानी त्वात्मैव मे मतम् । आस्थितः स हि युक्तात्मा मामेवानुत्तमां गतिम् ॥१८॥ बहूनां जन्मनामन्ते ज्ञानवान्मां प्रपद्यते । वासुदेवः सर्वमिति स महात्मा सुदुर्लभः ॥१९॥ कामैस्तैस्तैर्हृतज्ञानाः प्रपद्यन्तेऽन्यदेवताः । तं तं नियममास्थाय प्रकृत्या नियताः स्वया ॥२०॥ यो यो यां यां तनुं भक्तः श्रद्धयार्चितुमिच्छति । तस्य तस्याचलां श्रद्धां तामेव विदधाम्यहम् ॥२१॥ स तया श्रद्धया युक्तस्तस्याराधनमीहते । लभते च ततः कामान्मयैव विहितान्हि तान् ॥२२॥ अन्तवत्तु फलं तेषां तद्भवत्यल्पमेधसाम् । देवान्देवयजो यान्ति मद्भक्ता यान्ति मामपि ॥२३॥ अव्यक्तं व्यक्तिमापन्नं मन्यन्ते मामबुद्धयः । परं भावमजानन्तो ममाव्ययमनुत्तमम् ॥२४॥ नाहं प्रकाशः सर्वस्य योगमायासमावृतः । मूढोऽयं नाभिजानाति लोको मामजमव्ययम् ॥२५॥ वेदाहं समतीतानि वर्तमानानि चार्जुन । भविष्याणि च भूतानि मां तु वेद न कश्चन ॥२६॥ इच्छाद्वेषसमुत्थेन द्वन्द्वमोहेन भारत । सर्वभूतानि संमोहं सर्गे यान्ति परंतप ॥२७॥ येषां त्वन्तगतं पापं जनानां पुण्यकर्मणाम् । ते द्वन्द्वमोहनिर्मुक्ता भजन्ते मां दृढव्रताः ॥२८॥ जरामरणमोक्षाय मामाश्रित्य यतन्ति ये । ते ब्रह्म तद्विदुः कृत्स्नमध्यात्मं कर्म चाखिलम् ॥२९॥ साधिभूताधिदैवं मां साधियज्ञं च ये विदुः । प्रयाणकालेऽपि च मां ते विदुर्युक्तचेतसः ॥३०॥ इति श्रीमद्भगवद्गीता० ज्ञानविज्ञानयोगो नाम सप्तमोऽध्यायः ॥७॥

अर्जुन उवाच ॥ किं तद्ब्रह्म किमध्यात्मं किं कर्म पुरुषोत्तम । अधिभूतं च किं प्रोक्तमधिदैवं किमुच्यते ॥१॥ अधियज्ञः कथं कोऽत्र देहेऽस्मिन्मधुसूदन । प्रयाणकाले च कथं ज्ञेयोऽसि नियतात्मभिः ॥२॥ श्रीभगवानुवाच ॥ अक्षरं ब्रह्म परमं स्वभावोऽध्यात्ममुच्यते । भूतभावोद्भवकरो विसर्गः कर्मसंज्ञितः ॥३॥ अधिभूतं क्षरो भावः पुरुषश्चाधिदैवतम् । अधियज्ञोऽहमेवात्र देहे देहभृतां वर ॥४॥ अन्तकाले च मामेव स्मरन्मुक्त्वा कलेवरम् । यः प्रयाति स मद्भावं याति नास्त्यत्र संशयः ॥५॥ यं यं वापि स्मरन्भावं त्यजत्यन्ते कलेवरम् । तं तमेवैति कौन्तेय सदा तद्भावभावितः ॥६॥ तस्मात्सर्वेषु कालेषु मामनुस्मर युध्य च । मय्यर्पितमनोबुद्धिर्मामेवैष्यस्यसंशयम् ॥७॥ अभ्यासयोगयुक्तेन चेतसा नान्यगामिना । परमं पुरुषं दिव्यं याति पार्थानुचिन्तयन् ॥८॥ कविं पुराणमनुशासितारमणोरणीयांसमनुस्मरेद्यः । सर्वस्य धातारमचिन्त्यरूपमादित्यवर्णं तमसः परस्तात् ॥९॥ प्रयाणकाले मनसाचलेन भक्त्या युक्तो योगबलेन चैव । भ्रुवोर्मध्ये प्राणमावेश्य सम्यक्स तं परं पुरुषमुपैति दिव्यम् ॥१०॥ यदक्षरं वेदविदो वदन्ति विशन्ति यद्यतयो वीतरागाः । यदिच्छन्तो ब्रह्मचर्यं चरन्ति तत्ते पदं संग्रहेण प्रवक्ष्ये ॥११॥ सर्वद्वाराणि संयम्य मनो हृदि निरुध्य च । मूर्ध्न्याधायात्मनः प्राणमास्थितो योगधारणाम् ॥१२॥ ओमित्येकाक्षरं ब्रह्म व्याहरन्मामनुस्मरन् । यः प्रयाति त्यजन्देहं स याति परमां गतिम् ॥१३॥ अनन्यचेताः सततं यो मां स्मरति नित्यशः । तस्याहं सुलभः पार्थ नि-

[illegible]

इति श्री[illegible] [illegible]ऽध्यायः ॥ ८ ॥

श्रीभगवानुवाच ॥ [illegible]

[illegible]

इति श्री[illegible] [illegible]ऽध्यायः ॥ [illegible]

श्रीभगवानुवाच ॥ [illegible]

[illegible]

अर्जुन उवाच ॥ [illegible]

[illegible]

मया हतांस्त्वं जहि मा व्यथिष्ठा युध्यस्व जेतासि रणे सपत्नान् ॥३४॥

संजय उवाच ॥ एतच्छ्रुत्वा वचनं केशवस्य कृताञ्जलिर्वेपमानः किरीटी । नमस्कृत्वा भूय एवाह कृष्णं सगद्गदं भीतभीतः प्रणम्य ॥३५॥

अर्जुन उवाच ॥ स्थाने हृषीकेश तव प्रकीर्त्या जगत्प्रहृष्यत्यनुरज्यते च । रक्षांसि भीतानि दिशो द्रवन्ति सर्वे नमस्यन्ति च सिद्धसङ्घाः ॥३६॥ कस्माच्च ते न नमेरन्महात्मन् गरीयसे ब्रह्मणोऽप्यादिकर्त्रे । अनन्त देवेश जगन्निवास त्वमक्षरं सदसत्तत्परं यत् ॥३७॥ त्वमादिदेवः पुरुषः पुराणस्त्वमस्य विश्वस्य परं निधानम् । वेत्तासि वेद्यं च परं च धाम त्वया ततं विश्वमनन्तरूप ॥३८॥ वायुर्यमोऽग्निर्वरुणः शशाङ्कः प्रजापतिस्त्वं प्रपितामहश्च । नमो नमस्तेऽस्तु सहस्रकृत्वः पुनश्च भूयोऽपि नमो नमस्ते ॥३९॥ नमः पुरस्तादथ पृष्ठतस्ते नमोऽस्तु ते सर्वत एव सर्व । अनन्तवीर्यामितविक्रमस्त्वं सर्वं समाप्नोषि ततोऽसि सर्वः ॥४०॥ सखेति मत्वा प्रसभं यदुक्तं हे कृष्ण हे यादव हे सखेति । अजानता महिमानं तवेदं मया प्रमादात्प्रणयेन वापि ॥४१॥ यच्चावहासार्थमसत्कृतोऽसि विहारशय्यासनभोजनेषु । एकोऽथवाप्यच्युत तत्समक्षं तत्क्षामये त्वामहमप्रमेयम् ॥४२॥ पितासि लोकस्य चराचरस्य त्वमस्य पूज्यश्च गुरुर्गरीयान् । न त्वत्समोऽस्त्यभ्यधिकः कुतोऽन्यो लोकत्रयेऽप्यप्रतिमप्रभाव ॥४३॥ तस्मात्प्रणम्य प्रणिधाय कायं प्रसादये त्वामहमीशमीड्यम् । पितेव पुत्रस्य सखेव सख्युः प्रियः प्रियायार्हसि देव सोढुम् ॥४४॥ अदृष्टपूर्वं हृषितोऽस्मि दृष्ट्वा भयेन च प्रव्यथितं मनो मे । तदेव मे दर्शय देव रूपं प्रसीद देवेश जगन्निवास ॥४५॥ किरीटिनं गदिनं चक्रहस्तमिच्छामि त्वां द्रष्टुमहं तथैव । तेनैव रूपेण चतुर्भुजेन सहस्रबाहो भव विश्वमूर्ते ॥४६॥

श्रीभगवानुवाच ॥ मया प्रसन्नेन तवार्जुनेदं रूपं परं दर्शितमात्मयोगात् । तेजोमयं विश्वमनन्तमाद्यं यन्मे त्वदन्येन न दृष्टपूर्वम् ॥४७॥ न वेदयज्ञाध्ययनैर्न दानैर्न च क्रियाभिर्न तपोभिरुग्रैः । एवंरूपः शक्य अहं नृलोके द्रष्टुं त्वदन्येन कुरुप्रवीर ॥४८॥ मा ते व्यथा मा च विमूढभावो दृष्ट्वा रूपं घोरमीदृङ्ममेदम् । व्यपेतभीः प्रीतमनाः पुनस्त्वं तदेव मे रूपमिदं प्रपश्य ॥४९॥

संजय उवाच ॥ इत्यर्जुनं वासुदेवस्तथोक्त्वा स्वकं रूपं दर्शयामास भूयः । आश्वासयामास च भीतमेनं भूत्वा पुनः सौम्यवपुर्महात्मा ॥५०॥

अर्जुन उवाच ॥ दृष्ट्वेदं मानुषं रूपं तव सौम्यं जनार्दन । इदानीमस्मि संवृत्तः सचेताः प्रकृतिं गतः ॥५१॥

श्रीभगवानुवाच ॥ सुदुर्दर्शमिदं रूपं दृष्टवानसि यन्मम । देवा अप्यस्य रूपस्य नित्यं दर्शनकाङ्क्षिणः ॥५२॥ नाहं वेदैर्न तपसा न दानेन न चेज्यया । शक्य एवंविधो द्रष्टुं दृष्टवानसि मां यथा ॥५३॥ भक्त्या त्वनन्यया शक्य अहमेवंविधोऽर्जुन । ज्ञातुं द्रष्टुं च तत्त्वेन प्रवेष्टुं च परंतप ॥५४॥ मत्कर्मकृन्मत्परमो मद्भक्तः सङ्गवर्जितः । निर्वैरः सर्वभूतेषु यः स मामेति पाण्डव ॥५५॥

इति श्रीम० विश्वरूपदर्शनं नामैकादशोऽध्यायः ॥

अर्जुन उवाच ॥ एवं सततयुक्ता ये भक्तास्त्वां पर्युपासते । ये चाप्यक्षरमव्यक्तं तेषां के योगवित्तमाः ॥१॥

श्रीभगवानुवाच ॥ मय्यावेश्य मनो ये मां नित्ययुक्ता उपासते । श्रद्धया परयोपेतास्ते मे युक्ततमा मताः ॥२॥ ये त्वक्षरमनिर्देश्यमव्यक्तं पर्युपासते । सर्वत्रगमचिन्त्यं च कूटस्थमचलं ध्रुवम् ॥३॥ संनियम्येन्द्रियग्रामं सर्वत्र समबुद्धयः । ते प्राप्नुवन्ति मामेव सर्वभूतहिते रताः ॥४॥ क्लेशोऽधिकतरस्तेषामव्यक्तासक्तचेतसाम् । अव्यक्ता हि गतिर्दुःखं देहवद्भिरवाप्यते ॥५॥ ये तु सर्वाणि कर्माणि मयि संन्यस्य मत्पराः । अनन्येनैव योगेन मां ध्यायन्त उपासते ॥६॥ तेषामहं समुद्धर्ता मृत्युसंसारसागरात् । भवामि नचिरात्पार्थ मय्यावेशितचेतसाम् ॥७॥ मय्येव मन आधत्स्व मयि बुद्धिं निवेशय । निवसिष्यसि मय्येव अत ऊर्ध्वं न संशयः ॥८॥ अथ चित्तं समाधातुं न शक्नोषि मयि स्थिरम् । अभ्यासयोगेन ततो मामिच्छाप्तुं धनंजय ॥९॥ अभ्यासेऽप्यसमर्थोऽसि मत्कर्मपरमो भव । मदर्थमपि कर्माणि कुर्वन्सिद्धिमवाप्स्यसि ॥१०॥ अथैतदप्यशक्तोऽसि कर्तुं मद्योगमाश्रितः । सर्वकर्मफलत्यागं ततः कुरु यतात्मवान् ॥११॥ श्रेयो हि ज्ञानमभ्यासाज्ज्ञानाद्ध्यानं विशिष्यते । ध्यानात्कर्मफलत्यागस्त्यागाच्छान्तिरनन्तरम् ॥१२॥ अद्वेष्टा सर्वभूतानां मैत्रः करुण एव च । निर्ममो निरहंकारः समदुःखसुखः क्षमी ॥१३॥ संतुष्टः सततं योगी यतात्मा दृढनिश्चयः । मय्यर्पितमनोबुद्धिर्यो मद्भक्तः स मे प्रियः ॥१४॥ यस्मान्नोद्विजते लोको लोकान्नोद्विजते च यः । हर्षामर्षभयोद्वेगैर्मुक्तो यः स च मे प्रियः ॥१५॥ अनपेक्षः शुचिर्दक्ष उदासीनो गतव्यथः । सर्वारम्भपरित्यागी यो मद्भक्तः स मे प्रियः ॥१६॥ यो न हृष्यति न द्वेष्टि न शोचति न काङ्क्षति । शुभाशुभपरित्यागी भक्तिमान्यः स मे प्रियः ॥१७॥ समः शत्रौ च मित्रे च तथा मानापमानयोः । शीतोष्णसुखदुःखेषु समः सङ्गविवर्जितः ॥१८॥ तुल्यनिन्दास्तुतिर्मौनी संतुष्टो येन केनचित् । अनिकेतः स्थिरमतिर्भक्तिमान्मे प्रियो नरः ॥१९॥ ये तु धर्म्यामृतमिदं यथोक्तं पर्युपासते । श्रद्दधाना मत्परमा भक्तास्तेऽतीव मे प्रियाः ॥२०॥

इति भक्तियोगो नाम द्वादशोऽध्यायः ॥

अथ क्षिप्तः श्लोकः ॥

'अर्जुन उवाच ॥ प्रकृतिं पुरुषं चैव क्षेत्रं क्षेत्रज्ञमेव च । एतद्वेदितुमिच्छामि ज्ञानं ज्ञेयं च केशव ॥१॥'

श्रीभगवानुवाच ॥ इदं शरीरं कौन्तेय क्षेत्रमित्यभिधीयते । एतद्यो वेत्ति तं प्राहुः क्षेत्रज्ञ इति तद्विदः ॥१॥ क्षेत्रज्ञं चापि मां विद्धि सर्वक्षेत्रेषु भारत । क्षेत्रक्षेत्रज्ञयोर्ज्ञानं यत्तज्ज्ञानं मतं मम ॥२॥ तत्क्षेत्रं यच्च यादृक्च यद्विकारि यतश्च यत् । स च यो यत्प्रभावश्च तत्समासेन मे शृणु ॥३॥ ऋषिभिर्बहुधा गीतं छन्दोभिर्विविधैः पृथक् । ब्रह्मसूत्रपदैश्चैव हेतुमद्भिर्विनिश्चितैः ॥४॥ महाभूतान्यहंकारो बुद्धिरव्यक्तमेव च । इन्द्रियाणि दशैकं च पञ्च चेन्द्रियगोचराः ॥५॥ इच्छा द्वेषः सुखं दुःखं संघातश्चेतना धृतिः । एतत्क्षेत्रं समासेन सविकारमुदाहृतम् ॥६॥ अमानित्वमदम्भित्वमहिंसा क्षान्तिरार्जवम् । आचार्योपासनं शौचं स्थैर्यमात्मविनिग्रहः ॥७॥ इन्द्रियार्थेषु वैराग्यमनहंकार एव च । जन्ममृत्युजराव्याधिदुःखदोषानुदर्शनम् ॥८॥ असक्तिरनभिष्वङ्गः पुत्रदारगृहादिषु । नित्यं च समचित्तत्वमिष्टानिष्टोपपत्तिषु ॥९॥ मयि चानन्ययोगेन भक्तिरव्यभिचारिणी । विविक्तदेशसेवित्वमरतिर्जनसंसदि ॥१०॥ अध्यात्मज्ञाननित्यत्वं तत्त्वज्ञानार्थदर्शनम् । एतज्ज्ञानमिति प्रोक्तमज्ञानं यदतोऽन्यथा ॥११॥ ज्ञेयं यत्तत्प्रवक्ष्यामि यज्ज्ञात्वामृतमश्नुते । अनादिमत्परं ब्रह्म न सत्तन्नासदुच्यते ॥१२॥ सर्वतः पाणिपादं तत्सर्वतोऽक्षिशिरोमुखम् । सर्वतः श्रुतिमल्लोके सर्वमावृत्य तिष्ठति ॥१३॥ सर्वेन्द्रियगुणाभासं सर्वेन्द्रियविवर्जितम् । असक्तं सर्वभृच्चैव निर्गुणं गुणभोक्तृ च ॥१४॥ बहिरन्तश्च भूतानामचरं चरमेव च । सूक्ष्मत्वात्तदविज्ञेयं दूरस्थं चान्तिके च तत् ॥१५॥ अविभक्तं च भूतेषु विभक्तमिव च स्थितम् । भूतभर्तृ च तज्ज्ञेयं ग्रसिष्णु प्रभविष्णु च ॥१६॥ ज्योतिषामपि तज्ज्योतिस्तमसः परमुच्यते । ज्ञानं ज्ञेयं ज्ञानगम्यं हृदि सर्वस्य धिष्ठितम् ॥१७॥ इति क्षेत्रं तथा ज्ञानं ज्ञेयं चोक्तं समासतः । मद्भक्त एतद्विज्ञाय मद्भावायोपपद्यते ॥१८॥ प्रकृतिं पुरुषं चैव विद्ध्यनादी उभावपि । विकारांश्च गुणांश्चैव विद्धि प्रकृतिसंभवान् ॥१९॥ कार्यकारणकर्तृत्वे हेतुः प्रकृतिरुच्यते । पुरुषः सुखदुःखानां भोक्तृत्वे हेतुरुच्यते ॥२०॥ पुरुषः प्रकृतिस्थो हि भुङ्क्ते प्रकृतिजान्गुणान् । कारणं गुणसङ्गोऽस्य सदसद्योनिजन्मसु ॥२१॥ उपद्रष्टानुमन्ता च भर्ता भोक्ता महेश्वरः । परमात्मेति चाप्युक्तो देहेऽस्मिन्पुरुषः परः ॥२२॥ य एवं वेत्ति पुरुषं प्रकृतिं च गुणैः सह । सर्वथा वर्तमानोऽपि न स भूयोऽभिजायते ॥२३॥ ध्यानेनात्मनि पश्यन्ति केचिदात्मानमात्मना । अन्ये सांख्येन योगेन कर्मयोगेन चापरे ॥२४॥ अन्ये त्वेवमजानन्तः श्रुत्वान्येभ्य उपासते । तेऽपि चातितरन्त्येव मृत्युं श्रुतिपरायणाः ॥२५॥ यावत्संजायते किंचित्सत्त्वं स्थावरजङ्गमम् । क्षेत्रक्षेत्रज्ञसंयोगात्तद्विद्धि भरतर्षभ ॥२६॥ समं सर्वेषु भूतेषु तिष्ठन्तं परमेश्वरम् । विनश्यत्स्वविनश्यन्तं यः पश्यति स पश्यति ॥२७॥ समं पश्यन्हि सर्वत्र समवस्थितमीश्वरम् । न हिनस्त्यात्मनात्मानं ततो याति परां गतिम् ॥२८॥ प्रकृत्यैव च कर्माणि क्रियमाणानि सर्वशः । यः पश्यति तथात्मानमकर्तारं स पश्यति ॥२९॥ यदा भूतपृथग्भावमेकस्थमनुपश्यति । तत एव च विस्तारं ब्रह्म संपद्यते तदा ॥३०॥ अनादित्वान्निर्गुणत्वात्परमात्मायमव्ययः । शरीरस्थोऽपि कौन्तेय न करोति न लिप्यते ॥३१॥ यथा सर्वगतं सौक्ष्म्यादाकाशं नोपलिप्यते । सर्वत्रावस्थितो देहे तथात्मा नोपलिप्यते ॥३२॥ यथा प्रकाशयत्येकः कृत्स्नं लोकमिमं रविः । क्षेत्रं क्षेत्री तथा कृत्स्नं प्रकाशयति भारत ॥३३॥ क्षेत्रक्षेत्रज्ञयोरेवमन्तरं ज्ञानचक्षुषा । भूतप्रकृतिमोक्षं च ये विदुर्यान्ति ते परम् ॥३४॥

इति क्षेत्रक्षेत्रज्ञविभागयोगो नाम० ॥१३॥

श्रीभगवानुवाच ॥ परं भूयः प्रवक्ष्यामि ज्ञानानां ज्ञानमुत्तमम् । यज्ज्ञात्वा मुनयः सर्वे परां सिद्धिमितो गताः ॥१॥ इदं ज्ञानमुपाश्रित्य मम साधर्म्यमागताः । सर्गेऽपि नोपजायन्ते प्रलये न व्यथन्ति च ॥२॥ मम योनिर्महद्ब्रह्म तस्मिन्गर्भं दधाम्यहम् । संभवः सर्वभूतानां ततो भवति भारत ॥३॥ सर्वयोनिषु कौन्तेय मूर्तयः संभवन्ति याः । तासां ब्रह्म महद्योनिरहं बीजप्रदः पिता ॥४॥ सत्त्वं रजस्तम इति गुणाः प्रकृतिसंभवाः । निबध्नन्ति महाबाहो देहे देहिनमव्ययम् ॥५॥ तत्र सत्त्वं निर्मलत्वात्प्रकाशकमनामयम् । सुखसङ्गेन बध्नाति ज्ञानसङ्गेन चानघ ॥६॥ रजो रागात्मकं विद्धि तृष्णासङ्गसमुद्भवम् । तन्निबध्नाति कौन्तेय कर्मसङ्गेन देहिनम् ॥७॥ तमस्त्वज्ञानजं विद्धि मोहनं सर्वदेहिनाम् । प्रमादालस्यनिद्राभिस्तन्निबध्नाति भारत ॥८॥ सत्त्वं सुखे संजयति रजः कर्मणि भारत । ज्ञानमावृत्य तु तमः प्रमादे संजयत्युत ॥९॥ रजस्तमश्चाभिभूय सत्त्वं भवति भारत । रजः सत्त्वं तमश्चैव तमः सत्त्वं रजस्तथा ॥१०॥ सर्वद्वारेषु देहेऽस्मिन्प्रकाश उपजायते । ज्ञानं यदा तदा विद्याद्विवृद्धं सत्त्वमित्युत ॥११॥ लोभः प्रवृत्तिरारम्भः कर्मणामशमः स्पृहा । रजस्येतानि जायन्ते विवृद्धे भरतर्षभ ॥१२॥ अप्रकाशोऽप्रवृत्तिश्च प्रमादो मोह एव च । तमस्येतानि जायन्ते विवृद्धे कुरुनन्दन ॥१३॥ यदा सत्त्वे प्रवृद्धे तु प्रलयं याति देहभृत् । तदोत्तमविदां लोकानमलान्प्रतिपद्यते ॥१४॥ रजसि प्रलयं गत्वा कर्मसङ्गिषु जायते । तथा प्रलीनस्तमसि मूढयोनिषु जायते ॥१५॥ कर्मणः सुकृतस्याहुः सात्त्विकं निर्मलं फलम् । रजसस्तु फलं दुःखमज्ञानं तमसः फलम् ॥१६॥ सत्त्वात्संजायते ज्ञानं रजसो लोभ एव च । प्रमादमोहौ तमसो भवतोऽज्ञानमेव च ॥१७॥ ऊर्ध्वं गच्छन्ति सत्त्वस्था मध्ये तिष्ठन्ति राजसाः । जघन्यगुणवृत्तिस्था अधो गच्छन्ति तामसाः ॥१८॥ नान्यं गुणेभ्यः कर्तारं यदा द्रष्टानुपश्यति । गुणेभ्यश्च परं वेत्ति मद्भावं सोऽधिगच्छति ॥१९॥ गुणानेतानतीत्य त्रीन्देही देहसमुद्भवान् । जन्ममृत्युजरादुःखैर्विमुक्तोऽमृतमश्नुते ॥२०॥

अर्जुन उवाच ॥ कैर्लिङ्गैस्त्रीन्गुणानेतानतीतो भवति प्रभो । किमाचारः कथं चैतांस्त्रीन्गुणानतिवर्तते ॥२१॥

श्रीभगवानुवाच ॥ प्रकाशं च प्रवृत्तिं च मोहमेव च पाण्डव । न द्वेष्टि संप्रवृत्तानि न निवृत्तानि काङ्क्षति ॥२२॥ उदासीनवदासीनो गुणैर्यो न विचाल्यते । गुणा वर्तन्त इत्येव योऽवतिष्ठति नेङ्गते ॥२३॥ समदुःखसुखः स्वस्थः समलोष्टाश्मकाञ्चनः । तुल्यप्रियाप्रियो धीरस्तुल्यनिन्दात्मसंस्तुतिः ॥२४॥ मानापमानयोस्तुल्यस्तुल्यो मित्रारिपक्षयोः । सर्वारम्भपरित्यागी गुणातीतः स उच्यते ॥२५॥ मां च योऽव्यभिचारेण भक्तियोगेन सेवते । स गुणान्समतीत्यैतान्ब्रह्मभूयाय कल्पते ॥२६॥ ब्रह्मणो हि प्रतिष्ठाहममृतस्याव्ययस्य च । शाश्वतस्य च धर्मस्य सुखस्यैकान्तिकस्य च ॥२७॥

इति गुणत्रयविभागयोगो नाम० ॥१४॥

श्रीभगवानुवाच ॥ ऊर्ध्वमूलमधःशाखमश्वत्थं प्राहुरव्ययम् । छन्दांसि यस्य पर्णानि यस्तं वेद स वेदवित् ॥१॥ अधश्चोर्ध्वं प्रसृतास्तस्य शाखा गुणप्रवृद्धा विषयप्रवालाः । अधश्च मूलान्यनुसंततानि कर्मानुबन्धीनि मनुष्यलोके ॥२॥ न रूपमस्येह तथोपलभ्यते नान्तो न चादिर्न च संप्रतिष्ठा । अश्वत्थमेनं सुविरूढमूलमसङ्गशस्त्रेण दृढेन छित्त्वा ॥३॥ ततः पदं तत्परिमार्गितव्यं यस्मिन्गता न निवर्तन्ति भूयः । तमेव चाद्यं पुरुषं प्रपद्ये यतः प्रवृत्तिः प्रसृता पुराणी ॥४॥ निर्मानमोहा जितसङ्गदोषा अध्यात्मनित्या विनिवृत्तकामाः । द्वन्द्वैर्विमुक्ताः सुखदुःखसंज्ञैर्गच्छन्त्यमूढाः पदमव्ययं तत् ॥५॥ न तद्भासयते सूर्यो न शशाङ्को न पावकः । यद्गत्वा न निवर्तन्ते तद्धाम परमं मम ॥६॥ ममैवांशो जीवलोके जीवभूतः सनातनः । मनःषष्ठानीन्द्रियाणि प्रकृतिस्थानि कर्षति ॥७॥ शरीरं यदवाप्नोति यच्चाप्युत्क्रामतीश्वरः । गृहीत्वैतानि संयाति वायुर्गन्धानिवाशयात् ॥८॥ श्रोत्रं चक्षुः स्पर्शनं च रसनं घ्राणमेव च । अधिष्ठाय मनश्चायं विषयानुपसेवते ॥९॥ उत्क्रामन्तं स्थितं वापि भुञ्जानं वा गुणान्वितम् । विमूढा नानुपश्यन्ति पश्यन्ति ज्ञानचक्षुषः ॥१०॥ यतन्तो योगिनश्चैनं पश्यन्त्यात्मन्यवस्थितम् । यतन्तोऽप्यकृतात्मानो नैनं पश्यन्त्यचेतसः ॥११॥ यदादित्यगतं तेजो जगद्भासयतेऽखिलम् । यच्चन्द्रमसि यच्चाग्नौ तत्तेजो विद्धि मामकम् ॥१२॥ गामाविश्य च भूतानि धारयाम्यहमोजसा । पुष्णामि चौषधीः सर्वाः सोमो भूत्वा रसात्मकः ॥१३॥ अहं वैश्वानरो भूत्वा प्राणिनां देहमाश्रितः । प्राणापानसमायुक्तः पचाम्यन्नं चतुर्विधम् ॥१४॥ सर्वस्य चाहं हृदि संनिविष्टो मत्तः स्मृतिर्ज्ञानमपोहनं च । वेदैश्च सर्वैरहमेव वेद्यो वेदान्तकृद्वेदविदेव चाहम् ॥१५॥ द्वाविमौ पुरुषौ लोके क्षरश्चाक्षर एव च । क्षरः सर्वाणि भूतानि कूटस्थोऽक्षर उच्यते ॥१६॥ उत्तमः पुरुषस्त्वन्यः परमात्मेत्युदाहृतः । यो लोकत्रयमाविश्य बिभर्त्यव्यय ईश्वरः ॥१७॥ यस्मात्क्षरमतीतोऽहमक्षरादपि चोत्तमः । अतोऽस्मि लोके वेदे च प्रथितः पुरुषोत्तमः ॥१८॥ यो मामेवमसंमूढो जानाति पुरुषोत्तमम् । स सर्वविद्भजति मां सर्वभावेन भारत ॥१९॥ इति गुह्यतमं शास्त्रमिदमुक्तं मयानघ । एतद्बुद्ध्वा बुद्धिमान्स्यात्कृतकृत्यश्च भारत ॥२०॥

पुरुषोत्तमयोगो नाम पंचदशोऽध्यायः ॥

श्रीभगवानुवाच ॥ अभयं सत्त्वसंशुद्धिर्ज्ञानयोगव्यवस्थितिः । दानं दमश्च यज्ञश्च स्वाध्यायस्तप आर्जवम् ॥१॥ अहिंसा सत्यमक्रोधस्त्यागः शान्तिरपैशुनम् । दया भूतेष्वलोलुप्त्वं मार्दवं ह्रीरचापलम् ॥२॥ तेजः क्षमा धृतिः शौचमद्रोहो नातिमानि-

PUBLISHERS
TILAK BROS.
LOK. TILAK MANDIR
568 NARAYAN PETH
POONA CITY, (INDIA).

PREMIER OFFSET WORKS BOMBAY 4

These blank pages have been included in this volume for the convenience of the reader, if he wishes to make any notes.